"In the end, *Explaining Hitler* therefore achieves something more than what it sets out to do. Rather than merely explaining the explainers, it brings alive again the sordid story of Hitler himself, reinvigorating our memory of him and his milieu. For one more generation, Mr. Rosenbaum has prevented Hitler from passing into history as a caricature, and that is an achievement worth admiring." —Anne Applebaum, *Wall Street Journal*

"Remarkable. . . . Drawing on his considerable skills as an investigative journalist, Rosenbaum interviews many of the historians and other researchers, professional and amateur, who have looked into these matters. He has a sympathetic ear, a knack for classification, and a sharp, critical mind." —Michael R. Marrus, *New York Times Book Review*

"Brilliant. . . . richly researched and eminently readable." —Milton Rosenberg, *Chicago Tribune*

"Reading this book is like having a long conversation with someone who's passionate, brilliant." —John Dorfman, *Philadelphia Inquirer*

"Restlessly probing and deeply intelligent. . . . In this brilliantly skeptical inventory of the world's Hitler-thinking, Rosenbaum analyzes not only the multiple Hitler theories but also the agendas and fantasies that the theorizers bring to their subject. His book may be useful to the surprising number of people—Flat-Earthers of the moral realm—who, even now, refuse to believe in the existence of evil." —Lance Morrow, *Time*

"A truly brilliant book." —Frank McLynn, *Irish Times*

"It is both thoughtful and deeply felt and in some ways its personal freewheeling qualities enable Rosenbaum to get closer to the demonic element in Hitler." —John Gross, *New York Review of Books*

"Rosenbaum's bracing, rigorous, exhilarating, and beautifully written book is an amazing voyage into what must be one of the most confounding areas of scholarly inquiry." —Lev Raphael, *Detroit Free Press*

"Ron Rosenbaum brilliantly explores the origins of Hitler's evil. . . . Few contemporary writers are better equipped to pull off this task. Rosenbaum is a rare triple threat: He is a first-rate thinker, a fine reporter, and a superb writer. He is also, as this volume proves, in control of a massive body of scholarly work on Hitler. . . . Personal without being self-indulgent, erudite without being pedantic, written with passion and moral engagement worthy of its momentous subject, *Explaining Hitler* is an exemplary work of intellectual journalism, an idiosyncratic classic."   —Gary Kamiya, *Salon*

"A journey of considerable enlightenment. . . . Rosenbaum comes up with what is real news even for those of us who claim to be knowledgeable about the era."   —Fred E. Katz, *New Leader*

"Vintage Rosenbaum: a blend of a newshound's investigative reporting with a literary critic's close textual reading, all wrapped in an elaborate (if gingerly proffered) bundle of theories."   —David Greenberg, *The Forward*

"*Explaining Hitler* blossoms into an absorbing, occasionally suspenseful and exciting, and genuinely fresh look at a man who already ranked as perhaps the most thoroughly analyzed public figure in history."
    —*San Jose Mercury News*

"Rosenbaum has one of the most interesting minds and compelling voices in contemporary journalism. . . . The result is an extremely contemporary book that uses Hitler as a way to address the most profound questions of Western philosophy."   —Robert S. Boynton, *New York Newsday*

"Rosenbaum lays claim to no final answers, but by deploying and interweaving techniques proper to both history and literature, he uniquely illuminates one of the darkest corners of modern experience."
    —Steve Dowden, *Boston Sunday Globe*

"It is toward understanding the ways our culture has tried for more than half a century to make sense of Hitler and what he wrought that this book makes its real contribution."   —Michael Andre Bernstein, *Los Angeles Times*

"A remarkable study, as rich in humanity as a fine novel."
    —Algis Valiunas, *American Spectator*

"A thinking person's blockbuster."   —*Austin American Statesman*

"Smart, scrupulously reported."   —*Newsweek*

"A superb history."   —*Miami Herald*

"Profound and provocative. . . . A resourcefully imaginative examination of our desperate search for an explanation of ultimate evil."   —*Kirkus Reviews*

"Offers groundbreaking insights into the enigma of Hitler's psyche."
—*Publishers Weekly*

"Bold and provocative. . . . Illuminates the most perplexing unsolved mystery of the twentieth century. In *Explaining Hitler*, profound historical questions spring urgently and hauntingly to life."
—Sam Tanenhaus, author of *Whittaker Chambers*

"A work of exceptional scholarship. Ron Rosenbaum has written a fascinating and thought-provoking study that is a must-read for anyone interested in trying to understand Hitler."
—Gerald Posner, author of *Case Closed* and *Hitler's Children*

"A remarkable book, a major contribution. Ron Rosenbaum gives us his often dramatic discussions with the major analysts of Hitler's career and personality. While highly readable, it goes deep into the basic issues of ethics, of free will, and the problem of evil."
—Robert Conquest, author of *Stalin* and *The Great Terror*

"This is a wonderfully thoughtful investigation. The great strength of the book is the empathy Rosenbaum displays for the points of view he examines. It's a masterful job of listening, of tuning in to some great intellects of our era as they debate the subject—one that allows us all to participate in our own search for Hitler."   —Charles L. Mee, Jr., author of *Meeting at Potsdam*

"Ron Rosenbaum has brought his searching style of inquiry to the darkest of twentieth-century questions—the nature of evil in one man, in Adolf Hitler. By visiting and examining the experts and their testimonies, he has written a bewildering *Rashomon* tale, seen in a multifaceted mirror. *Explaining Hitler* is a remarkable journey by one of the most original journalists and writers of our time."   —David Remnick, author of *Lenin's Tomb*

EXPLAINING HITLER

EXPLAINING HITLER

THE SEARCH FOR
THE ORIGINS OF HIS EVIL

UPDATED EDITION

RON
ROSENBAUM

Da Capo Press
A Member of the Perseus Books Group

Printed in the United States of America.

For information, address Da Capo Press, 44 Farnsworth Street, 3rd Floor, Boston, MA 02210.

Designed by Tanya M. Pérez-Rock 1998
Set in 10-point Photina by the Perseus Books Group

Portions of this work were originally published in *The New Yorker* in different form. Grateful acknowledgment is made to the following for permission to reprint previously published material:

Basic Books, a subsidiary of Perseus Books Group LLC: Excerpt from *The Psychopathic God: Adolf Hitler*, by Robert G. L. Waite. Copyright © 1977 by Robert G. L. Waite. Reprinted by permission of Basic Books, a subsidiary of Perseus Books Group LLC.

Diane Cole: Excerpts from an interview between Diane Cole and Lucy Dawidowicz.
Used by permission of Diane Cole.

Neal Kozodoy, Literary Executor for the Estate of Lucy Dawidowicz: Excerpts from *The War Against the Jews*, by Lucy Dawidowicz, Reprinted by permission of Neal Kozodoy, Literary Executor for the Estate of Lucy Dawidowicz.

Cataloging-in-Publication data for this book is available from the Library of Congress.

First Da Capo Press Edition 2014
ISBN: 978-0-306-82318-3 (paperback)
ISBN: 978-0-306-82319-0 (e-book)

Published by Da Capo Press
A Member of the Perseus Books Group
www.dacapopress.com

Da Capo Press books are available at special discounts for bulk purchases in the U.S. by corporations, institutions, and other organizations. For more information, please contact the Special Markets Department at the Perseus Books Group, 2300 Chestnut Street, Suite 200, Philadelphia, PA 19103, or call (800) 810-4145, ext. 5000, or e-mail: special.markets@perseusbooks.com.

10 9 8 7 6 5 4 3 2 1

To those who survived, and to those who did not

The more I learn about Hitler, the harder I find it to explain.

—Alan Bullock

There will never be an adequate explanation. . . . The closer one gets to explicability the more one realizes nothing can make Hitler explicable.

—Emil Fackenheim

Hitler is explicable in principle, but that does not mean that he *has* been explained.

—Yehuda Bauer

He [God] owes me answers to many questions.

—Holocaust survivor
at Auschwitz, 1985

CONTENTS

Part Six
The War over the Question Why

Part Seven
Blame and Origins

PREFACE TO
THE UPDATED EDITION

Bear with me a moment. I'm not sure you need to read this Preface, but I feel like I need to write it. I need to say something about the title, *Explaining Hitler*. To dispel any doubt, clear up any ambiguity, the unfortunate shadow that irony casts. And by the way, in general, I *like* ambiguity. My longtime favorite work of literary criticism is William Empson's classic *Seven Types of Ambiguity*. I often see eight or more.

And I *like* irony—as long as people get it. But how can one be sure? There was that encounter with one interviewer who kept asking, about this book, "But what's *your* explanation, what's *your* explanation?"

Without much success I tried to explain *Explaining Hitler*. Explain that it was a book about the enterprise, the process, the *attempt* to explain Hitler. Something the subtitle—*The Search for the Origins of His Evil*—seemed to make clear. Not about *my* Answer. Not the final solution to The Final Solution. Not my PowerPoint slideshow drawing a clear line from the baby picture of Hitler (on the cover) to the exterminationist Führer in the bunker.

It was (it is) about the *search*. About the differing ways people seek to answer the question "Why?" The differing modes of interpretation, the differing lenses through which one can look at Hitler. And what they reveal about the explainers—about the eyes of the beholders—and the nature of their *failure* to explain Hitler. The way Hitler escaped the nets of the systems brought to bear upon him.

The hopelessly confused and conflicting psychoanalytic modes (was it the bad father or the overprotective mother?). The "psychohistorical" (the discredited "Jewish blood" theory), the psychosexual (the largely discredited Geli Raubal rumors). The ideological (was Hitler's anti-Semitism the result of nineteenth-century German "racial science" or nineteen centuries of Christian anti-Semitism, or a fusion of both?). The theological (what do the savants of Holocaust theodicy—the search for a *reason* for ultimate evil in a universe supposedly ruled by a just and loving God—tell us?). And the metaphysical: What do we make of George Steiner's "threefold blackmail of transcendence"?

Not neglecting the disease models (Nazi hunter Simon Wiesenthal's lifelong, unsupported belief that Hitler contracted syphilis from a Jewish prostitute in Vienna). A sad symptom of the recurrent effort to find a Jew to blame, such as the Australian obsessive who wrote a thick book based upon the supposition that Ludwig Wittgenstein—probably, though not definitely, a classmate of Hitler in middle school and the product of a family that converted from Judaism to Christianity—was somehow to blame.

Or did it all come down to a mosquito bite (the deferred "psychopathic" symptomology of epidemic encephalitis, a disease Hitler supposedly contracted in the World War I trenches)? Just to name a few, examined skeptically, herein.

Everyone seems to want to have one pet theory of Hitler, almost like a talisman against "the horror of inexplicability" as I call it. A talisman they hold closely, guard jealously. No need to think about it anymore. I can't tell you how many times I've had to answer the question, "Oh, have you read Alice Miller?" (the psychoanalyst whose error-filled Hitler thesis dressed up the discredited "Jewish blood" theory in Freudian terms to explain Hitler).

I came to examine these theories, however flawed as Hitler explanations they might be, for what they reflected of the explainers' predispositions and concerns. One critic described the book as being about "the cultural processes by which we try to come to terms with history."

About the flaws, the hidden agendas, the explanations that serve as consolations, or even exculpations ("the perversion made him do it," "the mosquito made him do it"). The meaningless ascription to him of the term "psychopath" or "sociopath." The way Hitler had somehow "escaped" all the terminologies, the overconfident theories that sought to pin him down, like some insect specimen. Escaped not in the manner of the "Hitler alive in Argentina" myth but escaped *explanation.*

Why was that? Was he the sort of "exceptionalist" phenomenon that *transcended* explanation—or had we just not *found* the events obscured by history, the missing piece of the puzzle that might constitute evidence for an explanation?

Explaining Hitler, in other words, is not my got-it-all-nailed-down instruction manual. It's not a biography; it's more a dissection, well, an examination of biographies—an essay in intellectual history. I do not have the hubris to declare discovery of a Unified Field Theory of Hitler. No Higgs Boson of Hitler. No "Theory of Everything" Evil. That doesn't mean there won't—or can't— ever be one, or that it's not worth the attempt to further clarify what we mean by Hitler, by evil, by origin. Indeed, as I've tried to point out in the book, the attempts often tell us more about ourselves, our own self-images, and our cultural predispositions than some indisputable truth about Hitler. "Cultural self-portraits in the negative" was the phrase I used: Hitler is everything we (hope) we are not. Thus the desire for explanations that put him beyond the range of "normal" human beings. Beyond the range of *us*.

I don't believe all explanations lack any merit and I go to great lengths to evaluate what they may have added to our understanding. And yet, and yet. . . . So often so many explanations fall maddeningly, and sometimes even comically, short.

For the record, my approach in *Explaining Hitler* grew out of the intellectual training I had in the practice of "close reading"—the search for resonant ambiguities and conflicts in texts inculcated in me by the last of the so-called New Critics at Yale (Robert Penn Warren, William K. Wimsatt, and the like). A method initially evolved for the study of literature, but which I've found transferable, if used with care, to the study of history or as I described it:

> close reading of documents, memoirs, police reports, and close listening to the voices of the explainers I sought out, in an effort to hear the unspoken subtext, the significant allusions, the hidden agendas, conflicts, and in particular, the doubts beneath the surface. To sense the nature of the longing that drives the explainers, and the kinds of solace explanations offer.

The problem to which I applied this was the one posed by the Hitler Baby Picture on the cover of this (and the initial) edition of the book. My emphatic choice of cover image. Because it asks the crucial question: How do we get from here (the innocent infant) to there (the genocidal monster)? In other words, what factors shaped the metamorphosis? Or was it a gradual evolution? At what point did Hitler become *Hitler?*

It's a controversial question. Is it "an obscenity in itself" to ask this question as Claude Lanzmann—the director of *Shoah* and would-be dictator of discourse about Hitler—argues? An obscenity even to try to explain? I don't agree. I don't believe one should stifle the innate human desire to make sense of things, even if some things elude our grasp. I don't believe Hitler and the Holocaust should be removed to some sacralized space apart from history.

Nonetheless, I think I understand where this rage at explanation comes from: because to explain is (always, according to Lanzmann) to excuse—to exculpate. To displace guilt from Hitler to the metaphorical mosquito. To offer a reason for the unreasonable. A step down the path to "to understand all is to forgive all." I don't see that this necessarily follows or calls for stifling the human impulse to ask "why."

In any case, by the time I finished the book, I may have gotten too close to the contradictions in the explanations. All too sure of themselves, yet all too contradictory and often tunnel-visioned, they couldn't all be true. My friend, the filmmaker, Errol Morris likes to cite what he claims was the dying declaration of the last survivor of an eccentric monastic community in nineteenth-century Ohio: "It just isn't possible that all religions can be true, but it *is* possible they all can be false."

And so I may have, perhaps, been too confident in assuming that readers would not take the title *Explaining Hitler* without an ironic grain of salt. Especially with the subtitle, *The Search for the Origins of His Evil.*

I still like the title, though I'm not sure now to whom I owe the credit. One of the editors I worked with at *The New Yorker* when preparing a ten-thousand-word early version of the Introduction, Robert Vare, Rick Hertzberg, or David Remnick? Still grateful to all of them.

But it's true I did have a moment of doubt when I wondered if it was a safe assumption that the irony would be apparent. I even talked my publisher (and Amazon, right before publication, in an unusually self-destructive move) into changing the title to *The Search for Hitler*, then changed it back to *Explaining Hitler* at the last minute.

The great aphorism for many writers is from Gide: "Do not understand me too quickly." For me, "do not misunderstand me too quickly." Perhaps I should have paid more attention to the possibility of misapprehension. In fact, it was only when I undertook writing a new Preface and Afterword updating the book that I realized the explanatory subtitle was *not* on the cover, only on the inside title page.

I'm glad this new edition has the subtitle on the cover. Just to remove the shadow of a doubt. Meanwhile, the search goes on and I'll have more to say about new developments in the Afterword. But perhaps the best way to explain *Explaining Hitler* is that, at its deepest level, it's an attempt to grapple with the project of explaining evil.

The Baby Pictures
and the Abyss

In the realm of Hitler explanations, it's come to be called "the survival myth," and though no one believes it now, it struck a chord in the post-war popular imagination. The image of a Hitler who had escaped—escaped the Berlin bunker, escaped the flames that were said to have consumed him, escaped *judgment*—turned out to be a curiously seductive one, inspiring fantasists from the lowbrow (the legendary *Police Gazette* "Hitler Alive in Argentina!" series) to the highly cerebral (George Steiner's challenging parable *The Portage to San Cristóbal of A.H.*). Seductive, perhaps, because it reflects a feeling that although Hitler did not escape us physically, in certain important respects he may have eluded us. The survival myth suggests a persistent anxiety that Hitler has somehow escaped *explanation*.

Similarly suggestive is the debate that erupted in 1995 over the discovery of a few curved shards of bone reposing in a Moscow archive, said to be the surviving remains of Hitler's cranium. The controversy over the identity of the skull fragments—an important one because they could perhaps tell us something about the circumstances of Hitler's suicide, his final act of self-definition—may be a symptom of a more disturbing truth: Regardless of what became of his skull, a sure sense of Hitler's mind has escaped us.

The real search for Hitler—the search for who he was, who he *thought* he was, and why he did what he did—has been an expedition into a realm far more inaccessible than the rain-forest jungles of Argentina or the remote haciendas of Paraguay, supposed hideouts of the escaped Hitler in the survival myth. It's not a search for where Hitler has hidden but for what he hid within him. It's a trek into the trackless realm of Hitler's inwardness. A realm disguised by his own deceitfulness, camouflaged by thickets of conflicting evidence, a tangled undergrowth of unreliable memory and testimony, of misleading rumor, myth, and biographical apocrypha. A terra incognita of ambiguity and incertitude where armies of scholars clash in evidentiary darkness over the spectral shadows of Hitler's past and the maddening obscurities of his psyche.

Is it conceivable, more than half a century after Hitler's death, after all that's been written and said, that we're still wandering in this trackless wilderness, this garden of forking paths, with no sight of the quarry? Or, rather, alas, with too many quarries: The search for Hitler has apprehended not one coherent, consensus image of Hitler but rather many different Hitlers, competing Hitlers, conflicting embodiments of competing visions. Hitlers who might not recognize each other well enough to say "*Heil*" if they came face to face in Hell. The mountebank Hitler of Alan Bullock's initial vision might well not see himself in the possessed true believer, the mesmeric occult messiah of H. R. Trevor-Roper. Nor would the contemptuously laughing Hitler Lucy Dawidowicz limned in the seventies find much in common with the dithering, hesitant Hamlet Hitler of Christopher Browning, the state-of-the-art Hitler of the nineties.

Yes, an enormous amount has been written but little has been *settled*. And certain things have been lost and forgotten. Just to touch upon that which has not been settled: There is the question of the origin of Hitler's anti-Semitism, the degree of its "sincerity." (Was he a true believer, as H. R. Trevor-Roper has always insisted, or a cynical opportunist who merely manipulated hatred of Jews for his own advancement, as Alan Bullock and the theologian Emil Fackenheim have argued?) There are unsettled issues about such basic questions as Hitler's ancestry (did he fear he was "infected" by Jewish blood?), his sexuality (its relation, if any, to his political pathology), and the moment of his death. (Did he die "a soldier's death," shooting himself with his own hand? Or was it a coward's death—a kind of assisted suicide with the help of cyanide and a valet—as a controversial Russian autopsy report argued?) If his end is in doubt, so is the question of his advent and his success: Was it inevitable or resistible? Were Hitler's crimes the consequence of irresistible historical forces or an implacable personal will?

At the heart of these questions is the elusive, perhaps unfathomable object of the search for Hitler: the nature of Hitler's "thought-world." Was he "convinced of his own rectitude," as Trevor-Roper firmly insists—did he believe in some deeply deluded way that he was doing good? Or was he deeply aware of his own criminality, as the philosopher Berel Lang has gone to great lengths to establish? Beneath this vexed question is the even more vexatious debate over Hitlerian exceptionalism—is Hitler on a continuum with previous and successive mass murderers, explicable within the same framework, on the extreme end of the same spectrum of the human nature we supposedly share with Jeffrey Dahmer and Mahatma Gandhi? Is there a potential "Hitler within" all of us, as some like to say? Or is he off the grid, beyond the continuum in a category of his own as Emil Fackenheim—who rejects the "Hitler within" notion—argues.

Then there is the question of Hitler's precise role and his degree of personal responsibility for the Holocaust. Powerful tendencies in contemporary scholarship have cumulatively served to diminish the decisiveness and centrality of Hitler's role. There is, first, the predisposition to look upon Hitler as the pawn of larger, purportedly "deeper" and more profound forces of history and society, forces that made the Holocaust "inevitable" with or without Hitler's agency. It's a predisposition expressed by the president of the United States, when at the dedication of the U.S. Holocaust Memorial, Bill Clinton spoke of the way the German "culture, which produced Goethe, Schiller, and Beethoven, then brought forth Hitler and Himmler"—Hitler as cultural *product* rather than (im)moral agent.

And there is a concomitant tendency to regard anything that hints of a "Great Man" theory of history as unsophisticated compared with the resort to explanation by Great Abstractions such as "Western racism," "eliminationist anti-Semitism," or even (still) "dialectical materialism." The Great Abstraction theorists are certain that if it hadn't been Hitler—given the historical circumstances of Germany—such forces would have produced someone *like* Hitler to execute the Final Solution.

It's a view that tends to deprecate or make relatively irrelevant the motive and psychology of the Hitler we *did* get. It's a tendency heatedly disputed by (among others) the influential polemicist Milton Himmelfarb, who took arms against Great Abstraction theories in a powerful 1984 essay entitled "No Hitler, No Holocaust." Himmelfarb's particular target in that essay was the theory that singles out Christian anti-Semitism as the true source of the Holocaust. Himmelfarb argues that abstract ideological or theological animus is not sufficient: "All that history [of Christian persecution of the Jews] could have been the same and Hitler could as easily, more easily, not have murdered the Jews. He could more advantageously have tightened the screws of oppression, as anti-Semitic tyrants had done in the past," without pushing for (and nearly achieving) utter extermination. That decision was Hitler's alone, Himmelfarb insists: "Hitler murdered the Jews not because he *had* to," not because he was impelled by abstract historical forces toward an inevitable end but because of his own personal will and desire, "because he *wanted* to" (emphasis added).

He wanted to. It's a bit surprising that Hitler's desire should have become so controversial, but in fact it is another one of the cruxes that has embroiled Hitler explainers, particularly in the last decade: Just how badly did Hitler want to proceed with the extermination, and just when—on what day, in what week, or what year—did he give an irrevocable signal to proceed with the Final Solution?

The controversy over timing is more than a mere pettifogging squabble over days and weeks; those who argue different decision dates for the final authorization are in effect proposing different Hitlers, differently motivated, possessed by altogether different priorities and substantially dissimilar mentalities. Here again the tendency of contemporary scholarship has been to diminish Hitler as a motive force, to downplay his personal zeal for the slaughter, to portray him as a reluctant, indecisive, even dithering figure, inhibited by conflicting wartime priorities—perhaps even by timidity in the face of the "enormity" of the crime, as Christopher Browning suggested to me—from giving the final go-ahead.

This recent tendency runs directly counter to the powerful argument elaborated by the late Lucy Dawidowicz in *The War Against the Jews* back in 1975: that Hitler had made mass murder his mission, his highest priority as far back as November 1918 in an army hospital at Pasewalk on the western front, where, in the throes of a still-mysterious episode of (depending on whose account you believe) gas blindness, a nervous breakdown, hysterical blindness, a hallucinatory episode in which he heard "voices," or a providential vision from on high (Hitler's version), he resolved to avenge the "stab in the back" he believed caused the German defeat by exterminating the Jews he held responsible, all of them.

The controversy over the episode at Pasewalk is itself a subset of a larger schism among Hitler's explainers over two distinct modes of explanation: evolution or metamorphosis. Is it possible to find in the thinly distributed, heatedly disputed facts of Hitler's life before he came to power some single transformative moment, some dramatic trauma, or some life-changing encounter with a Svengali-like figure—a moment of metamorphosis that made Hitler *Hitler*? It's a search impelled by the absence of a coherent and convincing evolutionary account of Hitler's psychological development, one that would explain his transformation from a shy, artistically minded youth, the dispirited denizen of a Viennese homeless shelter, from the dutiful but determinedly obscure army corporal, to the figure who, not long after his return to Munich from the war, suddenly leapt onto the stage of history as a terrifyingly incendiary, spellbinding street orator. One who proceeded to take a party whose members numbered in the dozens and used it to seize power over a nation of millions; made that nation an instrument of his will, a will that convulsed the world and left forty million corpses in its wake. Missing, metaphorically then, is something that will help us explain Hitler's baby pictures.

Those baby pictures: If I had to choose a single defining moment in the course of researching and thinking about the search for Hitler, it might have to be that evening in Paris when I witnessed—when I was on the receiving end of—French filmmaker Claude Lanzmann's angry tirade over Hitler's baby pictures. When I witnessed the way the acclaimed director of *Shoah*, the nine-and-a-half-hour Holocaust documentary, metaphorically brandished the baby pictures, brandished the scandalizing *idea* of the baby pictures in my face as weapons in his personal, obsessive war against the question "Why." It was a moment that exposed both the passion behind the controversy over the problem of explaining Hitler—and the question at its core.

It might come as a surprise to many that the very notion of attempting to explain Hitler should seem not merely difficult in itself but dangerous, forbidden, a transgression of near-biblical proportions to some. And, in fact, Lanzmann does represent an extreme position, the end point of a continuum, what I would call third-level despair over explaining Hitler. The point at which the despair turns to outright hostility to the process of explanation itself. The point at which the search for Hitler doubles back on the searchers.

The depth and extremity of despair I encountered in the course of talking to Hitler explainers was one of the most surprising things I discovered in the process of writing this book. I began to get an intimation of what might be called first-level or evidentiary despair in some remarkable pronouncements by mandarins in the field such as Alan Bullock and H. R. Trevor-Roper. After fifty years, Trevor-Roper avers, Adolf Hitler "remains a frightening mystery." After fifty years, Alan Bullock could only say, "The more I learn about Hitler, the harder I find it to explain." Jewish-studies scholar Alvin Rosenfeld is even more definitive: "No representation of Adolf Hitler has seemed able to present the man or satisfactorily explain him."

But no one summed up the case for evidentiary despair more briskly and conclusively than Yehuda Bauer, a founder of the discipline of Holocaust Studies and widely regarded as the most authoritative historian of the Holocaust. Hitler is not inexplicable, at least *in theory*, Bauer told me in his Hebrew University office in Jerusalem. It's not impossible to explain Hitler, but it might just be too late. Too late, because too many crucial witnesses have died without giving testimony, because too many crucial documents have been destroyed, too many memories have faded, because all too many gaps in the evidentiary record will never be filled, too many ambiguities can no longer be resolved. "Hitler is not inexplicable" in theory, Bauer told me. "But the fact that something is explicable in principle does not mean that it has been explained."

It was in Jerusalem as well that I was initiated into second-level despair, not evidentiary but a deeper, epistemological futility, by Emil Fackenheim, perhaps the foremost "theologian of the Holocaust" (as an essay in *Commentary* characterized him). Fackenheim argued, contrary to Bauer, that Hitler is not explicable even "in theory," that even if we *had* all the facts, Hitler was in some way beyond explanation. That no amount of biographical and psychological data about a difficult childhood, a dysfunctional family, no concatenation of trauma and deformation, no combination of bad character and evil ideology, could add up to *enough*. Enough to explain the magnitude of Hitler's crimes. The systems of explanation, historical and psychological, that we employ to explain ordinary human behavior, however extreme, cannot explain Hitler, who represents, Fackenheim believes, a "radical evil," an "eruption of demonism into history" that places him beyond even the extreme end of the continuum of human nature. Fackenheim sees Hitler as more than just a very, very, very bad man, in the sense of ordinary human badness, but something else again entirely, something beyond that, the meaning of which we need to search for not in psychology but in theology. The explanation for which, if there is one, can be known or fathomed only by God.

But Claude Lanzmann goes further even than that, goes deeper to a third-level despair—to a revolt against explanation itself, to a personal war against the question Why. For Lanzmann, the attempt to explain Hitler is not merely futile but immoral—he calls the very enterprise of understanding obscene.

"There are some pictures of Hitler as a baby too, aren't there?" he has said. "There is even a book written . . . about Hitler's childhood, an attempt at explanation which is for me obscenity as such."

Obscenity? I tried to explore with Lanzmann the strength of conviction that would compel him to use "obscenity" as a term of abuse for investigators who, however misguided they might be, were at least well-intentioned. Why should the maker of a nine-and-a-half-hour documentary on Hitler's death camps become so incensed about a book on Hitler's childhood? What was it about the baby pictures? I sensed they disturbed, they scandalized him not because they conjure up a specific theory of Hitler's childhood, but because they give us Hitler as an innocent, Hitler before he becomes *Hitler*, "a Hitler without victims," as the phrase coined by the scholar Alvin Rosenfeld has it. A Hitler whose baby-faced innocence lures us down the path Lanzmann condemns, seduces us into constructing explanations for the evolution of innocent child into mass murderer—explanations that are, Lanzmann argues, inevitably obscene rationalizations, not merely exculpations, but virtually justifications for Hitler's behavior.

It's worth noting that when Lanzmann tells us "there are some pictures of Hitler as a baby," Hitler's baby picture has an interesting history as a pawn in the politics of Hitler's image making, his stage-managing of his self-presentation. The baby picture appeared publicly first in a photo book published by Hitler's personal photographer, Heinrich Hoffmann, in 1932, a book disingenuously titled *The Hitler Nobody Knows.*

Despite the title's seductive intimation of confidences revealed, *The Hitler Nobody Knows* was in fact designed to counter the subcurrent of scurrilous speculations and gossip, the whispered Hitler apocrypha, the rumors fueled by Hitler's Austrian-born foreignness, by some indefinable alienness he radiated, a sense of strangeness and peculiarity, the vague impression of unwholesomeness he made on many Germans, a sense exacerbated by rumors about his private life, his confirmed bachelor status, and the well-known sexual scandals among his closest aides. Hoffmann's book of photos was a bait-and-switch tactic, a strained attempt to make the point that the *real* hidden Hitler, the Hitler nobody knew, was—surprise!—a paragon of family-values normality, of wholesome German comradeliness: It was Hitler's own, preferred, Hitler explanation. In a sense, it could be said Hitler's strategy has succeeded: He remains a figure that in some profound ways *nobody knows.*

The baby picture served a special purpose in this strategy. Along with the formal, somewhat mournful shots of his parents, it was designed at least in part to counter rumors that Hitler was illegitimate (it was not he but his father who was), that there was some shameful mystery about his family origins, perhaps "Jewish blood." The particular baby picture in question looks like it was taken when Hitler was less than two years old. In a snowy white, Dr. Denton-type outfit, complete with white booties, we see a round-faced, ruddy-cheeked child, a mildly pensive cherub. We could, considering what we know of what became of him, "backshadow" (the useful term coined by the scholar Michael André Bernstein to characterize this dubious but hard-to-resist habit of thought) into his dark, questioning eyes, into those lips pursed into what looks like a pout or a frown, a premonitory, melancholy, even a haunted and hurt expression. We could project upon that impressionable baby face the stirrings of some deep emotional disturbance in embryo. But we could just as easily see there not incipient demonism but a kind of gentleness and sensitivity. We could just as easily predict this child would turn out to be Albert Schweitzer.

One can sense why Lanzmann finds in the impressionable plasticity of the baby pictures a fatally alluring invitation, an invitation that lures the unwary into the seductive labyrinth of ratiocination, the deceptive and dangerous promise of understanding. Dangerous perhaps because at the heart of the labyrinth, the forbidden fruit on this particular tree of knowledge, lurks the logic of the aphorism "To understand all is to forgive all." To embark upon the attempt to understand Hitler, understand all the processes that transformed this innocent babe into a mass murderer, is to risk making his crimes "understandable" and thus, Lanzmann implies, to acknowledge the forbidden possibility of having to forgive Hitler.

It shouldn't be done, Lanzmann insists, it can't be done: Pacing the floor of his office, Lanzmann declaimed: "You can take all the reasons, all the fields of explanation . . . and every field can be true, and all the fields together can be true. But . . . even if they are necessary, they are not sufficient. A beautiful morning you have to start to kill . . . massively."

No, Lanzmann insists, you can't get from there to here. You can't "*engender* the killing, the mass murders, the destruction of six million people," from the baby picture. No finite number of explanatory facts—psychological traumas, patterns of bad parenting, political deformations, personal dysfunctions—can add up to the magnitude of the evil that Hitler came to embody and enact. No explanation or concatenation of explanations can bridge the gap, explain the transformation from baby picture to baby killer, to murderer of a million babies. It is not just a gap, Lanzmann argues; it is an *abyss*.

Fritz Gerlich's Bloody Spectacles

This is a book about those who have searched for a way to bridge that abyss. About the passion of those who construct explanatory bridges, about those who seek to burn them, about the images we project upon the surface of the abyss, about those who become lost in it searching for Hitler. Some have been lost, literally, to memory. I'm thinking in particular of the First Explainers, as I've come to think of them. The heroic anti-Hitler Munich journalists who from 1920 to 1933 (when many were jailed or murdered) bravely went about the daily task of attempting to tell the world about the strange figure who had arisen from the Munich streets to become leader of a movement that would seize power and inscribe a new chapter in the history of evil.

My fascination with these largely forgotten figures, the reporters who were the first to investigate the political and personal life, the criminality and scandals of Hitler and "the Hitler Party," as they astutely called it, began to grow as I first began to pick up echoes and traces of their struggle with Hitler, buried in the footnotes of postwar historians, those attempting to somehow get past the nearly impassable barrier of the Auschwitz Hitler to the Munich Hitler, the Weimar Hitler from which the mass murderer evolved.

My fascination deepened when I came upon a nearly complete collection of flaking and yellowing, seven-decade-old back issues of the anti-Hitler *Munich Post* moldering away in the basement of Munich's Monacensia library archives. They've since been transferred to microfilm, but there was something about communing with the actual crumbling copies of the newspaper Hitler's party called "the Poison Kitchen," issues in which Hitler was a living figure stalking the pages, that served to give me a painfully immediate intimation of the maddeningly unbearable Cassandra-like frustration the *Munich Post* journalists must have felt. They were the first to sense the dimensions of Hitler's potential for evil—and to see the way the world ignored the desperate warnings in their work.

As a journalist, I felt simultaneously a growing awe at what they'd accomplished, how much they'd exposed, and how completely they'd been forgotten. Theirs was the first sustained attempt to fathom the depths of the Hitler phenomenon as it began to unfold. One of the things I hoped to accomplish with this book was to begin in a modest way, at least, to rescue them from the limbo of historical oblivion, to begin to restore their vision of Hitler, a vision that has been, perhaps understandably, obscured by the post-Holocaust retrospective view that focuses primarily on the Berlin Hitler, the Auschwitz Hitler. The vision of the First Explainers was the vision of the men and women who were critical witnesses to the now-lost spectacle of Hitler becoming *Hitler*.

In addition to the courageous reporters and editors of the *Munich Post*, there were others such as Rudolf Olden, Konrad Heiden, and Walter Schaber, the last still alive at age ninety-two and living in Manhattan's Washington Heights when I interviewed him. And Fritz Gerlich, a strange, enigmatic figure of brilliance, courage, and contradiction. The iconoclastic editor of a conservative anti-Marxist, anti-Nazi opposition paper called *Der Gerade Weg* (the right way, or the straight path), celebrated as a journalistic nemesis of Hitler in his time, largely forgotten now, Gerlich was murdered in Dachau for attempting to print a damaging exposé of Hitler five weeks *after* the Nazis had seized power and crushed the rest of the opposition press. A fascinating figure, Gerlich, a scathing Swiftian satirical scourge of Hitler, he possessed an uncanny insight into the racial dynamics of Hitler's pathology. A skeptical historical scholar, Gerlich, nonetheless, came to believe in the prophetic powers of a controversial, probably fraudulent, Bavarian stigmatic and found in her a source of the faith that led him to gamble his life on a last-ditch effort to bring Hitler down with his pen and printing press. With an exposé to end all exposés of Hitler, he hoped: one final story that would shock the public and cause President Paul von Hindenburg to depose the newly installed Chancellor Hitler before it was too late.

It was a desperate gamble that failed. On March 9, 1933, storm troopers burst into Gerlich's newspaper office, ripped his last story from the presses, beat him senseless, and dragged him off to Dachau, where he was murdered on the Night of the Long Knives in June 1934. The nature of the exposé he'd been about to publish—some said it concerned the circumstances of the death of Hitler's half-niece Geli Raubal in his apartment, others said it concerned the truth about the February 1933 Reichstag fire or foreign funding of the Nazis—has been effectively lost to history; it is one of the evidentiary trails I've pursued to the bitter end.

But there was a moment in the course of that pursuit that crystallized for me what I was trying to accomplish with what might seem like a quixotic pursuit of a quixotic lost Hitler exposé: what I wanted to recover as much as the lost exposé. I had managed to track down in Munich one of Gerlich's last living colleagues, Dr. Johannes Steiner, a retired publisher in his nineties who had been a partner in Gerlich's doomed anti-Hitler attack sheet *Der Gerade Weg*. Dr. Steiner's memory of that awful time, particularly the last days of Gerlich, when they were all on the run, was fragmentary. But there was one moment, one memory he'd preserved with frightening clarity for six decades: a memory of the Gestapo and Fritz Gerlich's spectacles. Gerlich's steel-rimmed glasses had become a kind of signature image for the combative newspaper-man among those who knew him in Munich, an emblem almost of his steely determination and clarity of vision.

But after a year in Dachau, after the Gestapo had dragged him out of his cell and shot him in the head on the Night of the Long Knives, Hitler's thugs chose a cruel and chilling way to notify Gerlich's wife, Dr. Steiner recalled. "They sent to his widow, Sophie, Gerlich's spectacles, all spattered with blood."

It's an arresting image, an acknowledgment perhaps of Gerlich as a man who'd seen too much, who knew too much to live, a token of how much his vision was feared and hated by the Hitler inner circle, for having seen through them. Something about that image stayed with me, once I'd heard it, kept me in Munich for weeks paging through the last fragile copies of Gerlich's newspaper and those of the *Munich Post*. It made me want to know more intimately—as much as possible across the abyss—these men who knew Hitler most intimately. It made me want to begin to restore to light the vision they had: the view of Hitler through Fritz Gerlich's bloody spectacles.

The Escape Artist

In a sense, this book is as much about the spectacles, the explanatory lenses through which we look at Hitler, as it is about Hitler. About the way those lenses color, distort, and shape our perceptions. About the way explanatory lenses often project our own preconceptions and agendas upon the shadowy shape-shifting images of Hitler. About the way what we talk about when we talk about Hitler is often not the Hitler of history but the meaning of evil. Not evil as some numinous supernatural entity but evil as a name for a capacity of human nature. To what degree does Hitler represent some ultimate, per-haps never-before-seen extension of that capacity? Or does he represent not a qualitative leap in that capacity but rather a figure whose distinctiveness and importance in this regard have been inflated by the quantity of his victims?

In many ways, it doesn't matter what *word* we choose to apply to Hitler. The use or nonuse of the word "evil" changes nothing about what happened, about how many died. The choice of the word does not change a fact of history, but it is a fact, a facet, a reflection of culture: How we think about Hitler and evil and the nature of Hitler's choice is a reflection of important cultural assumptions and divisive schisms about individual consciousness and historical causation, the never-ending conflict over free will, determinism, and personal responsibility.

That some choose to use the word "evil" for Hitler's choice (no one doubts the *deeds* were evil in the sense of being horrifically, inarguably *bad*, but it's the nature of the mind and motivation of the perpetrator that's in contention) and some choose not to use the word doesn't make the former more virtuous or the latter less. Some historians, such as John Lukacs for instance, exhibit a positive aversion to the discussion of the word or its implications in relation to Hitler. While others, even an atheist such as Hebrew University's Yehuda Bauer, widely regarded as the most authoritative historian of the Holocaust and a polemical foe of "mystification," have little hesitation in using the word "evil." Yehuda Bauer told me he believes Hitler represents "near-ultimate evil," and his choice of the words "near" and "ultimate" are as carefully considered as his choice of the word "evil" is.

I found such choices, the reasons behind them, the assumptions they reflect as worthy of pursuit as the contentious debates over Hitler's ancestry and sexuality, say. In fact, I found the debates over Hitler's ancestry and sexuality worth pursuing *because* they were, beneath the surface, enactments of debates about exactly these questions—the way in which we explain or explain away evil—in disguised form.

In any case, at the very least the word "evil" turned out to be useful in a heuristic sense: as a catalyst, as a Rorschach test, as a way of bringing to the surface crucial distinctions and defining schisms.

One thing that surprised me in the course of speaking to Hitler explainers was that Yehuda Bauer turned out to be in a distinct minority among scholars. I found remarkable, at least at first, the pronounced reluctance of so many of them to call Adolf Hitler evil. It sounds strange even to say that, Hitler having become such an icon, an embodiment, a stand-in for ultimate evil in popular discourse. But that reluctance exposes the imprecision of our thinking on the subject of evil, reflects the difficulty we—both philosophers and laymen—have in defining what evil is, despite an intuitive sense that it exists and must exist in Hitler.

"If *he* isn't evil, who is?" Alan Bullock exclaimed to me. It's a somewhat backhanded endorsement of the idea, one that suggests a kind of definitional desperation in which Hitler is summoned to rescue a term that can't be defined or defended without him. And yet Bullock's exclamatory affirmation is an exception to the logic of most modes of contemporary discourse on both Hitler and evil, modes in which Hitler, ever the escape artist, escapes the category of evil. Yes, Hitler has become a personification of evil in popular culture, to the point where philosophers take pains to deplore what is now called *argumentum ad Hitlerum*—the resort to Hitler to end discussion on everything from capital punishment ("Well, *Hitler* deserved it, didn't he?") to vegetarianism ("It didn't improve *Hitler*'s character, did it?").

But in the realm of scholarship, it's remarkable to discover how many sophisticated thinkers of all stripes find themselves unwilling to find a principled rationale for calling Hitler evil, at least in the strict sense of doing wrong *knowingly*. The philosophical literature that takes these questions seriously makes a distinction between obviously evil *deeds* such as mass murder and the not-always-obvious nature of the *intent* of the doer, preferring the stricter term "wickedness" to describe wrongdoers who do evil deeds *knowing* they are doing wrong. I was drawn to the philosophical literature on the problem of wickedness (such as Alvin Plantinga's symbolic-logic discourse on the theodicy of "transworld depravity") by another defining moment in my encounters with Hitler explainers: my conversation in London with H. R. Trevor-Roper, former Regius Professor of Modern History at Oxford, one of the first and most widely respected postwar Hitler explainers. I'd asked him the deceptively simple question I'd begun asking a number of the Hitler explainers: "Do you consider Hitler consciously evil? Did he know what he was doing was wrong?"

"Oh no," Trevor-Roper declared with great firmness and asperity. "Hitler was convinced of his own rectitude." Hitler was wrong, in other words, dreadfully wrong to be so convinced; his *deeds* were evil, but he committed them in the deluded but sincere belief that he was taking heroic measures to save the human race from the deadly plague he believed the Jews to be. In taking this position, Trevor-Roper is doing no more than affirming the tendency of twenty-three centuries of Western philosophic thought on the question of evil. It is a tendency first articulated in Plato's *Protagoras*, in which it is argued that no man does wrong knowing he's doing wrong but does so only out of ignorance or delusion.

And Trevor-Roper is not alone. Perhaps the most unexpected echo of his "rectitude" argument—evidence that it's more than an academic quibble—is one I found in the excited rhetoric of the chief Nazi hunter in Israel, Efraim Zuroff, the director of the Simon Wiesenthal Center's Jerusalem headquarters. When I asked Zuroff, a big, tough, outspoken Brooklyn-born Israeli, whether Hitler was conscious he was doing wrong, he was even more emphatic than Trevor-Roper. "Of course not!" he practically yelled at me. "Hitler thought he was a doctor! Killing germs! That's all Jews were to him! He believed he was doing *good*, not evil!" To Zuroff, real evil is something he reserved for certain of the war criminals he was hunting, the middle managers of the Holocaust, the ones who participated in mass murder without conviction, for reasons of career advancement, not "banality" but selfish viciousness, cold-blooded personal ambition.

But the most characteristic contemporary escape from calling Hitler evil, escape from calling him a knowing, responsible agent, is the therapeutic evasion, in which Hitler is seen less as consciously evil than as an unconscious *victim*. If evil is defined as conscious wrongdoing, UCLA psychoanalyst and psychohistorian Dr. Peter Loewenberg (who's written cogent and influential studies of the mass psychohistorical trauma afflicting the German populace after the World War I defeat) told me, Hitler can't be said to be consciously evil, because he was so much a prisoner of his unconscious impulses—the dark, chthonic, unanalyzed forces that drove him to mass murder. The unspoken implication is that Hitler was *himself* a kind of victim, a helpless prisoner or pawn of those unconscious Freudian drives. Only a person who has fully owned, made conscious his unconscious impulses can choose evil freely, Loewenberg told me—although I'd suggest this implies that only fully and successfully analyzed clients of Freudian psychoanalysts are capable of committing evil.

One of the continuing subtexts of the conversations in this book is precisely this struggle, this difficulty so many thinkers have of finding a way to call Hitler evil. It's not merely a question of words and names; it's a question about who Hitler really *was*, what his attitude was toward the crimes he committed.

I was particularly drawn to the struggle of a few rigorous philosophers and theologians to find a way to reclaim Hitler for evil (or "wickedness"). It's something theologian Emil Fackenheim is concerned with in his critique of explanation; it's something the philosopher Berel Lang makes a sustained and impressively rigorous case for in his attempt to place Hitler in the context of a "history of evil."

But it was fascinating to observe the discomfort the notion of calling Hitler consciously evil caused in so many thinkers. I have a notion why that might be, a conjecture that occurred to me when thinking about Trevor-Roper's crisp, emphatic rejection of the idea that Hitler was consciously evil; that beneath the Socratic logic of the position might be an understandably human, even emotional, rejection—as simply *unbearable*—of the idea that someone could commit mass murder *without* a sense of rectitude, however delusional. That Hitler could have done it out of pure personal hatred, knowing exactly what he was doing and how wrong it was. Trevor-Roper's position on evil can be looked upon as more than a matter of logic, more than a theory about the nature of evil, but as an article of faith about human nature: an unwillingness to *conceive* of a human nature capable of that degree of conscious wickedness. It was an early indication to me of the way a stance on explanation can serve as consolation.

I don't pretend in this book to offer definitive answers to such ultimate questions. Rather, I'm interested in the range of solutions that a range of thoughtful explainers offer, focusing in particular on the way they construe Hitler's subjectivity, his inwardness, his "thought-world," to make their arguments. "Thought-world" is the useful term Albert Schweitzer employed to describe the object of *The Quest of the Historical Jesus*. Indeed, if there is a model for my approach, it might be Schweitzer's work, published nearly a century ago, once widely known, now rather neglected, a fading copy of which I came across in a secondhand bookstore in Jerusalem at the time I was interviewing theologian Emil Fackenheim and historian Yehuda Bauer. Schweitzer's work helped crystallize what most intrigued me about the controversies over Hitler I'd immersed myself in. It's a work about the attempts to explain another larger-than-life figure in history, Jesus, whose mythic, apocryphal, and supranatural dimensions have, somewhat like Hitler's, interpenetrated and obscured the fragmentary, conflicting scraps of evidence about his actual existence.

I have a sense that the mention of Schweitzer will for many readers conjure up the warm and fuzzy veneration for the sainted doctor who abandoned the comforts of Europe to tend to lepers in equatorial Africa. But there is another Albert Schweitzer, the brilliant, caustically critical historian of theology who sparked a worldwide controversy when his landmark book about Jesus explainers was first published in 1906. This Schweitzer, before he became a doctor, was nonetheless a surgical intellect: He was taking a scalpel to a couple of centuries of efforts to explain Jesus by the methods of modern thought, in particular the "scientific" positivism of German Protestant "Higher Criticism."

Schweitzer's was by contrast a work of explanatory pessimism, if not despair. He argued that the grail of the "quest of the historical Jesus"—to get beneath Jesus' transfiguration by nineteen centuries of post hoc dogma, beneath what those who came later made of him, to who *he* thought he was, his own sense of himself, his thought-world—might be irretrievable now even to the best efforts of historical inquiry. Instead, Schweitzer's examination of attempts to explain Jesus suggested that such theories revealed less about Jesus than they revealed about his would-be explainers and their culture, the kinds of needs their explanations fulfilled.

What they were often doing, Schweitzer believed, was not explaining Jesus but explaining *away* some disturbing unresolved elements in his biography, ones that were discomfiting to the modern sensibility—elements, in particular (from what Schweitzer believed were the earliest sources), that made Jesus look too Jewish, too primitive, too apocalyptic, too resistant to easy assimilation to the "rational religion," the etherealized spirituality of nineteenth-century liberal German Protestantism.

They were, in effect, turning their portraits of Jesus into self-portraits: Jesus as a nineteenth-century liberal German Protestant. I'd argue that Hitler explanations, similarly, are cultural self-portraits; the shapes we project onto the inky Rorschach of Hitler's psyche are often cultural *self*-portraits in the negative. What we talk about when we talk about Hitler is also who *we* are and who we are not.

The Escape from Hitler

Previous examinations of the literature of Hitler explanations have tended to be preliminary brush-clearing operations to make room for the author's own candidate for explicatory primacy. One brilliant exception is a work by Professor Alvin Rosenfeld, chairman of the Jewish Studies Department of Indiana University, but his book *Imagining Hitler* focuses primarily on fictional representations of the Führer—on novels, film, pulp mythologizing.

Gordon Craig and John Lukacs have done great services in their thoughtful studies of the rationalizations of postwar German historians, although in his book *The Hitler of History* Lukacs has an explanatory agenda of his own: discrediting revolution by portraying Hitler as the very model of a modern revolutionary rather than as a "reactionary."

Both Saul Friedländer and Ian Kershaw have produced important works that emphasize multifactorial rather than single-pointed explanations for Hitler, the complex interrelation between Hitler's consciousness, his projected image, and the German people's creation and reception of it. And, more generally, David H. Fischer offers an absolutely invaluable guide in *Historians' Fallacies* to the ways in which the longing for certitude, the wish to have some explanation, has led many to press premises beyond the logic of causality.

If there is one thing that distinguishes my effort from previous literature on the subject, it is my desire to examine the nature of those wishes and longings, the subtexts and agendas of Hitler explanations in face-to-face encounters with some of those engaged in the search for Hitler. Not just with historians and biographers but with philosophers, psychologists, and theologians as well. I am concerned less with defining absolutely the (perhaps irretrievable) truth about Hitler as I am with the meanings projected upon the unknowable, the agendas that shape the accounts of those obsessed with it.

In any case, as I proceeded in this fashion, I found myself surprised and struck, prompted to think more deeply about certain questions, by the kinds of observations, conjectures, and self-revelations that emerged in such face-to-face encounters with the explainers—ones often unexpressed in their published work, ones that might have escaped me or not emerged at all if I'd relied only upon their written words.

I'm thinking, for instance, of George Steiner describing with great candor his anxiety that the highly controversial Hitler character he created in his novel *The Portage to San Cristóbal of A.H.*, a Hitler who had escaped from the bunker to South America, had, in fact, escaped in some way from *him*, from Steiner, had taken on a disturbing life beyond his control. There was Hyam Maccoby, Steiner's intellectual foe, the chronicler of Christian anti-Semitism, explaining why he's come to believe Christmas is "a sinister festival."

There was Emil Fackenheim wrestling out loud with the conflicting impulses: to question God—to demand from God an explanation for Hitler's dreadful succcss—and to limit such questioning, because to hold God fully accountable (to the point of rejecting faith) might violate Fackenheim's own commandment against giving Hitler a "posthumous victory."

There was Alan Bullock, the most scrupulously sober-minded and restrained of Oxford historians, being driven to struggle with the same question—the problem of theodicy, the silence of God—in the vocabulary of mysticism, in terms of Incompleteness, the incompleteness of our understanding of Hitler and the incompleteness of God's omnipotence.

Then there was the wonderful Viennese expatriate Gertrud Kurth supplying me with the missing testimony, perhaps the last word, on Hitler's alleged genital incompleteness—what Bullock calls "the one-ball business"—testimony that seems to pull the rug out from under a number of elaborate psychosexual explanations of Hitler.

I'm thinking as well of the notion of the art of evil that emerged in my conversation with Berel Lang, a conversation that considered the relationship between Hitler's self-image as an artist and the character of the Nazi regime in which evil became a kind of art. And there was the time when David Irving (whom I witnessed revising aloud his "Revisionism") conjured up one of the single most chilling images of Hitler's cold-bloodedness: the moment in the aftermath of the June 1934 Blood Purge when Hitler emerges from a shower and, in effect, brandished his own baby picture, ostentatiously washing off the blood of his victims and declaring himself "clean as a newborn babe."

I'm thinking also of the way firsthand encounters with the explainers led me to seek out some firsthand experience of certain Hitler sites, the most haunting of which—the one that somehow embodied, in its fragmentary ruined desolation, the state of the art, or at least the state of evidence of Hitler explanations—was a shell-blasted ghost town, the ruins of the Austrian village once called Döllersheim in the hill country near the Czech border, a region local Nazis once proudly boasted of as Hitler's "ancestral home."

Döllersheim is the "foul rag and bone shop" of Hitler origin questions, the site of certain curious Hitler-family genealogical ceremonies that were memorialized in the parish register of the Döllersheim church and have been provoking questions and controversies ever since Hitler became a public figure. These questions and controversies may have doomed Döllersheim to its grim fate, blasted out of existence by artillery shells—some claim on Hitler's express order, some claim by the Russians later on—to erase his past from the map.

If the ruins of Döllersheim are an implicit allegory of the escape of Hitler from explanation—the absence or erasure from the record of a factual foundation upon which to construct an explanation—the edifice of contemporary scholarship on the Holocaust can be said to be founded upon an implicit attempt to escape *from* Hitler.

It could almost be said that "two cultures" of Hitler discourse have emerged. While the specter of Hitler looms ever larger as an icon and embodiment of ultimate evil in popular culture, on the other hand, in academic and scholarly literature a focus on Hitler (often characterized as a quaintly "Hitler-centric" perspective) has become increasingly unfashionable and déclassé, regarded almost disdainfully as a relic of the much-reproved Great Man Theory of History. Disparaged in favor of purportedly more sophisticated explanatory modes—Great Abstraction theories, the ones that emphasize "deeper" trends in history, society, and ideology.

While the satiric vision of "Hitler studies" in Don DeLillo's brilliant novel *White Noise* was one of the inspirations for this book (why not take a look at what passes for "Hitler studies" in the academy?), in actuality the study of Hitler (as opposed to the study of the Holocaust) in the academy is notable more for its absence, for Hitler's presumed irrelevance, rather than his presence. The disparagement and diminishment of Hitler's role accords with a phenomenon the historian Michael Howard has observed about explanation in history: Speaking of the efforts to explain the cause of the First World War, Howard noted the tendency to believe that "any event so great must have a cause equally grave or great or deep." Hitler, that Chaplinesque caricature, is surely not grave or great enough. No one could be.

The preference for great and grave abstraction is an explanatory strategy that can itself serve as a kind of consolation. Great abstractions have an appearance of inevitability and irresistibility that can be consoling: Nothing could have prevented the Holocaust. No one's to blame for the failure to halt Hitler's rise. If it hadn't been Hitler, it would have been "someone like Hitler" serving as an instrument of those inexorable larger forces. The alternative is to believe that a single soul had the power and the will to bring about the war and the Holocaust—that a single individual *wanted to;* that the human nature we presumably share with Hitler could have produced such a being. A notion that some might find both irrational and possibly unbearable.

One of the first, most perceptive reviews of postwar Hitler literature took note of this flight, this escape from the person of Hitler into impersonal abstraction. In 1948, less than three years after Hitler's death, Irving Kristol, then a leftist litterateur, later the godfather of neoconservatism, published a remarkably prescient essay in *Commentary* under the title "What the Nazi Autopsies Show." By Nazi autopsies, Kristol meant the first wave of postwar, postmortem examinations of Hitler and the Holocaust—the first attempts to explain Hitler in the light of full knowledge of the magnitude of his crimes. Attempts, Kristol says, that shied away from crediting Hitler with full responsibility and tended to view him as a "pawn" of larger forces.

Kristol speaks of the unpleasant shock he felt upon hearing "the distinguished British historian H. R. Trevor-Roper say in an aside that [Hermann] Rauschning's *Revolution of Nihilism*—that vulgar and sensational book authored by a former Hitler ally—has turned out to be a more reliable portrait of the Hitler regime" than the more sophisticated "prewar explanations which produced the 'delusion,' as Trevor-Roper calls it, that Hitler was only a pawn."

Kristol makes a point of declaring—in support of Trevor-Roper's view that Hitler was no pawn but the "sole maker," prime mover, and final cause of the Final Solution—that "the longer we stare at Nazism, the more our eyes focus on Hitler. . . . Hitler *was* Nazism" (emphasis added). It's an observation which might sound obvious to some but which, in fact, was much disparaged before the war and has become even more disparaged in the past two decades with "functionalists," inevitabilists, and abstractionists arguing Hitler's relative irrelevance to what went on around him. It's a tendency that Saul Friedländer, a believer in complex causality, nonetheless argues has "gone too far" in removing Hitler from the picture.

Explanation as Consolation: Billy Goats and Scapegoats

The continuing controversy over the decisiveness or the importance of Hitler's personal responsibility, his own desire to commit the crimes he committed, is due in part to the doubt that still remains about the origin and nature of that desire. The inaccessibility of the "black box" of Hitler's inwardness has resulted in a consequent inability to assess how much of that inwardness was shaped or constructed by outer forces—the pressures of bad history and bad ideas—and how much it was the product of internal psychology and will, of (one hesitates to use such an inappropriate, old-fashioned-sounding term) bad character, evil inclination, knowingly wicked choice. In part, it is the egregrious failure of psychological and psychoanalytic explanations of Hitler, which have discredited any effort to locate the origins of Hitler's evil within him, within his psyche.

Here Schweitzer on Jesus is a particularly useful model. His long-untranslated doctoral dissertation, "The Psychiatric Study of Jesus," is a fascinating examination of the desperate efforts of fin-de-siècle "scientific psychiatry" to diagnose—at nineteen centuries' distance—the figure of Jesus as a "psychopath" who suffered from clinical delusions, heard voices, claimed to talk to God and foresee the end of the world. Jesus as, thus, a paranoid schizophrenic whose mystery and beliefs could be reduced to a psychiatric case history. Similarly, the long-distance psychoanalytic study of Hitler relies heavily on certain unprovable, poorly corroborated, questionable "facts"—such as Hitler's alleged monorchism, a purported "primal scene," his alleged obsession with his own purported "Jewish blood," his alleged indulgence in an outré excretory sexual perversion. Hitler's psychoanalytic explainers contradict each other and give new life to the old phrase "often in error, never in doubt." Still, if psychoanalytic theories of Hitler are unsatisfying in explaining Hitler, they remind us again of the powerful function of explanation: as consolation, as insulation, protection against having to face not just the inexplicability of horror, but the horror of inexplicability.

Consider, for instance, two particularly revealing explanatory patterns that emerge in the popular and scholarly literature, patterns that involve two remarkable reversals: the tendency to see Hitler as a victim, and the apparent need to find a Jew to blame. Let's begin with a classic instance of the former: Hitler seen through the lens of contemporary American popular culture, Hitler integrated into the explanatory framework of pop victimology—Hitler as a serial killer suffering from low self-esteem. In November 1991, *Unsolved Mysteries*, the enormously popular "reality" TV series, devoted a "special edition" to a topic that was something of a departure from their usual fare of Lindbergh-baby and psychic-healer probes: a special edition devoted entirely to the mystery of "Diabolic Minds." It turned out to be a series of three portraits of possessors of said diabolical minds: Ted Bundy, John Wayne Gacy—and Adolf Hitler.

So there we have it: Hitler as serial killer. An all-time, most prolific one, yes, but basically a kind of workaholic Hannibal Lecter, explicable in the psychobabble of serial-killer pseudoscience as the victim of a dysfunctional family: "He had a stern father and was unable to establish a healthy relationship to his mother," we are told by *Unsolved Mysteries*. Had there been more time, problems with Hitler's "inner child" might have been invoked. But the real "explanation" for Hitler turns out to be that terrifying contemporary plague: low self-esteem. Thus, the segment concluded: "He subjugated and killed millions because he could not overcome his feelings of inferiority."

Silly as it might seem on the surface, the explanation does offer a kind of consolation on a couple of levels. For one thing, it makes Hitler a more familiar figure: We know serial killers, or feel we do by now; we've seen their families on *Geraldo*; they don't spring out of some demonic abyss; some of us are charmed by Hannibal Lecter—if you set aside the cannibalism, he seems like good company. Hitler was far worse, we remind ourselves, but—the implication is—we know his syndrome. That alone, that he *is* a type, not a sui generis singularity, is to some degree comforting.

And beyond that, he's a type we know, we feel a bit sorry for—perhaps even identify with—painful feelings of low self-esteem and bad parental bonds being not uncommon. And even more consoling is the implicit premise that Hitler was a victim/product of a *preventable* syndrome. A better society with better parenting, self-esteem programs in schools, equals no more Hitlers.

Another comic but instructive manifestation, really a kind of barnyard reductio ad absurdum of Hitler psychological explanations, is the Billy-goat Bite Theory, an extremely bloody variant of what might be called the Genital Wound school of Hitler interpretation, a mode of explanation that has at various times been employed to elucidate the prose of Henry James and the sanguinary appetite of Jeffrey Dahmer. It has led some to look for the source of Hitler's evil or pathology in a putatively absent left testicle, in the aftereffects of a case of syphilis, or in a malformation of his penis. Some might say it's the ultimate instance of phallocentric thinking to insist that whatever was wrong with Adolf Hitler had to originate with his genitalia. But genital-wound theories of Hitler have been rattling around in "Hitler studies" for decades.

The billy-goat bite story first came to light in 1981 in a memoir published in Germany under the title *Tödlicher Alltag* (Deadly Routine). Its author, Dietrich Güstrow, who was then a prominent attorney in West Germany, and whose book was widely and respectfully reviewed, tells us that in 1943 he served as a military court-martial defense attorney for a certain Private Eugen Wasner before a secret military tribunal that tried the soldier for "maliciously slandering the Führer." In fact, according to Güstrow, Private Wasner was being tried for an embarrassing *explanation of* Adolf Hitler. According to the lawyer's memoir, the occasion of Private Wasner's slander was a barracks bull session in which Wasner boasted that as a youth he had attended the same school as Adolf Hitler, in Leonding, Austria. Bitter about recent defeats on the eastern front, the private told his buddies, "Adolf has been warped ever since a billy goat took a bite out of his penis."

Wasner proceeded to give a graphic description of the bloody consequences of young Adolf's attempt to prove he could urinate in the mouth of a billy goat—a preposterous story on the face of it. And yet Güstrow declares forty years later, "Regarding the truth of Wasner's report, I never had any doubts." (Subsequently, doubt has been cast upon *Güstrow's* reliability.) But Güstrow goes further than merely vouching for the truthfulness of the story. He makes explicit the implication of Wasner's report: the traumatic billy-goat bite as an explanation for Hitler's subsequent derangement. To Güstrow, that billy-goat bite was—like the single "shudder in the loins" in Yeats's "Leda and the Swan," like the single bite of the apple in Genesis—an act of appetite from which whole histories of sorrow and tragedy would ensue. In a sense, Güstrow's own appetite—his hunger to find in this incident a single satisfying explanation for Hitler's psyche—is more revealing than the uncorroborated, secondhand story he tells about the billy goat. It's an example of the hunger for single-pointed explanation, the yearning to find some decisive turning point, some moment of metamorphosis that can explain Hitler's crimes as the result of a terrible trauma that made him "crazy"—a moment of metamorphosis that could "engender" the Holocaust from Hitler's "craziness" alone rather than his willful determination. Such a yearning tells as much about the explainer as about Hitler. For Güstrow, pillar of the postwar German Federal Republic, believing that a billy-goat bite explains Hitler, that a preposterous, obscene accident created Nazi Germany, can be seen as a way of absolving German society and culture—absolving himself—of implication in Hitler's crimes. The billy goat becomes a kind of *scapegoat* upon which he projects—and thereby purges—his own guilt.

If the Billy-goat Bite Theory is a reductio ad absurdum of the search for Hitler, the range of purportedly more sophisticated psychological explanations is often not much more impressive. Consider the attempt of the renowned Swiss psychoanalyst Alice Miller to portray Hitler as a victim of an abusive father. It was Miller's "book on Hitler's childhood" that so incensed Claude Lanzmann, triggered his tirade on the baby pictures, his incendiary attack on explanation, in my encounter with him. While I would not characterize it as "an obscenity as such" as Lanzmann does, the fifty-five-page Hitler explanation Miller included in *For Your Own Good*, an otherwise admirable plea against corporal punishment of children, had raised serious problems in my mind as well.

In seeking to advance her crusade against the evil of corporal punishment, Miller strains to prove that Adolf Hitler's evil can be traced to brutal corporal punishment by his father. Unfortunately, to accomplish this she employs dubious evidence. (We have mainly Hitler's self-pitying word for it that he was the victim of savage paternal beatings, an account contradicted by some who remembered his father as a far milder sort. In addition, harsh corporal punishment was widespread at the time—Chekhov suffered from paternal beatings, for instance—and only Hitler grew up to be *Hitler*.) Miller proceeds to use dubious evidence in the service of dubious psychologizing: She takes at face value the controversial, unproven theory that Adolf's father's father was a Jew; she argues that Adolf's father's beating his son and the son's subsequent anti-Semitism can be attributed to self-lacerating rage about this putative "Jewish blood." And a final leap from explanation to exculpation actually sees her rising to the *defense* of Hitler's veracity. In seeking to swat away the doubts raised by some about the portrait of Hitler's father as an abuser, she dismisses evidence to the contrary by saying, "As if anyone were more qualified to judge the situation than Adolf Hitler himself."

Yes, and who more deserves our trust and confidence? I recall being stunned when I came across that passage. Here Adolf Hitler himself has been appropriated into the rhetoric of victimology used on behalf of kids talked into accusations of satanic ritual abuse: *Believe the Children*. Believe the child even if he's Adolf Hitler, even if the account of abuse comes not from Hitler as an innocent child but from the adult hatemonger who spoke about his childhood beatings not in some tearful therapeutic confessional but in the *Führerbunker*. Believe him because he was *once* that innocent in the baby picture.

An inadvertently parodic counterpoint to Miller's demonization of Hitler's father can be found in the work of Erich Fromm, an equally respected and even more renowned psychoanalytic thinker, who singles out not Hitler's father but his mother, Klara. Fromm's version of father Alois is not the abusive monster Miller gives us. Fromm assures us that Alois was a well-meaning, stable fellow who "loved life," whose devotion to his honeybees was admirable, and who was "authoritarian" but "not a frightening figure." Instead, Fromm tells us, Hitler's mother Klara was the catalyst of his neuroses. In his retrospective psychoanalysis of Hitler (published in his 1973 book, *The Anatomy of Human Destructiveness*), Fromm confidently assures us that Hitler can be explained by Fromm's own "necrophilous character system" theory, which postulates a love of death and dead bodies and, consequently, the inclination to commit mass murder. Fromm asserts that this "necrophilous development" had its origins in the "malignant incestuousness" of Hitler's attachment to his mother. "Germany became the central symbol for mother," Fromm writes. Hitler's fixations, his hatred for the "poison" (syphilis and Jews) that threatened Germany, actually concealed a deeper, long-repressed desire to destroy his mother.

Fromm's serene confidence in these grandiose abstractions and his unsupported leaps of logic based on them are breathtaking as he proceeds to his conclusion: Hitler's deepest hatred wasn't Jews—it was Germans! Germans symbolized his mother. He made war against the Jews because his real goal was to ignite a worldwide conflagration in order to cause the destruction of Germany—to punish his mother.

Theories of Hitler as a victim of bad parenting (the Menendez defense of Hitler, one could say) are extensions of the common, careless attempt to explain (or explain away) Hitler as a victim of a mental disease, dysfunction, or syndrome—Hitler as "madman," "psychopath," "demented," "criminally insane." All of which tend to exculpate if not excuse the crimes he perpetrated on grounds of what the courts call "diminished capacity," an inability to know right from wrong. Popular notions of Hitler as "the carpet chewer," the thrower of frothing fits, a man not in control of himself but in the grip of some madness, suggest he is someone to be pitied rather than reviled, someone who could have been rescued by therapeutic intervention.

To these mental-illness theories can be added a strain of explanation that attributes Hitler's state of mind to a physical illness, thus removing him even further from conscious culpability. One of the most seriously argued recent versions of these might be dubbed, in view of the Oliver Sacks title: the encephalitic "awakening" hypothesis about Hitler.

A 1975 paper in the *Journal of Operational Psychiatry*, "Hitler's Encephalitis: A Footnote to History," reviewed the widespread reports of "post encephalitic sociopathy" in the medical literature of the 1920s and 1930s, when the phenomenon began to show up. A number of English and European physicians had noted profound personality changes in war veterans who had been stricken with Epidemic Encephalitis in the trenches. Years after they had recovered from the physical symptoms of the disease, they suddenly began to manifest disturbing personality shifts. The literature of the time used terms such as "moral insanity" and "moral imbecility" to describe these post-encephalitic sociopaths. They also noted that these sociopaths weren't classic loners but often were possessed of a manic charisma. The journal cites a 1930 article, "Zur Kriminalitaet der Encephalitiker" in *Acta Psychiatrica*, for instance:

> The post encephalitic moral imbecile is often possessed of cleverness and brilliance . . . an exceedingly plausible and ready liar . . . devoid of all moral and altruistic feelings . . . knows neither shame nor gratitude . . . [displays] viciousness and maliciousness with a gloating over the misfortunes of others . . . a coldly egotistical, vengeful, base, vile impertinence . . . truly explosive outbursts . . . criminal actions . . . wanton destructiveness . . . murder . . . arson . . . mythomania . . . cruelty as well as fraud . . . malicious denunciations . . . grandiloquent and ecstatic states . . . inclination to lie . . . to confabulate past adventures . . . to simulate and deceive.

The author of the 1975 paper is convinced he's found The Answer: He's explained Adolf Hitler's charismatic political persona as product of reawakened disease. However dubious that conclusion, the doctor's list of symptoms captures uncannily well the central contradiction in attempts to explain the duality of Hitler's thought-world: the apparently simultaneous presence of spell-like, unconscious possession ("explosive outbursts . . . ecstatic states") and conscious calculation, cynical manipulation—a dichotomy that the two great English-language Hitler biographers, Alan Bullock and Hugh Trevor-Roper, have debated for decades after Hitler's death.

The 1975 review article takes seriously the notion that Hitler's charisma, the spectacular mass appeal that transformed him from obscure grumbler in the trenches to world-bestriding conqueror, was the product of an infection: "The newly acquired charisma made such individuals, if as gifted, able and ambitious as Hitler, a mortal but as yet unfathomable danger to society." An unfathomable danger but in some ways a more comforting, easier-to-live-with one. The germ theory of Hitler suggests that the source, the magnitude of evil manifested in him, comes not from his humanness (thus implicating ours) but from an external microbial intervention. Unfathomable evil becomes, if not fathomable, diagnosable—indeed, perhaps curable, or at least preventable. The encephalitic-sociopath theory of Hitler is a paradigm of explanation as consolation: the impulse to find a way to avoid facing the possibility that Hitler *chose* to be who he was, that he was a deliberate perpetrator rather than a victim.

But encephalitis is not the only microbe to have been diagnosed as the true explanation of Hitler's criminal derangement. One of the most curious and revealing Hitler explanation quests has been Simon Wiesenthal's persistent if quixotic effort to explain Hitler's psyche as the product of a case of syphilis. For decades, Wiesenthal, famed as the preeminent hunter of Nazi war criminals, tried to track down the spectral spirochete he believed responsible for Hitler with the same relentless determination he applied to tracking escaped SS men in South America.

Wiesenthal's devotion to this of all possible Hitler-explanation theories is puzzling at first glance, because the syphilitic explanation of Hitler, while a frequent feature of prewar rumor and speculation, had long fallen into neglect until Wiesenthal attempted to revive it in the 1980s. His persistent propagation of it is puzzling also because of the particular variant of the story he chose to pursue: one in which the putative source of Hitler's infection was not just a prostitute in the Viennese lower depths (as in some versions of the story) but a specifically *Jewish* prostitute. Her Jewishness then becomes Wiesenthal's explanation for the elusive grail of Hitler studies—the origin of his anti-Semitism. And the syphilis—the mentally deranging effects of the final, tertiary stage of the disease—becomes the source of the deranged virulence of his Jew-hatred. Which makes Wiesenthal's syphilitic-Hitler theory an example of *both* the Hitler-as-victim trend and the concurrent tendency to find a Jew to explain his derangement.

But Wiesenthal was deadly serious in his search for the source of Hitler's putative syphilis. He first heard about the story, he says, from a now-deceased expatriate Austrian doctor who told him that he'd known another doctor from Austria whose father *might* have actually treated Hitler for syphilis. While the thirdhand evidence for the truth of this is sketchy at best, the evidence for the existence of a Jewish prostitute who had sex with Hitler is nearly nonexistent. Yet Wiesenthal seems to abandon the strict standards for evidentiary identification he applies even to despised war criminals to convict—virtually to *create*—this alleged Jewish whore. How does he know she was Jewish? Even if the source was Hitler (perhaps in a statement to the phantom doctor), must we take *his* word here? Is she supposed to have identified herself as Jewish to him in the act? But Wiesenthal accepts it and even suggests it as an explanation for another unresolved mystery in Hitler's biography: the mysterious death of his half-niece Geli Raubal. She killed herself, Wiesenthal told one writer, because Hitler infected her with the syphilis he'd gotten from the supposititious Jewish prostitute.

Consider these other instances of what seems to be the proliferation of Jewish suspects singled out by various explainers as the true source of Hitler's metamorphosis, most often as the true origin of Hitler's anti-Semitism.

Among them we find:

The Seductive Jewish Grandfather Explanation: The conjecture, which has been the subject of a bitter, unresolved debate among historians and biographers for four decades now, that Hitler believed a spectral Jewish seducer impregnated his paternal grandmother, Maria Schicklgruber, fathering Hitler's father and engendering in Hitler a pathological fear that he was poisoned by "Jewish blood"—and a need to exterminate that doubt by exterminating the Jews.

The Seductive Jewish Music Teacher Theory: The belief that the true cause of his half-niece Geli Raubal's death was Hitler's discovery that she was engaged to or impregnated by a figure variously described as a "Jewish music teacher" or "a Jewish violinist" she met in Vienna, whereupon Hitler either drove her to suicide or had her murdered. The corollary of which is that grief or guilt for her death led to his transformation into a grim murderous figure obsessed with vengeance against the Jews. In other words, to parody this interpretive tendency: After Geli's death, it was No More Mr. Nice Guy.

The Bungling Jewish Doctor Theory: The belief that the defining trauma of Adolf Hitler's life was the agony of his mother's death in 1907 when he was eighteen, an agony Hitler witnessed firsthand, an agony caused and prolonged, some believe, by the well-meaning but misguided ministrations of Dr. Eduard Bloch, the Jewish doctor whose alleged malpractice, in one caricature of this explanation, "caused the Holocaust."

Of course, Hitler's own deeply disingenuous effort to trace the origin of his anti-Semitism to a single Jew should not be neglected. In *Mein Kampf* he claims that until he came to Vienna in 1907, when he was eighteen, he had little or no contact with Jews and that he looked upon anti-Semitism as a rather vulgar, déclassé prejudice. Until a kind of revelatory, visionary conversion experience: his first sight of, he asks us to believe, or the first time he came face-to-face with, an *Ostjuden*, an Eastern European Jew in shtetl garb: "Once, as I was strolling through [Vienna's] Inner City," he tells us, "I suddenly encountered an apparition in a black caftan and black earlocks. Is this a Jew? was my first thought . . . but the longer I stared at this foreign face, scrutinizing feature for feature, the more my first question assumed a new form: Is this a German?"

The claim that this shocking apparition, this one Jew, suddenly, powerfully jolted him, opened his eyes to some truth about Jews, into seeing them, as he hadn't before, as alien and threatening—impelled him into searching out the dark truth about their malign influence on the world in anti-Semitic literature—does not survive close examination. It seems, in fact, to be a forged, retrospective construct designed to give the impression that there was some powerful, unmistakable, intrinsic evil essence emanating from this Jew that shocked Hitler into awakening out of a previous innocence about Jews in general. When, in fact, the scholar Helmut Schmeller has pointed out the presence in Linz, where Hitler had spent his youth before Vienna, of a rabidly anti-Semitic newspaper, the *Linzer Fliegende Blätter*, which featured malicious caricatures of caftaned and earlocked Jews. It's likely, then, that, had there been any such first encounter in Vienna, it would have been construed, seen through the lens of Hitler's previous familiarity with sinister caricatures of Ostjuden.

But there is something *echt* Hitler, one might say, in the spiteful focus on a single hapless wandering Jew guilty of nothing more than wearing traditional garb; in the maliciously spiteful delight he takes in making it seem that there might be, somewhere still living, perhaps reading his words, a single Jew who bears responsibility for his murderous hatred, who made Hitler Hitler. It is a cautionary instance, a warning against the perils of shifting the responsibility for Hitler's hatred from Hitler himself to some person, trend, or tendency supposedly responsible for it.

A most recent instance of this explanatory tendency focuses on the behavior of a few Jewish Bolsheviks in Munich back in 1919. It is an inference about Hitler's "crystallization," as John Lukacs calls it in *The Hitler of History*. It's an inference Lukacs draws from some recent studies of Hitler's behavior in the murky nine-month period after he returned to Munich from the army hospital in Pasewalk in January 1919 and before he joined the embryonic Nazi Party in September 1919 and emerged transformed into an electrifying charismatic hatemonger.

Most Hitler explainers have him undergoing a transformation, metamorphosis, crystallization, whatever you choose to call it, before he returned to Munich in 1919: as far back as Vienna during his "lost years," or in any case not later than November 1918 at Pasewalk, where Hitler himself claimed he received a visionary impetus to redeem Germany's betrayal by Jews and Bolsheviks. But a recent book by an Austrian scholar, Brigitte Hamann's *Hitlers Wien*, argues strenuously from an exhaustive study of the extant testimony that there is little reliable evidence of Hitler expressing anything but friendly feelings for Jews during his sojourn in Vienna (contradicting those historians who believe the claim by the anti-Semitic pornographer Lanz von Liebenfels— that Hitler visited his Vienna offices in 1909 and personally expressed to him his admiration for Liebenfels's scurrilous anti-Semitic hate sheet *Ostara*).

But certain recent, ambiguous discoveries in Munich archives have led some scholars to argue that when Hitler returned to Munich in early 1919, he still lacked the passionate intensity of the sort he did not display until the autumn of that year when he joined what became the Nazi Party. One piece of evidence adduced for this view documents Hitler's successful candidacy for a position on the soldier's council in a regiment that remained loyal to the short-lived Bolshevik regime that ruled Munich for a few weeks in April 1919. Another is a piece of faded, scratchy newsreel footage showing the February 1919 funeral procession for Kurt Eisner, the assassinated Jewish leader of the socialist regime then in power. Slowed down and studied, the funeral footage shows a figure who looks remarkably like Hitler marching in a detachment of soldiers, all wearing armbands on their uniforms in tribute to Eisner and the socialist regime that preceded the Bolshevik one.

Hitler a designated mourner for a Jewish socialist? Even if true, does his presence in that army detachment or his candidacy for a loyalist regimental post prove anything about his convictions or lack of them at the time? Does it prove that—if he wasn't a *sympathizer* with Jewish socialists—he was at least still an empty vessel lacking the hate-filled rage at Jews and Marxists he manifested a few short months later? Was Hitler still a man without qualities at that late date?

John Lukacs views evidence such as this as testament to his belief that Hitler's ideas were still "inchoate" as late as March 1919 and that he lacked passionate conviction until something happened to "crystallize" it in April: the brief bloody advent of the hardline Bolshevik regime in Munich that succeeded the murdered Eisner's democratic socialists and that, also, prominently featured Jewish leaders. This short-lived Bolshevik regime became notorious for the summary execution of some prominent right-wing nationalists (members of the wealthy occult racist Thule Society who bankrolled the birth of what became the Nazi Party). A regime that was itself overthrown by right-wing militia forces who visited even more bloody reprisals on the Bolsheviks.

All of which leads Lukacs to argue that "it is at least possible (in my opinion probable)" that what crystallized Hitler the inchoate into Hitler the hate-monger and scourge of Jews "were his experiences during the winter and spring of 1918–1919: the German collapse, but even more, his witnessing of the ridiculous and sordid episode of the Munich Soviet Republic with its Jewish and lumpen intellectuals et al."

There are a couple of problems with this conjecture. First, there is no need to believe that Hitler's "allegiance" to the socialist regime was anything more than pro forma. His presence as a designated mourner could be little more than a case of a soldier—in a phrase that later became infamous—"following orders." Either that or acting in an undercover intelligence capacity on behalf of right-wing officers in the army, a role he might have been playing when he ran for a position on the soldier's council, since he proceeded to inform on his "comrades" to the nationalist regime that succeeded the Bolsheviks. He was, of course, playing an undercover role in September 1919 when he first visited a meeting of what soon became the Nazi Party.

The other problem with Lukacs's conjecture—that Hitler didn't "crystallize" until April 1919 when he witnessed the "ridiculous and sordid" behavior of Jewish Bolsheviks—is the unspoken implication. It's one Lukacs himself is too sophisticated to endorse explicitly, but it's there in the tone of his condemnation of the "ridiculous and sordid" behavior of Jews and intellectuals in the brief reign of the Munich Soviet regime: that what crystallized Hitler was *something deplorable done by Jews*. That if those "Jewish and lumpen intellectuals et al." had only behaved better, Hitler might not have become Hitler. That up until that point he might have gone on mildly disliking Jews, but the horrors of the Jewish Bolshevik rule (barely three weeks! a handful of casualties!) gave birth to a genocidal monster. Made Hitler's transformation from mildly anti-Semitic slacker to mass murderer of Jews at least "understandable." It is this kind of understanding that makes Claude Lanzmann's crusade against *all* explanation—emotionally at least— "understandable." Particularly when we repeatedly find attempts to explain Hitler focusing not on what *Hitler* did but on what Jews did.

Some of the more sophisticated postwar explainers avoid the tactic of trying to find a Jew who personally affronted or aggrieved Hitler but instead find reasons to point fingers at Jews Hitler never knew. George Steiner, for instance, in his disturbing novel, *The Portage to San Cristóbal of A.H.*, aroused angry attacks from some fellow Jews over the way his fictional Hitler explains himself as the product of what might be called Jewish mental inventions, those of three Jews in particular: Moses, Jesus, and Karl Marx. Steiner's Hitler argues that the tolerance, the secret approval, the permission he received from the rest of the world to exterminate the Jews can be explained by the universal hatred mankind has for the Jewish "invention of conscience," for the torment inflicted on man by the ethical demands of Moses, Jesus, and Marx, three Jews guilty of the threefold "blackmail of transcendence."

(What's striking about the efforts to find a Jew to "blame" is the neglect it entails of a far more obvious class of suspects as decisive sources of Hitler's anti-Semitism: other anti-Semites. While Daniel Jonah Goldhagen in *Hitler's Willing Executioners* offers an exhaustive array of nineteenth-century German anti-Semitic predecessors to Hitler, there is perhaps an even more important

American source of Hitler's hatred of Jews. A crucial source of his vision of a Jewish world conspiracy and a perhaps crucial source of funding for Hitler's own conspiracy to seize power in Germany: Henry Ford. It's remarkable how easily—or conveniently—Ford's contribution to Hitler's success has been lost to memory in America. It wasn't lost to Hitler, who demonstrated his gratitude by placing a life-size oil portrait of the American carmaker on the wall of his personal office in party headquarters in Munich and by offering, in the twenties, to send storm troopers to America to help Ford's proposed campaign for the presidency. The worldwide publication of Ford's vicious anti-Semitic tract, *The International Jew*, which Hitler and the Nazis rhapsodically read, promoted, and distributed in Germany, the influence of Ford's work and fame—he was an icon of the Modern Age in Germany—helped validate for a gullible German public Hitler's malignant vision of the sinister "Elders of Zion" Jewish conspiracy.)

With Steiner's threefold "blackmail of transcendence," we've come a long way to a far more rarefied and sophisticated realm of explanation than the billy-goat and encephalitic-sociopath theories. But I am not sure all would agree it's brought us closer to satisfactorily explaining Hitler. Still, there is an earnestness in Steiner's search for an answer I cannot gainsay—an earnestness, a near desperation apparent in the work of a number of the explainers I respected, however skeptical I might be of their explanations. I found myself empathizing in particular with Simon Wiesenthal, in his eighties when I spoke with him, taking time away from his restless hunt for the last living escaped Nazi war criminals to try to hunt down the last, lost traces of that syphilitic Jewish prostitute story, the supposedly historical episode that Wiesenthal believes can prevent Hitler's escape from explanation.

It's clear that Wiesenthal desperately wanted to believe in this phantom woman, this spectral Jewish succubus purportedly responsible for Hitler's metamorphosis, despite the lack of any real evidence for her existence. If he could find the proof for it, he once told an interviewer, "I would be very happy because this would give the whole story of Hitler and the Jews a different picture." Would it really, even if it were true? What's the explanation for his focus on such a shaky conjecture? Even if he found the phantom Jewish prostitute, somehow identified her as the carrier, the bearer of the germ of Hitler's anti-Semitism, what could be the point? Wouldn't it inevitably tend to do something utterly unjust: make it seem as if the whole weight of the Holocaust should come down on the fragile shoulders of one poor woman of the streets?

One answer is that, yes, it *is* utterly unjust, but that, for someone like Wiesenthal who faced the horror in person, felt the horrific force of the hatred that killed millions all around him, it might in some way be preferable to have an unfounded explanation of that hatred than an utterly inexplicable hatred.

Perhaps for him bad logic, a flawed explanation for an unbearable tragedy, is preferable to no logic. The Jewish prostitute story might be cold comfort but some consolation.

The Lost Safe-Deposit Box

In taking note of agendas beneath the surface of explanations, I don't wish to seem unsympathetic to explainers who seek solace in some certainty rather than none. Indeed, the hope of finding some satisfactory way of explaining Hitler was what initially drew me to the literature, an impulse similar to Simon Wiesenthal's—the hope that I could track down something, somewhere, something buried in some archive, in some dying witness's memory, in some long-lost unpublished memoir, in some document never seen before, in some connection never made before, at the end of some tantalizing evidentiary trail never exhaustively explored before, a glimpse of some truth, some answer to the question "What made Hitler *Hitler?*"

Two factors, two progressive realizations, led me to shift course. First, there was a recognition, a concession to the reality of evidentiary despair, the evidentiary impoverishment Yehuda Bauer had described: the fact that there are certain crucial Hitler questions that, because of the incompleteness of the evidence, might never be resolved with any certitude. And second was my growing curiosity about another, contradictory phenomenon: the remarkable confidence, despite the shakiness of the evidence, of so many schools of explanation. And not just among scholars: I found it fascinating how many educated people cited Alice Miller's Hitler explanation as gospel, for instance, despite its dubious premises; remarkable how often, in discussing the subject with nonspecialists, how confident so many seemed that they'd figured Hitler out, usually citing one book they'd read, such as Miller's or Erich Fromm's or one apocryphal theory such as the "Jewish blood" or the sexual-perversion story. My own experience had been that the more I looked into such stories, into the range of explanations and the evidence to substantiate them, the less certain I became. But it began to seem to me that the less people knew, the more important to them it was to seem certain about Hitler, to be able to dismiss any mystery with simplistic pronouncements such as "he was a paranoid" or a pawn of big-business interests—much the way he had been dismissed and disparaged and underestimated before 1933. I became fascinated with this phenomenon, with the recurrent abandonment, when it came to Hitler, of "negative capability" (the quality first defined by John Keats as the ability to tolerate uncertainty without "irritable reaching" for certainty). I was stunned by what seemed to be a compulsive assertion of certainty, or of contradictory certainties, by the psychohistorians in particular. It was Hitler's *father!* No, it was Hitler's *mother* who caused the trouble! It was his missing testicle! No, it was a primal scene! "Irritable reaching" devolved into a desperate lurching after a single answer, a single person, none of which on closer examination was nearly sufficient or convincing.

All of which led me to shift my focus—with Schweitzer's *Quest* as a model—from a search for the one single explanation of Hitler to a search for the agendas of the searchers, an attempt to explain the explainers. From hoping I could find some previously unknown ultimate truth about Hitler to the more modest hope of critically assessing the claims of some explainers and seeing what I could learn from the struggle of those I admired. Finding in the efforts of scholars and explainers of all sorts if not *the* truth about Hitler, then *some* truths about what we talk about when we talk about Hitler. What it tells us about Hitler, what it tells us about ourselves.

"The Nazi genocide is somehow central to our self-understanding," Michael André Bernstein has written. It could be said as well that one's way of understanding or explaining Hitler can reflect a characteristic way of understanding the nature of the self. In particular, a position on the decisiveness of Hitler's personal role in the Holocaust frequently reflects a position on the possibility or relevance of autonomous agency, of free will, of freedom to choose evil, and responsibility for the consequences of such a choice.

"So many modernist thinkers wish to persuade us," Robert Grant, a lecturer on political philosophy at the University of Glasgow, has written, "that our subjectivity," our ability to choose, our reasons for choosing a course of action, are "wholly contingent, a mere epiphenomenon, historical deposit or social construct, in short an illusion and the real source of our actions and motivations lie elsewhere." Elsewhere in Great Abstractions, in deeper "inevitable" forces of history that make Hitler, that make us, nothing but particles borne forward on waves of powerful forces that make our power to act or choose on our own a virtual illusion. And absolve Hitler, absolve us, of responsibility for such illusory choices.

It might be said that the marginalization of Hitler in contemporary thought is an analogue of the "death of the author" vogue in contemporary literary theory: the Holocaust as a "text" produced not by human agency but somehow, autonomously, inevitably, by culture and language.

Even among some "intentionalists" who believe Hitler's desire to commit genocide was decisive, that intention is often portrayed as less a knowing choice than something shaped, *dictated to him*, by irresistible internal or external pressures beyond his power to resist to intend otherwise.

Of course, Hitler's will, his intention and choice alone were, if necessary, not sufficient for his success. As sophisticated explainers such as Saul Friedländer and Ian Kershaw emphasize, his success was the product of multiple

factors—of the interaction and interrelationship between Hitler and other historical figures and forces including the Nazi Party, the German people, and the
complicity and passivity of those in power inside and outside Germany.

But those forces, too, are necessary but not sufficient, and the tendency
of much recent literature has been to deny and diminish Hitler's freedom to
choose, to have chosen, the murderous course he did. Denying him that freedom permits him another kind of escape, an escape from responsibility.

In examining these questions, in thinking about my own role, I'd cite a
remark made to me by Milton Himmelfarb. In an article I wrote for *The New
Yorker* on Hitler theories and the Bullock/Trevor-Roper dispute over Hitler's
"sincerity," I'd referred to him as "the scholar, Milton Himmelfarb." When I
met the author of the important—indeed, defining—polemic "No Hitler, No
Holocaust" in his White Plains, New York, home, he gently and with great
humility suggested he'd like to amend the record. No, he told me, he didn't
think of himself as a scholar. He was attached to no university. Rather, when
he thought of how he'd describe himself, he conjured up for me the name of
a discount-clothing chain in the New York area called Syms, one that heavily
advertised itself with the slogan "an educated consumer is our best customer."
With a wry grin, Himmelfarb told me he thought of himself less as a scholar
than as "an educated consumer of scholarship." What I've attempted in this
book is to approach not all but certain aspects of Hitler scholarship with the
eye of an educated consumer. This is a selective and subjective study, focusing on certain currents and subcurrents, certain thinkers whose work I was
drawn to exploring in depth and often in person. I have many regrets about
others I would have liked to have spoken directly with, and several more volumes of this kind could well have been written without exhausting the subject,
although not without exhausting this writer.

In any case, if the particular nature of the way this Himmelfarbian consumer was educated has any bearing upon the book that resulted it may lie
in a predisposition to Empsonian ambiguity and uncertainty rather than the
certainties of theory. A preference for close reading (of documents, memoirs,
police reports) and for close listening (to the voices of the explainers) in an
effort to hear the unspoken subtext, the significant elision, the hidden agendas,
conflicts, and in particular the doubts beneath the surface—to sense the nature
of the longing that drives the explainers and the kinds of solace explanations
offer.

Consider, in this respect, one further excursion into a particularly poignant
subcurrent of Hitler-explanation apocrypha in which the sense of something
missing, something lost, something escaped finds an echo in a deeply resonant, recurrent image: the lost safe-deposit box. It's remarkable how often it
turns out that the evidentiary trails of certain arcane, apocryphal, but persis-

tent Hitler explanations disappear into a limbo that is not exactly a dead end so much as a lost end, the dead-letter box of historical truth: the lost safe-deposit box. A place where allegedly revelatory documents—ones that might provide the missing link, the lost key to the Hitler psyche, the true source of his meta-morphosis—seem to disappear beyond recovery.

Take the case of the lost Hitler exposé of Fritz Gerlich: the last stifled effort by the last of the anti-Hitler Munich journalists left at large in the weeks fol-lowing the Reichstag fire; a desperate attempt to get into print a purportedly devastating Hitler scandal in time to wake up the world to the truth about the new Reichschancellor before it was too late.

But it *was* too late, as I've noted. Gerlich's final exposé was ripped off the presses by a squad of SA storm troopers on March 9, 1933, just as Gerlich's newspaper *Der Gerade Weg*—then the last surviving, openly anti-Hitler paper in Germany—was about to go to press. Because of the respect Gerlich had earned from his contemporaries both for his courage and for his intellectual integrity, a mystique has grown up around the lost scoop, about its content and its ulti-mate fate. In fact, it's developed a kind of survival myth of its own—about the escape and survival of the lost truth about Hitler. The lost Gerlich scoop has become a symbol for all the lost secrets about Hitler, for the dark explanatory truths whose revelation might have—but did not—save history from Hitler.

No copy of Gerlich's investigation has ever come to light, but there are at least two stories about copies of the scoop escaping. According to the postwar biography of Gerlich by his colleague Erwin von Aretin, while the Brownshirts were busy sacking the place, a duplicate set of Gerlich's press-ready copy and the documentary material supporting it was spirited out of the newspaper offices by a Count Waldburg-Zeil. Von Aretin reports that Waldburg-Zeil car-ried the materials off to his estate north of Munich and buried them on the grounds for safekeeping. But, Von Aretin dishearteningly adds, "during the war, Waldburg-Zeil dug them up and destroyed them because they were too dangerous to possess."

Nonetheless, there is a second survival story about the fate of Gerlich's final exposé, a more open-ended one. One of Gerlich's last surviving colleagues, Dr. Johannes Steiner, directed me to this story. Dr. Steiner was the one who pro-vided me with the unforgettable image of Gerlich's bloody spectacles. He put me back on the trail of the lost exposé by referring me to the son of Gerlich's biographer, the late Von Aretin. The son, Professor Karl-Ottmar Freiherr von Aretin, had become a historian in his own right, specializing in aspects of the German resistance in Munich and Bavaria. He had a distinct memory of his father telling him about what sounds like the escape of a *different* set of Gerlich documents from the ones Waldburg-Zeil destroyed.

According to the younger Von Aretin's státement to me:

There was a state's-attorney inquiry into the matter of Geli Raubal. My father had a copy of the documents on his desk [in Gerlich's office] in February 1933. When the situation became difficult, my father gave these documents to his cousin and co-owner of the *Münchener Neueste Nachrichten*, Karl Ludwig Freiherr von Guttenberg, in order to bring them to Switzerland and deposit them in a bank safe. As my father remembered, these documents showed that Geli was killed by order of Hitler. Guttenberg carried the documents to Switzerland but kept secret the number of the safe-deposit account because he thought it would be too dangerous to tell anyone. Guttenberg engaged in the 20 July 1944 [anti-Hitler coup attempt], was killed in 1945, and took the secret [of the account number] with him to the grave.

The implication: somewhere in Switzerland, perhaps even now, a lost key to Hitler lies locked away in a long-neglected safe-deposit box, slowly turning to dust. But this is not the only instance of a tenuous evidentiary trail leading to an ambiguous survival in a lost safe-deposit box. The image, or a close variant of it, recurs several times in Hitler-explanation lore.

There is the purported fate of the Pasewalk case notes, for instance, a story about the doctor who treated Hitler's hysterical blindness in 1918—the treatment that, some Hitler explainers believe, might have been responsible for Hitler's metamorphosis from insignificant, obscurity-seeking corporal to charismatic, mesmerizing führer-in-the-making. Hitler biographers Rudolph Binion and John Toland have both adopted a version of the speculation first put forward in thinly veiled fictional form by émigré German novelist (and friend of Franz Kafka) Ernst Weiss, who argued that the episode represented one of the great tragic, Kafkaesque ironies of history. Weiss claimed to have learned, through sources in the émigré community, the true story of the "voice" Hitler heard at Pasewalk in the feverish extremity of his breakdown at the time of the German surrender, the voice Hitler claims to have heard summoning him to a mission to avenge Germany. It was that moment, that vision in which, Lucy Dawidowicz believes, Hitler defined the mission of his life: to murder the Jews.

According to Weiss's account, much of which Toland and Binion and the German historian Ernst Deuerlein have lent credence to (although others, such as Robert Waite, dispute it), that voice was actually the voice of a staff psychiatrist at Pasewalk, a Dr. Edmund Forster, who sought to cure Hitler's hysterical blindness by putting him in a hypnotic trance and implanting the posthypnotic suggestion that Hitler had to recover his sight to fulfill a mission to redeem Germany's lost honor. Weiss seems to have befriended Dr. Forster when Forster fled Germany after 1933, shortly before his suicide. According to Weiss's novelistic account of Forster's story, the Pasewalk psychiatrist had discovered, in the course of his hypnotic sessions with Hitler, a profound and shameful secret of Hitler's psyche, the key to his pathology. A secret so shameful that as soon as Hitler took power, Forster was pursued, harassed, and ultimately driven to his death by the Gestapo, which was determined to recover from him his case notes on the medical treatment of Patient Hitler at Pasewalk, to silence him, and to erase that secret from history.

According to Weiss's fictionalized account, a fearful Forster, desperate to preserve the truth about Hitler from destruction, crossed the border to Switzerland shortly before his death and locked the Pasewalk case notes in a safe-deposit box in a bank in Basel. Purportedly quoting Forster, Weiss says, "The most important part [of Forster's records are] the part concerning [Hitler's] relationships with women." Weiss has Forster giving special treatment to this secret: "'I wrote it down in hieroglyphics which no one but me can decipher.'" Unfortunately, Forster killed himself before confiding whatever secret he may have learned, and with Weiss dead, we cannot be sure how much he fictionalized.

Forster's death again leaves us with no key to his Swiss safe-deposit box and no key to Hitler, leaves us with the image of the truth stranded, abandoned, or moldering away in some basement bank vault, perhaps untranslatable even if recovered, because of Forster's hieroglyphics.

The unreadable cipher in the lost safe-deposit box: an irresistible metaphor for the explanation of Hitler that has eluded us, for the irretrievable enigma of his psyche. There have been similar disappearances of other phantom proofs purportedly crucial to deciphering Hitler's mind. There were, for instance, Hitler's alleged pornographic drawings of Geli Raubal, which were said to have disclosed the truth about his psychosexual nature, drawings which, once recovered from a blackmailer, were said to have disappeared into a safe in Nazi Party headquarters in Munich. There was the rumored "Austrian secret-police dossier" about Hitler's alleged Jewish ancestry, said in one version of the apocryphal story to have been stashed in a safe in the home of the Austrian chancellor's mistress until stolen by Hitler's minions.

We are clearly in the realm of folklore here, not verifiable history. And yet there's something in the image common to these tales, the image of the locked safe or the lost safe-deposit box that seems to capture in the way folklore sometimes can—and history sometimes can't—some deeply felt collective longing, a shared myth about a figure who was himself as much a piece of self-created folklore as history.

Some light may be shed on the deeper source of this image by its manifestation in a different context. Once, in the course of investigating a shady cancer-cure clinic south of Tijuana, Mexico, I came upon a smooth-talking "metabolic technician" who told me he was seeking to recover a lost cancer-cure formula devised by a certain Dr. Koch, a formula said to have disappeared after Koch's death in the 1930s. The metabolic technician believed he knew what had become of it, however; he'd had some indications that the formula for this philosopher's stone of health might still be found "in a safe-deposit box in a bank in Detroit," although he worried about reports that—like the secret of Hitler's sex life hieroglyphically entombed in a safe-deposit box by the Pasewalk mesmerist—the formula might be in code, and that without the actual begetter of the formula, the safe-deposit box might contain nothing but an indecipherable matrix of meaningless numbers.

These lost safe-deposit stories clearly serve as expressions of anxiety about—and talismans against—an otherwise apparently inexplicable malignant evil. In fact, despite the despairing tone of the safe-deposit box myths, they represent a kind of epistemological *optimism*, a faith in an explicable world. Yes, something is missing, but if we don't have the missing piece in hand, at least it exists somewhere. At least somewhere there's the lost key that *could* make sense of the apparently motiveless malignancy of Hitler's psyche or the cancer cell. A missing piece, however mundane or bizarre—a Jewish grandfather, even a billy-goat bite—but something here on earth, something we can contain in our imagination, something safely containable within the reassuring confines of a box in a Swiss bank. Something not beyond our ken, just beyond our reach, something less unbearably frightening than inexplicable evil.

When the recent controversy over Swiss-bank holdings of gold and valuables stolen from murdered Jews hit the press, for a brief moment a part of me felt a frisson of what I knew was false hope. That somehow, some lost and long-forgotten safe-deposit box would come to light and yield up one or another of the apocryphal grails of Hitler explanations. That the search for the stolen legacies of the dead would somehow materialize the missing key, the lost link needed to bridge the abyss between the baby picture and the baby killer. Needless to say, this was not a realistic expectation. But it made me think of a term of art in the philosophic literature on epistemology, the study of the nature and limits of knowledge: "the mind of God." It's a term used even by nonbelievers to express the idea of a realm in which the truths that elude human investigation—the answers to mysteries we fail to solve for lack of evidence—exist, even if they exist beyond our grasp. That's what the lost safe-deposit box folklore gestures at: the missing explanation of Hitler locked up tight in the inaccessible, indecipherable mind of God.

PART ONE

THE BEGINNING OF
THE BEGINNING

In which theories about Hitler's "racial origins" become the
origin of a debate about Hitler's psyche

CHAPTER 1

The Mysterious Stranger, the Serving Girl, and the Family Romance of the Hitler Explainers

In which the author makes an expedition to the Hitler family "ancestral home" and meditates upon the romantic life of Maria Schicklgruber, as imagined by historical fantasists

I was ready to give up and turn back. A surprise mid-autumn snowstorm had blown out of Russia and was blanketing Central Europe, making the relatively primitive back roads of this backwoods quarter of Austria increasingly impassable.

We were only about twenty miles short of our objective, but our rented Volkswagen was beginning to skid, once bringing us perilously close to the brink of one of the woody ravines that crisscrossed the otherwise featureless reaches of snow-covered farmland stretching north to the Czech border.

I'd timidly suggested to my Austrian researcher, Waltraud, who was at the wheel, that we ought to consider abandoning our quest for the day because of the risk. But she wanted to press on, declaring that, as a native of the mountainous Tyrol, she had experience navigating the far more treacherous mountain roads of the Alps.

Not entirely reassured, I nonetheless felt there was something appropriate about the blizzardy circumstances of this venture: The storm we were heading into was an autumnal version of the blitz of snow that had halted Hitler's panzer divisions just short of Moscow in the winter of 1941—the beginning of the end for him. The place we were fighting through the snow to find—a ghost town called Döllersheim—was the beginning of the beginning: the primal scene of the mysteries behind the Hitler family romance.

The disappearance, the apparently deliberate *erasure*, of Döllersheim is one of the most peculiar aspects of the deeply tangled Hitler-genealogy controversy. The tiny village was literally blasted off the map and out of existence sometime after Hitler annexed Austria. An effort—some partisans in the controversy contend—to erase all traces of certain irregular and disreputable Hitler family events that took place there. Irregularities that have long cast a shadow over accounts of Hitler's origins. Irregularities that had given rise to repeated pilgrimages to Döllersheim in the prewar years by journalists and other interested investigators, news of which invariably provoked Hitler into near-apoplectic rages.

"People must not know who I am," he was reported to have ranted when he learned of one of the early investigations into his family history. "They must not know where I come from."

And there are those who insist that after 1938 he made Döllersheim pay the price for being the site of such inquiries, made it *disappear*. Whatever the cause of the erasure, there can be little doubt of its effectiveness. That morning in Vienna, as the snow began gusting in from the east, I searched in vain for a map that still had the hamlet of Döllersheim on it, until I happened on a little shop belonging to a rare-book dealer who was able to dig up a musty 1896 German atlas of the world which still had the hamlet of Döllersheim on its map of Austria. While the map showed no roads, it did provide a means of triangulation: The dot on the map for Döllersheim was just north of a bend in the river Kamp and just east of another little dot on the map called Ottenstein.

Ottenstein: That name conjured up a peculiarly memorable phrase, "scion of the seigneurial house of Ottenstein." This Heathcliffian heroic epithet appears in a catalog of candidates—list of suspects, one might say—for the shadowy figure at the heart of the Hitler family romance: the man who fathered Hitler's father. The identity of the man who impregnated a forty-two-year-old unmarried serving woman named Maria Schicklgruber sometime in late 1836 was not disclosed on the baby's baptismal certificate filed in her parish church in Döllersheim when the child (christened Alois Schicklgruber) was born on June 7, 1837. That blank line on the baptismal certificate, in the space where the name of the father of the child should be, has become a kind of blank screen onto which journalists, intelligence agencies, historians, psychoanalysts, and other fantasists have projected a wild array of alternative candidates to the man named in the official Nazi genealogies as Hitler's paternal grandfather, Johann Georg Hiedler.

Hundreds and hundreds of pages in scores of books have been devoted to trying to divine the sexual choice behind that blank line, to read the mind of the woman who made the choice: Maria Schicklgruber. She was, in fact, the first of three generations of Hitler-related women whose unfathomable erotic liaisons cast a powerful spell over Hitler's life—and over his subsequent biographers. After Maria, there was Hitler's mother, Klara, and then his half-niece Geli Raubal. Three women—all, interestingly, serving girls—whose greatest service has been to the Hitler explainers.

The flavor of the speculation over Maria Schicklgruber's sexual choices is captured by the partial catalog of candidates for the role of Hitler's paternal grandfather offered by the impressionable German biographer of Hitler, Werner Maser.

"Various candidates have been suggested," Maser writes. In addition to the official nominee on the Nazi Party family tree for Hitler, Johann Georg Hiedler, and Maser's own candidate, Johann Georg's wealthier brother Johann Nepomuk Hiedler, there are "a 'Graz Jew' by the name of Frankenberger, a scion of the seigneurial house of Ottenstein, and even a Baron Rothschild of Vienna." Maser doesn't believe Adolf Hitler was a Frankenberger, an Ottenstein, or a Rothschild descendant (the latter astonishing suggestion seems to be traceable to the pre-*Anschluss* anti-Hitler Austrian secret police). But he has concocted an elaborate theory of rural sexual intrigue and greed over a legacy to bolster the candidacy of his man, Johann Nepomuk Hiedler.

One can argue with Maser's Brueghelian explanation of the Döllersheim ambiguities, but it's hard to deny his summary of the confused state of Hitler studies on the paternal-grandfather question: "If there is one fact on which at least some biographers are agreed, it is that Adolf's paternal grandfather was not the man officially regarded as such, namely the journeyman miller Johann Georg Hiedler." (A "fact" only "some" biographers agree upon is hardly a fact to rely upon.) The more judicious Alan Bullock says, "In all probability, we shall never know for certain who Adolf Hitler's grandfather, the father of Alois, really was. It has been suggested that he may have been a Jew, without definite proof one way or the other."

The closer we got to our destination, to Döllersheim, the more empty and remote from civilization the countryside began to look, the further back in time we seemed to be going. This part of Austria, the Waldviertel (the sector northwest of Vienna, between the Danube and the Czech border), and its scattered peasant-farmer inhabitants have remained relatively isolated from cosmopolitan civilization for centuries. With the heavy blanketing of snow shrouding the occasional ancient barn and farmhouse and obliterating almost all remaining visible traces of modernity, the lonely look and feel of the countryside could not have differed much from the way it looked some 156 years earlier. When someone—either a local-yokel miller or a mysterious stranger with "alien blood"—bedded down a middle-aged peasant woman named Maria Schicklgruber, leaving her pregnant with Hitler's father and leaving subsequent historians a legacy of doubt. Doubt that may have haunted Hitler as well as those who tried to explain him.

As we pulled into the courtyard of a three-century-old inn to ask for directions to Döllersheim, the remote snowbound setting and the nature of our search for Maria Schicklgruber's shadowy secret lover recalled to me the opening of Mark Twain's peculiar, posthumously published fable of evil, *The Mysterious Stranger*: "It was in 1590—winter. Austria was far away from the world, and asleep. . . . And our village was in the middle of that sleep. . . . It drowsed in peace in the deep privacy of a hilly and woodsy solitude . . . news from the world hardly ever came to disturb its dreams."

Of course, someone does then come to disturb the dreams of this insulated Austrian fastness in Twain's tale, "a mysterious stranger" who turns out to be Satan, although Twain's Satan is both more angelic and more diabolical than the conventional Prince of Darkness.

I was surprised when, after I returned home from Döllersheim and reread *The Mysterious Stranger*, to find in it the following passage from Twain's 1916 fable: "We had two priests [in the sleepy village]. One of them, Father Adolf, was a very zealous and strenuous priest. . . . [No one] was held in more solemn and awful respect. This was because he had absolutely no fear of the Devil. Father Adolf had actually met Satan face to face more than once."

It's remarkable how accurately Twain evoked the drowsing remoteness of this countryside, the sense of the sinister potential in somber, muffled silence. The little inn we'd stopped at was built sometime around 1600, one of the men huddled in front of the fireplace in the dining room told us. And aside from a poster on the wall announcing a "*Disco Abend*" next Saturday night at the local parish hall, it didn't look like much had changed in the centuries since. We ordered some wursts and asked the locals if they could help us find Döllersheim. It was they who gave us our first intimation of the nature of the *verfallen* world we were heading into.

The *verfallen* world, the ruined wasteland that was once Hitler's "ancestral homeland": It is the ur-source of Hitler's strangeness, the original locus of his alienness, his foreignness, an uncertainty of origins that was more than geographical. Throughout his life, wherever he went, Adolf Hitler was always a Mysterious Stranger. From the moment he first came to public notice, this uncertainty served to generate scurrilous rumors, whispers, and slanders. To some, the aura of strangeness, alienness was a source of his mystique—something that helped give him a mythic dimension, something that elevated him above the ruck of ordinary politicians, a quality of apartness he manipulated to his own advantage. To others who have tried to explain Hitler, the strangeness grew out of a haunting uncertainty about himself—an uncertainty in his own mind—that manipulated him, twisted him, was in fact the wellspring of the deformity of his psyche.

Ambiguity was built into the very geography of Hitler's origins; he was the product of not one but two borderlands: First, there was his actual birthplace in western Austria at Braunau on the river Inn, the river that separates Germany from Austria. (His father, Alois, was, in fact, a customs inspector who commuted back and forth across the riverine border every day.) But more significantly for the psyche of a fanatic believer in the determinism of racial ancestry, Hitler's family came from (and in his childhood he returned to) an "ancestral homeland" (as the local Nazis later proudly called it) two hundred miles east of Braunau, here in the Waldviertel, in a landscape that was for centuries disputed borderland between Austria and Czechoslovakia. It was a no-man's-land between one realm that was Germanic and another that was Slavic—the same Slavic people Hitler professed to loathe as subhuman and would later enslave and slaughter. Indeed, the very name "Hitler" and its older variants "Hiedler" and "Hüttler" are more Slavic than Germanic, a fact that certainly rankled Hitler, casting as it did a shadow on his claim to Aryan purity—although not so dark a one as the rumor that the mysterious stranger who wandered through this borderland was a wandering Jew.

Sir Isaiah Berlin once elaborated a kind of borderland theory of charismatic political genius. Citing Napoleon, Joseph Stalin, and Theodor Herzl as well as Hitler, he speculates that the peculiar psychology of many of the most charismatic, fanatic, possessed nationalist political leaders can be traced to their borderland origins: to the fact that they came "from outside the society that they led, or at any rate from its edges, the outer marches." The borderland syndrome, Berlin argues, has given rise to a disproportionate number of "men of fiery vision, whether noble or degraded, idealistic or perverted," men who developed "either exaggerated sentiment or contempt for the dominant majority, or else over-intense admiration or even worship of it . . . which leads both to unusual insights, and—born of overwrought sensibilities—a neurotic distortion of the facts."

It's a description that fits Hitler but only in part. There always was—there still is—a sense of strangeness about him that surpassed such a borderland syndrome, a persistent sense even among his allies that there was a deeper sort of aberration, a less explicable alienness than that of Napoleon, even Stalin. He certainly didn't fit, didn't seem to come from the one place to which he should have been native, this countryside, this "ancestral homeland of the Führer" we've been traveling through.

A number of Hitler biographers have made a point of noting that for centuries the peasant farmers inhabiting this isolated quarter of Lower Austria have stuck to their less-than-lush land, intermarrying frequently and producing generation after generation of more farmers—conspicuously failing to give birth to anyone who attracted the notice, much less disturbed the dreams of history. And then suddenly: Adolf Hitler.

One postwar German historian, Helmut Heiber of the highly regarded Munich Institute for Contemporary History, examining this phenomenon in his Hitler biography, voiced the unspoken implication: "The aberrational quality of the Hitler family beginning with the ambitious and enterprising father of Adolf shows that *other blood* must have entered the Lower Austrian Waldviertel stock which had been weakened by years of inbreeding" (emphasis added).

Other blood: the Hitlerian ring to this phrase is, one hopes, ironic. But the specter of "other blood" is at the heart of the highly charged Hitler family romance. "Family romance," of course, was the term first coined by Freud in 1909 as a way of characterizing a not-uncommon romantic fantasy: that one's parents are not one's real progenitors, that one's real parents are "others who as a rule are of higher social standing" such as "the Lord of the Manor or some member of the aristocracy." The family romance frequently involves a fairy-tale-like myth of origins in which one has been dispossessed of one's royal, exotic, or privileged origin by misfortune or sinister conspiracy—a theme common to myth, folklore, Shakespeare's late romances, eighteenth-century picaresque novels, and the paranoid fantasies of contemporary schizophrenics who proclaim they're heir to the Rockefeller fortune or they're Howard Hughes's love child.

While its form might evoke fairy tales, the core of the family romance is sexual mystery—the eternal disturbing truth that is at the heart of so much family and literary drama: "Pater semper incertus est," the identity of the father is always uncertain, as the Latin saying quoted by Freud goes. The nature of our reproductive biology has, built into it, an eternal mischief-making source of uncertainty. Men must trust the word of women about the paternity of their child, Freud lamented. In some special circumstances, even the woman cannot know.

Freud argues that the family-romance fantasy arises as soon as the child learns the truth "about sexual process." He "tends to picture to himself [in] erotic situations and relations . . . situations of secret infidelity and . . . secret love affairs" that, typically, bring his mother together with a more romantic, more exotic, higher-born mysterious stranger of a father.

Setting aside for a moment the question of whether Hitler himself entertained family-romance fantasies, there is little doubt that his explainers have. The proliferation of candidates for the mysterious stranger who fathered Hitler's father—in particular such high-born candidates as "a Baron Rothschild" and the "scion of the seigneurial house of Ottenstein"—and the persistent speculation about secret infidelities, illicit love affairs, and ambiguous "erotic situations" involving Maria Schicklgruber represents *the family romance of the Hitler explainers.*

Like glancing at the head of Medusa, staring too closely at the entangled strangeness of Hitler's origins has its dangers to the would-be explainers, one of them being the need to imagine that their extraordinary subject has a more exotic, more romantic origin than this grim peasant landscape could produce. It's a need that engenders the hope of finding an explicatory elixir such as "other blood" to account for the spectacular anomaly Hitler was, not only in the Waldviertel but in world history.

One reason the temptation to construe fragmentary genealogical evidence into a family romance has been hard to resist is the presence of such classic folkloric, fairy-tale-like elements in the mysterious-stranger-like setting. There's a wandering miller (Georg), an ambitious bastard (Alois), a rumored legacy, a (not quite) Cinderella-like peasant serving girl (Maria), a disappearing village (Döllersheim), rumored assignations with the prince of a nearby castle (Ottenstein), and whispers about intrigue with a powerful prince of "other blood" (Baron Rothschild).

At the epicenter of all these alleged intrigues and family-romance liaisons is that all-but-erased dot on the map that marks the disappearing village of Döllersheim. And at the center of the Döllersheim intrigues is a kind of sacred erasure, the now-obliterated parish church that was the scene of three peculiar, ambiguous ceremonies in the Hitler origins controversies. That church was, first of all, in 1837, the place where Maria Schicklgruber filed the baptismal certificate for the child who would become Hitler's father, the document with the mischief-making blank line. That same church was also, five years later, the site of a curious wedding ceremony between Maria, then forty-seven years old, and forty-three-year-old Johann Georg Hiedler, the wandering miller, who would later, without much solid evidence, assume prominence in Hitler's official genealogies as his paternal grandfather.

What made the wedding curious was what it *didn't* entail. It didn't entail the wandering miller adopting Maria's five-year-old son, Alois, the future father of Adolf—an adoption that might have been expected if, in fact, Johann Georg was the biological father of the boy. It didn't involve the son going to live under the same roof as his mother and putative father, Johann Georg. Instead, Hitler's father, Alois, went to live with Johann Georg's brother, Johann Nepomuk Hiedler (one reason Maser believes Nepomuk is his real father), a somewhat more settled and prosperous (but already married) peasant.

It seemed to be a marriage of convenience, but whose convenience? What made the ceremony even more curious in retrospect was yet a third ceremony enacted in the Döllersheim parish church thirty-five years after the marriage, a transaction of dubious legitimacy based on questionable affidavits: the name-change ceremony. This was the one by means of which Maria Schicklgruber's child—Alois Schicklgruber up till then—in his fortieth year suddenly reappeared in his home parish to claim, retroactively, that the long-dead wandering miller Georg, who'd never formally acknowledged paternity during his life, *had* been his biological father. And that the poor dead dad had dearly wanted him to bear the Hicdlcr name (although after the change Alois styled it "Hitler").

The questionable circumstances of these three Döllersheim ceremonies and the strange fate of Döllersheim itself would be of no concern to anyone if the newly minted Alois Hitler had not gone on to father a child named Adolf—and perhaps if Adolf had not shown such an exaggerated sensitivity to these Döllersheim aspects of his background.

But not long after he became a player on the world stage with the failed coup attempt of November 1923, another set of mysterious strangers began to show up in Döllersheim, poking into the records in the parish church registry, trying to find out what secret lay behind them. First, there were opposition journalists, then intelligence operatives, then private investigators, and ultimately the Gestapo itself making pilgrimages to the parish church. (At Himmler's request, Gestapo officers made no less than four expeditions to Austria to see if they could get to the bottom of the irregularities in accounts of Hitler's origins.)

The name change was the first issue to surface publicly and the first to provide an indication of Hitler's reaction to the questions shadowing his family history. According to Rudolf Olden's prewar Hitler biography, sometime in the mid-twenties, "an ingenious journalist published the fact in a liberal newspaper in Vienna, that Hitler's father had changed his name from Schicklgruber to Hiedler." Olden added a malicious (and, technically, inaccurate) twist of the knife, to the effect that "it was not correct to say 'Heil Hitler!' it should be 'Heil Schicklgruber!'"

This line in Olden's book has been taken up by several Hitler biographers, who have tended to build up the significance of the name change to world-historical proportions. Olden himself tells us, "I have heard Germans speculate whether Hitler could have become the master of Germany had he been known to the world as Schicklgruber. It has a slightly comic sound as it rolls off the tongue of a south German. Can one imagine the frenzied German masses acclaiming a Schicklgruber with their Heils?" John Toland, in similar language, tells us, "It is difficult to imagine seventy million Germans shouting in all seriousness, 'Heil Schicklgruber!'"

While too much can be made of the name-change explanation of his destiny, clearly Hitler was extraordinarily sensitive to any probing into a family history that was most likely terra incognita to himself. Olden adds that the fury of Hitler over the Schicklgruber disclosure took the form of a brutal assault: "Two young party members attacked the editor of the Vienna paper which printed the 'Heil Schicklgruber' story with truncheons in the café where he used to sit after dinner. The incident had no further consequences except that the change of name was now reported in all the newspapers." But, in fact, there may have been further consequences of which Olden, writing in 1936, could not have been aware. Consequences for the little town of Döllersheim, which was the scene of the dubious Schicklgruber/Hitler name change and which soon became the victim of a far more brutal assault with weapons worse than truncheons, was an assault that nearly obliterated all traces of its existence.

Such at least is the theory first advanced in 1956 by Franz Jetzinger, the Austrian archivist and author of a widely respected study (Bullock and Fest cite it frequently) called *Hitler's Youth*, which was the product of an exhaustive search of parish-church baptismal records and other long-forgotten depositories of documents on Hitler's ancestry and youth.

In his discussion of the controversial assertion, in a pre-execution Nuremberg memoir by Hitler's one-time private attorney Hans Frank, that Frank had uncovered evidence to support the view that the mysterious stranger/paternal grandfather of Hitler was a Jew, Jetzinger cites "this curious fact which may be interpreted as bearing out Frank's story":

> Not two months after Hitler invaded Austria, in May 1938, an order was issued to the Land Registries concerned to carry out a survey of Döllersheim (Alois Hitler's birthplace) and neighbourhood with a view to their suitability as a battle training area for the Wehrmacht. In the following year the inhabitants of Döllersheim were forcibly evacuated and the village together with the surrounding countryside was blasted and withered by German artillery and infantry weapons. The birthplace of Hitler's father and the site of his grandmother's grave were alike rendered unrecognizable, and today this whole tract of what was once fertile and flourishing country is an arid desert sown with unexploded shells. But an area so closely associated with Hitler's family could not have been used for battle training without his knowledge and permission. Then why did he give it? Or did Hitler himself initiate the order for the destruction of Döllersheim out of insane hatred of his father and the desire to erase the "shame" of his Jewish blood?

While Jetzinger's account has been challenged, primarily by Werner Maser (who argues that it was the Russians who destroyed Döllersheim after 1945 to eliminate a possible future shrine for neo-Nazis), in either version the goal was the elimination of the problematic archival nexus of Hitler's origins—a sanitizing, cleansing operation designed to exterminate the rats' nest of ambiguities that had its origin there, to exterminate the possibility of hostile or empathetic explanation.

Döllersheim delenda est. Nor was it just Döllersheim. No—as we learned from the proprietors of the inn we stopped at—who became our guides to what I came to call the *verfallen* landscape of Hitler's past—the entire area around Döllersheim, including the little village of Strones where Maria Schicklgruber was born and the cemetery she was buried in, was blasted, leveled, or, to extend the Nazi-inflected metaphor of sanitation, cauterized.

We warmed up and finished our wursts at a table beneath the "Disco Abend" poster before approaching the gaggle of locals clustered around the fireplace to ask them what they knew of a place called Döllersheim. He'd heard of it, yes, said the proprietor wrapped in winter clothes and wearing his Tyrolean hat indoors against the drafts from the storm outside. He'd heard about it, but it was . . . complicated. A map was summoned up, a big folded map of Austria that, Waltraud later informed me, bore the markings of the Austrian Freedom Party; it was an election-year giveaway of the party of Jörg Haider, the charismatic former male model and führer of Austria's far right (some call it neo-Nazi) movement.

The proprietor traced his finger from our location at the inn north and west along the road we were on. "You pass the castle of Ottenstein," he said. "It's up on a hill to the left, then continue on across the river until," his finger reached a shaded region where, he said, all is "*verfallen.*"

Alles verfallen?

He began pointing to a dotted line around a shaded area. Next to the name of each tiny village and town within it, there appeared the word "verfallen." Strones verfallen, Spital verfallen, a half dozen or so towns verfallen—that is destroyed, ruined. Finally, in the midst of it all there was Döllersheim—verfallen.

"Ruined how?" Waltraud asked.

"Long ago" was all he said.

The snow was still pelting the countryside as we skidded back onto the road from the courtyard of the inn. The number of barns and habitations had thinned out, the piney woods had thickened. At last, we saw a small sign that read "Ottenstein," and up on a cliff loomed the snowy outlines of a *Schloss*, the castle of Ottenstein.

The family-romance genealogical speculations might be conceptual castles in the air, but here were the snowy turrets of the *real* castle in Maria Schicklgruber's life, the only castle the peasant serving girl was ever likely to see—unless, of course, one believes the story spread by the Austrian secret police that she'd gone to work in the Vienna palace of Baron Rothschild. But seeing the snowy desolation that settled as early as autumn upon Maria's native land, it would not be impossible to imagine an unmarried forty-two-year-old domestic serving woman vulnerable to an intrigue with the type of exotic or wealthy employer envisioned by the family romances.

Who was this woman, Maria Schicklgruber, who left such a maddeningly ambiguous legacy to Hitler and to history? It is easy to project too much retrospective mystery upon her due to the disproportionate importance of her grandson. What is more interesting is how the serving-girl seduction romances of the two other Hitler women to figure prominently in subsequent Hitler-explanation controversies—his mother, Klara, and his half-niece, Geli Raubal—seem to reflect, even recapitulate the sexual mystery Maria Schicklgruber left behind. What is it about the amorous master/ambivalent serving girl relationship that causes it to figure in three successive generations of Hitler women and the controversies surrounding them?

Consider Hitler's mother, Klara, often portrayed by chroniclers (taking their cue from her devoted son's description of her) as a simple, saintly, self-sacrificing servant of her husband and children. In fact, a closer look at her role reveals Klara—a serving girl in the Alois Hitler household during his first two marriages—was capable of participating in complicated, illicit, clandestine (and borderline incestuous) intrigues with the imperious head of the household. We know, for instance, that at sixteen Klara was willing to move into the cramped quarters of a married man (Alois) twenty years older than she, a man not so distantly related to her (she was his niece), under pretext of being his serving maid.

It was 1867, and Hitler's father was then living with his first wife, a relatively wealthy woman thirteen years his senior, who was ailing when he married her, most probably for her money. As John Toland describes it, Klara, an attractive teenager "with abundant dark hair . . . was installed with the Hitler's in an inn where Alois was already carrying on an affair with a kitchen maid, Franziska," who would become his second wife when his first finally expired. After his first wife died, developments in the Alois Hitler né Schicklgruber household began to take on the appearance of a maimed French farce. After a period of living conjugally but without benefit of clergy with the kitchen maid, while simultaneously enjoying the services of the even younger maid (and niece) Klara, he married the older one. Only to find wife number two "was only too aware of how tempting a pretty maid could be to the susceptible Alois," Toland says, and one of Franziska's first acts after the wedding "was to get rid of Klara."

But not for long. Wife number two developed tuberculosis. As soon as

Franziska left to seek treatment elsewhere, "it was only logical for [Alois] to seek help from his attractive niece [Klara]." Even when the wife returned— soon to die—young Klara remained, "and this time," says Toland, "she became housemaid, nursemaid and mistress."

It was shortly after this that the incest problem arose, and the sordid comedy in the Hitler apartment became a matter of official concern to the papacy in the Vatican.

When wife number two died, Alois sought to legitimize his live-in liaison with his maid/mistress Klara, but there was a barrier: "bilateral affinity in the third degree touching the second" as Alois's petition to the local bishop (prepared with ecclesiastical assistance) described his complicated family relationship to Klara. (If we accept the official version of Hitler's descent, then Alois's father and Klara's granduncle were the same person: Johann Georg Hiedler.) The local bishop thought this "third degree affinity touching the second" too touchy to approve on his own authority and instead forwarded the petition to Rome with a plea for a papal dispensation. But even after the Vatican granted the dispensation, Klara continued to call her new husband what she called him when she was still his maid/mistress: "uncle."

"Uncle." That's exactly what Adolf Hitler's own housemaid/niece Geli Raubal called *him* when she moved into his apartment in 1929 and they began their intense, controversial (then and now), and ultimately fatal relationship, the third erotic serving-girl drama in the Hitler saga.

I'll return later to look more closely at the Geli Raubal tragedy, pausing here to note only those elements that make it such an uncanny recapitulation of the family romance of Maria Schicklgruber and the mysterious stranger. There was, in Geli's case, a suspected Jewish seducer, a (rumored) pregnancy, and a tormented affair with the master of the house in which she served. And with Geli, as with Maria, there is the abyss between two conflicting views of the essential nature of the serving maid in question: Was she an innocent, a blameless maiden, an "angel" (as many called Geli), or was she a scheming, intriguing seductress who used provocation and deception to advance herself?

Further evidence for how highly charged the serving maid–Jewish master fantasy was in Hitler's own mind can be found in its prominence as a pornographic motif in Julius Streicher's *Der Stürmer*, in Hitler's peculiar ecstasy over Streicher's coverage of the Hirsch case, a celebrated 1920s trial of a Jewish master for the rape of his Aryan serving girl. And in Hitler's denunciation of Matthias Erzberger, one of the "November Criminals" (the men who signed the "stab in the back" November 1918 armistice), as "the bastard son of a Jew and a serving girl."

And then, as Robert Waite has pointed out, there is the serving-girl codicil which Hitler insisted on including in the 1935 Nuremberg racial laws, a codicil that not only specifically outlawed intercourse between Jews and Aryans but also explicitly forbade Jews even to employ Aryan women under the age of forty-five in their homes. It is a bizarre legislative provision, in that it seems to have a pornographic fantasy embedded within it. It's a subversively ambiguous fantasy at that: While it seems to say that Jews could not be trusted with nubile Aryan women in their employ, the fact that the prohibition extended not just to the act of miscegenation but to the possibility of a Jewish master and Aryan maidservant being in each other's *presence* carries an implicit hint that the Aryan maids themselves might not be trusted. This deeply embedded distrust, or at least deeply divided view of the serving girl and her relationship to the shadowy *pater incertus* who may be her master, is at the heart of the enigma of Maria Schicklgruber and the fantasies projected upon the blank line on the baptismal certificate she filed in Döllersheim.

No explicit eyewitness or documentary evidence has survived to support this dark view of Maria. The rumored paternity correspondence that would document the story of a liaison between Maria and a wealthy Jew she served, the "Jew from Graz" cited by Hitler's personal attorney Hans Frank in his Nuremberg memoir, has never surfaced. There is no testimony from Maria's contemporaries to indict her, to indicate she was anything other than a simple good-hearted peasant woman, even a courageous single mother who defied poverty and advancing age to bear a child without benefit of clergy or paternal support at an age, forty-two, when other peasant women might have resigned themselves to declining years of childless drudgery.

And yet there is testimony, reported testimony, from a descendant. A story about Maria, a sordid story of low, mean sexual intrigue, fraud, and blackmail that makes her out to be a cunning and deceitful anti-Semitic extortionist. It's a story we might otherwise ignore were it not for its source—a man specifically assigned by Adolf Hitler to investigate the circumstances of Maria's pregnancy, an attorney who claimed he got his seamy, disreputable portrait of Maria from a member of her own family. To be more precise: from Adolf Hitler himself.

CHAPTER 2

The Hitler Family
Film Noir

*In which we meet two generations
of Hitler family con artists*

It was still a shock to see it, or what was left of it, when we finally found it.
We'd been traveling—snowplowing really—for about five miles into the *ver-fallen* world, on a road lined with barbed wire and marked conspicuously with frequent signs warning unsuspecting motorists about the hidden danger of venturing into the seemingly innocent pastoral landscape. There were unexploded shells lurking beneath the snowy fields. One translation of Jetzinger's Döllersheim-destruction hypothesis describes this realm as a "once flourishing and fertile region [that] is today a ghastly desert where malevolent death lurks in the form of unexploded shells. Its former inhabitants have been dispersed to all points of the compass."

Buried bombshells: Throughout Hitler's political career, his emissaries and his enemies made pilgrimages to Döllersheim to search for metaphorical bombshells buried in the church registries, in the memories of local residents and relatives, for explosive revelations that might expose or explain the source of Hitler's strangeness. And at last, around a bend in the road, there it was, all that was left of it.

A small sign on the side of the road announced "Döllersheim." As we pulled to a halt, we could see, up the snowy slope of a small hill, the pale ruins rising out of the deep drifts; a maimed Stonehenge of worn stone walls standing alone without buildings. Less a ghost town than an archaeological ruin. Rising over the bare ruined choirs of the parish church was one lonely, relatively intact rectangular wall. Into the top of it were inset two stone-arched window frames, empty of glass, eyeless sockets through the vacancies of which the snow-clouded sky stared.

On the last leg of the drive, I'd been reviewing the maddeningly unresolved testimony that had brought me here, the controversial Hitler explanation that has kept obscure events at Döllersheim a century and a half ago in the forefront of furious debate ever since the story surfaced in 1953. It has become *the fabula incerta*, the unfathomable crux, the veritable curse of the Hitler explainers: the Hans Frank story.

I'd been researching the Hans Frank story and its reception for some years by the time I arrived at *verfallen* Döllersheim. And in reviewing my files and the preliminary study I'd done of the Hans Frank story and a compilation of four decades of polemical arguments over it by an array of Hitler explainers, I found myself struck by three strong impressions:

1. How widely this uncorroborated tale has been accepted despite the numerous efforts to refute it. And how frequently it's become the very cornerstone of larger efforts to explain the origin of Hitler's anti-Semitism. That a story of this bizarre and improbable nature—a story about a mysterious Jew named Frankenberger whose nineteen-year-old son supposedly impregnated Maria Schicklgruber—has crept so far into the status of received wisdom is testament as much as anything to the poverty and inadequacy of other rival explanations for Hitler's psyche.

Most enthusiastic in their reception have been psychoanalysts and psychohistorians such as Alice Miller and Robert Waite. But even those who are obviously uncomfortable with the Hans Frank story, such as Bullock and Fest, can't feel confident enough about the facts to dismiss it; they feel compelled to cite it as a possibility and declare it neither proved nor disproved. And so, after the polemical smoke has cleared, the Hans Frank account of Maria Schicklgruber's liaison with a Jewish lover remains standing, albeit by default, as the most ambitious contender for the ultimate prize of Hitler studies—the explanation for the origin, the special virulence of his anti-Semitism.

2. And yet what also remains clear is the enduring reason for resistance to the Hans Frank story: that it is too neat, too symmetrical. One hesitates to call it too good to be true, but its suspiciously symmetrical ironies, its plentitude, its patness as explanation inspire distrust.

3. If it's overvalued as a disclosure of the hidden truth about Hitler's origins, as the missing explanation of Hitler's anti-Semitism, the Hans Frank story may be undervalued as an evocation of the Hitler mind-set, of the blackmail-riddled Munich demimonde he arose from. In its gritty specifics of sexual blackmail, sleazy small-time extortion, it's far different from the vague and grandiose Rothschildian variants of the Hitler family romance. The Hans Frank story is the Hitler family film noir.

Of all the war criminals executed at Nuremberg, none had a more peculiar posthumous life than Hans Frank. He was, in life, little more than a murderous flunky, a Nazi Party lawyer who sucked up to Hitler so successfully in Munich that he was elevated to chief party attorney. More important and less publicly, he gained Hitler's confidence as a *personal* attorney, the man Hitler called upon to deal with the recurrent sleazy blackmail and extortion plots that dogged him and the seedier members of his entourage, such as SA chief Ernst Roehm, who repeatedly had to contend with homosexual lovers peddling his pornographic correspondence to the press.

Hitler himself called on Hans Frank in September 1931 when he was desperate to stop his journalistic nemesis, the socialist *Munich Post*, from printing scandalous speculation about the nature of his relationship to his young half-niece Geli Raubal and the nature of his role in her mysterious death. For such efforts, and perhaps because of the secrets he became privy to, Frank was elevated to national prominence after Hitler came to power, first as Reichsminister for Justice. Then, after the conquest of Poland, Hitler made him governor-general of the occupied sector. It was chiefly for the crimes he committed in this post—his eager participation in the extermination process—that he was convicted at Nuremberg for crimes against humanity, sentenced to death, and executed.

Frank's behavior during his confinement at Nuremberg was unusual. He underwent a conversion to Catholicism and—unlike the other defendants, who tried either to minimize their own guilt or that of the Nazi regime—Frank at first publicly flagellated himself and his cohorts for their guilt over the extermination of the Jews. He proclaimed in open court "a thousand years shall not suffice to erase the guilt brought on our people by Hitler's conduct." After the court condemned him to death, he ostentatiously waived his right to appeal (although he permitted his lawyer to do so and began to speak of the Allied devastation of Germany as "balancing" the crime of the Nazis). With his appeal denied, Frank spent the remaining months of his life before he was hanged composing—with the encouragement of his priest confessor and a secular confessor, the American psychologist G. M. Gilbert—a memoir of his career with Hitler.

Hans Frank's thousand-page handwritten memoir (the original of which now reposes in the files of Jerusalem's Yad Vashem Holocaust Memorial) would probably have been forgotten completely had it not been for the bombshell buried in it. Amid Frank's ostentatiously tormented reflections on how he came to be mesmerized by Hitler, amid his post hoc critique of Hitler's excesses (which is still in thrall to the notion of Hitler's "greatness"), Frank includes a two-page account of a highly charged blackmail case he handled on Hitler's behalf back in 1930. One that involved the sensitive subject of Hitler's "family history," one in which, Frank claims, he went beyond his role of private attorney to become a kind of genealogical private eye.

The threat emerged at a crucial moment in the course of Hitler's resurgent political career. Frank recalls it as the latter half of 1930, a time when Hitler was in the midst of a political campaign that would mark his first giant step back from obscurity and marginality, the Reichstag elections that would raise the party's strength in the national legislature from 12 to 107 seats and make Hitler, in the midst of the Depression-induced political crisis, a serious contender for national political power. It was a moment also when Hitler—for many years a forgotten, near-comic figure outside Germany since the failed 1923 putsch—had suddenly become the subject of worldwide press scrutiny and was reacting to it with a furious defensiveness, particularly to any inquiries into his family history.

The Hans Frank story begins with just such an unwelcome intrusion. Word reached Hitler that his two troublesome relatives by marriage in Liverpool were negotiating with the Hearst syndicate to sell a story about the famous German führer they were related to. They were troublesome in that they'd already brought embarrassing attention to his family: Mrs. Bridget Hitler had been married to Adolf's wayward half brother Alois Jr. when the latter, a traveling salesman and waiter, settled in Liverpool, England, in 1910. He'd disappeared from Liverpool shortly before World War I, leaving behind his wife and a son, William Patrick Hitler. The mother and son thought him dead until the Hitler name hit the headlines with the failed putsch attempt in 1923. Their attempt to find news of Alois Jr., their long-lost husband and father, through Adolf led to the discovery that Alois was alive and well, living bigamously with a German wife and child. The trouble and the court case that ensued put Adolf on his guard against the English branch of the family. And when he learned in late 1930 of their attempt to sell a story about the Hitler family, Hitler hastily summoned the half-nephew to Munich, where he dressed him down and ordered him to deny he was related to the famous Nazi Party leader—to tell Hearst he'd been mistaken, his relative was a *different* Hitler.

In an interview some years later, the half-nephew claimed that Hitler yelled at him, "These people must not know who I am. Nobody must know where I come from."

But according to Hans Frank's account, some elements of which are corroborated by the nephew's interview, this was not the end of the relationship between the black-sheep British relative and the German führer.

According to Frank, the nephew, perhaps sensing there was financial advantage to be gained from the Führer's sensitivity to questions of family history, sent what Hitler described as a blackmail letter to him: "One day, it must have been towards the end of 1930," Frank wrote in his memoir, "I was called to the residence of Hitler at Prinzregentenplatz. He told me, with a letter lying before him, [of] a 'disgusting blackmail plot' in connection with one of his most loathsome relatives, with respect to his own ancestry."

Hans Frank tells us the source of this blackmail was

> a son of Hitler's half-brother Alois who was gently hinting that in view of certain allegations in the press it might be better if certain family matters weren't shouted from the roof tops. The press reports in question suggested that Hitler had Jewish blood in his veins and hence was hardly qualified to be an anti-semite. But they were phrased in such general terms that nothing could be done about it. In the heat of the political struggle the whole thing died down. All the same, this threat of blackmail by a relative was a somewhat tricky business. At Hitler's request I made some confidential inquiries.

Confidential inquiries: The language is that of the confidential operative, the private eye. The language and the role are uncharacteristic for the usually self-aggrandizing Frank, who saw himself as an Aryan jurisprudential visionary, not a common peeper.

Frank does not describe the details of his confidential inquiries or how he was led to the potentially explosive cache of documents, the purported smoking gun in the Hitler-ancestry controversy. He says only that he found them "in the possession of a woman living in Wetzlsdorf near Graz [Austria] who was related to Hitler through the Raubals"—Geli Raubal's family.

All Frank says about the process is that

> intensive investigation elicited the following information: Hitler's father was the illegitimate son of a woman by the name of Schicklgruber from Leonding near Linz who worked as a cook in a Graz household. . . . But the most extraordinary part of the story is this: when the cook Schicklgruber (Adolf Hitler's grandmother) gave birth to her child, she was in service with a Jewish family called Frankenberger. And on behalf of his son, then about nineteen years old, Frankenberger paid a maintenance allowance to Schicklgruber from

the time of the child's birth until his fourteenth year. For a number of years, too, the Frankenbergers and Hitler's grandmother wrote to each other, the general tenor of the correspondence betraying on both sides the tacit acknowledgment that Schicklgruber's illegitimate child had been engendered under circumstances which made the Frankenbergers responsible for its maintenance. . . . Hence the possibility cannot be dismissed that Hitler's father was half Jewish as a result of the extramarital relationship between the Schicklgruber woman and the Jew from Graz. This would mean that Hitler was one-quarter Jewish.

There are some obvious problems with this story, or at the very least with Frank's recollection of it seventeen years later at Nuremberg. Maria Schicklgruber came not from "Leonding near Linz" (where Hitler later went to school) but from Strones, near Döllersheim. Nor is there any independent evidence that Maria Schicklgruber worked for a Jewish family in Graz. Researchers have found no traces of a Frankenberger family living in Graz, although Werner Maser did locate evidence that a forty-two-year-old butcher and tripe boiler named Frankenreither was residing there in 1836, the year of Maria's mysterious conception.

Was Hans Frank serving up tripe himself? Maser, who disbelieves the story, suggests that Frank's conversion to Catholicism led him to invent a Jewish ancestor for the nominally Catholic Hitler "to foment unrest, anxiety and a lasting sense of guilt" among Jews, as if somehow the possibility of one Jew's murky liaison in 1836 with Hitler's grandmother should somehow make all Jews feel responsible for Hitler's crimes. Others have suggested that Frank was projecting his own family romance—his apparent belief he might have been descended from a Jewish grandfather named Frankfurter—onto Hitler.

Nonetheless, those who have challenged the factual basis of Frank's account of his confidential inquiries and his claim to have discovered paternity correspondence to corroborate it have for the most part ignored or failed to refute the even-more-surprising coda to his story: Frank's description of Hitler's *reaction* to Frank's report on his confidential inquiries, his recollection of Hitler's attempt to refute its potentially devastating implications. A reply in which Hitler, according to Frank, conceded the essential truth of the Frankenberger story, did not dispute the authenticity of the paternity correspondence with the Jewish family, but added an ugly twist to it, one that blackened his own grandmother Maria Schicklgruber's character, in an effort to absolve himself of the imputation of Jewish blood, which the bare facts of Hans Frank's "intensive investigation" seemed to establish.

"Adolf Hitler," Frank recalled in his memoir,

said he knew . . . that his father [was not the child of] the Schicklgruber woman and the Jew from Graz. He knew it from what his father
and his grandmother told him. He knew that his father sprang from
a premarital relation between his grandmother and the man whom
she later married [Georg Hiedler]. But they were both poor, and the
maintenance money that the Jew paid over a number of years was an
extremely desirable supplement to the poverty-stricken household.
He was well able to pay, and for that reason it had been stated that
he was the father. The Jew paid without going to court probably because he could not face the publicity that a legal settlement might
have entailed.

Setting aside for the moment the question of the origin of the story—
Hitler's actual words or Hans Frank's imagination—consider it as a story of
origins. At the very least it's Hans Frank's "just so" story, his explanation of
how Adolf Hitler became an anti-Semite. And what a sordid, degrading story
of origins it is. Beneath Frank's compressed, clinical recitation is a seamy tale
of sexual blackmail in which Hitler's grandmother engages in a sordid shake-
down scheme, one that left a legacy of sexual and racial ambiguity Hitler could
not extricate himself from, one that doesn't even fully exempt him from the
imputation of Jewish blood.

The Hitler family film noir, as Hans Frank recalls Hitler telling it, begins
with sexual tension and ends with sexual ambiguity. She is forty-two and he
is nineteen; she is a servant, he the son of the master. Something transpires
between them, perhaps something calculated in advance on her part. Perhaps as little as a look, perhaps much more. She gets pregnant, she tells her
shiftless local-yokel wandering-miller boyfriend that the child is *his*, not the
Jewish boy's, which might or might not be true; only she knows. Or does she?
The two of them, Maria and the miller, can barely support themselves much
less a child, so they cook up a scheme to extort funds from the wealthy Jew by
accusing his son of getting her pregnant. Whether she actually seduced the
son in order to use him as a pawn in her scheme or cold-bloodedly lied about
the actual sexual contact is irrelevant. Because at some point there comes the
showdown, the sit-down, the squeeze is put on. The extortion threat is made
explicit. The specter of pogrom is invoked as the ultimate threat: If the Jew
doesn't begin making payoffs, the conniving couple will make sure there's a
public outcry about the lustful Jewish sexual predator staining the honor of a
helpless Aryan maiden. The result, as Frank laconically puts it: "The Jew paid."

Recall that this sordid intrigue is, according to Frank, the way Hitler
wanted him to view his grandparents. Better to see them as petty-crook grifters, a whore-and-pimp extortion team, than envision the possibility that his

father was fathered by a Jew, although Hitler's "alibi" in Frank's account does not rule out the possibility that there *was* a sexual relationship between Maria and the boy.

It's astonishing how much mischief this one story has caused since it came to light in 1953 when Hans Frank's family published an edition of his memoir in Germany, astonishing how many years of research, years of debate have been devoted to disentangling the ambiguities embedded in it. Taking the story on its own terms as told by Frank—before attacking the problem of its credibility—there are two crucial questions left unresolved: Did Maria Schicklgruber actually sleep with the nineteen-year-old boy, or was a threat of the public accusation of violation enough to extort the money from the Jewish family for all those years? And if she did sleep with the Jewish boy about the time she conceived a child by her partner (and later husband) Johann Georg Hiedler, could she be *certain* the child was Hiedler's and not Frankenberger's? The early-nineteenth-century peasant's lack of sophistication about reproductive timing argues that, even for Maria Schicklgruber herself, pater incertus est.

Some of the most sophisticated late-twentieth-century Hitler explainers have tried to make a virtue out of the necessity of uncertainty here: They've taken the uncertainty at the heart of the seedy intrigue over Maria's pregnancy and made it the essence of their explanation of the otherwise inexplicable virulence of Hitler's anti-Semitism. They postulate a kind of chain of uncertainty, a communicable uncertainty that leads from Maria Schicklgruber's inability to be sure which of the two men, Aryan or Jew, got her pregnant, to the galling uncertainty in Adolf Hitler's mind over whether or not he was "infected by Jewish blood."

Crucial to understanding the link between Maria's uncertainty and her grandson Adolf's uncertainty, in this view, is the dynamic of Hitler's crackpot physio-mystico sexology. His favorite anti-Semitic theorist, Julius Streicher, ran admonitory stories in *Der Stürmer* about Aryan women who'd had intercourse with Jewish men discovering to their horror that, after repeated exposure, "Jewish seed" had insinuated itself into their blood, and that as a consequence they were *turning* Jewish.

Robert Waite, the Williams College historian who is the most energetic advocate of the Hans Frank story as an explanation for Hitler's anti-Semitism, cites a passage in *Mein Kampf* in which Hitler speaks of the peculiar potency of even the fractional presence of Jewish blood, the way it can infiltrate and subvert the Aryan component, a passage in which Waite believes Hitler is speaking of a struggle going on within *himself*. Hitler describes the struggle within the "racially divided being," between the Aryan and Jewish components, and the infallible signal by which the power of the Jewish blood can be detected: "The first products of such cross-breeding, say in the third, fourth, and fifth generation [he, of course, was third generation] suffer bitterly. In all critical moments in which the racially unified being makes the correct, that is, unified decisions, the racially divided one will become uncertain; that is, he will arrive at half measures."

The legacy of uncertainty over Maria Schicklgruber's sexual choices would, in Waite's view, consign Hitler to a state of hypervigilance: always searching his consciousness for the telltale signal, the slightest indication of hesitation, of uncertainty, of the infirmity of will that would indicate his Aryan blood was adulterated with sinister Semitic serum. And thus—and herein lies the heart of Waite's Hitler explanation—always seeking to prove his purity, his freedom from infirmity, by the unrelenting, uncompromising ferocity of his war against the Jews, exterminating the doubts about the Jew within himself by murdering all the Jews within his reach.

The problem with building such a dauntingly elaborate superstructure of explanation upon the uncertainty within the Hans Frank story is that such attempts ignore the uncertainty *about* the Hans Frank story. Waite and others have attempted to evade this question by stressing that they are concerned not so much with the actuality of Hitler's genealogy—whether he really had a Jewish grandfather—as with whether he *believed* he might have and thus generated the obsessively anti-Jewish hypervigilance that belief entailed. But this assumes that Hitler had actually heard a version of this story that led to an early, festering, lifelong obsession.

While in fact, there's no evidence that Hitler even heard this rumor, aside from Frank's story; and we only have Frank's word that he presented Hitler with "proof" of it. And the evidence for a lifelong obsession with his own ancestry is thinly corroborated, if at all, conjectural at best, almost wishful thinking. There is some external corroboration of the Hans Frank story but only for the very beginning of it; the letter to Hitler from "the loathsome relative," the one Hitler characterized as "a disgusting blackmail plot." As we'll see in more detail shortly, the OSS debriefing of Hitler's black-sheep English nephew William Patrick Hitler seems to confirm that he did send Hitler a letter that disturbed the Führer, and to confirm that the cause of the disturbance was Hitler's sensitivity on the subject of family history. But the OSS debriefing makes no mention of a specifically Jewish problem in the family history.

The search for further corroboration of the Hans Frank story has led to wild-goose chases, red herrings, and every other cliché of futility. The correspondence, supposedly reflecting paternity payments from the Frankenbergers to the Schicklgruber/Hiedler ménage, has never turned up. Archival searches in Graz have found no traces of the spectral Frankenberger family.

On the other hand, unfortunately, it has turned out to be difficult to prove the absolute *im*possibility of the story. No sooner had an archivist named

Nikolaus Predarovich claimed to have established that Jews had been barred from living in the province of Styria (which encompasses Graz) through the middle of the nineteenth century than Werner Maser, who doubts the Hans Frank story in general, nonetheless proved that Jewish traveling salesmen were permitted entry to the September fair at the Feast of Saint Giles held annually at Graz in the 1830s, which would have permitted an encounter between Maria and a traveling salesman in September 1836, the month in which Hitler's father was conceived.

Those who have attempted to prove on the basis of his character that Hans Frank fabricated this story have not had a much better time of it. If one watches Hans Frank's fiery, fist-shaking, rabble-rousing performance at the Nuremberg Party Day rally in Leni Riefenstahl's *Triumph of the Will*, one sees someone who looks like a brutal thug, capable of great cruelty and viciousness, but not—at least on the surface—the type capable of the diabolic subtlety, the history-destabilizing mischief that crafting such a story out of whole cloth, insinuating a counterfeit Hitler explanation so successfully into the historical stream of consciousness, would require.

On the other hand, a different version of Frank emerges in the brilliantly vicious, utterly unforgiving portrait of him by his son, Niklas Frank, who (in a memoir called *In the Shadow of the Reich*) depicts his father as a craven coward and weakling, but one not without a kind of animal cunning, an instinct for lying, insinuation, self-aggrandizement. For *this* Hans Frank, disgraced and facing death on the gallows for following Hitler, fabricating such a story might be a cunning way of ensuring his place in history as the one man who gave the world the hidden key to the mystery of Hitler's psyche. While at the same time revenging himself on his former master for having led him to this end by foisting a sordid and humiliating explanation of Hitler on him for all posterity. In any case, it was one Frank knew the victors would find seductive.

And it has continued to be seductive. It remains, years later, one of the two great temptations of Hitler explanation lore (the other being the Geli Raubal perversion story), tempting because it offers the gratification of a totalizing, single-pointed explanation of Hitler's psychology.

Not surprisingly, psychologists in particular have been drawn to it. Perhaps the first to be seduced—and the most important witness for Frank's credibility—was the American psychologist and confidant who guided Frank through the process of producing his memoir, Dr. G. M. Gilbert. Gilbert, an army captain with a Ph.D. in psychology, was the man whose job it was to observe the working of Frank's mind, to get beneath his defenses. He came away convinced that Frank did not manufacture this story.

I'll never forget listening to the tape of the interview Gilbert gave to John Toland. I'd found the tape in the research material Toland had donated to the archives of the FDR Library in Hyde Park, New York. On the tape, you can hear the urgency in Toland's voice as he questions Gilbert about Hans Frank's story. Toland seems to want to believe Hans Frank was telling the truth about his investigation into Maria Schicklgruber's love life. He wants to believe there's an explanation for Hitler he can credit. But he's aware how much depends on questions of belief.

"You believe this investigation [into Hitler's ancestry] *did* take place?" Toland implores Gilbert. "You're *the only one* in the world who can tell us." It's a dramatic moment: Toland is saying he believes Gilbert holds the key to the last best hope of explaining Hitler.

In fact, he exaggerates somewhat: There's really *no one* in the world, not anymore, who can tell us that with certainty. Still, Gilbert does have a strong feeling on the matter: He believes Hans Frank.

"While he was prone to exaggerate many things, and of course to glamorize his own role," the psychologist says, "this is something he thought of no great consequence and he said, 'Well, I guess stranger things have happened than hatred of one's own race.' [Frank] was inclined to believe the results of his investigation. He [Hitler] wouldn't acknowledge having Jewish blood but the mere fact that she [Maria] was in a position to blackmail a Jew, evidently having had relations with him, is enough to stir up this violent anti-Jewish sexual hatred in Hitler."

Not only was Gilbert the first to believe Hans Frank's story, he was the first psychologist to adopt it as a possible explanation, the hidden key to Hitler. It has a built-in attraction to psychologists because it makes the otherwise apparently unfathomable source of Hitler's crimes so interestingly *intrapsychic*. Indeed, Gilbert is the first to "improve" upon Hans Frank's own interpretation, developing what would become a paradigm of the psychologizing of the Hans Frank story: the shift from seeing Hitler's anti-Semitism as something driven by an external ideology or hatred to seeing it as a product of internal *self*-hatred.

Gilbert sees that moment in 1930 when Hans Frank purportedly told Hitler he had come upon documentary proof that his father was fathered by a Jew as a profound turning point in the evolution of Hitler's anti-Semitism. "Especially when he [Hitler] was already committed to being a violent anti-Semite with his whole ego structure depending upon this," Gilbert told Toland, "the idea that it [the Jewish grandfather story] could have been true could have been resolved in his sick mind only by showing, as Frank said, that he was the worst anti-Semite in the world, so how could he possibly be a Jew?"

Hans Frank's own explanation is both more tentative and more simple-minded than his psychologist's. At first, Frank sounds skeptical. "That Adolf Hitler certainly had no Jewish blood in his veins seems to be so strikingly evident that it needs no further explanation." But returning to the question again, he decides, "I must say that it is not absolutely impossible that Hitler's father was in fact half Jewish. Then his hatred of Jews would have arisen from outraged blood-relative hate psychosis. Who could interpret all this?"

Of course, he's already delivered his own off-the-cuff interpretation: Adolf Hitler is outraged at the violation of his blood relative Maria by a Jew, which explains his "hate psychosis" about the entire Jewish people. In other words, Frank seems to be saying, Hitler killed the Jewish people because of his hatred for one nineteen-year-old boy who might or might not have made advances to his grandmother a century ago.

Gilbert gives it a more complex, reflective interpretation: It's not hatred for the boy or for living Jews, it's hatred for the spectral Jew that might be *within* him and the need to eradicate even the suspicion of an internal presence by proving to the world—and to himself—that he was "the worst anti-Semite in the world." And all of it—all these increasingly elevated scenarios of internal psychodrama—come spiraling out of an uncorroborated story about the sexual choices of a little-known peasant woman. The maddening growth of this unverifiable speculation led me to understand—metaphorically—the impulse to destroy the primal scene of this uncertainty: Döllersheim.

Of course, it's unfair to blame the inanimate stones of Döllersheim. One might as well blame the Rothschild family: The Rothschild variant of the Jewish-blood explanation of Hitler's psychology rears its head in the work of another American psychologist who circulated his analysis at least five years before Hans Frank gave birth to the Frankenberger variation.

It was Dr. Walter C. Langer, a psychoanalytically trained Harvard psychologist recruited by Office of Strategic Services (OSS) chief William J. Donovan to analyze the mind of Adolf Hitler, who seized on the Rothschild rumor and spun it into a Hitler family romance. The report he prepared on Hitler's psychology—based on an array of raw material from published literature to confidential diplomatic reports—was circulated within the U.S. government at the highest levels, reportedly up to President Roosevelt himself, in 1943, although it wasn't declassified until the late 1960s, nor published until 1972.

Langer, relying on the often undependable, partly spurious memories of industrialist Fritz Thyssen and SS defector Hans Jürgen Koehler, clearly believes there is merit in their accounts of the Rothschild rumor. He summarizes his sources as follows:

> [Austrian] Chancellor Dollfuss had ordered the Austrian police to conduct a thorough investigation into the Hitler family. As a result of this investigation a secret document was prepared that proved that Maria Anna Schicklgruber was living in Vienna at the time she conceived. At that time she was employed as a servant in the home of Baron

Rothschild. As soon as the family discovered her pregnancy she was sent back to her home in Spital where Alois was born. If it is true that one of the Rothschilds is the real father of Alois Hitler, it would make Adolf a quarter Jew. According to these sources, Adolf Hitler knew of the existence of the document and the incriminating evidence it contained. In order to obtain it he precipitated events in Austria and initiated the assassination of Dollfuss. According to this story, he failed to obtain the document at that time since Dollfuss had secreted it and had told Schuschnigg of its whereabouts so that in the event of his death the independence of Austria would remain assured.

Here, the Jewish-blood story in its most extreme version is elevated to a wellspring of power politics, the crux of a geopolitical blackmail intrigue that raises the petty-criminal transactions to world-historical levels. A fantasy undoubtedly, but what's fascinating about it is that this fantasy was destined for the hands of FDR, who was himself the subject of Jewish-blood rumors widely publicized by the Nazi propaganda chief Joseph Goebbels, who, like Hitler, might have actually believed that the Roosevelt family was descended from Dutch crypto-Jews whose real name was Rosenfeld or some such variant. Was the titanic struggle between the two leaders of the opposing forces in the Second World War conducted by two men, each of whom mistakenly thought the other was a secret Jew?

Langer gives every indication he wants to adapt the Rothschild story in toto. You can see him struggling with the temptation in the prose that follows his account of the Rothschild variant. "This is certainly a very intriguing hypothesis," he says, and "much of Adolf's later behavior could be explained in rather easy terms on this basis."

Only at the last moment does he pull back slightly, saying, "It is not absolutely necessary to assume that he has Jewish blood in his veins in order to make a comprehensive picture of his character. . . . From a purely scientific point of view, therefore, it is sounder not to base our reconstruction on such slim evidence. . . . Nevertheless, we can leave it as a possibility that requires further verification."

Nonetheless, he immediately enumerates no less than six reasons that "favor its possibility," most notably reason number four:

"That the intelligence and behavior of Alois, as well as that of his two sons [Alois Jr. and Adolf], is completely out of keeping with that usually found in Austrian peasant families. . . . Their ambitiousness and extraordinary political intuition are much more in harmony with the Rothschild tradition."

Note that the moment Langer gives in to the temptation to explain Hitler's character on the basis of the Rothschild thesis, subtle anti-Semitic characterizations begin to be applied *to Hitler*. The "ambitiousness and extraordinary political intuition" Hitler has "inherited" from the Rothschilds can be seen as a euphemistic way of calling them—and Hitler—pushy, scheming Jews.

The Jewish-blood story has been a veritable curse, an affliction for Hitler biographers and explainers—the elephant in the living room that is both impossible to ignore and impossible to accept. Freudians in particular have been profoundly conflicted about it. The psychoanalyst Norbert Bromberg, for instance, coauthor of the 1983 book-length monograph *Hitler's Psychopathology*, refers conspicuously to the Hans Frank story, at first declaring very responsibly, "without proof, the facts of this report remain a mystery."

Yet when they come to the next-to-last chapter, "Behind the Intensity of Hitler's Anti-Semitism," Bromberg and his coauthor Verna Small reveal themselves to be virtually unable to analyze the subject without it: "It may be that [Hitler] believed his own blood was 'poisoned' by Jewish blood because of the rumors that he had a Jewish grandfather," they say.

Bromberg and Small adopt the strategy used by those such as Robert Waite and Joachim Fest to *almost* have it both ways about the Hans Frank story. Fest, journalist author of the most popular German biography of Hitler, calls it "a rather wild story," the contents of which "can scarcely bear close scrutiny." But he's actually casting doubt only on the factuality of someone named Frankenberger impregnating Maria Schicklgruber; he's accepting as truth Hans Frank's claim that he told this tale to Hitler: "The *real significance* [of Frank's report] is independent of its being true or false. What is psychologically of crucial importance is *the fact* that Frank's findings forced Hitler to doubt his own descent" (emphasis added).

Influential Swiss psychoanalyst Alice Miller quotes from Fest but utterly ignores even Fest's faint reservations about the Hans Frank story. She assumes it's true and, not only that, assumes that Maria Schicklgruber's son Alois *knew* his father was probably Jewish.

How does she know that Alois knew he was a half-Jewish bastard? "These facts were so well known in the village that they were still being mentioned a hundred years later," she says. Her evidence for this is the Hans Frank story, which *nowhere* ascribes the Jewish-blood story to village talk. Still, Miller insists, "it is scarcely . . . conceivable that the villagers would believe such generosity [the supposed paternity payments from the Frankenberger family that Miller assumes were the talk of the town in Döllersheim] was unmotivated."

With a final, halfhearted stab at displaying some reservations about the story, she plunges on to her conclusion: "Whatever the truth actually was, a fourfold disgrace weighed upon Alois: being poor, being illegitimate, being separated from his real mother at the age of five, and having Jewish blood."

She veers back from the brink of total credulity—or tries to—by saying.

"*Even if the fourth* [Jewish blood] *was nothing but a rumor*, this did not make matters any easier [for Alois]" (emphasis added). In fact, she uses its problematic rumor status as a reason for making the Hans Frank story even *more* powerful and important as an explainer: "If not consciously acknowledged and mourned, uncertainty about one's descent can cause great anxiety and unrest, all the more so if, as in Alois's case, it is linked with an ominous rumor that can neither be proven nor completely refuted."

The problem is that neither the *existence* of this rumor nor Alois's consciousness of it have ever been proven.

Undaunted, Miller goes on to construct a kind of Great Chain of Uncertainty, something akin to Waite's but incorporating Miller's preoccupation with corporal punishment of children as the root of all evil: Uncertainty about the responsibility for Maria's pregnancy begat Alois's uncertainty about his own identity, which begat in Alois "great anxiety." This psychic pain of possible Jewishness begat Alois's habit of beating little Adolf, inflicting physical pain on his son out of psychic pain for the sin of his uncertain father. The physical pain Adolf suffered, when transformed into psychic trauma, is what drove Adolf to inflict genocide on the Jews.

The remarkable persistence of the will to believe the Jewish-blood theory, however shaky the foundation it's built on—despite the fact there might be no foundation for it at all—suggests it fills some deeper need. In a darker sense, it might fulfill some need to find some Jew, any Jew, even an apocryphal nineteen-year-old boy, to blame for the Holocaust. Alternately, it might fill a need to believe that the Holocaust was caused by something a Jew had *done*, however insanely disproportionate the punishment, rather than the more unbearable notion that it was not for an act but just for *being* that they were exterminated.

In any case, there's no doubt of the appeal of the Hans Frank story to the imagination of anti-Semites. When I first began the frustrating task of reinvestigating the Hans Frank story, I came across a deeply delusional fantasy growing out of it in a relatively obscure Saudi Arabian publication, the Saudi *Gazette*, published in Jedda. I'd found a reference to the Saudi paper in a letter to the editor of New York City's *Jewish Press*, and the letter writer supplied me with the complete text.

The author of the letter to the English-language weekly circulated among foreign workers in the Saudi kingdom identified himself as "A. Dusseldorf, Riyadh." The *Gazette* editor headlined "Dusseldorf's" letter with the inflammatory question in half-inch-high type:

WAS HITLER A JEW?

He had learned, the letter writer begins, that there is "evidence to prove that Hitler himself was a Jew. . . . Hitler's mother was a poor Austrian woman, a Christian employed as a maidservant in a wealthy Jewish household. . . . The actual father . . . was one of the Jewish sons of the old man."

Clearly, a garbled version of the Hans Frank story has entered into the venomous slipstream of anti-Semitic literature, the identifying fingerprint of the source being the characterization of the Jewish seducer as one of the "sons of the old man." The malicious twist the letter writer gives to the story is to construct an argument that holds that since Hitler was a Jew, "the Jews should pay Germans reparations for the War, since *one of theirs* caused the destruction of Germany."

This sick misuse of the Hans Frank story should not obscure the fact that there can be legitimate, or at least understandable, reasons for its persistent appeal. The Hans Frank story has both a deeply Freudian and a grandly Wagnerian dimension that makes it more tempting than, say, Simon Wiesenthal's belief that an accidental encounter with a syphilitic Jewish prostitute explains Hitler's anti-Semitism. The Hans Frank story has a plentitude of Wagnerian motifs: a "hero" with poison-maddened blood plunged into a frenzied Götter-dämmerung of world-destroying self-destructive fury. And it's Wagnerian in another sense: There are those who believe that a study of Wagner's own "Jewish problem" demonstrates that Wagner, who was a key source of Hitler's mystical blood-and-race rationale for his anti-Semitism—what Saul Friedländer calls his "redemptive anti-Semitism"—suffered himself from the very syndrome many attribute to Hitler.

In his Cambridge University study, George Steiner made the Wagnerian parallel explicit for me: "The two great figures of modern German Jew-hatred may have suspected—*may*—that they were themselves tainted with Jewish blood. In Wagner's case, the obvious resemblance to the actor Geyer [his mother's Jewish paramour] is overwhelming. As to Hitler himself, it's not the facts, alas, that are very important, it's the possibility that he believed it. In which case, you have two self-doubting beacons of anti-Semitism whose self-hatred spiraled into an objective loathing of Jews."

It's a grand poetic vision, that spiral of self-hatred: it creates the image of a Dostoyevskian, literary Hitler, one that satisfies a hunger for profound explanations for profound events. But the facts, alas, are that we cannot even be sure Hitler suspected his grandmother of sleeping with a Jew, the alleged point of origin of the "spiraling self-hatred" Steiner suspects may lie beneath the objective loathing.

I've come to feel the Hans Frank story has been seized upon by the explainers for the wrong reason. Succumbing to the temptation to find a single-pointed theory, one that explains the single most significant and mysterious aspect of his psyche—his anti-Semitism—they've ignored the *kind* of story Hans Frank's tale is.

It's a blackmail story. Actually, it's two blackmail stories, one nested within the other. One, perhaps fictional, is set in 1836; the other, at least partly real, is set between 1930 and 1933. Two blackmail stories featuring two sets of Hitler-family blackmailers—as well as the spectacle of one Hitler blackmailed by another, indeed, one descendant of Maria Schicklgruber blackmailing another.

I believe that there is, in this more neglected aspect of the Hans Frank story, a window into a more neglected aspect of the Hitler thought-world: the pervasiveness of blackmail consciousness. Consider the *kind* of Hitler who emerges from the Hans Frank story. This is a Hitler steeped in the nuances of small-time sleaze, a Hitler who can think both like a blackmailer and like a blackmailer's victim. When approached by one of the Hitler-family grifters— the Liverpool-based William Patrick Hitler, who makes "a disgusting blackmail threat"—when Hans Frank then supposedly produces documents to corroborate it, Adolf then conjures up, *on the spot*, a century-old blackmail scenario involving his own grandparents as an escape hatch from the imputation of the blackmail documents he's confronted with.

It's a remarkable performance under pressure, some fancy footwork that suggests a deep understanding of the mind of the blackmailer and the deep structure of the blackmail transaction. This is a Hitler for whom the feints and counterfeints of the blackmail relationship seem like second nature. This Hitler is a different one from the demonic, Wagnerian mass-mesmerist, the grandiose Svengali, the German Expressionist Hitler—the Caligari Hitler, one might say (after the demonic mesmerist figure in the Weimar Expressionist film *The Cabinet of Dr. Caligari*). The Hitler Hans Frank saw (or created in the image of the one he knew) is the film noir Hitler, the Munich-demimonde Hitler, one whose relentlessly seedy, small-time character has been forgotten if not erased. This Hitler provides a useful corrective to a postwar Hitler who has grown ever more grandiose and all-powerfully demonic to match the gravity of the horrors he left in his wake. The Hitler known to Munich associates such as Hans Frank, the one that persists in Frank's memory or imagination despite the subsequent horrors, is the resolutely small-time conniver who was forever enmeshed in petty blackmail schemes, devious subterfuges: Hitler as sleazy con man, small-time crook.

While the truth of the Maria Schicklgruber blackmail intrigue must remain suppositious—did it happen in fact, did Hitler invent it, did Hans Frank invent a Hitler who invented it?—there does exist a peculiar kind of corroboration of this seedy *vision* of Hitler, confirmation that the blackmail transaction is somehow at the heart of who Hitler was—a recurrent Hitler family trait in fact. Confirmation that blackmail rather than Jewishness may be the hidden defining hereditary strain in Hitler's blood.

I'm speaking of the Hitler-versus-Hitler blackmail intrigue that erupted two generations after the events in Döllersheim: the blackmail plot involving another shadowy Hitler family couple, this one initiated by the shady mother-son team of Bridget Hitler and her son William Patrick Hitler, whose attempt to extort money from Adolf represents an uncanny recapitulation of the notional extortion plot of the previous Hitler couple: Maria Schicklgruber and Johann Georg Heidler.

The "loathsome relative" (as Hans Frank quotes Hitler calling William Patrick Hitler) as much as admitted it himself in a debriefing interview he gave to the OSS. The never-published summary of the OSS debriefing of this black-sheep Hitler nephew reveals a kind of low-comic duel between two Hitler family grifters, both playing for high stakes. The debriefing took place on September 10, 1943, in New York City. The nephew had arrived in the United States in 1939, after fleeing from Germany to France and then France to England, spreading insidious rumors about his Uncle Adolf along the way. Later, he mysteriously dropped out of sight, although John Toland hinted to me that he'd located William Patrick Hitler living in New York in the 1970s under a different name—one which Toland refused to disclose to me—and that he'd confirmed the substance of what he had told the OSS.

Before disappearing, William Patrick left behind with the OSS his own version of a sleazy standoff with his uncle, the outlines of which roughly match Hans Frank's account—a sordid, occasionally black-comic saga that gains some credibility because the younger Hitler is quite cheerful about assigning himself a rather disreputable mercenary role in the affair.

Money was his motive from the start, he admits to the debriefing officer. "In the late 1920s," the OSS summary records,

> when Adolf began to rise in popularity sufficiently to get into the English newspapers, they [William and his mother, Bridget] wrote to Adolf. [Then,] in 1930 when Hitler suddenly became famous with over 100 seats in the Reichstag they thought it was an opportunity of making some money by giving an interview to the Hearst press. Negotiations were underway but they felt the need of additional information and wrote to Alois [Jr., then living in Germany] asking for further details about Adolf's youth. The reply came in the form of a demand from Adolf to come to Munich immediately for a conference. . . .
>
> Upon their arrival in Munich they found Adolf in a perfect rage.
>
> The gist of what Adolf said was now that he was gaining some importance the family need not think that they could climb on his back and get a free ride to fame. He claimed that any release to the Hearst newspapers involving his family would destroy his chances for success in view of Alois' record.

The "record" Hitler was referring to was Alois's arrest for bigamy in 1924. This was embarrassing to Hitler, but did he really believe that was enough to "destroy his chances for success"? Or was his concern for Alois's petty misdemeanor a screen for a *real* family scandal he didn't wish exposed, the dubious Döllersheim transactions?

Hitler concluded his tirade, the nephew told the OSS, with the demand that "negotiations with the Hearst syndicate . . . be stopped immediately. . . . The great problem was how this could be done without arousing suspicion" that Hitler wasn't suppressing skeletons in the closet of his family history.

Hitler's first attempt to devise a solution to this problem—the mistaken-identity cover story—was laughable and reflects the short-term thinking of the petty criminal that backfires in the long run. Hitler

> suggested that William Patrick and his mother return to London and tell the Hearst people that it was a question of mistaken identity, and that they had discovered that the Adolf Hitler who was the leader of the Nazi party was *not* the uncle they had supposed, but an Adolf Hitler who was no kin of theirs whatever. Hitler was pleased with this solution . . . handed Alois 2,000 pounds to cover their expenses . . . [and] instructions to give Mrs. [Bridget] Hitler what was left over when their expenses had been paid.

It's hard to believe Hitler thought this "Oops! Wrong Hitler!" strategy would hold up for any length of time. But it reflects a certain desperation (as does the two-thousand-pound payoff, a considerable sum of money for "expenses") to keep reporters away from the English Hitler relatives, from any discussion of family history.

Having temporarily silenced his relatives, Hitler then supplied to Hearst a family figure he could control, the bigamous half brother Alois Jr., safely within Germany's borders, who dutifully penned—or allowed to be penned under his byline—a short, pious story that appeared in the November 30, 1930, issue of Hearst's New York *American*, entitled simply "Adolf Hitler." It's a brief, sanitized substitute for the one proposed by the English relatives, a story that admiringly details Hitler's rise from poverty to lead a movement to save Germany and omits all mention of the Schicklgruber side of the family history.

But the bought-off black-sheep nephew would not stay bought off. Sometime in the following two to three years, most probably in the summer of 1932, William Patrick Hitler put the squeeze on again. In his debriefing, he gallantly tried to shift the responsibility for this more overt and explicit extortion attempt to his mother:

> Mrs. [Bridget] Hitler chafed more and more under the poverty and thought Adolf might be willing to pay something to keep her quiet. . . . [She] wrote Hitler with a thinly veiled demand. Hitler replied and

invited William Patrick to Berchtesgaden for a summer vacation. . . . Hitler . . . told William Patrick that . . . since he insisted on making demands on Hitler, that he could see no way out of it except to tell him the truth . . . that his father Alois Jr. was not really the son of Hitler's father but a boy who had been orphaned as an infant and whom Alois Sr. [Adolf's father] had taken into his home. . . . [Adolf] only wanted to make it clear to William Patrick that he had absolutely no claim on him as an uncle and that they were, in fact, not related at all.

If we were not dealing with Adolf Hitler, this latest ploy would be a great comic moment in a small-time way. First, he tells William Patrick Hitler that he should tell people he had the *wrong* Hitler in mind as his relative; now, he's suggesting to him that Adolf is the right Hitler, but he, William Patrick, is not; they're not really relatives, not blood relatives, at all.

It's the comic inversion of the family romance; William's father was not a prodigal who turned out to be related to royalty (i.e., Adolf Hitler), he's someone who thinks he's related to royalty but who turns out to be an orphan of nonroyal (non-Hitler) blood. In a sense, Hitler's incredibly strained attempt to retrospectively detach the loathsome, troublesome relatives from his blood echoes the calculation attributed to Hitler by Hans Frank in his strained attempt to detach his grandmother Maria Schicklgruber from the taint of Jewish blood.

One suspects an undertone of deadpan satire in William Patrick's account of Hitler's latest attempt to erase the relationship between the two Hitlers. His description of Hitler's feigned reluctance to "break the news" that William's father was not a *true* Hitler—"he could see no way out of it except to tell him the truth"—is particularly nice. One wants to know if there was an attempt on Hitler's part to say this with a straight face, or whether there was a complicit smile between the two practiced Hitler-family con men, as one of them revealed his next move to the other in a duel of professionals.

The next move was William Patrick's, and he proved himself no novice; he was an investigative con man: "After his return to London," the OSS summary continues, "William Patrick and his mother checked on this report [that Alois Jr. was an orphan] through the British Consul General in Vienna who, after some time, said the story was impossible because no adoption papers were on record and the baptismal certificates were clear [that he *was* in fact a blood relative]. . . . William Patrick has also a photostatic copy of Adolf's baptismal certificate."

Once again, William Patrick says he was summoned for a conference, apparently after renewing his blackmail threats and demands. Again, he says, "over and over again, Hitler warned him about trying to cash in on their relationship." Unfazed by this onslaught, the nephew says he produced his trump card: "He said he then acquainted Hitler with the fact that he had documents from the British consul to the effect that his story about his father [being no blood relation to Adolf] was not true and that copies of these documents were deposited with the English government as well as with his mother in London."

If we can believe the nephew—and at a certain point (perhaps here) I suspect his imagined vision of himself defying the Führer feared by the world exceeds the reality—Hitler could not have relished the notion of the British government and the loose-cannon mother having his personal genealogical documentary touchstones in their hands. The deal that followed was, according to the nephew, an uneasy truce of mutual hostage taking and reciprocal threat. First, "Hitler arranged a job for [William Patrick] at the Opel Auto Company" in Berlin. (Pictures exist to confirm his employment there.) This provided the nephew with the cash flow he'd sought; it gave Hitler the nephew as a kind of hostage (now that he'd come to power in Berlin) within watching distance; and it gave the English relatives a kind of counterthreat with the documents they supposedly held hostage in London.

With an eerie ability to echo his Uncle Adolf's characteristic fusion of cravenness and boastfulness, William Patrick Hitler bragged to the OSS that, with the deal sealed, he had Hitler in the palm of his hand. He depicts himself as the kind of fellow who could stroll into Hitler's Reichchancellery and make the raging Führer of the German people quail into quiet submission: "From that time on," he told the OSS, "Hitler became more tolerant of him and whenever he began to rage about William Patrick's activities he [William Patrick] had only to mention the documents in order to get Hitler to calm down."

Although the OSS summary makes no skeptical comment, one really has to laugh at this picture for its peculiarly Hitlerian self-aggrandizement: the preening little blackmailer supposing he's got the world-conquering Führer wrapped around his finger. If there's something Adolfian in William Patrick, there's also something William Patrickian in Adolf: that combination of low cunning and grandiose imagination. The glimpse William Patrick Hitler gives us into the thought-world of the blackmailer—his own and that of his uncle— brings us closer to the Munich Hitler. This is the Hitler his disreputable Brown House cronies knew. This is the film noir Hitler, the poison-pen Hitler, the Hitler exposed with pitiless clarity by the journalists of his chief newspaper enemy, the paper called "the Poison Kitchen."

CHAPTER 3

The Poison Kitchen:
The Forgotten First Explainers

In which the heroic but doomed reporters of the Munich Post *capture the essence of a "political criminal" in the blackmail consciousness of the Munich demimonde*

Hitler's party called it the Poison Kitchen. That was the preferred epithet for his newspaper nemesis, the persistent poisoned thorn in his side, the *Munich Post*. The running battle between Hitler and the courageous reporters and editors of the *Post* is one of the great unreported dramas in the history of journalism—and a long-erased opening chapter in the chronology of attempts to explain Adolf Hitler.

The *Munich Post* journalists were the first to focus sustained critical attention on Hitler, from the very first moment this strange specter emerged from the beer-hall back rooms to take to the streets of Munich in the early 1920s. They were the first to tangle with him, the first to ridicule him, the first to investigate him, the first to expose the seamy underside of his party, the murderous criminal behavior masked by its pretensions to being a political movement. They were the first to attempt to alert the world to the nature of the rough beast slouching toward Berlin.

But the drama of their struggle has largely been lost to history. The exposés they published are remembered, if at all, only in obscure footnotes; the names of those who risked their lives to report and publish those exposés rarely appear even there. Their full story has never really been told, even in Germany, or perhaps especially in Germany, where it's more comforting for the national self-image to believe that nobody *really* knew who Hitler was until it was too late, until after 1933, when he had too much power (or so it's said) for anyone to resist.

But the writers of the *Munich Post* knew, and they published the truth for those who cared to see it. While their opposition to Hitler grew initially out of ideology (the *Post* was founded and sponsored by the Bavarian Social Democratic Party), their struggle with Hitler became extremely personal. They came to know Hitler in a way few others have known him; they knew him and his circle as intimate enemies, grappling at close range with them in the streets, in the courtrooms, in the beer halls, attacking Hitler with a combination of *Washington Post*–like investigative zeal and *New York Post*–like tabloid glee— and a peculiar streetwise, wised-up *Munich Post* edge all their own.

Their duel with Hitler lasted a dozen years and produced some of the sharpest, most penetrating insights into his character, his mind and method, then or since. Much of their work has been forgotten, but not much has been surpassed. And, as the name Poison Kitchen suggests, they succeeded in getting under Hitler's skin.

The Poison Kitchen: Let's linger a moment on that epithet. As a metaphor, its literal meaning is probably intended to convey the notion of a kitchen "cooking up" poisonous slanders, poison-pen journalism. But "poison" was not a word Hitler used lightly—it was one he reserved for his most profound hatreds. In his final testament, the last words he addressed to the world before committing suicide in his Berlin bunker, he enjoined the German people above all else never to cease from the "struggle against the Jews, the eternal poisoners of the world."

Hitler's final epithet for the Jews: "poisoners." It's an appellation with medieval roots in the accusations of well-poisoning that were used to incite pogroms in plague-stricken Central Europe. But "poison" and "poisoning" are more highly charged words than that; "poison" most often took on a racial, sexual meaning when referring to Jews, as in "blood poisoning": the sexual adulteration, pollution, tainting, and infection of Aryan purity. Jewish blood for Hitler was a sexually transmitted poison. It's hard to think of another word in his vocabulary more fraught with hatred and loathing.

And Hitler's hatred for the Poison Kitchen nearly matched in self-destructive fury the hatred he had for the "eternal poisoners." An argument can be made (and has been made by J. P. Stern, Lucy Dawidowicz, and others) that Hitler sabotaged his chances to hold the eastern front against the Red Army in 1944 because he insisted on withdrawing troop trains from his fighting forces in order to use them to accelerate the delivery of Jews to Auschwitz and other death camps, where he used poison gas to poison the "poisoners."

Similarly, at the crucial turning point in his putsch attempt in November 1923, at the moment Hitler most needed to mobilize maximum armed support for his march on the government center, Hitler's strongest and most fanatically devoted cohort—the Stosstrupp Hitler (the personal-bodyguard troops who were to evolve into the SS)—were dispatched instead to Number 19 Altheimer Eck, the building that housed the *Munich Post*, where they spent crucial hours sacking and looting and ripping apart the offices and presses of the Poison Kitchen. In what sounds like an early instance of the tactic of deniability that Hitler would employ to distance himself from the order for the Kristallnacht pogrom (and the Final Solution itself), he later proclaimed himself shocked, *shocked* at the assault on the Poison Kitchen by his personal bodyguards.

On that occasion, the Poison Kitchen rebuilt itself and rejoined the struggle. But ten years later, in March 1933, the moment the Nazi takeover in Bavaria was completed, a vicious troop of SA thugs burst into the *Munich Post* building, gutting it completely, dumping trays of broken type onto the streets, and dragging writers and editors away to prison.

This savage attack is a perverse tribute to just how galling the *Post* had been to Hitler from the very beginning. They knew how to get to him, get under his skin. They had his number in a sense far deeper than skin-deep: in the sense that they'd seen into him, through him, in a way that few others had or would. They'd seen the Hitler within Hitler, and—I believe—he knew they knew. It's been largely lost or forgotten to history, their vision of Hitler, but it's still there, it's still possible to retrieve it, or at least to glimpse, in the crumbling pages of the issues of the *Munich Post* decaying in Munich archives, some elusive truths about the Munich Hitler that have largely been eclipsed by the postwar focus on the Berlin Hitler, the Auschwitz Hitler.

The battle between Hitler and the Poison Kitchen began as far back as 1921, before Hitler had succeeded in solidifying his control over the fledgling Nazi Party. In August of that year, the *Post* found a way to cause Hitler severe embarrassment, enough to provoke a howl of outrage and a resort to the courts. They'd obtained the text of a vicious attack on Hitler by an internal faction of the Nazi Party.

This poison-pen polemic, entitled "Adolf Hitler, Traitor," had been circulating privately until the *Post* made it available for all to see. And it struck home, raising what would become persistent questions about Hitler and persistent themes of the *Munich Post*'s reporting: Hitler's alienness, his strangeness, both of origin and personality, his mysterious sources of support ("Just what does he do for a living?" the pamphlet asked), and, most woundingly, the question of his possible Jewishness or of some subterranean relationship to Jews. In his sudden grab for dictatorial power over the party, in his scheming divisive behavior, the anonymous Nazi authors of the poison-pen pamphlet claimed, Hitler was not only serving "Jewish interests" but acting "like a real Jew" himself.

Hitler's response was typically twofold, licit and illicit: Nazi death threats against the writers of the *Munich Post* in the night; by day, he took them to court, suing them for libel and fraud, taking advantage of the right-wing nationalist character of the Bavarian judiciary, as he would repeatedly in the twelve-year struggle that followed.

When the libel suit came to trial later that year, Hitler shamelessly accused the *Post* of fabricating, counterfeiting the poison-pen polemic that originated within his own party. The verdict, as would become the pattern, went against the *Post*, and a fine of six hundred marks was imposed. The headline on the story the *Post* ran about the verdict starkly defined the combat in the epic duel that would ensue:

HITLER GEGEN DIE MÜNCHENER POST

Hitler against the *Munich Post*. It was an unfair, uneven struggle. They were a small band of unarmed scribblers taking on a well-financed army of murderous thugs. But in ways large and small, they made his life miserable. Hitler "has no secrets from us," they liked to boast. And throughout the extraordinary, nightmarish last-ditch war they waged in the final years of Hitler's ascent to power, they found a way to obtain and publish one damning secret after another, often internal memos and correspondence of Hitler's inner circle that linked him and his cronies to sexual scandal, financial corruption, and serial political murder. They had eyes everywhere: If Hitler went to Berlin and spent lavishly at a luxury hotel, the next morning the *Post* would print the hotel bill under the derisive headline "How Hitler Lives." More grimly, they printed a running total of another kind of Hitler bill: the growing number of political murders credited to the account of the "Hitler Party," as they preferred to call the National Socialist gang.

"The Hitler Party": Their repeated use of the term was a relentless reminder to their readers that the crimes they reported on by Nazi Party members were the personal responsibility of one man, that the party they reported on was less a serious, ideologically based movement than an instrument of one man's criminal pathology.

At the close of the *Post*'s 1932 exposé of the death squad within the Hitler Party known as "Cell G," a story that was picked up by newspapers all over the world (and soon forgotten, alas), the *Munich Post* writers appended a revealing quotation from Adolf Hitler about his personal responsibility for his party's acts, a remark that has resonance beyond that particular scandal: "Nothing happens in the movement without my knowledge, without my approval," Hitler boasted. "Even more, nothing happens without my wish."

The Nazi Party and its crimes were Hitler's personal responsibility, the

Poison Kitchen always insisted. And they had no hesitation about making their attacks on Hitler relentlessly personal. They never, for instance, let Hitler or his followers forget Hitler's notorious belly flop in the face of hostile fire at the climactic moment of the November 1923 putsch attempt, the march on the Munich Odeonsplatz. As soon as loyal government troops fired at his mob, Hitler dived to the street and used the corpses of comrades to shield himself from bullets. There are conflicting interpretations of the belly flop: Some say Hitler was deliberately or inadvertently dragged down out of the line of fire by the grasp of a falling comrade, others that it was the instinct of a combat soldier to hit the deck when shots were flying. But it's also true that Hitler's chief ally, General Erich Ludendorff, picked himself up and marched straight into the hostile fire after that first volley, while Hitler, suffering from a dislocated shoulder, slunk away in pain before being carried off into hiding.

But for the *Post*, Hitler was always *on his belly*, a creature both craven and dangerously serpentlike. In reviewing the *Post* issues from the final months of the struggle against Hitler, I came across a cartoon they published in November 1932. It was a moment of heartbreaking false hope. After surging for two years, Hitler's vote in the final free national election, the one held on November 7, plummeted. There were those, even at the *Post*, who believed that at last Hitler's threat was fading, short of takeover. The cartoon showed a Hitler having been kicked out of a door by voters and landing ignominiously on the pavement. The prematurely triumphant caption read:

ON HIS BELLY AGAIN!

There was something about seeing that cartoon that brought home to me the exhilaration and tragedy of the *Munich Post* struggle. They always seemed to be one more story, one more exposé away from scotching the serpent. Once it seemed they were one story away from driving him to suicide. At the time of Geli Raubal's death, the questions the *Post* raised about the nature of Hitler's relationship to his attractive half-niece and about his role in her death and the suggestion that her nose had been broken in a quarrel brought Hitler close to the brink of shooting himself, according to several associates who were with him at the time. According to Hitler's attorney, Hans Frank, whom he'd dispatched to threaten the *Post* with a lawsuit over its Geli Raubal coverage, Hitler was moaning that "he could not look at a paper any more, the terrible smear campaign would kill him."

Alas, it didn't: In the end, in the sixteen months following Geli's death, as their pitched battle with Hitler and the Hitler Party reached a peak, they were still one story shy of bringing him down on January 30, 1933, when it became too late.

There were other journalists engaged in the same struggle. There was Konrad Heiden, Munich correspondent for the *Frankfurter Zeitung*, who went on to found an anti-Nazi press syndicate based in Berlin, and Rudolf Olden, Munich correspondent for Berlin papers, both of whom escaped with their lives to write scathing books about Hitler in an attempt to warn the West. And there was Fritz Gerlich of *Der Gerade Weg*, who did not escape.

But the *Munich Post* reporters—men such as Martin Gruber, Erhard Auer, Edmund Goldschagg, Julius Zerfass, among others—were in the trenches every day, taking on Hitler, facing down his thugs and their threats, testing the power of truth to combat evil, and sharing the Cassandra-like fate of discovering its limits. They lost, but there is more to their legacy than the heroism they displayed (although that in itself deserves far more recognition than it's received from their contemporary successors among German journalists). They also left behind a vision of Hitler, a coherent explanation, a perspective on him that's been lost, for the most part, to history and to the debate over who Hitler was. It's a perspective they never had the leisure to sum up in so many words in a tract, but it's one that emerges clearly from an immersion in their day-to-day coverage of Hitler and the Hitler Party.

Those hectic, nightmarish final two years were dominated in the *Post* coverage by a series of serial, detonating, closely linked Hitler Party scandals that began with a relatively small-time sexual-blackmail plot that, when exposed by the *Post*, led to escalating revelations of far more serious and deadly Hitler Party scandals: First, the exposé of "Cell G," the Hitler Party's secret death squad, which had been caught red-handed trying to assassinate the party members who'd brought them embarrassment in the original sexual-blackmail scandal. This led to an even more frightening and unfortunately prophetic exposé: secret Hitler Party plans for a bloodbath, a massacre of their political enemies once they came to power, a mass murder in embryo for all to see.

They even glimpsed, through a glass darkly, the shadow of the Final Solution. In fact, they picked up on the fateful Hitler euphemism for genocide—*endlösung*, the final solution—in the context of the fate of the Jews as early as December 9, 1931, in a chilling and prophetic dispatch called "The Jews in the Third Reich."

More than a year before Hitler came to power, the *Post* reported it had uncovered "a secret plan" from an inside source in Hitler's SA. A secret plan in which the Hitler Party had "worked out special orders for the solution of the Jewish question when they take power, instructions that are top secret. They have forbidden discussion of these in public for fear of its foreign policy effects."

What followed was an extremely detailed list of a score of anti-Jewish measures that foretold with astonishing precision all the successive stages of restrictions and persecutions the Nazi Party was to take against the Jews in the period between 1933 and 1939. And then the *Post* hinted at more: It spoke of a further "*final* solution."

The list of restrictions it predicted seems familiar now: removal of Jews from the courts, from the civil service, the professions; police surveillance, including residency and identity permits; confiscation of Jewish enterprises and property; detention and expulsion of "unwanted" Jews; Nuremberg-type laws against intermarriage and sexual and social intercourse.

All of this leading up to a further "final solution" beyond that: "for the final solution of the Jewish question it is proposed to use the Jews in Germany for slave labor or for cultivation of the German swamps administered by a special SS division."

One feels a chill reading this: the division between the ratcheting up of legal and civil restrictions and something beyond that—a final solution that involves removal of the Jews physically from German society for a worse fate in "the swamps" at the hands of the SS. That invocation of the final solution in the swamps carries with it a premonitory echo of an ugly euphemistic jest about the Final Solution Hitler, Himmler, and Heydrich would share ten years later as recorded in Hitler's "Table Talk": Isn't it terrible the "rumor" that we're exterminating the Jews when we're only "parking them" in the swamps of Russia.

Were the *Munich Post* writers aware then that those swamps would become euphemisms for the mass graves to come? One can only guess at what they sensed beneath the swamps of the "final solution" they reported on in 1931. (A survey of contemporary German and foreign newspapers for that period shows no evidence that any of them thought this premonitory report on a "final solution" worthy of further investigation.) But in the concatenation of their exposés and investigations, in the chronicling of the string of political murders committed by the Hitler Party, the *Munich Post* reporters left little hidden about the party's murderous nature and intent. They saw it as a homicidal criminal enterprise beneath the facade of a political party.

The emphasis on the down and dirty criminality of the Hitler Party is a signature of the *Munich Post* writers' vision: They were, in effect, enlightened police reporters covering a homicide story in the guise of a political one. This point was brought home to me vividly in a conversation I had with a son of one of the foremost chefs of the Poison Kitchen, their star political reporter, "the Prussian Nightingale." The Prussian Nightingale was the nickname his *Munich Post* colleagues gave to Edmund Goldschagg, one of the most visible point men in the *Post*'s war against Hitler—"Prussian" because he had come to the *Post* in 1928 after a long stint writing for a Berlin paper and "Nightingale" because he was known for his exuberant, convivial, often musical way with words, the way he would brighten the *Post Stammtisch* (communal table) at the Café Heck with his high spirits and songs.

When I spoke to Goldschagg's son Rolf in Munich, I found him largely unaware of the details of his father's most dramatic clashes with Hitler. They had, it's true, taken place before Rolf was born. But the limited-edition memorial volume Rolf had commissioned about his father dwelt for little more than a chapter on the pre-1933 struggle. In part, this can be attributed to the fact that his father's life *after* the Hitler takeover was so eventful—and also quite heroic. After the *Post* was sacked, the Prussian Nightingale was arrested and drafted into the army. But after being expelled for his political views, he went to ground in Freiburg, where, despite his own suspect status, he risked his life harboring a Jewish woman for a year until she could escape to Switzerland. Afterward, he became one of the founders of what was to become the powerful South German daily, the *Süddeutsche Zeitung.*

In part, the son's lack of detailed knowledge about his father's anti-Hitler journalism might be due to his temperamental distance from the flamboyant, socialist, anti-Hitler firebrand his father was. But the son of the Prussian Nightingale did make one memorable, defining remark to me about his father's vision of Adolf Hitler. I'd asked him a question I'd put to a number of survivors and chroniclers of the Hitler period: Did he think Hitler's evil could be explained by some insanity or mental derangement?

"No," the son insisted to me, with more passion than he'd summoned for any other comment on the Poison Kitchen, "my father did *not* think Hitler was crazy. He always referred to him as a *political criminal.*"

Not a criminal politician; a political criminal. When I first heard it, I thought this phrase had the ring of sterile Marxist rhetoric. But after spending time in the archives with their back issues, it was clear to me the *Post* was not a captive of Marxist orthodoxy; they were, in fact, anticommunist and contemptuous of the police terror masquerading as Marxism in the Soviet Union, a contempt embodied in the derisive name they gave to the death-squad infrastructure they exposed in the Nazi Party: "The Cheka in the Brown House," Cheka being at one time the informal name of the feared Soviet secret police. The *Post* was more liberal and populist than Marxist.

And, in fact, after immersing myself in their reportage on Hitler and the Hitler Party, I came to see that "political criminal" was not an empty epithet but a carefully considered encapsulation of a larger vision: that Hitler's evil was not generated from some malevolent higher abstraction or belief, from an ideology that descended into criminality and murder to achieve its aims; rather, his evil *arose* from his criminality and only garbed itself in ideological belief.

One sees this in the paper day by day, not so much in the big scandals, the headline-making events, but in the daily log of murders. "Feme [Death Squad] Murder in Thuringia," "Brown Murder in Stuttgart," "SA Killing in Halle," "Brown Terror in Magdeburg," "Nazi Murders in Lippe." Scarcely an issue went by in those final two years without one and usually two, three, or four brief dispatches reporting the blatant cold-blooded murder of political opponents by Hitler Party members. Cumulatively, what one is witnessing is the systematic extermination of the best and bravest, the most outspoken opponents of the Hitler Party as they're gunned down or clubbed to death with truncheons or as bodies are found stabbed, strangled, drowned, or simply never found at all. Followed frequently by reports of how one court after another has allowed the murderers to go free or get off with sentences more appropriate for petty theft.

Reading the *Post*'s despairing daily drumbeat of murder adds a missing dimension to the account of Hitler's rise, one that has been lost in some of the grand postwar explanations, which tend to assume some deep causal inevitability to Hitler's accession to power—economic conditions, generational psychic trauma, Christian anti-Semitism, fear of modernism, the techniques of mass propaganda, the torch-lit Nuremberg rallies, the manipulation of emotional symbols, the mesmerized crowds, the rhetoric, and, above all, the ideology.

All of these may help explain Hitler's appeal, but they do not necessarily explain Hitler's success. As Alan Bullock was the first to demonstrate, Hitler came almost as close to failing in his drive to seize power as he did to succeeding; what's missing from the grander explanations is what one sees on the ground, so to speak, the texture of daily terror apparent in the pages of the *Munich Post*, the systematic, step-by-step slaughter of Hitler's most capable political opponents, murdered by his party of political criminals.

But there are two other crimes that emerge from the seamy web of political criminality the *Post* exposed, two types of crimes that, if less violent and bloody than murder, cumulatively emerge in the pages of the *Post* as the peculiar, metaphoric *signature* crimes of the Munich Hitler and the Hitler Party: blackmail and counterfeiting.

Perhaps the best way to get a feel for the Poison Kitchen vision of the Hitler Party is to look closely at one of the emblematic blackmail scandals they exposed and then move on to the sources of their preoccupation with counterfeiting, not just the small-time forgery of documents but the Hitler Party's wholesale counterfeiting of history itself.

It began, the two-year-long final protracted battle between Hitler and the Poison Kitchen, with the June 22, 1931, issue and a sardonic banner headline that read:

WARM BROTHERHOOD IN THE BROWN HOUSE

followed by the subtitle: **SEXUAL LIFE IN THE THIRD REICH.**

What followed was a plunge directly into the seamy heart of Hitler Party blackmail culture, a thriving criminal subculture preying on itself, which raised the blackmail letter to a black art.

The focus of the story is an elaborate masterpiece of a blackmail missive directed to SA chief Ernst Roehm in the guise of an investigation by the letter writer *on behalf of Roehm* into another blackmail plot against Roehm. Here we have the characteristic syndrome of Hitler Party blackmail intrigue: Every blackmail plot generates, hives off, a parasitical doppelgänger blackmail plot leeching off it. It's a Hobbesean vision of predators preying on predators in a jungle of criminality. This one features, in addition, a Watergate-like break-in to retrieve the deeply embarrassing pornographic correspondence that gave rise to the original blackmail plot.

But before presenting its sensational report on "Sexual Life in the Third Reich," the *Munich Post* carefully defined its own ostensibly high-minded motives for bringing to light this sordid material. The epigraph opening the article is a quotation from Nazi Party ideologist Gregor Strasser attacking the attempt by parties on the left to abolish the Weimar Constitution's famous paragraph 175, the clause that made homosexual acts serious crimes. "But," the article begins, "every knowledgeable person knows, especially Gregor Strasser, that inside the Hitler Party the most flagrant whorishness contemplated by paragraph 175 is widespread."

"Now," they continue, "Hitler is making Roehm [who'd spent several years in semiofficial exile in Bolivia to let previous homosexual scandals die down] his chief commander, [which] is like trusting the cat to guard the cream." The *Munich Post* is *not*, it goes to great length to make clear, condemning homosexuality but rather "the disgusting *hypocrisy* that the Nazi Party demonstrates— outward moral indignation while inside its own ranks the most shameless practices . . . prevail." It is for this reason "we feel the need to denounce the shocking events inside the Hitler Party. Herewith we publish a report by a press officer of the Nazis, Dr. Meyer in Regensburg, sent to Roehm in Munich. . . . This report is both a letter of confirmation [of tasks completed], at the same time it is a blackmail letter addressed to the commander in chief, making him aware of his own words about his illegal homosexual activities—in order to gain further promotion [for the letter writer] above others in the party."

It's a brilliantly insidious piece of work, Dr. Meyer's letter. The talented Restoration rakes and poets were once famously described as "a mob of gentlemen who wrote well" in the late seventeenth century. Meyer was one of the mob of educated thugs among the Hitler Party inner circle who wrote blackmail literature well.

Meyer's letter to Roehm, obtained by and published in full in the *Post*, begins with an ostentatiously detailed recounting of his previous meeting with Roehm, a recounting that would be unnecessary if he had not wanted to put his potential leverage against Roehm in written form. It was a night, he recalls, in which the well-oiled SA chief was flushed with the triumph of his return to head Hitler's private army. He gives us Roehm joking boastfully that "homosexuality had been something unknown [in Bolivia] until [he] arrived, but [he'd] been working to produce rapid and lasting changes in *that* situation."

Then, according to Meyer's "reminder" to Roehm, the SA chief commissioned Meyer to intervene in a blackmail attempt against him, which initiates the spying and break-in mission Meyer proceeds to describe—ostensibly for Roehm's benefit, but more to demonstrate the dirt he has on him.

Meyer proceeds to take us on a tour of Roehm's demimonde as he tries to trace Roehm's blackmailer back to its source. First stop is a den of iniquity passing as the offices of a certain Dr. Heimsoth, a figure out of later Raymond Chandler. "You mentioned," Meyer meticulously and unnecessarily recalls to Roehm, that "inadvertently you have visited some homosexual pubs together with Dr. Heimsoth to get to know some homosexual boys. You also have been, several times, to Dr. Heimsoth's doctor's office and had the opportunity to see his 'artistically precious' collection of homoerotic photographs. You called my special attention to the fact that Dr. Heimsoth has some letters from you that you are very anxious to get back."

It's useful to consider, as we accompany Roehm's designated blackmail troubleshooter to the office of the blackmailing doctor, how such an account would play if it was an American newspaper publishing the results of an investigation into the chief aide of a homophobic American presidential candidate.

At the doctor's office, Meyer accuses Heimsoth of being the source of previous scandalous articles about the Hitler Party that appeared in the *Munich Post*. Heimsoth plays it cool and reads to Meyer his own thinly veiled blackmail letter to Roehm "asking for the organization of a news service and the provision of funds to supply it"—a blackmail letter within a blackmail letter.

"I calmed him," Meyer deviously reassures Roehm, "and asked him to consider that you are completely occupied with the Stennes case" (an internal rebellion within the SA). This does not satisfy the anxious Roehm. When Meyer returns empty-handed, without the doctor's stash of Roehm's love letters, Roehm tells him the letters "have to be recovered *a tout prix* and you [Roehm— he's still ostentatiously recalling these events that Roehm needs no reminder of] asked me to arrange 'the payoff.'" He further inflames Roehm's paranoia by telling him that "according to my judgment [there are] relationships between Dr. Heimsoth and Dr. Strasser," referring to Otto Strasser, a Hitler Party defector and now opponent (and Gregor Strasser's brother).

Not wishing to neglect any opportunity to embarrass Roehm should this letter become public (i.e., should Roehm fail to pay him off), Meyer then reports some of Roehm's bitter denunciations of Goebbels. Then he comes to the break-in: "The room in Bayreuther Strasse in which Dr. Heimsoth runs his doctor's office and keeps the letters can be opened without difficulties by a skillful toolmaker after seven o'clock in the evening," he reports.

The canny Meyer, obviously not wishing to incriminate himself—and perhaps wishing to keep Roehm guessing about who has the letters now—leaves it ambiguous as to whether he went ahead and executed the burglary. This dizzying whirl of break-ins, extortion, counterextortion, and primary, secondary, and tertiary overlapping blackmail threats, suggests a web entangling Hitler's chief of staff like the snakes around Laocoön—all of it laid out in the words of Roehm's "friend," Dr. Meyer, on the front pages of a Munich newspaper.

Roehm and the Hitler Party responded the following day by claiming that the letter from Meyer was forged or counterfeit. In the complicated litigation that dragged on afterward for many months, it emerged that Meyer did write the letter, that he may not have sent it to Roehm directly but used it to blackmail the SA chief with the threat of giving it to the *Munich Post*, which he eventually did. In the end, eight months later, Roehm withdrew his charges against the *Munich Post* over the letter and agreed to pay all the costs of the proceeding and those of *Munich Post* editor Martin Gruber.

But the repercussions of this story went beyond litigation. It exposed and further provoked a deadly schism in the party between Roehm and his blackmailing enemies within; it led to the formation of the Nazi Party death squad, "Cell G," which provided sensational material for another *Post* exposé, and ultimately brought the swamp of murder, prostitution, and blackmail to Hitler's doorstep: *"Nothing happens in the movement without my wish,"* as the *Post* reminded the people of Munich and a world that wouldn't listen.

What's revealing about these scandals is not so much the specific misdeeds as the culture of blackmail it opens a window into—a swamp of secret shames, a web of covert, coercive bonds with Hitler in the center. *That* is the unspoken assumption: Hitler can't act, he can't purge the tainted players in this sordid farce, because he, too, is caught in the web. They all have something on *him*, too.

Consider the comment of the Bavarian weekly *Die Fanfare* on Hitler's relationship to the blackmail stew within his party. In September 1931 (three months after this scandal broke), in an editorial addressing the rumors about the perverse nature of Hitler's relationship to Geli Raubal that arose in the wake of her mysterious suicide, *Die Fanfare* asserted that "leaders of subordinate rank know so much about their top leader that Hitler is, so to speak, their hostage and thus unable to intervene and conduct a purge if party leaders are involved in dark affairs."

Here we have the quintessential vision of the Munich Hitler: Hitler as

Laocoön, utterly enmeshed in serpentine blackmail plots, unable to extricate himself from his own implication in "dark affairs."

I've devoted scrutiny to the texture of the blackmail consciousness in which Hitler was enmeshed because I believe that there is something more serious than tabloid sensationalism to the dogged attention the *Munich Post* reporters paid to the concatenation of blackmail scandals that plagued the Hitler Party. I've come to believe that they found reflected in them a defining truth about the party and movement Hitler created, a truth that emanated from something essential about Hitler himself. It's the Hitler we've seen enmeshed in the minutiae of blackmail negotiations with his black-sheep nephew, a Hitler who we'll see enmeshed in blackmail intrigues that arose from his relationship with his half-niece Geli Raubal, a Hitler for whom blackmail has become more than second nature but an aspect of his *primary* nature, his defining relationship to the world.

While the term "blackmail" is most often employed today to describe a threat to reveal shameful secrets, a threat to harm by exposure such intangibles as reputation and image, I'm speaking here of blackmail in its original, more expansive sense of "any payment extorted by intimidation or pressure" (as the *Oxford English Dictionary* puts it), which includes the threat of physical or economic harm as well as damage to image. The essence of the blackmail relationship is a threat of future harm to extort present compliance. And one truth about Hitler which the *Munich Post* journalists were the first to capture in their reporting was the way he saw the world, the way he rose to power—the way he'd go on to manipulate statesmen and nations—with the mentality and the method, with the hard-won experience, and the discerning art of the blackmailing extortionist.

It was crucial in almost every stage of his rise to power. In the final, feverish months of vicious factional infighting, street warfare, political murder, and cynical deal making that led to Hitler's capture of the chancellorship on January 30, 1933, many (not all) historians believe blackmail played a crucial role in sealing the deal. Particularly in overcoming the reluctance of Reichspresident Hindenburg—who'd famously dismissed Hitler as "that Bohemian corporal"—to appoint Hitler to the chancellorship.

Many historians believe that a secret meeting between Hitler and President Hindenburg's son, private secretary, and factotum in charge of intrigue, Oskar von Hindenburg, resulted in a significant shift in the attitude of the revered but rapidly weakening octogenarian president. Many believed that the implicit threat Hitler held over the Hindenburgs' heads was the power of the Nazi Party in the Reichstag to support or kill the parliamentary investigation into the "East Help" scandal (allegations of massive, corrupt misappropriation of parliamentary subsidies for the aristocratic but impoverished Junker land barons in East Prussia, who numbered among them, as beneficiaries, the Hindenburgs). It had been widely rumored that the scandal could reach as high as Hindenburg and his closest allies and financial angels among the Junkers. The Nazi Party had initially supported the Reichstag corruption investigation—Hindenburg had, after all, been Hitler's chief opponent in a bitterly contested presidential election. But after Hitler's secret meeting with Oskar von Hindenburg and after Hitler took power with Hindenburg's blessing, the East Help investigation was quashed entirely.

And then in early 1938, at a crucial moment in Hitler's quest for unchallenged internal control of Germany, a crucial moment as well in his quest for the upper hand in the external power struggle over the map of Europe, two sordid blackmail episodes made all the difference. In January 1938, before forcing the *Anschluss* with Austria, before making his final extortionate move on Czechoslovakia, and before blackmailing the British and French into the Munich appeasement surrender, Hitler first needed to consolidate his personal control over the German army, whose relatively conservative officer corps had been reluctant to back up Hitler's threats to reoccupy the Rhineland in 1936 (only the inaction of the French army had allowed Hitler to succeed in his gamble then). The conservative army General Staff was convinced that Hitler's ambitions for Austria and Czechoslovakia would touch off a war they could not win. In particular, the resistance of the two top commandants of the German army, Generals Blomberg and Fritsch, was frustrating Hitler, because without the credible threat or bluff of armed invasion, he could not make his blackmail stick even with peace-at-any-price statesmen.

Hitler and his minions had an archetypal Hitlerian solution to the problem: sexual blackmail. Two shocking, successive blackmail intrigues apparently engineered on Hitler's behalf by Reinhard Heydrich. First, pornographic photographs of General Blomberg's new young wife illustrating her recent past in the sexual demimonde were dredged up and presented to Blomberg, then the highest ranking officer in the Reich. He resigned rather than face scandal. And then a homosexual prostitute known as "Bavarian Joe" materialized to make secret accusations to army authorities that he had observed General Fritsch, the second highest officer in the army, paying for the services of boy prostitutes in Berlin dives. Although this accusation (unlike the photographs of General Blomberg's wife) seemed to have been fabricated from whole cloth, General Fritsch, either from a horror of scandal or from something else real to hide, promptly resigned as well. Leaving Hitler free to appoint puppet generals Brauchitsch and Reichenau to replace them and to proceed with the successful extortion of Austria and Czechoslovakia from their Allied protectors without having to fire a shot.

It could be said as well that extortion was critical to Hitler's control over

Germany's captive Jewish population in the years between 1933 and the invasion of Poland in 1939. In the first months after his takeover in January 1933, when anti-Semitic rampages and boycotts by the SA led some groups in the world Jewish community to press for a worldwide boycott of German goods, Hitler skillfully undermined the unity and power of the external threat by threatening to ratchet up internal persecution of Jews even more brutally if German Jews didn't try to dissuade their fellows abroad from pressing the boycott. He threatened, in other words, to hold "his" Jews hostage to the behavior of foreign Jews, in effect blackmailing both into relative paralysis. And he blackmailed those few non-Jewish nations and statesmen who spoke out against Hitler's tightening noose on German Jews by threatening to expel them all and deposit them on the shores of nations whose statesmen and population were only (barely) willing to show concern at a safe distance—and certainly not ready to make them welcome as refugees.

I should perhaps note that I'm not arguing that blackmail and counterfeiting are in any sense Hitler's *worst* crimes, that they compare to the serial political murders his party committed in Munich and elsewhere in Weimar Germany or the mass murder he would commit after 1939. Rather, they were in some way *signature* crimes, signatures of something essential about Hitler's psyche, reflecting some truths about his mind and his method. And beyond that, I have a feeling that in their focus on these particular crimes, the reporters of the Poison Kitchen were aware that the blackmail and counterfeiting were crucial accessory crimes, the ones that made the larger crimes possible.

I think this is particularly true in their obsessive animus against counterfeiting—the counterfeiting not so much of currency but of history, of the past—against "political counterfeiters" as they recurrently called Hitler and the Hitler Party. It was something I began to grasp more deeply, this obsession with counterfeiting, after spending some harrowing days scrolling through microfilm of the final nine weeks of the *Munich Post*'s existence and experiencing with the Poison Kitchen reporters, day by day, those sickening last weeks that began with Hitler seeming like a politician on the wane (still suffering from an electoral setback in November). Until the last week—indeed, the last day—of January, when a collusion among corrupt and stupid right-wing party leaders, division on the left, and the maneuverings of amoral intriguers such as Franz von Papen with the acquiescence of the Hindenburgs suddenly and unexpectedly brought Hitler to power. I scrolled on, into the desperate final five weeks after the Hitler takeover when the *Post* continued to fight on futilely against the onrushing darkness, until March 9, when the Nazis banned the last opposition papers still publishing, and turned the *Munich Post* offices over to an SA squad to pillage.

I had, perhaps unwisely, wanted to try to recapture what it was like to experience those last weeks through the eyes of these tragic eyewitnesses. I say unwisely because even at one or several removes, through the scrim of the microfilm, it was a nightmarish experience to suffer with the courageous writers of the *Post* the shocking, crushing realization that despite their best efforts, their sacrifices, the years of struggle against Hitler, the ridicule, the exposés, the crimes, the death toll they'd pinned on him, Hitler had won—and all he'd threatened was about to come horrifically true.

The first thing one notices in the papers from the first two weeks of January 1933 is the way the drumbeat of political murder dramatically steps up its tempo. Beneath a banner headline radiating New Year's bravado in the January 3 issue—"*It's Our Duty to Beat Hitler in the Coming Year*"— the inside pages of the paper chronicle the grim and growing toll: "*Feme Murder Comes to Parliament*" (the murder of a socialist Reichstag deputy), "*Police and Feme Murders*" (lenient treatment for Nazi death-squad killers), "*Feme Murder Comes to Frankfurt*," "*Feme Murder in Thuringia*," the list goes on, and to document its magnitude they inaugurate a weekly "political murder summary."

These murders—political assassinations, really—became too frequent, too often, too awful for the *Post* to report on in detail. Instead, I was intrigued by the way they chose to focus on the continuing chronicle of one individual murder in particular to epitomize the depredations of the death squads they had taken to calling, with understandable stridency, "Hitler's murder beasts."

I was puzzled at first about why they'd chosen this case, the Hentze case, for intensive coverage; it was anomalous in the sense that the victim was not an anti-Hitler activist, as so many of the daily toll of feme murder victims were, but rather a teenage SA recruit named Herbert Hentsch who was murdered by SA thugs for some alleged deviation from party discipline—murdered, the *Post* reported, by executioners who "shouted 'Heil Hitler'" as they beat him to death.

"*What Have You Done Hitler?*" was the headline for a follow-up report on the Hentsch murder, the plaintive headline question coming from the slain boy's stricken mother.

What *have* you done Hitler: embedded in that question is, I believe, the larger reason for the close focus on this particular case. The naïve youth seduced by Hitler's propaganda into becoming a follower and then beaten to death by the "murder beasts" he's fallen in with—he's a stand-in, young Herbert Hentsch, for all Germany, all Germans who have fallen under Hitler's spell, and a kind of harbinger of the destruction Germany and Germans will suffer for having fallen for and unleashed the chief murder beast, Hitler himself.

Meanwhile, with each passing week, the murder rate continues to make sickening leaps, the reports of individual feme murders give way to increasing numbers of multiple murders or "bloodbaths." January 23: "*Bloodbath in Dresden.*" January 26: "*19 Shot in Terrible Political Bloodbath.*" Systematic assassination escalates to mass murder as Hitler comes closer to power. Hitler takes power, and socialist newspapers in Berlin are hit with temporary bans. But the *Munich Post* bravely, defiantly soldiers on. It's often forgotten, this strange terror-filled interlude after Hitler became chancellor of a coalition cabinet on January 30 and before the Reichstag fire on February 27 and the truncated snap election in early March gave him the undisputed power of a führer to ban the opposition and the opposition press completely. Those last few weeks when Hitler ruled but an opposition press still published gave the world a glimpse of what was in store for Germany, for all Europe.

After one week with Hitler in power, the *Munich Post*'s weekly political murder summary: eighteen dead, thirty-four badly wounded in death-squad attacks. February 9: "*Nazi Party Hands Dripping with Blood.*" February 10: "*Germany under the Hitler Regime: Political Murder and Terror.*" As the murderous days went by, the rhetoric understandably grew more strident, more horror-struck: "*Blood Guilt of the Nazi Party.*" "*Germany Today: No Day Without Death.*" "*Brutal Terror in the Streets of Munich.*" "*Outlaws and Murderers in Power.*" "*People Allow Themselves to be Intimidated.*" "*Bloody Matters on Sunday.*"

The headlines, the murders, build to an almost unbearable crescendo until abruptly something strange happens in three issues beginning February 13. Suddenly, the murders are off the front page, the chronicle of the desperate struggle of persecuted opposition parties in the Reichstag is downplayed, and the *Munich Post* gives over its pages to what seems at first a quixotic if not irrelevant plunge into the past with a long, unsigned three-part series bannered THE NOVEMBER CRIMINALS: WHAT HITLER DOESN'T TELL HIS LISTENERS.

It was, on the surface, an obsessively detailed history lesson, a response to now-Chancellor Hitler's repeated vengeful boasts that he had come to power to rectify the betrayal of Germany by the "November Criminals," the politicians who signed the armistice/surrender of November 1918. The series was an obsessed, intensive, remedial history lesson, yes, but it was more than that: It was an all-out frontal assault on what was the first, and in some ways most sinister instance of Nazi revisionism: the stab-in-the-back myth.

Of course, the myth was a lie; the German armies were collapsing in November 1918, Germany's borders were about to be overrun, the generals who later claimed to be on the verge of victory before being stabbed in the back were eager for the politicians to save them from ignominious rout, to make some deal that would permit them to march home at the head of their troops rather than flee home behind them. The generals forced the politicians to do the deal to save face for them, and then they turned around and stabbed the *politicians* in the back by claiming they had been betrayed.

It was an obvious lie, but it was a lie Hitler rode to power on. More than that; it was not just a lie Hitler exploited, it was a lie that in some very important way *created* Hitler, made him who he was. It was, you'll recall, in November 1918 at the army hospital in Pasewalk that Hitler experienced some kind of transformative vision or hallucination. It was a life-changing moment of metamorphosis brought on by the news of the German army surrender—a surrender that, he makes clear in his own account of the moment in *Mein Kampf* and elsewhere, was accompanied by a simultaneous sickening sense that the November surrender was a betrayal, a sellout, a stab in the back. In that moment of utter collapse (personal and national), total despair, and then subsequent visionary (or hallucinatory) summons, Hitler conceived the mission and the myth that would bring him to power fifteen years later. And so to the journalists of the *Munich Post*, the spiritual heirs of the socialist November Criminals, the stab-in-the-back myth was not merely a revisionist distortion, a historical fabrication, it was the lie that made Hitler Hitler. And a lie about *them*.

I believe it was an acute sense of the centrality of this lie to the tragedy unfolding around them in the weeks after Hitler became chancellor that led the Poison Kitchen reporters to abandon for a full three issues the daily chronicle of horror, to return to 1918, to what might be called the primal scene of the crime, the lie of Hitler's self-creation. It's a lie they'd been fighting from the beginning, one they'd fought a veritable war over back in 1924. My sense of the doomed urgency they devoted to refighting the war over the stab-in-the-back lie in February 1933 was deepened by a discovery I'd made in the basement of the Institut für Zeitgeschichte, Germany's repository of historical memory about the Nazi period, several days previously: the transcript of the epic 1924 "Stab-in-the-Back Swindle" trial, a discovery that made possible my tentative identification of the bitter, impassioned voice behind the unsigned November Criminals series in February 1933.

In the last few years before the Hitler takeover, as the murder toll of political opposition rose, most *Munich Post* stories were published without bylines, the better to make responsibility collective and protect individual reporters from being singled out for reprisal from the death squads. The February "November Criminals" articles were unsigned as well, but I thought I recognized the distinctive, enraged, and eloquent voice of the author from the transcript of the 1924 Stab-in-the-Back trial, the first bitter battle the Poison Kitchen had fought against Hitler's defining lie.

It was a war they provoked deliberately, almost recklessly, when a right-wing pamphleteer named Nikolaus Cossman published a revisionist analysis of the events of November 1918, an attempt to give a fig leaf of scholarly legitimacy to the stab-in-the-back myth. Cossman had spun out a poisonous conspiracy theory accusing some of the politicians who signed the November armistice of being in the pay of the French secret service, alleging they'd turned traitor for foreign bribes.

The *Munich Post* responded with a devastating attack on Cossman's research and on Cossman himself in a manner so vicious and personal it seemed deliberately designed to provoke a libel suit. The attack was penned by the *Post*'s political editor, Martin Gruber, who called Cossman "a political poisoner," a highly charged epithet in which the Poison Kitchen turned Nazi well-poisoning imagery on itself. While ridiculing Cossman's research, Gruber insisted Cossman was not merely deluded: "If he was only an idiot, his writing would be enough to make him ridiculous, but he's worse than an idiot," he was sinister, and in a very particular way—as a "counterfeiter of history." Gruber did more than characterize Cossman as a counterfeiter, he linked him with one of the most sinister and destructive historical forgeries ever fabricated: *The Protocols of the Elders of Zion*, the counterfeit minutes of a meeting of the secret Jewish world conspiracy (forged by the czarist secret police) that had been the bible of anti-Semites since 1905. A forged document that achieved mass worldwide distribution in Henry Ford's popularization, *The International Jew*, it was a forgery that indelibly shaped Hitler's own vision of the Jews. A forgery that one historian called a "warrant for genocide," which paved the way for Hitler's rise and the mass murder to come.

If the *Protocols* were the warrant for genocide, the stab-in-the-back lie was the local justification in Germany: Jews and Jewish money interests were behind the stab in the back in Hitler's version of the myth. As far back as 1924, Gruber's rhetorical rage against the counterfeiter Cossman seems fired by an awareness of the dire future consequences of counterfeiting history. He rails at Cossman as "a degenerate literary stock swindler, peddling false goods," a falsifier of history who "deserves not to be hanged but locked up in an insane asylum." Some of Gruber's personal abuse is clearly designed to force Cossman to sue for libel and give Gruber a public judicial forum to combat the stab-in-the-back swindle. But the emphasis on counterfeiting and forgery, on the link with the *Protocols*, repeated in Gruber's impassioned address to the court in the trial, comes from a serious political analysis of the dangerous consequences of allowing history to be falsified to justify murder.

The libel trial was briefly a national sensation in 1924, though almost forgotten now. Scrolling through the 2,500-page-long microfilm transcript of the trial, I was able to locate defendant Martin Gruber's final appeal to the court, a long, eloquent, caustic, emotional plea that revealed him to be a man possessed, driven nearly mad by single combat with the hydra-headed historical error he was grappling with. Up to the very last minute of the trial, he was desperately trying to introduce new evidence, memoirs and diaries of dead generals he'd discovered, to refute the November Criminal lies and forgeries.

He practically had to be dragged out of the courtroom kicking and screaming before he'd rest his case, before he'd cease from the near-hopeless task of trying to sweep back the tide of counterfeit history. He won the case on the evidence, but he lost it in the judgment of the right-wing nationalists who presided as judges. (Even they only fined him a nominal amount plus court costs.) But nothing succeeded in silencing him on the subject.

And given one last chance in 1933, as time was running out, even after time *had* run out, to strike a final blow against Hitler, Gruber, then editor in chief of the *Post*, preempted all other coverage to take on once again the counterfeit fabrication that by then had been virtually canonized as the official state truth of the new Third Reich. Gruber attacked Hitler personally this time as a "political counterfeiter," a forger of the past, a murderer of historical truth.

I found myself profoundly stirred by the doomed passion of Martin Gruber, the voice of the Poison Kitchen, making a final desperate plea against the poisoner of history. And I found myself thinking more deeply about the pervasiveness of counterfeiting as a defining element of Hitler's mind and method.

It recalled to me the regrettably neglected vision of the origin of Hitler's rise with which another Munich journalist Konrad Heiden opened his still memorable but out-of-print 1944 biography of Hitler, *Der Fuehrer*. It was a vision that seemed, when I first read it, a bit overwrought and melodramatic, but a vision which the *Munich Post*'s focus on counterfeiting made me reconsider: an utterly unexpected vision of the relationship between Adolf Hitler and the most sinister historical counterfeit of the century, *The Protocols of the Elders of Zion*.

Heiden had followed Hitler and the Hitler Party since 1921, when he began attending their meetings to report on them for a student socialist newspaper and then later for the *Frankfurter Zeitung*. He was so familiar to the Hitler Party that it was said Hitler himself would not begin a speech until he saw Heiden there to record and report it, however unfriendly the coverage. As time went on, there was less jocularity and familiarity in the relationship, and with death threats following him Heiden was forced to take flight across the French border after Hitler took power in 1933.

What had always struck me in reading and rereading the biography of Hitler that Heiden wrote in exile was the melodramatic opening passage, a dramatic reconstruction of the moment in 1917 when Heiden envisions a shadowy representative of the czarist secret police, the Okrana, the malign agency that created the forgery known as *The Protocols of the Elders of Zion*, slipping a copy of their deceitful document to a student in Moscow named Alfred Rosenberg. Heiden sees Rosenberg bringing it to Munich when he fled the Bolshevik Revolution, bringing it to the attention of Hitler through the circle of German mystical anti-Semites and Russian émigré haters of "Jewish Bolshevism" who became the nucleus, the source of funds for the Hitler Party and of Hitler's conspiratorial vision of the International Jewish Bolshevik threat. To Heiden, Hitler was first of all a handmaiden, a construct of the counterfeiters who created the *Protocols*. But Heiden believed Hitler's relation to the counterfeit conspiracy went beyond that.

Heiden is not alone in his emphasis on the centrality of the *Protocols* to Hitler and the Hitler Party vision, but he *is* alone in going on to posit a startling and ingenious relationship between Hitler and this counterfeit history—one that no one else, to my knowledge, has imagined. And yet it is one I believe worth rescuing from oblivion for the kind of paradoxical metaphorical way it illuminates a truth about Hitler: Hitler as a product, a virtual creation of a counterfeit of history, and history as a creation of this counterfeit.

Heiden reminds us that the *Protocols* didn't merely imagine a secret world-wide Jewish cabal. In fact, it posed as an actual tactical and strategic *manual* for such a conspiracy: how to subvert traditional institutions and values: how to manipulate public opinion and the media, and so on, all these supposed Jewish techniques lifted by the Okrana counterfeiters of the *Protocols* from an 1864 satire on the Machiavellian methods of Emperor Napoleon III of France.

Heiden's stunning conjecture, which deserves attention because of his intimate acquaintance with the Hitler Party from the very beginning of the Führer's rise, was that the secret of that rise lay in Hitler's adapting the modernized Machiavellian tactics attributed to his archenemy, the Elders of Zion, and *putting them to his own use* in manipulating the media, subverting the institutions of the state, and crafting his own successful conspiracy to rule the world. Heiden argues that Hitler did not merely adopt the counterfeit Jewish conspiracy as his vision of the world, he adopted the *tactics* falsely attributed to Jews by czarist forgers as his own—and used them with remarkable success. A success that made Hitler himself a kind of creation of a counterfeit.

It was an argument that left me intrigued but skeptical until I discovered how obsessed with counterfeit history the *Munich Post* reporters' vision of Hitler was, with counterfeiting as some primal aspect of Hitler's character.

And if one examines Hitler's behavior after he assumed power, one realizes he didn't merely use counterfeit documents and forged interpretations of history, he counterfeited the very *stuff* of history itself, a practice best exemplified in the ruse Hitler used to excuse his invasion of Poland in September 1939. The act that launched the war and the genocide to come was a charade in which a squad of Hitler's troops dressed up in Polish army uniforms in order to stage a "raid" on a German installation on the Polish border. Hitler then used the raid by the counterfeit Poles, complete with staged photos of counterfeit German "casualties," as the false excuse for the blitzkrieg that followed.

Not long after I returned home from Munich, I happened across a curious, slim volume in a private library—a remarkable polemical pamphlet entitled *Hitler's Counterfeit Reich*, written pseudonymously in 1940 by an author who described himself as "a German political refugee." The author goes to great lengths to find counterfeiting the essential metaphor for every aspect of the Hitler regime: the counterfeit of a justice system that masked state terror; the counterfeit of diplomacy that masked systematic blackmail and lying; and especially the counterfeit of economic success that masked the use of forced labor, and impoverishment of political enemies and Jews, an economy artificially inflated by secret, illegal expansion of an army preparing for war. The analysis of the economy was particularly valuable because it gives the lie to the counterfeit history, the myth that persists in some accounts still, that Hitler had pulled off a genuine economic miracle in the thirties.

It was heartening to feel somehow that the Poison Kitchen analysis, their focus on Hitler as a counterfeiter, had not fallen on deaf ears, that I was not alone in seeing it as an illuminating way to look at Hitler and his regime. But it was disheartening in a way as well, when I considered how successful Hitler had been in erasing his first, most brilliant, and intimate explainers from history and memory. Who knew of Martin Gruber anymore, who remembered him in Germany, much less the rest of the world?

His words and those of his colleagues crumbled away in the basement of the Monacensia library, faded on the microfilms in the Institut für Zeitgeschichte, echoed perhaps in the obscure *Counterfeit Reich* pamphlet, but otherwise . . .

I thought of that moment in November 1991 when I'd first searched the little crescent-shaped street in Munich for number 19 Altheimer Eck, hoping to pay tribute somehow to the place where the *Munich Post* was published. The moment when I found that number 19 no longer existed as a street address anymore, when I found a printing shop inside a courtyard that seemed to be the place where the *Post* premises had once been. There was a plaque on the printing-shop wall that explained how it had moved into this space back in 1934 when the address had still been number 19. The plaque made no mention of the newspaper that had been there, that had been pillaged and ousted, and offered no explanation for why the number had been changed. (As it turned out, the street had been renumbered after the war.)

One hope I had in writing this chapter was to challenge contemporary German journalists to do justice to the men of the Poison Kitchen, men who brought so much honor to the profession with their courage and investigative zeal. To challenge them to restore the Poison Kitchen's work to print again, to give German readers of today the experience of living through the coming of Hitler through the eyes of Martin Gruber and his heroic colleagues. To restore the Poison Kitchen vision to history and to historians whose attempts to explain Hitler could not help but benefit from exposure to the kind of investigative intimacy the *Munich Post* achieved in its hand-to-hand, eye-to-eye combat with him.

And one more thing I believe ought to be restored: their street address. Number 19 Altheimer Eck should become a memorial and shrine to the Poison Kitchen.

PART TWO

TWO POSTWAR VISIONS: SINCERITY AND ITS COUNTERFEIT

In which the question of Hitler's inwardness—was he conscious of his criminality or convinced of his rectitude—becomes the subject of a provocative dispute between two of the first and most influential Hitler explainers

CHAPTER 4

H. R. Trevor-Roper:
The Professor and the Mountebank

In which a historian's exposure to the Hitler spell prompts a suggestion of possession, and we find, in Hitler's own "Hitler diary" hoax, his defining lie

The death sentence was postmarked Lisbon. Hugh Trevor-Roper (now Lord Dacre) remembers that detail well. Recalling it one autumn evening, in front of a fireplace in an upstairs common room of the Oxford-Cambridge Club on Pall Mall, he treats the threat, which he received not long after the 1947 publication of *The Last Days of Hitler*, as an amusing footnote now, although he seems to have taken it seriously at the time.

"It was from the Stern Gang," he says, the Zionist underground guerrilla group that had demonstrated its seriousness by assassinating Mideast mediator Count Folke Bernadotte. The death sentence was their way of expressing their disapproval of Trevor-Roper's vision of Hitler in *The Last Days*, he believes.

But it was more than a footnote, it was a signal, a symbol of how highly charged Hitler explanations were to become in the postwar period. And of what was really at stake: the nature of Hitler's posthumous survival.

Trevor-Roper's *Last Days of Hitler* is not only one of the most famous and influential postwar Hitler books—still in print a half-million copies and a half century later—it was one of the first. And it was the work of a man whose superb intellect would destine him to rise to perhaps the most prestigious post in his field, Regius Professor of Modern History, at Oxford. And so the narrow time frame of the title is somewhat misleading: While the last days in the Berlin bunker are the focus, in fact Trevor-Roper's book offers a comprehensive vision of Hitler. A mode of explanation that constitutes one of the two opposing poles of Hitler interpretation in the first decades after the war. Poles that might be designated the Romanticist and the Classicist, or perhaps the Gothic and the Ironic. Visions of Hitler as monster or mountebank, believer or cynic, possessed or manipulator—these are some of the oppositions expressed in the dueling visions of Trevor-Roper and Alan Bullock, two of the most highly respected pillars of the historian's profession. An almost irreconcilable opposition until recently, as we'll see, when Bullock shifted his position in a crucial way and produced a synthesis of the previous thesis and antithesis he and Trevor-Roper represented.

Trevor-Roper's *Last Days* began as an intelligence mission. In September 1945, Soviet officials began deliberately to spread the lie that Adolf Hitler was still alive, perhaps even being harbored in the British zone of occupation in Berlin for nefarious future purposes. The Soviet decision to resurrect Hitler, one of the first harbingers of the bitterness of the embryonic cold war, fed what has come to be called "the survival myth," the belief that Hitler had escaped alive from the bunker in Berlin in which his body was first reported to have been found. The confirmation of Hitler's death had come first from Soviet troops, but the decision to spread the survival myth came from Stalin himself.

In any case, British intelligence took upon itself the task of establishing once and for all that Hitler was dead. Sir Dick White, then deputy director of MI6, dispatched Hugh Trevor-Roper to Berlin. Trevor-Roper brought to the task the skills of the professional historian and the abilities of an intelligence analyst familiar with the figures in the German high command through his wartime work monitoring the anti-Hitler elements among them.

Trevor-Roper proceeded to document meticulously the days, hours, and minutes of Hitler's final months in the bunker from the eyewitness testimony of officers and aides who were there, including those who'd soaked the dead body with kerosene and set it on fire. He also succeeded in discovering—perhaps in rescuing from oblivion—a profoundly illuminating document: Hitler's "final testament," the one in which he enjoins his followers to continue to wage war on the Jewish "world poisoners," a document that has become a touchstone in the debate over whether Hitler was an actor (as the theologian Emil Fackenheim argues and as Alan Bullock initially believed) or a true believer (as Trevor-Roper and Robert Waite, among others, insist) in his crusade against the Jews.

The irony of Trevor-Roper's mission is that while he succeeded in his intelligence task, in documenting the fact of Hitler's physical death, the book that he later wrote about Hitler's last days ended up becoming an important source of Hitler's metaphorical and mythic survival.

The source of this resurrection, however inadvertent and certainly unintentional on Trevor-Roper's part, was something he discovered in the ruins of the bunker, in his interviews with the defeated followers of Hitler, something he hadn't expected to find, a deeper mystery than whether Hitler survived: the survival of the Hitler *spell*. While one might have expected to encounter the power of the spell when Hitler was a demagogue on the rise or after he'd become the triumphant Führer, Trevor-Roper was surprised at the extent to which the spell still held sway even after ignominious defeat.

"Even in the bunker," he told me, "with all the buildings of Berlin falling down on top of him. Even when he was dead, they carried out his wishes. They stayed behind—they stayed there until he was dead, and when he was dead they exposed themselves [to bombs] carrying out Hitler's last wishes."

"People have described this as a mesmeric power," I said. "Do you think it's literally mesmerism?"

"I don't know. He certainly had an extraordinary power. It didn't work on everybody; it didn't work—to put it crudely—on the aristocrats or people who were sensitive to the vulgarity of his behavior or surrounding. But when he wanted to mesmerize, he did have the wherewithal."

Despite this flash of what might seem like snobbery, Trevor-Roper is humble enough to concede that even someone who was his peer, a virtual aristocrat, could have succumbed to the spell: Albert Speer, for instance. His encounter with Speer struck him with particular force, he says, because Speer was a man for whom he felt a certain admiration, even a kind of identification.

"He wasn't much older than me, he was only a little over forty-two at the time. I felt that we had a level conversation in which he talked to me like a rational person. He was a man highly intelligent, educated, but a man who was obviously, deeply still under Hitler's spell. Even when Speer was out of power, when the war was lost—he'd known the war was lost since December 1943, and he regarded Hitler as having caused all the wreckage. He'd got out of Berlin on the twentieth, I think, of April [1945] and yet made a special journey *back* to Berlin, when it was cut off, in order to take formal leave of Hitler. And that's an instance of the extraordinary spell which he exercises. And if you read Goebbels's diaries, you'll find the same. Goebbels periodically had doubt or has cold feet and becomes impatient with Hitler, and yet every time Goebbels goes back and sees Hitler, he's spellbound. 'Hitler's so wonderful, he'll pull something out of the bag. I am filled with confidence.' Every time, right up to the very end."

What Trevor-Roper sought to do in *The Last Days* was describe the spell as an inescapable fact of any account of Hitler's life. He does not try to explain it so much as evoke it. And yet by evoking it so eloquently, he came to be accused of perpetrating, indeed of falling under, the spell, of giving it, giving the Hitler myth, a posthumous life.

Now Trevor-Roper is, in every respect, the last person one can imagine falling under some gothic romantic spell of a dead dictator. To look at him is to see skepticism elegantly embodied: From his waspish donnish demeanor (thin as a rail in his Oxbridge tweeds, with a dyspeptically skeptical squint to the brow beneath his snow-white thatch of hair) to the tart, eloquently acerbic, bone-dry ironies of his speech and the touch of world-weary cynicism he might have developed from serving in wartime British counterintelligence, he does not seem the sort to have been easily mesmerized.

But, as he says, in an essay revisiting *The Last Days of Hitler* in a 1988 issue of *Encounter*, "I have been accused of having exalted Adolf Hitler and having created a public image of him as a genius of National Socialism. Indeed," he adds, "of being the prime *author* of that myth, almost a positive successor to Dr. Goebbels" (emphasis added).

I read him that quote and asked him who had accused him of that.

"Uh, well, I was condemned to death by the Stern Gang for one thing. And it was clear that this was the assumption [they'd] based the death sentence on, I was out of their reach, of course. The sentence of death was sent to me by airmail from Lisbon. It was signed Wilhelm ben Israel."

A sentence of death for writing a book about Hitler? It should be stressed that in no way is Trevor-Roper's book a defense of Hitler or sympathetic to him. His distaste for Hitler and his deeds is obvious throughout. No, it's not that he praised or exonerated Hitler but that in carrying out his mission to prove him dead, he was too successful; as a writer, he brought him back to life again.

If the Stern Gang (or whoever signed "Wilhelm ben Israel" in their name) was Trevor-Roper's most dramatic critic, the most thoughtful and thorough-going critique of *The Last Days of Hitler* comes from Professor Alvin Rosenfeld, the author of *Imagining Hitler*, a study of postwar fiction featuring Hitler. Trevor-Roper, of course, is not writing fiction, but Rosenfeld argues that the dramatic, cinematic image of Hitler in *The Last Days* was the defining image of Hitler, the ur-Hitler for the decades of fiction that followed, and the chief source of the overheated gothic, demonic vision that has dominated postwar literature, pulp, and film.

The essence of Rosenfeld's critique of Trevor-Roper and of his influence on the pop-culture vision of Hitler he helped create is that, in attempting to describe Hitler's spell, the historian fell under it. In trying to explain how this happened to the respected, skeptical Oxford scholar, Rosenfeld himself seems drawn to a subdued version of the occult rhetoric of possession he criticizes in Trevor-Roper: "The fiction writer within the scholar *seemed to come alive*" (my emphasis), as if some dark being within was awakened by exposure to the Caligari Hitler and took possession of the otherwise scrupulously rational historian.

Rosenfeld argues that in the process of describing Hitler in his "inspired, almost celebratory prose," Trevor-Roper "could not altogether resist the symbolic lure of his subject, and he was to contribute his share to some of the more striking aspects of the Hitler legend . . . [a] legend [that] was to be shaped . . . by a fascination with the most irrational sides of Hitler's personality."

The irrational sides: the mesmeric occult Svengali, the possessed, somnambulist Hitler. In describing the irrational mode of Hitler's appeal, Rosenfeld believes, "Trevor-Roper took recourse not only to the language of biblical theology and Middle Eastern and oriental legend but to the special language of the occult sciences. Thus Hitler is described repeatedly as a 'wizard' and 'enchanter,' a leader who could command unconditional obedience from his subjects because of 'the mesmeric influence' he had over them."

Rosenfeld cites in particular a Trevor-Roper description of Hitler's hypnotic eyes, the eyes of the Caligari Hitler: "The fascination of those eyes, which had bewitched so many seemingly sober men. . . . Hitler had the eyes of a hypnotist which seduced the wits and affections of all who yielded to their power. . . . This personal magnetism remained with him to the end; and only by reference to it can we explain the extraordinary obedience which he still commanded in the last week of his life, when all the machinery of force and persuasion had disappeared . . . and only his personality remained."

While Rosenfeld objects to Trevor-Roper's language, I feel it's his *logic* that is the real problem here. Trevor-Roper maintains that "only by reference" to Hitler's hypnotic, mesmeric eyes can his hold on the inner circle in defeat be explained. Was it his eyes, or was it the warping effect of proximity to absolute world-shattering power? Those in Hitler's Munich circle in the twenties—those who knew him before he came to power—often mock the self-conscious Svengali mannerisms Hitler adopted, the "penetrating" stare, the self-induced trance frenzies. Once in power, however, once at the center of the greatest drama in history, it was his armies, not his eyes, that counted. Even in defeat, he was a titan to those around him, a demigod, a celebrity beyond parallel. And those in his orbit could not help but be overcome: It was the so-called Stockholm syndrome in spades. It was not that *he* was nothing without his spell; *they* were nothing without believing it. Or worse than nothing—the gullible dupes of a defeated mass murderer. But if they kept the faith, then even in defeat, they could believe they were living out a noble Wagnerian Götterdämmerung.

That they should continue to be under the spell even after the war shouldn't have surprised Trevor-Roper as much as it seemed to, but it did. And it was clear from my conversation with Trevor-Roper that, despite the death threat and the attacks, he has not backed down from his belief that there is something irrational at the heart of Hitler's appeal, something not explicable by the ordinary tools and methods of rational historical and psychological analysis. The words he used to describe his belief in the failure to explain came as a jolt in the midst of the comforting firelit surroundings of his club: "Hitler remains," he told me, "a frightening mystery." Nor does he apologize for his resort to the language and imagery of the occult in describing Hitler, although he qualifies the connotation somewhat.

"You use the term 'demonic' repeatedly," I said to him.

"By 'demonic,'" he said, "I mean having demonic energy, having more than human power. I'm not using moral language."

It is, then, not demonism in the sense of Satanism; it's rather, he seems to be saying, demonic in the sense William Blake used the word: the Romantic exaltation of unbounded energy for its own sake. And by "more than human," he's affirming the implications of his imagery: that the "frightening mystery" of Hitler's psyche exceeds the powers of ordinary psychological analysis to grasp.

"I despise psychohistory," he told me, and while he has an arsenal of academic objections to it, his deeper objection may be his conviction that the psychological tools to analyze human behavior are inadequate to grasp a "more than human" Hitler.

But the thrust of Trevor-Roper's defense against the criticism of his vision of Hitler consisted—at least in my conversation with him—of a counterthrust: an attack on the rival school of Hitler explanation embodied by fellow Hitler biographer Alan Bullock. In fact, Trevor-Roper returned repeatedly and vigorously to what he believes is the key inadequacy of the Bullock school: the belief that Hitler can be understood by certain preexisting models of rational historical explanation.

To be fair to both Trevor-Roper and Bullock, neither Trevor-Roper nor I was aware at the time how dramatically Bullock had shifted his view of Hitler to incorporate the irrationally possessed aspect. So Trevor-Roper's attacks on Bullock's views are really aimed at the vision of Bullock's first book, of the 1952 *Hitler: A Study in Tyranny*, still (in its 1962 revised form) the single most popular and influential Hitler biography ever written.

"It's a good book," Trevor-Roper says, politely prefacing his critique of Bullock with mild praise. It's the explanatory tradition it grows out of that he objects to: the mountebank adventurer vision.

"This was influential right after the war," Trevor-Roper told me, "from Sir Louis Namier, who was a great historian and who really understood Central Europe—he was a Polish Jew. And yet after the war, he wrote an essay which was actually about Napoleon III" (the self-made adventurer who created himself Emperor of France in the mid-nineteenth century and whose Machiavellian cunning and ambition made him the target of the satire that later became the template for the anti-Semitic forgery *The Protocols of the Elders of Zion*).

"Namier," said Trevor-Roper, "described Napoleon III as the first *mounte-*

bank dictator, the implication being that he regarded Hitler as a mountebank dictator. And in Alan Bullock's book, he described Hitler as an opportunist who was solely concerned with acquiring power. I felt that none of these people had read or understood *Mein Kampf.*"

"Mountebank" is a word little used these days (although it does seem to be the root of the cardsharp street hustle known as "three-card monte")—which is unfortunate because it does have an expressive power to conjure up a whole worldview, a whole thought-world as well. Derived from the old Italian phrase for "mounting on a bench," a mountebank is defined by the *OED* as "an itinerant quack who from an elevated platform appealed to his audience by means of stories, tricks, juggling and the like." More generally a mountebank is "an impudent pretender to skill, a charlatan, one who resorts to degrading means to obtain notoriety." A mountebank is a grander, more pretentious figure than a mere con man or a charlatan—he's a figure of public life, often a politician, one who practices his charlatanry from a public platform.

What's essential about the mountebank characterization is the core of cynicism and manipulativeness. The mountebank may pose as a true believer, as one possessed by vision, conviction, a grand mission, but it is all "tricks, juggling and the like"—there is no real conviction. This is the actor Hitler that theologian Emil Fackenheim insists on (see chapter 16).

But the essence of Trevor-Roper's vision of Hitler is that he was *not* an actor but a believer, above all else a man of conviction, however wicked those convictions were, a man who was not a cynic but horrifically "sincere." It's a view Trevor-Roper articulated most strikingly when I asked him whether he thought Hitler knew that his actions were evil.

"Oh, no," Trevor-Roper said firmly. "Hitler was convinced of his own rectitude."

Convinced of his own rectitude. One has to hear Trevor-Roper pronounce the word "rectitude" with such plenitude of rectitude himself; he almost succeeds in endowing a sincere belief in genocide with a kind of dignity. This is not intentional, of course. He certainly means—but does not feel it necessary to say—that Hitler was dreadfully, mistakenly convinced of his own rectitude. But nonetheless, sincerely, honestly convinced the Jews were the deadly enemy of the Aryan race and needed to be destroyed for the superior race to survive.

Sincerity is not an excuse, an exoneration for the crime of genocide. Not in Trevor-Roper's mind. But in the eyes of Anglo-American jurisprudence, sincerity *can* mean mitigation. It was not long after I spoke with Trevor-Roper that I thought I heard his language about Hitler echoed in a California judge's charge to the juries in the first trial of Lyle and Erik Menendez. In his explanation of what the two juries would have to believe to convict the brothers of a lesser charge of voluntary manslaughter (rather than murder) for killing their parents, the judge told them that if they believed the brothers were honestly but mistakenly convinced that their parents were going to kill them, then killing their mother and father could be considered an "imperfect" form of self-defense, not murder. Half the jurors in the first trial voted to let the brothers off on the lesser offense because they believed the brothers were, in effect, "convinced of their own rectitude."

By that logic, if Hitler had survived to be put on trial for murder in California, say, he might theoretically have been able to argue that he was "honestly convinced" the Jews were trying to destroy him and thus had to be destroyed in self-defense. This is literally an absurd reductio from Trevor-Roper's argument (although not entirely dissimilar from the tack taken by neo-nationalist German historians in the mid-eighties, some of whom argued—in the famous *Historikerstreit*, "the historians' battle"—that Hitler's atrocities were a kind of preemptive self-defense against genocidal Stalinist atrocities and a supposed Jewish "declaration of war" against Hitler).

Trevor-Roper certainly did not intend his provocative remark about Hitler being "convinced of his own rectitude" to be taken that far. But he clearly, sincerely believes that Hitler was a sincere believer. He traced for me the origin of his belief in Hitler as a true believer to a moment in 1938. He spoke of an essay by a British diplomat, Sir Robert Ensor, in the *Spectator*.

"In the course of this article," Trevor-Roper told me, "Ensor said that he had the advantage, which was rare, in having read *Mein Kampf* in German. Hitler wouldn't allow *Mein Kampf* to be published in English. Or in any foreign language. There was a very highly abbreviated authorized text, but that was for propaganda. And Ensor used the words, 'To read *Mein Kampf* in German is the beginning of wisdom in international affairs.' So I thought I'd better read *Mein Kampf* in German. And I did."

What *Mein Kampf* revealed about Hitler to Trevor-Roper was something that few took seriously before the war and even after: "a powerful, horrible message which he had thought out, a *philosophy*. He obviously took it very seriously. He was *not*, as Bullock calls him, an adventurer. Hitler took himself deadly seriously—all this comes out in *Mein Kampf*. He considers that he was a rare phenomenon such as only appears once in centuries. And reading it in 1938—I'd been in Germany, and I couldn't help but being impressed by the fact that *Mein Kampf* had been published in 1924 or '25 and he'd *done* all these things that he said he would do. And it was not a joke he was selling. It's a serious work."

"Not a joke he was selling: That is, he was not a mountebank?"

"Well, the conventional wisdom about Hitler was always—before the war, at least until Munich—that he was a sort of clown, that he was taking off from the music hall. He looked ridiculous. He had this Charlie Chaplin mustache and he made these ranting speeches and people couldn't take him seriously."

It occurred to me as Trevor-Roper conjured up the Chaplinesque prewar film footage of Hitler how much the accelerated speed of prewar newsreel footage must have helped create the burlesque, comic, Chaplinesque impressions of Hitler. Herky-jerky, sped-up newsreels made him almost impossible to take seriously, and contributed to the deadly serious error of underestimating the threat he posed.

"And when, after Munich they *had* to take him seriously, the opinion changed. And then it became the demagogue and the menace. The point is that he was still really not taken seriously. He was a figure of fun. That's perhaps being a little extreme. But even after the war, when it was all over, he was regarded as an adventurer who had led Germany spellbound into the war. He was not regarded as a man of genius. He was seen as powerful, no doubt disastrous—but not as a man to take seriously."

Again and again in the course of our conversation, Trevor-Roper returned to the attack on what he believed was the wrongheadedness of the mountebank adventurer Hitler he believes Bullock bequeathed the postwar world. Almost as if Bullock's Hitler, the *false* Hitler, was the real enemy. "He was *not* an adventurer," he repeated to me at one point. "At the end of the war, the Allied line was Hitler was an adventurer, an irresponsible opportunist—it's just *not enough*."

Why would the postwar "Allied line" favor this Hitler over Trevor-Roper's or other Hitlers? For one thing, it was more convenient. Faced with the cold-war task of legitimizing a West German regime, most of whose citizenry had happily followed Hitler, it was more convenient to believe they'd been tricked into it by a mountebank than that they'd *shared* the poisonous delusions of a true believer.

But this is "not enough" for Trevor-Roper. "The notion arises: Would the Germans follow a mere irresponsible opportunist? Could he have gone so far? And the fact is he nearly won the *war*. It was by a whisker he didn't. If he had won the war—and I think there were three or four moments when he really could have won it—historians would be saying to you he was, as he saw himself, this great historical figure."

I found it fascinating Trevor-Roper could become so impassioned on the subject; it seemed more than an embattled academic position, more like an article of faith. Hitler explanations offer contradictory comforts. For Emil Fackenheim, it is important to believe Hitler was insincere and opportunistic precisely because he doesn't want to exempt Hitler from the gravest degree of responsibility, from conscious, premeditated knowing evil. Perhaps for Trevor-Roper, that degree of knowing evil, evil without the fig leaf of rectitude, is inconceivable or unbearable to contemplate.

In any case, Trevor-Roper's predilection for believing in Hitler's sincerity is nothing if not consistent. It's certainly there in what is otherwise his most illuminating essay on Hitler, the one entitled "The Mind of Adolf Hitler," which appeared as the introduction to the so-called Secret Conversations, also known as Hitler's "Table Talk," the transcripts of his wartime pontifications.

"You believe," I asked him, "that the Hitler of the Table Talk is the *real* Hitler, that he's not posing."

"Oh, it's the real Hitler. Oh, yes, oh, yes, no doubt about it," he told me unequivocally.

My response to the Table Talk is far more equivocal, that at best it's the real *counterfeit* Hitler: That even though the words are (for the most part) really Hitler's, nonetheless it's almost as false a creation as the "Hitler Diaries." In a sense, the "Table Talk" is Hitler's own Hitler-diary hoax.

First of all, while the Table Talk seems to be Hitler's words, the best that can be said of it is that it's an edited reconstruction of Hitler's speech. It's worth recalling the way the process of reconstruction verged on fabrication. Beginning in mid-1941, when Hitler established his underground command post for running the war on the eastern front, his nightly routine was highly consistent. After midnight, tea and cakes were served, and Hitler relaxed with his personal staff, including several young secretaries, a couple of congenial aides, and a guest or two from the outside world. Then, beginning around 2 A.M. and sometimes continuing until dawn, when he finally went to sleep, Hitler would hold forth to his captive audience for hour upon hour, pontificating upon the world situation, history, art, philosophy, literature, opera, culture, and, above all, his vision of the Brave New Aryan Future.

Prevailed upon by the flattery of his increasingly powerful aide, Martin Bormann, to permit a stenographer to attend these sessions so that none of the pearls of wisdom he dispensed would be lost, Hitler relished the idea that he was speaking for history. Bormann would then take the transcripts from the stenographer and knit together the raw flow of Hitler's words, editing, refining, polishing, constructing a testament to Hitler's thought process—his stream of consciousness as he wanted history to see it.

Consider, for instance, the counterfeit of piety Hitler gives us in the entry for October 24, 1941, when he piously declares, "The Ten Commandments are a code of living to which there is no refutation. These precepts correspond to the irrefragable needs of the human soul; they're inspired by the best religious spirits."

Is this a Hitler "convinced of his own rectitude" or a Hitler consciously, deceitfully posing as someone convinced of his own rectitude, the charade or counterfeit of the real thing? Perhaps the best answer to that comes in the Table Talk entry for the very next evening, an extremely telling and revealing discussion of the Final Solution that might be Hitler's consummate lie.

What makes this lie so astonishing is that it is delivered to the two men who are in the best position to know what an enormous falsehood it is—the "special guests" in the command post that night, the SS chief, Heinrich Himmler, and his chief accomplice in mass murder, Reinhard Heydrich. To them, Hitler's two closest confederates in carrying out the Final Solution (which in the preceding months had accelerated to programmatic mass extermination), Hitler, in an obviously staged performance, delivers himself of these chilling reflections:

> From the rostrum of the Reichstag, I prophesied [in 1939] to Jewry that, in the event of war's proving inevitable, the Jew would disappear from Europe. That race of criminals has on its conscience the two million dead of the First World War and now already hundreds of thousands more. Let nobody tell me that all the same we can't park them in the marshy parts of Russia! Who's worrying about our troops? It's not a bad idea, by the way, that public rumor attributes to us a plan to exterminate the Jews. Terror is a salutary thing.

This is not the language of a man "convinced of his own rectitude" in exterminating Jews. This is a man so convinced of his own criminality that he must deny that the crime is happening (it's only a "rumor" which, though "salutary," is not true); a man who must surround that backhanded denial with disinformation (we are merely "parking" the Jews in the marshy parts of conquered Russian territory, not murdering them en masse and burying them in pits); a man who must preface that disinformation with a justification for the act disingenuously denied ("That race of criminals has on its conscience the two million dead"—and therefore if the "rumor" was true, the killing would be just). It is perhaps the supreme Hitlerian counterfeit.

One can imagine the glances that Hitler, Himmler, and Heydrich must have exchanged during the orchestration of this elaborate charade for the stenographer, perhaps even the silent laughter. The three Holocaust perpetrators here become the first Holocaust deniers, establishing the pattern for the "Revisionists" who followed: The Holocaust didn't happen, but if it did, the Jews deserved it. If this is "the real Hitler," as Trevor-Roper declares, the realness is to be found in his slippery, conniving falseness, not in the sincerity that Trevor-Roper persists in finding in him.

But Trevor-Roper believes in the Table Talk and enjoys telling the tale of intrigue entailed in bringing the Table Talk manuscripts to light. It's a cloak-and-dagger document hunt that found him enmeshed with Nazi-sympathizing mountebanks, one that in a way foreshadowed the Hitler-diary fiasco and might have predisposed him to his initial disastrous misjudgment of those counterfeits.

From his reconstruction of the last days in the bunker, Trevor-Roper was familiar with Hitler's nightly habit of expounding to his flunkies for Bormann's stenographic record. He'd assumed the transcripts of these sessions had been lost or destroyed, and so he was intrigued when—after the publication of *The Last Days of Hitler*—suggestive-sounding excerpts from what appeared to be Table Talk discourse surfaced in Germany.

"Then I discovered that Bormann's whole text existed in the hands of a rather curious Swiss citizen called François Genoud, a businessman, very secretive. I know him quite well; Genoud [who committed suicide in 1996] is a Nazi sympathizer. He had a picture of Hitler in his house, and Genoud at the end of the war came to the rescue of some of the Nazi leaders, and he made bargains, and he bought Hitler's copyright, if it existed, which was very dubious, from Hitler's sister [Paula]. He also bought Bormann's copyright from Frau Bormann. He also bought Goebbels's copyright from, I think, his sister. And so Genoud has been sitting for nearly fifty years on these valuable copyrights. And whenever anyone attempts to publish anything by Hitler, Goebbels, or Bormann, suddenly Genoud pops up and says, 'Hi, I own the copyright,' and he does. He has to be bought out.

"Anyway, I discovered Genoud, and I went and saw him. And he showed me the text [of the Table Talk]. He wouldn't part with the German text for good reasons: There was always a question who owned Hitler's copyright. Hitler's property was confiscated by the state. Was it owned by the Austrian state or the German state? The sister was an Austrian. That was one question. Then did confiscation of his assets include copyright? That's another question. So Genoud rushed out a French translation to establish a copyright. You *can* claim copyright to a translation, but he wouldn't let the German text out."

What followed was more hugger-mugger, mountebanks galore. Trevor-Roper's publisher, Macmillan, was leery of the copyright problems. Trevor-Roper enlisted George Weidenfeld, who hired a translator who, Trevor-Roper believes, ended up collaborating with Genoud behind Trevor-Roper's back. Instead of translating the German manuscript into English, he translated the *French* translation of the German into English, a subterfuge Trevor-Roper didn't twig to until he found a curious locution in the Table Talk in which Hitler supposedly said, "I feel quite confused about" something.

"Now, Hitler was never *confused* about anything," Trevor-Roper told me, "but he was subject to embarrassment and I realized [the translator] must have mistranslated [the] French '*confuse*,' which is 'embarrassed,' not 'confused.' And I looked up the German text, which by that time was a little more available, and I found that was true. He had only been allowed to use the French translation."

I was impressed by Trevor-Roper's confidence in his grasp of Hitler's thought-world—that he could be certain Hitler was a man *never* confused but sometimes subject to embarrassment—that he was willing to credit Hitler's profession of the latter sincere. I was impressed as well by his confidence that, in a translation of a translation of a heavily edited transcription, Trevor-Roper was sure he'd found "the real Hitler." Perhaps it's the pride of discovery, of being the first to authenticate—perhaps the same impulse that led him to his own episode of confusion and embarrassment thirty years later when he pronounced the "Hitler diaries" genuine—this time confusing genuine forgeries with the forged genuineness of the Table Talk.

Forged genuineness—the way Hitler strains in the Table Talk to seem the intellectual bon vivant, the generous dispenser of wide-ranging conversational gemütlichkeit, the grating graciousness—it rings false to me. But I believe that a close reading of the Table Talk does reveal something authentic, something unacted, but something that emerges only inadvertently, in bits and pieces, an awareness pushing itself up from beneath the surface of Hitler's words: a growing, progressively alarmed apprehension beneath the surface of denial that the tide of war has turned, that victory is slipping away, that the architecture of the future, the cloud castles he's so grandiosely constructing for the entertainment of his guests, are melting away.

If it could ever be said that one could derive *pleasure* from reading Hitler— and I'm not sure "pleasure" is the right word—it is in seeing the way the bad news about the war impinges on Hitler's self-serving monologues in the Table Talk, which begin saturated with self-satisfaction and slowly become more plaintive, more defiant, as he tries unsuccessfully to conceal the anger, bitterness, disappointment, the betrayal of his hopes that haunt him.

Still, Hitler's voice in the Table Talk never seems anything but an act. And except for occasional flashes of abstract hostility toward "the Jews," it's an act that is always concealing something beneath the bonhomie: the actual slaughter he's presiding over.

That's what's surprising about Trevor-Roper's faith that this is "the real Hitler," that what we hear in the Table Talk is the true unguarded "Mind of Adolf Hitler" (as Trevor-Roper called his introductory essay preceding the Table Talk) when it's more like—to mix metaphors of tyranny—a Potemkin village of Hitler's mind, about as truthful to the reality within as the sign on the gates of Auschwitz that proclaims "*Arbeit macht Frei*" (work will make you free).

Yes, one *can* weave together a coherent ideology from the self-infatuated philosophical passages in the Table Talk. So brilliantly does Trevor-Roper do so in his introductory essay that it has become the foundation document of an entire school of Hitler explanation: the ideological school that gained popularity and had occasional impressive expositors (J. P. Stern in England, Eberhard Jäckel in Germany) in the 1970s. A school which emphasized the importance of taking Hitler's ideas, his Weltanschauung, his philosophic worldview, seriously—very seriously. As if the *possibility* of finding coherence in the logorrhea of the Hitler corpus meant that his thought-world *was* coherent—and that *he* took his ideas as seriously as the ideological school does.

Trevor-Roper is a master at finding coherence, but that's another thing entirely from finding belief. But he insists on belief as well, on Hitler's belief in his own rectitude, and hammers theorists who deny it, almost as if *they* were the mountebanks. His faith in Hitler's good faith (for want of a better phrase) and his habit of finding sincerity in Hitler's words are perhaps the very things that made him vulnerable to the mountebanks who were peddling the counterfeit Hitler diaries in 1983.

Trevor-Roper (by then Lord Dacre) played a pivotal role in the Hitler-diary affair, as a consultant brought in to assess them by Rupert Murdoch's *Times* of London. He initially pronounced the fake diaries genuine on the basis of a brief exposure to a stack of them in a bank vault. And then, just as *The Times* was about to go to press with its first installment, with the eyes of a waiting world upon it, Trevor-Roper pivoted 180 degrees, called *The Times* and let them know he *now* had serious doubts.

When word of Trevor-Roper's shift was relayed to Murdoch, Murdoch's response—as first reported in Robert Harris's tragicomic account of the affair, *Selling Hitler*—has since entered the annals of newspaper legend. Reached in New York and told of Trevor-Roper's switch, Murdoch shouted across the transatlantic lines: "Fuck Dacre! Publish!"

The mystery is why Trevor-Roper believed the diaries in the first place. He maintains that he was conned deliberately by mountebanks on the German end of the transaction who falsely assured him that laboratory tests on the "diaries'" paper proved they were of pre-1945 origin, when the opposite was true, as real tests later showed. But it's also true that at crucial moments when doubts came up, Trevor-Roper trusted in the sincerity of the Hitler-diary mountebanks.

"I took the bona fides of the editors" of *Stern*, the German magazine whose reporter was a virtual accomplice of the forgers, "as a *datum*," a given, Trevor-Roper told Harris.

Later, challenged at the last moment by *Times* reporter Philip Knightley, who had doubts about the diaries, Trevor-Roper fell back on faith in those the next step up the ladder: "The directors of *Stern*," he told Knightley, "one must assume do not engage in forgery."

If the directors of *Stern* were not directly engaged in forgery, they at the least seemed to have conned themselves into acting as front men for the mountebanks behind the scheme, who did engage in forgery. And the mountebanks behind the scheme, whose counterfeit Hitler seemed to owe much to the rhythms and the persona of the Table Talk Hitler Trevor-Roper had already authenticated, were clever enough to have counterfeited just the kind of Hitler, a *sincere* Hitler, that Trevor-Roper would be most likely to find authentic.

When I listen to the tape recording of my conversation with Trevor-Roper and I hear him hammering again and again at "the mountebank Hitler," the false Hitler of Bullock and others, it almost sounds as if he has a personal grudge against the mountebank image of Hitler. A grudge, I suspect, that may reflect the animus he still feels for the mountebanks who sold him on the counterfeit Hitler of the diaries. That bank vault where he fell under the spell of the forgeries was Trevor-Roper's own bunker. And the most convincing evidence for the continuing power of Hitler's spell is that someone as astute as Trevor-Roper could have succumbed to such a bad counterfeit, succumbed in truth to the Hitler spell that persisted even in that bank vault.

Still, I think Trevor-Roper's critique of the mountebank theory addresses an important inadequacy: that gap again, the abyss between the small-time film-noir grifter, the mountebank criminal the *Munich Post* reporters knew, and the magnitude of the horror Hitler created when he came to power in Berlin. But unbeknownst to Trevor-Roper, Alan Bullock, too, had begun to believe that his original mountebank explanation of Hitler was, as Trevor-Roper insisted to me, "just not enough."

CHAPTER 5

Alan Bullock: Rethinking
Hitler's Thought Process

*In which the most prominent Hitler biographer changes his mind about
Hitler's mind and resorts to the mystical tradition to explain Hitler's evil*

"**I**f you ask me what I think evil is," Alan (now Lord) Bullock was saying as
we approached the soot-begrimed, gargoyle-encrusted facade of Oxford's
Ashmolean Museum, "it's the Incomplete."

"The Incomplete?"

"In the sense it has a yet-to-be-brought-into-being quality, yes," he said.

More than anything he disclosed to me, perhaps even more than the
radical shift in his vision of Hitler's thought process, this mystical streak of
Bullock surprised me. He was, after all, an Oxford classics professor before he
became a historian and Hitler biographer; he'd been a student of Thucydides
and Tacitus. The hallmark of his work had always been judicious restraint,
the scrupulous unwillingness to exceed the limits of the available evidence.
In his published work, he's the kind of writer who eschews overstatement,
speculation, and certainly avoids mystical formulations about Evil and Incompleteness. But in person, Bullock is a veritable fount of provocative speculation, ranging from his notion of Hitler's metaphysical incompleteness to rather
earthy thoughts about Hitler's physical incompleteness. Or, as Bullock put it,
the "one-ball business."

The "one-ball business" came up in the context of a question I'd asked Bullock about the death in 1931 of Hitler's young half-niece, Geli Raubal. In his biography, Bullock had stated his belief that Hitler "was in love" with Geli, that they'd shared a tormented relationship plagued by his jealousy and possessiveness. But Bullock does more than depict Hitler in love with Geli; he asserts that her still-puzzling death—an apparent suicide in her bedroom in Hitler's Munich apartment—was "a greater blow than any other event in his life" (a remarkable statement, considering what the life encompassed). Over a glass of wine in the common room of St. Catherine's College, I asked Bullock if he still believed that Geli's death was a moment of transformation for Hitler.

"Well, it seems so—I mean, the keeping of the room, the sentimentality," Bullock told me, referring to the Miss Havisham-like shrine to Geli which Hitler ever after maintained untouched in the room in which she died. Bullock then turned to the nature of their relationship. "But what did he want her to *do?*" he asked. "What did Hitler want from Geli he couldn't get, or she couldn't give? Did he want her to marry him? Be his mistress? But could he perform? I mean, it was suggested actually, I understand he, sexually . . ." Bullock at first appeared somewhat uncomfortable with the subject. "I mean, you come back to the one-ball business."

I asked him whether he believed the 1945 Soviet autopsy report that no left testicle had been found in Hitler's charred body.

"Oh, there's no question," Bullock replied.

In fact, certain questions raised by the Russian autopsy about Hitler's last moment of life have *not* been laid to rest—questions ranging from those about the one testicle that the Russians claim was missing to those about the one bullet that passed through Hitler's head. A long-standing dispute between Bullock and Hugh Trevor-Roper over the circumstances of Hitler's suicide reflects once again their profound disagreement about Hitler's essential character.

Most authorities agree that on the afternoon of April 30, 1945, with Soviet troops advancing on the bunker, Hitler and Eva Braun entered their private suite with two revolvers and some cyanide capsules. Shortly thereafter, a single gunshot was heard, and Hitler's aides carried the two dead bodies to a bomb crater just outside the bunker, soaked them with petrol, set them on fire, and then buried the charred remains in a shallow grave. Shortly thereafter, Soviet troops captured the bunker, dug up the remains, and called in pathologists. With the help of dental records, they identified Hitler's body and performed an autopsy. The results of the autopsy were kept secret by the Soviets until 1968. Before then, almost all historians agreed with the scenario that Trevor-Roper had pieced together from his interrogations and published in *The Last Days of Hitler*. According to that account, Eva Braun killed herself by crushing a cyanide capsule in her mouth, while Hitler chose the traditional death of a defeated German officer who wished to avoid being captured alive—shooting himself in the head with his service pistol. The crux of Trevor-Roper's view of Hitler's death is once again his unshakable faith in Hitler's sincerity. "Of Hitler at least it can be said that his emotions were genuine," he wrote in *The Last Days*—he died a soldier for the cause.

The Soviet autopsy findings, which came to light in *The Death of Adolf Hitler*, a 1968 book by the Russian journalist Lev Bezymenski, told another story. Soviet pathologists reported finding crushed glass shards of a cyanide capsule clenched in Hitler's badly burned jaw and thus concluded that he had died from cyanide poisoning. Bezymenski argued, on the basis of the pathologists' report and a story attributed to Hitler's valet, Heinz Linge, who was just outside the death chamber, that Hitler died not a soldier's death but a "coward's death." According to Bezymenski, Hitler, lacking the courage to pull the trigger on himself, bit down on a cyanide capsule: after Hitler's death, Linge entered the suite and fired Hitler's pistol into his head to create the illusion that the Führer took the soldier's way out.

But Trevor-Roper contends that the Soviet autopsy report shouldn't be taken at face value, that it was a political as well as a medical document, designed to diminish Hitler for history. Seen in that light, the Soviet report of Hitler's genital incompleteness could also have been concocted as a crude way of further denigrating Hitler. The missing testicle would then become the objective correlative of the lack of manliness that the Soviets imputed to his style of suicide.

Until recently, Bullock has adhered steadfastly to the findings of the Soviet autopsy on the suicide method in part because they validated his original conception of Hitler as a schemer up until his final moment—an actor even in his final act. But some time after I visited him, evidence in a new book, *The Death of Hitler* by Ada Petrova and Peter Watson, caused Bullock to alter his view. "What the book shows is that Linge's story is ruled out," Bullock now says. "This is what Trevor-Roper said from the beginning." Bullock now accepts Petrova and Watson's view that Hitler bit down on a cyanide capsule and then almost simultaneously fired a bullet through his head.

Bullock remains fascinated, however, not just with the conclusions of the Soviet autopsy but with the autopsied organs. He told me that he had added material to the paperback edition of his 1991 dual biography, *Hitler and Stalin*, to include an account of the bizarre odyssey of Hitler's organs, based on interviews with the Soviet soldiers who had disposed of Hitler's remains. "On Stalin's orders . . . Hitler's organs, which had been placed in jars during the autopsy, were removed to the Kremlin," Bullock wrote.

"Stalin had the organs sent to him in Moscow?" I asked Bullock at St. Catherine's.

"Yes, he had them sent," Bullock replied. "Ah, marvelous! But did he *eat* them is what I want to know!" he asked, grinning, as he conjured up a horrific primal communion between the two dictators. "I'm sure some psychiatrist is going to say, 'Yeah, he ate Hitler's ball.' I must say, his one and only ball. Just think of what they'll make of that one. Poor old Waite—he'd really go overboard on that one." In *The Psychopathic God*, Robert Waite built an elaborate castle of Freudian interpretive analysis on the slender foundation of Hitler's purportedly half-empty scrotal sac. Bullock doesn't buy Waite's Freudian theorizing about the one-ball business, but he does seem to believe it was a signal absence, a token of a larger incompleteness in our vision of Hitler.

One might say that Bullock has found an incompleteness of a similar sort in his original Hitler explanation. The Hitler who emerges from his 1952 volume, *Hitler: A Study in Tyranny*, is a deliberately diminished and deflated figure, metaphorically one-balled. And the new vision of Hitler he disclosed for me could be described as a shift from oneness to twoness, or duality.

It's rare for a scholar to speak so frankly about changing his mind so completely. Bullock is not repudiating his first book entirely, although he did show flashes of irritation when I brought up questions based on it: "But I've *changed*, don't you see!" he exclaimed at one point. To appreciate the nature of the change, it might help to recall the context in which his initial thesis emerged.

Bullock can still describe with enthusiasm the experience of plunging into the research for the first book, shortly after the end of the war. "All of us, I think, came back wanting to know *why*," he told me. Before the war, Bullock had been primarily a historian of ancient wars, conflicts chronicled by Thucydides and Tacitus. But after the invasion of Poland, he says, "I spent the war in London during the blitz, building up the broadcasting to Europe, so I was sensitized in a big way to the politics and history of Europe of that period. I think all historians in one way or another who were drawn into the war, like Hugh Trevor-Roper, Hugh Seton-Watson, came back with the question 'Why?—How did this happen?'"

What galvanized him to attempt to explain it was the transcript of the Nuremberg trials. "Chatham House, the Royal Institute of International Affairs, sent me twenty-six volumes of verbatim testimony from the trials. And I reviewed every one of them. And I became intensely excited about them because—you can argue whichever way you want about whether it's justice or not—but from the point of view of the historian the Nuremberg trials were an absolutely unqualified wonder. I mean, the greatest coup in history for historians. The capture of the records of the most powerful state in the world immediately after the event! So I became involved with the publication of those, and then out of the blue came an invitation to write the life of Hitler."

He went to Germany, and what he remembers most vividly was the silence: "I went there immediately at the end of the war. I was in Germany a lot, and I remember going to the Ruhr—this was the heart of Europe as far as industry was concerned. There wasn't a single smokestack. There was silence everywhere. There were no cars, no trains. Long lines of foreign workers wending their way home. It was like a remote agricultural country except for the ruins. I couldn't believe what happened. I mean civilization was destroyed."

One thing Bullock didn't do was retrace Trevor-Roper's steps and focus on the people in Hitler's inner circle. "Everybody you might want to interview," he said, "was either dead or in prison." While that sounds like a bit of an overstatement, it might help explain why Bullock ended up with a book, with a vision of Hitler that did not dwell on the uncanniness of the spell Trevor-Roper encountered in reflected form from the inner circle, a spell some say he perpetuated. Not that Bullock's book is devoid of drama: His reconstruction of the final months of 1932 and the first month of 1933, the final weeks and days of high-stakes, high-tension maneuvering that led to Hitler's capture of the chancellorship, is a tour de force of historical narrative, one whose subtext—how often, how close Hitler came to *failing*—goes directly against the grain of Trevor-Roper's emphasis on how close Hitler came to *winning* the whole war.

Bullock's is an enthralling account of near failure by a distinctly nonenthralled narrator. Indeed, one can almost calibrate the degree to which an author is in the thrall of the Hitler spell by the amount of time he or she has spent with the possessed of that inner circle. Bullock, at the furthest remove, analyzes Hitler's appeal in terms of his cold-blooded, Machiavellian manipulativeness—his own detachment matches that of the mountebank Hitler he gives us in his first book. Trevor-Roper spent time with the inner circle. He was in it but not of it, able to be among the possessed and to recapitulate the power of the spell in his prose with awe but distaste. And then there is David Irving, who (as we'll see in chapter 12) entered into the inner circle, called it "the Magic Circle," and, it seemed to some, never really reemerged.

Bullock's book was an instant success on publication, a bestseller on both sides of the Atlantic; it's sold three million copies so far, he estimated, and remains in print in a 1962 revised edition. I asked him about a remark he made about *A Study in Tyranny*: how in writing the original version he deliberately set out to combat the embryonic form of the "Hitler myth," the occult messiah myth Trevor-Roper helped create.

"The book struck a chord," Bullock told me. "I think, if you ask me what chord, I remember very much [the reception] in the popular press: 'Now we know Hitler wasn't a madman, he was an extremely astute and able politician.' I think that really did surprise people."

Not a madman but a politician. It doesn't sound, on the face of it, shocking, but in the context of the time it was a defiantly contrarian view. As the terrible reality of the Holocaust became more and more a fact of shared consciousness, Hitler became more than the hated enemy leader, a figure like the Kaiser, say, after World War I. He grew to something closer to evil incarnate. New words were being coined—genocide, Holocaust—to describe his crime, and the dimension of his persona became grotesquely inflated to match the grotesque dimensions of the slaughter. Bullock's Hitler, in that context, seems to be a deliberately deflated figure, particularly in contrast with the irrational, demonic Hitler Trevor-Roper had given the postwar world. Bullock's Hitler was, if not a rationalist, then a man of shrewdly rational calculation, a human-scale schemer, an astute and able politician, not a monster of madness or an evil genius of theological dimensions who burst the bounds of previous frameworks of explanation.

In fact, Bullock's book is more than a biography, it's a valiant effort to somehow fit Hitler into the more comforting or at least more familiar framework of classical historical portraiture. Literally classical: Bullock even defiantly affixes to the book an epigraph from Aristotle: "Men do not become tyrants in order to keep out the cold."

"Lovely remark," Bullock says when I asked him why he chose it. "Well, I'm a classics scholar and Aristotle's *Politics* is a wonderful book that I just thought has to be brought to bear."

But what about the significance of that particular line? I asked him.

"All right: Men become tyrants because they wish to exercise power. It is not for material betterment or comfort, but because they have an itch for power."

"The love of power for its own sake?"

"That was my view of Hitler then. It's changed, you know."

The original view, then, is one that envisions Hitler as an extreme case, but an extreme case of something comprehensible, something that fits into the explanatory framework of such foundational documents of Western thought about power and tyranny as Aristotle's *Politics*, something that has precedent in Suetonius's description of a bloodthirsty Caligula, say—an extreme manifestation of something known.

But is Hitler adequately known? Before getting deeper into the way Bullock shifted from his classicist framework, I wanted to take him through the unresolved controversies in the field to get a sense of his view of the state of the art of Hitler explanation. At first, I was surprised at how often he felt attempts at explanation had failed, although since he was a believer in Incompleteness as a principle of being, perhaps that shouldn't have been so surprising.

"The true reasons for Hitler's anti-Semitism?" he mused in response to my question. "I don't know. Nobody knows. Nobody's even begun. I mean, one supposes the metaphors in which he talks about that are so frequently sexual.

One wonders if there's something there . . ." But he drew back from pressing the point: "There are a lot of mysteries in life you could never be able to give an explanation for, and Hitler's one of them. I think there are more things that are mysterious than people seem to think."

On the question of Hitler's sexuality itself, however, Bullock did have some pronounced opinions. He described for me a strange encounter he'd had with Ernst "Putzi" Hanfstaengl, Hitler's onetime confidant and foreign-press liaison, who'd recounted, after fleeing to the United States in the late thirties, a number of scurrilous stories about Hitler. Bullock recalled a strange hand gesture Hanfstaengl made to symbolize Hitler's sexuality.

"The man really was odious," Bullock recalls of Hanfstaengl. "He really was unpleasant to be up close [to]. He was such a blackguard, he was a faker. At any rate, it so happens the studio in which we were conducting the interview, there was a piano there."

Hanfstaengl famously had established himself as one of Hitler's most intimate late-night confidants with the way he played Wagner on the piano; there were times, it was said, when Hitler could not get to sleep unless and until Hanfstaengl was summoned from across town to come and soothe him with his Wagner stylings.

Bullock continues: "I said, 'Come on, play like you played for Hitler.' My God, he played badly. And then suddenly he started this—" Bullock imitated Hanfstaengl's hand gesture by holding out his hand with forefinger and pinky extended. "And he said, 'You know, [Hitler] could only play on the black keys.' Now, what did he mean by that? I think that he [meant that Hitler] was sexually incapacitated. And I think that's plausible, because I suspect that what happened in the affair with his niece was voyeurism. I'm sure that Hitler was in some ways sexually abnormal."

If Hanfstaengl meant anything more explicit, Bullock didn't press him. With Hanfstaengl's death, the precise meaning, if there was one, of that hand gesture became the lost chord of Hitler explanation.

Bullock returned to the subject of Geli Raubal and the questions raised about her death. Did he believe the official verdict of suicide?

"Let's say the evidence doesn't incline one way or another. The plausibility is suicide, but the evidence is not persuasive, doesn't move you one way or another. I think the odds are on suicide."

"That he drove her to suicide?"

"I think he—especially after the affair she had with his chauffeur and then her wanting to go to Vienna and all the rest of it. . . . He was a real old monster. I mean, she just had to do what he wanted her to do, and, I think, love? Possibly, he wanted her to go through some kind of voyeur antics which she objected to. I think that's what happened. I mean, women had to undress and do all sorts of things in front of him rather than screw him. And I think it's . . . that's my feeling about it. It fits better than the others."

"Better than?"

"Well, better than—I don't know what to say about him sexually, but it seems to me there's *something* wrong there. Whether it was he contracted a venereal disease from a Jewish prostitute and then had become impotent and so all he could do was go through the motions, or he had the lust to do it but not the capacity—I think that could be the case."

It was the Jewish-blood question that brought from Bullock his most impassioned discourse on incompleteness and explanation.

"[Franz] Jetzinger and Waite credit the Hans Frank story," I began.

"Yeah, they do. It's a nice explanation. They *want* to explain. I can't explain Hitler. I don't believe anybody can. Because I think human beings are very mysterious. Let's get straight what we can get straight. I mean, it's pretty terrifying, and I think they want to explain it because they want to be more comfortable with it. Let's have the rawness of it, which is the fact that he was a person like you and me in many respects."

Bullock has said two important and potentially contradictory things here. First is his critique of explanation. As I understand it, it's a more modest one than Emil Fackenheim's and Claude Lanzmann's; he doesn't rule out the *possibility* of explanation. Like Yehuda Bauer, he seems to feel the problem is incompleteness: a sufficient critical mass of facts are lacking that, if they *were* present, might well provide the missing explanation.

But Bullock's reservations about the possibility of explanation are belied to a certain extent by the words he used to describe those who crave certainty: "They want to be more comfortable with it. Let's have the rawness of it, which is the fact that he was a person like you and me in many respects."

In declaring so offhandedly "the fact" that Hitler was "a person like you and me," Bullock places himself squarely on one side of a great schism among Hitler explainers: those who speak of Hitler as "one of us," of a "Hitler within" all of us, of a potential for Hitlerian evil in all human nature, in *our* nature—and those who maintain one of several varieties of Hitlerian exceptionalism. Exceptionalist arguments range from the belief that the magnitude of Hitler's evil (however that magnitude is measured) surpasses that of previous malefactors of history to the more sophisticated theses of those like the philosopher Berel Lang who argue that it is the quality of Hitler's intentionality, not the quantity of bodies, that makes the Nazi genocide a new chapter in a "history of evil." Beyond that are the more metaphysical and theological arguments of Emil Fackenheim, who rejects the idea of a Hitler "within us," who argues instead that Hitler is beyond the continuum, off the grid, not explicable by reference to any previous version of human nature. Rather, he represents some kind of "radical evil," even an "eruption of demonism" into history, one so unprecedented it must cause us to reconsider our conception of God's relationship to man.

While such views seem extreme, it could be argued that seeing Hitler as a "person like you and me" is not necessarily a milder or more mitigating vision but a darker and more disturbing one. It's a radically dark view of the potential of human nature that can find a Hitler, or Hitler-potential, even within Alan Bullock. In fact, that seems to be what Bullock's saying when he says let's have "the rawness of it"—the rawness inheres in finding Hitler not inhuman or demonic but in finding him somehow *human*. It's a rawness that goes beyond Prospero's saying of the fiendish Caliban, "this thing of darkness I acknowledge *mine*" at the close of *The Tempest*, because that still implies a kind of separation—a responsibility for, but not an identity with, the "thing of darkness." Bullock pushes that further, in saying Hitler was "a person like you and me in many respects." To a point where he almost seems to say, "This thing of darkness I acknowledge *me*."

It was at this point that I raised with Bullock the question about Hitler's evil I'd raised with Trevor-Roper and other Hitler explainers: Did he see Hitler as consciously, knowingly evil? I raised it in the context of the Bulger case, which was in the London headlines that morning. James Bulger was a two-year-old boy who'd been lured away from his mother in a Liverpool shopping mall by two ten-year-old boys who proceeded to take him to a railroad crossing, beat him to death with bricks, and leave him to be run over, hoping to create the counterfeit of a "tragic accident" to cover their deed.

I'd been struck by the language of the trial judge in delivering his guilty verdict. The words the judge used were shocking in the context of discussions I'd had with Hitler explainers on the question of Hitler's consciousness of evil. No, Trevor-Roper said, Hitler wasn't consciously wicked, Hitler was "convinced of his own rectitude." No, Dr. Peter Loewenberg, the psychohistorian at UCLA argues, Hitler wasn't consciously evil, he was a captive of his unconscious drives and thus did not fully *own* his conscious impulses, was to that extent prisoner or victim of them, and thus not capable of conscious evil in the sense that a fully and successfully analyzed patient might be.

Thus, the language of the judge calling the two boys "EVIL . . . WICKED," guilty of "UNPARALLELED EVIL," as the headlines blared, was almost shocking. The reluctance of the experts to call Hitler evil set off against a judge calling two prepubescent ten-year-olds evil was thought provoking, to say the least.

I asked Bullock if he felt the barriers Trevor-Roper and Loewenberg did to calling Hitler consciously evil.

"If *he* isn't evil, who is? That's all. I mean, if not he then who? The only defense you could make," he said, thinking out loud, "is that he believed it." He considered the question in relation to Heydrich: "He didn't believe . . . "

"You don't think Heydrich . . . "

"He didn't believe *anything*. Curiously, Hitler chose him as the man who might succeed him, while Himmler was almost ridiculous in his belief. He *yearned* to believe. Heydrich did, I think, quite enjoy cruelty."

"And Hitler also?"

"No evidence of it. Never went near it [meaning the death camps]. He never saw it. He never went near a concentration camp, he never went near a death camp. He took no actual part in it. He didn't actually organize it. He left that to Himmler and Heydrich."

But, Bullock said, if it comes to a question of responsibility, Hitler *was* conscious of his responsibility. "He was the inspirer of it all. The only man who— he would *take* the responsibility. He was willing to. . . . So if he isn't evil, then the word has no meaning."

I asked Bullock about a curious phrase he used in his first book to describe Hitler's mind: "moral cretinism"—which, depending on how one reads it, is either a disease metaphor for immorality or a moral symptom of a disease, something like the post-encephalitic theory of Hitler's hatred. To most, I believe, "moral cretinism" would sound like a kind of diminished-capacity defense of Hitler, making him as much victim (of a morally incapacitating syndrome) as perpetrator.

Bullock seemed a bit unsure himself how he used it but cheerfully reached up to a shelf above him (we were in his St. Catherine's study now) to bring down a dictionary. "I suppose there's a notion," he said, flipping through the *C*s to find "cretinism," "of the cretin as a person who is so undeveloped that he has no notion of good and evil. And I think one of the things that is extraordinary about Hitler—maybe he *protected* himself from it." The "it" he is referring to is the reality of the actual death camps and killing chambers Hitler refused to see. He took responsibility for them, "but he seems to be unmoved by the idea of it. And one hears this description of people whose emotions are dead inside them. They are literally cut off from any sense of compassion. I suppose that's what [moral cretinism] means. I suspect I was using it not very precisely, I don't think I say that in my second book."

He finds the page in the dictionary and reads the definition of "cretin": "'Person of deformity and mental retardation caused by thyroid deficiency'— well, he wasn't suffering from mental underdevelopment. He was functionally too damned clever."

"But suffering from *moral* underdevelopment?"

"Yeah, that's what one means by it—moral retardation."

This doesn't completely clarify the ambiguity in moral cretinism: Is it a willed, a conscious refusal to develop a moral sense, or a congenital deficiency, or a traumatically induced one, for which one is not "responsible" but merely born or afflicted with? But this is not necessarily Bullock being imprecise so much as being of precisely two minds on the subject. In fact, his new vision of Hitler's thought-world is about Hitler's own double-mindedness—a synthesis of two seemingly contradictory visions of Hitler's thought-world.

The first hint I had of how pronounced his change was came in Bullock's response to Emil Fackenheim's actor theory of Hitler. I'd mentioned something Fackenheim had told me in Jerusalem, his insistence that Hitler's hatred of the Jews was, like all his professed convictions, a cynical opportunistic *act*.

I'd assumed that Bullock might tend to agree. I'd assumed, indeed, that Fackenheim had derived his actor theory, at least in part, from a reading of Bullock's first Hitler biography with its vision of Hitler as a cynical, calculating politician, the adventurer with the itch for power for whom beliefs, like people, were only instruments.

But Bullock's response surprised me.

"Ah!" he said. "He was the great actor who *believed* in the part. *That*'s the unique thing about him. He's a great actor but he—there's a wonderful quotation from Nietzsche which I have . . . "

From another bookshelf in his office, he drew down a volume of Nietzsche and read aloud the passage (from *Human, All Too Human*) that, in fact, embodies Bullock's revised view of the dynamic of Hitler's thought-world:

> Men believe in the truth of all that is *seen* to be strongly believed. In all great deceivers a remarkable process is at work to which they owe their power. In the very act of deception with all its preparations— the dreadful voice, the expression, the gestures—they are *overcome* by their belief in themselves, and it is this belief which then speaks so persuasively, so miracle-like to the audience. Not only does he communicate that to the audience but the audience returns it to him and strengthens his belief [emphasis added].

The mental process he describes here is complicated, a kind of dynamic. It begins with what seems like a cynical, opportunistic calculation: What is most important is not to believe but to be *seen* to believe; that is, the acting of belief is more important than the sincerity. But if there is calculation behind the act initially (the calculation which for Fackenheim is essential to preserve a sense of Hitler as consciously evil), what follows is "a remarkable process" in which the actor-deceiver becomes carried away, possessed, overcome by his own act, a believer in his own deception. Possessed by himself.

Bullock's revised dialectical vision of Hitler's thought process, then, begins with his original vision of a calculating Hitler, call it Bullock I (a crafty, calculating actor-deceiver who has much in common with the calculating criminal counterfeiter envisioned by the *Munich Post* writers), then proceeds to incorporate the possessed, spellbinding "sincere" Hitler of Trevor-Roper, and, finally, through a meshing of thesis and antithesis, arrives at a synthesis, the Hitler of Bullock II: the actor who comes to believe sincerely in his own act.

The key change in his thinking, Bullock told me, was in his view of the role of ideology in Hitler's thought-world—Trevor-Roper's preoccupation. "I changed my mind about Hitler in that I originally took him as solely interested in power. . . . I now think the ideology *is* central. I think it's what armors Hitler against remorse, guilt, anything. Hitler was unmovable on this ideology, this belief that he was the man sent by providence. The belief in himself—I think I have brought that out much more in the second book *[Hitler and Stalin]* than I did in the first. In the first I was very much . . . I didn't grasp that."

I was impressed by Bullock's humility but still not absolutely clear about whether this new, more complicated model of Hitler's thought process didn't contain a contradiction.

"Are you saying," I asked him, "that there is calculation which then leads to a possession that is *then* authentic and not merely acted?"

"I think it's exactly the same with Stalin," he said. "Stalin was very different in many ways. Because he was no speaker, he'd absolutely no charisma, but the Stalin cult which he manipulated, he made sure that he's praised and all this praise is synthetic, it's not spontaneous. *To begin with.* It became spontaneous with a lot of people at the end. And with *him*, he is aware that he's doing it [creating a cult of his own genius], yet at the same time he's aware he's doing it, he knows that it's true—that he *is* a genius."

"Simultaneously?"

"I find nothing difficult in that," he said. "Men are perfectly capable in public life of holding two incompatible beliefs. And most of the day, I do."

"But can one be sincere and insincere at the same time?"

I thought I might have had him there, but he trumped me with a visual metaphor and a story about a funeral.

"It's like fast-moving water, isn't it?" he asked me.

Fast-moving water? I thought of light flickering off the peaks of rapidly moving waves. There was something intuitively convincing about the image, the flickering back and forth of calculation and belief in the fast-moving stream of consciousness.

As for the funeral, it took place that very morning, he said. A colleague had drowned in a swimming accident—in fast-moving water. Bullock had spoken at the interment that morning. "I experienced it this morning when I was speaking," he told me. "I was speaking with my whole heart, because I really was very distressed. The wife who had gone through this appalling experience was in front of me, looking at me. And at the same time I was saying to myself, 'Are they listening to me? Am I being a success?' I'm being frank with you. I don't think I'm an insincere man, but I'm perfectly aware of what I do, and I wanted to be a success. There's an element of the actor in many people. I mean, I know there's a little devil in me which will come up and say. 'Oh, you believe that do you? Aha, but you do rather *well* out of it, don't you?'"

"The imp of the perverse?" I asked. "Isn't that what Poe called it?"

"Absolutely. And that's been frequently described. Goethe tells us about him. You know, the little devil who comes up and says that. And I say, 'Bugger off, babe, I'm all right, I really mean it.'"

While I'm not quite convinced that Bullock's imp of the perverse is in any way usefully commensurate with Hitler's exterminationist urge, the dynamic Bullock was describing seemed more persuasive when he applied it to explain what he believes was the cause of Hitler's ultimate wartime failure. The turning point, the *real* beginning of the end, Bullock believes, came for Hitler after—perhaps because of—his first heady victories on the Russian front in 1941.

Before that, Bullock sees him as cautious and calculating enough—in 1936, for instance, he was ready to withdraw immediately if the French had shown any sign of military opposition to his reoccupation of the Rhineland. "Up to that point [in 1941], he's hesitant and *then* ruthless," Bullock said. "But once he gets the attack on Russia, then I think he thinks, you know, this is *it*." At that point, he becomes so overcome with belief in himself, in his destined invulnerability, that, Bullock says, "The man destroys himself. Which is so interesting. I mean, making the German army stand in front of Moscow and not retreat, getting rid of all these generals, insisting they stand. If only he'd been flexible, you see, if only he had been prepared to come back at him, it's quite conceivable Stalin could have made a compromise peace. That's one of the things that's a mystery. . . . But the extraordinary thing about this—and this is where the element of hubris comes into it—it's when he gets to that point where he no longer *manipulates* his image but believes in it *entirely*, when he drops the manipulation, then he's destroyed. He was destroyed by his own image. As long as he believed *and* manipulated, [he was successful,] but when he gets outside Moscow, he no longer manipulates, it's Will and Will alone afterwards."

"He loses the practical vision of the cynic?"

"All of that. Look, the man could have had half Russia on his side against Stalin. But look at the treatment of the Ukraine—ridiculous. [Foreign Minister] Ribbentrop sees this and remembers people saying it to him: 'That's the moment when he goes over. That's the moment he destroys himself.' Oh, it's a very satisfactory Greek tragedy."

Satisfactory? Here again, Bullock seems to return to his classicist roots, to the impulse to conceive a tragedy within an Aristotelian framework, Hitler and the Holocaust as part of a continuum of human tragedy, part of the continuum of human nature. And yet, like his model of Hitler's thought-world, he too flickers back and forth on the question: Shortly after his remarks about Hitler's hubristic downfall being so satisfactory, he raises the question of whether, in fact, Hitler *shatters* the old, Aristotelian, framework.

I'd asked him if his study of Hitler had resulted in a change in his view of the potential of human nature for evil.

"A lot," he said. "I mean, if you're brought up as most of us are, we live in a very protected society and we're confronted by that—I mean, I'll never forget coming out of Yad Vashem," he says of a visit to the Holocaust memorial in Jerusalem. "I was shattered. Shattered."

Does it require that we reconsider what the essence of human nature is?

At first, he seems to affirm that Hitler and the Holocaust were some-thing that the classical vision of human nature could have incorporated. "Is anything different? To go back in history—and also in scale—if you go back to some of the things that went on in antiquity, I think if you read Tacitus, if you read Thucydides, most of us who read these books haven't had this experience."

"The slaughter of the helots?" I suggested, recalling Thucydides' account of a Greek massacre of slave workers in Sicily.

"Yeah—it's on a different scale. But I think there's a pretty grim story."

"And what about the thought-world of those who commit these crimes? Does the impulse to kill one thousand make one equally culpable as someone who kills ten thousand? Or does there become a point where—"

"I think it's a very interesting question. I think there's an extra thing which comes into it when you mechanize it. Then it's suddenly—the accountants working on the cost-benefit of this and that method of killing—this is the hor-ror of the German Holocaust. This isn't done in hot-blooded fury of battle or revenge, all that. It's cold-blooded. The Jews were not a military threat. It's cold-blooded. When the Russians committed atrocities—by God, they had provoca-tion. That was revenge. This wasn't revenge. This was cold-bloodedness."

So, for Bullock, the state of mind behind the killing is one factor in the cal-culation of degrees of evil but not the only one. He returns to the question of scale. He's had trouble, he says, getting contemporary students to comprehend the scale of devastation wrought by Hitler's war and the death camps.

"You can't convince people. I mean, they're so horrified of what's going on in Yugoslavia. I know it's ghastly, but that's nothing compared to what was going on in Yugoslavia when Hitler was trying to destroy them."

"We have a tough time with comparative evil."

"It's a difficult one, isn't it? Scale—I'm afraid I think it *does* matter, but I resist that conclusion. And yet I think it's true. I mean, I feel it's somehow or other morally flawed, that judgment. And yet I do think if you see a million people killed, somehow or other it's worse than if ten are killed. It's troubling. But the Bullock philosophy is that there are a lot of troubling things in life that won't be explained."

"Does that philosophy come from the study of classics?"

"Yes. And from Machiavelli. Machiavelli was a moralist, you know."

But on the cusp of committing himself to the classicist view, Bullock raises the mystical question. "I must say I think the mystics have something to say on the question. I don't make a claim to be a mystic myself. But I think about the questions they raise. Extraordinary, the fact that they occur in every culture, Tao, Sufi, Zen Buddhism, Catholic, Protestant, Blake, Plato, Plotinus—extraordinary. And roughly—although they're so different, they all loved paradox: that which is and that which is not; that which is wholly united and that which is wholly divided."

It was his father who inspired his interest in the mystical path, and Bullock speaks movingly of his father's unorthodox spiritual trajectory:

"A Unitarian minister, he nonetheless came to feel after the [First World] war that religion was dying and that there were so many people on a sort of spiritual hunt he couldn't reach. That he just couldn't reach. So although he continued to preach, and a marvelous preacher he was, he did revive an old tradition, an alternative ministry. He completely severed himself from the church side of things, took a room which had no resemblance to a chapel— there was no ritual, no prayers, no hymns, he didn't wear any vestments or anything. And he called them psychology lectures. And he went on for about twenty to thirty years. And there he brought home many of his religious beliefs, stated them in some nonreligious terms. A lot of people came to listen to him. Totally without recognition because this was a town in the north which no one had heard of—Bradford. And he said, well, my luck is to talk to forty or fifty people. And he never complained. I think in the nineteenth century he would have been a great preacher. And the late twentieth century, he'd be on television. And, well, he was a lovely man, he really was."

Is there a sense here in which he is implicitly contrasting his unsung preacher father with the malevolent street preacher he's spent his life chronicling? He's now working, Bullock told me, on a memoir of his father, which he says he hopes will help make amends to his wife for all the years he's spent with Hitler and then Hitler and Stalin.

"We've been married over fifty years," Bullock told me. "I said to her, 'I'll see if I can make it up to you.' She adored him [his father]. Wait till she sees I'm working on that [the memoir of his father]. She's had Hitler and Stalin for the last seven years, she's kind of tired of it."

It occurred to me, after my talk with Bullock, that his new vision of Hitler's thought-world partakes of the mystical paradoxes his father was fond of: His revised Hitler, Bullock II, both is and is not an opportunist, both is and is not a possessed believer. Both qualities flicker back and forth like light on fast-moving water (the stream of consciousness), together forming a unifying conception. It also occurred to me that in his new synthesis Bullock is incorporating two sides of himself, two generations of Bullock: his own orthodox, classically trained vision and his father's unorthodox, nonconformist, mystical inclination. It is a classic instance as well of a phenomenon I came to find recurring in my conversations with some of the most conscientious Hitler explainers: the way the search for Hitler, the search to find coherence in the fragmentary surviving evidence, frequently led to a kind of searching *self-examination*, a reassessment of world history *and* of personal history.

It almost seems as if Bullock's love and respect for his father is what licenses him to look beyond the classical framework, the Oxford skepticism about such matters, to raise the question of faith, the questioning of God that Hitler has catalyzed in others. Over lunch at St. Catherine's Fellows' table, for instance, he surprised me when, in response to a reference I'd made to something he'd written about Hitler perhaps being "an expression of the Hegelian world spirit," he shifted the frame of reference from philosophy to theology, leaned over, and whispered to me in a genuinely impassioned tone, but one he evidently didn't wish the other fellows to hear, "Some days I ask God: '*If you were there, why didn't you stop it?*'" It's the problem Hitler and the Holocaust pose to theodicy—the attempt to reconcile the existence of God with the persistence of Evil.

He returned to the question again as we left St. Catherine's to cross the river Isis and headed toward the Ashmolean, where he was due at a meeting. It was on this walk that he first raised the notion of Evil as Incompleteness and then went on to advance a notion of God as incomplete. As the pillars of the Ashmolean loomed before us, Bullock expanded upon this vision of evil with reference to Jesus and Judas.

"The paradox of Jesus embracing Judas!" he exclaimed. "That's fascinating. You read it in the Bible, your hair stands on end! He kissed him on the lips!"

It took me a bit of time to parse out the relationship between Bullock's vision of evil as incompleteness, the embrace of Jesus and Judas, and Bullock's conception of Hitler. But there is a unity there. Consider first seeing evil as incompleteness. Evil then is not an alien, inhuman otherness as the Manicheans see it but a less highly evolved form of humanness. Lower, far lower on the Great Chain of Being but still part of the same continuum of creation that gave birth to us and emanates from or evolves toward God. Thus, even the most consciously evil figure in the New Testament can be embraced as part of creation, albeit the most singularly incomplete element of it. (For a far different vision of the Judas figure, see Hyam Maccoby's thesis in chapter 18.)

Bullock never goes so far as to suggest that *Hitler* must be embraced, but the unspoken assumption of his explanation of Hitler is that he, too, however extreme his evil, is on the same continuum of incompleteness that, in effect, embraces the rest of humanity. Hitler, that thing of darkness, was, then, one of us; can be explained as human, however incompletely so; requires neither Trevor-Roper's "more than human" formulation nor Fackenheim's "eruption of demonism." And where does Bullock's vision of evil leave God? As Himself a figure of incompleteness: "The one thing I would never say about God is that he's omnipotent," he told me. "He's botching along. Just trying to subdue the chaos that is still there."

I mentioned the conversation I had with Yehuda Bauer on this question: "Bauer told me one can't believe that God is both all-powerful *and* good because if he's omnipotent, then he's Satan for not having intervened."

"Yes, absolutely," Bullock said. "Never believe God is omnipotent."

If, in Bullock's belief, we need to acknowledge our kinship to evil and evildoers, he still believes evil should be confronted and combated. And, in fact, when in his early eighties, he nonetheless girded his loins and reentered the lists to take on the Holocaust deniers. It's a fascinating late development in his long career: the man whose biography defined Hitler for more people in the English-speaking world than anyone else in the past half century taking on not just the outright deniers such as David Irving was at the time, but also those who acknowledge the Holocaust but deny Hitler much personal involvement or responsibility—those among the "functionalists" who believe that the Holocaust was a kind of spontaneous combustion borne of bureaucratic exigency "from below" with complicity not extending above Himmler and Heydrich to Hitler.

He was summoned back to battle, Bullock says, after he published a review article in the *Times Literary Supplement* praising Christopher Browning's book (*Ordinary Men*) about the members of a Nazi police battalion and how they become mass murderers. This had come to the attention of the Holocaust Study Center at London's Yad Vashem Institute, which was engaged in combating the latest wave of Holocaust-denier publicity stirred up in Britain by David Irving.

Irving—long a controversial historian from the time he asserted in *Hitler's War* (1977) that since no written order for the Holocaust had been found with Hitler's signature on it, Hitler probably never ordered it at all—had, in the late eighties, shifted to the view that not only was it never *ordered* by Hitler, it never *happened* at all. Yes, Irving conceded, there were maybe hundreds of thousands of deaths due to disease, starvation, and scattered eastern-front atrocities, but no one was gassed because there were no gas chambers "worthy of note."

"Did they want you to respond to David Irving?" I asked Bullock.

"I didn't attack David Irving," Bullock insists. "I don't play his game."

What Bullock did was deliver a lecture at London's Yad Vashem Institute that was a methodical evidentiary assault against the two strains of denial. The lecture had a wide impact beyond the small hall in which it was delivered: A widely watched television segment on Bullock drew widespread attention to his stance (and hate mail as well, he told me).

In a sense, the address, entitled "Hitler and the Holocaust," is Bullock's final testament. And central to it is that quotation from Nietzsche about the mountebank who succumbs to belief in his own con game—Bullock's revised view of Hitler's thought process. ("No one," Bullock says in the address, "has described the charismatic power with which Hitler could project [his] belief to a German audience better than Nietzsche in a passage written with the insight of genius, more than ten years before Hitler was born.") A vision which, in fact, is central to his method of disposing of the "problems" raised by the deniers.

Hitler was, Bullock says in the lecture, "every bit as much a politician as a visionary: It was Hitler's mastery of the irrational psychological forces in politics which catches the eye [i.e., Trevor-Roper's Hitler], but it was . . . an opportunist's ability to conceal, disguise, and defer his long-term objectives" that was responsible for Hitler's "successes."

Here, Bullock, while insisting on the importance of both aspects of Hitler, seems to place greater emphasis on his earlier vision, the opportunist adventurer, the "mountebank" image Trevor-Roper rejects: Because what Bullock emphasizes in his analysis of Hitler's relationship to the Final Solution is the creation of a *counterfeit* detachment from the killing process.

Yes, Bullock believes killing the Jews was a central concern to Hitler (although he does not go as far as Lucy Dawidowicz, who viewed it in *The War Against the Jews* as virtually Hitler's *only* concern from as early as 1918). Bullock more tentatively says, "There may well have been the evil dream of a final solution [early on, but] this remains speculation. . . . What is clear is that, whenever he may have first conceived the idea, Hitler's judgment of what was *practical* in carrying out his fantasies . . . meant [that the idea for the Holocaust] developed by stages [and] was not programmatic but evolutionary."

Bullock, in what, to me, is the least convincing aspect of his thesis, pictures Hitler trying to placate two camps in the path to the Final Solution: his original "rabid or violent anti-Semite" supporters and the "much wider section of the German people" who were less concerned with going beyond discrimination and expulsion of the Jews to murder. (The evidence that Hitler was a relative *moderate* in his hatred compared to others is spotty to say the least.)

Bullock acknowledges that Hitler's programmatic anti-Jewish ideology was the sine qua non of the Final Solution, but, he argues, Hitler was not so utterly possessed by it, not so "convinced of his own rectitude" that he didn't feel the need to *hide* it. Bullock cites instance after instance in which Hitler, despite being "the moving spirit of this radical solution both in word and deed" (as Goebbels put it), nonetheless sought to preserve *deniability*, the deniability contemporary Holocaust deniers still assert on his behalf. It was not Hitler but Göring who wrote to Heydrich to arrange the massive organization of the Final Solution. It was Himmler who "prepared a report for Hitler on the progress made with the Final Solution during 1942," but it was also Himmler who, upon returning that note to Adolf Eichmann, wrote on it: "The Führer has taken note: destroy"—erase the evidence of Hitler's involvement.

Destroy any note of Hitler taking note to preserve the counterfeit of detachment. "Even in the 1930s," Bullock writes, "Hitler distanced himself from the execution of measures against the Jews; [in the forties,] he was still mindful of the lesson of the euthanasia program and the importance of his image . . . [and] could not afford to let his image be sullied by association with the dirty work of systematic mass murder."

It is in the very charade of distance, the counterfeit of detachment that, Bullock's argument suggests, we find the most damning evidence for the degree to which Hitler was *consciously*, knowingly evil. The degree to which he was not "convinced of his own rectitude" as Trevor-Roper believes, but committed the crime knowing it was a crime, suggests he did it out of a pure hatred that masked itself with the illusion of idealistic rectitude—and that he covered it up with a counterfeit of detachment like the conscious criminal, the "political counterfeiter," first defined for posterity by the reporters of the *Munich Post*.

Which still leaves the question: What lay beneath the counterfeit? Was there something human, and if so what sort of human? Is there anything retrievable and true to be said about Hitler's human nature? I think that's why the Geli Raubal episode still exerts a fascination. I was surprised at first to find Bullock, certainly one of the most sober and judicious of historians, expressing a fascination with the nature of Hitler's "love" (Bullock's word in *Hitler: A Study in Tyranny*) for Geli Raubal, a fascination with the nature of that passion, with the mystery surrounding Geli's death.

There is a forensic mystery at the heart of the Geli Raubal question—the circumstances of her death, Hitler's role in the suicide or murder. But the larger mystery, the one that has made it such a contested site of Hitler-explanation debates, is whether it offers a window into Hitler's inwardness, into the question of his humanness, of whether he was an utterly demonic aberration or whether—in some perhaps even *more* disturbing ways—Hitler could be considered "normal." It raises the question as well of whether the evil in Hitler had been there always, intrinsically, from the time he entered politics. Or whether we can conceive of an *evolution* of Hitler's evil, of a Hitler whose evil was at one time less absolute, more incomplete (as Bullock would have it) than its final form. And if so, what factors conspired to produce the final Hitler, the Hitler of the Final Solution?

PART THREE

GELI RAUBAL AND HITLER'S "SEXUAL SECRET"

A skeptical investigation into a persistent tradition

CHAPTER 6

Was Hitler "Unnatural"?

*In which we meet Mimi Reiter, Hitler's forgotten "first love,"
glimpse Hitler attempting to explain himself to a homicide detective,
and consider "Hitlerism as a sex problem"*

Chief Archivist Weber stops in the midst of reading the document he has dug up for me. "This is very strange," he says. "Listen to what Hitler says here."

The document he's been reading from, the fragile, yellowing six-decade-old six pages he's unearthed from the basement of the Bavarian state archives in Munich, is a police report: the report prepared by Munich police detective Sauer on his investigation into the gunshot death of Geli Raubal, Hitler's half-niece, who was found dead in a bedroom in Hitler's apartment with Hitler's gun by her side.

Archivist Weber had been reading aloud to me from the document in his office on the third floor of the Bavarian state archives. The "strange" remark that stopped him dead came from Detective Sauer's interview ("interrogation" would be too strong a word) with Hitler at the death scene several hours after the body was discovered. An interview in which Hitler was attempting to explain to the detective why the attractive twenty-three-year-old woman chose to blast a hole in her chest with his 6.5 caliber Mauser pistol.

This police report has been much speculated upon but rarely seen in the decades that followed Geli Raubal's death. And that "very strange" thing Hitler said—his bizarre remark to the detective about a fateful prophecy at a séance he claimed his young niece had attended—has escaped careful examination.

The circumstances of the detective's interview with Adolf Hitler couldn't have been more highly strained. It was mid-September 1931, Hitler was on the verge of an electoral breakthrough that would bring him to the brink of power. In the legislative elections the previous year, the Nazi Party had leapt out of fringe status: Its representation in the Reichstag had risen from 12 to 107 seats, making it the second largest party in the 600-seat body. For years after the failed putsch of 1923, Hitler had been regarded as a kind of crank, far outside the mainstream, a figure of fun; now, building upon the economic collapse of the Depression and the Reichstag electoral surge, he was contemplating a run for the presidency against Hindenburg in the next national election in early 1932. Suddenly, he was a serious contender. And just as suddenly, the level of press scrutiny of him and his party had intensified. The death of Geli Raubal climaxed a summer of sexual scandals in the Munich Nazi Party. The opposition *Munich Post* had exposed a sordid nexus of prostitution, blackmail, and murder plots involving Ernst Roehm and other Hitler cronies.

Now Hitler himself had a body on his hands, a body in a bedroom in his own apartment, a body whose identity raised the possibility of both a sexual and a murder scandal. Although the particulars differed, the parallels to an episode in American politics nearly forty years later may put the peril candidate Hitler faced in perspective: the suspicious death of a young unmarried woman; a presidential contender who'd been close to her; frantic advisers convening; inconsistent early statements about the circumstances of the death; police suspicion; press speculation about a cover-up. The death of Geli Raubal had the potential to become the death of Adolf Hitler's political ambitions, to become—to employ a deliberate anachronism—Adolf Hitler's Chappaquiddick. His entire career was riding on the outcome of Detective Sauer's investigation.

Of course, Detective Sauer's career might have been in jeopardy as well. The police and prosecutorial bureaucracy in Munich was dominated by rightwing nationalists, such as Minister of Justice Franz Gürtner, many of them Hitler sympathizers. Already, strings were being pulled behind the scenes to minimize Hitler's embarrassment. Already, party officials were keeping a tight rein on Detective Sauer's investigation.

In fact, one very prominent party official was there on the scene Saturday morning, even before Detective Sauer arrived. His name was Franz Xaver Schwarz, the party treasurer and one of the closest confidants of Hitler among the old comrades from the party's "struggle period" in the twenties. Schwarz had apparently been summoned to the death scene even before the police that morning. Schwarz made clear to Detective Sauer that Hitler had been far away from his apartment when his niece had taken Hitler's gun and shot herself:

He'd left on the previous afternoon for a campaign trip to the north; Hitler had no knowledge the tragedy had even occurred, although efforts were now under way to reach him and bring him the terrible news, Schwarz told the detective.

Detective Sauer and his partner, Detective Forster, viewed the body along with the police doctor. They found the young woman in her bedroom with a large hole in her chest and a large gun by her side. The doctor estimated that the bullet had been fired at close range and that it had missed the heart but passed through a lung. The gun, they were told by the household staff, belonged to Hitler and had been kept in his bedroom, the one down the hall. There was no suicide note, just a half-finished letter to a friend in Vienna discussing an upcoming visit.

In the absence of the master of the house, Detective Sauer began taking statements from the five members of the household staff. The story the staff told, under the vigilant supervision of Party Treasurer Schwarz, was that the previous afternoon, a Friday, about fifteen minutes after Hitler left for his campaign trip, Geli had been glimpsed rushing out of Hitler's bedroom, looking agitated. That was the last they'd seen of her, they all said, until the following morning, when she didn't respond to a knock on her bedroom door. The door was locked (it could be locked from either side), and the husband of the housekeeping woman had jimmied it open, revealing the dead body. She must have, they said, taken the gun Hitler kept in his bedroom and used it on herself.

None of them had heard a shot, they said. The wife of the housekeeping couple thought she'd heard a thud, like the sound of something heavy falling or breaking, in Geli's room shortly after Geli rushed out of Hitler's bedroom and locked her door behind her. But the housekeeper hadn't thought of that thud as a gunshot or a body falling at the time, she said.

Detective Sauer took the statements and conferred with the police doctor. Neither the body itself nor the statements of the household staff gave an indication of foul play, but there was one factor missing from a suicide judgment; the motive. Here the household staff had been distinctly unhelpful. None of them would hazard a guess about why the vibrant, attractive young woman who lived such an enviable life at the side of her famous uncle would suddenly have stolen Hitler's gun and fired a bullet into her chest. Indeed, they went out of their way to declare their helpless bafflement in almost identical terms.

"She shot herself—why, I can't say," the husband of the housekeeping couple told Detective Sauer.

"Why Geli Raubal took her life, I don't know," the cleaning woman told Detective Sauer.

"Why she shot herself, I cannot say," the wife of the housekeeping couple told Detective Sauer.

That was why Detective Sauer needed to speak to the absent Adolf Hitler.

If he was going to close down this investigation to the satisfaction of his superiors—and, more problematically, the press—with a suicide verdict, it would be helpful to have a motive.

He was told Hitler was being notified and that undoubtedly he would race home to mourn his niece. Detective Sauer returned to Munich police headquarters to report to his superiors and await word from Hitler. At approximately 2 P.M. the call came. Adolf Hitler had arrived back at his home and was prepared to answer questions about his niece's death.

We cannot, of course, intuit what might have been going through Detective Sauer's mind when he approached the princely residence that was home to Hitler and his half-niece. Perhaps he was already aware of the pressure being brought to bear by Bavarian Minister of Justice Franz Gürtner to limit the police investigation and of the decision of the police doctor that the body should be released without a formal autopsy for embalming and hasty shipment across the border to Vienna.

Still, he knew he had to have *some* explanation from Adolf Hitler for the record. Perhaps if Detective Sauer was aware of the rumors already racing through Munich, rumors about the nature of the relationship between Hitler and the young woman, rumors about the nature of the quarrel between them, he might have wondered if Hitler *was* the explanation.

In the decades since that day, tens of thousands of words have been devoted to that question, to the nature of Hitler's role in the Geli Raubal tragedy, to the effect of that tragedy on Hitler's future role in history. Buried beneath the layers of analysis are Hitler's own words that day to Detective Sauer. According to the detective, this is what Hitler had to say:

> His niece was a student of medicine, then she didn't like that anymore and she turned toward singing lessons. She should have been on the stage in a short time, but she didn't feel able enough, that's why she wanted further studies with a professor in Vienna. Hitler says that was okay with him but only under the condition that her mother from Berchtesgaden accompany her to Vienna. When she didn't want this, he said he told her, "Then I'm against your Vienna plans." She was angry about this, but she wasn't very nervous or excited and she very calmly said good-bye to him when he went off on Friday afternoon.

Then Hitler added the remark that struck Archivist Weber as so strange:

> She had previously belonged to a society that had séances where tables moved, and she had said to Hitler that she had learned that one day she would die an unnatural death. Hitler went on to add that she could have taken the pistol very easily because she knew where it was,

where he kept his things. Her dying touches his emotions very deeply because she was the only one of his relatives who was close to him. And now this must happen to him.

Setting aside for the moment the question of its truth, that strange séance story was a brilliant if somewhat desperate stroke on Hitler's part. Flourished at the last moment like a magician's cloak, it was clearly designed to obscure with a flash of fatalism what he must have known were the conspicuous inconsistencies and the overall inadequacy of the rest of his attempt to explain his half-niece's death.

Even the timid, closely supervised statements of the household staff seem to contradict Hitler's statement on a key point: *They* report Geli looking agitated and excited, rushing from Hitler's bedroom with a gun, scarcely a quarter hour after Hitler reportedly departed. Hitler, on the contrary, declares Geli was neither nervous nor excited but rather said good-bye to him "very calmly."

This appears, on the face of it, to be a feeble attempt to detach the quarrel he admits to having had with Geli—the dispute over whether she could travel to Vienna alone—from her decision to kill herself. As if, in the fewer than fifteen minutes between the time he left and the moment she raced into his room to steal his gun, something *else* had come up, something unrelated to Hitler, to cause Geli to decide to shoot herself.

He's trying unsuccessfully to have it both ways. He wants to minimize the importance of the quarrel between them, but in doing so he undercuts its potency as an explanation for her suicide, thus raising questions about what the real motive might be—or whether the death might not have been suicide at all.

And Hitler's account of the quarrel itself strains credibility, suggests darker possibilities. Perhaps a young woman of twenty-three would resent being told her mother had to accompany her on a trip to a voice-instruction lesson in Vienna. But would a young woman of twenty-three end her life over that issue? The disparity between the explanation and the act inevitably raised questions about whether there was something more to the Vienna trip than voice lessons, something that required close family supervision to forestall. The disparity gave rise to rumors that—as newspapers in Berlin, Munich, and Vienna would soon speculate—the trip to Vienna was for an elopement with a forbidden fiancé or an attempt to escape an intolerable relationship with Hitler.

But Hitler was shrewd enough to realize that, on the face of it, his account of Geli's purported motive for killing herself fell short of being compellingly convincing. Thus, the séance story: a masterful touch which *seems* to be a spontaneous emotional coda to his statement but which, in fact, when the whole statement is examined carefully, seems more like a capstone of what is a carefully calculated subtext of character assassination.

Who is Geli in Hitler's portrait for the detective? She's someone who fatally, fickly abandoned serious plans for a medical career just because "she didn't like that anymore." Only to impulsively take up a singing career, where she displayed similarly fickle instability: "She should have been on the stage in a short time, but she didn't feel able enough." Always trouble with Geli!

Then Hitler shamelessly depicts himself as the real victim of Geli's act: "She was the only one of his relatives who was close to him. And now this must happen to him." To him; not to her.

And, finally, there is the most ingenious and insidious touch: the séance. Characterizing her as the type who attends "table-moving" sessions serves to portray her as unstable, emotionally immature. If she's impulsive enough to have been influenced by some mountebank posing as a departed soul who declares she would die an unnatural death, she might well have been motivated by the "prophecy" to give in to the impulse to kill herself at the slightest, most trivial provocation. After all, it was—or she believed it to be—her fate. Perhaps Hitler hoped to strike a respondent chord of superstition in Detective Sauer so that he would shift his focus from the gaps, the absences in Hitler's story and write Geli's death off to fate, the invisible working of the Other World, a matter of karma, not homicide.

Before proceeding further with the problems with Hitler's explanation, with the questions that have been raised about the degree of his responsibility for her death, it is worth lingering over the phrase Hitler used to describe the purported séance prophecy about Geli: She would die a death that was "*keines natürlich.*"

"Keines natürlich": Conjoined with the word for death, the literal meaning is "unnatural," as in an "unnatural death." The implication in context is murder or suicide as opposed to a "natural" death from old age or disease. But the phrase "nicht natürlich" has been used to characterize not just Geli Raubal's death but her relationship to Hitler. And it evokes the truly troubling question raised by the whole Geli Raubal affair: how natural or unnatural, how normal or abnormal, Hitler himself was.

It's troubling because the temptation in sifting the evidence for what really went on between Hitler and Geli Raubal is to believe the darkest rumors—and some of them are *extremely* dark—because it is somehow more comforting to view Hitler as a monstrous pervert in his private life. Then his public crimes can be explained away as arising from private pathology, from *his* unnaturalness, from a psyche that isn't in any way "normal," that isn't in any way akin to ours, one whose darkness we don't have to acknowledge as in any way related to ours. Paradoxically, it may be far more disturbing to find Hitler "normal"—capable of "normal" love, for instance—because it would in some way make it seem that there was something of us in him. Or worse: something of him in us. But a whole explanatory industry has arisen—and not just among

Freudian "psychohistorians"—predicated on the assumption that with Geli Raubal, Hitler was most "himself" and most psychosexually "unnatural."

There are those who believe that with Geli Raubal, Hitler experienced the closest he came to real love, the closest he came to the emotional life of a normal person. But there are also those who believe that in his relationship with Geli Raubal, Hitler expressed the true, profound deformity of his moral nature in perverse sexual practices (we call them paraphilia these days) that either drove Geli to suicide or led to her murder to prevent her from talking about them.

Rumors of some deep-rooted psychosexual unnaturalness shadowed Hitler long before they crept into print at the time of the Geli Raubal affair. The pioneering photojournalist Nachum Tim Gidal, who covered Hitler for the *Munich Illustrated News* in the 1920s (and who claims to have taken the only unguarded, unauthorized intimate photograph of Hitler in the Munich period) before barely escaping with his life in 1933, told me offhandedly in his Jerusalem apartment sixty years later that "everybody in Munich knew" that Hitler was "some kind of sexual pervert."

Hermann Rauschning, onetime mayor of the Free City of Danzig, one of Hitler's earliest agitational targets (Danzig had been removed from German sovereignty by the Treaty of Versailles), who had contact with Hitler in the crucial years just before he came to power, later wrote a memoir of his conversations with Hitler. While his reminiscences have been challenged on the grounds he exaggerated his access, they were enormously influential and helped create the image of Hitler relied upon by the OSS and historians such as H. R. Trevor-Roper. Rauschning described the atmosphere around Hitler as a "reeking miasma of furtive unnatural sexuality that fills and fouls the whole atmosphere round him like an evil emanation. Nothing in this environment is straightforward—surreptitious relationships, substitutes and symbols, false sentiments, secret lusts—nothing has the openness of a natural instinct."

And attempts to explain Hitler's political malevolence as an outgrowth of sexual unnaturalness arose quite early as well and quickly spread beyond Germany. Consider, for instance, the remarkable essay that appeared in London's *Spectator* on January 19, 1934. I cite this essay, entitled "Hitlerism as a Sex Problem," not for its analytical persuasiveness but as a symptom of a persistent, almost wishful strain of Hitler explanation.

The author, Rodney Collin, begins by attempting to explain the German turn to Hitler as the result of a mass, generational "sex starvation": The enforced abstinence of World War I turned, after 1919, he says, "to promiscuity, a neurotic state. . . . Unemployment and the terror of it" made "German males less willing to contemplate marriages." Military fanaticism, "the recognized enemy of full heterosexuality," led to "the literary preoccupation with perversity, the notorious nightclubs for men only; these stories showed how deep went the underground currents."

Then, "after the 1931 depression," this analysis continues, "sex starvation turned guilty and flamed into fanaticism, cruelty and bitterness. Distorted sex showed itself in Jew-baiting, persecution and ultrapuritanism."

Finally, then, enter Hitler. The psychohistorical situation in Germany "threw up representative leaders—Hitler in whose life there has been no other woman but his mother." Hitler, a "sexual abnormal with a childhood fixation . . . unable to conceive the normal ideal of full and ideal heterosexual love and marriage. . . . The tragedy lies in the power wielded by such abnormals over . . . average people." (A contemporary, less homophobic descendant of this kind of argument can be found in Klaus Theweleit's *Male Fantasies*, a study of the sexuality of the proto-Nazi *Freikorps* militias heavily influenced by Freudian heretic Wilhelm Reich's sexual analysis of fascism.)

Collin laments the fact that "a psychoanalytical interpretation of history and politics which should naturally follow from any acceptance of Freudianism remains unwritten." In fact, it would not remain unwritten for long. It crops up nine years later in the psychoanalytically oriented report on "The Mind of Adolf Hitler" prepared for the OSS by Dr. Walter C. Langer, the centerpiece of which is an assertion about the nature of Hitler's relationship with Geli Raubal.

"From a consideration of all the evidence," Langer wrote, in a report destined for the eyes of FDR, "it would seem that Hitler's perversion is as Geli described it." Although this purported description by Geli, while certainly colorful, is not very well corroborated, nonetheless it became, in effect, the official diagnosis of the U.S. government: that Hitler had an extremely perverse sexual psychopathology, one he acted out with Geli Raubal, and one which was in effect a source of his murderous political pathology because "it isolated him from the normal love of human beings."

A key document upon which the OSS diagnosis is based, one that might be the missing link between the prewar stew of rumor and gossip about Hitler's sexuality and the postwar formulation of the psychohistorians who raised these speculations to pretensions of science, is a report in the OSS files: the naval-intelligence debriefing of Dr. Karl Kronor, who had a story to tell about Hitler and Geli Raubal.

The Kronor document (OSS number 31963, dated 1943) was prepared by a naval-intelligence analyst stationed in Reykjavík, Iceland, where he debriefed Kronor, a German refugee doctor; the analyst prefaced the refugee doctor's diagnosis of Hitler thus: "The following report on Hitler prepared by Dr. Karl Kronor, a German refugee living in Reykjavík and a former nerve specialist in Vienna is forwarded for information. A tentative evaluation of B-3 has been placed on the report. Dr. Kronor is supposed to have been present at the original medical examination of Hitler."

Hitler's original medical examination? Since Kronor is identified as a Viennese "nerve specialist," that would seem to suggest an examination that took place before Hitler left Vienna for Germany. But since the medical treatment Kronor proceeds to describe focuses on Hitler's treatment by a "nerve specialist" for hysterical blindness at the end of the First World War and since Kronor claims to be familiar with the circumstances of this treatment at firsthand, it suggests he meant to say Hitler's original *psychiatric* treatment at Pasewalk in November 1918, when he had his alleged encounter with the "nerve doctor" Edmund Forster who some believe imbued Hitler with a vision of his calling. Perhaps Kronor was detailed there, or perhaps he heard the story in émigré circles. In any case, he professes great familiarity with, and strong opinions about, Hitler's blindness.

In the first place, Kronor is skeptical that Corporal Hitler's blindness had anything to do with gas poisoning, as Hitler had claimed, because "blindness is not normally cured without trace," and in Hitler's case there were no known aftereffects. Indeed, Hitler is known for his "studied hypnotic stare" and "there is no recorded example of gas poisoning having had so favorable an outcome." In such a case, he insists, "there are only two possible explanations: 1) simulation (i.e., faking), 2) hysteria or psychopathy (or, of course, a combination of both, for hysterics can simulate and, in fact, tend to do so)."

This brings him to the Geli Raubal case, which he describes as one that will "prove that even in private life, the psychopath Adolf Hitler belongs to the class of psychopathic criminals":

> His own niece, a certain Fraulein Raubahl [*sic*] was found dead with a bullet wound in the head and a revolver by her side. Suicide was declared to be the cause of death (as in the case of Professor Forster). Actually, she was shot because she refused to surrender to the perverse desires of her uncle. (Hitler like many psychopaths is sexually abnormal. He is not, however, as is commonly supposed, homosexual but a pervert of another kind.) . . . The murderer, usually so clever, had failed to remember in this instance that young girls very rarely commit suicide by shooting, and never by a shot in the head.

Again, while we can question the accuracy of his evidence (Geli was shot in the chest, not the head), we have here encapsulated the linkage of perversion and murder Geli Raubal's death gave birth to, from almost the first moment it became public. Indeed, the very first skeptical newspaper report—the one that appeared in the *Munich Post* the Monday following the Saturday when the death was announced—raised questions about the suicide verdict, suggested a violent quarrel with Hitler had preceded the death, raised the specter of sexual possessiveness, and in effect accused Hitler of lying to cover up the damaging truth about this "dark affair." It went so far as to suggest that, if the truth came out, the scandal could spell the end of Hitler's political career.

The headline on the *Post* story read: "A Mysterious Affair: Hitler's Niece Commits Suicide," and the insidiously suggestive story went as follows:

> Regarding this mysterious affair, informed sources tell us that on Friday, September 18, Herr Hitler and his niece had yet another fierce quarrel. What was the cause? Geli, a vivacious twenty-three-year-old music student, wanted to go to Vienna, where she intended to become engaged. Hitler was decidedly against this. That is why they were quarreling repeatedly. After a fierce row, Hitler left his apartment on Prinzregentenplatz.
>
> On Saturday, September 19, it became known that Geli had been found shot in the apartment with Hitler's gun in her hand. The nose bone of the deceased was shattered, and the corpse evidenced other serious injuries. From a letter to a girlfriend in Vienna, it appeared that Geli intended to go to Vienna.
>
> The men in the Brown House [Nazi Party headquarters] then deliberated over what should be announced as the cause of the suicide. They agreed to give the reason for Geli's death as "unsatisfied artistic achievement." They also discussed the question of who, if something were to happen, should be Hitler's successor. Gregor Strasser was named.
>
> Perhaps the near future will bring light to this dark affair.

It was the allegations and insinuations in this story that would cause the Munich chief of police to order Detective Sauer to reopen his hastily closed investigation.

But what's remarkable is how widespread, how public, and how ugly and damning the publicity about Geli Raubal's death was—and not just in Munich. It was as if her death suddenly unleashed or legitimized the expression of the unspoken, the publication of the most vile and virulent whispers about Hitler, embodying the belief, even the wish, by his opponents that he was as much a monster of perversion privately as he was in his politics—a belief, a wish that had already spread beyond the borders of Germany.

Consider what turned up from a survey of the newspaper archives in Hitler's native Vienna in the week following Geli Raubal's death. No less than six newspapers ran stories about the case, stories that mixed fact, error, and dark speculation about the story behind the story. Two in particular caught my attention. The *Neue Wiener Tageblatt*, in a dispatch datelined Berlin, indicated skepticism about "the official version of her suicide: over anxiety and fear of her first public appearance in a music recital."

The *Tageblatt* also echoed the whispers that found their way into the Munich press, the ones that raised the specter of a Jewish (often Viennese) cuckolder: "Hitler was reported to have reproached her for a relationship with a music teacher of alien race."

And the account of Geli's death in Vienna's *Der Abend* (which reprinted the story published in Berlin's left-wing *Neue Montags Zeitung*) reflects how widespread and public were the rumors about the aberrational nature of Hitler's relationship to his half-niece. The suicide is attributed to the young woman's "bitter disappointment at the nature of Hitler's private life," which echoes the euphemism employed by the Bavarian weekly *Die Fanfare*, which explained, "Hitler's private life with Geli took on forms that obviously the young woman was unable to bear. Leaders of subordinate rank know so much about their top leader that Hitler is, so to speak, their hostage and thus unable to intervene and conduct a purge if party leaders are involved in dark affairs."

This image of Hitler and his party leadership poised in an embrace of mutual blackmail over an abyss of scandal might, perversely, have contributed to the fatal underestimation of Hitler's prospects on the part of his political opponents: The widespread belief that he was so hopelessly compromised, so "unnatural," so deeply enmeshed in dark affairs that were almost an open secret, led to the expectation that sooner or later exposure of them in episodes like the Geli Raubal affair would cause Hitler to self-destruct in disgrace over his private life and spare his opponents the task of defeating him politically. The sexual explanation of Hitler may have had unforeseen and unfortunate historical consequences even before it became a red herring for psychohistorians.

But there was another detail further down in the *Der Abend* account that caught my attention: the earliest reference I'd seen in print to a previous woman's suicide attempt over Hitler. One that took place several years before Geli Raubal's death, one that became, along with that of Geli and several others, the basis for what might be called "The Legend of Hitler's Suicide Maidens," a legend that became enshrined in postwar psychohistorical explanations of Hitler's sexual pathology.

Der Abend referred to "another incident about three years ago when a young woman in Berchtesgaden committed suicide on account of Hitler. The girl hanged herself out of fear after having accused Hitler in a letter to her parents as the only one to be held responsible for it." While a crucial detail is either deliberately or inadvertently reported incorrectly here—in fact, it was not an actual suicide but an unsuccessful suicide *attempt*—there can be no mistaking the reference. The young woman in question was one Mimi Reiter, a name that has since become enshrined in the realm of shadow-Hitler apocrypha as the first of the suicide maidens.

The litany of Hitler's suicide maidens appeared first in Robert Waite's psychoanalytical biography, *The Psychopathic God: Adolf Hitler.* Waite, now an emeritus professor of history at Williams College, broke new ground in Hitler studies by succeeding in getting Walter Langer's secret wartime OSS report on the mind of Adolf Hitler declassified.

Waite adapted Langer's conclusion that Hitler practiced an outré sexual perversion so repellent it drove women to suicide. He buttressed his belief by a kind of grim roll call: "The idea that Hitler had a sexual perversion particularly abhorrent to women is further supported by a statistic: of the seven women who, we can be reasonably sure, had intimate relations with Hitler, six committed suicide or seriously attempted to do so." In addition to Geli Raubal, he reports, "Mimi Reiter tried to hang herself in 1928; . . . Eva Braun attempted suicide in 1932 and again in 1935; Frau Inge Ley was a successful suicide, as were Renate Mueller and Suzi Liptauer." (The seventh—nonsuicide—maiden was Leni Riefenstahl, Waite believes.)

The clear implication of this catalog is that Mimi Reiter was the first to know the awful truth about Hitler's unnatural sexuality and the first to prefer death to living with the indelible memory of her humiliating participation in his perversion. And yet Mimi Reiter's *own* account of her romance with Hitler, which surfaced in 1959, does not bear out Waite's implication.

Reiter's description of her romance with Adolf Hitler, a complete version of which has never appeared in English, is certainly disturbing, even profoundly disturbing, but in a different way from the one Waite suggests: It's disturbing because it gives an impression of something we may be far more squeamish about accepting than some excretory perversion; it gives a disturbing impression of something close to normality. And it is worth examining more closely for the context it gives to the subsequent affair with Geli Raubal and the pervasive reports that a horrible perversion drove her to kill herself or led to her being killed to silence her about Hitler's shame.

The Mimi Reiter story came to light in a chance conversation between Hitler's sister Paula and *Stern* reporter Günter Peis. Peis had worked on a 1959 British documentary called *The Hitler Years*, which featured interviews with close Hitler associates, including Paula. Driving Paula (who then called herself Paula Wolf) home from the interview in his Volkswagen, Peis reported the following remarks from her: "'The autobahn and the VW are probably the best things my brother left behind.' And then she . . . suddenly mentioned a visitor she had a few days before. The visitor was a woman, 'maybe the only woman my brother had ever loved. Who knows, maybe everything would have happened differently if he had married her.'"

This was Mimi Reiter. Peis proceeded to track down Mimi Reiter and draw her out on the details of Hitler's courtship and romance, an account (printed in *Stern*) that suggests some striking similarities to—and significant differences from—Hitler's later, fatal affair with Geli Raubal.

Mimi was only sixteen and Hitler thirty-seven when they met (Geli was nineteen and Hitler thirty-eight when he began keeping company with her). She was the daughter of a Social Democratic Party official in Berchtesgaden, site of Hitler's mountain retreat. Her account is a curious mixture of naïve schoolgirl romanticism on her part—and a curious, stilted, almost crippling courtliness on his part that often seems to verge on the abnormal or unnatural but, at least in Mimi's account, never quite does. In fact, in 1959, over thirty years after the affair, even after Hitler's defeat and demonization, she describes the affair in the language of a Harlequin romance novel. Hitler is the stiff, somewhat ruthless stranger who first appears with a dog and whip but is later melted into a schoolgirl-fantasy lover by her charms.

"There is the famous Hitler recently released from prison," she's told, when she first glimpses him in 1925 on the street outside the family shop where she works.

"He was wearing breeches and a light velour hat," she recalls. "In his hand was a riding whip, he had warm light-gray stockings and a windbreaker that was held together by a leather belt . . . beside him walked a beautiful shepherd."

He sees her, too, and is theatrically captivated. He asks Mimi's sister, "Could you introduce me to this bliss?"

Mimi is brought over. "He transferred his riding whip from his right hand into his left . . . gave me his hand and looked at me with a piercing gaze." And praised her dog: "The dog is really beautiful and well trained. You are really good at that."

They talked about dogs for an hour. Hitler "did not take his eyes off Mimi," Peis reports. "Then he very formally asked [her sister] Anni whether she would permit him to take Mimi for a walk sometime. At that she [Mimi] got up and ran away."

Still, she was fascinated in a starstruck way. "He looks quite dashing, with his breeches and his riding whip." There is one note that spoils the picture: his mustache. "The funny flies," she calls the black, hairy growths beneath Hitler's nose. I'm tempted here to introduce a digression on Hitler's mustache styles, prompted by a viewing in Munich of the recent "Hoffmann on Hitler" exhibition, a collection of some of the thousands of Hitler photographs taken by Heinrich Hoffmann, Hitler's personal photographer and for many years the man with an absolute monopoly on Hitler's image, the *only* person authorized to photograph him in the Munich years. One of the revelations of the Hoffmann exhibit is how calculated Hitler was in every aspect of his pose, how in the Munich period he experimented ceaselessly with details of his image, his physical appearance, especially his mustache.

It is interesting that Mimi Reiter describes the mustache as "flies" at that point, because a study of Hoffmann's portraits shows that, at that very period,

Hitler was making a transition in mustache styles. Up till then he had preferred a thick, bushy, taller rather than wide look.

But a Hoffmann portrait of Hitler in lederhosen which is dated very close to the time he met Mimi Reiter shows his first rather unsuccessful experiment with a different look. He seems to have chosen to trim away thin patches directly beneath the septum and above the upper lip to give his mustache a more horizontal, less overgrown and furry look. Unfortunately, in this early photograph of the new look, he seems to have trouble avoiding the ragged and unsymmetrical appearance that conjured up two black flies nesting on his upper lip. Still, she did not permit her discomfiture with the "flies" to dissuade her from seeing him again. This time, Hitler, sensing the source of his attraction, began to lay on the political-celebrity bit rather thickly. He invited her to a dinner and speech he'd be giving at a private political meeting in Berchtesgaden (his parole conditions still forbade him from making public speeches).

That evening, Mimi and her sister were shown to the head table, to a place of honor next to Hitler. "I was very embarrassed and blushed. It was as if he had organized the meeting just for me," she said, waxing rhapsodic in her Harlequinesque way, "as if all that counted for him now was just to conquer me."

Hitler then applied even thicker layers of Viennese charm like impasto. At a private dinner after his speech, "he fed her pieces of cake like a little child. He treated her like a child and then again like a grown woman"—an alteration that had a powerful effect on the sixteen-year-old.

Then he invoked his sainted mother. Hitler talked "about the death of Mimi's mother," then he "repeatedly told her that she reminded him of *his* mother and that they had the same eyes. These words," Peis says, "deeply impressed the young, inexperienced girl."

Hitler followed these tender sentiments about his mother's eyes, Mimi told Peis, with a "coarse" sexual advance. While another dinner guest asked Hitler why he hadn't gotten married (he answered that he had to save the German nation first), "Hitler touched my legs with his knee and heavily stepped on my toes with his shoe . . . a funny and rude hint at what he wanted to say." Reading this account is problematic to say the least. One is tempted to give in to the crude, clownish, bucolic comedy of it, the combination of cartoonish sentiment and oafish coarseness, but one is unable to forget, to reconcile it with the later horror, the high tragedy with the low comic idyll.

When, soon thereafter, a darker note enters the account, one almost begins to hope its portents will be fulfilled by even darker ones:

> We went out into the night. . . . Hitler was about to put his arm around my shoulders and pull me toward him when the two dogs suddenly attacked each other. . . . Hitler suddenly intervened, like a maniac he hit his dog with his riding whip . . . and shook him violently by the

collar. He was very excited. . . . I did not expect that he could hit his dog so brutally and ruthlessly, the dog which he had said he could not live without. Yet he beat up his most loyal companion.

"How can you be so brutal and beat your dog like that?" I asked. "It was necessary," Hitler said.

It was after midnight now, and brutality was succeeded by tenderness. They return to Mimi's sister's apartment. "Hitler came up very close to me and looked at me for a very long time. I could feel his breath. Tenderly, he touched my shoulders, his mouth changed, his voice sounded sad, 'Don't you want to kiss me?' he asked."

She forces herself to say no, that they shouldn't see each other again. Hitler takes the rejection badly, he "turned cold . . . kindness disappeared from his face . . . abruptly he turned away . . . said '*Heil*' and left."

But he had not given up. He sends a confidant around to Mimi's store the next morning. The surrogate tells Mimi, "I have never seen him like that. Herr Hitler poured his heart out to me. Believe me: The man is on fire."

Mimi agrees to another meeting. Hitler arrives in the store "radiant with joy." Mimi accedes to an excursion to the picturesque Starnbergersee, which is to be the scene of their first kiss, although Hitler begins the intimacy on the drive itself. With his chauffeur, Emil Maurice, up front at the wheel, Hitler sits very close to Mimi in the back. "He took my hand and put it into his lap, then he took my other hand as well and pressed it: 'Now I have your hands, and I have you, and I will keep you now.'"

Next he does his mesmerist act: "He puts his right arm around me and tenderly placed his hand on my temple, pulled my head toward his shoulder and wanted to close my eyes with his fingers. He said I should dream." This combination of coarseness (the hand in the lap) and tenderness works its magic on Mimi. "I think that during those first minutes on our ride to Starnberg my reserve was broken."

Next date: the graveyard. Hitler takes Mimi to her mother's grave. Hitler is overcome, thinking of his own mother, "moved by something he did not want to tell me. What he said sounded very grave, in utmost distress: 'I am not ready yet.'"

Hitler, holding on to his riding whip, comforts a sobbing Mimi and strangely chooses that moment to tell her, "I want you to call me Wolf" (a favorite pseudonym for him when he traveled incognito).

One wants to read in portents of abnormality here, a Hitler so mesmerized by his memory of his mother, he is incapable of a normal sexual relationship, which seemed to be in prospect then. But again, this is contradicted by Mimi's account, which becomes suddenly less courtly and more explicitly sexual.

Hitler takes Mimi for a walk in the woods, which she describes like some sappy cinematic love-in-bloom montage: "Lightheartedly, we ran across a meadow as if driven by the sun." Hitler leads her to a fir tree, poses her in front of its, steps back, and gazes at her "from top to bottom. Then he stretched out both hands and begged me to come to him, 'You know what you are now? Now you are my "*Waldfee*" [wood nymph or fairy].'"

She laughs at the extravagant theatricality of it, which provokes him to come close. "He gripped me and kissed me. For the first time, he kissed me wildly and passionately. He pulled me toward him and said, '*Mimilein*, my dear, beautiful girl, now I cannot resist any longer.' He embraced my neck and kissed me. He did not know what to do. He said, 'But, Mimilein, I like you too much. What I am feeling for you is everything. Kiss me.'"

Even three decades later, even after the crimes she knows he's committed, Mimi Reiter seemed swept away by Hitler's passion in her Harlequin-novel way. "I was so happy, I just wanted to die. Again and again, Hitler stopped and gave me a startled stare, then kissed me again, my forehead, my mouth, my neck."

She does report there are some disturbing or disconcerting aspects to his expression of passion: "I could feel how he clenched his fists. I could see how he was fighting with himself. 'My child, I could squash you in my arms at this very moment.' I did not resist any longer, his true self had come out." (Mimi's blinkered notion of Hitler's "true self" is astonishing if one considers it in the 1959 context of her remark.) Next, according to Peis, Hitler "told her that he wanted her to be his wife, to found a family with her, to have blonde children, but at the moment he had not even the time to think of such things. Repeatedly, Hitler spoke of his duty, his mission."

At this point, a curious period of delay ensues before any further physical consummation—a long period, in fact, when Hitler is away in Munich. Finally, when Mimi's ice-skating club makes a trip to Munich, she and Hitler have a rendezvous at Hitler's favorite spot, Café Heck. There are endearments and caresses, but Hitler puts her off with grandiose talk of his search for a new apartment: "In between caresses, Hitler again and again mentioned that he had to look for a bigger apartment . . . and that he needed it for himself and Mimi," Peis reports.

Mimi recalls that "Wolf pressed his forehead against my neck, 'You must not leave me, Mimi, do you hear? When I get my new apartment you have to stay with me . . . forever. We will choose everything together, the paintings, the chairs, I already can see it all: beautiful, big lounge chairs of violet plush.'"

Mimi is still entranced by the violet plush of Hitler's love rhetoric, but again there is no actual proposal, no actual consummation, and the bewildered young woman is driven to distraction and ultimately to a dangerous course of action.

She returns to Berchtesgaden, and Hitler begins to ignore her. He returns there himself some months later, but he does not visit her. She waits despairingly for word from him. Alone, she starts weeping desperately. "My whole world started tumbling down. I did not know what had happened, nothing that explained" his inattention. "All sorts of pictures appeared in my mind . . . faces of other women and Hitler smiling at them. I did not want to go on living."

"In this depressed mood," Peis reports, "she went to find a clothesline. One end of it she slung around her neck, the other around a door handle. Slowly, she glided to the floor. Slowly, she lost consciousness." At the very last moment, her brother-in-law arrived to bring her word from Hitler and "saved her life at the last minute."

I dwell upon this account because, for all its ludicrous sentiment, it serves as a kind of counterstatement to the School of Perversion in Hitler studies (and it is at least as well, in fact, slightly better corroborated—if we take the word of sister Paula—than those accounts). Waite has attempted to make Mimi into the first woman driven to suicide by outrage and humiliation over Hitler's alleged "perversion." It's a vision of Hitler that has crept into the literature, into popular culture without much serious critique, a popular vision because it offers an easy explanation for Hitler's political monstrousness. But in Mimi Reiter's version, the suicide attempt seems more like the melodramatic act of a teenage girl with an unrequited crush on a celebrity, a love that is exploited by the celebrity for a limited amount of physical gratification and fantasizing. But up to this point—unfortunately, one wants to say—there are few hints of abnormality, much less of monstrous perversion.

One darker note does enter here. When Mimi recovers, her brother-in-law tells her Hitler's explanation for his sudden silence and absence: poison-pen letters. According to Mimi, "Hitler told [the brother-in-law] that anonymous letters had been mailed to the party office saying that Hitler was having a relationship with a girl who was underage. The letters said, 'Hitler seduces young, inexperienced girls. He just found a sixteen-year-old girl in Berchtesgaden who obviously will be his next victim.'"

Threatened with the possibility of a scandal, Hitler told her, via this emissary, he could not see her for some time in order not to "jeopardize the success of his party." As it turned out, Mimi says, the poison-pen letters were actually written by a woman within Hitler's circle who was either concerned about Hitler's infatuation as a potentially threatening scandal or jealous of it: one more instance of how Hitler's every move, his entire existence in the Munich period, was enmeshed in blackmail, poison-pen consciousness, often generated by his own intimates.

Still, the long-promised consummation was postponed once again. This time, two years and a marriage intervened. Mimi marries an Austrian hotelier, moves to Innsbruck with him. But then, two years later, she quarrels with her husband, decamps to Munich, and calls Hitler's adjutant Julius Schaub. Informed that Mimi is in town, Hitler tells Schaub, "Bring her over."

Mimi places the episode that follows in the summer of 1931, when Hitler was living in his big, new apartment with Geli Raubal. Peis believes it's possible Mimi has the date wrong and that the visit occurred after Geli's death; however, if it happened while Geli was alive, Peis suggests it "would for the first time shed some light on Geli's mysterious suicide. She might have heard of Mimi's visit." Because on this visit, Mimi insists, "I let everything happen."

In fact, since Geli's death was so public and so scandalous and since Hitler turned Geli's room in his apartment into a lugubrious shrine to the departed, it's unlikely Mimi would have forgotten such details if the visit had taken place after Geli's death.

In any case, this is Mimi's reconstruction of the night of consummation: She confesses to Hitler she's left her husband. He professes himself shocked. "Not for any moral reasons" but for fear he might be publicly linked to a divorce scandal. She asks Hitler if he can find her a job. Instead, Hitler laughs and invites her to stay with him. He now had the big apartment with the violet plush chairs. Now he could offer her everything.

"He told me, 'From now on, I will take your life into my hands.'"

And at last, she says, he took her body into his hands: "He pulled me toward him and kissed me. It was well after midnight. He leaned back on the sofa, further and further. He held me more and more firmly. I let everything happen. I had never been as happy as I was that night. . . . Around 2 A.M. he got up. After a while he said, 'Mimilein, I am rich now. I can offer you everything. I can remove any obstacles for you. Stay with me. My beautiful darling, dear Mimi. You must stay with me.'"

She tells him she cannot be an illicit live-in lover. At which point, "he suddenly turned on me. 'What do you want from me?' he shouted. 'I want to have you. I want to have you here. Why don't you understand I have never had such a relationship with any woman but you?'"

Still Mimi refused to move in, although when she returned to Austria, Hitler had his lawyer Hans Frank help her initiate divorce proceedings on her behalf. "When they parted," Peis reports, Hitler "assured her once more that she was the only woman he loved."

Their final scene played itself out three years later. She recalls it as a 1934 visit to Munich, although Hitler was then in power in Berlin. "Once again," Peis reports, "the relationship came to life, once again he asked her to stay with him as his lover." She insists she will not be part of an illicit relationship; she wanted to be married and have children. "Suddenly, Hitler had a fit of rage. He shouted, 'Why do you women only think of having children?' . . . He kept shouting—it was around 3 A.M.—that he could not take care of a woman. He shouted he had a big mission to fulfill. They argued for two more hours, then they departed, never to see each other again."

What do we make of this? Peis characterizes it as "a ridiculous, sad, miserable episode." It is certainly all these things, and yet it falls far short of the monstrousness attributed to Hitler, far short of the kind of monstrousness many long to attribute to him. Here he's a cad, a roué, with perhaps an unhealthy interest in underage girls. There is something halting, hesitant, obsessive, yet repressed about his courtship and lovemaking style. There is something disturbing about the mixture of stilted courtliness and crude brutality. There is a whip, yes, but he uses it to beat his dog, not Mimi. And if we believe Mimi's account, there is, ultimately, "normal" sexual consummation: "I let everything happen."

One can find reasons to be skeptical of her account (the romance-novel sensibility; the fact that if there had been "unnatural" acts, she might be reluctant to identify herself as a participant). Yet nothing has emerged to contradict her, and, according to Peis, Paula Hitler confirms Mimi's importance to her brother: "maybe the only woman my brother had ever loved."

If those who have debated the nature of Hitler's sexuality can be divided into a Party of Normality, a Party of Perversion, and a Party of Asexuality, Mimi Reiter's account must be considered exhibit A for the Party of Normality. If it doesn't necessarily refute the rumors and hearsay about the nature of Hitler's relationship with Geli Raubal, it is reason to examine them more closely and skeptically, to see if they might be the product of a kind of perverse wishful thinking—the wish to believe Hitler "unnatural" in order to avoid the consequences of thinking he was in any way "normal."

CHAPTER 7

Hitler's Songbird and the Suicide Register

What was so "frightening" about Geli Raubal?

A rchivist Weber has another surprise for me: another Geli Raubal police document he's unearthed from the basement of his fortress of Bavarian archival rectitude. This one suggests that not everyone in the Munich criminal-justice system was satisfied with the police investigation into Geli Raubal's death.

It's a dusty, faded blue-green ledger that looks like an accounts record for a small business. It is, in a sense, a ledger of lost souls: Munich's *Selbstmörder* (self-murder) register for 1931, the record of all suicides or suspected suicides the Munich police have investigated that year. Inside this *grimoire* of despair, between hand-ruled lines spread across two pages, spidery black handwriting inscribes in mournful detail the truncated lives of the 334 men and women who have hacked, stabbed, shot, hung, poisoned, or flung themselves to death within the city limits that year.

Archivist Weber opens the ledger to the page on which the details of suicide number 193, Angela Raubal, are listed. The first two entries, date of birth (June 4, 1908) and place of birth (Linz, Austria), are both true. There follows one entry which is only half true.

This one identifies Geli as a "medical student," perhaps wistful misinformation supplied by a mother who felt the tragedy wouldn't have happened if Geli had not abandoned her medical-student ambitions for a singing career. (Geli's mother told an officer of U.S. Army Intelligence in 1945 that the source of Geli's quarrel with Hitler was her relationship to a singing coach in Vienna— not the first or last time this spectral Viennese seducer makes an appearance.) Or perhaps "medical student" was preferred by Hitler himself, sounding as it did less lurid than "singer" with its overtones of "siren."

But before I could focus on further details in the Selbstmörder register, Archivist Weber directed my attention to the final entry on the far right-hand side of the page, in the column devoted to the disposition of the police investigation into the death. Weber points to the second of two numerical entries in the column. "This shows the investigation was reopened by someone in the public prosecutor's office," he tells me. "When I saw that, I looked for the file in the archives of the public prosecutor's records. It was not there. I believe it has been removed."

While Weber had initially been skeptical about my inquiries into the Geli Raubal case, his conviction that a file has been removed has made him less so. It's an old story, he says, but one he can still summon fresh bitterness about. When the Hitler Party took over in Munich, one of the first things they tried to do was erase history, remove and destroy the records in the Munich archives of a number of embarrassing police investigations and prosecutions against party leaders.

Archivist Weber has a touchingly proprietary devotion to the integrity of the archival history of the period. He regards gaps in the records almost like wounds in his own body. Particularly, the criminal-justice archives. He feels that a neglected explanation for Hitler's success can be found in fragmented form in the police-blotter history of the Nazi Party: the way the right-wing nationalists who dominated the criminal-justice system in Bavaria and Munich allowed the Hitler Party to get away literally with murder—the murder, beating, and terrorizing of political opponents. Time after time, perfunctory arrests would be made by the police, he says, only to see the cases dismissed by Nazi-sympathizing judges or disposed of with laughably light sentences. A system of justice that allowed the Hitler Party to murder their way to power with impunity.

In pursuit of restoring this mutilated history, he's been working on a biography of one of the heroes of the legal history of the time, Klaus Hirschberg, the embattled lawyer for the *Munich Post*, the point man for the *Post*'s running legal battles with Hitler and the Hitler Party.

I believe one of the reasons Weber was so helpful to me was our mutual interest in what was one of the most gaping wounds in the archival record until Weber restored it: the transcript of the stab-in-the-back trial of 1924. I'd spent the previous afternoon in the basement of the Munich Institute for Contemporary History, scrolling through the microfilm transcript of that epic courtroom war, one in which the reporters and editors of the *Post* fought a libel action against them for their devastating exposure of the lie behind Hitler's version of history.

As soon as I mentioned that I'd followed Hirschberg's embroilment in the stab-in-the-back battle, Weber's intense, saturnine demeanor softened into a pleased grin.

"I found that," he said of the trial transcript. He'd located the long-missing transcript himself and restored it to its rightful place in the archives—and in history. With so many German historians and political thinkers arguing over the importance of "restoring Hitler to history," of "normalizing" him as part of history, I found myself more impressed by Archivist Weber's mission, his conviction that what should come first is the restoration of the history *of* Hitler, the history Hitler erased.

Thus, his interest in evidence of what he believes is the missing public prosecutor's investigation of Geli Raubal's death. I pressed him on the issue: Detective Sauer's police report indicated that he had reopened *his* investigation. The *Munich Post* forced him to: the Monday following the Saturday discovery of the body, the *Post* came out with a report that there had been signs of violence on Geli Raubal's dead body, including a broken nose. Signs of violence and reports of a violent quarrel preceding the suicide—the clear implication being that Hitler had beaten her, thus driving her to suicide, or that a struggle between them had led to her murder.

All the witnesses Detective Sauer had interviewed that Saturday, including Hitler, had denied any violence or signs of violence. With public attention now focused on him by the *Munich Post*, Detective Sauer reopened the case by interviewing several more witnesses, including the woman at the mortuary who had cleaned and prepared the now-departed body of Geli Raubal for its hasty shipment across the border to Vienna, where it was then out of reach of a detailed autopsy.

The funeral-home woman and the police doctor who'd made the initial snap judgment that it was a suicide and not murder insisted that Geli's nose was not broken, that what appeared to be bruises from violence were the result of postmortem lividity due to the body lying nose down on the floor. Detective Sauer closed this brief "reopened" investigation with his conclusion on the cause of death unchanged. Was this what the inscriptions on the Selbstmörder register were referring to?

No, Archivist Weber insisted to me, the letters and numerals scrawled on the very edge of the page in the Selbstmörder register indicated a public prosecutor, not a policeman, had reopened the case.

I must admit I was surprised to find apparent archival confirmation of the existence of a document I'd consigned in my mind to the limbo of the lost and the legendary—one of those Swiss safe-deposit-box stories I spoke of in the Introduction. You might recall that the son of a colleague of crusading Munich newspaper editor Fritz Gerlich recalled that his father had actually seen a copy of "a state's attorney inquiry into the matter of Geli Raubal" in Gerlich's office, one that purportedly "showed that Geli was killed by order of Hitler." A document that was said to have been deposited for safekeeping in a Swiss safe-deposit box, the account number for which was lost during the war. The lost-safe-deposit-box twist to the story had left me thinking the whole account of a lost Geli Raubal murder investigation must also have been apocryphal, despite or because of a variant appearing in the not always reliable memoirs of Otto Strasser: "an inquest [into Geli's death] was opened in Munich," according to Strasser. "The public prosecutor, who has lived abroad since Hitler's accession to power, wished to charge him with murder, but Gürtner, the Bavarian minister of justice, stopped the case."

When I read that passage to Weber, he scowled. Gürtner is his bête noire, one of the men he believes most responsible—but held least accountable—for Hitler's success. The degree to which Gürtner's solicitude for Hitler and his henchmen kept them out of jail—and helps explain Hitler's ultimate accession to power—has been hard to measure, Weber believes, because so much of the crucial evidence of complicity has been removed from the archives. The entry in the Selbstmörder register discloses further evidence of Gürtner's handiwork, he now believes.

Archivist Weber leads me down to the musty basement storage room where the registries of the public prosecutor's office are kept, shows me where the missing file should have been. Tells me he believes Gürtner may have had it removed. Was there a lost file? Proof by absence wasn't enough to satisfy me completely. It was another one of those frustrating moments in the search for Hitler where one is forced to acknowledge an investigative dead end, yet another of those gaps that deepen cumulatively into an abyss that may never be fathomed.

Before getting deeper into the terra incognita of Hitler's role in Geli Raubal's death, it might be useful to attempt to restore her to life—to flesh out a figure who has become ever more mythical in the decades succeeding her death. The last image of Geli Raubal in Konrad Heiden's account of her final hours is a striking and memorable one. Heiden, you'll recall, was the Munich-based reporter for the *Frankfurter Zeitung* whose inside sources in the Hitler entourage make his 1944 biography, *Der Fuehrer*, a still-valuable source of Suetonian detail about that Caligula's court. Heiden sets the scene for his final image of Geli Raubal's life on the Friday afternoon, just sixteen to eighteen hours before the official discovery of her body. There had been a quarrel between Hitler and

Geli over the issue of the planned trip to Vienna, Heiden says. In the aftermath, Heiden depicts Geli disconsolately wandering, Ophelia-like, around the Hitler apartment, "with a little box bearing a dead canary bedded in cotton; she sang to herself and wept a little and said she meant to bury poor dead 'Hansi' [the canary] near the house on the Obersalzberg. . . . Next morning she was found shot to death."

That sense of Geli, too, as a songbird freed from her cage only by death seems a bit too sentimental, perhaps the product of those who—like Hitler—wanted to depict her as a suicide-prone sentimentalist about death. But the image of Geli as a songbird of one sort or another is a persistent one. Indeed, the very earliest eyewitness description of Geli I've been able to discover, from perhaps the last living witnesses to her childhood, was one of Geli as a kind of songbird, singing to herself. The source was the Braun sisters. Sixty-five years later they still remembered their first vision of Geli Raubal singing. The Braun sisters (no relation to Eva) lived in the same apartment building as Geli's family in the early 1920s; the apartment building still existed when I visited it, a solid, dignified five-story walk-up not far from Vienna's West-bahnhof railway station. I was introduced to the Braun sisters, who were living in a senior-citizens' pension, by Hans Horvath, a Viennese amateur historian who is obsessed with Hitler artifacts—and with Geli as perhaps the most exquisite artifact of them all.

The eyes of the elder Frau Braun lit up when she recalled that first encounter with Geli: "I was walking down the street outside our apartment building, and I heard her singing. I saw her, and I just stopped dead. She was just so tall and beautiful that I was speechless. And she saw me standing frozen and said, 'Are you frightened of me?' And I said, 'No, I was just admiring you.' She was just so tall and beautiful, I'd never seen anyone like that."

Are you frightened of me? Geli's near-terrifying beauty has become a kind of fetish for those who were exposed to it firsthand and for many who have written about it. And yet, when one looks at the photographic record of her brief four-year span in the limelight, her image doesn't correspond to classical notions of beauty, nor does she seem to have the intimidating, "frightening" beauty those who saw her face-to-face often report. An appealing vitality radiates from certain images, but the round-faced, chubby-cheeked, heavy-limbed, mousy-haired figure in many of the photographs seems to fall mystifyingly short of the supernaturally seductive loveliness attributed to her by much of the literature of the period. There is little hint in the photographs of a sirenlike ability to freeze in their tracks with one glance those she cast her spell upon.

Perhaps whatever mesmerizing power Geli had that so affected Hitler did not express itself in the stasis of silver-nitrate still life. But after reading repeated rhapsodic descriptions by those contemporaries who'd come under her spell, I came to feel they were, in effect, displaced meditations—displaced from the political to the erotic realm—upon the power and mystery of the *Hitler* spell. About the pronounced disparity between the paltry physical being of the person and the absurd and terrifying—*Are you frightened of me?*—mystery of the magnified *persona*.

"One has to take on trust the astonishing oratorical power Hitler was supposed to possess," the writer Jenny Diski remarked in an essay in the *London Review of Books*. "Such film as remains of his speeches leaves you shrugging." While I'm not sure that's entirely true of *all* film footage of Hitler (the later newsreels that don't suffer from Chaplinesque sped-up jerkiness convey a sense of brute gestural power), the remark reemphasized for me that maddening disparity between person and persona echoed in descriptions of Geli Raubal's spell—and impelled me to proceed with what might seem a quixotic pursuit: the attempt to track down the only woman alive who embodied in one person both Hitler and Raubal genes. To see if there might be something about her, perhaps some family secret she knew, that might offer a clue to the idiosyncratic appeal of her two mysterious progenitors.

Well, not exactly progenitors: Hitler has no direct descendants, despite Werner Maser's exploded claim two decades ago that he had located a Hitler son alive and living in France, a claim which caused the poor fellow, supposedly the result of a World War I liaison between Hitler and a French girl, considerable embarrassment and discomfort. But the woman I found *was* a descendant of Hitler's father. Geli, you'll recall, was Hitler's half-niece. This woman is Geli's niece, the daughter of Geli's younger sister Friedl. One of her great-grandfathers was Hitler's father. I'd come upon "Anna," as I'll call her (since she is understandably not eager to call attention to the Hitler side of her lineage), in the course of trying to track down her mother, Friedl. The last address I had for Geli's sister placed her in a tiny Austrian hamlet not far from Hitler's birthplace at Braunau, on the German border. I'd gotten the address from an amateur historian in Munich, Anton Joachimsthaler, author of an opinionated, disputatious study of the biographical data on Hitler's life up until 1920, which is largely an attack on Werner Maser's Hitler biography and which is, in fact, entitled *Hitler: Correction of a Biography*. This cranky but useful volume demonstrates how slippery some of the most basic information about Hitler is. It was Joachimsthaler who helped uncover the still puzzling fact of Hitler's participation as a designated mourner in a funeral parade for a murdered Jewish socialist in Munich in February 1919, just a few short months before he joined the Nazi Party. Joachimsthaler's dogged research figures as well in the investigation of the Geli Raubal case, since he is the one who unearthed the one document that substantiates Hitler's alibi: a speeding ticket Hitler received on Saturday, September 19, while racing back to Munich to deal with Geli's death. A speeding

ticket that places him two hours north of Munich and to some degree corroborates his story that he'd spent the night Geli died in a hotel in Nuremberg.

In pursuing the Geli case further, Joachimsthaler told me, when we met in
Munich, that he'd written, asked for, and been refused an interview by Geli's
sister Friedl several years ago. I'd thought there was enough of a chance, however slight, that a visit to Friedl in person might provoke some final thoughts
on the fate of her sister—and perhaps a clue to, or echo of, Geli's charisma—to
seek her out at her last known Austrian address.

I was too late for that. When I arrived at the little collection of cottages
just south of the German border (feeling a bit like the obsessed detective in
Laura) and found the correct house, I learned from a woman leaning out her
window that Friedl had died several years previously. Still, she had a surprise
for me: She was Friedl's daughter, Geli's niece—and even more surprisingly, an
absolute dead ringer for Geli herself.

She was nearly two decades older than Geli was when she died, but the
resemblance to the Geli of photographs was uncanny. And so was the hint,
the echo of what had eluded capture in the photographs of Geli: an irresistible
glint of mischief, an extraordinary animation which—almost from the first
moment of our conversation—her husband tried to mute or repress (a benign
version of the same problem her great-uncle Adolf had with Geli?).

I'd explained to Anna I was interested in unresolved questions about the
circumstances in which Geli had been shot. She picked up immediately on the
mild ambiguity in the way I'd phrased the question. "I'm glad you said she had
been shot," she said defiantly, meaning shot by someone else.

She seemed eager to expand upon her beliefs right then, but at this point
her husband reached out, pressed his hand down on hers to halt, at least temporarily, the expression of what were obviously strong feelings on the question.

First, the husband felt the need to put me through a test, a kind of catechism on the cruxes of the case, which he, too, seemed extremely familiar with;
they were Geli *buffs* who wanted to test my knowledge and point of view. After
quizzing me carefully on the variant descriptions reported of Geli's Viennese
lover—the one she seemed to be seeking to escape to at the end but who has
been described variously as a music teacher, a voice instructor, a drawing master, a Jew, and a violinist—the husband permitted his Geli-look-alike wife to reveal two important pieces of previously unknown Raubal-family information.

First, there were letters, letters never seen before, perhaps the last letters
Geli Raubal finished (the one found in her room ended in the middle of a sentence), letters mailed to Friedl in Vienna shortly before Geli's death. Anna's
husband would not let her read them to me, but she described them as letters
from "someone excited about her life, not someone who wanted to end it."

And, second, she insisted she knew the truth about another matter of dispute in the case: the attitude of the two women closest to Geli, her mother and

sister. She had heard, Anna told me, from Friedl's own lips that Geli's sister did not believe Geli's death a suicide. And, she told me, Friedl had heard the same from Geli's mother, Angela.

The visit with Geli's look-alike niece left one seemingly trivial but perhaps symbolic mystery in the literature on the case unresolved: how so many chroniclers came to call Geli Raubal blond. Most of the photographs show a woman who, though fair of skin, is definitely brown-haired. And yet, even among those contemporaries who could have seen her face-to-face, there is a tropism of error that turns her brown hair blond.

The usually reliable Heiden, for instance, conjures up a Geli with "an immense crown of blonde hair." His description of Geli as a blonde is picked up by a number of postwar writers; as late as 1989, Louis Snyder's *Encyclopedia of the Third Reich* gives us a Geli with the "immense crown of blond hair" of Aryan royalty. But Werner Maser, though he never saw her, insists she had "black hair and a distinctly Slavonic appearance." The evidence of the photographers seems to favor Maser over Heiden; the appearance of the dead-ringer niece makes it clear: Blond would be all wrong.

That there should even be a controversy on this question is perhaps testament to the power of the aura Hitler bestowed upon Geli, to the way his spell clouded the minds of those in his orbit. Hitler endowed Geli with the image of perfect Aryan maidenhood that transmuted her brown locks to gold in the minds of some. It's an example of how uncertain, in an almost Heisenbergian sense, any observation made within the orbit of the Hitler spell can be.

More important, descriptions of Geli's *character* are deeply divided between golden and much darker hues. Many observers recall her reverently as "a deeply religious person who attended mass regularly," a "princess" whose regal bearing and beauty "would cause people on the street to turn around and stare at her." The golden-girl school of Geli's character sums her up as "the personification of perfect young womanhood . . . deeply revered, even worshipped by her uncle. [Hitler] watched and gloated over her like some gardener with a rare and lovely bloom."

Others saw her as quite another kind of bloom. Less a princess than a sorceress, less a churchgoing Aryan vestal than a calculating opportunist, "an empty-headed little slut, with the coarse bloom of a servant-girl." This stinging phrase comes from Ernst "Putzi" Hanfstaengl, the Harvard-educated artbook publisher and long-time confidant of Hitler, who may have been as close to him as anyone in the 1920s. Hanfstaengl took quite a violent dislike to Geli Raubal, as apparently a number of males in the Hitler inner circle did, perhaps because they were envious of her growing sway over him or fearful for the consequences of their intimacy, the potential for scandal.

Hanfstaengl attempts to buttress his slur on Geli as a slut by reporting that—despite Hitler's "moon-calf" obsession with her—Geli betrayed him sexually with his chauffeur, Emil Maurice. And, even more woundingly, that she planned to leave him permanently to marry a man whom Hanfstaengl describes as "a Jewish art teacher in Linz."

Some women, too, described Geli resentfully. She was "coarse, provocative and a little quarrelsome," Henrietta Hoffmann (the daughter of Hitler's personal photographer, Heinrich Hoffmann) told John Toland. But to Hitler, Henrietta sniffed, Geli was "irresistibly charming," and she took advantage of it: "If Geli wanted to go swimming it was more important than the most important conference."

There is little doubt that, golden or dark hearted, Geli by the end had incited in Hitler what Alan Bullock calls a "jealous possessiveness" that would have fatal consequences. But possessiveness of what?

In the beginning, in the early twenties, the relationship was no doubt wholly avuncular. Still, to the barely teenaged Geli, living in straitened circumstances with her widowed mother in Vienna, a visit from her famous Uncle Alf must have been a rather special occasion. The man emerging from the powerful, chauffeured Mercedes, a man already making headlines, must have cut a dashing if not romantic figure in the military-style cloak he favored then. He came cloaked as well with an aura of destiny—he was a man with a mission embarked on a daring and dangerous crusade.

And then, in the mid-twenties, he invited Geli to become part of that mission. Released from prison with restrictions on his political activities, he'd retreated to his aerie amid the Obersalzberg peaks to recoup his strength for an eventual comeback. The summons came from the mountains to Geli and her mother, who was then working in the kitchen of a Jewish school for girls in Vienna. It was the chance to escape from the anonymous drudgery of their life and join Hitler as live-in housekeepers in the stunningly picturesque Alpine retreat.

Suddenly, at age eighteen, Geli was in the hall of the mountain king. In the crystalline air of the Obersalzberg, Hitler was living the life of a Nordic demigod, drawing on the purity of his surroundings to restore his strength for a return, the revenge, the Götterdämmerung to come. And Geli, now a young woman, became drawn into the drama, rising from Cinderella-like servant girl to full consort at the court of the exiled prince, a role that seemed to fuel romantic fantasies on both sides.

Before long, Geli's mother was left behind with the housekeeping chores while Geli was put on display at Hitler's side. Konrad Heiden describes Hitler squiring Geli around the bucolic mountain villages "riding through the countryside, showing the blonde [*sic*] child how 'Uncle Alf' could bewitch the masses." It soon became evident that "Uncle Alf" was becoming "bewitched" as well.

Before long, Hitler's preoccupation with Geli causes Henny Hoffmann to tut-tut about the meetings he missed to take Geli swimming. And party officials such as one Gauleiter Munder, a district leader from Württemberg, complained that Hitler was "being excessively diverted by the company of his niece from his political duties." (Hitler fired Munder shortly after his complaint became known.)

Photographs from the period show Geli blossoming into womanhood, affecting the marcelled wave of the Germanic flapper, leaning over a tanned arm in a sleeveless dress at a dinner party to engage in earnest conversation with stern-looking SA chiefs, playing the role of the Führer's hostess to the hilt.

This was their public relationship; the nature of the private one is less clear. There were, at Berchtesgaden, barriers to the kind of intimacy they could enjoy. For one thing, they were not alone. They were living under the same roof but under the eye of Geli's mother. And then, of course, there was Hitler's rather public dalliance with local maiden Mimi Reiter.

No, if things changed between them from the avuncular to the sexual, it is unlikely to have happened until later, when Geli moved to Munich, leaving her mother behind to tend to the Obersalzberg house while Geli took up residence with Hitler, ostensibly to serve as his housekeeper and take music lessons for the singing career she'd suddenly declared she wanted to pursue.

The question of the nature of Hitler's affection for Geli Raubal has dominated the literature on the question. Many accounts paint a picture of her as the unwilling prisoner of a drooling pervert, or at the very least captive of a twisted Platonic possessiveness. But there is some testimony that indicates a different view: that although Geli may have been in Hitler's thrall, she was also enthralled by him in a starstruck way. One of the most interesting observations on this question can be found in the postwar recollections of Geli's Munich voice instructor, Albert Vogel, who claimed that Geli told him repeatedly how thrilled she was to be Hitler's companion and how she hoped and expected they'd get married.

And Toland suggests that it was *Geli's* jealousy of Hitler rather than his of her that led to her impulsive suicide. Toland interviewed many of the same members of the household staff as Detective Sauer did and found them more talkative long after the war than they had been in 1931. One of them told Toland a story about the reason for Geli's distress when she'd run out of Hitler's bedroom the final afternoon of her life: that she'd found in there a gushing note to Hitler from Eva Braun about an evening at the theater she'd spent with him. It's an anecdote that seems dismissable for its second-rate, *Dynasty*-like, plot-point sentimentality. But the second-rateness of the Hitler milieu is often underrated, the Wagnerian themes overrated as explanation.

Whoever was in thrall to whom, the relationship was *nicht natürlich* in at least one specific sense: ecclesiastical legality. Because of their tangled family relatedness, if they had contemplated marriage a papal decree would have to be obtained to evade the stricture against the borderline-incestuous consanguinity of the two of them. If the possibility of legal consummation of their relationship was problematic, the question of whether and what kind of physical consummation took place has been the subject of endless wrangling among writers on the subject, a fractious debate which has evolved into roughly three schools of Hitler Sexuality: the Party of Normality, the Party of Asexuality, and the Party of Perversion.

Even within the Party of Perversion there are divisions. Konrad Heiden, the highly respected though somewhat Suetonian biographer of Hitler who had contacts within Hitler's Brown House demimonde, will only go so far as to say that Hitler entertained perverse *fantasies* about Geli; only Otto Strasser goes so far as to suggest they were consummated, although he claims he heard the details from Geli herself.

Heiden places the moment of change in the relationship at a point sometime before Hitler moved into his princely new residence with Geli. Indeed, Heiden believes Hitler's approach to Geli led to an elaborate hushed-up scandal that became "one of the reasons for Hitler's change of lodgings."

Here, then, in Heiden's words is the locus classicus of the Hitler perversion legend. The story Heiden tells has had a remarkable longevity and influence; it echoes in the subcurrent of Hitler rumor and gossip that was picked up by the OSS's Walter Langer, who gave it the imprimatur of official intelligence. It's a story gloated over "like some gardener with a rare and lovely bloom" (as it was said Hitler gloated over Geli) by psychohistorians and psychoanalysts who have felt that *here* must be the dark, hidden, repressed *truth* about Hitler's psyche. It's been picked up and mythologized in the fictions of Thomas Pynchon (his Geli-like figure in *Gravity's Rainbow*) and Steve Erickson (Geli, the veiled central figure in *Tours of the Black Clock*, is a kind of Scheherazade of pornography for Hitler).

Heiden calls the story he tells—the affair of the purloined pornography—the opening act of "the tragedy of Hitler's private life." It has become the second great temptation of Hitler explainers (the first being the Hans Frank Jewish-blood explanation).

"One day," Heiden begins, Hitler's

parental relations to his niece Geli ceased to be parental. Geli was a beauty on the majestic side . . . simple in her thoughts and emotions, fascinating to many men, well aware of her electric effect and delighting in it. She looked forward to a brilliant career as a singer and expected "Uncle Alf" to make things easy for her. Her uncle's affection, which in the end assumed the most serious form, seems like an echo of the many marriages among relatives in Hitler's ancestry [in its borderline incestuousness].

At the beginning of 1929, Hitler wrote the young girl a letter couched in the most unmistakable terms. It was a letter in which the uncle and lover gave himself completely away; it expressed feelings which could be expected from a man with masochistic coprophilic inclinations bordering on what Havelock Ellis calls "undinism" [the desire to be urinated upon for sexual gratification]. . . . The letter probably would have been repulsive to Geli if she had received it. But she never did. Hitler left the letter lying around, and it fell into the hands of his landlady's son, a certain Doctor Rudolph; perhaps this was one of the reasons for Hitler's change of lodgings. The letter was in no way suited for publication; it was bound to debase Hitler and make him ridiculous in the eyes of anyone who might see it. For some reason, Hitler seems to have feared that it was Rudolph's intention to make it public.

Feared his intention: Implied here is a blackmail threat. According to Heiden, this initial blackmail scheme engendered—as frequently seemed the case in the Hitler demimonde—a second-level blackmail plot by those Hitler employed to pay off the first blackmailer.

Let's examine Heiden's story more closely, since it is the ur-source of the Hitler perversion myth—and of the temptation to believe it. One thing to note about Heiden's account is that it's a description of a purported fantasy in a letter that probably never reached Geli. It is not the report of an *act*, and nowhere does Heiden suggest the act was ever consummated. This story is often conflated with another, later story from Otto Strasser in which Strasser claims Geli weepily confessed to him her unwilling participation in extremely degrading practices with Hitler, practices which seemed to include "undinism."

Heiden's story has an echo if not corroboration (because the echo is a less-reliable source) in the memoirs of Putzi Hanfstaengl, who describes a somewhat similar blackmail attempt on Hitler and includes as a key intermediary one Franz Xaver Schwarz, the party treasurer and longtime Hitler crony who appeared in his apartment before the police did on the morning Geli's body was found.

In Hanfstaengl's version, the "first indication that there was something wrong with the relationship [between Hitler and Geli] came, as I recall, fairly early in 1930 from Franz Xaver Schwarz." Hanfstaengl says that one day he ran into Schwarz on a Munich street and found him "very down-in-the-mouth." Schwarz took him to his flat and "poured out what was on his mind.

He had just had to buy off someone who had been trying to blackmail Hitler, but the worst part of the story was the reason for it. This man had somehow come into the possession of a folio of pornographic drawings Hitler had made. . . . They were depraved, intimate sketches of Geli Raubal, with every anatomical detail."

Hanfstaengl says he was surprised when he found Schwarz still had possession of the ransomed Geli drawings. "Heaven help us, man! Why don't you tear the filth up?" he asked the party treasurer.

"No," he quotes Schwarz replying, "Hitler wants them back. He wants me to keep them in the Brown House safe."

There might well be some underlying, lost, earlier Q source for these not-quite-matching versions of the story. But Heiden's version bears closer inspection because, unlike Hanfstaengl, Heiden enjoyed throughout his life a substantial reputation for journalistic probity. He remains one of the most frequently cited sources for anecdotal material about the Munich Hitler by explainers of all persuasions, including Bullock and Fest. And he is the source for a highly influential school of postwar Hitler explanation, the one embodied best in Alan Bullock's first biography: the personally corrupt, politically cynical, yet classically explicable Hitler, with Heiden as his Suetonius and Bullock as his Tacitus.

Consider some excerpts from the highly respectful *New York Times* obituary of Heiden in 1966:

> Until other scholars began their work on Nazi documents after World War II, Mr. Heiden was the best-known authority outside Germany on the party and its leaders. . . .
>
> To the leaders of the Third Reich, [Heiden] was a hated and sought-after enemy. One of the Nazis' acts upon taking over a country was always to ban and burn his books.
>
> Mr. Heiden is sometimes given credit for popularizing the word "Nazi." The National Socialists were known in their earliest days by the conventional abbreviation "Naso" until Mr. Heiden, it was said, began using "Nazi"—Bavarian slang for "bumpkin" or "simpleton"—in his articles. . . .
>
> The writer was a propagandist of a special kind—one who used objectivity and documents to destroy the object of his derision. . . .
>
> As a writer for the liberal Frankfurter Zeitung . . . his special assignment was the Nazi party. It was said that Hitler sometimes refused to start meetings until Mr. Heiden arrived.
>
> In 1930 he left the paper to manage an anti-Nazi newspaper syndicate in Berlin. In 1932 his first book, "History of National Social-

ism," was publicly burned by the Nazis, who were then on the brink of gaining power. When they took over . . . in 1933, he fled.

The obituary doesn't report the fact that Heiden was among the first to publicly air the rumor that Hitler had Jewish blood, and not surprisingly there is no mention of the perversion question, which first appeared in Heiden's 1944 *Der Fuehrer*.

But as the source of two of the most wounding and embarrassing anecdotes about Hitler, Heiden clearly was a target: the obit gives a brief account of his exile and pursuit and last-minute escapes, first from Germany in 1933, then from the Saarland in 1935 (after a Hitler plebiscite restored it to German control), then from Paris in 1940, by way of Lisbon under a false passport, and, finally, to the safety of America.

The *Times* concluded its summation of his career by noting "his masterwork was *Der Fuehrer: Hitler's Rise to Power* . . . still a standard source for biographers."

Would Heiden have adulterated his "masterwork" by inserting a smutty story he fabricated about Hitler's sexuality, a sensational story that is both defiling and defining? It's a powerfully explicit explanation for Hitler's strangeness, alienness: Heiden calls his chapter on Hitler's personal life, the one containing this anecdote, "The Unhappiest of All Men," and here, purportedly, is the core of Hitler's unhappiness.

Brandeis scholar Rudolph Binion has a skeptical view of Heiden's story. Binion, a staunch partisan of the Party of Asexuality in the Hitler sexuality debate, believes Hitler had *no* sexual life, only idealized unconsummated infatuations, because of his overpowering devotion to his mother. He contends that Heiden, founder of the rival Party of Perversion, "can't be trusted" because he "exaggerated to sell books."

But a mercenary motive for a putative fabrication of the perversion story doesn't ring true. I have come to believe that it's possible to imagine another kind of motive, however: explanation as revenge, as a radical *idealistic* act of defacement.

I came to this notion reluctantly and still tentatively. Reluctantly first out of my respect for Heiden, whose work is in many ways indispensable: It offers a more intimate feel for the Munich Hitler than any other subsequent biography. Read in the context of the overabundant wealth of seamy detail Heiden provides about the Caligula's court surrounding Hitler—a profusion of sexual blackmail and murder scandals often centered around possession of pornographic letters—the story Heiden tells about Hitler's pornographic letter to Geli and the blackmail plots that it generated doesn't seem all that unthinkable. In Heiden's account, Hitler's perversion is not something that reads as if it's artificially slapped on but rather as if it's the hitherto-unseen dark star whose emanations of secrecy and shame influence the visible matter. It made a certain kind of sense, it was tempting to believe.

But before giving in to the temptation, two alternate possibilities must be considered: (1) that Heiden invented the story; (2) that he might have believed it but adapted it from a source who invented it.

The *Times*, it will be recalled, described Heiden as "a propagandist of a special kind—one who used objectivity and documents to destroy the object of his derision." As a description, it points two ways: The means are objectivity and documentary truth, but the end is to destroy with derision for propaganda's sake. Could Heiden have felt justified in his struggle against a man he knew capable of ultimate evil to use fair means *and* foul to destroy him? Recall the lesson the anti-Hitler journalists had learned in the pre-1933 period: Truth and objectivity alone had failed to stop Hitler from coming to power.

Could Heiden, Hitler's longtime nemesis, his most knowledgeable biographer, his most intimate explainer, driven into exile by Hitler's triumph, have seized the opportunity to take a very personal kind of revenge upon Hitler, to brand him, stain him with a story that, once heard, sticks almost indelibly to its subject? It would be a gesture that he might also have rationalized on political grounds—mobilizing hostility and disgust against a Hitler whose genocidal potential he may have sensed, using the classic tactic of "black propaganda."

I thought there might be a clue to Heiden's intent in the apparently gratuitous inclusion of coprophilia in his account. As we'll see, the only other contemporary source who links Hitler to an excretory perversion, Otto Strasser (who may well have been Heiden's source for the perversion story), mentions only undinism. Heiden gratuitously adds coprophilia. It's almost a metaphor for what the whole Heiden story is doing—smearing Hitler's image with excrement. A metaphor perhaps for the defilement Heiden wanted to inflict on him? In telling this story, Heiden assumes the position of Geli Raubal in Hitler's alleged fantasy: pissing on him, shitting on him. If the Jewish-blood story is the family romance of the Hitler explainers, the Heiden-Strasser stories can be seen as the sexual fantasy of the Hitler explainers, with Geli Raubal as their stand-in.

In a sense, the preoccupation of the explainers with Geli Raubal can be seen as a kind of envy of Geli for another reason: She just might have achieved the explainer's fantasy: seeing Hitler unmasked, Hitler close up, with his defenses down, the "real" Hitler. It is probably not an accident that when Heiden describes the purported pornographic letter Hitler wrote to Geli, he calls it one in which Hitler "*gave himself completely away*"—the grail of the explainer, the moment of naked self-revelation.

What about Otto Strasser's version of the story, the second pillar of the case for the Party of Perversion? Strasser's version omits coprophilia, but it does two things Heiden's doesn't: It describes consummated acts, not fantasies. And it claims the description comes firsthand from Geli Raubal herself.

What makes Strasser's account even more significant historically is that it is *this* version of the perversion story that was adopted almost in its entirety by the OSS. It is, in fact, then, the paid-for, classified, officially stamped U.S. government sexual fantasy about Adolf Hitler.

But, like Heiden, Otto Strasser had, at the very least, an equal motive to want to revenge himself on Hitler, to defile his person: Hitler murdered his brother Gregor. The two Strasser brothers had been founders of the Nazi Party in northern Germany, at least as responsible for its success outside Bavaria as Hitler, who for a long time was regarded as a clownish Bavarian anomaly in the more cosmopolitan urban centers of the north.

Gregor Strasser was the public man, the politician; Otto the journalist, propagandist, pamphleteer. Hitler had always resented them as an independent power in the party, and by the late 1920s strains had grown between him and the Strassers. At first it was over ideological issues: The Strassers, who had always stressed the socialist side of National Socialism, were alarmed at Hitler's sacrifice of populist principles in order to court the contributions of big-money industrialists and Junkers as he got closer to power. Otto quit the party first, late in 1931 (shortly after Geli's death, in fact), and began to wage an increasingly active opposition to Hitler. Gregor remained the nominal number-two figure in the party until shortly before Hitler took power, when he was dismissed for attempting to broker a power-sharing deal with the short-lived government of Kurt von Schleicher. Hitler never forgot what he regarded as a betrayal; he had Gregor murdered amid the carnage of the Night of the Long Knives in June 1934. By then, Otto had gone into exile in Czechoslovakia, where he'd formed an anti-Hitler underground group known as the Black Front to engage in sabotage and black propaganda against the man who killed his brother.

Before the split, however, the Strassers were part of the Hitler inner circle in Munich, close to both Hitler and Geli. Otto would later claim, in fact, that Gregor was the one who took the gun from Hitler's hand as he was about to commit suicide in the aftermath of the ugly publicity surrounding Geli Raubal's death. And Otto claimed to have socialized with Geli herself. According to a story told by Hanfstaengl as well as Strasser, Otto even aroused Hitler's "jealous possessiveness" over Geli on more than one occasion.

"I liked the girl very much," Strasser told a German writer. "And I could feel how much she suffered because of Hitler's jealousy. She was a fun-loving young thing who enjoyed the Mardi Gras excitement in Munich but was never able to persuade Hitler to accompany her to any of the many wild balls. Finally, during the 1931 Mardi Gras, Hitler allowed me to take Geli to a ball." It was on that occasion that Otto claimed Geli disclosed to him exactly what went on between her and Hitler in his bedroom.

"Geli seemed to enjoy having for once escaped Hitler's supervision. On the way back . . . we took a walk through the English Garden. Near the Chinese Tower, Geli sat down on a bench and began to cry bitterly. Finally, she told me that Hitler loved her, but that she couldn't stand it anymore. His jealousy was not the worst of it. He demanded things of her that were simply repulsive. . . . When I asked her to explain it, she told me things that I knew only from my readings of Krafft-Ebing's *Psychopathia Sexualis* in my college days."

Again, as with Heiden, we have the pseudovalidation of a sexologist tossed in. But Strasser, in his OSS debriefing, becomes as specific as Havelock Ellis or Krafft-Ebing, providing details of what Heiden had only alluded to in Latinate euphemism before.

That night "at the Chinese Tower in the English Garden," Strasser says, Geli told him that, when night came, "Hitler made her undress [while] he would lie down on the floor. Then she would have to squat down over his face where he could examine her at close range, and this made him very excited. When the excitement reached its peak, he demanded that she urinate on him, and that gave him his sexual pleasure. Geli said that the whole performance was extremely disgusting, and although it was sexually stimulating [to him], it gave her no gratification."

It's a story that can give no one any gratification. But over the years it has satisfied a kind of need among explainers, the need for some hidden variable, often a sexual secret, some dark matter, that could help illuminate the otherwise inexplicable enigma of Hitler's psyche.

CHAPTER 8

The Dark Matter:
The Sexual Fantasy of the
Hitler Explainers

A critical evaluation of certain hidden variable theories

The putative sexual secret: It's the "dark matter" in the universe of Hitler explanations. Like the invisible, only indirectly detectible dark matter of cosmology—whose existence, whose powerful gravitational pull physicists are obliged to believe in without seeing in order to account for otherwise inexplicable behavior of visible matter—the notion that Hitler had a profound, concealed, and deeply disturbing sexual secret that explains his otherwise inexplicable pathology is a persistent one.

In fact, to exploit another analogy from physics, Hitler explanations can be divided into distinct genres: field theories and hidden-variable theories. Field-theory explanations of Hitler are analogous to the way the Copenhagen school of quantum physics explains radioactive decay. In a given field, with the right preconditions, a disciple of Danish physicist Niels Bohr will tell you that a certain number of particles will inevitably decay (split), releasing fragments that can, for instance, spark a chain reaction. However, the school of quantum-field theorists founded by Bohr will absolutely deny that there is anything about any *individual* particle that would allow an observer to predict that it is the unstable particle that will decay next. You could theoretically investigate an individual particle "in depth" forever without being able to find some "hidden variable," some internal instability that will make one more likely than another to decay.

Similarly, in historical explanation, field-theorist types tend to argue that it is the preconditions in the field—societywide poverty, desperation, depression, panic, poisonous ideas, and ideology—that create the preconditions for *some* individual like Hitler to emerge, to crystallize the field of discontent, to start a chain reaction. The readiness is all to field theorists; it hardly matters what hidden variables within an individual psyche cause him to emerge as a catalyst; the societal critical mass produces its own trigger. Or as Daniel Goldhagen, a field-theorist type, suggests: if not Hitler, someone *like* Hitler would emerge.

On the other hand, Albert Einstein resisted to the end of his life the Copenhagen school's insistence that "hidden variables" within particles did not exist or were not causally significant. Einstein insisted there had to be some as-yet-undiscovered hidden variable within that caused one particle as opposed to another to decay. Most but not all contemporary physicists believe Einstein was on the losing side of the argument, and many but not all contemporary theorists of historical explanation regard the search for hidden variables within Hitler (or "Hitler-centric" explanations of any kind) to be irrelevant. The search for the origins of the Holocaust has been shifting—not without opposition—from the search within Hitler to the fields of social forces and ideological currents into which he was born. Why history was ready and waiting for *a* Hitler is seen as more important than why *he* turned out to be *the* Hitler.

Ironically, when Einstein specifically addressed the question of Hitler he adopted an uncharacteristic field theory for his rise: "As soon as economic conditions improve, Hitler will sink into oblivion," Einstein said in *The Cosmic Religion*, a collection of his remarks published in 1931. He sees Hitler as an aberrational particle: "Hitler is no more representative of the Germany of today than are the smaller anti-Semitic disturbances." But Hitler is a particle whose aberration is the product of a disturbance in the larger field: "Hitler is living—or shall I say, sitting?—on the empty stomach of Germany," Einstein maintained. Hitler is, then, the product of a rage generated by societal deprivation rather than someone who conjured up, catalyzed, a rage that might not otherwise have materialized in the malevolent form it took without his literally particular impetus.

In any case the putative sexual secret Hitler may have concealed from the world can be envisaged as perhaps the last best hope of the hidden-variable theorists of Hitler—the most hidden hidden variable. Does it really matter to anyone if Hitler had a sexual secret? In practice, it seems to have mattered most to two remarkably disparate groups. It mattered to Freudians as a vindication of the belief that the defining truth about the unanalyzed person can be found in what is hidden rather than what is apparent; that the important truths are always beneath the surface and that they are almost always sexual truths. Hitler was one of the first living world leaders to be subjected to prolonged long-distance analysis by Freudians, and it became a kind of crucial test for the discipline: If they could not offer a specifically psychoanalytic explanation for Hitler's twisted psyche, how relevant could Freudian theory be to history and human nature?

And so, from the beginning, psychoanalytic writers (and subsequently in the sixties and seventies a whole school that came to be known as psychohistorians) have had a go at Hitler, most trying to locate the source of his problems in his infantile erotic life, the preferred breeding ground for problems in Freudian theory. Curiously, Freud himself does not seem to have pronounced on the source of Hitler's pathology (at least in print), although he suffered directly from it, being forced by the Gestapo to flee from Vienna in 1938 to escape a climate hostile not just to Jews but to psychoanalysis as a pernicious "Jewish science." But generations of his successors have tried to make the analysis of Hitler's psyche a demonstration and confirmation of the ability of Freudian theory to diagnose the origins of evil.

The other group that has joined the Freudians in promoting the notion of a sexual secret—indeed, formed, in effect, a strange explanatory alliance with them—consists of a number of embittered ex-Nazi defectors from Hitler's inner circle, former intimates such as Otto Strasser, Ernst Hanfstacngl, and (to a lesser extent) Hermann Rauschning. If the mostly Jewish Freudians lacked inside information and the former Nazi insiders lacked objectivity and theory, the two groups found—at a distance—common ground in their vision of Hitler, with the Freudians frequently adapting the Strasser and Hanfstaengl perversion stories as confirmation for their speculations.

What the two groups have in common is a tendency to focus on the Geli Raubal relationship (rather than the later Eva Braun relationship, considered by most to be of far less decisive significance) as the episode in which the dark secret of Hitler's true sexual pathology came closest to declaring itself—the closest to the light the dark matter has come. But some psychoanalytical explainers have gone further than making the Geli Raubal relationship the revelation of Hitler's sexual pathology; they have tried to make it the moment in which his sexual pathology engendered his *political* pathology. When his anti-Semitism metamorphosed from a common opportunistic political device—from a disposition to exploit the Jews—to a determination to exterminate them.

This is the thrust of the only book-length purely psychoanalytic study of Hitler, Norbert Bromberg and Verna Volz Small's *Hitler's Psychopathology*. The two authors (the former a psychoanalyst and professor at the Albert Einstein College of Medicine, the latter a medical writer) specifically link Hitler's alleged sexual perversion—the nature of which they adopt from Strasser's excretory version—to the crystallization of the exterminationist version of his anti-Semitism.

For them, the secret sexual pathology is the missing link. It was not so much the specifics of the perversion (although they account for the alleged undinism in Freudian infantile-erotic terms) that made it decisive, as it was, they argue, that only in the freedom of his intimacy with Geli Raubal was Hitler able to fulfill his paraphilic desires fully. And, they contend, it was this very fulfillment that led to a profound shift in the gravitational center of his pathology. They characterize the three-year period (1928–1931) that they say encompassed the Hitler-Geli Raubal relationship as one that saw "a striking shift" in Hitler's psychic constellation: *"the displacement of his fear from women to Jews"* (emphasis added). "Around 1928," they write:

> Hitler was deeply, and more openly than ever, involved with a woman: his niece, Geli. About the same time he was preparing a work which became known as *Hitler's Secret Book*, published for the first time thirty-three years later. In this book he associated his hatred of Jews with ideas about blood and race for the first time. His sexual interest in his niece must have inevitably stirred in Hitler thoughts of incest and fears of harming her and possible progeny by what he believed might result: the corruption of her blood [by the putative "Jewish blood" Hitler believed he'd been tainted with, in their view]. All these ideas and wishes he projected onto the Jews, and by universalizing, as was his wont, he made the Germans, the Motherland, and the whole world their victims instead of Geli.

To parse out the complicated dynamic they claim obtained within Hitler: The combination of the intensity of the sexuality (his first fulfilling experience) and the near incestuousness of Hitler's relationship with Geli exacerbated what Bromberg and Small believe was his obsession with his Jewish blood—the Jew "within" him; exacerbated Hitler's sense of himself *as a violating Jew*, specifically an identification of himself with the Jew whose original predatory sin violated, poisoned the blood of his grandmother Maria Schicklgruber. Hitler's relationship with Geli was then, Bromberg and Small imply, a kind of *recapitulation* of the relationship between his putative Jewish grandfather and his Aryan grandmother. The anger he projected outward at the Jews was, they conclude, derived from the hatred of the sexual predator, the predatory Jew within himself. He had to exterminate them because he *was* them. As overcomplicated, uncorroborated, and speculative as it seems, it was this self-hating dynamic that, the psychoanalytic authors maintain, generated the Holocaust.

I cite this not for its persuasive power (it falls far short of convincing me) but as an example of the way explainers strain for the ultimate explanatory prize, the missing link, the key hidden variable in Hitler studies: the link between his purportedly aberrant personal pathology and his abhorrent political ideology—between his sexuality and his anti-Semitism.

Which isn't to say the authors don't sincerely believe in their solution. (Although, from my conversations with Verna Volz Small, I believe she has a more highly nuanced view of the question than the more dogmatically Freudian Dr. Bromberg). But there are several problems with the way they've forged this connection that betray an overeagerness to explain everything. For one thing, singling out 1928 as the year the missing link materialized is important to them, since 1928 is the year Hitler wrote the so-called Secret Book (rants mainly on race and foreign policy initially planned as a sequel to *Mein Kampf* but never published in his lifetime because of changes in the foreign situation). But Bromberg and Small's ambiguous characterization of the Hitler-Geli relationship in 1928 may betray their own doubt (and the doubt in the evidence) about how real the involvement between Hitler and Geli was at that point. In one sentence, the authors claim there was a "deep and open involvement" between Hitler and his half-niece as early as 1928. But there is still considerable dispute about how deep (in the sense of mutual and consensual) and how open (if it was deep in the sense they suggest, it was *never* open) it was even as late as 1931, when Geli was found dead. And yet a few sentences later, they back off from "deep and open" to suggest that Hitler's sexual "*interest* in" (as opposed to involvement with) Geli in 1928 would have been enough to trigger the poisonous dialectic they envisage ensuing.

But even more questionable is the insistence that it was in Hitler's "Secret Book," as it's come to be called, that Hitler *for the first time* linked hatred of Jews with ideas of race and blood. Overly eager to make the Geli secret and the Secret Book the key nexus of Hitler's psychological and political evolution, they ignore evidence that Hitler became a racial anti-Semite (as opposed to a traditional "religious" anti-Semite who would theoretically accept a Jew who converted to Christianity—the racial anti-Semite is convinced "Jewish blood" is an inherited evil no conversion can change) long before 1928. They ignore, for instance, a 1919 letter Hitler—then a political-information officer for the defeated German army who'd yet to join the Nazi Party—addressed to a Munich man, in which he specifically characterized Jews as a "racial tuberculosis" that would have to be "amputated" or exterminated because Jews were, in effect, an incurable genetic evil, not a mere religious threat that could be "cured" by conversion. If the authors were unaware of the 1919 letter, they could hardly ignore the many passages in *Mein Kampf* (written in 1924) in which Hitler explicitly defines himself as an anti-Semite of race and blood, long before any involvement with Geli Raubal.

The extent to which Bromberg and Small ignore this evidence to bolster a connection between the sexual and the political in Hitler is testimony to the conceptual prize they seek: the source of Hitler's exterminationist impulse.

Others have found more simple and direct ways to integrate the putative Geli Raubal sexual secret into their Hitler explanations: Hitler's alleged rage, for instance, his sexual jealousy over a rumored Jewish seducer of Geli. Several gossipy contemporary sources suggested that Geli's attempt to escape Hitler's ménage for Vienna shortly before her death was motivated by her plan to marry a Viennese Jew who seduced her and possibly made her pregnant. Which, if true, would not only have made Hitler the victim of a Jewish cuckolder but also have "poisoned" his beloved Geli with "Jewish blood." Indeed, considering Hitler's fearful view of Jewishness as a kind of sexually transmitted disease, he might have felt it had poisoned *him*—sufficient fuel, supposedly, to ignite an exterminationist urge against all Jews as violators. Or, in other versions of this theory, it was not so much jealousy of Geli's affection for the spectral Viennese Jew but fear of what she might *confide* to him—fear that knowledge of Hitler's shameful and disturbing sexual secret would be placed in the hands of his worst enemies.

The problem with these theories is that they beg the question of whether there *was* a sexual secret, some hidden pathological abnormality that made Hitler *nicht natürlich*. Perhaps it might be best, before assessing the role the Geli Raubal relationship played in the evolution of Hitler's pathology, to examine the competing explanations of Hitler's sexuality from the ground up, so to speak, beginning with the genital-wound theories.

There is an almost comic disproportion to the amount of attention, the amount of weight, the amount of potency that has been projected upon Hitler's genitalia in general and on his purportedly absent testicle in particular. Like the lost safe-deposit box, the lost testicle has become a repository for the hope that some singular solution—an explicatory single-bullet theory—exists somewhere to explain *everything*. The lost-testicle myth serves as a metaphor for the urge to find some freakish, idiosyncratic abnormality in the person of Hitler—to explain the magnitude of his crimes as a freak of nature rather than something that arose from the "normal" human nature we would otherwise share with Hitler.

The missing-testicle question poses, first of all, a perplexing problem of origins: The rumor preceded the supposed factual confirmation by some thirty years. The rumor is best known in the doggerel line of the popular World War II marching song: "Hitler—has only got one ball." The problem this presents is that, of all the scurrilous rumors about Hitler's sexuality and Hitler's genitalia that circulated up to the time of his death—rumors that were assiduously compiled regardless of reliability in the 1943 OSS "Hitler Sourcebook"—none suggested monorchism or cryptorchism. (The latter is the condition in which both testicles are present, but one *intermittently* retracts up into the inguinal canal from the scrotum.)

Homosexuality, syphilis, excretory perversion, impotency, freakish under-development—all these were whispered about, some even published, before the war. The missing testicle did not become the subject of serious historical speculation (to the point that Oxford's Lord Bullock can chattily discourse to me upon the import of "the one-ball business," as he called it) until three decades *after* the war. The missing-testicle theory might have gone the way of the others into the realm of the unprovable conjecture had not the Soviet government, in 1968, permitted the release of the 1945 autopsy report prepared by Soviet doctors shortly after Hitler's body was found in the Berlin bunker.

The forensic description of Hitler's remains by the head of the Autopsy Commission, the wonderfully named Doctor Faust Shkaravski, is detailed and disturbing to read. Of an organ that, metaphorically, has been the subject of even more speculation than his genitals—Hitler's heart—he observed: "The cardiac ventricles are filled with coagulated reddish brown blood. . . . The heart muscle is tough and looks like boiled meat." The last words on Hitler's heart: boiled meat.

Moving on to the sexual organs, the Soviet doctor records that "the genital member is scorched. In the scrotum, which was singed but preserved, only the right testicle was found. The left testicle could not be found in the scrotum or in the inguinal canal, nor in the small pelvis."

Much about the Soviet autopsy revealed since its 1968 publication has made it suspect, revealed it to be as much a political as a medical document. The chief focus of its distortions has been its attempt to prove that the method Hitler used to kill himself revealed he died "a coward's death" rather than a "soldier's death." That he lacked the nerve (colloquially, the balls; that he wasn't *man enough*) to put a bullet into his head with his revolver, the traditional way defeated German generals cheated the enemy of a captive. But rather that he cravenly chewed a cyanide capsule, having first arranged for an aide to enter his death chamber and put a bullet in his head *after* cyanide killed him—to make it appear that he died a soldier's death. Most experts now agree that the Soviet theory (particularly the posthumous gunshot by the aide) was falsified to prove Hitler's lack of manhood. Wouldn't it be equally possible that they falsified the autopsy details to show that his "manhood" was physiologically impaired as well—confirmation for the literal minded?

One almost suspects the fine hand and black humor here of one of the British moles consulting for the KGB in Moscow in the sixties. Guy Burgess or Kim Philby would have been familiar with the "one-ball" line in the Colonel Bogie song parody about Hitler; they could easily have been called in to consult when the results were being prepared (or doctored) to be released to the world in 1968.

My own skepticism about the one-ball report in the Soviet autopsy has been strengthened by my discovery of a hitherto-unknown, or at least long-ignored, source on the subject, one with what one might say was firsthand knowledge of the question. But before introducing this source, I think it's worth looking at what a mountain of signification has been piled upon the putatively absent testicle. Psychoanalytic explainers, in particular, have made it a foundation for their posthumous analysis of Hitler. An analysis that begins, in the most ambitious psychoanalytic vision—that of psychohistorian Robert Waite—with Hitler's mother Klara's hands:

"Klara was not only worried about her son's feeding and toilet training," Waite tells us.

> While cajoling (or forcing) him to eat more food, to move his bowels regularly and on schedule, and to control his bladder, she also *could* have fretted about an anatomical defect she *may* have detected in her son: one of his testicles was missing. One *can speculate* that she periodically felt the little boy's scrotum, checking anxiously to see if the testis had descended. Such solicitous concern *would have* heightened Adolf's infantile sexual feelings and increased the difficulty of a healthy mother-son relationship [emphasis added].

It's a passage so riddled with conjecture and tentative speculation—she *could* have fretted . . . she *may* have detected . . . one *can* speculate . . . solicitous concern *would* have heightened—that it's hard to imagine it serving as anything but a cryptofoundation for a cryptorchid or monorchid theory.

In placing such great emphasis on the destiny-shaping role of an absent testicle, psychoanalytic explainers rely on the work of a psychoanalytically oriented child analyst, Dr. Peter Blos, who did a small study of emotionally disturbed eleven- and twelve-year-old boys who were missing a testicle. Blos concluded that when mon- or cryptorchism occurs "within the matrix of a disturbed parent-child relationship . . . profoundly detrimental" consequences result, among them: "Hyperactivity, learning difficulties, compulsive toying with physical danger, social inadequacy, chronic indecision, and tendencies to exaggerate, to lie, and to fantasize. . . . A bisexual sense of identity and an interest in architecture, as a symbolic substitution for the absent testicle in concrete objects in the outer world." Taking this list as a blueprint or as a lens through which to view the supposed facts of Hitler's childhood, psychoanalyst Dr. Norbert Bromberg claims, "Adolf's need to continue playing cowboy-and-Indians and war games after his playmates had become bored with them attest to his youthful hyperactivity."

Waite dutifully adduces rages and poor report cards at a crucial age ("learning difficulties") as further evidence for the monorchid hypothesis. And, of course, there is the architectural obsession later on. But Waite is only getting started. He goes on to link Hitler's monorchism to his notoriously mesmeric stare, the way he'd attempt to fix those in his presence with the power of his gaze: "Monorchid boys favor symbolic substitutes for the missing testicle.... Patients may be excessively concerned about eyes. Hitler's eyes were particularly important to him.... The adult Hitler was aware of their power and practiced 'piercing stares' in front of the mirror. He also played games with his eyes. He would slowly cross them in looking at people, or he would stare them down."

While some might see this as Hitler attempting to exercise hypnotic self-aggrandizing power over individuals the way he did with crowds, Waite, steeped in the supposed insights yielded only to the adepts of psychoanalysis, sees something deeper going on: Hitler "may have been saying to them and to himself, 'See I do have two powerful (potent) testicles, and I can penetrate and dominate others.'"

Is *that* really what Hitler was saying? On any level, conscious or unconscious? Waite's book was written at a time when it was still common to give the insights of psychoanalysis an almost touching credulity and power. But Waite carries his monorchid theorizing so far, his Hitler explanation almost becomes a replication of it: Compensating for a conspicuous absence (here not of testicle, but of hard evidence), the crypto-explainer claims to have eyes, to *see*, to penetrate into matters further than others with his potent insights.

In fairness to Waite's monorchid preoccupation, he does adduce one possible consequence of the condition that has a suggestive resonance. He cites the report of an American child analyst "that his young monorchid patients have a desire 'of an almost frantic or feverish type' for redesigning and reconstructing buildings. They hope to quell their anxiety about defects in their own bodies by making other kinds of structures whole." (This sounds like a hyperbolic way of saying they liked playing with building blocks.) Hitler's lifelong preoccupation with architecture fits the pattern, Waite asserts, citing his architectural ambitions and fantasies that go back to his first years in Vienna and the frenzy for redesigning and reconstructing entire cities he indulged himself in in partnership with Albert Speer once he came to power. Waite has even discovered a previously unpublished passage from Hitler's wartime Table Talk in which Hitler goes to great lengths to define himself, as a youth, not as an aspiring painter but as an aspiring architect. He disparages the watercolors he painted to raise money from tourists and lauds his "*architectural sketches . . . [as] my most valuable possessions*, my own brainchildren which I would never have given away as I did the pictures" (emphasis added).

The problem with this insight is that while it might be an important aspect of Hitler's self-definition, there's no basis in evidence for believing it's explained by monorchism, unless we're compelled to believe that all impassioned architects must be driven by missing testicles.

Bromberg takes another tack: In his analysis of the monorchid effect, he suggests that all wicked rulers must be suffering from a physical defect that is the true source of their wickedness. "Freud cited Gloucester in *Richard III*," Bromberg writes, "who argues that since he cannot play the lover because of his [hunchback], he will be a villain, intriguing and murdering as he pleases. For the physical wrong done him, he claims the right to exemption from the scruples inhibiting others. . . . The similarity to Hitler's feeling of justification for any behavior is striking."

Striking, if one takes Richard III's words literally, if one believes that in *fact* he is offering a sincere "victim defense" of himself, rather than offering, say, a transparently cynical parody of the victim defense—by someone whose predilection for evil is far deeper and more complex than some all-too-easily-understandable compensation for his conspicuous hump. Similarly, it seems to miss a dimension of Hitler's capacity for evil to define him by his absent lump; it tends to make him a figure of pity for his psychological suffering, someone who couldn't help himself.

But Bromberg believes he can explain just about *everything* about Hitler from this single-pointed, single-testicle theory. He cites another Freudian study, "of narcissistic adults with minor physical anomalies," that found additional features that also stand out in Hitler's life record:

> These include a secret fantasy life replete with narcissistic-exhibitionistic-aggressive themes, sadomasochistic fantasies, eroti-cized megalomanic daydreams, conscious or semiconscious aspirations to greatness and immortality; compensatory self-aggrandizement; heightened aggressiveness, often accompanied by outbursts of ag-gression and hate in word and deed . . . revenge fantasies. . . . Particu-larly intense in male patients in whom inguinal or genital anomalies such as testicular malformations exist.

Finally, Bromberg makes the monorchid theory jump through its tricki-est hoop of all and explain the exact nature of the perversion Hitler allegedly practiced with Geli Raubal—the extreme version of the alleged perversion described most explicitly by Otto Strasser, the version Strasser claims to have heard from Geli herself, the one involving undinism. The way Bromberg ex-plains it, "a perversion itself bespeaks extreme castration anxiety." And Hit-ler's extreme castration anxiety can be traced in a large part to the missing testicle: "Monorchism would lend an element of reality to castration anxiety."

There is, at best, a conjectural quality to this assertion; at worst, a projec-tion of the explainer's own *epistemological* castration anxieties—his incapacity to fully *know*—on the thought process of the monorchid child. Such questions do not trouble Bromberg, who moves from monorchism to castration anxiety to the engendering of Hitler's perversion:

Fear of his father's imagined castration threat because of the Oedipus complex added to anxiety, as did identification with his mother while she was also perceived as a phallic castrating figure. All these converged in an unconscious acceptance of an image of himself as castrated and also resulted in the feminine passive inclinations which he disavowed so disastrously. . . . An extreme, even degrading form of the passive feminine inclination was *obviously expressed in the submissive situation Hitler chose for himself in the perversion* [emphasis added].

Perhaps I would have been less inclined to be skeptical of the interpretive castles in the air the architects(!) of the monorchid Hitler theory have built upon the slender foundation of Hitler's purportedly half-empty scrotal sac, had I not come across what seems like a fairly convincing refutation of the whole premise of their arguments. It came to me in a communiqué from a woman named Gertrud Kurth, who played a little-known but important role in the development of postwar psychological theories of Hitler. She'd written to me in response to Alan Bullock's comments on the "one-ball business" which appeared in my *New Yorker* essay on Hitler theories. She had something to add, she said.

Hearing from and then meeting with Dr. Kurth (she has a Ph.D. in psychology) was both extremely rewarding and rather a surprise. Until I received her letter, I'd carelessly assumed she was no longer alive. But, in fact, at age ninety-two, she was still very much alive, very much alert, still enthusiastically practicing psychotherapy part-time in her apartment on the Upper West Side of Manhattan.

She was more than alive, she was one of the last living embodiments of the thrilling, febrile world of Viennese Jewish culture that the resentful Viennese tramp, Adolf Hitler, so loathed he destroyed. A culture exemplified by Dr. Kurth's mother, for instance. Toward the end of our conversation in her West End Avenue office, Dr. Kurth began to talk a bit about her family—about her mother in particular, a talented, emancipated woman who'd not only been the first woman ever to earn a doctoral degree in Vienna but who had, in addition, as an eighteen-year-old, written a novel that became a sensation from Vienna to Moscow because it touched upon the anxieties unleashed by the newly open discussion of sexuality in Vienna.

The novel, called *One for Many*, took the form of the diary of a young Viennese woman named Vera, who makes the shocking and demoralizing discovery that her beloved fiancé has been sexually promiscuous before their betrothal. The revelation of his crude sexuality is unbearable to her, and she ends up committing suicide. As a novel, it was both sexually frank and morally censorious, not dissimilar in that sense from the Freudian fusion of the two that emerged from Vienna. And, like Freud, the novel spawned a cultlike following, at least for a while. In Russia, for instance, earnest young men formed "Vera clubs" (not unlike today's fundamentalist men's group the Promise Keepers) in which they ostentatiously pledged themselves to the ideal of premarital chastity to spare the Veras in their midst the shock that led to Vera's suicide.

Dr. Kurth herself had ambitions to be a writer and had published short stories in Viennese magazines before she and her family were forced to flee to escape Hitler's 1938 homecoming march into Austria. Arriving in New York, she got work first as a translator for German-speaking émigré professors at the New School for Social Research but soon became an editor at the New School's book-publishing arm, International Universities Press, whose output was renowned in scholarly circles throughout the world. After a distinguished career there, she decided in the 1960s (in her sixties as well) to get a doctorate and become a psychotherapist. It was work she'd already demonstrated a remarkably precocious talent for in her unofficial role as analyst of Hitler's psyche in Walter Langer's secret OSS study of the mind of Adolf Hitler.

Dr. Kurth had been recruited by Langer in 1942 to do research and translation work, although her contribution turned out to be much more influential. And it was in Langer's company that she made a journey up to the Bronx to interview Dr. Eduard Bloch, the Hitler family's Jewish doctor, the man who had the only firsthand testimony about "the one-ball business."

My own journey to interview Dr. Kurth was not an easy one to arrange. She had bouts of severe emphysema, she told me, and was concerned whether her breathing difficulties would permit her to talk. Finally, after one postponement for that reason, she called to say I should come visit her in her office. "You'll find a woman who looks very old," she told me in her delightful Viennese accent, "but the noodle is still working."

The noodle proved, in fact, to be quite sharp. She received me in what looked like a fairly typical Upper West Side analyst's office. She was a small woman with a steely bun of hair, bright eyes, a strong voice, and a mischievous wit. And, in fact, her memory was quite sharp and detailed in recalling her encounter with Hitler's family doctor. Much of her work for the secret OSS Hitler study had involved library research and translation, but she'd been called upon to accompany Dr. Langer for this important interview because, for one thing, Hitler's family doctor was also part of *her* family, the Kafka clan.

Dr. Kurth was the third person I'd spoken to in the extended Kafka family who was related in some way to Hitler's Jewish doctor—and to Franz Kafka. In Dr. Kurth's case, she was related by marriage to Dr. Bloch's daughter Gertrude. It was Gertrude Bloch who, along with the Washington-based relative of Dr. Bloch, Dr. John Kafka, had led the attack on Rudolph Binion's theory, the one that singled out Dr. Bloch's painful treatment of Hitler's mother's cancer as a source of Hitler's hatred of the Jews (see chapter 13). Dr. Kurth was familiar with the controversy; in fact, she admits to being somewhat responsible for it, because it was her influential 1952 paper in the *Psychoanalytic Review*, entitled "The Jew and Adolf Hitler," that first focused attention on Dr. Bloch as the one actual Jew Hitler had come close to in the formative period of his life, and moreover, the one Jew who had been most closely enmeshed in the most powerful relationship of Hitler's life, the one with his mother. (That Hitler's doctor was also a relative of Franz Kafka is an irony only Kafka could comprehend.)

In that influential paper, Dr. Kurth was the first to suggest that Hitler's curious public treatment of Dr. Bloch—after his mother's death, Hitler wrote him grateful missives thanking him for his devoted care; and after Hitler annexed Austria in 1938, he singled out this one Jewish doctor for special praise and special protection—did not tell the whole story. "Hitler's conscious and unconscious attitudes [to the doctor] were diametrically opposed," Dr. Kurth argued in her paper. She believed that Hitler "experienced a father transference to the doctor" that was responsible for the public, surface expression of warmth. But that beneath the surface, repressed into Hitler's unconscious, the anguish and horror of his mother's fatal illness, which Dr. Bloch's treatments failed to abate, was displaced: "The attribution of all positive traits to the [Jewish] doctor and of all negative ones to the Jew [in general]."

Binion took this idea and ran with it, ran much too far with it, according to Dr. Bloch's outraged relatives, who argue that Binion's version of this theory—which goes beyond Dr. Kurth's in the way it characterizes Dr. Bloch's primitive, painful, and ineffective chemotherapy treatments as verging on malpractice—virtually blames their beloved Dr. Bloch for the Holocaust.

"It is not about blame," Dr. Kurth told me when I asked her about this controversy. "A child reasons not the same as an adult." In other words, she suggests, the problem was not Dr. Bloch's treatment decisions, but the child (actually, eighteen-year-old) Hitler's unconscious, irrational overreactions to them, which tapped into the reservoir of Jew-hatred seething beneath the surface of Austrian culture, a cultural disposition that gave the adult Hitler sanction to vent his displaced rage upon the Jews.

Although she will defend Dr. Bloch from any alleged blame for the Holocaust, Dr. Kurth is decidedly less than enthusiastic in her memory of the man himself in that encounter in the Bronx (the refuge to which Hitler had permitted him to emigrate). What struck her most about him at the time—since the controversy over the putatively absent testicle did not really arise until a quarter century later—was something Dr. Bloch said about Hitler as they took their leave.

"At the end of the interview as we were leaving, Bloch made a point of telling us 'what a nice pleasant youth' Hitler was." More than fifty years later, Dr. Kurth can't get over this. "Outside in the street, Langer and I laughed and laughed at that—bitter laughter," she told me, shaking her head.

It is not that she disputes the possibility that Hitler *was* "a nice pleasant youth." That has always been the crux of the problem for Hitler explainers—how and why a youth who was remembered by many as pleasant, at least gentle and harmless seeming, could turn into a bloodthirsty mass killer. It was, rather, she says, Bloch's insistence on clinging to, selectively emphasizing, in 1943, the nice, gentle aspect which provoked the bitter laughter.

Still, she had no doubt whatever about the truth of Bloch's answer to the question Langer put to him about Hitler's genital normality. He examined Hitler as a youth, Bloch said, and found that, in fact, there was *no* genital defect or testicular deficit. "Langer asked him whether the examination included the genitals," she recalls. "And he said 'absolutely, they were completely normal.'"

In which case, bitter laughter might indeed be in order *now*, considering all the elaborate theorizing psychoanalysts and others have erected on the shaky foundation of an assumption that Hitler was monorchid, all that cogitating about the probing fingers of his mother Klara, anxiously searching for the missing testicle in the child Hitler, thus disturbing forever his sexuality and paving the way of his murderous political pathology.

How, then, would she explain the Russian autopsy? I asked Kurth.

She laughed. "You know, when I read about it, I thought—you know, the German slang word for testicles is 'eggs'—so I thought 'maybe one of the eggs had been cooked.'" That is, consumed by fire when the corpse was burned. The language of Dr. Faust Shkaravski's autopsy report suggests otherwise, though: It reports that the scrotum was "singed" rather than burned.

Still, it is conceivable that with a corpse so badly burned overall, a corpse hastily buried and then dug up, the missing testicle or the burned fragments remaining from it fell off or dropped out in the shallow pit in which the body was initially hidden. And that in the years following, as more and more grandiose theories were being fabricated about the implications of its absence, more and more meanings were projected upon the absent "egg" as the metaphysical demon seed of Hitler's pathological evil, the actual physical remains of the left testicle were quietly disintegrating into organic molecules in the subsoil of Berlin. It is also marginally conceivable that—if Hitler had been suffering from cryptorchism rather than monorchism—both testicles might have been present on the occasion Dr. Bloch examined him, but the left one was AWOL on other occasions, such as those when Klara's probing fingers sought it.

Neither Hitler's World War I service records nor interviews with fellow soldiers have turned up any mention of a genital wound suffered during the war, subsequent to Dr. Bloch's examination, so we are left with the contradiction between Dr. Faust Shkaravski and Dr. Bloch—one testicle or two. If we cannot resolve it with absolute certainty, it is possible at least to suggest why analysts of all kinds are drawn to the notion of a genital wound: for reasons that are as much mythic and Wagnerian as they are Freudian. It is a Wagnerian figure, Amfortas, who suffers from a genital wound whose cure is crucial to the quest for the Grail. The genital wound gives a Wagnerian dimension to the figure of Hitler that on the face of it the man himself, the fumbling dissembler, the bumbling hand kisser, seems to lack. The genital wound suits as well the explanatory preferences of a century that has preferred to believe that what is most hidden and most shameful (i.e., sexuality) is most essential and true. And it serves as well the disposition to see Hitler as not normal, not "whole"—that is, not like us.

Of all the genital-wound variants offered, the only one that holds out a slender hope of reconciling the reports of Dr. Bloch and Dr. Faust Shkaravski is the cryptorchism diagnosis. It has at least a certain power as a self-referential metaphor for the slippery, elusive state of fact and interpretation in the realm of Hitler studies—a field plagued by crypto-explanations that depend on truths that appear and then, the more one probes them, seem to disappear or elude the efforts of researchers seeking to grasp their significance.

But to move on from the physical to the psychological genital-wound theories of Hitler, we find the diminutive Dr. Kurth once again casting a giant shadow, because it was she who made the controversial discovery of that grail of Freudian interpretation—an alleged primal scene!—in a veiled, overlooked passage of *Mein Kampf*—a discovery that, like the monorchid theory, was responsible for giving rise to an entire explicatory industry that has subsequently had the rug pulled out from under it.

"That was my big scoop" is the way Dr. Kurth recalls her primal-scene revelation. She found it when reading over a passage in *Mein Kampf* in which Hitler seems, on the surface, to be diagnosing the familial origins of societal ills, tracing them back to the oppressiveness of an impoverished childhood. Here, in the redaction of Hitler's words by Robert Waite—who became a vocal champion of the primal-scene theory (in addition to the monorchid theory)— is the controversial passage Dr. Kurth singled out, in which Hitler invites us to join him in a fantasy:

> Let us imagine the following: In a basement apartment of two stuffy rooms live a worker's family. . . . Among the five children there is a boy, let us say, of three. This is the age at which a child becomes conscious of his first impressions. In gifted people, traces of these early memories are found even in old age. The smallness and overcrowding of the rooms do not create favorable conditions. Quarreling and nagging often arise because of this. In such circumstances people do not [so much] live with one another, [as] push down on top of one another. Every argument . . . leads to a never-ending, disgusting quarrel. . . .

But when the parents fight almost daily, their brutality leaves nothing to the imagination; then the results of such visual education must slowly but inevitably become apparent in the little ones . . . especially when the mutual differences express themselves in the form of brutal attacks on the part of the father towards the mother or to assaults due to drunkenness. The poor little boy at the age of six, senses things which would make even a grown-up shudder. Morally infected . . . the young "citizen" wanders off [to become one of the dangerous disaffected members of society].

It is a fascinating passage in which, on the surface, Hitler seems to take on the guise of a concerned liberal social reformer probing the roots of social pathology in the poverty and misery that produce dysfunctional families and spousal abuse. Hitler as a caring feminist; Hitler as Jane Addams.

But Dr. Kurth saw something more in this passage, a darker vision lurking beneath the surface of the social reformer's prose. She interprets the "brutal attacks" that would make even an adult "shudder," the assaults that leave "nothing to the imagination," as specifically *sexual* assaults: the child witnessing his drunken father forcing himself on his shuddering mother. She believes that in writing about this scene, Hitler is consciously or unconsciously recalling, recreating the primal scene of abusive parental intercourse that he himself witnessed as a child: Alois forcing himself on Klara.

Until Dr. Kurth made this interpretation, no one had taken any particular notice of the passage. But once she brought it to the attention of Dr. Langer, he incorporated it as his own into the summary of his secret OSS wartime report on the mind of Adolf Hitler. Langer's report, of course, was not declassified until the late 1960s; and the first public adumbration of the primal-scene theory of Hitler's sexuality appeared in Dr. Kurth's 1947 *Psychoanalytic Review* paper.

She recalls that the response to it was immediate. "Menninger [Dr. Karl Menninger, head of the renowned Menninger Clinic] wrote me offering me a job," she says. Other psychoanalytic explainers fell in line; in addition to Langer, Bromberg and Waite agreed that *here* was the origin of the pathological disturbance of Hitler's psyche that gave rise to both sexual perversions and perverted political views. For Waite, this primal-scene trauma gave rise to "severe castration anxiety," which, in conjunction with his monorchism, made Hitler the psychopathic pervert Waite believes he was. Waite even went so far as to connect the primal-scene vision of parental sex with that other primal visual trauma Hitler describes so dramatically in *Mein Kampf* as a turning point in his life: his first glimpse of the spectral, black-caftaned, black-earlocked Jew-as-alien in the streets of Vienna.

Unfortunately, like so many other "scoops," so many other eureka concepts in Hitler studies, just as the primal-scene interpretation was settling in as received wisdom among psychoanalytic and psychohistorical Hitler explainers, a Johns Hopkins scholar, Hans Gatzke, threw cold water on it, debunking Langer's use of the passage on the grounds that he depended on a strained and skewed translation of the actual German phrases Hitler used. Gatzke insisted the passage referred to physical assaults—beatings—but not *sexual* assaults.

Dr. Kurth herself now has second thoughts on the *weight* Freudians give to the alleged primal scene. She's spent some time researching a reconsideration of Freud's view on the traumatic potential of the child witnessing parental sex. The great majority of people living in poverty (i.e., the great majority of people who live or have lived on the planet) have routinely lived and slept together in a single room, she points out, so that primal scenes have inevitably been a far more frequent feature of "normal" childhood experience than Freud conjectured from the perspective of his genteel Viennese milieu. In addition, Dr. Kurth points to some recent research into the culture of childhood which suggests that those who spent their infancy in the same room as their parents are at least as likely to have derived comfort and strength from the closeness of parental presence as they are to have been scarred by witnessing parental sex.

Still, there is one assertion in Kurth's 1947 paper that has appeared persistently in almost every succeeding attempt to explain Hitler's psychology, one persistent belief that has consistently drawn explainers back to the Geli Raubal relationship as somehow able to supply a crucial revelation about his psyche: the belief that Kurth called "inescapable" in her paper, "that Hitler's anti-semitism . . . was 'unmistakably of sexual origin.'" A tortured sexual origin that was engendered in Vienna and somehow finally revealed itself floridly in the bedroom where Geli Raubal's body was found.

Even the cautious Alan Bullock told me he believed there was "probably something sexual" to Hitler's anti-Semitism. In other explainers, the longing to find a sexual explanation is almost sexual in its intensity. And almost all those who posit a sexual explanation for Hitler's psyche end up arguing that, but for his nicht natürlich sexuality, Hitler would have been not only "normal" sexually but (the implication goes) normal morally as well, at least not driven to mass murder. It is a forlorn echo of Wilhelm Reich's belief that the origins of evil can be found in the failure to achieve wholesome, "normal" orgasmic release. It is the last forlorn echo of the Romantic faith that liberation from sexual repression would free us from the Dark Ages, the dark impulses within us. In the realm of Hitler studies, it is expressed as the hope that a sexual explanation will liberate us from the darkness of inexplicability, from the darker implications of a "normal" Hitler—release us from implicating ourselves, implicating "normal" human behavior in the mystery of what made Hitler so profoundly unnatural morally.

It is rare to find a Hitler explainer who does *not* make an occluded sexual secret the hidden variable of Hitler's psyche. Which is perhaps why, after having encountered so much speculation about the unknowable sexual dark matter, I found myself drawn by contrast to the more sedate, less fevered vision of Hitler's sexuality proposed by the historian John Lukacs.

In his book-length study of the Hitler-Churchill relationship (*The Duel*), Lukacs argues that "sexuality and its appetites seem to have played a less than decisive part in their [Hitler and Churchill's] lives." He calls Hitler "undersexed" not in the sense of a deformity or dysfunction but in a temperamental lack of interest. "In my considered view," Lukacs argues, Hitler's "relations with women were fairly normal"—a shocking statement in the context of a literature consumed with an obsession with Hitler's alleged abnormalities.

Lukacs called the evidence of unnatural sexuality "rare, inauthentic and difficult to judge." Lukacs's view is a useful corrective in its argument that Hitler's sexuality does not necessarily have to be the linchpin of a theory of his personality, however normal or abnormal that sexuality was. It reminds us that Hitler's monstrousness is no less frightening—in fact, in certain ways, far more frightening—if we don't regard him as sexually deformed or monstrous as well.

To deny or doubt there was some shameful sexual secret at the core of Hitler's psyche does not diminish the mystery of Hitler's soul. For many years, those who have investigated the Geli Raubal affair have looked to Dr. Fritz Gerlich, a nearly forgotten figure from the world of opposition journalists in Munich, as perhaps the only person who had gotten to the bottom of the Geli Raubal mystery (and perhaps that of Hitler's psyche as well). Some believe Gerlich had discovered a secret about Hitler so dangerous he was murdered for it before he could publish what he'd learned. I'd come to doubt, finally, that Gerlich *did* find proof that Hitler murdered Geli Raubal. But in searching for Gerlich's apocryphal secret, I came upon what I felt was one of the earliest, most powerful attempts to explain the secret dynamic of Hitler's soul.

PART FOUR

HATRED: COMPLEX AND PRIMITIVE

*Suggestive conjectures retrieved from the work of
Fritz Gerlich and the raw files of the OSS*

CHAPTER 9

Fritz Gerlich and
the Trial of Hitler's Nose

*In which we unearth a lost classic of Hitler
explanation by a murdered explainer*

It still has the power to shock: Adolf Hitler married to a black bride. More than six decades after this extraordinary photocomposite image of Hitler in top hat and wedding tails, arm in arm with a black bride in a scene of wedding-day bliss, appeared on the front page of one of Munich's leading newspapers, this mocking representation of Hitler—in a context of decapitation, miscegenation, transgressive sex, and violent defacement—still gives off an aura of recklessness, of danger.

And, in fact, there can be little doubt that this sensational visual and verbal attack on Hitler did turn out to be dangerous, fatally so, to its creator, the courageous, possessed anti-Hitler journalist, Dr. Fritz Gerlich. The mocking headline over the Hitler "wedding" photo—"Does Hitler Have Mongolian Blood?"—was published in July 1932, a scant six months before Hitler came to power, and may well have ensured Gerlich's later death in Dachau. Although Gerlich went even further some five weeks *after* Hitler came to power and attempted to publish something perhaps even more dangerous: a story that would have—by some accounts—linked the newly installed Reichschancellor in a scandalous way to the death of Geli Raubal. That March 1933 story, which was confiscated by the Gestapo before it could be printed, was the immediate cause of Gerlich's arrest and later murder. But the way he wounded Hitler with the "Mongolian-blood" front page in July 1932 probably sealed his fate, regardless of what was in the Geli Raubal story. The unpublished story may have had greater potential to damage Hitler, but the one Gerlich *did* publish had already succeeded in wounding him, in surgically exposing his psyche with a well-honed scalpel. It was a brilliant piece of character assassination as well as an unmatched work of character analysis that captures as well as or better than any subsequent one a powerful truth about Hitler and Hitler's racial psychology.

Yes, caricatured images of Hitler had appeared in opposition papers and on posters for years, but this was different. Prewar Hitler caricatures tended to focus on the mustache and the forelock, to exaggerate the contorted face in paroxysmal oratorical fury. But this image struck closer to home; it struck at Hitler's deepest, most obsessive anxiety: his blood.

The depiction of the champion of racial purity, of pure blood, in a wedding photo with a bride of an "inferior race," the combination of that scandalous image with the sensational question raised about his own racial purity was designed not merely to shock the paper's tens of thousands of casual readers but to wound, to draw blood from one reader in particular: Adolf Hitler. To draw blood by conjuring up the seamy congeries of sexual and racial rumors that had arisen around Hitler, rumors that arose from his persistent unmarried state, the rumors about his racial heritage that arose from the emphatically non-Aryan appearance of this champion of Aryan purity. And there can be little doubt it was designed as well to raise the specter of the most deeply inflammatory rumor, for which the allegation of Mongolian blood would be, in the minds of many readers, a euphemistic stand-in: the rumor that Hitler had in his ancestry another variation of "oriental" racial origin—"Jewish blood."

Consider the political circumstances in which this assault appeared. In July 1932, ten months after Geli Raubal's death in September 1931, Hitler had made the transition from much-ridiculed Bavarian crank to a national political figure campaigning on equal terms for the presidency of the German Republic with the venerable Reichspresident Hindenburg. He was now not merely a local or a national figure, but one who attracted worldwide attention, commanded a huge private army (the SA, which was terrorizing and murdering his political and journalistic opponents), and seemed to embody the future.

To publish an attack as vicious as this one, an attack that was more far reaching and deeply wounding in the body of the text than even the sensational photo and headline would indicate, was an act of great personal courage by a desperate and doomed prophet.

What Gerlich does in "Does Hitler Have Mongolian Blood?" is adopt the unctuously concerned tone and mock-scholarly rhetoric of Swift's *Modest Proposal*. He modestly proposes first that we apply the "racial science" of one of Hitler's favorite quack racial theorists, Dr. Hans Günther—who had prescribed the precise shape and dimension of each and every head and facial feature of "the Nordic type"—to Hitler's own head and face, especially to his nose. Gerlich proceeds to demonstrate in excruciating detail, with the accompaniment of photographic close-ups and comparisons, just how abysmally Hitler failed to live up to the standard of his own racial criteria.

But even more wounding was the way Gerlich proceeded from the analysis of Hitler's facial features—the highlight of which is a hilarious Swiftian Trial of Hitler's Nose—to a brilliant critique of the essential features of Hitler's personal and political identity. A critique which resulted in the devastating conclusion that Hitler—by his own lights—not only lacked Aryan physiognomy, he lacked an Aryan *soul*.

Before getting deeper into the vision of Hitler beneath the mockery of the Mongolian-blood lampoon, a vision that represents one of the most sophisticated attempts to explain Hitler by one of his Munich-period contemporaries, it might be valuable to see it in the context of the time when it was published, in the context of the fatal trajectory of the brave man who wrote it.

While the black-bridal image and the Mongolian-blood headline seemed shocking when I came upon them, it was difficult to gauge how transgressive it would have seemed in mid-1932, in the final few months of Hitler's ascent to power. It certainly seemed to me a quantum leap beyond what I'd seen in the other Munich opposition papers I'd seen for that period. The courageous anti-Hitler *Munich Post* tended to rely more on reason, on ideology and investigation; there was pointed satiric commentary and, yes, the occasional pointed visual image, usually a caricature of Hitler, but nothing like the brutal mockery of Hitler's racism in the bridal photomontage. Elsewhere, there were whispers and insinuations about Hitler's appearance; there was underground humor (in which the Nordic ideal was mocked as "thin like Göring, tall like Goebbels, blond like Hitler"). But I'd never seen anything so openly, so sensationally, so contemptuously ridicule the physical body of Hitler and the political/metaphysical fraudulence it symbolically betrayed.

I decided to test this impression with one of the few people who could put Gerlich's assault in the context of its moment, one of the last living veterans of the anti-Hitler opposition press in Weimar Germany. His name is Walter Schaber. He was in his nineties and a resident of Washington Heights in New York City, where he continues to write for the *Aufbau*, the venerable German-Jewish émigré weekly. He'd edited socialist newspapers in Thuringia and Saarfeld, directed the Socialist Worker Press Association in the late 1920s, and ended up in a Munich jail in March 1933 after the Hitler takeover. Schaber managed to escape to Czechoslovakia and then to America, where he went on to become an editor of the *Aufbau*. I brought my photographic reproduction of Gerlich's Mongolian-blood lampoon to Washington Heights to get Schaber's perspective on it in the context of the anti-Hitler journalism he knew.

Schaber takes a lively if also melancholy interest in the work of the opposition press in the years before the 1933 takeover. Outside Munich, he told me, with few exceptions (most notably the editor of the Berlin weekly *Weltbühne*, Carl von Ossietzky), the socialist opposition press was so distracted by internal factional fighting (primarily between the pacifist and pro-rearmament wings of the party) that they failed to focus the attention they should have on the struggle against Hitler. (Alfred Kazin told me of his disappointment in learning from émigré German socialists in the thirties how certain leaders of the party—unlike its reporters—had been pensioned off by Hitler. Kazin added that he believes the ideological roots of Hitler's success in the struggle between a divided left and a militant fascist right have been neglected.)

Perhaps this retrospective regret was why Schaber's face lit up with such evident pleasure when I showed him Gerlich's "Mongolian Blood" screed. He laughed out loud as he devoured the acidulous headlines, the mocking captions, interrupting his reading with exclamations such as, "This is amazing! . . . July 1932! . . . This is wonderful! How did you find it?" (It was a tip from photojournalist Tim Gidal, who'd known Gerlich and recalled the satire, which I found in the Monacensia library in Munich.)

It seemed to give him great satisfaction that at least here, one anti-Hitler journalist had gone all out, had gone for the jugular, had given vent to the anger and contempt they all felt before they were all silenced. I suspect this no-holds-barred fatal recklessness has something to do with my own fascination with Gerlich. It's surprising to discover, when you look at the literature on Hitler and the Nazi leadership before and after the war, inside and outside Germany, how little outright, heartfelt hatred and loathing is expressed in print.

The tone and tendency of prewar explainers was to condescend to Hitler, to treat him as a phenomenon beneath contempt, much less serious consideration. Rather than urge the necessity of combating Hitler, prewar explainers acted as if he could be wished away with words, belittled into oblivion. They diminished him to the point where he was not even a worthy target for antagonism. Postwar literature tends to diminish Hitler in a different way; knowing well what he wrought, the tendency is to argue it wasn't really *him*, it was the deeper and more profound forces behind and beneath him, the wave on which he rode. He is, once again, then, barely an agent himself worthy of being blamed and loathed and held responsible so much as an instrument of abstract forces, hatred of whom is virtually irrelevant.

This is particularly true of German literature on the subject, and the rare exception to it like Gerlich throws the absence of passion elsewhere into stark relief. Is hatred a legitimate response? I'm not sure it's always helpful analytically, but the reckless yet exquisitely well-honed hatred beneath the surface of Gerlich's satire gave me the kind of satisfaction I'd found in one of the few genuinely hate-filled postwar accounts of the period, *In the Shadow of the Reich* by Niklas Frank, the son of Hitler lawyer and mass murderer Hans Frank. Niklas's "biography" of his father is filled with a kind of joyful cleansing hatred and contempt. The son grew up in the castle in Kraków, Poland, that his father used as governor-general of occupied Poland—the place of evil from which Frank presided over and profited from the Final Solution.

The son portrays his father in acid, scathing tones as a conniving, vain, priggish, and piggish predator, squeezing the Jews for their valuables before sending them off to be incinerated. The drama of the Niklas Frank book is in the conflicted tone, the way the son's effort to keep a distance between himself and his loathing for his father (by portraying him as a comic monster) recurrently collapses into pure hatred, drives him to devise new heights of obloquy and abuse—the prose can barely contain his rage and contempt. But for all its venom, it felt to me a cleansing rage, one that burned the accretions of pity and "understanding" away from the doors of perception. Certainly a healthy emotion when set against the torturous temporizing of Albert Speer, pitilessly captured by Gitta Sereny, wrestling with his conscience and the truth to account for Hitler's hold over him; or compared with the ritualistic rationalizations the postwar German historians perform to "historicize" and distance themselves from Hitler, the wrestling with the notion of Hitler's "greatness" in a way that trivializes his crimes. Niklas Frank's work meant more to me than all of this ratiocination—a pure howl of hatred.

Gerlich's hatred of Hitler was more than a howl, it was a razor-edged analytic tool that cut to the heart of Hitler's pathology before anyone else did, before it was too late—if anyone had listened. Which is why I feel it's important to rescue Gerlich, his life and work, from archival oblivion, to begin to restore him from footnotes to full-blooded memory.

Just who was this man, Dr. Fritz Gerlich? Restoring him to history is a particularly complicated task, because in the rare cases he does get mentioned, he's often used to serve the agenda of fictionalists or factionalists. To put the mystery of Gerlich's last scoop into better perspective, it's helpful to look more closely at Gerlich's path toward that final moment when the Gestapo ripped his last story off the presses. It is the story of a man who was driven by his obsession with Hitler from the rational to the irrational—but not without reason. What makes his trajectory in the Munich years so unusual is that Gerlich was an early, credulous supporter of the extreme nationalist politics Hitler represented.

Born to a staunchly Protestant family in 1883, six years before Hitler, Gerlich was something of an outsider when his family moved to heavily Catholic Bavaria. A naturally studious type, at university in Munich he began studying natural sciences but shifted to history, receiving a doctorate for a dissertation on an eleventh-century Germanic emperor. When his age and eyesight prevented him from serving in the German army during the war, Gerlich began a career in the state archives and sought an outlet for his nationalist fervor in patriotic newspapers. In the aftermath of the German defeat, he abandoned the archives for the front lines of polemical combat as editor of nationalist newspapers, rising quickly to become editor in chief of one of the most conservative Munich papers, the *Münchener Neueste Nachrichten*, in the early twenties.

By 1923, he'd become such a respected and influential figure in the nationalist movement that, in the spring of that year—as destructive inflation and strife over war reparations led to the French reoccupation of the Rhineland—Gerlich received a special visit in his apartment from the controversial rising star of the right-wing nationalist forces: Adolf Hitler. Something happened at that spring 1923 meeting between Gerlich and Hitler, something that, in conjunction with Hitler's actions six months later during the beer-hall putsch, turned Gerlich—who might have become an ally of Hitler—into a bitter, implacable, lifelong enemy.

The way I've been able to reconstruct it from fragmentary sources is that, for Gerlich, it became a matter of faith and faithlessness. What seems to have happened is that at some point in the run-up to the putsch, perhaps in that face-to-face meeting, Hitler gave his word of honor to Gerlich that, while he would support the national aspirations of Gerlich's man, the right-wing Bavarian prime minister Von Kahr, he would not resort to illegal, putschist methods to push his agenda. After that, however, Gerlich personally witnessed the beer-hall putsch at the Bürgerbräukeller and saw Hitler publicly place Von Kahr under arrest and extort an oath of support from him at gunpoint. Gerlich never forgave this betrayal. In his newspapers, he called it "one of the greatest betrayals in German history." Forever after, of the many epithets he hurled at the Nazis, among them "criminals" and "sexual degenerates," the one that was for Gerlich the first among all sins was *"oath breakers."* In pronouncing them oath breakers, it was as if he were a medieval pope casting their souls into eternal torment.

And eternally torment them he would. Gerlich and a close-knit group of colleagues, first at the *Münchener Neueste Nachrichten* and later at Gerlich's own breakaway anti-Hitler paper, *Der Gerade Weg*, became in the decade from the 1923 putsch until the 1933 Hitler takeover the most outspoken center of anti-Hitler journalism on the conservative side of the political spectrum.

The importance of the Gerlich group was brought home to me during a visit to Dachau where, in an exhibit devoted to the first months of the Hitler takeover in neighboring Munich, the Dachau Museum had blown up reproductions of Munich newspaper stories about the manhunt for the Gerlich-group members who'd escaped arrest in the raid on Gerlich's office in March 1933. They were hunted relentlessly because they had been genuinely dangerous. Some, like Gerlich, were murdered, some arrested; others, when released, went on to become the nucleus of the aristocratic anti-Hitler movement that culminated in Claus von Stauffenberg's failed assassination attempt in July 1944, after which they were all brutally executed.

But something strange happened to Gerlich and this little group in the late twenties: They forged a highly improbable alliance, one that became a source of the faith that fueled their courageous anti-Hitler campaign. Gerlich and his friends became deeply involved with a holy stigmatic—a highly controversial, probably fraudulent, yet widely worshiped Bavarian peasant woman.

Her name was Therese Neumann, and it still seems remarkable to me that a skeptical, Protestant, rationalist historian such as Gerlich, the no-nonsense newspaper editor with the gimlet eye behind the steel-rimmed glasses, would be taken in by this primitive, bedridden, Catholic mystic whose own church was skeptical, who claimed she lived for years on no food but Eucharist wafers, who produced great gouts of blood in the pattern of Christ's wounds on Good Fridays, claimed to have been transported back in time to the scene of the Crucifixion and to have received visitations on a regular basis from the Virgin Mary, who issued dire apocalyptic warnings about the dark fate that awaited contemporary Germany. But the strange affinity between the skeptical newspaper editor and the possessed or perhaps counterfeit stigmatic had its roots in the peculiar apocalyptic temper of the time.

The peasant girl who changed Fritz Gerlich's life began having visitations from Jesus and Mary about the same time Geli Raubal began getting visits from her Uncle Adolf. Therese Neumann was a twenty-seven-year-old farm girl living in Konnersreuth, north of Munich, when in 1925 she took to her bed, claiming to be paralyzed by mysterious spasms, spinal injuries, and—the story goes—the trauma she suffered when she tried and failed to rescue farm animals from a burning barn.

After a year of bedridden paralysis that mystified doctors, she suddenly began having visions: She went into an ecstatic trance and, when she awoke from it, claimed she'd been transported back to Jerusalem during the final twenty-four hours of Jesus' Passion. She'd seen him praying on the Mount of Olives; she'd witnessed the stations of the cross. He'd actually spoken to her from the cross even as he bled from the nails in his hands and his feet, and the spear through his side.

It was on Good Friday 1926 that a new element was added to these visions: stigmata. Blood suddenly appeared on the palms of *her* hands and the soles of her feet, and blood seemed to ooze from her side—bloody wounds imitating the pattern of Christ's wounds on the cross. With one idiosyncratic addition: blood seemed to ooze from her eyes as well.

Her local Catholic priest became convinced a true miracle, a visitation from the Savior, was occurring. Excitable priests and peasants spread the word. Soon, devout Catholics from all over came to her bedside to witness the stigmata that had begun to appear not just on Good Friday but *every* Friday. Along with the stigmata, her conversations with Jesus became more urgent: Some claimed she tried to *warn* Jesus of the bloody end he was facing, to help him escape the Crucifixion.

In return, Jesus and Mary would issue warnings through Neumann about the condition of Germany. It was this quasi-political dimension of her visions that began to attract sophisticated and otherwise skeptical visitors from Munich, some of whom were journalistic colleagues of Fritz Gerlich. They came to see the bloody wounds and came back with her bloody prophecies ringing in their ears, prophecies that captured the preapocalyptic mood of late Weimar Germany.

One of the visitors—an aristocratic Catholic conservative, Count Erwin von Aretin, who survived to become Gerlich's postwar biographer—became a believer. Von Aretin wrote a breathless two-part feature on the Konnersreuth stigmatic in August 1927 for Gerlich's *Münchener Neueste Nachrichten*— a series that created a nationwide, then international sensation over the peasant-girl visionary. Translated into thirty-two languages, it made the bed of the bedridden stigmatic the focus of an international cult of followers who fervently wanted to believe that at last God was trying to make his presence, his advice felt in the historical travail they were experiencing, choosing this innocent soul as a medium.

Finally, after repeated urgings from his colleagues, the skeptical Protestant Gerlich decided to pay a visit to the stigmatic. To the surprise of just about everyone, he came back deeply impressed. More than that; he returned, returned repeatedly, found himself drawn deeper and deeper into the peasant girl's circle, would transcribe her visionary utterances, and try to translate them into warnings and prophecies about the growing crisis in Germany.

In November 1927, he wrote his own enthusiastic account of the Konnersreuth phenomenon in his newspaper, which was surprising enough. But then, three months later, he shocked everyone by quitting his influential and prestigious position as editor of the *Nachrichten* and devoting himself for the next two years to writing a two-volume biography of the Bavarian stigmatic and her prophecies. He climaxed that period by formally converting to Catholicism in 1930.

At first I found myself puzzled by Gerlich's apparently wild swerve from engagement in the ongoing crisis of the German polity, the ongoing struggle against Bolshevism and Hitlerism he'd been so deeply committed to. My puzzlement grew deeper when I looked a little further into the actual nature of the stigmatic phenomena that had so mesmerized the hard-nosed newspaper-man Gerlich.

In his reverent biography of Therese Neumann, Dr. Johannes Steiner, Gerlich's colleague, portrays Gerlich first going to Konnersreuth "determined to unmask every fraud he encountered . . . if there were any to be found." Instead, "he was favored with a very special grace. He immediately recognized the events at Konnersreuth as unexplainable in the natural order of things and went back to Munich like a second Saint Paul."

Not in the natural order of things, *nicht natürlich*, yes, but in a very different sense from the sinister unnatural aura around Hitler. And yet other investigations of the phenomena suggest other explanations than the supernatural. Consider the fascinating 1949 report by an Oxford-educated Catholic writer, Hilda Graef, *The Case of Therese Neumann*. Aside from Neumann's local parish priest and bishops who became caught up in the worldwide celebrity of their parishioner, many Church authorities were resolutely skeptical about these "miraculous manifestations," and Graef exhumed some of the early investigations by physicians dispatched by the Church to look into the Konnersreuth claims.

What their reports and Graef's summation of the evidence amounts to—however indirectly and politely phrased (out of a tenderness of feeling for the genuinely reverent sentiment of the believers)—is that the little peasant girl was a complete fraud, a con artist. Her stigmata were produced, most probably, by concealing little vials of blood under her bedclothes and applying them to her stigmatic "wounds" surreptitiously or when her parents ushered visitors out during a "coughing fit" or with the excuse that the chronically bedridden Therese needed to relieve herself in a bedpan. When the visitors returned they found the charismatic peasant girl's visage suddenly smeared with blood; she'd dramatically throw off the bedcovers to display wounds on her hands, feet, and side that mimicked the pattern of the bloody holes in Christ's body.

To read the results of Graef's inquiry is to encounter a mystery more perplexing than the shabby conjurer's tricks used to perpetuate the illusion of stigmata: the mystery of how a hard-bitten, embattled newspaperman such as Gerlich could have been taken in by such an unsophisticated, homespun hoax. (It's a question not dissimilar to the one asked about Hitler: How could a sophisticated culture such as Germany fall for a shameless counterfeit such as Hitler?) There is a cynical explanation for Gerlich's conversion for those so inclined in Steiner's worshipful account of Gerlich's Saint Paul experience at Konnersreuth. "In Konnersreuth," Steiner writes, Gerlich

became acquainted with Prince Erich von Waldburg zu Zeil. He later discussed with him the foundation of a newspaper that would be independent of any control by financial powers, with himself as editor and the prince as financial backer. The prince was moved by Gerlich's words that "Hundreds of souls are hanging in the balance" . . . and in the course of the years 1930–1933 he [the prince] sacrificed some half million marks for the newspaper that they then published: "The Straight Way." The publishers were known as the "Natural Law Publishing House" because their chief program was an expression of the fight for recognition of human rights.

A cynic might rush to assert that Gerlich's "conversion" to belief in the peasant-girl stigmatic was a convenient way of ingratiating himself into the circle of wealthy aristocrats conned by her, a way of conning them (for a good cause) into financing his anti-Hitler paper. But I'm inclined to credit Steiner's depiction of the relation between Gerlich and the stigmatic prophet: "As publishing adviser" to *Der Gerade Weg*, Steiner says, he was

> once or twice directed by Gerlich to travel to Konnersreuth and ask Therese questions when she was in a state of ecstasy. . . . The answers that Therese gave in her state of ecstasy always renewed [Gerlich's] courage in his battle against National Socialism and also Bolshevism. There were never any definite orders. . . . But there were insights and hints that put him in a better position to hit upon the correct decisions himself. Words like, "Look, in the last analysis this [meaning Hitlerism and Bolshevism] is all directed against our Savior," were enough for him. . . . Clear statements of the justice of the stand he was taking.

Why, though, would a man such as Gerlich, who prided himself as a rationalist, scholar, and skeptic, need to have his courage sustained by such a suspect source of reassurance? Some further perspective on the nature of the relationship between the crusading anti-Hitler journalist, the local stigmatic, and the meaning of Hitler for Germans was provided in the course of my conversation with Walter Schaber, one of the last living survivors of the Weimar press wars.

"What you have to remember," he said, in his Washington Heights apartment as his wife served us coffee and cake, "what people forget about that time, is that everyone was searching for a *Heiland*."

"A Heiland?"

"Yes—healer, holy man. It was a time when you had healers, seers, prophets emerging all over the countryside. There were seers here, prophets there, all over." He spoke of a certain Louis Hausser, a former champagne maker who set himself up as a prophet and called upon Germans to do penance for their sins, to heal themselves, to avert apocalyptic retribution. He spoke of a Joseph Wiesenberg in Berlin. "He claimed to heal people by laying hard white cheese on them," and despite such dubious claims attracted a fanatic following of believers. "And then there was Hanussen the mystic and astrologer, who was in Munich with Hitler. They were all around, these people promising the messiah, all of them together created a mood from which Hitler could arise. An apocalyptic mood all over Germany."

He told me that he was only vaguely familiar with Therese Neumann but that she fit the pattern: "One Heiland after another, and after all the small Heilands came the big Heiland, Hitler."

"You're saying, then, that there was a pervasive appetite for *some* kind of apocalyptic figure, some kind of healer/messiah/savior, a longing that paved the way for them to accept Hitler, however strange and outlandish he seemed—in fact, *because* he was as strange as he was?"

Yes, Schaber said, the very things that led conventional politicians and statesmen to underestimate and dismiss Hitler as outlandish and unsuitable, a hopeless outsider—that nicht natürlich strangeness, that alienness—were the very things that constituted the subterranean power of his appeal. Hitler's other stigmata of strangeness, the apocalyptic fits, the trances, the occult, somnambulistic, mystic ravings, then—while they may have alienated some rational citizens—were perfectly attuned for the wider, deeper longing for a figure of higher irrationality, a Heiland, to rescue Germany. People who'd lost faith in conventional politics were looking for a political faith healer.

Something about this aspect of my conversation with Walter Schaber stayed with me for some time after I'd left Washington Heights. Something about the way he spoke of the longing for a Heiland led me to consider further the root in German of the word "Heiland," holy man, healer: *Heil*. To consider further the deeper purpose behind the ritualized incantation of "Heil Hitler," the all-purpose greeting, bond of solidarity, mass chant in the Hitler movement. To consider whether it might not have been designed deliberately to evoke the longing for a Heiland, for a healer, a holy man. Was that effect a deliberate creation, an example of Hitler's conscious genius for manipulating mass psychology, or a fortuitous reflection of the preexistent unconscious longing for a Heiland it tapped into—or both? Was there always a deeper level than mere salutation, mere hailing, in the incantation "Heil Hitler"? A sense in which the speaker, the chanter, was imploring, urging the Führer: *Heal Hitler*, Heal Us Hitler, Heal Germany, Hitler. Less a salutation than a prayer.

When I asked Schaber for his reaction, as someone who lived through the awful period when "Heil Hitler" grew from the tribute of misfit sociopathic sycophants of a barbaric crank to a massive roar of near-religious national assent, he was skeptical at first. It struck him as a novel idea, "Heil Hitler" as

"Heal, Hitler," but after considering it, he told me, "I think there may be something to it."

If the longing for a Heiland helps explain the perverse attraction of Hitler's strangeness, the way its very irrationality worked in his favor, might an analogue of that attraction help explain why Gerlich, the secular, rationalist doctor of history, found himself drawn to the irrational, supernatural pronouncements of a stigmatic peasant girl? Perhaps for someone like Gerlich—witness to the failure of reason, argument, and polemic to stop the rise of an evil Heiland such as Hitler—a figure such as Therese Neumann, a kind of anti-Hitler Heiland, might be both a counterforce and a comfort in a struggle that was causing him to doubt the efficacy of the weapons of rationality.

The irony of Therese Neumann is that even if she was a fraud, she was a fraud who helped galvanize a group of courageous men to risk their lives in opposition to Hitler, both before and after his takeover. Even after Gerlich's 1934 murder in Dachau, the Gerlich–Therese Neumann circle continued their sub rosa participation in the loose and ineffectual but nonetheless morally significant activities of the anti-Hitler opposition—until many of them were executed in 1944. The Gestapo made efforts to close down the circle, but Therese and her cult survived to flourish again after the Hitler defeat, even among American GIs of the occupation force.

It could be argued, then, on the basis of admittedly fragmentary evidence, that what made Gerlich and his group unique, what inspired the exceptional courage they exhibited, was the sense of a divine sanction, an apocalyptic role the prophecies of Therese Neumann gave them. One could even speculate that in Gerlich's mind there was a kind of relationship between Hitler and Therese Neumann: Although he was the demonic obverse of her, they *shared* certain characteristics. Both Therese Neumann and Hitler presented themselves as prophets who heard voices, voices which enjoined them to embark on divine missions (Hitler's bedridden vision at Pasewalk and Neumann's bedridden vision at Konnersreuth). Both exhibited their afflatus in ecstatic, histrionic trance-state fits of prophesying. Both were Heilands, and both were obsessed with blood. For Hitler, it was blood in the sense of the racial essence that was the true defining force in human destiny—blood as the sign and stigma of superiority and inferiority. For Therese Neumann, blood was the visible stigma of her invisible link to the holy family. It's easy to see how to Gerlich Therese Neumann could be seen as a kind of divinely sanctioned anti-Hitler. And how for Gerlich and Neumann, Hitler had become a kind of Antichrist.

The metaphoric blood relationship might go some way to explain Gerlich's reported preoccupation with the bloody fate of Geli Raubal. A young woman close to Therese Neumann's age, not an innocent, but still not much older than a schoolgirl. A woman whose bloody stigmata Gerlich apparently sought to trace to Hitler. And there is something haunting about that final image of

Gerlich, the one related to me by his colleague Dr. Steiner, about the way the Gestapo "sent to his widow, Sophie, Gerlich's spectacles, all spattered with blood": the way the final bloody stigmata of his vision of Hitler, the blood that burst from his eyes when the Gestapo beat him, morbidly mimics the stigmata of Therese Neumann when she had her Good Friday visions of the bloody spectacle of the Crucifixion.

But the mystical sources of Gerlich's vision of Hitler should not distract from the incisive surgical dissection of Hitler's mentality he left behind. Initially, I feared that his vision of Hitler had been lost with the lost Hitler exposé of 1933, but it's *there*, in his long-forgotten, brilliant, Swiftian summa, perhaps the most penetrating and insightful explanation of Hitler's racial pathology in the Weimar era, it's there in the vicious and hilarious 1932 satire, "Does Hitler Have Mongolian Blood?"

The more I read and think about it the more impressed I am, not just with its passion, but with its dispassionate analytic vision, the way it managed in mid-1932 to anticipate two of the most sophisticated postwar explanatory tendencies: the aesthetic and the Asiatic. All this in a mock-scholarly lampoon that offers a hilarious, deadpan set piece that might be called "The Trial of Hitler's Nose."

The tone Gerlich adopts in his prose is crucial. Assuming the mantle of scholarship and a pedantic tone that mimicked the magisterial German tradition of critical scholarship, he directs his readers' attention to the peculiar phenomenon he proposes to explicate: the picture of the Hitler-headed black bridal couple.

He did not create this outlandish photocomposite image himself, he assured us, I suspect disingenuously. Rather, it was sent to him by a reader who had noticed some compelling connection between two separate photographs—one of a snarling Hitler, the other of a grinning black bridal couple—in a recent issue of Gerlich's paper and had ingeniously combined them.

"The resultant composite perplexed me greatly," Gerlich avers with deadpan formality. Not because of any black and white disharmony, the photo miscegenation, but rather, surprisingly, because of what seemed to him an undeniable "inner harmony" between the bride and the Hitler-headed groom, between the noggin of the purported avatar of the master race and that of his Negro marital partner, representing a purportedly inferior race.

This unexpected "inner harmony" haunts him, Gerlich says; he finds himself driven to apply scientific techniques to search for its source. It's a quest he's particularly qualified for, he tells us, because in his university days he studied anthropology and ethnography. But before setting out on this scientific quest, he wishes, as the cautious, unprejudiced observer he is, to eliminate the possibility that the impression of inner harmony was the accidental result of that one particular Hitler pose.

So begins a hilarious and scathing inquest. Stage One of the trial of the nose consists of Gerlich's painstaking efforts to ensure that he has arraigned the right nose for analysis. The nose on the Hitler head in the Negro-wedding composite seems so "peculiar," so insistently non-Aryan, that, as a judicious-minded student of racial science, he wants to ensure that this impression is not a mere accident of camera angle in that one particular photo. And so, he says, he will turn for further comparative nosology to the array of Hitler nose images that appear in a then-famous book of photographs of Hitler called *The Hitler Nobody Knows*.

The sly subtext of this entire judicial inquest into Hitler's nose, of course, is an exercise in satiric metonymy, the figure of speech in which a part substitutes for the whole. The effort to understand, classify, and explain (ridicule) the anomaly of Hitler's nose is really the attempt to explain (ridicule) the anomaly of Hitler himself. Which is why his initial resort to *The Hitler Nobody Knows* is so apropos, because the book was central to Hitler's extremely shrewd, extremely well-controlled effort to manipulate his image—specifically, his physical appearance—to turn his notoriously non-Nordic-looking foreignness, his much-remarked-upon strangeness, into assets to his charisma.

It's often forgotten how closely Hitler guarded the dissemination of his physical image, particularly in the early stages of his career. Dramatic illustration of the degree to which obfuscation was practiced can be found in a rather remarkable sidebar to a story in a 1923 issue of *American Monthly*, a sidebar entitled "What Does Hitler Look Like?" It's remarkable because it was illustrated with an array of Hitlers: fat Hitlers, thin Hitlers, blond Hitlers, bald Hitlers, bearded Hitlers, *every* Hitler but the actual Hitler. The premise of the article—which was written in a disingenuously naïve tone and which seemed to be willingly complicit in Hitler's manipulative strategy—was to depict Hitler in the spirit of "that damned elusive Pimpernel." Mysterious, daring, a man of so many disguises (because he was so controversial and made so many enemies) that his baffled opponents could not decide on what Hitler looked like, much less what the dashing rogue was up to. And so the story quoted various alleged misleading descriptions of him in the German and the world press and then illustrated these conjectures: blond Hitler, fat Hitler, and so on.

And, in fact, while it's true Hitler exposed himself to public view in street rallies and beer-hall assemblies, places where perhaps he felt confident of the personal mind-clouding charisma, the power of *Führerkontakt*, to make his physical appearance irrelevant, he was *extremely* careful from the beginning to limit and control any photographic mass reproduction of his image. From the very earliest moments of his emergence, he strictly limited the number of people who could take his picture to exactly one: his trusted acolyte Heinrich Hoffmann. No outsiders, no insiders were allowed to photograph Hitler other than Hoffmann. And even Hoffmann was almost never permitted "candid" unrehearsed shots. As a recent museum exhibit of Hoffmann's outtakes demonstrates, Hitler carefully rehearsed, edited, studied, and crafted the few poses he would permit the world to see.

Even after the "What does Hitler look like?" period of deliberate obfuscation (ostensibly for security reasons), unauthorized photographs of Hitler, certainly unauthorized close-ups, were almost nonexistent, so much so that few have disputed Munich photojournalist Tim Gidal's contention that he took the *only* unauthorized candid shot of Hitler in existence.

The year was 1929, and Gidal, who went on to become a pioneering photojournalist for *Life*, was then the photographer for the *Munich Illustrated News*. I'd tracked Gidal down to a suburb in Jerusalem where, at ninety, he'd recently had a one-man show and a retrospective of his work published. We had a fruitful conversation about the world of anti-Hitler Munich journalists in the twenties—it was Gidal, in fact, who not only recalled Gerlich but alerted me to the existence of the Mongolian-blood attack on Hitler. Indeed, Gerlich had occasionally joined Gidal at his newspaper's *Stammtisch* at the Café Heck, a place also frequented by Hitler. And it was in the garden of the Café Heck that Gidal had taken his unique photo of Hitler unguarded. He showed me the photo; there is something not only unfamiliar but disturbing about it. It shows Hitler conferring with three stout figures at a garden table beneath a leafy shade tree. With their backs to us, it's hard to identify the others; one looks like a banker, two of them have tanklike military builds and brutal crew cuts. (The thick neck of one of them suggests it might be SA Commander Ernst Roehm.) Hitler gazes out, chin in hand, looking pensive, tentative, as if in the midst of crafting a thought, when he catches sight of Gidal and his camera, glances up with a dawning troubled awareness that he'd been *caught*. It's a troubling image. One is tempted to say that this rather than any image by Heinrich Hoffmann is "the Hitler Nobody Knows," the Hitler no one is permitted to see. It's disturbing because that tentative, half-formed quality of surprise and curiosity on Hitler's face makes him look more "human" than we are comfortable with. The pictures Hitler authorized Hoffmann to release almost all tended to project what Hanfstaengl called Hitler's "Napoleonic" mode, which gave him an air (at least in retrospect) of somewhat ridiculous martial pretentiousness. Gidal's picture reaffirms that Hitler is most frightening now when he seems in any way human, tentative, seems even slightly *like one of us*. Which in Gidal's stolen Café Heck shot he does.

Perhaps that was the calculation behind the release of *The Hitler Nobody Knows*. At a certain point in the early thirties when Hitler had emerged from post-putsch disgrace and ridicule to become a major figure in German politics, the calculus of image control changed. The aura of mystery that worked for him was threatened by the rumors of alienness, of a nicht natürlich persona that undermined his newly prominent public role. A decision was made to permit a kind of authorized candor, photos of officially licensed informality to demonstrate there was nothing abnormal about the man. And so *The Hitler Nobody Knows* showed him engaged in "normal" gemütlichkeit pursuits, friendly interchanges with fellow citizens, relaxing in casual Bavarian (as opposed to militaristic) garb. The title—*The Hitler Nobody Knows*—played upon the air of mystery, seeming to promise disclosure of secrets, to reveal a Hitler that Hitler didn't want revealed. When, in fact, it was an authorized unauthorized Hitler, carefully calculated to "disclose" the secret that there was no (shameful) secret.

While release of more photographic images would inevitably make people more aware of how short he fell of the Nordic racial ideal he was espousing so furiously, by that time he'd created such an aura of mystery about himself that the revelation of a non-Nordic physiognomy had less impact than the revelation that Hitler was otherwise relatively "normal" looking, that he engaged in normal-seeming German activities.

Gerlich is pressing upon the sensitivity with which the Hitler image had been managed in his arch reference to the supposedly "real" Hitler revealed in the Hoffmann book. But Gerlich solemnly pretends to take seriously the claim of *The Hitler Nobody Knows* to depict the unguarded truth because he has his own satiric agenda. He turns Hoffmann's book into a treatise on "The Nose Nobody Knows" and submits to the jury four smiling images of Hitler from the Hoffmann book.

"Here, then," he says, "we find a series of photographs that differ significantly" from the snarling image of Hitler's head atop the body of the Negro groom. Different poses, yes, he points out, but the same "peculiar nose," which proves that the one in his bridal composite was not an accident of camera angle but "his real nose."

Now that the authenticity of the specimen has been verified, Gerlich, the inquiring scientist, brings in a fellow scientist to consult on its peculiarities: "We now present two illustrations of persons with Nordic noses, from *Racial Characteristics of the German People* by Dr. Hans F. Günther, who, as is well known, has been named professor of racial research at the University of Jena by the Thuringian National Socialist Minister Frick."

Frick was famous then for being the first Nazi to become a cabinet minister in one of the states that made up the Weimar Republic. Günther was in the forefront of the "racial scientists" who purported to give academic coloration to Nazi racism, an avatar of the discredited quackery of nineteenth-century racial theorists Hitler admired, such as Houston Stewart Chamberlain. Günther then will be Gerlich's "expert witness" in the trial of Hitler's nose.

"The racial research of these scientists," Gerlich gravely tells us, "informs us that the nose of a Nordic Aryan human being has a small bridge and a small base." He then submits to the court "two illustrations of persons with Nordic noses," two photographs of Aryan individuals with their small-bridged, small-based noses.

Triumphantly, he invites us to compare the Hitler noses with the Nordic noses, helpfully pointing out that "the noses of the Ostic [Eastern] and Mongolian type are based widely, have flat bridges and, in general, have a little break in their bridge that puts the end of the nose a little bit forward and higher." Hitler's nose, he needn't add, fits the latter description—a description by Hitler's own racial theorists of Oriental noses—far better than it fits the description of the more delicate bridges and bases of the Nordic nose.

Relentlessly, Gerlich presses his case. Look again at Hitler's nose, he urges the reader. Notice the resemblance to one of Günther's examples of the Slavonic or Bohemian-type nose. The Slavic type, he points out, "was formed by the intermingling after the Hun invasion of Mongols with original Slav bloodstock."

Now Gerlich's off to the races, taking wicked delight in rubbing his readers' noses in the ugly truth about Hitler's nose. What follows is a detailed demonstration, in the quack rhetoric of Hitler's own racial scientist, that Hitler's nose is not only at best Slavonic rather than Nordic, but Slavonic in a very special way: Slavonic in a way that reflects the Mongolian invasions of Europe by Attila the Hun's hordes. Hitler's nose, then, is not even compatible with pure, albeit "inferior," Slav stock, but with the mongrel, mixed-blood Slav types who are the bastard offspring of the rape of Slav women by invading Mongol horsemen.

"The war-strategy of those times," Gerlich the mock pedant writes, "made it customary for the victorious armies to have sex with the women and girls of the defeated peoples. . . . We have to suppose that in the home region of Hitler's family foreign, no Nordic blood remained."

Helpfully, Gerlich reminds us that his sustained attention to the minutiae of nose forms is justifiable because, "according to the racial science of Günther" and thus Hitler himself, the nose is the "most important symptom of the racial descent of a person." And so, yes, the nose stands for the man, metonymically and racially, but one also has to wonder if there is not a kind of sly comic displacement going on here as well in which—as it does in *Tristram Shandy*'s long mock-scientific disquisition on the differences between long- and short-nosed people—there is some salacious displacement of one body part for another. In the same way, one wonders if in Gerlich's "scholarly" attribution of Mongolian blood to Hitler there is also a kind of displacement going on—a subtextual allusion to Hitler's more widely rumored "Jewish blood."

But overtly at least, Gerlich has a different kind of displacement in mind:

the shift from the question of whether Hitler has a Nordic nose to the one of whether he has a Nordic soul. The nose analysis is mainly malicious fun (although it anticipates an important strain of Hitler-explanation theory, the one that focuses on the aesthetic-eugenic origins of racial anti-Semitism). But Gerlich's inquest into the question of whether Hitler has a Nordic soul is deadly serious.

He begins by citing the other avatar of Nazi racial science, Alfred Rosenberg, who decreed that the worldview (Weltanschauung) of an individual is a consequence of his race and blood. Gerlich then proceeds to work backward to examine the Hitlerian worldview to determine just what racial-blood composition gave birth to it. It should be emphasized that, in pursuing this line, Gerlich is not accepting the validity of Rosenberg's race-based theory any more than he's accepting Günther's nose-based classification system; rather, he's using these crackpot theories to hoist Hitler by his own petard.

What Gerlich does first is define what he believes to be the true, primal meaning of the Germanic soul—or at least what he somewhat wishfully defines as the German soul: "We are in the fortunate position through having the law books of the old Germans available of knowing exactly their conceptions, which have long since been expressed in the phrase 'Germanic common liberties.'"

He expands upon the concept of these liberties by observing that it is the characteristic of the true old Germans that "they didn't even give total obedience to their own leader or king. And, in fact, in times of peace, the king actually is the servant of the wishes of the people." He cites the words of the racial-science quack Günther on the nature of ancient Aryan-Germanic freedom: "To be free means for the German or Nordic individual living according to his own individual judgment; [he displays] a passion for intellectual liberty and his own independent belief . . . a bluff independence" that led to Germany becoming a stronghold of Protestantism in Catholic Europe.

This Germanic conception of the relationship between leader and people is, Gerlich then slyly asserts, "the absolute opposite of the Asiatic-despotic conception. Even in times of war, the Germanic duke didn't have the power of life or death but is still completely indebted to the will of the people. He never has a role comparable to the one of the Asiatic-despotic emperor—or in the terminology of today, the dictator."

Who could he be thinking of? Who fits the definition of the "Asiatic-despotic" soul, the one that stands in sharp contrast to the true Germanic one?

"Adolf Hitler," he says, "explains that in his political movement there is only *one* will and that's his. . . . He never has to explain what he does . . . his followers have to carry out his commands without any information. . . . *The contrast between the real Nordic ideal and the one of Hitler cannot be expressed any more dramatically. Hitler's attitude is absolutely un-Nordic and un-Germanic. It is, racially, pure Mongolian"* (emphasis added).

It should come as no surprise that in the capstone of Gerlich's parody of racial science, Hitler has a Mongolian weltanschauung; after all, he has a Mongolian nose, Mongolian blood, and the great theorist Rosenberg himself has proclaimed that the soul is a "consequence" of the blood. Hitler's Mongolian attitude is "prefigured by the great Mongolian leaders Genghis Khan and Tamerlane," Gerlich argues in a more serious vein. "It is Mongolian absolute despotism that is expressed in Hitler's attitude and that can be explained by the fact that this man is a typical bastard who has mainly non-Nordic blood in his veins." Framing his conclusion in the creepy blood rhetoric of the newly hatched vampire-horror-film genre, he declares: "With Adolf Hitler, the Mongolian blood that has migrated here for two thousand years is making an effort to take over the power of the state and the people."

The Nazi movement itself betrays its "mongolian essence," Gerlich declares, in its "Asiatic" idol worship of its leader. And, finally, he directs the reader's attention to a portrait of Stalin he reproduces in the text following the comparative-nose photos. Stalin, Hitler's Bolshevik Antichrist, nonetheless, Gerlich says, shares with Hitler both Asiatic features and an Asiatic soul, ruling Russia as a Khan-like despot. Hitler has more in common with his Marxist archenemy physically—and philosophically in his worldview—than with true Germanic ideals, Gerlich concludes.

In using this satiric conceit to redefine Hitler, in using Hitler's ridiculous "racial science" to prove Hitler was not Aryan but Mongolian in blood and weltanschauung, Gerlich risks being misinterpreted as somehow *endorsing* the hierarchy of values of the "racial scientists" and merely placing Hitler lower on the racial hierarchy than Hitler would place himself. In fact, of course, Gerlich's endorsing a very different hierarchy of values—one that places liberty, autonomy, and independent thought above all else—beliefs that could be held by anybody of any race regardless of "blood"—and is trying to redefine the Germanic ideal as *that* ideal, not some pathetic nonsense about nose shape.

And in a follow-up article in the next week's issue of *Der Gerade Weg*, he makes his antiracialist stance explicit. In it, he discusses the violent reaction to the Mongolian-blood issue. Nazi thugs stoned his apartment building, and some Hitler-sympathizing readers expressed particular outrage at the pairing of Hitler and the Negro bride.

"We can't," Gerlich replies, speaking for his paper's Catholic editors,

> understand how people who call themselves righteous Catholics could feel upset by the juxtaposition of Hitler and a Negro woman. What exactly bothers you, dear ladies and gentlemen? Didn't you

learn, in the first principles of our religion's catechism, not only that
all men have their souls bestowed on them by God but also that we
are all descendants of one father and one mother, children of Adam
and Eve? According to our own Catholic principles, Negroes are our
brothers and sisters *even by blood*? It is totally impossible for those of us
with Catholic worldviews to "degrade" a Central European like Adolf
Hitler by pairing him with a Negro woman. A Negro woman isn't a
person of inferior race. . . . We regard a Negro woman as our sister in
blood [emphasis added].

It is acerbic, arch, acidulous, designed to further offend Hitler sympathizers by demanding they admit that their religious principles require them to
hold Hitler on the same level as a woman they, in their racist mind-set, believe
inferior—thus pitting their religion against their racism. It could just be a rhetorical tactic, this assertion of the spiritual (and blood) kinship of blacks and
Germans. But I can't help sensing that on Gerlich's part there is something
that rings true and seems heartfelt: A genuine, not rhetorical, religious belief
in true human brotherhood and the irrelevance of race lies beneath his contempt for Hitler and his "racial science."

But there's something else impressive, even prophetic about Gerlich's
Mongolian-blood conceit. For some time after I'd uncovered Gerlich's Mongolian-
blood satire, I'd assumed the Mongolian aspect of it was more than anything
an arbitrary conceit, that he had chosen it for its outré alienness, for the displaced suggestion, in its orientalism, of the far more commonly rumored
Jewish blood.

But then I came across, in historian Richard Breitman's study of the
Himmler-Hitler relationship (*The Architect of Genocide*), some startling indications that Gerlich's Mongolian conception of Hitler's mentality was far more
prescient than I'd imagined. As it turns out, in the mind-set that produced
the Final Solution, the specter of Genghis Khan and the murderous Mongol
hordes were highly charged figures.

Breitman calls attention to the 1934 publication in Germany of a two-
volume biography of Genghis Khan, *Genghis Khan: Storm out of Asia* and *The
Legacy of Genghis Khan*. Both books were taken up by Himmler, who ordered
up a special one-volume edition of them for the SS. The Russian émigré author
of the works described the Khan's progression in murderous brutality from
the execution of enemy leadership to the extermination of entire populations.
He emphasized the Khan's clinical, unemotional approach to the necessity of
mass murder. He exterminated cities "as we destroy rats when we regard them
as noxious." The author saw the Khan as an exponent of the racial superiority
of his Mongol warriors, as a conscious eugenicist who "improved" his horde's

genes by mating them with the strongest and most beautiful of the captive women.

Himmler, Breitman reports, even came to believe that the Khan's Mongols were not garden-variety Asiatics but descendants of émigrés from ancient Atlantis who may have been the forebears of Aryan Germans. While there is no decisive evidence on whether Hitler read this particular work as well, Breitman believes that at the very least he received a distillation of it from Himmler. And evidence exists that the Khan's Mongolians were in the forefront of Hitler's meditations about mass murder.

In fact, the Khan and the Mongols are at the heart of a famous "secret speech" Hitler gave to SS troops shortly before he launched the invasion of Poland in August 1939, the invasion that would, for the first time, place millions of Jews in his hands. Here is what Hitler said:

> Our strength is in our quickness and our brutality. Genghis Khan had millions of women and children killed by his own will and with a gay heart. History sees in him only a great state builder. Thus, for the time being, I have sent to the east only my Death's Head units with orders to kill without pity or mercy all men, women, and children of Polish race or lineage. Only in such a way will we win the vital space that we need. Who still talks in our day of the extermination of the Armenians?

I'd previously seen this speech referred to, but only the Armenian reference excerpted. I hadn't realized that the context for this chilling assertion of forgetfulness as assurance of genocidal success was an invocation of Genghis Khan and Mongolian bloodshed. The Mongolian reference goes further than the Armenian: mass murder is not merely forgotten (as in the case of the Armenians) but becomes (in the case of the Khan) the foundation for an exalted reputation as "a state builder." Hitler was then invoking Genghis Khan as a role model for the successful, triumphal mass murderer, the ur-precedent for genocide, the model he commended to the troops who would carry it out. Suddenly, Gerlich's vision of Hitler's "Mongolian soul" (which also invoked Genghis Khan as a progenitor) seems more than a mere satiric conceit but a powerfully intuitive insight into Hitler's mind and soul.

Breitman argues that Himmler and Hitler adapted a special genocidal technique from what they construed as the practice of the Mongol Khan: the creation of "blood cement," the solidarity that comradely complicity in mass killing brought to those who got blood on their hands. Increasingly, studies of the question of Hitler's role in the Final Solution emphasize the way he and Himmler relentlessly drew an entire upper layer of the SS leadership into active complicity with the genocide—reinforced their participation and their silence—with such blood cement and guilty knowledge, when abstract ideological enthusiasm alone might not be enough.

But Breitman's study of the Hitler-Himmler conception of the extermination suggests that the highly charged resonance of the Mongolian model served two superficially contradictory purposes in the minds of the murderers. Not only did Hitler and Himmler identify themselves with the Mongol killers, they also excused themselves, justified, legitimized wholesale murder by identifying their *enemies* with Mongol mass murderers.

Himmler was particularly fond of describing the Soviet foe as "Asiatic." In a 1942 speech to SS troops, Himmler spoke of an ideological battle and a struggle to the death between Aryan Germans and Soviets whose "physique" is so mongrel-like "one can shoot them down without pity and compassion.... When you fight you are carrying out the same struggle against the same subhuman, the same inferior races that at one time appeared under the name of Huns and still another time under the name of Genghis Khan and his Mongols. Today they appear as Russians under the political banner of Bolshevism."

If Hitler and Himmler did not have actual Mongolian blood, they were in one way or the other mesmerized by Mongolian bloodshed. They identified with the Mongol aggressors *and* with the victims of Mongol aggression; they sought to find the Khan within and to fight the Khan without. They became Mongols in order to exterminate the Mongols.

What's even more remarkable is the continuing potency, even today, of the Mongol/Asiatic signifier first adumbrated by Gerlich. It was taken up three decades after Hitler's death by the neonationalist historians of the German *Historikerstreit*—the battle of the historians over reconceptualizing Hitler and Germany's guilt over the war and the Holocaust. It was the historian Ernst Nolte who first introduced the "Asiatic" rationale for "normalizing" German history. The Hitler slaughter must be looked at not in isolation as an unprecedented act of evil, Nolte argued, but as a response to the "Asiatic" methods of Stalinism that exhibited themselves, long before Hitler began shedding blood, in Stalin's extermination of the kulaks, in the mass killings of the purges in the thirties, all of which, in Nolte's view, were precedents if not exactly excuses for the Hitler mass murder. Once again, the Asiatic/Mongol specter of Stalin as Khan is invoked to excuse Asiatic methods adapted by Germans in response to the "Mongol" threat.

The Hitler-Genghis Khan comparison continues to be a highly charged one, serving as a kind of Rorschach-test image upon which conflicting visions of Hitler are projected. Consider two recent instances. In January 1996, a member of the Iranian Parliament, incensed by a recently disclosed U.S. plan for covert operations, denounced the United States as "a renegade government whose logic was no different from Genghis Khan or Hitler." While in the very same week, in an article on waning Jewish identity, the director of the Anti-Defamation League, Abraham Foxman, was quoted saying, "to the next generation, Hitler might as well be Genghis Khan."

In the former instance, Hitler is linked to the Khan; in the latter, he is distinguished from him. In the former, the linkage has the effect of "historicizing" Hitler, of making him one of a company of barbaric rulers, rather than a uniquely murderous creature. To liken Hitler to Genghis Khan before the war, before the Holocaust, before he even took power, as Gerlich did, was to take a figure with few murders to his credit and prophetically assert his true kinship with one of the greatest murderers in all history up till then. But to link Hitler to Genghis Khan *after* the war, after the Holocaust, Foxman is saying, is a conscious choice to diminish and distance him. To diminish him by historicizing him, making him just another bloody ruler, as opposed to the *novum*, the new thing many post-Holocaust philosophers insist on defining him as. Particularly in the case of the German historians, it is a way of distancing him from German culture by defining him as some orientalized Other, attributing his unprecedented murderousness to an oriental precedent, to an Asiatic rather than German element in his thought if not his blood.

Fritz Gerlich was employing the Mongol metaphor to try to change the minds of Germans about Hitler, to save their souls by redefining the Germanic soul. The postwar German historians who sought to relativize Hitler were using the Asiatic rhetoric not so much to change the mind of Germany as to change its *image*.

If Gerlich was, as it turned out, unsuccessful in changing enough minds, he was nonetheless more successful than almost any other Weimar-era explainer in capturing the nature and complexity of Hitler's mind. In giving us his own far more revealing vision of "the Hitler nobody knows," in giving us the Hitler with the Mongolian nose, he was the first to explore a dynamic that has come to preoccupy many postwar explainers: Hitler's racial hatred as a manifestation of displaced self-hatred: the argument that the disparity between Hitler's metaphysical idealization of Nordic nature and his own non-Nordic physical appearance was more than a matter of mere irony but somehow a motive force in Hitler's psyche, the secret engine of his hatred in a poisonous dynamic in which he projected upon the external non-Nordic polar opposite (the Jew) the hatred he felt for the non-Nordic Other he knew or feared himself to be.

Gerlich stops short of asserting that Hitler was conscious of the disparity between himself and the Nordic ideal; it's almost as if he wants to *make* Hitler conscious of it, however, to rub Hitler's nose in nose typology, hold up the mirror of his own racial science in which Hitler would have to see his true self. Gerlich desperately wants to force Hitler to realize that he must reject the "science" or himself—that each is the refutation of the other. Gerlich's brilliant analysis raises an unanswerable but provocative question about Hitler's thought-world: Beneath the subterfuge and media manipulation of What Does Hitler Look Like and The Hitler Nobody Knows, how conscious *was* Hitler of the disparity between his own features and his racial ideal—and how did he rationalize it? Did he become a murderer to exterminate the sense of the Other he feared he was?

Gerlich's is one of the first in what would become a persistent tradition in the subsequent debate over the origin and nature of Hitler's hatred, one that tends to suggest a complex dynamic Hitler was unaware of, or at the very least couldn't *face*—it was literally self-refuting. But the magnitude of Hitler's hatred does not necessarily require a corresponding magnitude of complexity, a highly complicated psychogenesis. It is also possible to suppose that such a murderous hatred might have a primal, obdurate primitive quality not easily analyzed or sourced but no less virulent.

CHAPTER 10

The Shadow Hitler, His "Primitive Hatred," and the "Strange Bond"

In which the author explores his own lost safe-deposit box

Before conceding defeat in my effort to resolve definitively the riddle of Geli Raubal's death, there was one more carton of documents I felt I had to get to the bottom of: a carton I'd come to think of as my own personal lost safe-deposit box—one I began to realize served a similar function for me as those folkloric safe-deposit boxes in Switzerland that were said to have held (or still hold) crucial lost documents that might somehow explain what was otherwise inexplicable about Hitler: the Pasewalk case notes, the Fritz Gerlich exposé, the Austrian secret-police dossier on Hitler's ancestry. Documents that embodied the very inaccessibility of Hitler's inwardness that they purported to explain—because we've lost the account number, the key to unlock *their* inwardness.

The carton reposing so long in a corner of my office was not strictly speaking inaccessible. Far from it, it was, rather, one whose depths I had been strangely reluctant to plumb to the very bottom, blocked, I suppose I should say, for nearly three years for reasons that were for some time obscure to me. The contents of the carton were a thousand or so pages of printouts from microfilms I'd obtained from the National Archives, microfilm copies of the raw

179

files of what's known as the "OSS Sourcebook" on Adolf Hitler, what I'd come
to think of as the lost safe-deposit box of the Shadow Hitler realm.

The Shadow Hitler. I take the term from Thomas Powers, from his book
Heisenberg's War—an attempt to find the locus of Werner Heisenberg's inwardness, to divine from ambiguous clues just what the brilliant German physicist's
intentions were in his role as director of Hitler's atomic-bomb development
program. (Did he deliberately stall it or dutifully, if unsuccessfully, advance it?)
Powers evokes the subterranean world of rumor, myth, and speculation about
Heisenberg's intentions, the cloud of uncertainty that cloaked the truth about
the position of the author of the Uncertainty Principle. A nimbus of doubt
that nonetheless was, or became, a fact of history, because the Allies had to
make decisions about those inaccessible intentions—decisions such as the one
to send an agent to attempt to assassinate Heisenberg.

If we want to know the truth, Powers writes in a chapter entitled "What
Happened?" at the close of his five-hundred-page investigation, "if we want
to know what Heisenberg actually thought about the bomb at the time, *we
must turn to the shadow history of the war*—what he and his friends said to each
other in the small hours of the night, as recorded in memoirs, private letters,
diaries, remembered conversations and the files of intelligence services" (emphasis added).

The shadow history of the war: Powers's definition of the nimbus of
shadow surrounding Heisenberg can be extended to a similar Cloud of Un-
knowing, a cloud of fact, fiction, and contradiction that surrounded the elusive figure of Adolf Hitler and the inaccessible truths about his inwardness.
The Shadow Hitler was embodied in fragmentary rumors, second- and thirdhand hearsay, whispered speculations and slander, questionable documents,
counterfeit anecdotes, the fevered imaginings of suspect sources.

But unlike the Shadow Heisenberg Powers had to painstakingly re-create
from recovered fragments, in the case of the Shadow Hitler we are fortunate
(and in some ways unfortunate) to have what amounts to a historic snapshot,
an X ray, or, if you prefer, a frozen fossil record of the Shadow Hitler at a certain crucial moment: a raw file that culled and sampled the visible evidence
of the Shadow Hitler, both fact and apocrypha, as it existed in 1943, drawing
on sources that ranged from intelligence reports and confidential diplomatic
memoranda to the debriefing of a suspect Austrian "princess" in a Texas detention camp. One that includes documents exfiltrated from Germany (such
as the report by Hitler's parole officer in 1924, warning against his early release for fear of his inevitable return to rabble-rousing politics) and transcripts
of cozy chats in wartime Hollywood with émigré directors who recalled tales
told by Berlin actresses about nights in the Reichschancellery with Hitler. All
collected and preserved in unevaluated and apparently indiscriminate order

under top-secret seal until the late 1960s on spools of microfilm in the OSS section of the National Archives in the "Hitler Sourcebook" file.

The Sourcebook should not be confused with the more widely known, book-length analysis, *The Mind of Adolf Hitler*, the one psychoanalyst Walter Langer prepared, largely based upon the Sourcebook materials, the Shadow Hitler universe. Although both figure and ground, so to speak, have been declassified, only the Langer book has been published. Some who have written about the Langer analysis have assumed that Langer's work is a distillation of the Sourcebook, but in fact it's rather a distortion of it, in that Langer has reduced all ambiguity, collapsed all contradiction in order to lash the numinous Shadow Hitler to a Procrustean couch of Freudian significance. While indicating only mild awareness of the dangers of trusting his sometimes dicey sources, Langer falls headlong for the two great temptations of Hitler explainers: the alleged "undinism" perversion story and the alleged Jewish grandfather/Jewish blood legend. But Langer neither exhausts nor reflects accurately the more protean shape-shifting of the Shadow Hitler in the Sourcebook.

Physically, the Sourcebook is *very* raw material. When I had the microfilm spools (which I purchased from the National Archives) printed out, the result was a thousand-page-plus file of poorly typed extracts from blurry photostats of documents that vary widely in source and value. The indiscriminate and haphazard catchall quality of the Sourcebook is captured by this excerpt from the somewhat casual index, under the heading of WOMEN: Hitler

> ... relation to
> ... not attracted by
> ... abstinence
> ... immune to human weakness
> ... no proof Hitler ever slept with one
> ... accused of excessive intercourse.

That last index couplet—"no proof Hitler ever slept with one" followed by "accused of excessive intercourse"—fairly well sums up the state of unresolvedness characteristic of the Shadow Hitler, an unresolvedness that persists today.

There are many reports, rumors, and speculations about Geli Raubal in the Sourcebook, of course. So familiar did she become to the OSS analysts compiling the index for the Sourcebook that they rather casually list her alphabetically under G for "Geli" rather than by last name as Hitler's other rumored paramours are.

The microfilm printouts were fascinating to read though difficult to trust, and at a certain point—about 650 pages into the thousand or so total—I found I had to stop. Cumulatively, the experience of reading the Sourcebook was to pile Pelion on Ossa, rumor upon speculation upon hearsay, leaving one, if anything, less certain about *any* assertion about Hitler, because for any assertion ("no proof Hitler ever slept with one") there was likely to be an equal and opposite contradictory speculation ("excessive intercourse"). One can still find in much of the current Hitler literature second-, third-, and fourth-generation traces of anecdotal adumbrations that had their origins in the Shadow Hitler, a kind of evidentiary game of Telephone played with historical reality.

But there was another reason, I believe, I'd been putting off getting to the bottom of the box. A variation on the lost-safe-deposit-box syndrome that has haunted the search for Hitler: the temptation to believe that Hitler could be explained if only we could get our hands on some lost or locked-away cache of documents, the location of or key to which is forever beyond our reach. It's a vision that, while despairing on the surface, represents, I'd come to believe, in folkloric form, a kind of epistemological optimism: Hitler at least *might* have been explicable at one time if we had that lost document, that missing piece of the puzzle now just beyond our reach.

My reluctance to reach to the bottom of that carton of OSS microfilm printouts could be attributed to the same dynamic: By refraining from reaching the bottom, some primitive prerational part of me could preserve the illusion that there might still be some previously overlooked clue, some fragmentary piece of testimony in there whose potential significance had gone unnoticed by others, some observation, conversation, some intimation that might make sense of the Geli Raubal riddle—the answer to the questions that surround the circumstances of Geli Raubal's death—or to the larger questions that surround the nature of Adolf Hitler's life. On some level, I think I knew that by actually plunging into the unread material, that illusion would probably be dispelled, and I might be compelled to confront an even more chilling inexplicability.

But, finally, I knew I'd have to complete that task. And so, I retrieved those 350 pages and began dutifully searching through them.

There was, in fact, some Geli Raubal material I hadn't seen before. For one thing, there was another nominee for the role of spectral seducer, the shadowy fiancé boyfriend or putative impregnator of Geli, a figure said to be the source of Hitler's final fatal jealous quarrel with her. In most other accounts, the man who purportedly cuckolded Hitler tends to be an unnamed "drawing master from Linz," a "Jewish music teacher from Vienna," a Viennese voice coach, or a "Jewish art student." Here, however, for the first time I'm aware of in the literature we are given a name: Emil Baumann, described as "a Munich student who'd become Geli's fiancé until Hitler heard about it and broke up the relationship." And broke up her plans to run away with him—at least according to the fairly suspect-sounding tabloid-tinged 1940 book by one Felix Gross entitled *Hitler's Guns, Girls and Gangsters*, which the OSS analyst duly (and heavily) excerpts. Gross, of course, cites the usual suspect sources like Otto Strasser, and further appends the chilling (if true) detail that the "mutilated body" of the hapless Baumann was found dumped in the street, dead, just days after Hitler's 1933 accession to the chancellorship.

Another fairly useless rumor, it appeared. If you believed everything in the OSS Sourcebook, Geli Raubal's time was so ceaselessly engaged in *getting* engaged, in planning elopements with multiple partners in Vienna and Munich, she could not have had a moment to spare to participate in the fairly time-consuming perversion she was also supposed to be engaged in after-hours with Adolf Hitler.

But there was, of course, far more in the Sourcebook than Geli Raubal rumors. Much seemed unreliable on its face, but there were certain items that had acquired a kind of semilegendary stature in the life of Shadow Hitler intrigues. And so it was fascinating to see that some were quite real. There was, for instance, a copy of the extremely curious article that appeared in Hearst's New York *American* on November 30, 1930, entitled simply "Adolf Hitler" and bylined "Alois Hitler." It's the manifest visible product of the Hitler family film noir, the product of the collaboration of Adolf Hitler and his half-brother Alois, who manufactured a distancing, counterfeit cover story about their relationship for the Hearst press.

It's an article the black-sheep nephew William Patrick Hitler had initially tried to peddle to Hearst before Hitler summoned him to Munich and demanded that he deny any blood relationship with his Uncle Adolf, demanded he even tell Hearst that he (the nephew) had mistakenly fingered the "wrong Hitler" for his relative.

Once William Patrick was bought off—at least for a while—Alois Jr., the half brother of Adolf and father of William Patrick, was rushed into the breach to give Hearst *something*. What I hadn't realized until I dug the clipping out of my carton was that Alois had further collaborated with Adolf in subtly but deftly downplaying their blood relationship.

Buried in the apparently innocuous prose of Alois's loving evocation of Adolf's rise from poverty in Vienna to popularity in German politics is the false assertion Alois makes that he is "the son of a cousin of Adolf's father," when in fact he is the son of Adolf's father himself (by an earlier wife). Seeing the petty counterfeit in print was fascinating, the slippery small-time-crook aspect of Hitler at its most deviously detail oriented.

What struck me more forcefully, however, were two longer documents deeper down in the carton: the OSS analyst's memorandum of a debriefing session with a suspect adventuress who called herself Princess Stephanie von Hohenlohe, and extracts from the memoirs of an American correspondent in Berlin for United Press, one Frederick Oechsner. The anecdotes therein ranged from the trivial (Hitler's alleged nose job) to the potentially profound (the "strange bond" of intimacy that may help explain the nature of Hitler's "primitive hatred").

Consider first certain moments in the six-page single-spaced OSS "Interview with Princess Stephanie von Hohenlohe, June 28, 1943, at Alien Detention Camp Seagoville, Texas." Although she comes across in her own account as a figure out of a fictional spy adventure, Princess Stephanie was, in fact, a figure of very real interest to American intelligence agencies in the three years before her detention. FBI and army intelligence files reflect heavy surveillance of her activities in the United States. J. Edgar Hoover himself was convinced, not without reason and evidence, that she and her paramour, Captain Fritz Wiedemann, the German consul in San Francisco, were high-level operatives of Nazi intelligence detailed to America to make contact with influential Hitler sympathizers among the American elite who were conspiring to keep the United States out of the war in Europe.

Princess Stephanie appears to have been born a half-Jewish woman named Richter who insinuated herself first into the Austrian princely house of Hohenlohe, then into the grace and favor of British press baron Lord Rothermere. It was as his personal representative to Hitler's court that she managed to become intimate with certain figures very close to Hitler—most particularly with a very significant figure in Hitler's life, Captain Wiedemann. And, according to several observers within that court, with Hitler himself.

Wiedemann had been close to Hitler longer than almost anyone else in Germany—as far back as 1914, in fact, when Hitler was then a twenty-five-year-old immigrant from Austria who'd enlisted in the German army as soon as the war broke out. Wiedemann was Private Hitler's superior in the List regiment and apparently took a liking to the somewhat strange soldier with the Austrian accent and the air of a bohemian artist. Hitler, in turn, became attached to Wiedemann, according to fellow soldiers.

In 1934, shortly after Hitler's accession to power, he summoned Wiedemann to Berlin to serve as his personal adjutant. As such, he became part of the gossipy inner circle of Hitler aides and intimates. Wiedemann even seems to have been enlisted (with the connivance of Princess Stephanie and her British contacts) as a secret emissary from Hitler to Britain's foreign secretary, Lord Halifax, at the height of the Czechoslovakian crisis.

But according to Princess Stephanie, Hitler took a more-than-diplomatic interest in her, becoming so enamored, in fact, that in order to have her for himself alone he abruptly exiled Wiedemann to San Francisco. (She subsequently followed Wiedemann to America, and some intelligence analysts believed the Hitler-jealousy exile story was a cover for his spy mission to America.)

But buried in the Princess's somewhat defensive, somewhat self-promoting account to the OSS of her experience in the Hitler court are certain observations that struck me as worth rescuing from the Shadow Hitler realm. She starts out by protesting a bit too much that her inside information on Hitler was gleaned in an official capacity, not as some glorified groupie. She goes on at length, the OSS analyst noted, declaring that "as Lord Rothermere's personal representative in his dealings with many European statesmen, a position she held for a period of seven years, she was called upon to interview Hitler several times, as well as Göring, Ribbentrop and other leading Nazis."

The anonymous OSS interviewer notes, "This differs markedly from the Hanfstaengl account of the relationship," according to which the Princess "was one of Hitler's favorites—in fact so much so that Hanfstaengl had to caution him about his association with her on the grounds that . . . the Princess was half Jewish." Hanfstaengl also appears to believe the claim that Hitler "became insanely jealous" of the Princess's relationship to Wiedemann and sent him to San Francisco in order to get him out of the way. The OSS analyst notes that it seems "reasonable to suppose that her contact with Hitler had a social as well as an official side. How far the social went it is difficult to say." The analyst says her information about Hitler "corroborates much of the material obtained from numerous other sources," but a few incidents in particular deserve attention because they "throw further light on [Hitler's character]."

Some of the stories the OSS analyst singles out are less than illuminating. I'll mention one as an example of the curious tenor of Princess Hohenlohe's intimacy with the Hitler inner circle, her value-neutral way of characterizing Hitler and Göring as two men who Can't Express Their Feelings to Another Man.

Hitler at one point confesses to her, the Princess says, his profound and deep devotion to Göring, a devotion that extends to him worrying that Göring drives too fast because "It would be too dreadful to think . . . " he begins, but can't go on, so choked is he with emotion at the idea of a Göring car crash. It turns out, she says, the two men "are probably tongue-tied when they try to say to each other what they think of each other"—afraid to share their feelings. Because when she reports the Führer's sentiments to Göring, it causes "a veritable explosion of joy" in Göring; he's "thrilled to the core. . . . His radiance and delight shows such words from Hitler mean more to him than even uniforms and jewels"—which means they meant a *lot* to the uniform- and jewel-obsessed Göring. "The Bavarian braggart and brute disappeared and a proud little boy came to the surface."

However touched we might be by this display of shy mutual hero worship that daren't speak its name, it is an observation of another relationship the Princess's OSS debriefing sheds light on—a relationship in some ways more intense and sinister than Hitler's relationship with Göring, one that precedes it in time and intensity—that struck me as far more significant:

"In spite of all this"—she says, meaning in spite of Göring and Hitler's shy mutual hero worship, they "have never reached the intimate stage of *brüder-schaft* where they address each other with the familiar '*du*'"—the second-person singular German pronoun for "you"; an intimate form of address reserved for only the most intimate of friends, the equivalent in English of the archaic "thou."

"Göring was always very jealous because [Rudolf] Hess had this privilege," the Princess goes on. "There is only one Nazi besides Hess who has been granted that privilege and that, of all people, is Julius Streicher, editor of *Der Stürmer*. This, too, is a most peculiar relationship about which we know very little. It is quite certain that Streicher is one of the most hated of all the Nazis by all the other Nazis and yet Hitler has steadfastly resisted all pressure to remove or demote him. *A strange bond seems to hold these two together*" (emphasis added).

The strange bond with Streicher: It's referred to with the same mixture of wonder and dread that Hitler's strange bond with Geli Raubal evoked in some observers. But here, in the strange bond of brüderschaft, might be a far more significant locus of Hitler's *nicht natürlich* nature. I might perhaps have been less inclined to make too much of the report, buried as it is in the debriefing of a suspect adventuress (despite the OSS analyst's belief that her closeness to Captain Wiedemann gave her account credibility), had I not come upon another reference to the strange bond between Hitler and Streicher in another document in the Sourcebook.

The second reference appears in a passage excerpted from a memoir by Frederick Oechsner. Oechsner arrived in Germany in 1929 as Berlin correspondent for the New York *Sun*. He became Berlin bureau chief of United Press in 1933 and stayed on until 1942, condemned to spend the last six months of his stay in Gestapo-supervised detention with a number of other American journalists and diplomats who'd been interned shortly after Hitler's December 1941 declaration of war against the United States.

In any case, after a kind of hostage exchange in 1942, which permitted Oechsner and his colleagues to return to the United States (where he went to work for the OSS psychological-warfare division), he began preparing a memoir of Hitler and his cronies that he'd begun in Nazi detention. Oechsner had had several personal encounters with Hitler in the thirties, when the Führer was still courting American public opinion through correspondents for American papers; he was also tuned in to the rumor mill of the Shadow Hitler.

Oechsner's memoir is notable for its sober, no-nonsense, unsensational tone, for his wide range of German sources, and for the unexpected details that caught his eye and ear. Among the apparently trivial ones that show up in the OSS Sourcebook is Oechsner's report on Hitler's alleged nose job.

He introduces the subject by remarking that

Hitler is indeed vain, perhaps this is the reason why, shortly after he became Reichschancellor he had the shape of his nose corrected by a well-known plastic surgeon. The nose had been a little bulbous at the end and fatty on the bridge, so Hitler got a Berlin medical man to recommend a colleague in Munich, and the operation was performed, the superficial flesh removed. Thereafter, he was always posed by his official photographer Professor Hoffmann to bring out the best points of his remodelled nose.

Such are the snares of the Shadow Hitler that I was almost tempted to believe the nose-job report, to believe even that Fritz Gerlich's brilliant and caustic "Trial of Hitler's Nose" had exacerbated Hitler's self-consciousness enough to prompt him to have his nose done over. Oechsner is a good reporter, but unfortunately there appears to be no other corroboration in the literature for the nose-job story, and I'd suggest it's more likely that the appearance of remodeling Oechsner perceives was a matter of mustache-contour design or redesign. As we've seen from Heinrich Hoffmann's photographic outtakes over the years, that was Hitler's way of creating the illusion of a new nose.

More to the point is a story Oechsner relays from another medical doctor, an observation about the nature of Hitler's hatred. According to "a well-known German physician," Oechsner tells us, Hitler's attitude toward the Jews is "a primitive hate typical of half civilized or even uncivilized persons." Oechsner himself then goes on to evoke the nature of Hitler's relationship with the most inflammatory of primitive anti-Semites, Julius Streicher: "Der Führer is always greatly quickened in his anti-Jewish feelings by his contact with the notorious Julius Streicher. It is often noticeable that after he has been with Dr. Streicher for a time he is apt to come out with some new anti-Jewish measure or speech."

What we have here is a reversal of the famous *Führerkontakt* effect—the often-reported experience that personal exposure to Hitler's charismatic presence had a profound transformative effect on those so exposed. Here the Führer himself is depicted as vulnerable to what might be called *Streicherkontakt*. But what struck me as most significant in that paragraph was the notion of primitive hatred in itself and the linkage of primitive hatred to the Hitler-Streicher relationship.

The question of the nature and origin of Hitler's hatred is perhaps the crucial one at the heart of the heart of the search for Hitler. And primitive hatred is a notion that the most sophisticated recent literature has shied away from. Note how the "well-known German physician" makes an effort to distance himself and presumably civilized German culture from the "half civilized" and "uncivilized persons" in whom primitive hatred is to be found. He portrays Adolf Hitler as a kind of anthropological aberration in German society.

Would it were true that fully civilized people were incapable of manifesting primitive hatred: One of the things that made the Holocaust so unique and uniquely horrifying was precisely that it arose from a society widely regarded as the most civilized, in the sense of "learned" or "cultured," and philosophically sophisticated—convinced of its own rectitude—in the world.

"Convinced of his own rectitude," of course, was the phrase Hugh Trevor-Roper used to characterize Hitler's hatred as "sincere," based on rational belief. The notion of primitive hatred intrigued me as a way of embodying a missing term in the debate between Bullock and Trevor-Roper over the nature and sincerity of Hitler's hatred.

Alan Bullock initially argued that Hitler's hatred, his convictions about Jews, about anything, were counterfeit, or at least far less important than his *ambitions*: that the former served the latter, that his hatred was, if not a complete counterfeit, then a device to serve his drive for power. While Trevor-Roper contends that Hitler's convictions, including his anti-Semitism, were not only sincerely held but the source of his ambition, the reason he *wanted* power. But in fact, that dichotomy doesn't really exhaust the possible ways to construe Hitler's hatred. Bullock came up with a more complicated vision, a dynamic in which the actor who initially counterfeits passion and conviction becomes carried away with his own act. Yet there might be another, simpler way to look at the hatred at the heart of the controversy.

When Trevor-Roper characterizes Hitler as "convinced of his own rectitude," he is speaking of an ideologically based hatred, what one might have to call an "idealistic hatred," however deluded the idealist, however wicked the ideals on which it is based. But there is another kind of hatred, one that is neither counterfeited for manipulating the masses nor ideologically driven and well thought-out. There is another kind of hatred that is not intellectual but visceral, personal; an irrational hatred that can assume the guise, the mantle, of an ideological antipathy but which is primitive in the sense of being *prior* to ideology—its source rather than its product.

A primitive hatred does not necessarily need to cloak itself in the lineament of ideals or the pose of rectitude. A primitive hatred can manifest itself as a kind of primal, unresolved, ancient enmity, immune to reason, opaque to persuasion or even pragmatism. Pure pre-rational hatred, the kind of hatred Julius Streicher was notorious for. Streicher, of course, had founded an anti-Semitic political party in Nuremberg in 1919, months before Hitler joined the fledgling Nazi Party in Munich. A schoolteacher known for his brutality to more than just his pupils, known for his savage physical as well as verbal attacks on Jews and other opponents, the thuggish Streicher nonetheless deferred to Hitler once he became Führer of the Munich-based National Socialist Party; Streicher voluntarily relinquished his own primacy to merge his party with Hitler's and take up a subordinate position as Gauleiter (regional leader) of Franconia.

It was common for other members of Hitler's inner circle envious of the brüderschaft, the special relationship between the two men, to disparage Streicher's vulgar primitivism, to wonder aloud why Hitler appeared to protect and tolerate such a savage, primitive figure. To wonder aloud at Hitler's continued devotion to Streicher's vicious, pornographic hate sheet *Der Stürmer* with its compulsive focus on Jews as sexual predators upon innocent Aryan maidens. But in their efforts to distance themselves from Streicher, in trying to distance Hitler from him, they may have been ignoring or denying the possibility that the "strange bond" grew out of a deeper truth, a truth about Hitler rather than Streicher: that Streicher represented the true, unmasked face of primitive hatred that Hitler harbored.

It's interesting to see the way Streicher figures far more forcefully in the Shadow Hitler documents of the Sourcebook than he does in more sophisticated postwar ideological analyses of Hitler's anti-Semitism and its role in the Final Solution. Many postwar analyses emphasize Hitler's hesitations, his distance from the Final Solution decision, the way his genocidal intentions toward Jews played a perhaps lesser role in his hierarchy of priorities than more pragmatic considerations of battlefront exigencies, say.

Even Daniel Jonah Goldhagen, who does give priority to genocidal intentions in the Nazi (and more broadly German) mind-set, postulates those intentions as the product of a relatively sophisticated ideology—"eliminationist anti-Semitism"—which, however murderous, had a sort of debased intellectual genealogy in the thought of nineteenth-century racial theorists and "scientists." But primitive hatred, the kind manifested by Julius Streicher, the kind he perhaps shared in his strange bond with Hitler, is a different thing, not the product of thought and theory so much as unmediated emotional animus; it requires no grounding in theory and ideology but speaks, shrieks, for itself.

What's interesting in the comment of the "German physician" who diagnosed the strange bond and in Oechsner's observation of Streicherkontakt is the assumption that Streicher was the one who made Hitler more anti-Semitic, that Streicher was the senior partner, the more primitive hater. When, in fact, there's no reason not to entertain the opposite view. Hitler himself seems to suggest as much in an overlooked remark he made on the real relationship between his and Streicher's hatred of Jews. It's a line I first came across in John Toland's biography of Hitler, one I'd forgotten until I came upon the references to the strange bond with Streicher at the bottom of the Shadow Hitler box.

Toland frames this remark by painting the conventional portrait of Streicher as primitive: "A stocky, primitive man with bald head and gross features. . . . He had excessive appetites alike at table and in bed. . . . Like Hitler, he was rarely seen in public without a whip. . . . His speech was glutted with sadistic imagery. . . . [*Der Stürmer*'s] filth and virulence . . . was already a source of dismay to many of those close to Hitler."

This, then, is the conventional portrait of the Hitler-Streicher relationship: Hitler surrounded by "moderates" reflecting his own essential moderation, certainly by comparison with the extreme primitive vulgarity of Streicher's savage, sex-obsessed, primitive hatred which—curiously, for some inexplicable reason—Hitler would not reprove or restrain. But Toland is conscientious enough to quote a startling Hitler remark that seems to pull the rug out from under that conventional assumption, which calls into question who was the extremist and who was the moderate.

"Hitler had an unexpected answer for those who reproached Streicher for his gross exaggerations [about the hatefulness of Jews] in *Der Stürmer*," Toland reports. "The truth is the opposite of what people say," Hitler confided to one of his early party colleagues, Dietrich Eckart. In fact, to his mind, Streicher "*idealized the Jew. The Jew is baser, fiercer, more diabolical than Streicher depicted him*," Hitler declared (emphasis added).

The tone of this remarkable statement is not entirely clear but it suggests something unexpected about Hitler's hatred: that it is at once more primitive and more sophisticated than Streicher's. It suggests that Hitler's hatred was so primal that he could look at Streicher's hate-filled, poison-pen, pornographic *Der Stürmer* vituperation—which ostensibly appalled even thuggish Nazis in Hitler's inner circle—and call Streicher's image of Jews unjustly "idealized," too moderate and dainty for his taste, unwilling to go the full distance and tell the truth about how diabolical the Jews were.

So, one could say, on the face of it, Hitler is portraying his hatred as *more* primitive, "fiercer" (the word he uses for the Jews) than Streicher's. But one must also acknowledge the possibility that Hitler might have been making, as well, a kind of sophisticated, knowing in-joke for those of his inner-circle cronies with ears to hear it. By speaking ironically of Streicher as "idealizing" Jews, he's having it both ways: relegating the Jews to an even lower circle of diabolism while having a little joke on himself and Streicher for the extremity of their views. His hatred is more extreme, but he's sophisticated enough to joke about its extremity. It's almost like Charles Manson calling Jeffrey Dahmer "a sentimentalist," say, with a wink and a nudge, because Dahmer claimed to have loved ("idealized") the victims he killed and ate.

It is this combination of primitivism and knowingness that makes Hitler's hatred so wickedly distinctive to those, like the philosopher Berel Lang and the historian Lucy Dawidowicz, who pay more than casual attention to the nature of Hitler's hatred—something much of the current literature takes for granted or no longer finds relevant.

The "strange bond" with Streicher suggests a hatred both hot-tempered and cold-blooded, and thus all the more chilling and wicked (in the technical philosophical sense of the word *wicked*—as evil done knowingly rather than with a conviction of rectitude).

Why should the debate over the nature of Hitler's hatred be of particular relevance to the search for Hitler and his place in history, and how does it relate to the Geli Raubal literature? The answer to the first question is suggested in what might be the single most significant anecdote in the Sourcebook, one buried in the final paragraph of the Princess Stephanie debriefing, one about Hitler's role in the Kristallnacht pogrom of November 9, 1938. One that also has larger implications for how we construe Hitler's role in the Final Solution.

The OSS debriefer—making clear his belief that Princess Stephanie's account of the true origin of the Kristallnacht pogrom appeared to come from Captain Wiedemann, a source in a position to know, an intimate who might well have been privy to the Kristallnacht discussions—records Princess Stephanie's assertion that "*It was Hitler not Goebbels* who planned and instituted the November pogrom. He looked forward to it with the greatest relish and expected it would be a howling success among the German people and attract the attention of the entire world. When he discovered that the attention was not nearly as favorable as he had expected, he gave the impression that it was Goebbels' doing and Goebbels could do nothing but accept the responsibility to a large degree" (emphasis added).

It's purely anecdotal but noteworthy because it goes against the grain of much postwar analysis of Kristallnacht, analyses that buy into the idea that Hitler was somehow removed from unleashing the primitive hatred of that pogrom; that Hitler was appalled at its primitivism when he learned about it; that he tried to halt the violence once it was unleashed and regretted the damage the primitive Jew-bashing did to Germany's image; that he favored a more "rational" and "unemotional" sophisticated and systematic anti-Semitism.

This is not true of all postwar analysis of Kristallnacht and Hitler's hatred. The Hohenlohe/Wiedemann account of Hitler's instigator role in Kristallnacht corroborates the analysis of the episode by Lucy Dawidowicz, who in her *The War Against the Jews* argues that in Kristallnacht we can find a successful model of the deniability mechanism Hitler used to cloak his intentions, his similar prime instigator role in the Final Solution to come. It's a charade of deniability that some serious historians, not just Holocaust deniers, still give credence to.

The notion of primitive hatred has a particular relevance to the literature on the Geli Raubal case as well, to the literature, memoirs, and the like dominated by what I've come to think of as the "No More Mr. Nice Guy" school of interpretation. This is the notion that until he was overwhelmed by bitter grief over the death of Geli Raubal, his only true love, Hitler wasn't really *Hitler*. Adherents of this school, who include a conspicuous number of Hitler's own closest aides and colleagues, portray him as, if not a sentimental humanist up to that point, then certainly a far more human, less hardened, less ruthless and cruel a fellow than the one he became after Geli Raubal's death.

It is a line of thought that has persisted from the time Geli died until the current moment. It's a temptation, I must admit, I've given into myself in the past because of the very absence of a more convincing candidate for a moment of metamorphosis, a point of punctuated evolution in Hitler's life. It's a view a remarkable number of Hitler's Nazi colleagues promoted in the aftermath of Geli's death—which is one reason I came to distrust it. It clearly serves their purposes to split off the later genocidal Hitler from a purportedly nicer early Hitler, the Hitler they first knew and bonded with, the Weimar Hitler, the Munich Hitler, the Hitler without (mass quantities of) victims.

Göring himself pushes this view: "Geli's death had such a devastating effect on Hitler that it . . . changed his relationship to everyone else." And Hitler's photographer Hoffmann argued that "at this time the seed of inhumanity began to sprout in Hitler."

Only then! Just a seed!

Hanfstaengl in particular flogs the "No More Mr. Nice Guy" concept: "With her death the way was clear for his final development into a demon"— which absolved Hanfstaengl from full implication in the crimes of the putative predemonic fellowship he shared with his Wagner-loving friend and Führer. Because up to that time Hitler was strange, quirky, yes, but not demonic.

Demonizing Hitler has been criticized by some historians not with a view to minimizing Hitler's crimes so much as with an awareness that to demonize can mean to distance Hitler, in a falsely comforting way, from ourselves. In any case, the view that Hitler became a demon only after the death of Geli Raubal is not limited to old cronies of Hitler. It finds a contemporary champion in *Hitler and Geli*, a 1997 book by prolific British biographer Ronald Hayman. Hayman uses all three of these quotes from Hitler cronies—Göring, Hoffmann, and Hanfstaengl—to support his view that after Geli's death (which Hayman attempts to prove Hitler caused with his own hands) "the change must have been substantial."

Hayman goes much further; he tries to explicitly link Hitler's loss of Geli with the genocide to come: "[Hitler's] appetite for carnage grew monstrously after Geli's death," Hayman writes. He adopts for his purposes the Shadow Hitler realm's belief in the excretory perversion Hitler supposedly practiced with Geli. And he adopts as well Hanfstaengl's interpretation of the effect the loss of Geli had on Hitler: the abrupt loss of the fulfillment it had brought him removed the only inhibition he had to committing mass murder.

Hayman even seems to fault Eva Braun for failing to provide the crucial distraction or sublimation for Hitler's "appetite for destruction": Eva was "never his partner in the same sense as Geli," Hayman tells us. "Eva could never release his nervous energy nor restrain his destructiveness. Certain subjects had never been discussed with Geli, but at least there had been some human interaction. Eva's company never seemed to have much effect on him."

Setting aside all the suppositions rendered as fact here—about the nature of Hitler's small talk with Geli and the nature of his sexual relationship with Eva (which is the subject of a range of conflicting reports)—one could characterize the gist of Hayman's argument as the assertion that if Eva Braun had somehow been able to make more *meaningful* small talk with Hitler, he might have had an outlet to "release his nervous energy" and restrain his destructiveness. Small talk might have substituted for genocide.

In addition, Hayman makes much of the notion that Geli was Hitler's first murder: "If Hitler did shoot Geli, she was his first human victim. There is no evidence of his killing anyone during the First World War, in which his main job was to carry messages. But the boy who shot rats turned into the man who gassed Jews, and it looks as if Geli's death was a stepping stone" in that transformation or evolution.

There are two problems with calling Geli Raubal Hitler's "first human victim" in the sense Hayman uses the phase. First of all, by September 1931 the toll of dead who were, in a very real sense, Hitler's victims had reached into the hundreds if not thousands. I'm speaking of the near-daily toll of political murders, fatal beatings, stabbings, and shootings inflicted upon opposition-party activists and other opponents by Hitler's murderous SA thugs. Murders committed in his name, frequently accompanied by "Heil Hitler!" invocations, in fact. The toll is there in graphic detail in every issue of the *Munich Post* for that period. If those victims didn't make Hitler a mass murderer yet, they certainly made him a serial killer by proxy by the time Geli Raubal died.

These murders were Hitler's responsibility; the blood of those victims was on his hands long before the blood of Geli Raubal was spilled in his apartment. While some have argued that the death of Geli Raubal (whether she was murdered, killed herself, or was driven to kill herself by Hitler) made a crucial difference in Hitler's psyche, it was those other murders, the political murders, that made a more important difference: those bodies paved his path to power, those murders would certainly have given Hitler the feeling that he could get away with murder, with many murders. That he could have people killed to benefit him but escape the consequences because there was no written order—just as he may have left no written order for the Final Solution (and thus would, in the minds of some, escape full responsibility for that as well). It seems silly to have to say so, but after reading the lugubrious remarks of Göring and Hoffmann that Hayman cites—about the way their gemütlich Hitler turned cold and inhuman after Geli's death—perhaps it *does* need to be said that Hitler was not exactly a nice guy before the alleged "No More Mr. Nice Guy" moment.

The other problem with Hayman's assertion that Geli Raubal was Hitler's first victim is the literal sense in which Hayman intends that term: Hitler's hands-on role in her murder. Hayman goes to great lengths to proffer a scenario in which Hitler and Geli are struggling for possession of his gun in her bedroom, a gun Hitler has drawn to shoot either himself or her, and which goes off in her chest as she's trying to wrest it from his grasp.

Now, few would have any problem in thinking Geli Raubal was Hitler's victim in *some* sense—not necessarily his first victim, not necessarily by his own hand—but certainly in the sense of having been driven to her death by his oppressive attentions, whether perverse or merely possessive in the extreme. But Hayman is intent on proving a kind of Oliver Stone scenario involving Hitler's struggle for the gun in Geli's bedroom and an extensive conspiracy to cover up his role, his presence when the gun went off. A conspiracy that goes so far (in Hayman's view) that it involves concealing the body, concealing the murder for a day and a half while Hitler's tracks are carefully covered, alibis are set up, stories are concocted by dozens of complicit conspirators to keep the secret. A conspiracy so elaborate Hayman needs to posit a missing night of murder to account for it and then a missing day to fabricate the cover-up and coin the counterfeit stories to maintain it.

Hayman follows the Shadow Hitler literature in positing, as the cause of the fatal quarrel, Geli's relationship with a spectral (probably Jewish) seducer who posed a threat to poison her blood, father her child, expose Hitler's perversion to the Jewish press. But where Hayman departs from the Shadow Hitler (and from everyone else in the literature) is in altering radically the chronology of Geli's death.

I've come to think of Hayman's creation of a missing day as the temporal equivalent of the lost safe-deposit box, a place, a locus of a solution that is inaccessible or unimaginable otherwise. Just to place Hayman's missing-night gambit in the perspective of the case, let's briefly recall the conventional chronology of Geli Raubal's death, the one accepted by all previous commentators on the case, even those who believe Hitler murdered Geli.

On Thursday evening, the seventeenth of September 1931, Geli goes to the theater with the wife of Julius Schaub, one of Hitler's personal adjutants. In his postwar memoir, Schaub said his wife noticed that Geli seemed upset, even tearful, that night, but "they were used to mood changes in Geli."

On the next morning, the eighteenth, a Friday, Schaub reports in his memoir (using the third person to describe himself), "Schaub said goodbye to his wife because he had to go to Hamburg with Hitler."

Almost all accounts have Hitler eating lunch with Geli in his apartment that Friday, with the household staff present. A lunch during which there was something of a disagreement, quarrel, or unpleasantness over Geli's desire to make a trip to Vienna. Accounts vary as to the nature of the quarrel, but almost all accounts (including those of anti-Hitler newspapers such as the *Munich Post*) have Geli alive and lunching with Hitler on Friday the eighteenth.

Following which Hitler took off en route to Hamburg and spent the night in Nuremberg, two hours north, at the Deutscher Hof Hotel, while Geli went to her room, never to be seen alive again. Ambiguous noises heard in her room after Hitler left have led most accounts to have her shooting herself sometime after lunch on the eighteenth, her body not being discovered until the following Saturday morning, the nineteenth.

But Hayman is determined to offer a novel solution in which Geli had been dead for nearly two days by the time her body was discovered, in which Geli had been dead *all day* Friday when she'd been reported lunching with Hitler, a scenario in which Geli had been murdered Thursday night, the seventeenth.

How Hitler spent the missing day, the Friday between his supposed Thursday-night crime and the Saturday-morning discovery of the body, is not clear from Hayman's scenario. Did he go north to Nuremberg Thursday night, in which case the people at the Nuremberg hotel had to be coached to lie that he didn't arrive till Friday night? Or did he hang around his apartment all day Friday as Geli's body cooled and stiffened and an elaborate cover-up was concocted? And then slip out, drive north to Nuremberg so he could establish an alibi the morning the body was "discovered" (by getting a speeding ticket as he was racing back to Munich, supposedly after receiving the terrible news)?

It's not even clear Hayman *needs* this missing day to give his conspiracy theory more credibility—it makes it more suspect, it seems to me. But then he proceeds to add to his account an apocryphal story from a deeply discredited source: a story about Fritz Gerlich and a late-night final quarrel between Hitler and Geli in a public place. The story is told by Bridget Hitler in her long-unpublished and much-distrusted memoir, the one that contains at least one glaring, self-promoting fabrication—that young Adolf Hitler spent a missing year of his youth with Bridget and her husband, Alois Jr. (Hitler's half brother), in their Liverpool apartment in 1911.

Hayman uses the fabricator of a missing year to bolster his story about the murder night because Bridget Hitler purports to tell us the true story of Geli's last night, the truth (Bridget claims) that Fritz Gerlich himself uncovered: the long-lost, never published Gerlich scoop on Geli Raubal's death, the one Gerlich had been about to publish in his newspaper when he was dragged off by the Gestapo in 1933, the one thought lost to history or to some lost safe-deposit box.

But no, Bridget Hitler says, it might *not* have been lost. She doesn't reproduce it herself, it's not even in the Hitler documents she claims she and her son keep "in our safe deposit box at the bank." No, she says, Gerlich's lost scoop *did* get published, not in his newspaper but in a pamphlet, which she says was entitled by Gerlich *J'Accuse*, one in which he laid out his proof that Hitler murdered Geli. Bridget hasn't seen it herself, she tells us, rather she just heard about it in a conversation with her son William Patrick Hitler, who claims *he* heard about it from Geli's surviving brother Leo Raubal, who happened to run across Gerlich "by accident" and received from Gerlich's own hands the purported revelatory pamphlet.

If it ever existed, no such pamphlet has surfaced. It exists only in the Shadow Hitler realm, and no other person ever reports having seen it or heard of it, but Hayman wants to adopt Bridget Hitler's description of its contents, that "the evidence accumulated by Dr. Gerlich's investigation pointed inevitably to just one verdict: murder."

It is in this account of what we might call the Shadow Gerlich investigation that Hayman finds his missing night. He accepts the fabricator Bridget Hitler's account of William Patrick Hitler's account of the Gerlich investigation purportedly recalled by Geli's brother Leo (and ignores the fact that Leo, who survived the war, made *no* such report to any of the authors who interviewed him). But the missing night is there in the shadow affidavit in the Shadow Gerlich investigation, in the purported affidavit of a crony of Hitler, a Herr Zentner, the proprietor of the Bratwurstglöckl, one of Hitler's favorite restaurant hangouts. In the summary of Gerlich's *J'Accuse* pamphlet in Bridget's memoir, in the shadow of a shadow of a report Hayman relies on, Zentner "testified" that

> Adolf had come to his restaurant with his niece and remained there until nearly one o'clock occupying a private room on the first story. . . . Adolf was slightly intoxicated as a result of drinking beer, an extremely unusual practice for him. . . . After Adolf and Geli left the restaurant, they returned to the apartment about one o'clock. Happy to find himself alone with her, Adolf renewed his advances, which Geli opposed. During the discussion, he threatened her with the service revolver he habitually wore. Certainly there was a struggle and during it a shot was fired.

So Hitler shoots Geli, Hayman argues, after a Bratwurstglöckl quarrel on Thursday night, shoots her back at his place, in her bedroom. Not only is this missing-night theory not even necessary—there's no reason the Bratwurstglöckl quarrel couldn't have occurred late *Friday* (as Zentner's apocryphal affidavit has it) rather than Thursday night with less sneaking around and slipping in and out than a Thursday-night scenario requires. But Hayman has created the missing night from an extremely strained interpretation of the evidence—in what actually looks like a glaring *mistake* in dating the Thursday and Friday in question, a mistake in interpreting one single source: Julius Schaub's unpublished memoir.

Even Hayman calls the reference he uses to create the missing night "ambiguous," although one has to strain to find any ambiguity, if you ask me. For the record, here is all the evidence for the missing night, Schaub's two-decade-later recollection that "*On the day before the suicide (17.9.31)* he [Hitler] left Munich in his car to hold a meeting at Nuremberg." Hayman insists this "could mean either that Geli died on Thursday 17, September or that Hitler left Munich on 17, September." But *either* way, it means Hitler left Munich *before* Geli died (which contradicts Hayman's murder scenario).

It's difficult to rule *out* the possibility that Hitler murdered Geli or had Geli murdered. He certainly lied about the nature of his relationship and the nature of his quarrel with her, dissembled about the source of her supposedly suicidal proclivity (the séance story). But absent the emergence of a smoking gun from the Shadow Hitler realm or the materialization of some truth Fritz Gerlich dug up, absences I suspect will persist, there is no positive proof. The missing night Hayman pulls like a rabbit out of his hat cannot make up for the missing evidence he does not have.

The missing night is a phantom of the Shadow Hitler realm, but I understand the evidentiary despair that may have caused Hayman to want to believe in it. I, too, had hoped to find in the Shadow Hitler realm, supplemented by contemporary investigation—even exhumation of Geli's body—a solution to the Geli Raubal mystery that would pin her death directly—in a hands-on way or by personal order—on Adolf Hitler. It certainly seems he was capable of it, that he had the motive, means, and opportunity. And it certainly can be said that if he didn't do it himself or didn't order her murder, he was at least in some larger sense *responsible* for her death. But Hayman's missing-night gambit is akin to the lost safe-deposit boxes of the Shadow Hitler Switzerland—an illusion born of the hope that the solution not just to Geli Raubal's death but to Adolf Hitler's psyche can be found in some inaccessible place.

Such a solution would make Hitler's purported transformation from human to inhuman, the "No More Mr. Nice Guy" metamorphosis, explicable as a product of blood guilt over Geli as well as grief. It would suggest that killing Geli Raubal "blooded" him in some way he hadn't been personally blooded before, exterminated the last bit of humanness within him. And that the specter of a Jewish seducer of Geli behind their fatal quarrel then set him on a course that made extermination of the Jews inevitable.

In a certain sense, this increasingly strained argument is as unjust to Geli Raubal as Simon Wiesenthal's fantasy of a Jewish prostitute giving Hitler syphilis would be to that poor woman of the streets if she'd ever existed: appearing to place the whole weight of the Holocaust on her shoulders. More important, the whole line of No More Mr. Nice Guy speculation (which enjoys favor from sober and rational historians as well as conspiracy theorists) about Geli's death as a great divide is contradicted by the evidence that Hitler's primitive hatred burned with a hard, gemlike flame long before September 1931. Burned with sufficient virulence in Hitler to account for his subsequent exterminationist acts without any reference to Geli Raubal's character or fate. The primitive hatred Hitler shared in his strange bond with Streicher, the primitive hatred Streicher manifested, a hatred that might have been the true face of Hitler's *own* hatred, was in place in Hitler's heart long before Geli Raubal moved into his apartment. And whatever emotion he felt upon her death paled in comparison to the primitive fury of the entrenched ruling emotion of his existence.

If there was any real shift in the nature of the hatred Hitler harbored, if his primitive hatred could be said to have evolved or changed, it might rather have been in the way Hitler came to acquire and deploy a kind of ironic knowingness about his primitive hatred. The way he would come to make artful little knowing *jests* about it, virtually chuckle over the magnitude of his hatred by telling his cronies, with a nudge and a wink, that he thought Streicher—and the notoriously, savagely primitive hatred Streicher so shockingly and nakedly displayed—was in fact practically temperate compared to his own hatred; that to him, to Hitler, Streicher "idealized" the Jews.

The wickedly artful ironic consciousness of his own primitive hatred is a signature of Hitler to some thinkers. Bullock's notion of Hitler's duality sees him as the cynic who becomes possessed by sincere conviction, by "true" hatred. Here, though, it's the possessed, true hater who can be wickedly ironic if not cynical about the degree of his hate-filled possession, who can jest about his own murderousness.

The way Hitler jests, in the Table Talk, about the "rumor" he's exterminating the Jews; the way he can jest to Christa Schroeder about feeling "clean as a newborn babe" after the Blood Purge; the way he speaks of the Final Solution in the imagery of laughter Lucy Dawidowicz picks up on (see chapter 20); the way he jests to Goebbels about the suffering of his victims throughout the war—this mirthful knowingness, the laughter and relish, is a sign and signature to the philosopher Berel Lang of the peculiar way Hitler and his cronies raised the consciousness of evil to a veritable art: created what Lang sees as an art of evil.

PART FIVE

THE ART OF EVIL
AND THE
FUTURE OF IT

In which the perils of getting too close to the Führer are explored

CHAPTER 11

To the Gestapo Cottage;
or, A Night Close to the Führer

In which the philosopher Berel Lang closes in on
the locus of Hitler's evil in his identity as an artist

Night and fog on the Obersalzberg, Hitler's mountain retreat. We seem to have lost our way, although Herr H.—often in error, never in doubt—insists he knows exactly where we are. And so, despite the blowing fog that bounces the high beams of his BMW back into our faces, obscuring all but a few feet of the icy pavement in front of us, Herr H. presses on, up the mountain. He's on a mission. He wants to "spend a night close to the Führer." In a sense, so do I.

The problem is that the main road up to the top of the mountain that had once been Hitler's personal peak has been barricaded. Something to do with the preparations for the local Christmas market, not the dangerous ice, Herr H. insists, as he pilots us onto an even narrower, icier switchback route with no guardrails. The road seems dangerous to me and nothing less than terrifying to Herr H.'s Israeli girlfriend, Miriam, who has only recently recovered from a near-fatal car wreck on a similarly icy road and who is rigidly braced in the front passenger seat for a repetition of the horror.

But Herr H. has determined not to permit poor visibility, dangerous road conditions, or painful memories to deter him from the now-so-near fulfillment of a long-held fantasy, the goal of this pilgrimage to the mountaintop shrine.

In 1942, Martin Bormann announced with great fanfare a grand construction project on the mountain that had, since the 1920s, been Hitler's Alpine retreat, the place where Hitler built a sumptuous rustic palace for himself, the Berghof, his Hall of the Mountain King. Here, Hitler would escape from the embroilments of Munich (and then Berlin) politics to meditate amid breathtaking Alpine vistas, hike in traditional Bavarian lederhosen, and imbibe the crystalline mountain air. Here, he'd receive heads of state and host strategy conferences with his generals, dictating from that heady perspective the future map of Europe against the backdrop of snowcapped peaks visible through vast floor-to-ceiling picture windows.

It was here Hitler could ascend skyward to another aerie—to the tiny teahouse at the very top of the mountain where he could survey in lonely splendor the realm he commanded from his Eagle's Nest. And it was here, Martin Bormann announced, that, at the request of the Führer, he was constructing a grand guest house for the German people on Hitler's magic mountain.

"Here," the politically ambitious and slyly self-promoting Bormann proclaimed, "every German who participated in a pilgrimage to the beloved Führer would have the opportunity to spend one day and one night close to the Führer, for only one reichsmark."

As it turned out, construction was so expensive and demand for rooms so great on the part of middle-management Nazi officials that only the elite of the Third Reich could be accommodated, although the structure Bormann built was a vast, rambling behemoth whose rustic exterior concealed high-ceilinged Teutonic reception halls, banquet rooms, and an extensive, high-tech underground bunker.

Still, the dream of the pilgrimage, the goal of spending one night there, "one night close to the Führer," has not died. It's alive in Herr H.

Getting close to the Führer is Herr H.'s lifelong project. He's a forty-five-year-old Viennese furniture restorer and amateur historian of the variety one sarcastic German journalist characterized as the *Hitler mit Schlippern* (Hitler in slippers) school. They tend to be something more than serious memorabilia collectors (although they are that, too) and something less than serious historians. I'd first met Herr H. as a result of my Geli Raubal investigations: He had attracted some notice when he petitioned the city of Vienna to exhume Geli's body in order to see if further forensic evidence on the circumstances of her death could be garnered from the remains (the pro-Hitler public prosecutor had forestalled a full forensic autopsy in 1931). The Vienna city government had derailed Herr H.'s effort over the question of the certainty of the grave location. Geli's body had been moved from its pride of place in Vienna's Central Cemetery shortly after the war when the Hitler family had, perforce, stopped making payments on its upkeep. Her remains, in a zinc coffin, had been shifted to an unmarked field of paupers' graves. But Herr H. claimed to have dug up the moldering schematic diagrams of the cemetery that pinpointed Geli's new resting place. The city disputed Herr H.'s certainty, and there the matter rested, although not Herr H., who produced an elaborate, privately printed volume of Geli Raubal documents, recollections, and interviews he'd conducted with those still alive who knew her.

I found Herr H.'s attitude toward Geli and Hitler curiously inconsistent and sometimes self-contradictory. He claimed at one point he'd solved the case and that he knew the name of an SS man who'd murdered Geli at Hitler's orders. But I hadn't been convinced of the authenticity of the documentary evidence he'd shown me: an entry from a purported diary kept by Geli's supposed spiritual adviser, a Viennese priest named Father Pant; and Herr H. didn't take up my offer to have the diary-paper tested for historical authenticity. But despite trying to promote proof that Hitler had Geli murdered, he didn't seem to be too exercised over Hitler's other murders.

It was in keeping with the disturbingly serene view of the Hitler mit Schlippern school: not neo-Nazi, not denying the Holocaust, but choosing to focus instead on the memorabilia Hitler, the "personal" Hitler, the Hitler relaxing at home with his beloved dog Blondi in Eva Braun's home movies, the Hitler of the warm reminiscences by his secretarial staff and valets, who spoke of his fondness for their children, his delight in remembering their birthdays, the nightly tea parties in the command bunkers, the gemütlichkeit Hitler of the Table Talk.

Underlying Herr H.'s ability to sustain this attitude is the relativization, the historicization of Hitler accomplished by the German nationalist historians of the *Historikerstreit* in the eighties, the ones who made the comparative-evil argument: Stalin was worse; Stalin invented mass murder and concentration camps; Hitler's brutality was a *response* to the threat of the bloodthirsty "Asiatic" Bolsheviks in the east. Hitler was the lesser, or at least the *later* evil in world history.

Herr H.'s mother was a postwar refugee from Stalinist Czechoslovakia who'd fled to Vienna (where Herr H. was born in 1949) and imbued him with a horror of the Bolsheviks. At an early age, he began to collect Wehrmacht uniforms and Hitler memorabilia, building up his collection from a personal hobby to a thriving business supplying German uniforms and ordnance to movie companies making Nazi-period films.

This, along with his chain of antique-furniture restoration shops and some private dealings in Hitler watercolors and the like, have paid for the brand-new BMW and the expensive Armani jackets he wears over his carefully faded pressed jeans and his Gucci loafers. He's a relatively genial fellow, and we'd come to an uneasy truce over our respective attitudes after a clash over roast goose at his favorite Vienna restaurant. After drinking some wine, Herr H.

had been declaiming that the Russian people deserved their suffering under communism, because they'd put up with Stalin and his henchmen for so long. I countered by asking him if he then agreed with those who said the German people deserved *their* suffering for putting up with Hitler. For whatever reason, he had not wanted to progress beyond relativizing Stalin and Hitler's comparative evil to explicitly portraying Hitler as somehow *more* defensible than Stalin.

In a sense, Herr H. and I were using each other: He hoped that I would promote his "solution" to the Geli Raubal case (which, in fact, because of my skepticism over the "diary," I did not). And he had proved useful to me in getting access to certain Hitler landmarks in Vienna. He had, for instance, established a relationship with the director of the Männerheim, the still-functioning men's shelter Hitler had called home for three long years of his lost period in Vienna, when his artistic ambitions had been crushed and he'd been reduced to scraping together pennies by selling his stilted postcard renditions of "scenic views" of Vienna landmarks.

That despondent and disillusioned period in the men's shelter was a crucial one in Hitler's development, one that saw the destruction and loss of his romantic artistic illusions. Some believe it was the interlude when other, more sinister illusions took their place. Many have argued that it was in some encounter there in the Männerheim or in some moment of embittered introspection, some vision there, that triggered Hitler's metamorphosis from struggling artist and harmless bohemian to the grim hater he became.

The evidence on the question of a transformation at the men's shelter is mixed, corrupted in part by several con-artist inmates who tried to cash in on Hitler's later fame by claiming they'd been his soul mates there. I'd read all the Männerheim accounts but had been surprised to learn that it still was open, still served the same function it had eight decades ago. It was still home to vagrants and the barely working poor, the able-bodied homeless, the refugees, the restless and vagabonds who'd drifted in or had been driven to Vienna from all corners of Europe.

And so, one gray November morning, I found myself wandering through the halls of the Männerheim, trying to get a sense of the way it looked and felt to the youthful Hitler. Very little has changed, the director told me. He meant very little of the architecture, but it was true of more than that. There's a famous disputed photo taken of the interior of the Männerheim during the period when Hitler was in residence. It shows a dark-clad figure seated in front of a window off the kitchen area, staring out the window into the void. Some have said it's Hitler. It's probably not, but it could have been. Touring the ground floor, I came upon a figure seated in that same position staring out into the same hopeless void, wearing a black wool sweater and a black knitted watch cap, smoking a pipe and staring vacantly into space. A refugee, the director said, a fellow who'd fled from Macedonia after the political breakup of the Balkans, his home destroyed in the ethnic strife that ensued. In a pessimistic frame of mind (as who could not help but be in this place), one could imagine the same brew of bitter hatred secreting itself inside this man as it had in Hitler. As the director said, very little has changed.

After assisting me in gaining entrance to the Männerheim, Herr H. disclosed he had a favor he wanted to ask me, a dream he wanted me to help fulfill. He knew I was planning to leave Vienna for Munich by train; he offered instead to drive me to Munich with a stop at the Obersalzberg—if I could help make it possible for him to stay in the guesthouse Bormann had built in Hitler's compound, the place where, Bormann had promised, every citizen of the Reich would be able to spend "a night close to the Führer."

The reason he hadn't accomplished it before—the reason he thought I could help—was that after the war the Bormann guesthouse had been taken over by American army authorities. They'd dynamited Hitler's personal residence to destroy its possible future as a shrine for neo-Nazis. But it was felt the guesthouse was not itself imbued with the kind of numinous evil Hitler's own house had been. Instead, it was transformed into a kind of mountain-resort facility for American servicemen and their families stationed in Germany. Herr H. was under the impression that it was open to all American citizens and their guests as well, and so he asked me to make a reservation for me and him and his Israeli girlfriend at the Hotel General Walker, as the place was now called.

I know why Herr H. wanted to spend "a night close to the Führer," but I wondered what his Israeli girlfriend Miriam's attitude was. She seemed as normal a young woman as any of her generation; born in Austria, raised in Israel from age five to twenty, now returned to Vienna, where she was an apartment-rental agent. On the way to Munich from the Obersalzberg, when Herr H. stopped to gas up his BMW at a roadside stop in the heart of Bavaria, as lederhosen-clad villagers in peaked Alpine hats decorated with colorful turkey feathers picnicked outside the buffet, I asked Miriam what it felt like spending time with Herr H. in an apartment filled with Hitler and SS memorabilia.

She was enthusiastic about the opportunity it represented—an opportunity to learn about Hitler: "In Israel, you know, it was almost forbidden to talk ever of Hitler," she said. "It is too awful. But I want to understand, and through knowing H. I have learned very much."

It was hard to argue with the impulse she was expressing, although one might quarrel with the method. But, in a sense, she was pursuing the same quest as Herr H. and one not too dissimilar from mine. In mapping the labyrinthine thickets of Hitler explanations, in trying to disentangle the historical Hitler from the meanings projected upon him, from the adhesions of spurious facts and theories, I was, in my own way, trying to get "close to the Führer."

And so we set out from Vienna on a gloomy November Sunday afternoon, stopping for an early dinner on the way, crossing the border into Germany around dusk. It was after dark when we started up the Obersalzberg slopes and found ourselves diverted onto that icily treacherous back road; it was pitch black when we found ourselves turned away from the Hotel General Walker.

The cavernous reception hall was filled with a throng of buzz-cut GIs, their wives and babies wearing the Bart Simpson T-shirts that were all the rage that year. The clerk had my reservation and all seemed in order till she asked me for my army identification. No one had mentioned that on the phone, I said. It seemed they must have assumed I was in the service because—contrary to Herr H.'s information—the Hotel General Walker was not open to all Americans but only to military personnel. No amount of complaining about how we'd driven three hours just to spend the night sufficed: There was no room at the inn for us.

Outside in the cold, clear air of the mountain night, Herr H. pointed up to the Eagle's Nest, nestled in the snowy crevices just below the peak. "It's closed for the winter," he said. At first I thought he planned on us hiking up the mountainside to take shelter in that inaccessible shrine, but it turned out he had a more congenial—to him at least—backup plan in mind.

"Don't worry," he said. "We can always stay at the Gestapo Cottage."

The Gestapo Cottage. The place felt only slightly less sinister than it sounded. It was a compact little inn not far down the mountain from the Hotel General Walker, a place that had been built before Hitler began building his private preserve, a little inn known as far back as the twenties as Zum Turken because of the Turkish nationality of its original owners. In the thirties, to the great credit of the owners, their clear lack of Nazi sympathies caused Bormann to seize it from them and turn it into a dormitory residence for Hitler's Gestapo bodyguards. After the war it was returned to the ownership of the original family, whose descendants run it now, although to the likes of Herr H. it remains always "the Gestapo Cottage."

Despite the proprietor family's lack of sympathy, the place, because of its location, attracts those obsessed with and sympathetic to the era, who want to stay in a place that has changed less than any other Hitler landmark except perhaps the Männerheim. By the registration desk, one can find books filled with cheerful photographs of a relaxed, genial Hitler taken at various sites on the mountaintop: Hitler with his beloved dog Blondi (the one he killed with cyanide when he was testing the poison he would take himself); Hitler with blond children; Hitler with Eva Braun; Hitler posing with Alpine-garbed Nazi visitors; Hitler hiking through the wildflowers; Hitler relaxed in front of the breathtakingly picturesque crags. Hitler, in other words, in slippers. And in the Gestapo Cottage's cozy common room, where we had a beer before retiring, there is still a picture on the wall of Eva Braun, one that could well have been put there to brighten up the off-duty hours of the Gestapo bodyguards while she and Hitler were still alive.

The Gestapo Cottage was closed for the season, but the proprietors were only too happy to accommodate such a faithful repeat visitor as Herr H. They opened up the otherwise empty guest floor to make two rooms available to us. Despite their hospitality, it was not exactly a place in which I could get a comfortable night's rest. Alone in my room in the nearly empty Gestapo Cottage, I couldn't sleep, thinking about the previous occupants of the room, about the spectral seated figure in the Männerheim I'd seen earlier that day.

It was possible, if one allowed one's imagination free rein, to feel, here on Hitler's mountain, the presence of Hitler's evil almost literally thickening the night air. And to a much greater sense than I would care to admit, I did feel something almost palpable, however irrational that may sound. But giving in to it that night was a kind of turning point for the inquiry I was pursuing, one that dramatized to me the perils in the attempt to get "close to the Führer" and helped clarify for me what I was really seeking.

The most obvious peril was the kind that Herr H. embodied, the way a quest for closeness can devolve into a kind of comfortably engrossing intimacy, one that can metamorphose into the gargantuan nearsightedness of the Hitler mit Schlippern gemütlichkeit vision of the Führer.

But there was another kind of peril in the path I'd been pursuing, in immersing myself in the literature on the subject, in spending time with those who'd made explaining Hitler their lifework: getting *too* close to the Führer, so close that the magnitude of his evil became a distorting lens that makes any human perspective impossible. So close that the temptation, the inevitable tendency, is to begin looking at all history in terms of how it led to Hitler and the death camps. And a concomitant temptation to examine all human nature for the sources, the wellsprings of Hitler; to view all evil in relation to Hitler's evil. A process that eventually can end up turning Hitler into a kind of graven image—a defining, if not ruling, principle of all being.

One also has to question if, as a Jew, as someone who could have been one of his victims, one can look at the subject with any perspective. The tendency is to want to see one's own tragedy as something universal and ultimate—as all mankind's, all history's, all human nature's ultimate tragedy.

The German psychiatrist Helm Stierlin reports in the introduction to his psychohistorical study of Hitler that he was impelled to embark on the project, in part at least, by a question his eight-year-old child asked him: Was Hitler the most evil man that ever lived? It's a child's question, but still an important one because it raises the question of how we measure, judge evil: by quantity, by body count, or by the quality of consciousness with which the deed is executed, the malevolence of the intentionality, the conscious awareness of wrongdoing? It's the kind of question I'd been asking ever since H. R. Trevor-Roper had surprised me by declaring his belief that Hitler had no conscious awareness of doing wrong: that he was "convinced of his own rectitude."

One question I formulated that sleepless night on the Obersalzberg, and in the crystalline light of the following morning when the late autumn sun had burned through the fog, was a different one, although it addressed similar issues to that raised by Trevor-Roper and by Stierlin's child, issues that sophisticated post-Holocaust philosophers and theologians had been wrestling with for half a century: Do we have to redefine our conventional, centuries-old notions of evil to take into account the nature of Hitler; or do we have to redefine our notion of Hitler to account for him in terms of our previous notions of evil?

To put it another way, to use a familiar Jewish formulation: Why is this evil different from all other evils—*if* it is? Are we too close to know? These are questions I'd been asking, in one form or another, in my encounters with historians such as Bullock and Trevor-Roper, thinkers such as George Steiner and Emil Fackenheim, in talking to psychoanalysts, psychohistorians, and other explainers. They are questions that I found a despairing and disappointing number of times to have been begged, evaded, or glossed over.

"Well, if *he* isn't evil, then who is?" Lord Bullock harrumphed, as if that answered the question—when, in fact, it just opened it up.

Ultimately, however, I did find one philosopher who did not beg the question, did not claim it to be irrelevant or impossible to parse, who did not claim to have a final answer, but who wrestled with it with what I thought was scrupulous honesty, and who seemed to be suggesting a provocative new way of answering it. It came as a surprise to me, having read fairly extensively in the philosophical literature on the question of evil, both in the abstract and in relation to Hitler, to have found someone with something new to say. But I began to sense something both new and important being suggested in an understated, just short of explicit, way in a work called *Act and Idea in the Nazi Genocide* by Berel Lang, the chairman of the philosophy department at the State University of New York's Albany campus. And, in a more explicit way, in a preliminary essay Lang drew my attention to called "The History of Evil and the Future of the Holocaust."

It was a surprise, once I began to understand the implications of Lang's argument, that it had not caused more of a stir when he first published it, although I have a feeling its implications are only beginning to be assessed and debated. Certainly, Lang's book attracted favorable notice when it appeared. He was a fairly prominent writer and thinker on these questions, he'd chaired prestigious symposia and authored two previous books on the subject. And his newest work, *Act and Idea*, had attracted praise. Saul Friedländer, one of the most highly regarded thinkers on the question, called it "one of the most important attempts made to face the philosophic implications of the Nazi genocide," and Cynthia Ozick credited Lang with "an intellectual and technical force equal to that of Primo Levi."

But I fear the power and import of Lang's breakthrough might have been lost on some of his readers because of the reticent nature of Lang's style: In his prose, as well as in his person, he's self-effacing to the point of self-erasing. In part, it's a scholar's modesty and scrupulosity; in part, it's personal modesty, a reluctance to make claims for his own originality—so much so that I was not sure, until I drew it out from him in person, just how original his argument was.

Still, when we'd settled down in the comfortable living room of his West Hartford, Connecticut, home, even Lang expressed some surprise that many who reviewed and discussed his book had failed to react to his novel argument on the consciousness-of-evil question.

"I wondered about that, too," Lang told me.

He speculated that the attention of reviewers—because the audience for the book was primarily philosophers rather than historians—had been drawn to a later section of *Act and Idea* on Kant ("Genocide and Kant's Enlightenment"). That chapter was Lang's contribution to the debate over where to place the "philosophical blame" for Hitler and whether the sources of Nazi totalitarianism and racism might be more attributable to the Enlightenment rather than the Old Regime it rebelled against.

But, in fact, it is in the opening two sections of Lang's book, "Intending Genocide" and "The Knowledge of Evil and Good," that I believe Lang has made an even more profound and controversial contribution to the debate over the nature of Hitler's evil. Lang takes the problem Hitler poses to the language of evil, the problem raised by Bullock—if not Hitler, then who *can* we call evil?— very seriously. "It's absolutely essential," he told me, to find a way to fit Hitler into the framework of evil—or reassess whether that framework has any useful value. Finding a way is essential, but that does not guarantee it's possible.

And so, in his book, he takes on the two obstacles raised against calling Hitler consciously evil, ones that might be called the dysfunction objection and the rectitude objection. Of the first he says, "If everything is explained by some dysfunction, the one-ball theory—whichever one of them, or you put them all together, then of course—why would Hitler be responsible or accountable? What's evil about [a dysfunction]? It's grounds for a defense of insanity: 'It's out of my control. And if it's out of my control, then you can't blame me for doing it.'"

But even more problematic, Lang believes, is the argument from rectitude, the argument Trevor-Roper encapsulated by saying Hitler could not be considered consciously evil because he was "convinced of his own rectitude." It's an argument that dates back more than 2,000 years to Socrates' insistence in the *Protagoras* that people do wrong only if they have a defect that prevents them from knowing right or are deluded into mistakenly *thinking* they are doing right when actually doing wrong. Two millennia of argument have not found a way around the rectitude problem, sometimes called "the Socratic paradox." Even the most searching state-of-the-art philosophical discourse on the question of evil ends up resorting to literature rather than history when it seeks to hold up examples of people who do evil despite knowing it's so. Iago, Milton's Satan, Claggart (the persecutor of Melville's Billy Budd)—they are repeat performers in almost all such discussions, and while everyone would like to add Hitler to that list, precious few humans actually fit the description of knowing or believing they were doing evil and yet doing it anyway. Even the Marquis de Sade believed he was ultimately involved in a liberating project, not an evil one; political torturers claim to be acting out of ideology or theology. The problem is an embarrassing one for the philosophical profession, since it seems to have argued itself out of what so many people intuitively know or feel, and so almost argued itself out of history. But Lang feels we can't avoid or ignore the problem: We must revise our notion of Hitler or revise our notion of evil.

His most strenuous efforts are devoted to undermining the argument from rectitude: "Trevor-Roper buys into that," Lang told me, "maybe not blindly, maybe not completely—that they really believed their own metaphors. That the Jews were parasitic, were a microbe. And that they believed the implications to be drawn from that—that it's just as if they were doctors regarding germs that must be exterminated. And, here again, you have the Platonic tradition, which holds that people act in the name of what they *take* to be good. The question is whether this is an adequate explanation for all the instances of evil we find in the Nazi period. I mean, that's the crucial question."

To attack this crucial question, Lang zeroes in on one crucial locus of the rectitude argument, on one of the most famous statements about the Nazi genocide, Himmler's speech to SS officers at Posen on October 6, 1943. Essentially, this was a pep talk Himmler gave to the SS men directly responsible for organizing and executing the death-camp slaughter. This was a special group that, Himmler said, had to harden themselves against the human considerations that might call out to them from the mass graves, from the women and children:

> The hard decision had to be made that this people [the Jews] should
> be caused to disappear from the earth. . . . Perhaps at a much later

time, we can consider whether we should say something more about this to the German people. I myself believe that it is better for us—us together—to have borne this for our people, that we have taken the responsibility for it on ourselves (the responsibility for an act, not just for an idea) and that we should take this secret with us into the grave.

A chilling pronouncement, one that represents—in the absence of a signed order from Hitler—one of the most explicit statements on record of the intent and the mind-set behind the Final Solution. As such, it is often cited to refute the arguments of the so-called functionalist school, which holds that there was no central directive or determination to exterminate the Jews, that it just happened out of bureaucratic exigency—the difficulties of otherwise disposing of the millions of Jews in captured Polish and Soviet territory after the 1941 invasion; that it was cobbled together by middle managers rather than imposed from above.

But Berel Lang focuses on this speech as the crux of the rectitude argument: It offers within it suggestions for and against the notion that the top Nazis were convinced of their own rectitude in pursuing the extermination of the Jews. It seems, on the one hand, that Himmler is arguing to the SS men carrying it out that he believes that what they are doing is a noble and elevated mission on behalf of mankind. But, on the other hand, could not the injunction to silence or concealment, the necessity of taking the secret "to the grave," in fact come less from "noble" considerations than from Himmler's consciousness of the *criminality* of their actions?

It's worth dwelling on the way Lang deals with the contradictory implications of the Himmler speech because it illustrates the manner in which he brings to bear the insights of both history and philosophy on the question of the intentionality of Nazi evil. He takes up first the rectitude question: the argument that Hitler, Himmler, and the planners of the Final Solution thought they were engaged in a noble crusade. The strongest and most inflammatory argument deployed in support of this proposition—that in their own minds, at least, the top Nazis were idealists—is the Pasteur/Koch analogy, the germ theory of Jewishness. In this view, we must credit the sincerity of the self-image propagated by Hitler and Himmler—that in exterminating the Jews, they were acting akin to idealistic, self-sacrificing *doctors*, healers, trying to save the human race from a plague.

As early as 1919, Hitler wrote that "the effect of Jewry will be the racial tuberculosis of nations." The implication: doctors treating a germ-caused disease do not seek to reform or educate the germs but to exterminate them for the sake of the life of the patient. For the sake of the life of the Aryan race—if the Jews are tuberculosis germs—such germs must be exterminated. Hitler made this analogy explicit in February 1942 as the programmatic extermination of the Jews had gathered momentum: "The discovery of the Jewish virus is one of the greatest revolutions that has been undertaken in the history of the world. The struggle we are waging is of the same kind as in the past century, that of [Louis] Pasteur and [Robert] Koch. How many diseases can be traced back to the Jewish virus! We shall regain our health only when we exterminate the Jews."

Here, then, in its most refined form, is Hitler's preferred self-image, his self-explanation. He is Doctor Hitler, the crusading, germ-fighting hero virologist, trying to save the human race from a plague of deadly infectious germs. The grotesque enormity of the image does not prima facie exclude the possibility that Hitler believed it or deceived himself into believing it, in which case it validates Trevor-Roper's rectitude argument. While I am more inclined to see Hitler as a vicious, cold-blooded hater who fabricated, counterfeited a *mask* of rectitude for the sake of history and expediency, is there any way—aside from retroactive mind reading—to disprove this medical-crusader version of Hitler's self-image?

Lang scrupulously examines some of the weaker objections to the medical-rectitude model before going on to what I believe is his own stronger approach. Among the weaker objections is a policy shift that has become a famous crux in Hitler studies: the 1944 decision, when the eastern front against Stalin was on the verge of collapse, to withdraw railroad cars urgently needed to carry replacement troops to the besieged battlefront—in order to shift them instead to the task of carrying more Jews to the death camps.

Lang portrays this as an argument against the rectitude defense. If Hitler's idea was the preservation of the Aryan race and the German nation, it went against these alleged ideals to leave the front defenseless against a Soviet onslaught in order to pursue an apparently selfish personal passion (in this view) to kill Jews.

But, in fact, the opposite conclusion could be drawn: Hitler was so deeply, "sincerely" committed to the view that Jews were an infectious plague on humanity that he was willing to sacrifice the existence of the German nation itself as an independent state in order to preserve the "idealistic" goal of saving the Aryan race from the Jewish infection for all time—lose the war against Stalin, but win the war against the Jews. Which would make the 1944 train transfer evidence in support of the rectitude argument.

Another key objection to the rectitude argument, one made by Bullock among others, is the evidence of concealment and shame. Hitler and the Nazis went to great lengths to keep secret the Final Solution, which proves that they knew it was wrong, that they were ashamed of what they were doing—which would certainly contravene the view they were convinced of their rectitude.

On the other hand, there's nothing intrinsic in the fact of concealment to make it a necessary conclusion that concealment came from shame as opposed to, let's say, "idealistic" prudence. The kind of self-sacrificing, forbearing, idealistic prudence that Himmler purports to exhibit and urge on his troops in the Posen speech: We are the only ones with the strength and rectitude to see that our ideals require us to take radical, horrific-seeming measures before the rest of the population is fully aware of their idealistic necessity, their "medical" urgency, the ultimate healing goal of the killing.

These difficulties that Lang raises to his attempt to prove consciousness of *wrongdoing* (rather than rectitude) on the part of the top Nazis, ultimately, I believe, strengthen the case he does make. A case that goes beyond arguing that they did what they did despite knowing it was wrong, to considering the possibility that they did what they did *because* they knew it was evil.

He begins his journey to that remarkable conclusion by suggesting the "surprising" notion that "there may be differences among wrong doers in respect to the measures of humanity they acknowledge in victims." Acknowledging someone's humanity makes it more difficult to deprive that person of his humanity or his life. Which leads Lang to argue that the Nazi dehumanizing process, "the systematic brutality and degradation" inflicted on the death-camp inmates—instead of killing them right away, they first tried to reduce them to subhumans to make them less troubling to kill—"by a cruel inversion testifies more strongly even than extermination itself to *the essentially human status accorded the Jews to begin with*" (emphasis added).

Here is a refutation of the Hitler-as-Pasteur argument, that the Final Solution was executed by those with a self-image as idealists: In fact, they didn't think of Jews as infectious germs, embodiments of disease—they *first* had to deliberately, consciously reduce them to that subhuman state in order to make the subsequent killing "palatable" to humans.

Knowingness, deliberation, consciousness of the *process* of wrongdoing, these are the elements that for Lang mark the dehumanization process as evidence of conscious evil. One can conceive of a doctor killing germs, or, say, killing contagion-carrying rabid dogs out of some service to humanity, defending humankind; but a doctor who took what he regarded as a healthy human being and deliberately reduced him to subhuman level and *then* killed without compunction or moral scruple, or who claimed moral *worth* by virtue of that kind of killing, cannot be called anything but consciously evil.

"The process of systematic dehumanization requires a conscious affirmation of the wrong involved in it," Lang says, "that someone human should be made to seem less than human; here the agent of the act is voluntarily choosing to do wrong as a matter of principle—what is wrong by *his* lights" (emphasis added).

Wrong even by his own lights. This is the state of mind that the *Protagoras* argues is impossible; wrongdoers chose wrong out of delusion, from mistaken views of what was right, not from a clear view that they were doing wrong. Proof the Nazis knew what they were doing was wrong by their own lights can be found, Lang believes, in the stages of deliberation required for the carrying out of genocide: deciding that individuals are to be judged not by their merits but as a contaminated group, deciding that the contamination is an imminent threat, and finally, a third stage in which the decision is made that only extermination can avert the danger. "Each of these stages requires reflection, denial of the evidence against it, thoughtfulness and deliberation."

The dehumanization process is, itself, an elaborately staged one, requiring not just a highly conscious awareness of what is being done but an intention to provide false covering, false color for the subsequent killing—killing that might have looked wrong before dehumanization but "right" afterward.

It is at this point that Lang makes a leap in his argument that few historians and philosophers have been willing to make. The leap from saying that the perpetrators of the Final Solution did evil despite knowing it was wrong, to the suggestion that they did it *because* it was wrong.

Many philosophers question whether this degree of evil, this kind of person, exists at all, outside of literature, where we do have Milton's Satan vowing, "to do ill [will be] our sole delight," for instance, and Richard III and Iago rub their hands in glee over the evil they design. But even Iago offers a kind of explanation, feels he needs to excuse his evildoing: He's heard it whispered about that Othello had been sleeping with Iago's wife. Iago admits he doesn't necessarily believe it; rather transparently he concedes that this "explanation" is protective coloration for his delight in doing evil for evil's sake. But still, he's fictional; in real life, even Satanists reflect a kind of inverted morality, a need to explain: They believe *God* is the Evil Usurper, Satan a misunderstood force for human liberation and good. "To do evil *despite* knowing it's evil is one thing," I said to Lang in his West Hartford living room. "But to do it *because* it's evil is quite another, isn't it?"

His response to my question stunned me because it had not been suggested explicitly in his book; it was one I could not have imagined, but one that changed the way I've looked at the question ever after. It has something to do with the notion of evil as an art, the art of evil.

Lang introduced the subject by referring to the sheer inventiveness of Nazi lies about the genocide. We had been talking about a passage from Hitler's Table Talk I'd been fixated upon, the passage in which Hitler, Himmler, and Heydrich are ostentatiously debunking the "rumor" (which they know to be true) that the Jews are being exterminated. It's silly that people should say such things, Hitler piously avers, when we're only "park[ing the Jews] in the marshy parts of Russia," although he adds that if it *were* true, it would be no less than the Jews deserved.

It seemed to me a transparent charade, in which the three architects of the Final Solution were becoming the first Holocaust deniers, the first "Revisionists," so to speak, and doing so in a particularly repulsive, winking and nodding way. It's evidence both of concealing and revealing this charade, isn't it? I asked Lang. Concealing it for the record, but revealing, almost reveling in it, with those in on the "joke."

"That would be my take on it," Lang said. "The *inventiveness* seems to me in some ways really to come to the heart of the matter, even though it's subtler than the brutality. Primo Levi used the phrase 'needless violence,' which is not quite what I'm saying; it's the element of gratuitousness, but it's more than the gratuitousness. There seems to be this imaginative protraction, elaboration that one finds best exemplified in art forms and which in art we usually take to be indicative of a consciousness, an artistic consciousness, of an overall design."

An artistic consciousness in the design and enactment of evil? Yes, he says, in part because the notion of an art of evil implies a knowing awareness of wrongdoing. If the locus of evil is in the degree of consciousness of the evil nature of an act, artistic consciousness is almost, by definition, the most elaborate, the deepest kind of consciousness.

"It's the role of the imagination in the elaboration of their acts," Lang suggests, that indicates an artistic consciousness of evil at work in the perpetrators of the Final Solution. "Brutality is straightforward, it's not imaginative. This isn't just brute strength. It seems to me that there is a sense of irony constantly—the sign [over the entrance gate to Auschwitz], you know, '*Arbeit macht Frei*' [Work will make you free]. *It's like a joke*, it *is* a joke. The orchestra playing as these people go out to work." Ironic consciousness, artistic consciousness imply contemplation, deliberation, knowing elaboration. It's there in Hitler's ostentatiously artistic falsehood in the Table Talk about the "rumor" they're exterminating the Jews.

I had an intimation of a connection I thought Lang might be driving at: If the signature of self-aware evil in the genocide project was the artistic consciousness that went into its elaboration, execution, and concealment, might one source of that be Hitler's own lifelong conception of *himself* as an artist? Or, as I put it haltingly to Lang: "The notion that artistry or artistic imagination is what is distinctive about Nazi evil. . . . It makes sense in a way of what I hadn't been able to put my finger on. But when you spoke of the *art* of it, I found myself wondering—Hitler *as* an artist, was this the source, he thought of himself as—"

"Well, there is no question that in some ways, some very obvious ways, he was an artist," Lang replied. "I mean, those rallies and his presentation of himself in his speeches. Those are nothing if not art. Now as to whether at its depth, whether one could speak of the whole as artistry, I couldn't have a judgment on that."

But he then began to speak in a fascinating way about similarities between the thinking process of the artist and that of the conscious evildoer.

"There is an element of deliberation and pride. We think of style in artwork as presupposing the choice among alternatives, a systematic series of choices which excludes some and includes other alternatives and then builds on each other. And where moral issues are at stake, then one has to say, well, I mean one could speak of moral style using the moral as an aesthetic; there has to be at least the consciousness of evil which plays its role: consciousness of the road *not* taken, awareness that the road taken is one that's believed to be evil. And the presence of inventiveness, imagination."

This is not to say that at the level of the killing squads and the extermination chambers there was an artistic sensibility (although in the latter, there was a diabolical art of deceit). It is rather a sensibility that inheres in the minds of the designers and architects of the elaborate system.

Lang brings the point home dramatically with his critique of the now overly familiar but not clearly defined notion of "the banality of evil" that Hannah Arendt introduced in her book on the Adolf Eichmann trial. "Arendt says that Eichmann demonstrates the *lack* of imagination in evil. But I think it's *there*, an imagination in his acts. One doesn't require genius to have imagination. Nobody is so banal as to be without imagination."

While Arendt tries to define evil as "thoughtlessness," heedlessness of moral questions, Lang sees it as *thoughtfulness*, in the sense of literally being full of thought (of the roads taken and not taken), of deliberation, and imagination—at least in the case of the Nazis. Evil not as *lack* of imagination, but as too much, too artistic an imaginative consciousness of wrongdoing.

Let's consider provisionally what viewing Hitler's evil as an aspect of his self-image as artist might entail. We know he defined himself in his childhood as an artist; we know his assertion of that identity set him in conflict with his powerful father, who disapproved, and brought him closer to his mother, who encouraged the sensitive-soul side of young Adolf. We know that after his father's death he felt liberated enough to set out for Vienna to pursue his artistic dream—only to be brutally disillusioned when he was rejected as lacking the talent even to *study* art at the Vienna Academy of Fine Arts. It was a rejection that was to have a shattering and lasting impact on his life.

Of course, even after his rejection by the academy and his subsequent rejection by the school of architecture, the young Hitler continued to define himself as an artist. Even in the men's shelter, he continued to hand-paint postcards to sell on the street; in the trenches of the First World War, he tire-lessly sketched fellow soldiers and the ravaged wartime landscape. (He was not—as those inclined to ridicule and underestimate him mistakenly like to say—"a house painter." He might not have been a good painter, his landscapes are clichéd and depopulated, but he was a painter for all that.)

He was an artist not just in output but in personal temperament as well. In the Munich demimonde he inhabited in the Weimar era, in the salons of the disreputable bohemian aristocrats who cultivated him, Hitler adopted the pose of the temperamental artiste with much talk of Wagner and the need to restore the artistic ideals of Greek classicism. It is the pose that flourished into absurd grandiosity in the endless art-appreciation monologues in the Table Talk, in the conscious artistic design of the Nuremberg rallies, and in the monstrous totalitarian architectural fantasies he planned (and sometimes executed) with Albert Speer.

As Gordon Craig points out, Thomas Mann was one of the first to recog-nize that at the heart of Hitler's appeal to the German people was his presenta-tion of himself as a mythmaking artist rather than as a politician. And finally, at the bitter end, in the depths of the bunker, with Soviet troops and his own suicide just days away, Hitler could not be drawn into practical discussions of his dire situation because he could not be drawn away from contemplation of the scale model of his ultimate architectural fantasy: rebuilding his hometown of Linz into the cultural capital and art repository of the Thousand-Year Reich.

It was Hitler's vanity, as well, to surround himself with collaborators who saw themselves as artistic in some form: Heydrich was an accomplished classical violinist, Goebbels a novelist, Göring a predatory art collector, and, of course, there was Speer, Hitler's aesthetic soul mate. And not without de-liberation does Richard Breitman call Himmler the *Architect* of genocide. In a study of the architecture of Auschwitz, Debórah Dwork and Robert Jan van Pelt make the case that, to a greater extent than anyone had imagined, Lang's thesis about the death camps as a conscious work of the art of evil is confirmed by the actual theory and practice of the designers of Auschwitz.

In fact, in recent years a whole school of thinking about Hitler and the Holocaust has emerged which places its aesthetic and artistic focus at the heart of the matter: artistic consciousness not as a by-product of the Nazi project but as its source. A recent film called *The Architecture of Doom* by Munich's Peter Cohen traces the source of Nazi racism in perverted aesthetics (much as Fritz Gerlich suggested in his satire of Hitler's racial science). Others go further and see Nazi racist consciousness as an outgrowth of the mainstream Western tra-dition of idealizing aesthetics—a perversion at the heart of Western culture itself, as Yale's George Hersey argues in *The Evolution of Allure*. Hersey sees Nazi eugenics as a demonic art that tried to sculpt a racist idea of perfection from the flesh of the genome through primitive biogenetic engineering that entailed euthanasia, eugenics, and mass murder as racial sculpting tools.

Perhaps the *Munich Post* journalists were onto something when they chose as a signature epithet of abuse for Hitler the phrase "political counterfeiter." A counterfeiter, after all, is a forger—an artist of sorts even if an artist of falsity, of fraud. And perhaps the contemporary novelist D. M. Thomas was onto something when he ventured that in certain disturbing respects, Hitler and Kafka were fellow artists, almost psychic twins, both alienated figures on the margins of the German Reich who fashioned a vision, an art, out of despair and dispossession, both possessing imaginations capable of conceiving of a concentration-camp world, although Hitler had the evil dream and the will to bring into being Kafka's nightmare.

There's a passage in Thomas's novel *Pictures at an Exhibition*, a passage growing out of his meditation on Kafka and Hitler as twinned artists, in which a character writes to a friend, "I need to know more about Modernism. It seems to me you could consider the death-camps a form of repulsive art. They had a terrible beauty of pragmatic efficiency, with surreal overtones. I mean, the arrival by train, which you normally think of as a homecoming, or else opening up the excitement of a holiday. And the orchestras playing jolly music. The metaphors of purification, the bathhouses and the cleansing-furnace."

As we'll see, the Kafka-Hitler link has become a ground of great contention. But does this way of thinking add anything to our understanding of Hitler and the character of Hitler's evil? Looking at Hitler through the lens of artist and artistic consciousness does succeed in linking certain of his obsessive preoccupations. Consider the extremity with which Hitler urged a "war of extermination" against degenerate art and the degenerate modernists and Jewish artists who produced it. It's possible to see his vision of inferior peoples and degenerate races as perverted *artistic* judgments: Inferior races were the "degenerate art" of biological creation. One could argue that the singular, signature gesture of Nazi evil was a kind of act of demonic connoisseurship: The encounter between Nazi and Jew on the train-arrival platform at Auschwitz was an encounter of "selection," of a kind of murderous, connoisseurlike discrimination—an almost curatorial ritual. Indeed, the official Auschwitz term for the ritual of choosing between those destined to die instantly and those destined to be worked and tormented to death in a protracted "artistic" fashion had a chilling curatorial ring: the "selections."

At the very least, looking at Hitler's evil through the lens of the artistic consciousness it exhibited helps refute the rectitude objection; there is a conscious *relish* in the horrific transgressiveness of the dehumanization process—a kind of artistic process in reverse, a *decreation*, in which humans are reconfigured, resculpted into subhumans—a relish in the process that cannot be defended as a self-sacrificing descent to ruthless methods for an idealistic cause. The methods *were* the essence, the methods were the madness.

The creation of a unique art of evil raises another issue on which Lang has some provocative thoughts to offer: the question of whether there is an *evolution* of evil, a "progression" to previously unknown forms of wickedness in the Nazi era. I asked Lang if he believed it was Hitler's creation of an art of evil that made the Nazi genocide a new benchmark, a new *fact* in the history of evil.

Lang had first broached the idea of a progression in the development, an evolution in the gravity of evil, in a piece entitled "The History of Evil and the Future of the Holocaust," published in *Lessons and Legacies*, a collection of essays. In arguing that evil *has* a history, a development from the first intentional murder (of Abel or whomever) to Hitler's genocide, Lang had not made use of the artistic metaphor. But in discussing with me whether evil might have further stages to evolve *beyond* Hitler, he did:

"I suggested [in the essay] that this may not be the last phase of evil; I would use the artistic analogy. I mean, if one can talk about the future of art, we are speaking of the imagination. I think it does require an act of the imagination, of the immoral imagination, to conceive of genocide as they did. And if one speaks of the imagination, then one feature of it that distinguishes it, really, is the kind of unpredictability of it."

"You're saying, if you could predict the next stage, it really wouldn't *be* the next stage," I suggested.

Yes, he said, and shifted to the notion of genius. "If there is genius in art, in a Mozart, and there can be genius in morality, a Gandhi, is there not an analogy to artistic genius in the genius of evil? Genius shows us something we've never seen before."

A kind of evil we've never seen before? An evil that transcends Hitler's? It's a breathtaking notion. It's—by definition—beyond imagination. Or has it already made its presence felt?

I asked Lang if he thought the phenomenon of Holocaust denial, or "Revisionism," as it's sometimes called, might be the ingenious new development in the history of evil. After all, the Revisionists at heart not only are *pleased* about the Holocaust, they seek to add—in a diabolically inventive way—insult to injury by branding the survivors and victims as liars. They exterminate the exterminated all over again by saying their deaths never existed. In their counterfeit of history, these real deaths were counterfeit. Is there not a demonic art to this—a quantum leap in the imagination of evil—in devising a way to torment the already exterminated?

Lang resisted the idea. He argued that, since the Revisionists don't deny that *if* the Holocaust had occurred it would have been a crime, they are at least implicitly characterizing the notion of killing the Jews as something wrong, something one would *want* to deny.

I'd argue that the Revisionists are frankly lying when they say they think that it would have been bad if it had occurred. In fact (as the recent book on the German neo-Nazi movement by Ingo Hasselbach and Tom Reiss, *Führer-Ex*, demonstrates), in private, among themselves they express great delight it occurred and seek to deny it in public only as a way of tormenting the already tormented survivors by dishonoring the dead. They make dancing on the graves of the dead into an evil choreography, an art.

Lang suggests an alternate conception of the next step in the evolution of evil, an evil more highly evolved than Hitler's evil, albeit without the massive body count: the one embodied in the postwar attitude of Martin Heidegger, the philosopher who became a Nazi sycophant for purposes of academic self-advancement during the war.

"Heidegger," says Lang, who'd been studying his life and work for his book, *Heidegger's Silence*, "knew it happened and he didn't care. His silence—it wasn't even denial. For him it wasn't *important*. It wasn't important! It wasn't important," Lang repeats in an uncharacteristic outburst of impassioned bitterness. "Now if you ask which of them is worse. . . . The Revisionists deny it occurred—if one asks about their motives for denying it, one can say all kinds of things, but at least if it occurred it would have been wrong. But Heidegger knows it occurred, but it's just not important; it's not something to distort history to deny—for Heidegger, this is not history to concern oneself with."

For Lang, this unconcern with history is worse than falsifying it. Knowing and not caring is worse than the art of denying, forging, and counterfeiting.

I'd suggest he underestimates how highly evolved an art Revisionism has become. Lang has never met David Irving and tried to grapple directly with the avatar of "scholarly" Revisionism. I have.

Danger?
Adds to evil?

CHAPTER 12

David Irving:
The Big Oops

*In which we explore the mind of Hitler's "Ambassador to
the Afterlife," witness the "Hitler spell" in action, and meet,
once again, Hitler as a newborn babe*

Ringing the bell on the heavily fortified, high-tech-security-equipped
entrance to David Irving's living quarters on Duke Street in London, I
couldn't help recall Alan Bullock's words on Irving. Bullock had taken great
pains to make the point that his return to the polemical fray with a public lecture on Hitler's role in the Holocaust had not been a direct or ad hominem
response to David Irving's vigorous advocacy of Hitler's noninvolvement but
was, rather, a response to Revisionists and Holocaust deniers in general. He
didn't want to dignify Irving as an opponent, as a representative of a legitimate
rival school of historical explanation and interpretation.

But Bullock is fascinated or at least horrified by the phenomenon of Irving.

"He's a real rabble-rouser," Bullock says. "A real Hitler speaker."

"A Hitler speaker?"

"Aye," Bullock says, reverting to his native North Country accent in his
contempt for David Irving, Hitler explainer turned Hitler defender.

"Aye, he goes over the top. He goes to Germany and whips it up."

Bullock was referring to newspaper reports of David Irving addressing
rallies of German sympathizers. I had one of those reports in my possession,

a 1991 dispatch by Gitta Sereny, author of *Albert Speer: His Battle with Truth*. She depicts Irving telling a Hamburg audience that in two years "this myth of mass murders of Jews in the death factories of Auschwitz, Majanek and Treblinka . . . which in fact never took place" will be laid to rest. "Two days later," Sereny reports, Irving "delivered his message to a mob of tattooed flag-waving youths in the former East German city of Halle. The crowd shouted 'Sieg Heil' when he extolled the heroism of 'that great German martyr, Rudolf Hess.'"

For all his mystical contemplation of the notion of Jesus embracing Judas, Bullock seems to see Irving as an unforgivable Judas to historical truth. Clearly, he simply despises him. "Strange little rascal," Bullock said of Irving. We'd been talking about conscious evil. "I do think he was evil. He whips it up, and he *knows he's doing it.*"

Is David Irving evil? If evil is a destination, Bullock believes Irving has already arrived at the station. I'm not sure. I believe I saw him at a moment when he'd reached the last stop before the terminal and was in the process of deciding whether to step off or go the distance.

Indeed, the decision-making process seemed to be going on before my eyes. It's rare to see the defining moment of such a process enacted out loud, but that's what I felt I was watching as I listened to Irving struggle with a fateful dilemma over a manuscript, one he is proud of discovering and yet wants to repudiate, delegitimize. Because it contains within it a refutation of the last two decades of his work. Because it contains that which Irving had long insisted would never be found, did not exist: evidence of Adolf Hitler's personal order, the long-sought "*Führerbefehl*," the directive ordering the extermination of the Jews. It was this manuscript, this decision process that led me to overcome my reservations about speaking to Irving when I was in London to talk to Bullock and Trevor-Roper. I wanted to know if Irving was, as he seemed to indicate in an interview with the *Telegraph*, seriously considering revising his Revisionist views.

The manuscript is a purported memoir by Adolf Eichmann, and a foot-thick photocopy of it was sitting on Irving's desk and weighing heavily on his mind the afternoon I visited him in his study on Duke Street. Also on his desk was a bust of Goebbels and a tiny toy-soldier figure of Hitler.

Irving's a tall, florid-faced fellow in country tweeds whose face can twitch when he becomes agitated. Which he often seemed to be in the course of our conversation. Particularly when it came to the dilemma of the Eichmann memoir.

Irving had established his reputation as a Hitler controversialist with the publication in 1977 of *Hitler's War*, a book in which his professed aim was to describe the origin and conduct of the war through Hitler's eyes, "from behind his desk." Many acknowledge Irving's diligence in digging up from German sources a large number of private papers, diaries, and documents long thought lost. "Whatever allegations may be levelled at Irving as a historian—and there have been many—there is no doubting his ability to sniff out original documents," Robert Harris wrote in his account of the 1983 Hitler-diaries fiasco. Still, most rejected the conclusion Irving had been driving at ever since *Hitler's War*: that the absence of any written order from Hitler to pursue the Final Solution proves that he *didn't* order it and probably didn't know about it.

In taking that position, he was going further—but not much further—than the more extreme functionalists among the German historians in the intentionalist-functionalist debate of the 1980s. The functionalists argue that while Hitler *might* have known of it, the Holocaust happened almost by spontaneous combustion, that it was the bureaucratic by-product of wartime circumstances and the complicity of Nazi leaders lower than Hitler in the hierarchy—Himmler and Heydrich, Göring and Goebbels along with regional authorities in the occupied eastern territories, acting largely on their own initiatives.

But in the twenty years since the publication of *Hitler's War*, Irving's views have undergone a shift or several shifts back and forth: from mild dissident to apparent agreement with radical Holocaust deniers, back to apparent assent to the fact of mass murder, albeit murder ordered by others than Hitler. On that he's been consistent. Occasionally no Holocaust, always no Hitler.

And to an ever-increasing extent, Irving has come out from behind *his* desk to become a fiery rabble-rousing Führer of the Holocaust-denial movement, addressing adoring rallies in Germany and, not surprisingly, in Argentina. "He really whips it up," Bullock had said, and indeed, on Irving's desk is a videocassette whose slipcase is adorned with a graphic picture of Irving whipping it up in front of a crowd of cheering deniers, eerily conjuring up the figure he's obsessed with.

In any case, it was at one of those rallies in Argentina that someone handed Irving a time bomb of a manuscript. It was evidently meant as a gift, a tribute from one believer in the cause to its leader, but the gift turned out to be a poisoned apple.

"The Jewish community in Argentina was foolish enough to denounce me in the national press as being a national socialist agitator," Irving told me. "Whereupon things got interesting. I was immediately whisked out of my hotel and kept in an army villa because my host said that in Argentina when people call you names like that, they're not fooling. The beneficial consequence was that at the end of the next meeting a guy came out to me with a brown-paper package. And he said, 'You're obviously the correct repository for these papers that we've been looking after since 1960 for the Eichmann family.' See, the Eichmann family panicked when he was kidnapped in the streets. And they took all his private papers which they could find, that had any kind of bearing, put them into brown paper and gave them to a friend. Then he gave them to this man who gave them to me, who gave them to the German government. Who threw me in jail and called me all these things," Irving adds, getting distracted by more recent events. (He was imprisoned briefly in Munich before being expelled from Germany as a Holocaust denier. A Munich court convicted him in 1992 of "slandering the murdered Jews.")

"This is my photocopy of them," he says, indicating a stack of papers. "I gave the original to the German government, but I made a good photocopy before I gave it to them."

I asked Irving if he could show me the bombshell "Führer order" passage that's been tormenting him ever since he came across the alleged Eichmann memoirs. He flips through the stack to a passage flagged by a yellow Post-It note.

"It's rather mind-boggling. He [Eichmann] refers on many occasions to a discussion he had with Heydrich at the end of September or October 1941 in which Heydrich says, in quotation marks, these two lines [which Irving quotes from the manuscript]: 'I come from the Reichführer [Himmler]. He has received orders from the Führer for the physical destruction of the Jews.'"

It's fairly unequivocal and, more disturbing to Irving, it appears in a memoir he believes written *before* Eichmann's capture and trial testimony.

"He keeps coming back to it," Irving tells me. "Comes back to it again and again. These flags . . . " he indicates the Post-It notes with which he's marked other places where Eichmann recalls the order for the Final Solution.

"When did you first come upon this?" I asked him.

"Christmas Eve 1991," Irving recalls. "It gave me—it rocked me back on my heels frankly because I thought 'Oops!'" He laughs, trying to make a joke out of his discomfort. "How do you explain *this* one away?"

A good question. The quote, if authentic, knocks a hole not only in Irving's then-current no-Holocaust position but also in his earlier no-Hitler-involvement-in-the-Holocaust position. It was deeply disturbing, Irving admits. "I had to tell myself, 'Don't be knocked off your feet by this one.'"

The obvious solution was to declare the Eichmann memoirs a forgery, consigning their revelations to the trash bin with the Hitler diaries. But Irving was committed to the authenticity of the Eichmann find, and furthermore, he claims, the authenticity has been verified by the German Federal Archives at Koblenz. (This is only partially true. A spokesman at the Koblenz archives told my researcher that the "memoirs" appear to be cobbled together from interviews with Eichmann by a sympathetic journalist and other sources.) Irving's reputation as recoverer of lost Hitler treasures probably can't stand another flip-flop. In the 1983 Hitler-diaries affair, Irving at first denounced the purported diaries as forgeries and then at the last minute switched and pronounced them real, precisely reversing Hugh Trevor-Roper's switch but landing, unfortunately, on the wrong side.

Now, with the Eichmann memoirs, Irving portrayed himself as torn between his desire for vindication as a digger-up of authentic diary treasures and his position as a Hitler exonerator. He shared his dilemma with the London *Sunday Telegraph* in 1992 in a quote that made it seem as if he might be retreating from his no-gas-chamber position to a revision of his Revisionism: "Quite clearly this has given me a certain amount of food for thought and I will spend much of this year thinking about it. They [the memoirs] show that Eichmann believed there was a Führer order. . . . It makes me glad I've not adopted the narrow-minded approach that there was no Holocaust. I've never adopted that view. Eichmann describes in such very great detail that you have to accept there were mass exterminations."

By the time I saw him, however, Irving's year of reflection on the subject was over, and he was once again very close to denying the truth of the Eichmann memoirs rather than conceding Hitler had a role in the Holocaust. He unveils for me a strategy to discredit the Eichmann extermination-order statement without discrediting the memoirs as a whole: *They* aren't counterfeit, but Eichmann could have been *lying* when he wrote them. Irving's come up with a rather flimsy conceptual framework on which to hang his desire to disbelieve Eichmann's words: the Suez crisis.

"I tried to apply the three criteria that Hugh Trevor-Roper thought were indispensable to reading documents," Irving tells me. "Three questions you ask of a document: Was it genuine? Was it written by somebody who was in a position to know what he's writing about? And *why* does this document exist? The third one is the crucial one with the Eichmann papers. He's writing in 1956 at the time of the Suez crisis; we know because he refers to it. And 1956—he's aware that any day now his cover may be blown and he may be arrested."

It took me a while to figure out why the Suez crisis would suddenly cause Eichmann to believe his cover might be blown, but I believe Irving envisions Eichmann thinking that an Israeli conquest of Cairo (or capture of high-ranking Egyptian officers) might put Israelis in possession of intelligence files on the fugitive-Nazi network, from which Egypt had recruited scientists and weapons technicians—and thus lead them to Eichmann's location.

From this far-fetched projection of Eichmann's paranoia, Irving deduces that Eichmann "must have had sleepless nights, wondering what he's going to do, what he's going to say to get off the hook. And though he's not consciously doing it, I think his brain is probably rationalizing in the background, trying to find alibis. The alibi that would have been useful to him in his own fevered mind would be if he could say that Hitler—all *he* did was carry out [Hitler's] orders. And I'm certain that at some time Heydrich would have said something like that to assure him—Der Führer habt richt der Ausrottung der Juden befohlen—which is a typical Hitler phrase. When Hitler used the word '*Ausrottung*,' it didn't carry the connotation which the word 'Ausrottung' carries [now]. Which is very important to know. I've got a whole card index on Hitler's use of the word 'Ausrottung.' But of course 'Ausrottung' means extirpation—weeding out something and discarding it. Get rid of it."

It was only in reading over the transcript of this discourse that it occurred to me how transparently Irving was projecting his own dilemma about the Führer order onto his image of Eichmann's thought-world during the Suez crisis: "He must have had sleepless nights wondering what he's going to do, what he's going to say to get off the hook. And although he's not consciously doing it I think his brain is probably rationalizing in the background trying to find out alibis . . . in his own fevered mind."

As Eichmann confronted the possibility of discovery and capture, so in *his* "sleepless nights," in his fevered mind, David Irving confronted the possibility of refutation by his Eichmann discovery.

And the conclusion about the memoir he offers me now derives from his Suez fantasy: "The first thing one has to say, it's not a document with sufficient evidentiary value to weigh very much in the balance against the other documents from the other direction, which *are* of evidentiary value. It's one which gives me pause for thought, but having thought about it, I am inclined to say that it's not enough on its own to tilt the balance."

The pose, the rhetoric are that of the serious historian weighing "evidentiary value" in the balance, and yet the pose may be a counterfeit. According to a London paper, Irving confided that he is simply trying to manipulate the media. The balance has already been tilted. When he speaks of these "other documents from the other direction," he implies the existence of documents that somehow prove or state Hitler did *not* issue an extermination order. But, in fact, those who take that position argue *not* from other documents but from an *absence* of documents—the unavailability of a signed, notarized Führer order for the Final Solution—an absence that in any case might only prove Hitler's desire to conceal.

How did David Irving get to this point, tying himself into knots to exculpate Hitler? Some—not all—of the historians I'd asked about Irving spoke respectfully of his work in the seventies in unearthing previously unseen Hitler-era documents. I mentioned this to him.

"They think I've really gone round the bend now?" Irving half asked, half stated. He still has a peculiar concern for his reputation with other historians, a reputation which, as he put it to me, is "down to its uppers, but hasn't yet worn through to the street."

How did Irving go round that bend? From the way he described it to me, the crucial development was his attempt to break into the inner circle, or "the

Magic Circle," as he characterized it to me, of surviving former Hitler confidants. Once inside that Magic Circle, he encountered—he became a living example of—the continuing power of the Hitler spell.

There were, however, stirrings of skepticism about the conventional vision of Hitler as early as his wartime childhood, he tells me. "Unlike Americans, we English suffered great deprivations" during the Second World War, Irving tells me. He was born in 1938, and "we went through childhood with no toys. We had no kind of childhood at all. We were living on an island that was crowded with other people's armies." (The alternative to this irritating state of affairs, of course, was to live on an island occupied by Hitler's army.)

What disturbed Irving, he tells me, was not the deprivation but the rationing of truth. "We saw the losses in Allied air fleets by watching the formations take off and return with great gaps in them" after bombing missions, he said. "You know these things, but they wouldn't report them in the press." And in the papers, there were the caricatures of the Nazis which led him to question official truths. "There was a magazine at that time rather like *Life* but in England called the *Picture Post*. And every issue had a caricature box rather like 'Doonesbury'—that kind of layout—and it was called 'Arthur Ferrier's Search Light,' a box of various little caricatures usually dominated by the Nazi figures. There was fat old Göring and Hitler with his postman's hat, and there was Dr. Goebbels, who was shorter and had one leg shorter. And it seemed to me at that time, as a youngster, there was something odd in the fact that these cartoon characters were able to inflict so much indignity and deprivation on an entire country like ours. I said to myself, If they're such ludicrous people, then why are the Germans doing it for them?"

It's interesting that Irving raises the same objection here to the caricature Hitler as Trevor-Roper does to the pawn and mountebank theories: Such a diminished figure can't bridge the abyss between Hitler's apparent pettycriminal character and the unimaginable magnitude of the crimes he did perpetrate, the power of the spell he cast over the German people.

"And so," Irving continues, "I began to be skeptical, and emerging from university rather footloose and feckless with no particular aim, I became a steelworker in Germany. To help me learn the language. Then finding out about Dresden, which at that time was totally unknown in the outside world. Nobody had ever heard of the Dresden air raid," he says, exaggerating somewhat. "And I wrote a book on the Dresden air raid [*The Destruction of Dresden*] which imported Dresden into the vocabulary of war atrocities. People now speak about Hiroshima, Auschwitz, and Dresden, and that's thanks to me. So I decided to be a writer. And I went to my publisher and he said, 'What are you going to write next?' and I said, 'I've decided to pick Adolf Hitler.'

"And he said, 'Well, there have been lots of books about Hitler. How are you going to justify yours?' And I said, 'Well, I'm going to tell it from the inside. The way I did with the Dresden book.' You couldn't get access to the air-ministry records of the Dresden raid, so I circumvented that by advertising in the newspapers in Germany and in Britain and America for people who had taken part on one end or another of the air raid. And I'll do the same with Hitler. I'll spend five years interviewing all the Hitler people."

At this point Irving's wife, Suzie, a young woman from Denmark, entered and asked if we'd like tea or coffee. After we made our requests, Irving returned to the story of how he got entrée to the Magic Circle. In return for collecting documents for the archivist of the Munich Institute for Contemporary History, Dr. Anton Hoch, Hoch "gave me a lot of help identifying to me the important people and all the addresses of Hitler's private staff, who at that time kept their heads very, very low. They kept down. They were a small circle of very frightened people who were putting up with grave indignities and who had a very tough time. Christa Schroeder, Hitler's secretary, had been held in prison by the Americans for three or four years, and that's a very unpleasant experience for a young girl."

It's remarkable how easily Irving's sympathies are aroused for a young woman who spends three or four years in an American prison, and yet he can appear so unmoved by the hundreds of thousands of young women who died in concentration camps. But Christa Schroeder was the key to the Magic Circle.

He pursued Christa Schroeder like a suitor. "Even with her, it took me a couple of years to get through her front door. It took a lot of patience. But the entrée to the circle, the Hitler circle, was when I translated the memoirs of Field Marshal Wilhelm Keitel, who was the head of the German high command and hanged at Nuremberg."

He tracked down the field marshal's son and asked him about ellipses and omissions in the published versions of his memoirs. "And he obviously valued the fact that I had taken this trouble to do that, because he was indignant at what the German publishers had done to this book. And because I'd taken that trouble, on the second occasion I visited him, in about 1967, he said, 'If you like, I will introduce you to Otto Günsche.' Still alive. The only one of Hitler's adjutants still alive, living near Cologne. His significance was that he was the SS adjutant on Hitler's staff who burned his body at the end. That's where he comes in. He was Hitler's most faithful bulldog. And he has never spoken to anybody except me. I got ten hours of recordings of Günsche, which he's never given to anybody else."

With Günsche, Irving was at last home free: "That was the entrance to the Magic Circle. It *was* a magic circle. They met at the graveside. When one of them left"—his curiously euphemistic word for dying—"they would meet at the graveside. And to get into that magic circle was almost impossible."

Irving lost no time exploiting his entrée: "Having got into the ring, the next problem is winning their confidence. They had stories to tell, and a lot of them had private papers. This wasn't so easy but . . . half the battle was won because I was the Englishman who had written the book on the Dresden air raids that was, by this time, a big bestseller in Germany." While it's undoubtedly true that part of the success of the Dresden book was attributable to the way it helped buttress a moral-equivalence slaughter-on-both-sides complacency in postwar Germany, I was surprised to discover that Irving didn't encourage this view at the time he wrote his Dresden book. In fact, in the last sentence of the book Irving calls Dresden "a massacre carried out in the cause of bringing to their knees a people who, corrupted by Nazism, had committed the greatest crimes against humanity in recorded time."

But the more time Irving spent with the Magic Circle, the less he seemed to focus on these "greatest crimes in recorded time," the more he seemed to succumb to the spell. Irving describes himself as laboring to gain the confidence of the Magic Circle, but another kind of confidence game seemed to be at work—one in which Irving was, if not conned, then taken so far inside their confidence, so far inside the Magic Circle, that he could no longer look at it from without. Within the charmed circle, the Hitler spell still held sway, and Irving had fallen victim to it.

"I was talking to these people in '67, '68, and '69. I carried out major interviews with all these people on tape. I went into enormous detail with them. And what struck me very early on . . . is that you're dealing with people who are educated people. [Hitler] had attracted a garniture of high-level educated people around him. The secretaries were top-flight secretaries. The adjutants were people who had gone through university or through staff college and had risen through their own abilities to the upper levels of the military service. So they were educated people with insight."

I recall wondering at the time where this praise of the Magic Circle's résumés was leading. I didn't have long to wait: "This is the point. These people, without exception, spoke well of him. Coming as I did with an as-yet-unpainted canvas, this was really the seminal point, the seminal experience— to find twenty-five people of education, all of whom privately spoke well of him. Once they'd won your confidence and they knew that you weren't going to go and report them to the state prosecutor, they trusted you. And they thought, well, now at last they were doing their chief a service."

I believe Freudian slips are often overrated as tools of analysis. Nonetheless, Irving's slip here—"Once they'd won your confidence" when clearly in the context he means "once *you'd* won *their* confidence"—gives away the true nature of the confidence game going on. Irving's reasoning is fairly suspect on several other counts. First, his claim that he approached his Magic Circle sources with "an as-yet-unpainted canvas" is unconvincing—unpainted, perhaps, but not uncolored by that time.

More important, his claim to have been thunderstruck that people with excellent résumés still spoke highly of Hitler should scarcely come as a revelation. (He also tells me without a trace of irony that they told him Hitler was well loved by children and dogs.) More important than their degree of education in shaping their postwar view is their degree of association with Hitler: It serves their own self-image far better if the Hitler they present to the world, the Hitler they served so faithfully, is the congenial gemütlich host of the post-midnight dinner parties rather than the mass murderer of millions. All that happened outside the bunker, outside the Magic Circle's purview.

But Irving still maintains he was just absolutely astonished to find all this goodwill from the secretaries and flunkies: "That's what convinced me that obviously there was a book to be written here. That there were two Adolf Hitlers. There was the Adolf Hitler of Madison Avenue and Hollywood. And there was the Adolf Hitler that these people had experienced in flesh and blood. That he was a walking, talking ordinary human being with bad breath and largely false teeth."

What's false here is not just Hitler's teeth but the way Irving defines the two Hitlers: the true, flesh-and-blood, impressive-to-top-notch-secretaries Hitler, and the false Hitler "of Madison Avenue and Hollywood"—as if the flesh and blood of the fifty million casualties of Hitler's war were an invention of Hollywood and Madison Avenue. A better description of the "other" Hitler would be not the Hollywood and Madison Avenue but the Dachau and Auschwitz Hitler. The bizarre logic of this attitude inheres in the allusion to Hilter's "bad breath"—in the pretense that Irving is no slavish hero-worshiper but capable of seeing the unvarnished truth about Hilter's flaws: not the mass murder, of course, but the poor oral hygiene.

Here again, the question arose: Can Irving believe in the false logic of the two-Hitler argument, has he convinced *himself* of it? Or is he a cynical manipulator—a mountebank? The Bullock-versus-Trevor-Roper debate again, here not about Hitler but about the thought-world of his chief postwar defender. It was at this point that Irving told me a Hitler story I'll never forget, one that may go further to explain him—and perhaps Hitler—than any I'd heard. It's a story he heard from the woman who was his key to the Magic Circle, Christa Schroeder, a story about Hitler washing blood off himself.

"I was talking with Christa Schroeder one morning about 2 or 3 A.M. over a bottle of wine, and she says, 'You know, he [Hitler] could be quite cruel. I don't think you're right about Hitler's Jewish problem. He could be very cruel.' You sensed a story coming on. . . . Now, the problem with Christa Schroeder was I couldn't take notes. If she saw a piece of paper come out she would clam right up. I had to go straight round to a café and download my brain onto a sheet of paper for hours. You can discipline yourself to do that," Irving tells me.

"And she said, 'Well, you remember the Night of the Long Knives in June

1934? I was in Berlin, and the chief'—which she called him or 'A.H.'—'phoned me and said I had to go to the Rhineland immediately to join him—something had come up. And I flew over to the Rhineland and Dr. Goebbels was there. On our way to the chief, we flew down to Munich that same night, and we drove out in his car up to Bad Weisee, and I was with him when he arrested Ernst Roehm and all the SA leaders. And I was with him when he drove back, and I remember how—how impressed I was that on the way back, he personally got out of this big supercharger and stopped the oncoming cars of the other SA generals and had them arrested, too, and no concern with the risk that he was taking. . . .

"'Anyway, at the end of all this bloody day, when they were going to take them up to prison to be shot, we flew back to Berlin and I'd lost sight of [Hitler] in the Chancellory for a while. And I went to the cafeteria and I got myself . . . you know it was quite late . . . but he joined me because we were both vegetarians. He came in an hour later, stood in the doorway and he says, "So Fräulein Schroeder, now I have had a bath and I am as clean as a newborn babe again."'"

"'Clean as a newborn babe'—meaning from the blood?" I asked Irving.

"That's right. It jangled around her brain for forty years until she found an Englishman she could repeat it to."

"And why did she find that particularly cruel?"

"She found it symptomatic of the facility with which he committed mass murder," Irving says matter-of-factly. "That he just had to have a bath and was as clean as a newborn baby."

"He leaves it behind in—"

"Went down the plughole," Irving assents enthusiastically, "like the blood in *Psycho*."

This is an astonishing story, but one I'm inclined to credit despite its source because it certainly does Hitler no credit. I'm not quite sure what Irving makes of this story, but I think it can be seen as a defining Hitler story—and a defining David Irving story. A defining Hitler story because it's an image of Hitler in effect brandishing his own baby picture, pronouncing himself "clean as a newborn babe" and just as innocent in an utterly meretricious—almost *knowingly* meretricious—way: enjoying, laughing at the notion of himself as an innocent babe. Brandishing his baby picture to forge a counterfeit image of innocence, as the blood, the first trickle of oceans to come, spirals "down the plughole like the blood in *Psycho*."

And it's a defining David Irving story because he's made it his mission to wash the blood off Hitler's image, to restore him to history as a (relative) innocent, certainly one innocent of the blood of genocide.

Irving doesn't use the image of washing blood off and newborn babes, but he does use the rhetoric of cleansing—"stone cleaning," he calls it. One can trace his evolution from respected amateur historian to sporadic Holocaust denier in the way he redefines "stone cleaning" from erasing grime to erasing crime. The "stone cleaning" image came up when I asked Irving if his sympathetic attitude toward Hitler might be a reflection of his captivation, if not captivity, by the Magic Circle. "Is it possible there's a kind of 'Stockholm syndrome' going on?" I asked him.

He professed himself unfamiliar with the phrase; I explained its origin in the report of a Swedish bank robbery that turned into a prolonged siege after which hostages held by the robbers emerged from captivity speaking remarkably sympathetically of their captors.

"In the same way, did they [the Magic Circle] gain your sympathy and—"

"Oh, undoubtedly," he said without hesitation. "Every time I've written a biography, you find you become close to the character you're writing about because you're his ambassador then. You're his ambassador to the afterlife. Or to the next generation. And if you do your job conscientiously, then you bend over backward to do it." After a pause, he adds, "I don't think it should lead you to adapt an *unobjective* position," although it's hard to see how being Adolf Hitler's self-anointed Ambassador to the Afterlife conduces to objectivity. "I think that people who say I'm whitewashing Hitler," he continues, "or that I'm a Hitler apologist—these words I find deeply offensive. I'm stone cleaning, not whitewashing."

"Stone cleaning?"

"Cleaning dirt off." It's an English expression which, he says, came into use after the limitations on sulphurous coal burning cleaned up London's grime-affixing smog: "The buildings are being cleansed of sulfuric grime," he tells me. Similarly, with Hitler, he says, "There's been a lot of slime poured over him, both during and after the war."

For Irving, however, stone cleaning has meant far more than that. The turning point in the evolution of his views on the question of gas chambers and the extermination came in 1988, he tells me. Until then, he'd always adhered to the line that Hitler hadn't ordered extermination by gas. Then he came to question whether there had been any extermination or gassing at all. The occasion was the 1988 trial of Canadian Holocaust denier Ernst Zundel. Irving had come to testify there had been no Führer order. But "I was shown the reports on the tests on the walls of the gas chambers at Auschwitz"—these were tests performed forty-five years after the fact by America's self-proclaimed electric-chair expert Fred Leuchter, an engineer rather than a chemist—"and I became quite satisfied having studied forensic chemistry at university that this is an exact science and that there's no traces of cyanide compounds in the walls of those gas chambers." That was enough to convince him: "That was the turning point for me. That's when we decided we had to cut the word 'gas chamber' out of my book."

Irving says he doesn't "regard myself as a Revisionist because I'm not a Holocaust specialist." But he seems happy to take credit for the recent high visibility of Revisionism, arguing that his claim in *Hitler's War* that an absence of a written Führer order for extermination became the basis for a Revisionist view which denied that the killing process ever happened.

"So what started out as a historical footnote in my *Hitler's War* in 1977 has now become so important that prime ministers and presidents have to [denounce] it," he says proudly. He's proud, but surprisingly he's also somewhat ashamed, ashamed at least of some of the company he keeps in the Revisionist camp.

"Let me ask you about that," I said. "You know historians often speak of you as someone who's dug up a remarkable number of important documents, speak of that with great respect, but—"

"Then they say, 'Pity he flipped'?" he asked me almost plaintively.

"Well, they probably do say that in one way or another, but aren't you uncomfortable with the kind of people who are drawn to support you, many of whom are not interested in evaluating this objectively but are flat-out anti-Semites who would—"

"Yes—" he began, as our voices overlapped.

"—would, if there was no Final Solution, have *wanted* one anyway?"

To my astonishment, he said, "You're absolutely right. The word 'uncomfortable' I think is an understatement. I find it odious to be in the same company as these people. There is no question that there are certain organizations that propagate these theories which are cracked anti-Semites."

He then proceeds to make another amazing assertion: He's only *using* these "cracked anti-Semites" cynically. He plans to jettison them as soon as he can find more respectable forums.

"What else can I do?" he said, but speak at the gatherings of these "cracked anti-Semites" for the moment. "If I've been denied a platform worldwide, where else can I make my voice heard? As soon as I get back onto regular debating platforms I shall shake off this ill-fitting shoe which I'm standing on at present. I'm not blind. I know these people have done me a lot of damage, a lot of harm, because I get associated then with those stupid actions."

Fascinating: association with cracked anti-Semites experienced by Irving as the minor discomfort of ill-fitting footwear. Fascinating as well his candor about the manipulation he claims to be practicing upon the cracked anti-Semite allies he plans to discard like an ill-fitting shoe. He'll use them, these vile true believers, use them, manipulate them to give him a platform for his views and then when he—it's not clear how—becomes respectable again, he'll drop them. Why did this somehow remind me of a certain historical figure proclaiming himself "clean as a newborn babe again"? Perhaps it's the assumption that the taint of whipping up the cracked anti-Semites will all wash off, presumably just like the blood spiraling "down the plughole" in *Psycho*.

I must admit I found Irving's reasoning difficult to take seriously; it didn't make sense either as cynical, calculating opportunism (it seemed too pitifully transparent and inept to succeed) or as genuine, heartfelt rationalization of his behavior. I could not even find a Bullock-like synthesis of calculation and sincerity to make this argument seem coherent, especially (or because) he was confiding it to one of the "traditional enemy." ("Traditional enemy" is Irving's name for Jews in his *Action Report* newsletters, which seem to cater to his "temporary" cracked anti-Semite allies and Holocaust deniers. Therein one can find reports from enthusiastic home-experimenter Holocaust-deniers on their "scientific" experiments in which, for instance, they subject chickens and rabbits to diesel-exhaust gas in an attempt to disprove the possibility that such gases were used to kill Jews.)

Similarly, Irving's stance in relation to Holocaust denial has seemed to waver confusingly back and forth in the time since I encountered him in his supposed moment-of-truth deliberation over the Eichmann Führer-order revelation. In his controversial 1996 biography of Goebbels, which he was hard at work on when I spoke to him, Irving seems to argue that the Holocaust, or at least mass killings of Jews, *did* happen, but that it was the evil Goebbels who was more responsible than Hitler, still virtually innocent "as a newborn babe" of that blood. Or at least of deliberate killing, of premeditation.

That was the position he maintained when he spoke to me: that there was *some* deliberate killing of Jews, perhaps a hundred thousand or so, but mainly wildcat, unauthorized actions in the blood heat of the fighting on the eastern front. And as for the concentration camps, they were really there for concentration, not killing. It's a position he seems to hold in the somewhat schizoid biography of Goebbels: There *was* a systematic effort to eliminate Jews, but Auschwitz was not a place specifically designed to gas and kill, merely "the most brutal of all Himmler's slave labor camps and the one with the highest mortality rate"(!).

"What happened in the camps like Auschwitz and Treblinka," he told me, "was not murder except in the kind of generic sense that people were sent to camps where it was likely they would die" of starvation and disease.

"Generic murder" might qualify as one of the great evasive euphemisms of the late twentieth century. Irving makes it sound somehow less culpable than real murder, although its victims are just as dead. "There was a climate of hatred," he concedes, against Jews. "There was an atmosphere of brutality and mass murder" on the eastern front, an "atmosphere" whose origin he prefers to attribute to Allied bombing raids on the German homeland. As a result of the "atmosphere," there might have been a hundred thousand or so Jews killed there in spontaneous outbreaks by troops on the eastern front.

"You wouldn't apply the word 'criminal' to even one hundred thousand, or 'evil'—"

"Unquestionably a criminal action," he said. "But the criminal action, to my mind, wasn't genocide."

He finds an even more peculiar rationale for distinguishing the murder of Jews, even hundreds of thousands, from actual genocide. "To my mind, the crime wasn't killing Jews. The crime was killing *innocent* Jews. And it was the innocence that made it a crime rather than their Jewishness that made it a crime. But this is what the word 'genocide' is meant to blanket out. Because as soon as you abandon the word 'genocide' and call it 'innocenticide' instead, the Jewish community would oppose that."

I must admit with the introduction of the "innocenticide" concept, I lost the ability to fathom what Irving was talking about.

I tried to get past the semantics of "generic murder" and "innocenticide": "Setting aside the *name* genocide—" I began.

"The criminality is beyond doubt," he concedes. "These are innocent people being killed. And I even take it one step further than a lot of people [presumably he means a lot of people in the Revisionist camps or a lot of his crackpot anti-Semite followers]: If somebody's put in a camp where they're likely to die of typhus, this, too, is a crime, even though what happened to people who died isn't prima facie murder. Anne Frank died of typhus. She wasn't murdered. But it's still a crime. And if I'm writing a book about Adolf Hitler, I still have to absolve him of that particular crime. Because it wasn't—what's the word?—*premeditated.* Any more than the killing of all the people who died of starvation in Buchenwald wasn't premeditated at the end of the war. Emaciated corpses that television loves to show us. This wasn't premeditated. Hitler didn't go around saying, 'Okay, let's emaciate these guys.'"

But didn't how "these guys" got there to die in the first place have something to do with Adolf Hitler? I found myself fascinated by the kind of hairsplitting Irving indulged in, always with the aim of cleansing the blood from Hitler. It was somehow important to absolve Hitler of the charge of murder in Anne Frank's death from typhus, even though if typhus hadn't gotten her, one of Hitler's crematoriums would have. It was, ultimately, horrifying: It was like watching the Hitler spell in action as Irving tied himself in knots making a magic circle around the absent figure of the perpetrator, the Hitler he wants to envision "clean as a newborn babe."

I tried one final time. I quoted Irving's own words to him from something he'd written in the introduction to *Hitler's War*: "If this biography were simply a history of the rise and fall of Hitler's Reich, it would be legitimate to conclude: 'Hitler killed the Jews.' He after all created the atmosphere of hatred with his speeches, [which] even though never explicit, left the clear impression that 'liquidate' was what he meant."

"Exactly what I said to you today," Irving told me.

"But is there a practical difference between creating the *atmosphere* for extermination . . . and leaving the 'clear impression' he wanted liquidation?"

"Oh, I think a court can find the difference," he said cheerfully.

"A moral difference though?"

"It would be rather like killing somebody by negligence," he said. "Hitler was negligent in not realizing that this would be the outcome of his speeches. That would be one way of looking at it."

Holocaust by negligence; extermination as unintended consequence.

A big "oops!" by the newborn babe.

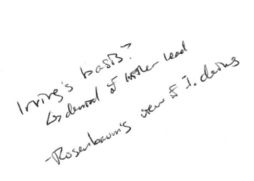

PART SIX

THE WAR OVER
THE QUESTION WHY

An inquiry into "the obscenity of understanding"

CHAPTER 13

A Tale of Three Kafkas:
A Cautionary Parable

In which the perils of pressing a Hitler explanation too far
are explored with a professor haunted by the descendants of Franz Kafka

> *Kafka moved in for the kill . . .*
> *Kafka will not give up!*
> *And I said to George, "Can't you stop Kafka?"*
> *Kafka will get you if it takes his last dying breath!*

Gazing at these lines I copied out of the transcript of my interview with Professor Rudolph Binion, it occurred to me that Kafka didn't just haunt the story of Binion's Hitler explanation, he stalked it.

In addition to the real Franz Kafka and a mysterious lodger in Hitler's Munich apartment named Kafka, the story features a relative of Kafka who was Hitler's mother's doctor; a friend of Kafka who rescued the story of Hitler's mysterious "nerve doctor" from oblivion. And a distinguished American psychoanalyst named Kafka, also a distant relative of Franz, who has become—in Binion's mind at least—the academic equivalent of a stalker. A Kafka who's been hounding Binion and his supporters at scholarly conclaves, relentlessly seeking to discredit Binion's Hitler theory—Binion's claim to have discovered, in the coded casebook of Hitler's mother's Jewish doctor, the secret source of Hitler's anti-Semitism. Or, to put it in more Kafkaesque terms, the source of Hitler's metamorphosis.

The mystery of Hitler's metamorphosis was what attracted Binion to Hitler studies in the first place. A promising young historian with a doctorate from Columbia, a professorship at Brandeis, and two well-received books—*Defeated*

Leaders (a study of three failed politicians of the Third French Republic) and *Frau Lou* (a biography of Vienna's modernist muse, Lou Andreas-Salomé)— Binion was casting about for a new subject to tackle when he came upon Bradley Smith's 1967 study of Hitler's childhood. (It should be noted that this is Professor Bradley *F.* Smith; to the professor's dismay, the eighties saw the emergence of a Holocaust-denier "Revisionist" named Bradley R. Smith.)

Binion had much respect for Smith's book on the young Hitler, but it also served to emphasize to him that something—the seed of metamorphosis— was still missing. "Smith says this young Hitler just isn't the man that we know as the fulminating Führer who's always spewing out hate and rage and so on. He's just another guy. He's sort of likeable. And something must have happened to him. I thought: *Something must have happened.*"

Binion is recounting for me the journey he embarked upon in search of that something during lunch at a deli in Brookline, Massachusetts, called Pick-a-Chick. Binion left Hitler behind long ago (his book *Hitler Among the Germans* was published in 1976 to respectful reviews in *The New York Times Book Review* and the *New York Review of Books*), although, as he put it, "you never *really* leave Hitler behind."

And, in a sense, Hitler has not left *him* behind. Binion's most recent work, *Love Beyond Death*, a study of the eroticizing of death in post-Enlightenment European culture, led him to his own highly fraught encounter with love and death. He'd fallen in love with the graduate student researching *Love Beyond Death* with him, a woman who was at the time suffering—in a haunting irony—from the very condition (metastasized breast cancer) that was at the heart of his Hitler explanation. The two became involved at a time when Binion himself was being treated for lymphatic cancer. He recovered, she died, and the harrowing emotions he experienced have found a place in a long verse play he's written called *The Patient*, a floppy-disk copy of which he handed me at his apartment before we headed out to Pick-a-Chick.

And Hitler has not left him behind in another sense: Binion's archenemy Kafka, the descendant of Franz, continues to wage unceasing war on his Hitler theory, forcing Binion to return to Hitler again and again to defend his thesis against Kafka's attack.

The recurrence of linkages of one sort or another between Hitler and Kafka throughout "Hitler studies" is rather remarkable—and controversial. In addition to the D. M. Thomas character's conjecture about the kinship of Kafka and Hitler as artists of the unthinkable and the unbearable, many have invoked Kafka as a prophet, seen the absurd logic of the death camps foreshadowed in "In the Penal Colony" and *The Trial*, and wondered whether only a Kafkaesque universe can explain the nightmare world Hitler made flesh. So many that a kind of scholarly backlash against Kafka-Hitler linkages has emerged: Michael

André Bernstein, author of *Foregone Conclusions*, has characterized the habit of reading Hitler intimations into Kafka as "backshadowing." And Holocaust-literature scholar Lawrence Langer has argued that the Kafka linkage is another instance of explanation as consolation: "Establishing precedents for the unprecedented allays the puzzled conscience of a dismayed generation that still has trouble living with the unaccountability of the history of its time."

Still, some of the little details and correspondences are striking. George Steiner, who, as we'll see, believes in some metaphysical sense that Kafka *invented* Hitler or at least Hitler's concentration-camp universe, points out, on a smaller scale, that *Ungeziefer*, the word Kafka used to describe the insect into which Gregor Samsa metamorphosed, is a favorite word of Hitler's, one he used to characterize the "vermin" of Europe, the Jews he wanted to exterminate like unwanted insects. But Binion was the first to apprise me of the very peculiar fact—meaningless except in a Kafkaesque way—that a man named Kafka once lived in Hitler's house.

"I have a friend who was a GI who'd been with the American occupation forces in Munich in 1946," Binion told me that afternoon. "And he was visiting Hitler's apartment on Prinzregentenplatz," where Hitler lived from 1928 till he took power in Berlin in 1933, the one in which Geli Raubal was found shot to death. "And he found it occupied by a lawyer named Kafka."

A coincidence certainly, but the Hitler-Kafka connections go deeper than happenstance. Were it not for Binion's Hitler explanation and the attack on it by a descendant of Kafka, the world might never have known that the Jewish doctor who treated Hitler's mother was a relative of Franz Kafka.

Is there something more to the link than these accidents of fate? It might be best to approach Binion's Kafka entanglement from the beginning. Over pasta and potato salad at Pick-a-Chick, I asked Binion if his initial interest in the Hitler question had something to do with his family background. Did he lose relatives in the camps? Having talked with him for an hour or so, I assumed by many cues that he was Jewish; he's a tall, lean, excitable *Shpritzer* type full of hostile, dismissive wisecracks about his academic antagonists; Philip Roth–esque, one might say. But apparently because of the ambiguity of his name, certain of his opponents assumed Binion was not Jewish. I don't think Claude Lanzmann—who virtually called him a "Revisionist"—knew. In fact, Binion says he's half Jewish. His father was Swiss, "but my mother was Ukrainian Jewish," he told me. "She had been in Austria and Germany in between wars," before coming to America. "After the war she rushed over to see her old friends as if nothing had happened. I remember her innocence and I thought, what's wrong with her? I had seen her cry, terribly, desperately, shortly after the war when the first revelations had come out about the camps saying, 'These were my people.' And then never another word. Until a year before she died. She'd fallen into a cellar door open [on a sidewalk in Brooklyn]. I rushed to New York, and my mother was semidelirious in her room, and she would say to me in a kind of hushed whisper, with terror in her eyes, when no one was within earshot, the doctors were gone, '*Get me out of here. They're gassing us. They're putting us into gas ovens, and we're here to be killed. Get me out of here!*'

"And in the year afterwards, I remember, when she was back in her normal mind and we were talking about her hospital experience, I said, 'Oh Mother, you don't know you were so far gone, you said *this*.' And she said, 'Are you telling me that your mother [is mad]? They *were* gassing us.' Completely insane," Binion says. "I mean there's a little corner of insanity in which she had been traumatized. But the rest, I mean in her conscious, waking, normal condition, she had no sense of being involved in the Holocaust even indirectly. You know. I think every Jew was hit in one way or another with this."

Certainly—right then and there—Binion had been hit. But he couldn't know when he began his investigation into Hitler's metamorphosis that it would bring him back to an eerily similar tableau: a tormented, delirious mother on a sickbed and her impressionable, traumatized son—not Rudolph Binion, but Adolf Hitler.

Accepting the challenge he found in Bradley Smith's book on Hitler's childhood—"something happened" to transform the "likeable" young Adolf into the later monster; what was it?—Binion began his search by immersing himself in Hitler's world, trying to get inside Hitler's head. This "method of empathy" would be a focus of Claude Lanzmann's attack on Binion's book; Lanzmann believes that to attempt to understand Hitler by putting oneself in Hitler's place, by in effect *becoming* Hitler, is a dangerous delusion that can lead ultimately to exculpation. But Binion had the courage of his convictions. He located what he believed was the key to Hitler's psyche in a cache of captured sound recordings of Hitler speeches he'd found in the National Archives in Washington.

What struck Binion most forcefully in listening to the recordings was how often Hitler articulated his hated of Jews as hatred of "*the* Jew." "It's so strange, in the first years he's inevitably using the singular—'the Jew.' I just felt there had to be *a* Jew. Now, at first, I thought maybe it was the guy who invented poison gas because Hitler was gassed. Then I saw a Gertrud Kurth," the analyst who'd worked on the OSS profile of Hitler for FDR. "Wonderful woman. She had written an article called 'The Jew and Adolf Hitler,' . . . saying just as I did that 'the Jew' was a person, and look, here's this guy [Dr. Bloch] who treated his mother, and [Hitler] didn't know what was involved in the treatment, but obviously patients always blame the doctor unconsciously when something goes wrong. And Hitler sent Bloch loving postcards afterwards with 'yours gratefully, Adolf,' and he became the protector of Dr. Bloch after the 1938 Anschluss."

The peculiar relationship between Hitler and the Jewish doctor intrigued Binion. "I thought, this is something worth investigating," he told me.

Binion then did what no previous historian had done, which was to scour the archival records and interviews for details of Dr. Bloch's treatment of Hitler's mother. And finally—his eureka moment—down there in the National Archives, in the collection of Hitler papers, he found a file labeled "Cassette de Hitler," private papers relating to Hitler that had been captured by the Allies.

Inside that, he found a Hitler document no one had ever remarked on before, that no one had imagined would have survived. It was the medical casebook of Dr. Eduard Bloch, with the record of his 1907 treatment of Klara Hitler. It had been procured by the Gestapo from Bloch in 1938 along with various other Hitler memorabilia (including those affectionate postcards from young Adolf) before Bloch left Linz for America—indeed, it turned out, as a condition for Bloch getting the precious exit visa denied to almost all the other doomed Jews of Austria.

The case notes on Klara Hitler were extremely hard to read, Binion told me. "It took a lot of deciphering."

"Was it in code or bad handwriting?" I asked Binion, little realizing I'd hit on a sore point—that this question was the occasion of the entry of Kafka into the tale.

"It turns out it was not his own handwriting, I think. There was a guy who was brought up by Bloch—was actually a nephew. But I think Bloch's brother died, and so he brought the kid up. And he is called now . . . his name is Kafka, John Kafka, a whole new person who has been persecuting me since my book came out."

"Persecuting you?" This was the first I'd heard of the Kafka-Binion war.

"Because he thinks that I blamed the Holocaust on Bloch, and he's got to deny everything that I ever said. And I was at a scholarly meeting in San Francisco, and all of a sudden this guy rose to condemn me, saying, 'And furthermore, [Binion] said in his book that it was Dr. Bloch's billing record, but it's *not* in his handwriting!'"

Before we get further into the bitter dispute between Binion and Kafka over Dr. Bloch's treatment of Hitler's mother, let's address the question: Did—does—Binion blame the Holocaust on Kafka's uncle, Hitler's mother's doctor?

This is how Binion reconstructs the situation. Adolf was not yet eighteen when his mother was diagnosed with breast cancer in early 1907. At the time, he was entertaining ideas of going to Vienna to become an artist. After his mother's operation in February and her apparent recovery, he did go off to Vienna, where he experienced his profoundly disappointing rejection by the Academy of Fine Arts. And then, in September, when he'd heard his mother had taken a turn for the worse, he returned to Linz to consult with Dr. Bloch, who told him the tumor had recurred in the surgical wound, the cancer was spreading, and only desperate measures had a chance of saving her.

Bloch proposed using iodoform, the disinfectant now mainly known as the source of "hospital smell" but then hailed as a kind of panacea in the medical literature. According to Binion, there were several things wrong with iodoform treatment for breast cancer in general: It was utterly ineffective, "ruinously" expensive, and the caustic solution caused unbearable agony for the patient it was administered to, usually in the form of iodoform-soaked gauze applied directly to the skin above the tumor.

In addition, Binion argues, on the basis of his deciphering of Bloch's medical casebook, the well-meaning doctor gave poor Klara extreme overdoses of the searing solution:

> Several decades of medical warnings were defied as iodoform gauze was packed onto the suppurating wound at an unexampled, intolerable rate (about a meter of fresh gauze containing some five grams of iodoform daily). Why did not Bloch, a compassionate "poor folks' doctor" and "benefactor of the indigent," kill the pain with morphine instead at small cost? For he recollected that Klara Hitler's sufferings "seemed to torture her son. An anguished grimace would come over him whenever he saw pain contract her face."

Why indeed? Binion proposes on the basis of somewhat sketchier evidence than he's employed up to now that Hitler himself urged the overtreatment on the doctor. He quotes Hitler's sometimes-reliable friend Kubizek recalling Hitler flaring up at the doctor's verdict that his mother's cancer was incurable. "Such a Hitler," Binion writes, "would have urged upon Bloch the drastic treatment that followed."

Binion, then, finds Hitler much implicated in the horrific and disastrous course of treatment—not Dr. Bloch alone. Nonetheless, if he does not ever explicitly blame the Holocaust on this one Jewish doctor, he's certainly critical of every aspect of the treatment the doctor supervised, from the dosage to the price. And few dispute that the results of this treatment were months of unbearable agony for Hitler's mother, suffering Hitler witnessed firsthand as she approached her painful death on December 21, 1907.

"I have never seen a boy so ineffably saddened," Bloch would say later. Adolf's suffering was intense. And transformative, Binion believes: "Hitler's experience of his mother's last illness," Binion concludes, "looms behind his later tireless diatribes against 'the Jewish cancer,' the 'Jewish poison,' the 'Jewish profiteer.'"

He cites telling examples from Hitler's rhetoric of the spectral presence of his mother's medical trauma: "How many diseases have their origin in the

Jewish virus! . . . [The Jews are] poisonous abscesses eating into the nation . . . an endless stream of poison . . . being driven by a mysterious power into the outermost blood vessels" of the body politic.

Binion deals with the obvious objection to this theory—Hitler's profusions of gratefulness to Bloch at the time, the singular protection he extended to Bloch when he absorbed Austria in 1938, the "undying gratitude" Bloch himself later described as Hitler's attitude toward him—by insisting that "consciously Hitler bore Bloch no grudges" because he was both traumatized *and* knew himself to be implicated in the "order to burn out the abscesses . . . to the raw flesh" of his mother.

But while the trauma had buried his resentment at the Jewish doctor deep in his unconscious, it festered and metastasized there, Binion insists. "Abusing 'the Jew'" in his speeches, Binion maintains, "was for Hitler a means of abusing Bloch." Murdering the Jews in the camps was the ultimate outcome.

It is perhaps an oversimplification to say that Binion blames the Holocaust on the malpractice of a Jewish country doctor, and his thesis involves more than just the Dr. Bloch episode. (Another essential triggering event of the metamorphosis, Binion believes, was Hitler's *own* medical trauma ten years later: his 1918 gassing and the treatment he received from the doctor at Pasewalk. Binion was the one who unearthed the story first circulated by Ernst Weiss, the émigré novelist and friend of Franz Kafka, that posthypnotic suggestion by a Pasewalk "nerve doctor" precipitated Hitler's metamorphosis.) Nonetheless, Binion's view of Dr. Bloch's management of Hitler's mother's treatment does lend itself to a blame-the-doctor oversimplification.

That was what most upset Dr. Kafka, Dr. Bloch's nephew and Binion's implacable nemesis, when I later spoke to him. Dr. Kafka brought to my attention the advance description of the first published form of Binion's thesis in the *History of Childhood Quarterly*:

> In 1907 a Jewish doctor poisoned Hitler's mother while treating her for breast cancer.

> In 1918 Hitler was himself hospitalized from gas poisoning in the War and hallucinated a summons from on high to reverse Germany's defeat.

> In 1941 Hitler personally ordered removal of "the Jewish cancer" from the breast of Germany through the use of poison gas. Six million Jews died as a result.

However oversimplified this may sound, in the years since Binion published his thesis, it has garnered a number of adherents, including biographer John Toland (in part) in the United States and, in Germany, the highly regarded historian Eberhard Jäckel, as well as the influential psychohistorical biographer Helm Stierlin.

Until Dr. Kafka materialized on Binion's case, those who objected to his theory tended to focus on the debatable persuasiveness of the unconscious dynamic of trauma Binion described—in which Hitler supposedly forced the Jews to pay the price for Dr. Bloch's prescriptions but spared the doctor himself. But Dr. Kafka's assault on Binion focused on his analysis of the *prescriptions themselves*, on Binion's claim that Dr. Bloch misprescribed, overprescribed, and overcharged for the searing poison he applied to Klara Hitler's breast and thus can be blamed for the Holocaust.

I'd read some vague reference to this objection to Binion's thesis in a scholarly journal, and asked Binion about it. "That's junk!" Binion told me. "This is so hopelessly stupid! No one has the patience to read through the literature as I did, but Kafka brought this up at that San Francisco meeting. And he said, 'Maybe you all think that just because he was my foster father, I'm defending him [Bloch]. But that's not true. It's because truth requires it.' Now," says Binion, "Kafka moves in for the kill. *Aargh.*"

Kafka moves in for the kill. . . . It should be noted at this point that the Kafka Binion refers to so casually and dismissively is not a lone, obsessive amateur. Dr. John Kafka, M.D., is, in fact, a scholar in his own right, a clinical professor of psychiatry and behavioral science at the George Washington University School of Medicine, a senior training and supervising analyst at the Washington Psychoanalytic Institute, and the author of *Multiple Realities in Clinical Practice*, a provocative book about the way "our personally meaningful realities are fluctuating and subtly diverging." The divergences in realities between Kafka and Binion are far from subtle, but Binion is not too far off, however, in his perception of Kafka's relentlessness, his implacability in pressing home, at every opportunity and in every forum, his attack on Binion's thesis.

But when he "moves in for the kill," he does so by entangling Binion in an unspeakably complicated and bizarre—indeed Kafkaesque—polemical embroilment over medical packaging as practiced nine decades ago in provincial Austria. Specifically, whether, back in 1907, Kafka's uncle Dr. Bloch used the "large economy size" of iodoform gauze and exactly how much use he made of it.

Binion argues on the basis of Dr. Bloch's billing notes in his Klara Hitler file that Bloch overapplied the iodoform-soaked gauze, thus causing Klara needless torture. At that San Francisco conference, where Binion was delivering a paper and Kafka "moved in for the kill," Dr. Kafka argued that while Dr. Bloch's records show purchases of forty packages of sterile iodoform gauze, Binion is mistaken in concluding he applied *all* the gauze in every package to Klara's breast.

"Kafka is saying, in effect, he bought large economy-size packages," Binion tells me, "used a little, and since he wanted the gauze to remain sterile, he would have discarded the unused balance. But the gauze *is* an antiseptic; it remains sterile. If you think it through," Binion says, "that means he would have bought a huge package, charged Adolf for it, and snipped off a bit and thrown the rest away. Completely insane! And nobody believed that."

Of course both positions are matters of retrospective conjecture, and Binion's argument didn't get Kafka to back off. Indeed, Binion says, Kafka has taken his Binion-baiting crusade international now and is stalking not just Binion but his scholarly allies. "I recently got a letter from Eberhard Jäckel," Binion told me. "Jäckel was speaking at some conference in Germany and along came Kafka to heckle him because he was one of my supporters. And he began with this business about the iodoform and the large economy size."

Binion sighs. *"Kafka will never give it up."*

I believe Binion might have lost something in translation, because the way I reconstruct the heckling-of-Jäckel episode, it took place at an international conference held in Frankfurt on the psychoanalytic and psychohistorical sources of anti-Semitism. Kafka was not present in person but was represented by what I've come to call Kafka's truth squad, a number of psychoanalytically oriented colleagues who've joined with him in his attack on the Binion theory of Hitler's anti-Semitism.

In any case, the heckling seemed to have had an effect on Jäckel, who evidently hadn't known the ins and outs of the large economy-size question and, under fire, left the conference early.

"Look, Eberhard," Binion recalls replying to Jäckel, "it's about time you looked at the problem yourself. I spelled it out as carefully and simply as I could to him, because people lose patience." And no wonder they do: If you try to follow Binion's "simple" explanation, he leads you into the thickets of his obsessively researched and calculated disquisition on the sizing and pricing of iodoform-gauze packaging in 1907 Austria.

"I went to the Austrian pharmaceutical registry, which had perfect records as far back as 1907. They sent me all the literature for that year: how much it costs, how it's sold. Iodoform gauze can be bought in three ways: small, medium, and large. And the larger was slightly more economical by so-and-so many centimeters. And you just cut off a little. And it's perfectly clear in all the books that you can just cut it off and then wrap the rest and it's reused indefinitely, it's absolutely specific." In other words, Binion is saying, Dr. Bloch *used up* all the iodoform gauze he charged the Hitlers for, which means, in effect, he *over*used, even abused it.

If we now seem a bit far afield from the quest for the source of Hitler's anti-Semitic metamorphosis, this episode is typical of how frustratingly elusive the search for certainty is about any of the fragmentary pieces of evidence that underlie grand Hitler explanations. And how bitter the battle over details can be.

Here, for instance, is the chart Binion has prepared to support his assertion that Dr. Bloch was overprescribing iodoform, excerpted from a terrifyingly complicated, four-page single-spaced response he made to Kafka's "large economy size" critique:

For his protracted treatment of Klara Hitler, Bloch certainly bought the iodoform gauze in 5-meter strips, these being the most economical. The price of 5-meter strips in Austria 1907 was:

% solution	price (Heller)	of which for: iodoform	(the rest)
10	375	13.2x10	(2.7x90)
20	480	13.2x20	(2.7x80)
30	580	13.2x30	(2.7x70)

(Calculated by Ed Green, Mathematics, Brandeis. He says the figures are slightly irregular—that 580 should be 585.)

The price of iodoform powder then was : 10 grams = 90 Heller.

Therefore, each application of iodoform gauze by Bloch involved:

solution	grams of iodoform 59 Kr.	or 35 Kr.	meters of gauze 59 Kr.	or 35 Kr.
10%	5.5	3.2	1.9	1.1
20%	8.6	5.1	1.5	0.9
30%	10.5	6.3	1.2	0.7

These are highest and lowest average quantities for 42 applications.

The maximal cost figure of 59 Kr. represents the total of the three "a conto" payments if the one for 3 October is 15 Kr.; if it is 18 Kr., then the results under 59 Kr. above should be increased by some 5%. The minimal cost figure (a) excludes the "a conto" payment for 3 October, the next "a conto" payment having been made before the iodoform treatment began, and (b) counts only 15 of the 24 Kr. paid "a conto" on 2 December, as these 24 Kr. may have been meant to last a month, or 31 days, whereas the patient lived only 19 days more.

It goes on and on, getting even more complex, virtually indecipherable. Still, I found myself returning again and again to gaze transfixed at the forest of figures, the cryptic hieroglyphs of century-old prescription protocols. I found myself feeling finally that there was something emblematic and tragic embodied in it—and in the heroically optimistic belief that pinning down with precision the mathematics of iodoform prescriptions will somehow bring us closer to the elusive spectral figure supposedly lurking in that thicket, the elusive truth about Hitler that has slipped away once again from yet another attempt to pin down the origin of his evil.

Even Binion's allies have shied away from following him into the labyrinth of his iodoform chart. Eberhard Jäckel, a historian renowned for his ability to penetrate the veils of even the minutest of Hitler minutiae to retrieve a valuable insight, resisted following Binion *this* far: just wouldn't read the insanely complex chart.

"'Don't you see what this man Kafka is doing?'" Binion wrote to Jäckel. "'He's trying to create an ambiguity where there is none!' So I get an answer from Jäckel saying, 'Oh I know you're right, so I can't be bothered with the details.'" (One German researcher who did bother with the details, Ernst Günter Schenck, author of a study called *Patient Hitler*, has claimed that Binion might have misinterpreted some of Dr. Bloch's abbreviations for iodoform, although Schenck, too, acknowledges the difficulty of finding any certainty in disentangling and deciphering the nearly century-old details of the prescription mathematics.)

By this time, the relentless Dr. Kafka had, it appeared, begun to wear down even the ceaselessly combative Binion. He described to me an attempt to reach out through the Kafka family to see if he could get Dr. Kafka off his back. He appealed to George Kren, the son of Dr. Bloch's daughter Gertrude, himself a well-known Hitler-era historian based at Kansas State University. Kren's mother had called Binion's book about her father "an international disgrace" for unfairly accusing her father of "malpractice" that "caused the Holocaust." But Kren himself had given Binion's book a fairly positive review, one that focused on Binion's belief that the overtreatment with iodoform was *Hitler*'s idea as much as Bloch's, that Hitler's implication in his mother's suffering was more important psychologically than the actual number of grams per yard of gauze Bloch used.

Then, according to Binion (in an account that is substantially confirmed by Kren and Kafka himself), Binion discovered that Kren *too* had been chastised by Dr. Kafka, his own great-uncle. When Dr. Bloch's daughter Gertrude Bloch Kren died in 1992, both George Kren and Dr. Kafka attended the funeral.

George Kren "stayed for the funeral in Trenton, New Jersey, with John Kafka," Binion told me. "And he said Kafka started in on him again. He'd attacked George at that San Francisco meeting for supporting me, and George had a terrible attack of emphysema—they had to carry him out on a stretcher! [Kren recalls the emphysema, not the stretcher.] We were all terribly upset about that."

In any case, after the funeral, in response to Binion's plea—"*George, can't you stop Kafka?*"—Kren did speak with Kafka about Binion. Only to report back, according to Binion, that Kafka said "there's no way" he'll *ever* stop. "He says that you have maligned his adored foster father," Kren told Binion, "*and he will get you if it takes his last dying breath.*"

You have maligned his adored foster father . . .

When I spoke to Dr. Kafka, I was impressed by his passion, which, he argued, came from more than a mere personal or familial motivation. He believes that Binion's psychoanalytic reasoning is simplistic and flawed; more important, he insists: "You cannot explain the Holocaust by saying some Jew is the cause of it in one way or another."

But still, something about Dr. Kafka's whole crusade recalled to me the opening lines of *The Trial*, in which Franz Kafka had written: "Someone must have been telling lies about Joseph K. for without having done anything wrong he was arrested one fine morning."

Somebody was spreading lies about *my* foster father, Dr. K. must have thought to himself on whatever fine morning he awoke to read the Binion thesis. Someone was spreading lies that the country doctor (another Kafka title, of course) was to blame for Adolf Hitler metamorphosing into *Adolf Hitler*.

The story of Binion's haunting by Dr. Kafka is in itself a kind of Kafkaesque parable of the danger, the consequences of too confidently trying to explain Hitler, of the way such explanation can almost inevitably involve shifting responsibility from Hitler to whoever or whatever supposedly "caused" his metamorphosis. In particular, it's an example of the danger of trying to trace, to pin the origin of his anti-Semitism on a hapless Jew. Binion doesn't go as far as George Steiner, who, as we'll see, not only seems willing to blame the Holocaust on Jewish ideas, he seems to want, in a more than metaphorical way, to blame it and Hitler on the power of Franz Kafka's imagination.

But Binion's Hitler explanation has become the symbolic focus, even the scapegoat, for a radical reaction against, a rejection of, the whole project of explanation itself, a rejection embodied in Claude Lanzmann's fervent denunciation of the "obscenity of the very project of understanding."

CHAPTER 14

Claude Lanzmann and
the War Against the Question Why

≈

In which the director of Shoah *tries to silence a*
Holocaust survivor who fails to understand his film

It was a moment of high drama. It left some who witnessed it stunned and angry. It was perhaps the signature moment in Claude Lanzmann's ferocious campaign against Hitler explanation, his crusade to silence the question Why.

It was a moment in which Lanzmann, the maker of *Shoah*, the highly respected nine-and-a-half-hour Holocaust documentary, turned on a Holocaust survivor—a man who had endured two years in Auschwitz—because the survivor had dared violate one of Lanzmann's commandments about how one should, and should not, speak about the death camps.

Some who witnessed it found Lanzmann's attack—his successful attempt to suppress the discussion the frail and gentle septuagenarian survivor wanted to have about certain troubling questions that arose from his Auschwitz experience—shocking. One of those present spoke up and compared Lanzmann's behavior to that of Nazi book burners. And four years after the attack, the target, the Auschwitz survivor, Dr. Louis Micheels, still sounded shaken when he spoke about it to me. He called the filmmaker's behavior "totalitarian." A strong term, but one that perhaps should not come as a complete surprise to those familiar with Lanzmann's position on the question. Because his central commandment—the one he enforced so harshly against Dr. Micheels, his imperious "Thou Shalt Not Ask Why"—is one Lanzmann has proudly adapted from a Primo Levi story about an SS guard at Auschwitz, a man who told Levi, "There is no why here."

Many will be surprised at how extreme Lanzmann has become in his holy war against the explainers, at the way he'll call their work "obscene," even "Revisionist," linking the Hitler explainers with Holocaust deniers. Lanzmann is a man deservedly much honored, even revered, by many for whom *Shoah* was the primary, even the defining evocation of this greatest of all human tragedies. To many, he is a sage, even a prophet or holy man, for having been the medium of transmission of a powerful, horrifying truth. To some, however, particularly among poststructuralist, American and French academics in the thrall of the theories and jargon of Jacques Lacan, he has become the center of what amounts to a literary theorists' Holocaust cult—academics whose response to Lanzmann's film is to celebrate it for embodying poststructuralist, theoretical fetishes such as "open signs" and "mimesis of representation" in his footage of death-camp witnesses.

Consider the introductory description of Lanzmann by one of his chief academic acolytes, a paean delivered on the very evening Lanzmann succeeded in suppressing the voice of the Auschwitz survivor:

> *Shoah* . . . was described by critics immediately upon its appearance as "the film event of the century." We know today that it is more than the film event of the century, because it is not simply a film but a truly revolutionary artistic and cultural event. . . . One of the things that has been most frequently remarked upon, especially in Europe about the film *Shoah* is the amazing psychoanalytic presence of Claude Lanzmann on the screen . . . a presence tangible both in the depth of his silence and in the efficacy of his speech, in the success of his interventions in bringing forth the truth.

I thought *Shoah* an impressive achievement when I saw it, although there were some aspects of it—Lanzmann's unquestioning adoption, for instance, of the point of view of an inmate witness who survived by keeping fellow Jews about to be murdered in the dark—that raised questions in my mind about his judgment. I was not aware until I began researching the literature that had arisen around Lanzmann and *Shoah* in the aftermath of its 1985 release how the film had raised him to the vatic, prophetic heights from which he now hurls thunderbolts at those who violate his commandments. It is not an exaggeration to call them commandments. Lanzmann uses explicitly Sinai-like rhetoric to articulate the rules for all who dare to discuss *his* subject. Consider the words he used in his published attack on Steven Spielberg's film *Schindler's List*: "After *Shoah*, certain things can no longer be done."

When I first heard that line, I was sure there had been a mistake. A researcher was reading to me over the phone a translation of the version of Lanzmann's attack on Spielberg that appeared in the Parisian daily *Le Monde* on March 3, 1994.

"You mean he's saying, after *the* Shoah, certain things are forbidden," I said, thinking Lanzmann might have been echoing Theodor Adorno's famous remark that "to write poetry after Auschwitz is barbaric."

No, my researcher insisted, "Lanzmann is saying that after *Shoah*, after *his film*, certain things are forbidden."

The most severe of the many strictures Lanzmann issued against Spielberg's film was the "forbidden" crime of "creating a false archive"—that he had transgressed by attempting to re-create scenes within the concentration camps, because any attempt at representation inevitably falsified the reality. Finding a true path through Lanzmann's commandments about recreation and representation is tricky. He, for instance, in order to provoke a sobbing breakdown on the part of his key death-camp witness, the Jewish barber in Treblinka, had rented a barber shop and instructed the reluctant ex-barber to pretend to be practicing a trade he'd long abandoned—to clip hair in order to force him to confront the barbering he'd done at Treblinka: shaving the heads of thousands of women before they were gassed. Lanzmann is proud of *that* representational re-creation. But on the other hand, he is equally proud of his own rejection of *genuine* archival footage. Not only did he refuse to use any actual film footage or still photographs of the death camps in *Shoah* (footage of the sort that Alain Resnais used with devastating effectiveness in his *Night and Fog*, for instance), Lanzmann made it a moral principle that such film was inferior to *his* method of reconstruction: talking-head interviews between Lanzmann and survivor witnesses, which gives *him* more screen time in *Shoah* than any of the survivors, makes him the hero of memory, makes him "the amazing . . . presence" to replace the absent images of real victims he's forbidden and banished.

But Lanzmann goes further: In his attack on Spielberg, he insisted that if he ever found a secretly made film that shows the actual killing of three thousand Jews in a death camp, say, not only would he refuse to use it, but he would seek to destroy it. There certainly are arguments to be made on both sides of these questions, but for Lanzmann, "after *Shoah*," there is no argument: Certain matters are settled, certain things are forbidden. His film is not merely superior to reality: it replaces, substitutes for, and demands the literal destruction of the merely real.

Of course, Lanzmann is not alone in his impulse to make post-Holocaust commandments. Emil Fackenheim offered one: Thou shalt not grant Hitler any posthumous victories. But Fackenheim has the humility not to insist that after his book further discussion is forbidden, nor has he forbidden actual survivors from raising questions about their experiences, as Lanzmann did when he used his celebrity power to silence Auschwitz survivor Dr. Louis Micheels in a humiliating public attack.

It was in preparation for a scheduled interview with Lanzmann in Paris that I came upon some disturbing transcripts and memoirs of that episode, which occurred on the night of April 11, 1990, at Yale's Becton Engineering Laboratory auditorium before an audience of one to two hundred academics and psychoanalysts. After immersing myself in it, I found myself forced to ask the forbidden "why" about Lanzmann: What could possibly explain his behavior that evening? Before describing my tense encounter with the sage in Paris, some further background is appropriate.

To begin with, Lanzmann was a latecomer to Jewish identity. According to the laudatory introduction at Yale by his admiring acolyte, "Claude Lanzmann was born in Paris . . . to a Jewish family that had cut its ties with the Jewish world. During the Second World War he was a student resistance leader in France organizing, at the age of seventeen, his fellow high school students as a resistance group against the Nazis."

There is something of the zeal of the late convert in his behavior. One observer of the crusades Lanzmann and his circle have pursued so relentlessly against those who violate the commandment against asking Why suggested that the "late-conversion phenomenon" might be responsible for the fanaticism of the cult surrounding him as well: "Many of them are Lacanian psychoanalysts who have lionized Lanzmann, having themselves only come to Jewish identification through *Shoah*." Again, not through *the* Shoah but through Lanzmann's film about it.

One source of the fanaticism on the question is the combative style of the engagé French intellectual. Lanzmann rose in that world by serving first as private secretary to Jean-Paul Sartre and then later as lover of Sartre's onetime great love Simone de Beauvoir, who anointed him editor of *Les temps modernes*, a position equivalent to that of pope of postexistentialist, poststructuralist Parisian intellectuals, one that encouraged the issuance of intellectual papal bulls and proscriptions.

The style calls for a kind of moralizing, even criminalizing rhetoric of ethical and aesthetic matters. My favorite example of Lanzmann's edicts in this respect is his reply to a questioner at a seminar at Yale about the "crime" of certain camera angles. "I wanted to show the village of Chelmno, and the cameraman told me there is only one way: by helicopter. I said, 'Never. There were no helicopters for the Jews when they were locked in the church or in the castle.' This would have been a crime—a moral and artistic crime."

Maybe yes, maybe no. One wonders if the dead of Chelmno would be as exercised as Lanzmann on this helicopter-shots issue or as appreciative as his self-congratulatory tone suggests they should be.

Still, the zeal of the convert and the arrogance of the Parisian intellectual are not sufficient to explain Lanzmann's rage, the violence of his attack on the idea of explanation. Certainly, the eleven-year ordeal of making *Shoah*, of living with the horror as he did, helps make the passion he brings to these questions understandable. Once, in the course of researching a story on the bitter controversies over the origin and meaning of the Dead Sea Scrolls—and the potentially momentous implications their decipherment might have for both Judaism and Christianity—a prominent Scrolls scholar, the head of the Princeton Theological Seminary Dead Sea Scrolls publication project, began ticking off for me a casualty list of some of the most brilliant of the Scrolls scholars, men who had been driven to madness, drink, religious conversion, suicide, and heretical visions by the long years they'd spent trying to piece together some meaning from the hellish jigsaw puzzle of the fragmentary scraps of scrolls that remained to be linked up. The attempt to find some ultimate Lost Revelation, perhaps the very fingerprints of God in these tattered scraps of ancient parchment, drove all too many over the edge. It's surprising it hasn't happened more often among those like Lanzmann trying to piece together the truth about the nature of ultimate evil from the fragmentary scraps of evidence that are our only clues.

But what's surprising about Lanzmann's post-*Shoah* crusade is not the passion of his own views but the violence of his attack against views of others. It's not enough to refute their logic or question their assumptions; they must be hounded into silence or oblivion, branded as guilty of virtual complicity in the Holocaust. Consider the way Lanzmann virtually branded Rudolph Binion of Brandeis, the son of a Jewish mother, as "a Revisionist"—a Holocaust-denying Nazi sympathizer. As editor of *Les temps modernes*, it wasn't enough for Lanzmann to publish an acolyte's vituperative assault on Binion's book *Hitler Among the Germans*, an attack that nearly caused cancellation of a planned French edition of the book. But Lanzmann could not resist putting a blood-red banner across the otherwise sedate cover of that issue for a promotional blurb:

RUDOLF BINION AND ADOLF HITLER: PSYCHOHISTORY AS FIG LEAF FOR REVISIONISM?

Binion believes the misspelling of his first name as "Rudolf" rather than "Rudolph" was a sly covert effort to make it conform visually with Adolf.

Whatever the case, the overt content of the promotional blurb is an assault in itself: In asking whether Binion's Hitler explanation is a "fig leaf for Revisionism," Lanzmann comes very close to branding Binion himself as a Revisionist, the clear implication being that his work is a deliberate attempt not merely to explain but to exonerate Hitler. Indeed, Lanzmann's belief is that all explanation *is*, de facto, exoneration; but he can't resist the imputation that in Binion's case the explainer's thinly veiled *goal* is the same as that of neo-Nazi Holocaust deniers. Binion told me he took Lanzmann to court in France for the Revisionist slur, but that after winning a preliminary judgment that he was entitled to a full-scale trial he had to drop the suit because he couldn't afford to pursue it on his Brandeis professor's salary.

"'Revisionist' is a strong word to use," I said to Lanzmann in the course of our encounter in his Paris office.

"I don't know if it's a strong word," he said, "but the ruling enterprise of Binion is obscene."

Why obscene?

"Because he believes you can explain it."

Obscenity: it is the epithet of choice for Lanzmann and his devotees when attacking those who ask the question Why. "Binion doesn't shrink from formulating the question . . . 'Why did they kill the Jews,'" writes Sabine Prokhoris, the author of the article heralded by the "fig leaf for Revisionism" blurb. "The obscenity of this question is stressed by Claude Lanzmann," she says, as if that settles the matter all by itself.

But obscenity only begins to limn the rhetoric of abuse that the Lanzmannites heap on those such as Binion who ask the question Why. Consider this partial catalogue of insults that Prokhoris heaps on Binion and his work:

- "confounding stupidity"
- "epistemological monster"
- "bizarre"
- "despicable"
- "active ignorance"
- "destruction of thought"
- "scandalous"
- "perversity"
- "de facto justification of the Holocaust"
- "his [Binion's] hero, Hitler"
- "annihilated history"
- "destroyed psychology"
- "fascist discourse"
- "poisonous imposture"

This catalogue of abuse, used to support the familiar Lanzmann argument that to attempt to explain Hitler psychologically is to empathize and excuse him, builds to a final vicious thrust. Binion is guilty, Prokhoris claims, of using explicatory "method *as* final solution," a charge that goes beyond calling Binion revisionist or an apologist for Hitler; it is tantamount to identifying Binion *as* Hitler: both of them executors of a horrific Final Solution, with Binion as what Prokhoris calls, in a final epithet, a "paper Eichmann."

And so I shouldn't have been surprised, I suppose, when it turned out that in person Lanzmann proved as combative and intemperate on the subject as the buzz-saw prose he and his disciples use to assault those who dare to ask Why.

It was an ill-starred encounter in several respects, beginning with what in retrospect seems like a symbolic misunderstanding over "the codes." Lanzmann's assistant had written me, in reply to my request for an interview, suggesting that I contact Lanzmann when I reached Paris. After several days of missed connections, Lanzmann instructed me to meet him in his office at 7 P.M. one evening. But when I arrived there, a little early, I found a darkened building. There were no names identifying the two dozen or so buttons on the intercom, and Lanzmann had not given me an apartment number. The outer door was locked. There was a numbered and lettered keypad beneath the buzzers that, I later learned, was used to punch in the access code to the building lobby.

I stared up at the unlit windows above me and, wondering if I'd gotten the address wrong, then repaired to a nearby brasserie to call Lanzmann. I reached only an answering machine, left a message about my problem, and returned to the building to see if Lanzmann might have been waiting downstairs to let me in, thereby missing my call. Still no sign of life, much less of Lanzmann. I returned to the brasserie to call, reached the answering machine again, repeated the fruitless trek several times for a full half hour, until finally I left a despairing message on Lanzmann's machine apologizing for any misunderstanding and telling him I was returning to my hotel, a good distance away in another district. Trudging unhappily through the streets in search of a taxi, I ducked into a laundromat and decided to give Lanzmann one more call.

This time, Lanzmann answered, but in a belligerent, annoyed voice asked me where I'd been, insisted he'd been waiting for me. I said I'd been waiting outside the building but didn't know how to get in.

"But I gave you the codes," he said, meaning the access code.

"No," I said truthfully. "You didn't give me the codes."

"I gave you the codes," he insisted.

When I asked him if I could come up and talk to him anyway, he said no, now it was too late.

But, I pleaded, I'd come all the way to Paris just to see him.

Finally, he relented, gave me the codes and the apartment number, and I headed back.

Later, after the interview had concluded and I had a chance to wonder about what went wrong, something odd about Lanzmann's version of the misunderstanding occurred to me. If he'd been waiting there for me, why hadn't he picked up the phone during the repeated calls I'd made over a half-hour period when I reached only his answering machine? And why did he only pick up the phone and answer *after* I'd left a message that I was leaving the district and returning to my hotel?

It's a minor thing. I've done it myself to avoid encounters. And it's possible that he really *did* think that he gave me the codes, but I found the episode puzzling, particularly in light of what seemed like a continuing hostility when I finally arrived. Out of breath and a bit flustered, I sat in one of the chairs across from Lanzmann's desk, put my overcoat on an adjacent chair, and, trying to make the most of the time remaining, hastily slotted a cassette into my tape recorder. Before I could begin, Lanzmann stopped me and ordered me to remove the overcoat from the chair and take it out of sight into another room.

I complied without asking the forbidden why. Perhaps Lanzmann was trying to establish an atmosphere of "Here There Is No Why," his primal commandment against explanation. Later, I came to think of our exchange about the codes as emblematic of Lanzmann's commanding voice-of-Sinai attitude toward all other discourse on the Holocaust: *I gave you the codes*, in *Shoah*. After the giving of the codes, all other attempts to gain access to the mystery are fruitless at best, obscene at worst.

And to ask why such attempts must be called obscene, as I did that evening, is to compound the obscenity: I suspect that in addition to the contretemps over the codes, my encounter with Lanzmann might have gotten off on the wrong foot because my first question involved the use of the word "obscenity" and veered directly into an uneasy discussion of that evening in 1990 when Lanzmann tried to silence the Auschwitz survivor.

"You have spoken of the obscenity of understanding—" I began.

"No, no, I never said this," Lanzmann barked at me. "Forget that quote."

I was a bit taken aback by this, but fortunately I had brought with me the account of that "Evening with Claude Lanzmann" entitled "The Obscenity of Understanding," from *American Imago*, the quarterly of the Association for Applied Psychoanalysis. I read to Lanzmann a passage from his spoken remarks that night.

"You said, 'There are some pictures of Hitler as a baby too, aren't there? I think that there is even a book written by a psychoanalyst about Hitler's childhood [Alice Miller's book, he later told me], an attempt at explanation which is for me obscenity as such.'"

"Where did I say this?" Lanzmann demanded.

I showed him the photocopied pages. "This is called 'An Evening with Claude Lanzmann,' it's entitled 'The Obscenity of Understanding.'"

"Show me this," he ordered me, "where did it appear?"

"In this publication, *American Imago*," I said, handing him the photocopied sheets.

At this point, two minutes after it had begun, Lanzmann tried to end the interview. "Explain to me," he said, using the forbidden word, "what are you doing exactly?"

I repeated to him what I'd written in my original letter to him that had resulted in the invitation to meet with him in Paris: that I was writing a book that would focus in part on the debate over the explicability of Hitler, a debate I first became interested in through my conversations in Jerusalem with Yehuda Bauer and Emil Fackenheim. "I thought it was an interesting debate about whether explanation is possible or explanation is perhaps wrong. That's why I was interested in your remarks—"

"You don't speak French," he said, interrupting me.

"No."

"You should. You should learn. I have written about this."

After agreeing with him that indeed I should, I explained that my book involved conversations with people in the controversy about questions they might *not* have addressed in written works.

At this point, he again tried to end the interview, claiming that he did not have time—because of my mistake about the codes, of course—to address this long and difficult matter, but finally he relented and began to respond to my original question about his characterization of the very attempt to explain Hitler as obscene.

He began by saying something surprising and paradoxical, something I hadn't seen, read, or heard him say before on the question. "I don't say that the Holocaust is an enigma," he told me. "I don't say this. I do not think so. It is an historical event which took place. It is not an event which took place out of history. In a way, it is a product of the whole story of the Western world since the very beginning."

Before going further, it's important to note that Lanzmann has made two important and perhaps contradictory points. First, he'd conceded that he *has* called the question Why an obscenity. And second, he had nonetheless offered a kind of answer to the forbidden question, offered an implicit explanation: Hitler and the Holocaust are "a product of the whole story of the Western world," which has engendered the six million murders. Implicit therein is the assumption that there is something built into the very mode of thought and feeling, into the institutions, language, the deep structure of Western civilization that inevitably *produced* the Holocaust, an event described specifically as a "product." Implicit as well is the assumption that Hitler himself is not an agent so much as a product. The formal cause of the mass murder is not the mind or will of Adolf Hitler but the mentality of Western culture.

Except that Lanzmann is somewhat inconsistent: Once having declared that it's not an enigma, that it *can* be explained as a product of history, he then turns around and reiterates to me his belief that the Why of explanation is obscene.

"You can take all the reasons, all the fields of explanation, whether it is psychoanalytic explanation, an opposition between the German spirit, the German *geist* and the Jewish one, Hitler's childhood, and so on. You can take the unemployment in Germany, the economic crisis, whatever you want. You can take all of these fields of explanation. And every field can be true, and all the fields together can be true. But these are conditions. Even if they are necessary, they are not sufficient. A beautiful morning you have to start to kill, to start to kill massively. And I said that there is a *gap* between all the fields of explanation and the actual killing. You cannot give *birth*—in French we say *engendre*—you cannot generate such an evil. And if you start to explain and to answer the question of Why *you are led, whether you want it or not, to justification.* The question as such shows its own obscenity: Why are the Jews being killed? Because there is no answer to the question of why." Because, in other words, any answer begins inevitably to legitimize, to make "understandable" that process.

Lanzmann leaps from the epistemological inadequacy of explanation to condemning the *moral* inadequacy of those who try to explain, assuming accusatorially that they're acting in bad faith, that in attempting to explain they *intend* to excuse.

One of Lanzmann's critics in France, an expatriate American psychoanalyst named Sean Wilder, who had observed the havoc Lanzmann and his acolytes have wrought over this issue—their assault on a respected Parisian psychoanalytic institute that had the temerity to invite Binion to speak resulted in the implosion and dissolution of the Institute over the question—offered a commonsense critique of Lanzmann's position: "I think the question of 'why' is a fundamental human function. For Christ's sake, what do they think people are going to do? You put food in somebody's mouth, and if he chews and swallows it, he is going to digest it. The question 'why' is the mental or intellectual equivalent to the process of digesting. You get information, and unless you are a bloody idiot you work on it, and one of the fundamental intellectual processes is this question Why. I think it is one of the nobler acquisitions of the human mind and should be considered as such."

Lanzmann's position in insisting that people ingest only raw information without digesting it is, to continue the metaphor, a kind of intellectual bulimia. Although he prefers a different sense-metaphor for his method: willed blindness. "When I was making *Shoah* I was like a horse with [blinders]," he told me. "I did not look to the side, neither my right side nor my left side. I was trying to look straight into this black sun which is the Holocaust. And this blindness, this voluntary blindness was—is—a necessary requisite, the necessary condition for the creation. And this blindness was the contrary of blindness, it was like *clairvoyance*, it was to see, to see absolutely clearly, you know. And the only way to cope with this blinding reality is to blind one's self to all kinds of explanation. To refuse the explanation. It is the only way. It was a moral attitude, an ethical touchstone."

Hearing Lanzmann rhapsodize in the eternal language of mystics (and French intellectuals) on blindness as insight and the ethical superiority of his position recalled to me another mystical formulation I'd seen him use: "Didn't you once say that there should be a sacred flame around the Holocaust?" I asked him.

"A *circle* of flame. Yes, one should not, should never try to cross this circle."

This seemed to me the very kind of language Yehuda Bauer was objecting to when he wrote his essay deploring the "mystification" of the Holocaust. If there's a circle of flame around it, how does one know what's inside the circle? Having spent considerable time with homicide detectives, I tried to imagine the reaction of those I've known if someone had said to them, "Don't cross the circle around the body, don't ask questions about the mind of the murderer." And yet the Holocaust, while vastly different in scale, is still a homicide. Exempting the mind of the murderers from scrutiny, *shielding* the murderers with a circle of flame, is a policy that could please only the murderers and their would-be successors.

"A circle of flame around Hitler's psychology, too?" I asked Lanzmann. "Don't try to cross? . . ."

"No, there is no circle of flame around Hitler. I don't look at psychology. I am not interested in it."

No circle of flame but still a willed circumscription of inquiry. "The SS men in your movie? Not interested in their psychology either?"

"I was not interested in the psychology. I always said [to them], 'I don't talk about you, I am not interested in you.' I wanted to ask them *how* it happened."

By "how" he means only how, mechanically, they accomplished it, not how they could have become inhuman enough to want to do it.

"Yehuda Bauer says that there's a danger of mystification if we set off the Holocaust and Hitler from the processes of history and psychology, there's a sacralization, mystification—"

"Mystification of . . . "

"Mystification of the Holocaust. If we say that it can't be explained, that it's a mystery beyond understanding."

"But I told you at the beginning that it is *not* a mystery beyond understanding," he said.

"But if we can't get from the people who did it to the actual event, if there's a gap as you've said, an abyss between the cause and effect—how did it happen?"

"How did it happen?"

"Yes."

"I have shown it, I think."

"You've shown that it *did* happen. But how did ordinary men come to this? Were they evil? Were they possessed by demonism?"

"No, I never said this. No, you don't understand me, that's all."

I believe the problem is not that I don't understand Lanzmann but that I do. That his position is philosophically inconsistent: Above all else, he insists it is wrong to try to explain the murders because inevitably that will excuse them, absolve them of responsibility. And yet, he insists that there is "no enigma" about why the Holocaust happened, he *has* the explanation, it is the product of "the whole story" of Western civilization. Which in effect *does* absolve individuals from responsibility: It is not the individual conscious—thus, culpable—decisions of the murderers that are responsible for the Holocaust; it is rather the machine, the engine of all of Western history that "produces" the crime.

If one is forbidden from inquiring into the psychology of the decision to murder, there is no way to account for it happening aside from spontaneous generation or some vague notion of everything causing everything, an abstract historic inevitability that excuses the murderers from individual responsibility. I don't believe Lanzmann *wants* to absolve or exculpate the murderers of responsibility—all the more reason for him to be cautious in ascribing exculpatory "Revisionist" motives to those who take different philosophical positions on explanation from his.

Even Lanzmann's professed devotion to the question "how" as opposed to why is called into question by his attack on a recent book that demolishes the no-gas-chamber arguments of the Holocaust deniers. The book, written by a former Revisionist, Jean Claude Pressac, is based upon documents Pressac found in the Soviet archives, documents described in a *New York Times* story on Pressac as "previously unpublished commercial correspondence and contracts linking Nazi officers at Auschwitz and the German engineering corporation that built the gas chambers, ventilation systems, elevators, crematories, and other devices that made murder possible."

The French Nazi hunter Serge Klarsfeld, the man who brought Klaus Barbie to justice, called the Pressac book "a major contribution to the literature" of the Holocaust. "A problem existed," Klarsfeld told the *Times.* "Exactly how did the gas chambers and the crematoria work? How could that number of bodies be disposed of? It was a question of explaining and documenting a criminal technique, and Pressac has now provided the most authoritative account."

One would have thought that Lanzmann, who eternally urges that we should blind ourselves to everything but the how, the criminal technique, would have *welcomed* the production of these revealing documents, which revealed precisely "how." Yes, the documents were discovered by a former Revisionist, but that does not make them less authentic. And in his film Lanzmann did not scruple to ask former SS men "how."

But according to the *Times*, Lanzmann was "enraged by the book. 'Mr. Pressac's work,' he wrote in the weekly *Le Nouvelle Observateur*, 'is pernicious and marked by the bizarre reasoning of people . . . who deny the Holocaust. By insisting on documentary proof, by discounting the emotional testimony of survivors, the book legitimizes the arguments of revisionists, who become the point of reference for future debate. . . . I prefer the tears of the barber from Treblinka in *Shoah* to a Pressac documentary on gas detectors.'"

He prefers then his own staged and crafted catharsis to documentary facts. But what about the importance of combating neo-Nazis' lies, which are used to justify contemporary violence against the Jews? Hitler rose to power on the back of Revisionist history, the stab-in-the-back myth that Germany didn't lose the war but was cheated out of victory by a conspiracy of Jews and Jewish-controlled "November Criminals." If Pressac helps pull the rug out from under contemporary liars and deniers, "shouldn't one try to combat neo-Nazi Revisionists in every way?" I asked Lanzmann.

"First of all," he says, "I didn't say this."

"The *Times* was misquoting you?"

"Yes," he said, "it is a journalistic thing." (The *Times* reporter told me he stood by his story when I read it back to him.)

"Okay, so tell me what you *do* feel about the Pressac book."

"What is the Pressac book? Pressac is a former Revisionist. He's convinced that the gas chambers did actually exist. And he's not discovering anything new in this. Absolutely nothing. He opens the door of the gas chamber. Everybody knew they were there."

Everyone knew, but a powerful and insidious claque of deniers is having disturbing success in convincing an alarming number of people they might not have been there. Klarsfeld, who has been on the front line of the fight against real Nazis and neo-Nazis rather than the battle over the aesthetics of filming them that Lanzmann is engaged in, believes the Pressac book is a useful weapon against the deniers.

Lanzmann purports to be interested in describing how the crime was committed but sees no particular value in studying how to prevent it from being committed again. "Yehuda Bauer told me," I mentioned to Lanzmann, "that if we don't try to understand how it happened, then we learn nothing about preventing it from happening again."

Lanzmann refused to believe Bauer could have said this. "I [have known] Yehuda Bauer for a long time. And I am astonished he talks like this." (In fact, in an essay entitled "On the Place of the Holocaust in History," attacking "mystifiers," Yehuda Bauer argued that "once [a catastrophe like the Holocaust] has happened, it can be repeated. . . . The Holocaust can be a precedent, or it can become a warning." A warning, that is, against the possibility of repetition that Lanzmann is so unconcerned with.)

"Don't you believe," I asked him, "that it's worth investigating the process of history in order to—"

"Okay, okay," he said disgustedly. "We do this. We do this. I did it. As I told you, the Holocaust is not something which is out of history. So it is an historical event."

"But you seem to be saying it's out of psychology—"

"I tell you you can take psychology, you can take economic conditions, you can take whatever you want. All of this might be true. But this doesn't give *birth* to the Holocaust. You cannot *engender* the Holocaust. As I told you, it's an ethical position."

Lanzmann is quick to define whatever choice he'd made as the only ethical one, but his self-proclaimed ethical position leads him to strange kinds of passivity in the face of the neo-Nazi movement in contemporary Europe.

"What about the neo-Nazis of Germany today?" I asked him. "One should not write about them? They want to kill Jews again."

"It is not complicated," Lanzmann says, to understand them. "And I don't think that history repeats itself. You can write about the neo-Nazis if you can convince them, and so on, yes," he allows.

"But can one do that without investigating the Nazis of the past?"

"Listen. What kind of investigation do you need? It has been done," he repeats. "I did it. I already did it."

It's been done. I have done it. After *Shoah*, it is forbidden to speak of certain things. Because I have already said what needs to be said. The rest should be silence. If Lanzmann's disciple can accuse Rudolph Binion of using "method as final solution," one can almost say Lanzmann wants *Shoah* to be the final solution of Hitler explanation; further discussion must be terminated if not exterminated.

Toward the close of our encounter, I asked him directly: "Is it *all* to be condemned—to write or even think about Hitler?"

"I think it is to be condemned," he said. "I think it is—all the way."

At this point, Lanzmann went to get some homework for me. He handed me a copy of a collection of essays on *Shoah* and instructed me to read the one he'd written, the one called "*Hier Ist Kein Warum*" (Here there is no why)—the locus classicus of his attack on explanation.

I was familiar with that essay already. I was familiar with the story Lanzmann tells in that essay, the story about an incident in Auschwitz which Lanzmann makes the very heart and soul of his commandment against explanation—the why of his attack on Why. And I still find myself amazed by his use of it. It's a story he takes from Primo Levi's memoir, *Survival in Auschwitz*.

Here is Levi's story. It's about his first disorienting day in the camp:

> The whole process of introduction to what was for us a new order took place in a grotesque and sarcastic manner. When the tattooing operation was finished, they shut us in a vacant hut. The bunks are made, but we are severely forbidden to touch or sit on them, so we wander around aimlessly . . . still tormented by the parching thirst of the journey. . . .
>
> Driven by thirst, I eyed a fine icicle outside the window, within hand's reach. I opened the window and broke off the icicle but at once a large, heavy guard prowling outside brutally snatched it away from me. "*Warum?*" I asked him in my poor German. "*Hier ist kein warum*" (there is no why here), he replied, pushing me inside with a shove.

And here is what Lanzmann makes of this story in his essay:

"It is enough to formulate the question in simplistic terms—Why have the Jews been killed?—for the question to reveal right away its obscenity. There is an absolute obscenity in the very project of understanding. Not to understand was my iron law during all eleven years of the production of *Shoah*. I had clung to this refusal of understanding as the only possible ethical attitude. '*Hier ist kein warum*'—Primo Levi narrates how the word 'Auschwitz' was taught to him by an SS guard. 'Here there is no why,' Primo Levi was abruptly told upon his arrival at the camp. *This law is equally valid for whoever undertakes the responsibility of such a transmission.* Because the act of transmitting [what happened in the Holocaust] is the only thing that matters and no intelligibility, that is to say, no true knowledge pre-exists the process of transmission" (emphasis added).

A truly astonishing thing has happened here. Set aside the fact that he comes close to asserting the position that the Shoah did not exist until its "transmission" by Lanzmann in *Shoah*. Even more bizarrely, Lanzmann has taken an SS death-camp guard's "grotesque and sarcastic" rebuke to a Jew asking why—and made that sneering mass murderer's command into *his own* commandment. He's made an insulting *description* (here there *is* no why) of a policy designed to keep the gas chambers running on time (without any troublesome Jewish questions harrying the murderers) into a moral injunction: Here there *should be* no why.

The SS guard tells the thirsty Jew he must suffer his torments without asking why; Claude Lanzmann tells those thirsty for knowledge, for an explanation, that they must suffer in a silence imposed by him. Perhaps it might be different if Lanzmann had been content to impose what he proudly calls his "iron law" on himself and his own work, as a kind of discipline. But, in fact, he and his acolytes have become a kind of gang of intellectual enforcers who don't merely disagree but seek to suppress those who break Lanzmann's law: Thou shalt have no Holocaust discussion that violates my iron law.

It's important to distinguish skeptical, even scathing critiques of Hitler explanations—in part, this book is about the follies and fiascoes of certain explanatory attempts—from Lanzmann's position. This ill-considered adaptation of the death-camp guard's abusive remark to a thirsty Jewish prisoner as a motto with which to silence *all* inquiry suggests Lanzmann has lost his sense of proportion. That staring too long into "this black sun" has blinded him to the identity of the real enemy. Or so it would seem from his treatment of Dr. Louis Micheels.

CHAPTER 15

Dr. Louis Micheels:
There Must Be a Why

In which an Auschwitz survivor fights for the right to ask Why

It all began, this memorable psychodrama, with a polite invitation Dr. Micheels sent to Claude Lanzmann. A softspoken gentleman, this survivor of a brutal hell is in every respect the soul of politeness. I began to get a sense of his extraordinary thoughtfulness in the very process of making arrangements to visit him to talk about his confrontation with Lanzmann.

Dr. Micheels told me he'd pick me up at the Westport station and then went to extraordinary lengths to ensure that we would not miss each other when the train from New York pulled in. I'd told him that since I have red hair, I'd be easy to recognize in a crowd, but he proceeded to describe his car in great detail and even made me write down his license-plate number.

It was, for one thing, an interesting contrast with Claude Lanzmann's behavior in arranging our rendezvous—neglecting to give me the access code for his building and then insisting that he *had*, practically accusing me of lying in denying he had.

But I also suspect there was more than mere politeness involved in Dr. Micheels going so far as to insist I write down his license-plate number. It was, I believe, a touching reflection of the lifelong sense of the fragility of human contact a Holocaust survivor must have. That sense of fragility haunts

Dr. Micheels's profoundly moving and sad memoir of his experience, *Doctor #117641: A Holocaust Memoir.*

In 1942, Micheels, a young Dutch medical student, and his fiancée, "Nora" (he doesn't use her real name in his memoir), fled a Nazi roundup in Antwerp only to be arrested on the run and sent to the first of several concentration camps. He and Nora were separated for a time but finally in mid-1943 found themselves—and found each other again—at Auschwitz.

Micheels's account of their time at Auschwitz is one of horror, yes, but also a story of how their relationship, their fleeting contacts, their notes from cell block to cell block, their love, kept their sanity and their humanity alive amid conditions of inhuman savagery. It's a story about the survival of humanity in hell, but it's also an account of the degrees of evil in hell, particularly as manifested by the camp personnel Micheels came to know best—the doctors of Auschwitz, the medical men who partook in healing and killing at the same time.

Men like Dr. Eduard Wirths, who personally sent tens of thousands to instant death by participating in the infamous "selections" at the railroad platform at Auschwitz, choosing which arriving Jews would be sent to be gassed immediately and which were fit enough to be "saved" for a brief living death as slave laborers. And Dr. Hans Munch, another doctor who played a more ambiguous role there, Micheels believes, refusing to participate in selections and, according to Micheels, demonstrating lifesaving "decency" to many of the prisoners under his medical care.

It was the appearance of Micheels's fiancée forty years later in a documentary film about Dr. Wirths that was the seed of the showdown between Micheels and Claude Lanzmann. He and Nora had been separated shortly after the liberation of Auschwitz in 1945, Micheels told me one autumn afternoon on the deck of his Westport home. When they found each other finally, it was not a storybook ending: "Our feeling of love could not be salvaged," Micheels wrote in a deeply saddening passage in his memoir.

He went to America, where he became a psychoanalyst, a professor of psychiatry on the faculty of the Yale School of Medicine and president of the Western New England Institute for Psychoanalysis. Nora remained in their native Holland, and, although Dr. Micheels married, they stayed in touch, and in the late eighties she wrote to tell him that she had appeared as a "witness" in a documentary two Dutch Jewish filmmakers had made about Dr. Wirths.

Micheels sent for a tape of the film (which was shown on Dutch television but never released commercially) and found it flawed but thought-provoking. In addition to Nora, among the witnesses was Dr. Munch, the one who'd refused to take part in the "selections" and who was the only Nazi doctor acquitted in a war-crimes trial, in part because of the testimony of Auschwitz survivors who believed they owed their lives to him.

"I thought Munch was important," Micheels told me, "because he demonstrated that it was possible to refuse to participate in some aspects of the killing process without being punished for it"—a fact that contradicts the exculpatory claims of many Nazis who said if they hadn't participated in the killing they would have been killed.

On the other hand, Micheels recognizes clearly that Munch did not resign from or resist the whole killing system. His behavior raises the question of whether there can be degrees of evil in hell. By staying where he was and saving some Jewish lives, was Munch doing "good" in the midst of evil? By refusing to participate in selections but following other SS orders, can it be said Munch was "better" than Wirths, or are such distinctions meaningless in Auschwitz? These are questions Robert Lifton addresses in his study *The Nazi Doctors* with his theory of "doubling"—the doubling of the Nazi doctors' personalities into killer and healer components, with little communication between the two.

The questions are valid, Micheels believed. So he wrote, politely, to Claude Lanzmann, inviting him to discuss these questions, never expecting the traumatic consequences of his request. Lanzmann was scheduled to be at Yale for a series of seminars with the French and history departments in April 1990. Micheels invited him to participate in a panel discussion with him at a meeting of the Western New England Psychoanalytic Association scheduled for the same week at Yale. Micheels proposed they discuss *Shoah*, Micheels's memoir, and the film about Wirths, which Micheels described in summary to Lanzmann.

Lanzmann accepted the invitation without commenting on the Wirths film, and Micheels heard nothing further from him until he arrived in New Haven two days before the panel discussion. Micheels first met Lanzmann that evening over dinner at the home of Dr. Dori Laub, a survivor and cofounder of the Yale Holocaust witness project.

"He behaved very strangely," Micheels said of Lanzmann, "both that night and throughout."

"At the dinner I attended," Dr. Micheels's wife told me, "he made so much trouble over food. First, it had to be a vegetarian meal, then he refused to eat the vegetarian food, then the wine was no good. I watched him take a swallow and spit it back into his glass. I think he was going to say something about how bad it was until he caught me looking at him with horror."

What Lanzmann did at the first dinner was essentially spit out the film Dr. Micheels wanted to show and discuss. Micheels ran a tape of it for him. "He saw the movie, but when I asked him for comments, he walked out of the room. I followed him and pressed him, but all he would say was, 'If you show that movie, I won't come.'"

Micheels was under some pressure. The panel discussion was heavily oversubscribed because of Lanzmann, whose renown far exceeded Micheels's. If Lanzmann withdrew, many would be disappointed.

So Micheels told Lanzmann, "'I won't show the movie. Let's talk about *Shoah*. I'll talk about some of my experiences.' He apologized for his behavior about the film, and I expected him not to talk about it. But when his turn came he began to talk about it, he began to attack it."

"Did you experience it as a personal attack?" I asked Micheels.

"Yes," he told me. Dr. Micheels is not one to overdramatize. Life has shown him far too much real drama for that. He is as mild-mannered a man as he is polite, so when he says that Lanzmann's attack on the film (and him) reminded him of the totalitarian methods of the camp guards, it is not something he says casually.

I've read the transcript of the public clash that evening over the film, and Lanzmann's attack on the film in front of an audience of Micheels's colleagues and friends cannot be seen as anything but a personal attack. Lanzmann conceded that he was "violent, very violent" in his denunciation of the film. And his public attack on the film that night was so full of fury and venom, it was difficult to interpret as anything but an attack on its sponsor—on anyone who believed the film should be shown and discussed and not simply burned and destroyed.

The panel discussion that evening, before an audience of psychoanalysts, Yale academics, and guests, began with Dr. Micheels speaking about his experience in Auschwitz. Speaking in particular about the Auschwitz phenomenon in which prisoners became *Geheimnisträgers*, bearers of secrets, secrets about what was really happening, secrets about what had become of the people who disappeared from within their midst, about the work many of them did keeping the machinery of death running. The silence was necessary in part because the secrets were literally unspeakable, in part because the penalty for talking about them was death, and finally because survival was possible only by a willed refusal to accept the truth.

Geheimnisträgers: At his home fifty years and half a world away from Auschwitz, I asked Dr. Micheels if the real secret too unbearable to utter was the truth about human nature.

"Yes," he said. "About how bad it could be. No one had known how bad."

But now, today, Dr. Micheels told the audience at Yale that evening, it is important for those who are the secret bearers to tell their secrets, to "make a breach in the wall of silence around the Holocaust."

He was followed by Claude Lanzmann, who felt it was more important to silence Dr. Micheels. After an effusive introduction ("[*Shoah*] is more than the film event of the century . . . but a truly revolutionary artistic and cultural event" in its own right), Lanzmann took the stage and, to Dr. Micheels's surprise, announced he would explain why he "forbade" the expected showing of the Wirths film and the discussion about it Dr. Micheels wanted to have.

In terms of contempt, using the jargon of Lacanian film theorists, Lanzmann told the audience, "It's a very bad film, in my opinion; one doesn't even know *who* did it (I think two people from Holland), but it's a film without any kind of *signature* . . . . There is no *desire* behind this film" (emphasis added).

Having dismissed it first of all for the sin of not fulfilling Lacanian film-buff criteria, Lanzmann goes on to make an even uglier charge: "I had to tell myself that *the purpose of the film was the rehabilitation of this Nazi doctor.* . . . [It is a] bad film that complacently sets out to explore a Nazi soul" (emphasis added).

At this point, Dr. Micheels, an Auschwitz survivor, stood accused in effect of being so morally obtuse that he would complacently sponsor a film that rehabilitated Nazis. One step away from the ultimate Lanzmann accusation: Revisionist. Although Lanzmann claimed to "respect very much" Dr. Micheels, he told his colleagues that the film Micheels wanted to show "represented for me all of the things I have always fought against, with all my strength. . . . What I have called the obscenity of the very project of understanding."

All this after Lanzmann had refused to tell Micheels to his face why he objected to the film when Micheels pressed him at their introductory dinner; all this after Lanzmann had indicated that he would *not* launch an attack on the film at the panel discussion.

"Did you feel betrayed?" I asked Micheels.

"Yes, I did," he told me. "He led me to believe he would not."

Not only was Dr. Micheels caught off guard, he was outmatched physically: At seventy-three, fragile and slender, Dr. Micheels said the six-foot-plus Lanzmann, an imposing figure in his black leather jacket, reminded him of "a German general" both in his physical stature and his aggressive, pounding assault on Micheels's position and judgment.

Indeed, Lanzmann was only getting started in an epic savaging of the film he wouldn't let the audience see. As he expanded on his accusation of the obscenity of (and thus the need to censor) the film he forbade, he focused first on its transgression of his commandment against studying Nazi baby pictures.

"I wish to give you the reasons for my revolt" against the forbidden film, Lanzmann says, adopting the pose of the heroic resistance fighter, rather than his actual role: a man who used his celebrity power to force the panel into dropping it under threat of refusing to appear. "The film . . . that I forbade, started with a picture of this Nazi doctor as a child, as a baby. He's a smiling child." Here, he invokes his dictum that you cannot engender the Holocaust by explaining how smiling babies become mass murderers. Not only can you not engender it, you cannot discuss the question of how it happens.

But they do, *somehow*. The babies in the baby pictures who do not seem to manifest a desire to murder *do* grow up to be baby killers. Some babies do, some babies do not. The ones who do must acquire the ability, the *desire* to do so, somehow. It doesn't happen by spontaneous generation. The fact that they do seems to be of some legitimate interest to those who live among babies and baby killers. But such interest is forbidden by Lanzmann; any such inquiry must, he insists, entail sympathy for the devil, for mass murderers. All explanation is excuse.

But, Lanzmann thundered on, the mind-set of such a film with its baby pictures "is not only obscenity, it is real cowardice. . . . It is a way of escaping, it is a way not to face the horror." It seemed more than a bit odd for Lanzmann, who has faced the horror of Auschwitz only on film, to lecture Dr. Micheels, who has faced it in person, about cowardice.

But still Lanzmann is not finished. To Dr. Micheels's horror, he's devoting his *entire* speech that night to denouncing the film Micheels wanted to discuss. And now, on top of obscenity and cowardice, he tosses out his favored trump-card insult: Revisionism.

He cites a discussion between Elie Wiesel and the archbishop of Paris (who was born a Jew but raised a Catholic by the French family that sheltered him during the war). In the context of a discussion with Wiesel on a French television show, the archbishop said, according to Lanzmann, "The true problem, the true question [of the Holocaust] is the problem of evil." An assertion Lanzmann insists is such a cowardly evasion of the horror that happened at Auschwitz that it amounts to Revisionism. Lanzmann accuses the archbishop not just of being a Revisionist but of being a Revisionist in "a much more perverse form" than that of a Holocaust denier.

Always Lanzmann insists on assuming bad faith (as the existentialists like to call it) on the part of of those who discuss the subject in any fashion that violates his commandments. The Jewish archbishop, he says—making a point of playing up his Jewishness—cannot be attempting, sincerely if misguidedly, to discuss the question; he must be a cowardly Revisionist.

Having announced the discovery of "a much more perverse form of revisionism," he finds evidence of it in the film Dr. Micheels wanted to simply discuss. The chief evidence, aside from the baby pictures: The film presents a discussion of the meaning of Dr. Wirths's suicide shortly after he was captured. Wirths's family members speculate about whether he killed himself in part out of consciousness of guilt. The presence of this footage in the film, the implication Wirths might be suffering pangs of conscience (when, in fact, the filmmakers might be taking just as jaundiced a view of the relatives' rationalization as Lanzmann does), makes it too *dangerous* to be shown, Lanzmann insists.

Lanzmann makes explicit his paternalist-censor role toward the close of his assault. He realizes, he says, that the intensity of his attack might give the audience "a strong desire to see this film." But, he jokes condescendingly, he's now "prepared that you see the film, because I have given 'directions for use.' And this was necessary because there are some virgin brains among you!"

The response of the audience to this tirade, when it finally concluded, was mixed. I felt worst for Dr. Micheels, most conscious of the sense of isolation and betrayal he must have felt, when I read in the transcript the way Micheels's colleague and fellow panelist Dori Laub suddenly and unexpectedly attacked the film.

Laub was, after all, the cosponsor of the evening. He'd seen the film but never raised any objections to it—certainly not to Dr. Micheels—until that very moment. But Lanzmann had been "violent, very violent" in his attack on the film to Laub before the panel convened, as well as in his attack on the film at the panel. And rather than defend Dr. Micheels or the plan to show the film, Laub felt compelled in his closing remarks to publicly take Lanzmann's side.

His rationale was curious. He announced that he'd been fooled, hoaxed. He said that when Dr. Micheels first showed him the film, he'd understood the German-speaking witnesses but not the Dutch. When he saw it again with Lanzmann, with subtitles for the Dutch, he had a revelation, a radical change of mind: "I realized that the film was . . . a hoax."

He doesn't explain very clearly why what the Dutch speakers had to say caused his hoax conviction. Here is how he tried to explain it: "There was no balance whatsoever between this feeble and fumbling attempt of German self-explanation and that of the [Dutch] survivors. The Germans' attempts were hardly substantive. They were not enough. There was a disproportion. And I thought it was right not to be exposed to this kind of information." As if it would be a better, less dangerous film to watch if the German self-justifications were *more* convincing.

And what of Dr. Micheels? After indirectly, implicitly being charged with the intention to promulgate a cowardly Revisionist work, he now seemed to stand accused of having perpetrated a hoax on his colleague Dori Laub, concealing from him the supposedly revelatory words of the Dutch witnesses.

I can understand the dismay Dr. Micheels must have felt at this moment, but fortunately Micheels did find at least one passionate defender that night. Late in the evening, one member of the audience rose and spoke out eloquently to Lanzmann:

What I have to say is very painful. . . . It has to do with the difficulty of learning from history and history repeating itself in different guises. . . . The Nazis started with a kind of book burning. By saying that there are things that people should not see because they are bad for people. Because they are too upsetting to the ideas that they have. Because they misrepresent. Because people cannot be allowed to make their own minds up about it. . . . The Wirths film . . . may be a terrible film. But I'm very disappointed and very angry that I was not given the opportunity to make my own mind up about it and that you used as justification for that an *ideological stance which is a repetition of exactly what it is that you're attempting to help us to understand.* And I find that very upsetting [emphasis added].

This was followed by "loud assent" from the audience. Then a second person in the audience was emboldened to challenge Lanzmann and, referring to the last speaker, told Lanzmann, "He feels that people should have been able to make up their own mind." A true revolt seemed to be brewing.

You can watch the film if you want, Lanzmann replies, he'll just "go into the corridor and . . . smoke a cigarette." It's "absolutely boring," he says dismissively. "I don't know what this film wants to convey."

Another audience member challenges him now, "Why should you have to know what it's going to convey before we can see it?"

Here Lanzmann adopts an ironic, paternalistic tone: "I really wanted to protect you [from it]."

Finally, an audience member says, "I would be very interested if Dr. Micheels—he's a soft-spoken man, but it's a film that personally, Dr. Micheels, you're involved in. . . . Could you make some comments on it?"

Four years later, Dr. Micheels and I are seated in his dining room overlooking Long Island Sound. He's just shown me the forbidden Wirths film, and he's telling me what he really wanted to say that night to Lanzmann and why he didn't.

He was, he says, taken aback by Lanzmann's assault. But there was something more: Lanzmann looked and acted so apoplectic, Dr. Micheels felt "he might have been about to break down or fall apart." And so, at the time, Micheels told me, he was reluctant to provoke further outbursts: "He looked out of control."

He confined himself that night to a dignified response: "One objection you [Claude] had to the movie [was] that it was an attempt to rehabilitate Wirths. I didn't see that in the movie. . . . Almost all of the participants were indicting Wirths."

I didn't see rehabilitation in the film when I watched either. I was alert for the kind of exculpatory psychologizing Lanzmann had indicted it for. Yes, there are the dangerous baby pictures whose insidious subtext Lanzmann warned against. And, yes, Wirths's surviving family members ramble on confusedly about whether Wirths's suicide after capture indicated a consciousness of guilt rather than mere knowledge, or certainty of imminent trial and execution. But if the family members want to rehabilitate Wirths, the film does not endorse their project; the film provides copious, sickening examples of Wirths's criminality from those survivors who witnessed it, including Dr. Micheels's dignified but impassioned former fiancée, Nora.

In any case, it scarcely seemed the sinister, quasi-Revisionist document Lanzmann portrayed it as, even with the subtitles for the Dutch. But, of course, the content of the film was not really the issue at all. Lanzmann is a man possessed by a rage against explanation. It is a rage I find much sympathy for when examining critically the often ludicrous failures of attempts to explain Hitler and the Holocaust. But it seems to me that for Lanzmann it has become a blind rage. Blindness has been elevated from a filmmaking tactic to a cosmic principle. It's an abstract rage about the crime of the Holocaust that blinded him to the feelings of one of its flesh-and-blood victims, a rage that made the victim rather than the perpetrators the object of his wrath that night. It has blinded him to the possibility that not all who seek answers or attempt to understand are knowing perpetrators of an obscenity.

I'd been surprised at the unquestioning obeisance Lanzmann's dictum on this question had received from his academic acolytes, and for a while felt alone in being disturbed by it until I found I had an ally in Tzvetan Todorov, the respected writer, critic, and director of research at the Centre National de Recherches in Paris. In his 1996 work about the death-camp experience, *Facing the Extreme*, which appeared about a year or so after my encounter with Lanzmann, Todorov remarks that "Primo Levi spent forty years after Auschwitz trying to understand why, so that he might fight the rule that harsh epigram [Here there is no why] conveyed, whereas Lanzmann prefers to make the moral lesson of the SS man his own."

But it was Dr. Micheels, that afternoon in Connecticut, who provided me with the most persuasive and eloquent defense of the question why. It was something he came up with after the showdown with Lanzmann had passed, the reply he would have made if he hadn't been stunned by the tone of Lanzmann's assault.

It's a reply to Lanzmann's appropriation of the line from the SS guard in Primo Levi's story: "Hier ist kein warum." A misuse of the line, Dr. Micheels insists. He reads me something he's written on the subject: "The word 'Hier' is the important one for my argument," Micheels told me. "It refers to the world of Auschwitz, which has become synonymous with the Holocaust. I have, as others, described this world from my personal experience as so different and so foreign . . . another planet, light-years away. It was inhabited by creatures that had little if anything in common with what we consider human beings. . . . In that world, I agree, 'ist kein warum.' However, in the civilized world to which so few of us, including Primo Levi, returned, there should be—da soll ein warum sein. Without an attempt, no matter how difficult and complex, at understanding, that very world, where truth is most important, could be lost again."

"Da soll ein warum sein": There must be a why.

PART SEVEN

BLAME
AND ORIGINS

The search for the source of the Final Solution

CHAPTER 16

Emil Fackenheim and Yehuda Bauer: The Temptation to Blame God

*In which contemplation of Hitler as an actor prompts the leading
theologian of the Holocaust to make a "double move"*

Icame to Jerusalem to speak about theology with a historian and about history with a theologian. In the time I spent talking with Yehuda Bauer and Emil Fackenheim—respectively the foremost historian of the Holocaust and the preeminent theologian of the Holocaust—I'm not sure which struck me more forcefully: their agreements or their disagreements.

Their disagreements were, certainly, more dramatic. There was their clash over Hitler's "normality." For Bauer, Hitler's murderousness was "not ordinary" but "unfortunately not abnormal," not in human history, not in Nazi Germany. While for Fackenheim, Hitler was beyond any previous notion of normal humanness—for Fackenheim, there is a radical disjuncture between human nature and Hitler nature, a radical disjuncture between ordinary evil and "radical evil."

Then there was their even deeper disagreement over the *theoretical* possibility of explaining Hitler. To Bauer, Hitler was, "in principle" at least, "perfectly explicable," as all men are. To Fackenheim, even the best explanations of Hitler are doomed to failure—only God can account for such radical evil, and he's not talking.

Wide as the gulf is between them on these issues, more remarkable to me are those matters on which—coming from such differing perspectives—they agree. Both historian and theologian agree that Hitler is still a mystery, that Hitler has *not* been explained in *practice*, as opposed to theory. "That something is explicable in principle," Bauer told me, "does not mean it has been explained already." And it hasn't been—Hitler hasn't been—this most thoughtful and searching student of Holocaust history insists: the evidence on Hitler's evolution is too thin to support a confident conjecture about the source of his evil. "I'd like to find it, yes," Bauer told me, "but I haven't. I just don't know."

Another surprising point of agreement: the use of the word *evil*. They agree on the applicability to Hitler of a term that so many are reluctant to use. This might not be surprising coming from a theologian such as Fackenheim, although he has wrestled at great length to try to redefine the nature of evil in the light of the radical evil he believes Hitler's regime brought into being. But it is somewhat surprising for a historian such as Bauer, a professed atheist, not at all given to unnecessary metaphysical speculation. But Bauer had no hesitation in employing the term contemporary sophisticates are reluctant to employ. "Hitler is not insane," Bauer told me. "He is evil. What I would call near-ultimate evil."

To reach Yehuda Bauer's office on the Mount Scopus campus of Hebrew University, I found myself crossing Nancy Reagan Plaza, passing by the Frank Sinatra Student Center, before winding down some steps to the more modest edifice that housed the Vidal Sassoon International Center for the Study of Anti-Semitism. The disjuncture between the styling-mousse aura of the Sassoon brand name and the seriousness of the center's mission (although Sassoon did serve in the Israeli army) disappeared once I found myself in the presence, the fiercely focused, intimidating presence, of Yehuda Bauer, whom I'd come to regard with some awe for the historical and moral authority of his work.

In addition to being founder and chairman of the Department of Holocaust Studies at Hebrew University, Bauer must be considered one, if not the chief, founder of the entire discipline. His work is prodigious in its scope and profusion. At the time we spoke, he was also serving as editor in chief of the scholarly journal he founded, *Holocaust and Genocide Studies*, serving on the editorial board of the Yad Vashem Holocaust Memorial publishing project, and all the while writing and publishing some dozen books of his own, including *The Holocaust in Historical Perspective, The Jewish Emergence from Powerlessness, American Jewry and the Holocaust*, and *A History of the Holocaust*. It was almost as if Bauer's remarkable output was in some way a personal response, an embodiment of "the Jewish emergence from powerlessness" in history, a way of regaining control over the history that in the past had made Jews powerless victims.

But it was not so much the quantity of his work as its intelligence and penetration that impressed me: the direct, unsparing clarity, the surgical precision with which he opened up and examined the most difficult, highly charged questions raised by the behavior of the perpetrators and the experience of the victims; the courage he had to confront such issues without sentimentality; his impassioned commitment to the subject combined with the scholarly dispassion with which he dissected ultimate questions of the relationship between the Holocaust and history, between the Holocaust and Hitler.

I was drawn initially to Bauer's work by a couple of powerfully argued polemics in *Holocaust and Genocide Studies* in which he attacked those he called "mystifiers." In "Is the Holocaust Explicable?" he speaks of "an increasing number of commentators—theologians, writers as well as historians—[who] argue that ultimately the Holocaust is a mystery, an inexplicable event in human history. Various expressions are used such as *tremendum*, with its theological connotations. . . . They all indicate a measure of final incomprehension." They've given up too soon, he says, in effect. It does not diminish the gravity and terror of the Holocaust to say that in some ways it can be compared to other tragedies and that in some ways it can't. But the fact that in some ways it can't, that in some ways it's unprecedented, doesn't remove it from the realm of human nature or human comprehension; it makes it a new disturbing *fact* of human nature, not necessarily a metaphysical mystery we must sacralize with the "circle of flame" around it, the barrier to thought Claude Lanzmann wants to erect.

Although Bauer doesn't name Fackenheim specifically as one of the "mystifiers," I had a sense he might have had in mind the man dubbed the preeminent "theologian of the Holocaust," and I wanted to see what the most searching historian of the Holocaust had to say about some of the issues raised by the leading theologian of the Holocaust.

A thin, intense, no-nonsense scholar in white shirtsleeves and black-framed glasses, Bauer grew up in post-Kafka Prague (he was born in 1926) until his family escaped to Haifa in 1939. And he might look at home as an actuary in Kafka's insurance office. His powerful and passionate commitment to historical truth is belied by a dry, dismissive, self-effacing style of discourse. Perhaps it's the bleak, bone-dry ironies of a desert kibbutznik. (Bauer had made his home in Kibbutz Shoval in the Negev desert since 1953.)

Bauer was, as usual, busy that day. He confined himself largely to short, compressed answers, ones that nonetheless frequently concealed slow-detonating shocks. It was difficult to draw him out at length on "Hitler-centric" questions because he believes the evidence is too fragmentary for conclusive judgments. But he did register agreement with Milton Himmelfarb's "No Hitler, No Holocaust" stance—that the tragedy was not an inevitable consequence of unstoppable forces. "Without the driving force of Hitler," Bauer told me, "there probably would not have been a Holocaust." Hitler "radicalized" a nation that was otherwise anti-Semitic enough to be complicit with his Final Solution but not enough so to have demanded or forced it themselves.

Bauer made an important distinction about Hitler: Although Hitler was not "ordinary," Bauer believes he was not "abnormal," not "inhuman—that's the problem we have with them [the Nazis], because they are like us and we are like them" in many ways.

He did offer a provisional judgment about the origin of Hitler's anti-Semitism, one he believes is originally traceable "to his Viennese environment that included extreme anti-Semitic ideologies, especially of the sort of half-occult groups like the *Ostara* group and others." And while, during his war-time service in the trenches, Hitler exhibited little hostility to Jews, after 1918 with "the trauma of the defeat, with the destruction of his world—he goes back to the explanation he found in Vienna."

To Bauer, the locus of the real mystery about Hitler and the Holocaust is the question of when Hitler made up his mind for extermination, when Hitler crossed what Bauer calls "the moral Rubicon" between imagining the Final Solution and ordering and implementing it. He finds the attempts to answer that question frustrated by what he believes was Hitler's deliberate obfuscation. He believes Hitler issued an oral order to proceed with a final solution in March 1941. But how long before that had Hitler envisioned extermination—did it lurk beneath ostensible plans for mass expulsion that were the public face of Nazi Jewish policy until then?

"Hitler's a very careful individual, very circumspect," with regard to that, Bauer told me. "He proceeds with that in a very crafty manner."

"Deliberately covering his tracks?" I asked.

"Well, maybe there were no tracks."

All the more reason, Bauer believes, not to dismiss him as insane, a psychopath. "You can only assume he's evil if he's not insane." And Bauer has no doubt Hitler is evil. Hitler is "what I would call near-ultimate evil."

The notion of near-ultimate evil was a bridge to Bauer's surprising, even shocking remarks about God. For someone who doesn't believe in God's existence—he'd told me he was an atheist—Bauer has some strong opinions of his character if he did exist. I'd asked Bauer if he'd become an atheist because of the "near-ultimate" evil he saw unleashed—unchecked by God or man—during the Holocaust.

"Post factum maybe," he said. "But I had no room for any relevance of a God, even if he existed, before that." He grew up in a nonobservant family, he said, his mother an atheist, his father nominally Reform. "I was religious at the age of seventeen," he said, which would have been in 1943, and he's still "very interested in religion, because I think it's a very important phenomenon historically, certainly among Jews, so you could call me a religion-loving atheist."

One who, he says, "looks at religion on the positive-negative scale in terms of what's good for the Jews or bad for the Jews. Certainly religion was good for the Jews for a very long period of time. It doesn't work too well today—you know, 'Where was God during the Holocaust?'—the record of God as far as the Jewish people is concerned is not too overwhelming of late. But you can talk in terms of Hitler's evil whether you are religious or not actually."

"What about certain Orthodox seers here in Israel who've said the Holocaust was part of God's plan, who even describe Hitler as 'the rod of God's anger' at the Jews of Europe who were falling away from strict Torah worship? Or the Holocaust as a way for God to set up the establishment of the State of Israel?"

"Well, that's idiotic, isn't it?" Bauer said with some of the kibbutznik's contempt for the seers who'd credit *their* pioneering courage and sacrifice to a God who supposedly needed the sacrifice of six million for his "plan." "I've just written about that," he told me. "What I say is that there's no way that Hit—" he stops, correcting an apparent slip, as if he was about to say "Hitler" when he meant to say "God." But, in fact, the syllogism he goes on to propose envisions God as a figure perhaps even more evil—ultimate rather than near-ultimate evil:

"There's no way that there can be an all-powerful *and* just God. He can either be all-powerful *or* just. Because if he's all-powerful, he's Satan. If he's just, he's a nebbish."

God as Satan? I've rarely heard a more radical formulation of the problem of theodicy (the attempt to reconcile the existence of a supposedly loving and just God with the persistence of evil). What Bauer is saying, to unpack the assumptions compressed in his God-is-Satan-or-nebbish syllogism, is this: An all-powerful God who was just and loving would not have permitted six million innocents to be slaughtered for any reason, any plan. If he's all-powerful, he could have intervened (as he did on so many lesser occasions of peril in the Bible), and if he's just, he *would* have intervened. If he's all-powerful and permitted near-ultimate evil to prevail, a million *children* to be slaughtered virtually in front of their parents' eyes, without intervening, he might as well be Satan. Which leads us to the second element of the syllogism: If God is just, he can't be very powerful, because if he's just, he would have wanted to intervene but just wasn't powerful enough to make a difference—he's a well-meaning but not very awesome God.

"A nebbish?" I asked.

"Well, you know, a poor chap who has to be *supported*, a God who needs to draw his strength from us, this is [theologian] Irving Greenberg's idea"—and that of *When Bad Things Happen to Good People* author Rabbi Kushner.

It doesn't work for Bauer.

"I don't need a God like that. What kind of God is that, you know, he's not an all-powerful being, he's all-*present*?"

That latter remark about an "all-present" God was a reference to Emil Fackenheim's tortured rationale for the absence of what Fackenheim called "The Commanding Voice of God" at Auschwitz, to Fackenheim's desire to find *some* presence of God in the death camps, even a silent witnessing presence. Bauer has no patience for a God who merely suffers silently with the victims: "When he's there, he cries—that's very nice of him, but it doesn't help me much. He's totally superfluous. There's no one to pray to in that concept."

God as Satan. Or an impotent nebbish. Are these the only alternatives open to us in the aftermath of the Holocaust? In fact, there is a strain of theodicy that attempts to argue that God is neither all-powerful nor impotent but has *limited* his own power to the extent necessary to give man free will, the freedom to choose good and evil. The most powerful argument for this—a contemporary symbolic-logic version of G. W. Leibniz's argument that this is the best of all possible worlds consistent with individual freedom (as opposed to determinism or predestination)—is the one made by the Notre Dame philosopher Alvin Plantinga, who insists that without God permitting the possibility of evil, of man choosing wrong, of what Plantinga calls "transworld depravity" (that in any world in which there is freedom *some* will choose evil), there can be no possible world in which free will or moral choice is meaningful.

But to many, the Holocaust is a challenge to the notion of the best-of-all-possible-worlds-consistent-with-free-will theodicy. Why couldn't God have created a *slightly* less depraved human nature? Does the necessity for transworld depravity require a human nature so depraved that hundreds of thousands would collaborate in the murder of millions of children too young to be paying for any imagined sins? Can Auschwitz be reconciled with *any* best-of-all-possible-worlds theodicy that doesn't require us to question the character of God's creation, the character of God's creative impulse? Or must we resort to what is known generally as an irenic (or "soul-making") theodicy—that catastrophic evils such as Auschwitz are painful moral *lessons* that God intends will lead ultimately to a less-depraved human nature? Must we then say, in effect, "Thank you, God, we *needed* that"?

Bauer is not satisfied with the alternatives to his syllogism, which merely make explicit the dramatic implications of the indictment of God that Fackenheim and other troubled believers and theologians have been wrestling with in the aftermath of Hitler. Believers like Fackenheim have been acting in effect as defense investigators for a silent, absent client, groping for the explanation of their client's conduct that he won't provide himself.

The use of legal rhetoric, the language of trial courts, to describe this ongoing investigation is not my invention. In a survey of the debate over "The Holocaust as a Challenge to Belief" that appeared in the *Journal of the American Academy of Religion* in 1989, we find the terms "indictment," "liability," "perpetrator," "complicity," "aiding and abetting" used in regard to God's role—as well as a remarkable line about "the spectator defense of God." The spectator defense, the legal strategy used by "good Germans" who said they didn't participate, they only stood by while the crimes were being perpetrated, has been attacked by Elie Wiesel and others who believe those who watched passively were just as guilty of murder as those who pulled the triggers. Therefore, the spectator defense, the Academy of Religion analyst remarks, "*does not remove God from the dock*" (emphasis added).

God in the dock: On trial is not God's existence—this is, for the most part, a more interesting controversy than the old one about whether God is "dead"—but his character, potency, and responsibility for the malignancy, the "radical evil" of Adolf Hitler.

What Emil Fackenheim does is attempt to vindicate a continued if altered Jewish relationship to God in the light of the indictment against him framed by Yehuda Bauer. Fackenheim concedes the validity of the indictment by attacking the adequacy of any other Hitler explanation, other than one that places responsibility on God's doorstep. But he does not concede the verdict.

"How do you explain a person anyway?" Fackenheim asked me after we'd settled ourselves into the patio chairs on the veranda of the small apartment in Jerusalem he shares with his second wife and their eleven-year-old son.

It was a hot June afternoon and Fackenheim, then an energetic sixty-seven, was dressed in Bermuda shorts, polo shirt, and sandals, looking a bit like an American grandfather at a kosher bungalow colony. He was speaking about the attempt to explain Hitler. But in revealing bits and pieces over the course of the afternoon, Fackenheim explained his explanation by explaining some things about himself.

He began with a phone call on Kristallnacht and an encounter with a playmate of Reinhard Heydrich's. On November 9, 1938, Kristallnacht, Fackenheim, then a twenty-two-year-old student of Old Testament studies and post-Kantian philosophy at the University of Berlin, called his parents' home in the north German city of Halle. "My father had been taken," he told me. "I told my mother I was coming. I came: I reasoned that the safest place was somewhere the Gestapo has already been. I forgot that they might have tapped the wire. They listened on the phone, and the next day they came for me."

"What was that like?" I asked him. "A whole squad?"

"No, no," he says, "just two fellows came and picked me up."

They took him to Sachsenhausen, the newly constructed concentration camp outside Berlin. It was there, Fackenheim has written, the SS invented what he calls "the groundwork of Auschwitz," the fictive "work battalions" that maintained a transparently false illusion that the camps were about work. Not that they succeeded in disguising the darker fate: "The fiction was still maintained even when the secret was out," Fackenheim says, making it "a Kafkaesque system in which there appeared to be meaning [but] was none. . . . Thus, a clear line of development leads from . . . Sachsenhausen in 1938 to the incredible and unprecedented legend on the gate of Auschwitz"—*Arbeit macht Frei* (Work will make you free).

It is interesting he should single out as the essence of the cruelty of the camps the enforcement of meretricious meaning: false explanation. It was there in Sachsenhausen that his lifelong distrust of deceptive explanation was born. As an illustration of the easy explanatory truisms he detests, he cites the commonplace sentiment about "the Hitler within" he encountered not long after his escape from Germany.

In 1939, he'd been released from Sachsenhausen and obtained an exit visa to Canada before the doors slammed shut on the Jews in Germany. He completed rabbinical studies in Canada, and it was as a fledgling rabbi that he first encountered the "Hitler within" explanation. "I was asked to speak to an interfaith group about Hitler," he told me. "To support the war effort. And the thing that struck me as being pretty terrible—here we are at war, and these nice Christian ladies would come and say, 'There is a Hitler in all of us.' They'd say, 'Christians are bound to say this. When we see other people's sins we look at our own sins.' I wanted to avoid just this," he says. "It just isn't true."

"It just isn't true": Fackenheim's conviction, one that he elaborates on in his theory of "radical evil," is that one cannot find an explanation for the horror perpetrated by Hitler on the familiar continuum of human nature. To say that Hitler was just a very, very, very bad man (or as Alan Bullock would have it, an incompletely good one) and that some version of that same badness, one that differs only in degree, is to be found in ourselves, diminishes the radical evil Hitler represented. Such evil cannot be explained, Fackenheim insists, by his having had a very, very, very mean father, or a very, very extreme manifestation of the same inclination to evil that is in all of us.

Fackenheim's strong reaction to the "Hitler within" argument is at the heart of what has become a radical stance that has defined one pole of the debate over explaining Hitler: that there is a radical disjuncture between human nature and Hitler nature—a disjuncture with human nature akin to the one that Fackenheim and others later came to insist obtained between the Holocaust itself and the rest of human history.

Even more radical was a subsequent decision Fackenheim made: twenty years of silence. Shortly after the war, after the magnitude of the tragedy became apparent, Fackenheim decided that to speak or write about Hitler, even to mention his name, could only magnify him, give him a posthumous life. And so, for twenty years, while becoming a much-laureled professor of philosophy at the University of Toronto, while publishing a much-admired synthesis of

Hegelian philosophy and twentieth-century Jewish theology, he maintained a determined silence on the twentieth-century Jewish tragedy, believing that to discuss Hitler was somehow to perpetuate him, that to speak his name was to broadcast an incantation of radical evil.

Then, in 1967, in the tense run-up to the Six-Day War, Fackenheim changed his mind and changed his life. The specter the possible destruction of the state of Israel raised of a second Holocaust convinced Fackenheim he needed to break his silence on the meaning of the first—on the implications of the radical evil it had introduced to the world. It was that year that he formulated the now widely known "614th commandment," the single sentence for which he has become most famous, the "post-Holocaust commandment" regarding Hitler, which Fackenheim felt compelled to add to the traditional 613 rules of worship and conduct in the Orthodox Jewish canon. He phrased it this way: "Jews are forbidden to grant posthumous victories to Hitler."

Later in our conversation, he would disclose the deeper role this commandment plays in the trial of God. Back then, however, in 1967, he decided that one practical way to fulfill the mandate of the commandment was to uproot himself from his comfortable Canadian exile, move to Jerusalem, and begin to study Hitler.

The immediate cause of his decision was an exchange of letters with writer Terrence Des Pres. Des Pres is the author of *The Survivor*, about the experience of the death camps. "I wrote him a letter in which I said it's a wonderful book," Fackenheim tells me, "but it's only half the story."

"Half the story?"

"The story of the survivors is half. But I told him now you have to write a book about the [something]."

"About the what?" I said, not making out his last word because of his still-pronounced Central European accent.

"About the criminals! The Nazis, the murderers!" he exclaimed, looking at me to see if I was deaf. "You know, *Hitler!*"

But *really* knowing Hitler was a kind of peril, Des Pres warned Fackenheim.

"He wrote me that the way to try to understand them is to identify with them. And the danger is you might like them—no, *become* like them. So he said he refused to write about the criminals as a lot of people have. And one particularly shocking case is that fellow David Irving, who wrote volumes about Hitler's war because he sympathized. This is the danger, once you try to explain it."

If there's a peril to empathy, a *danger* of explanation, the counterpart, he told me, "is the danger of objectivity. If you try to explain it clinically like Hannah Arendt does . . . the more you detach yourself—you can collect all the objective facts you want and explain less and less." He cited a "good German historian [Jäckel] who has a chapter which refers to 'the biological insanity of the Nazis.' That explains absolutely nothing! Insanity is the *smallest* explanation of what went on."

How then does one—how then did Fackenheim—avoid this Scylla and Charybdis of empathy and objectivity?

"You have to make a double move," he told me.

A double move?

Fackenheim then introduced a remarkable notion that reveals, if nothing else, how fraught the very idea of explaining Hitler is for him and for us. "There has to be an epistemological rejection, *a resistance to explanation*," he insists.

The double move then: Use the technique of empathy to understand the processes that produce evil in Hitler but at the same time resist the idea that an explanation can explain *away* his personal responsibility for evil.

"I read people like the Auschwitz commandant [Rudolf] Höss," he says by way of example (Höss is the author of memoirs called *Death Dealer*). "Höss is full of self-excuses, and all of them are lies, but I'm not sure whether he's conscious of the fact they're lies."

But resisting the "sincerity" of Höss's self-explanation was just a warm-up, he told me. "Then, finally, with a deep breath, I read *Mein Kampf*."

In fact, Fackenheim does not sound as if he experienced much difficulty in finding reasons to resist empathy with the Hitler of *Mein Kampf*. He seems to have first seized on Hitler's claim to be what Fackenheim really is, a philosopher in the grand tradition: Hitler's assertion in *Mein Kampf* that he possessed what post-Kantian German philosophy exalts above all else—a weltanschauung, a comprehensive, philosophically consistent worldview.

"The book is all so self-inflating," Fackenheim says contemptuously. But especially so "when he says he found his weltanschauung in Vienna. What does this mean? How did he find it? He became suddenly a philosopher in his own mind and a kind of philosopher that has a weltanschauung and everything fits. Never again would Hitler doubt."

But Fackenheim's certainty on this question is not shared by all Hitler explainers. The issue of whether Hitler *did* have a coherent worldview—an ideology if not a weltanschauung—has, like every other issue in Hitler studies, become a battleground. The seventies saw the emergence of two opposed schools of Hitler explanation. There was the "psychohistorical," which explained Hitler's actions as pathological irrationality, the product of mental disease if not madness. And there was the "ideological" school, which attempted to demonstrate that Hitler's actions *could* be construed as "logical," in the sense that they proceeded from a coherent structure of beliefs, a weltanschauung, and responded to a coherent if wicked analysis of actual German historical realities and an accurate assessment of the sentiments of the German populace.

Many of those who attempt to make this case are German Hitler explainers, but not all. J. P. Stern, for instance, the Czech-born British historian (who heard Hitler as a boy in Munich and escaped to England with his Jewish family in 1938) is one of those who took issue with Fackenheim's dismissal of Hitler's intellectual pretensions. In *Hitler: The Führer and the People* (1974), Stern contended, "the attempt to offer a fuller understanding of the Hitler myth does involve a new look at his intellectual equipment. With fuller evidence of his studies in Vienna and Munich it becomes clear that (to quote Bullock's phrase) to speak of Hitler as a 'moral and intellectual cretin' is no longer justified."

There is still a gulf, of course, between saying Hitler is not an intellectual cretin and crediting him with a coherent philosophical worldview, but Fackenheim has no doubt on that question: He calls the notion Hitler had a weltanschauung "a transparent lie."

But the big lie in *Mein Kampf*, the biggest lie about Hitler, Fackenheim believes, is the one he told about himself and the Jews. Not the obvious lies about Jewish evil—no, this was one of those moments in my conversation with Fackenheim in which one of his observations pulled the rug out from under certain familiar ways of thinking about Hitler to reveal not a floor but an abyss of uncertainty beneath; it occurred to me that this is why people used to pay attention to philosophers.

He broached the subject of the biggest lie by recalling something once said about Hitler's final words, his deathbed testament, which Fackenheim believes was actually his final, *defining* lie. "You know Robert Waite's book?" he says, referring to Waite's psychohistorical study, *The Psychopathic God: Adolf Hitler.* "It's a very good book," Fackenheim told me, "but I think he made a few mistakes. One thing Waite says is, 'Nobody goes to his death with a lie.'"

"Nobody goes to his death with what? . . ."

"With a *lie!*" (What Waite actually wrote is that the deathbed testament is the "quintessential Hitler.")

Waite, Fackenheim explains, makes this remark in discussing Hitler's famous final testament, the one he wrote in the bunker before his suicide, the one in which, even in the midst of the destruction he'd brought upon his own people with his war against the Jews, Hitler enjoins them and their successors to continue the war to the death with the "eternal poisoners of the world," the Jews.

"So, therefore, since Hitler went to his death with his famous testament of hating Jews, that must have been the *true* Hitler. But it's *completely false!* . . . I mean, it may be the case . . . [But] it may have been that Hitler, who posed all his life, who could never believe anything until he had the crowd before him to cheer him, went to his death like an *actor*. For posterity."

In other words, Hitler's deathbed testament was a big lie to maintain his pose of authenticity, the pose as a crusader who died for a passion he believed in, rather than a failed opportunist who believed in nothing but his own ambition and *used* Jew-hatred to advance it.

Hitler as actor. Actor as in liar/cynic/mountebank, whose biggest lie was that the apparent utter authenticity of his passion, which J. P. Stern calls the source of his appeal, was never real, only calculated. Hitler as an Iago whose "motiveless malignancy" was all cynically manipulative sleight of hand, not even faintly "redeemed" by a sincerity, however pathological.

"Look at his marriage," Fackenheim continues. "His wedding half an hour before his death. What does that mean? It was all a *performance*," says Fackenheim, who later told me he "had no doubt" Hitler was "a strange sexual pervert." The deathbed marriage was then also a lie, "theatrical from beginning to end."

I asked the implicit question: "Are you saying he didn't even believe in his anti-Semitism?"

"I don't think he knew the difference between acting and believing."

He goes on to recall a detail from one of the Hitler-crony memoirs, the fact that "Hitler would pose before a mirror before his speeches." He cites footage of an early rally in which "Hitler started out with a questioning look, and then he gets sincere approval, and then relaxes and smiles. Here was a man who was considered a nobody when he was with private people, especially women. And became a big god in front of the masses."

The public Hitler, he maintains, was a joint creation of actor and audience. "Of course," Fackenheim adds in a devastating fillip, "it's a shocking thing to consider that six million Jews were murdered because of an actor."

What I found particularly shocking coming from Fackenheim was not just his belief that Hitler's hatred of the Jews wasn't sincere but his almost casual dismissal of any certainty on the question. The deathbed testament is "completely false," he said first, and then added, "It may be the case." In other words, we have no basis for knowing one way or the other. For the foremost post-Holocaust Jewish philosopher and theologian to assert that after a half century we still can't come even to this basic conclusion about Hitler's thought-world was stunning enough when I first heard it that afternoon in Jerusalem. But it was only a year later, after a third reading of the transcript of my talk with Fackenheim, that I began to understand what was really behind the black-humored irony of that remark about six million "murdered because of an *actor.*"

It was Fackenheim's ultimate effort to rescue Hitler from explanation, to preserve him for evil.

By characterizing Hitler's apparently implacable hatred of Jews as merely an actor's trick, by thus denying him the "virtue" of passionate sincerity (or the pity perhaps due to a victim of a pathological mental disease), Fackenheim deflects, even derails one entire project of Hitler explanation—the focus on finding the psychological source of the white-hot virulence of Hitler's hatred of the Jews—by contending that the passion was *not* white-hot but pure, cold, calculated invention.

And, thus, all the more evil. Evil for evil's sake, evil inexplicable by pathology or ideology and all the more inexcusable. "Radical evil": a term Fackenheim uses to define a phenomenon that goes beyond the quantity of the victims, a new *category* of evil.

While it might seem at first glance not terribly controversial to call Adolf Hitler evil, Fackenheim was the first to make me aware of a fault line in the Hitler literature: the surprising reluctance of those who have written about him to consider Hitler himself as *consciously* evil. The argument against explaining away evil in Hitler is central to Fackenheim. His notion of radical evil (which is not the same as Arendt's or Martin Buber's use of the term) differs from the traditional Jewish conception of evil, which postulates not an absolute principle but an "evil inclination" within that can be overcome. It differs from the traditional Christian conceptions of evil, which vary from defining it as *non*being (the absence of good), to personifying evil in a demonic personage, as the prince of darkness struggling for the possession of the soul.

Fackenheim's notion of radical evil differs in that it is not contingent on, not the result of, a struggle within the human soul, but the kind of evil "that can never be overcome," evil that is "transcendent, unsurpassable, absolute," as one commentator on Fackenheim describes it, evil that cannot be explained away, even atoned for, but can only be "resisted" by its victims, however hopelessly.

One problem with Fackenheim's argument—the problem with others who, like him, strenuously argue that the evil of Auschwitz is absolutely unique, never before committed or experienced—is that it can seem to issue from a kind of inverse narcissism: My evil, the evil I suffered from, is worse than your evil, worse than his evil, any other evil. This can lead to tortuous ratiocination devoted to proving that, for instance, the Armenian genocide falls short or the Stalin-inflicted famine and slaughter is less worthy of uniqueness—a preoccupation with comparative demonology that divides rather than unites victims of evil—and can absolve the actual perpetrators of responsibility. "The insistence on the Holocaust's uniqueness and inexplicability," Elizabeth Domansky wrote of this position in the journal *History and Memory*, "allowed the West Germans to see the Holocaust as something that could not be explained even in the context of the Third Reich. The Holocaust thus [is] transferred to the realm of the a-historical and [thus] renders the question of responsibility obsolete."

Still, Fackenheim's insistence on the absoluteness of Hitler's evil defines one pole of the debate; it helps explain Fackenheim's resistance to the very *idea* of explanation. Explanation, in Fackenheim's view, if not evil itself, nonetheless can verge on ameliorating, excusing, even colluding with evil.

Which brings us to Fackenheim's point of attack on the Hitler-explanation enterprise: the "Jewish blood" crux. That was the next firecracker this contentious philosopher threw across my path that afternoon in Jerusalem: his peculiar take on this disturbing strain of Hitler lore—the attempt to explain Hitler's hatred of Jews as a form of self-hatred, as a product of the maddening doubt he had about his own "racial identity."

While more sophisticated versions of this long-standing but still outré and disturbing notion have been gathering adherents since the seventies—particularly among psychoanalytically oriented Hitler explainers—I was surprised to find Fackenheim not resisting but almost embracing it as an explanation. Until I saw how he turned it into the spear point of his attack on explanation itself.

The subject arose when I asked him about Milton Himmelfarb, and he responded with a story about a playmate of Heydrich.

"What is your view of the statement, 'No Hitler, No Holocaust?'" I asked him, in regard to Himmelfarb's insistence that Hitler's personal will alone, rather than abstract historical forces, was the necessary if not sufficient factor in making the Holocaust happen.

"Is that Milton Himmelfarb? Yeah, I think he's probably quite right. Although I recently wrote there might have been one exception—Heydrich could have done it. And that strikes very close to home. I came from the German town of Halle, and when I had to write my memoirs, which aren't complete yet, I entitled the first section about Halle 'From George Frideric Handel to Heydrich.' And did you know that for three weeks my mother lived under the same roof where Heydrich played?"

"Really?"

"Because when Kristallnacht happened and I was at school, my brother and my father were [taken] away, my mother was all alone, our best friends asked her to move in with them, the Levines—their daughter Ilse was just visiting me—well, Kurt Levine was the only Jew in the whole city who wasn't taken. Because he was protected by his neighbor Heydrich. So I just asked Ilse Levine recently, 'Did you know Heydrich when you were younger?' She said, 'Oh, sure, he came to our house all the time. When his sister was in trouble with her parents, we used to look after her.'

"And it shocks you absolutely. Because Heydrich was reputed to be the only man who could have followed Hitler. Incidentally, about Heydrich, they also say that he had a Jewish ancestor."

More than incidentally: Many accounts of the life of Reinhard Heydrich, "the evil young god of death," portray him as a kind of *double* doppelgänger of Hitler. He was a twin in the fanatical single-mindedness of his drive to exterminate the Jews—he was, after all, the man to whom Hitler entrusted the planning and execution of the Final Solution (until Heydrich's assassination by Czech partisans in 1942). But, also like Hitler, Heydrich was rumored to have had a special *Jewish* doppelgänger haunting *him*: a shadowy alleged Jewish ancestor, rumors of whose existence gave rise to the widespread reports that Heydrich felt personally plagued by a putative Hebraic shadow.

To some, then, Heydrich was not only a potential successor to Hitler, he might be a possible *explanation*—in the sense that his struggle with this Jewish-blood shadow might be a clue to a similar dynamic in Hitler's psyche. Rumors about "Jewish blood" pursued Heydrich from Halle to the Naval Academy at Kiel, where fellow midshipmen are reported to have taunted him as "Izzy Süss" (Süss being a derisive surname of caricatured Jews), followed him even into the SS, when Himmler put him in command of its intelligence division, the SD, in 1932, a post that would later lead to his being given command of the Gestapo in 1934.

Heinz Höhne, the historian of the SS, cites a communication from a local Gauleiter (regional party leader) in Halle who wrote to party headquarters in 1932: "It has come to my ears that in the Reich Leadership, there is a member named Heydrich. . . . There are grounds for suspecting that Bruno Heydrich of Halle, said to be the father, is a Jew."

Höhne reports that although no solid evidence was found in a subsequent investigation, "the higher Reinhard Heydrich . . . climbed on the National-Socialist ladder, the more persistent became the rumour that [he] . . . was of Jewish origin."

In a memoir, a League of Nations official who came to know Heydrich reported a probably apocryphal but nonetheless representative story: Heydrich had become so tormented by the fear of the "Jew within" that one night, in a drunken fit, he stared into a mirror, thought he actually glimpsed the shadowy Jew within somehow *emerge* in his reflection, and promptly fired his pistol into the mirror image, hoping to extinguish it. Unable to extinguish the doubt about a Jew within, the logic of this theory goes, Heydrich had to prove his purity by engineering the extermination of the Jews of Europe.

One reputed source of this theory was none other than Heydrich's boss Himmler. Fackenheim cites Himmler's belief that Heydrich's devotion to the Final Solution came from the "fact" that he had "overcome the Jew in himself . . . and had swung over to the other side. He was convinced that the Jewish elements in his blood were damnable; he hated the blood which played him so false. The Führer could really have picked no better man than Heydrich for the campaign against the Jews."

Despite the fact that these "thoughts" of Himmler come to us from his only-sometimes-reliable confidant, the masseur Felix Kersten, Fackenheim believes their essential truth. "You know Ilse said this, too," he told me, referring to Ilse Levine, whose home was spared Kristallnacht because the young Heydrich had frolicked there as a child. "She thinks [the Jewish blood rumor] is true. She knew, of course, Heydrich's father very well. He looked very Jewish and he ran a conservatory of music."

In fact, both Heydrich and his father were highly accomplished violinists, but according to my own analysis of the multiple, overlapping, and conflicting accounts of the Heydrich Jewish-blood question, the truth might be more absurd and ironic than even the presence of "actual" Jewish blood in this architect of the Final Solution.

It seems Bruno Heydrich had a stepfather who, although impeccably Aryan, bore the stereotypically Jewish surname Süss. A perhaps malicious music-world rival, compiling an entry for Bruno in a directory of Germany's musical elite, went out of his way to make it appear that Bruno's last name was Süss, as it apparently had been for a time when growing up in his stepfather's house (much as Hitler's father's surname for the first forty years of his life was Schicklgruber, after his unmarried mother's surname; Adolf's never was).

And it also seems that Bruno's strategy for deflecting the whispers about his heritage proved to be a self-defeating one. He was known to do a mean comic Yiddish accent at parties, perhaps to demonstrate he had nothing to fear or hide. If so, this penchant of his for playacting the Jew backfired: The more he did his Jewish impressions, the more he fostered the impression he really *was* a Jew.

The irony is that Reinhard, Bruno's son, fit every criterion Nazi "racial science" had established for pure Nordic appearance but was shadowed, plagued (perhaps even turned into a mass murderer) by a rumor based on his father's comic impressions. Of course, "irony" is an inadequate term for the idea that such horror could grow from such origins. In discussing this and the idea that a similar spectral struggle with a phantom Jew underlay Hitler's obsessive hatred, we have gone beyond conventional irony. We are really in Kafka territory again.

Fackenheim's take (his double take, it might be called) on the Jewish-blood explanation of Hitler and Heydrich is a concession to Kafka as description but a resistance to Kafka as explanation.

Fackenheim first addressed the question in his 1982 work *To Mend the World*, where he took up Robert Waite's formulation of the Jewish-blood theory. Waite's thesis (Hitler needed to exterminate the Jews to exterminate his doubts about a Jew within himself) "supplies solutions of sorts to problems which otherwise would seem totally intractable," Fackenheim writes. "Why did Hitler attack Russia, thereby wilfully creating the long-dreaded, unnecessary two-front war? Why did the plan to 'remove' the Jews turn into a vast system of murder, more important than victory . . . To such questions psychohistory gives more plausible answers than either psychology without history or history without psychology."

Having thus set up Waite's theory as the best of all possible explanations, Fackenheim then subverts any complacency about its having *really* "explained" Hitler. "It gives its answers, however, only at the price of raising still more intractable questions." Quoting Herbert Luethy's 1954 *Commentary* essay, he asks, "How shall one 'reconcile the gravity, the catastrophic magnitude of the event with the vulgar mediocrity of the individual who initiated them?'"

These questions, Fackenheim goes on to declare, "assume a dimension of utter absurdity. . . . Were six million actual 'non-Aryans' and many additional honorary ones butchered and gassed because the Führer hated his father and thought of him as a half-Jew?"

The disproportion between absurd cause and catastrophic effect is unbearable: Waite's thesis, then, is defective precisely because it pretends to the *possibility* of plausibility: "The more plausible psychohistory becomes the more it points to an ultimate absurdity." Fackenheim writes, "The mystery remains."

"Utter absurdity," "ultimate absurdity"—the abyss between the horror of the tragedy and the near-comic absurdity of the explanation—in other words, the illogic of the Kafkaesque, the rationale of irrationalism. Fackenheim both accepts and resists the Kafkaesque as Hitler explanation. The absurdity might be true, but it is not enough. Fackenheim dismisses the best of Hitler explanations in the same way Theseus dismisses the absurd clowning of the Mechanicals' play in *A Midsummer Night's Dream*: "The best in this kind are but shadows"—all actors are bad actors if they aspire to give us the "truth" of the world; similarly, all explanations are bad explanations if they aspire to give us the truth of Hitler.

Any explanation, however plausible in human terms, that pretends to proceed logically from comically finite human psychological sources to the tragic infinitude of the horror of the camps is prima facie absurd, Fackenheim seems to be saying. Fackenheim's almost visceral repugnance at the absurdity of explanation is a rejection of Kafka as the "author" of history, of the idea of God as Kafka. Still, Fackenheim recognizes that his unwillingness to see God as Kafka opens the way to the even more unthinkable notion Yehuda Bauer had broached: God as Satan.

"The mystery remains," Fackenheim says. The usual suspects have been rounded up and found wanting. The unusual suspects—a spectral Jew here, a medical mesmerist or a billy goat there—have been arraigned and dismissed for lack of evidence, leaving only the prime suspect standing, the Prime Mover, God himself.

Fackenheim's courage lies in following the logic of his attack on explanation, in following the logic of monotheism to frame an indictment of the God of monotheists. The refusal of God to speak in his own defense, his refusal to take the stand, so to speak, at his own trial, cannot be ignored by those who profess to believe in or worship him, Fackenheim insists. Caution rather than courage, however, is evident in how Fackenheim structures what might be called the jury-deliberation process in the trial of God.

Elie Wiesel is famous for a stunning image of what might be called the capital punishment of God. For having described in *Night* the horrific spectacle of a young boy hung from the gallows by the death-camp guards. And for having cried out that the hanged boy dying in the noose was, for him, God—God dying to him. (In a Yom Kippur 1997 essay, Wiesel wrote that, after half a century, he wanted to "make up" with the God he abandoned on the gallows, although "Auschwitz must and will forever remain a question mark" that no "theological answers" have yet explained.)

Fackenheim wants to get God down from those gallows. His vision of a God who was not a "commanding" presence in the death camps but a silent one is somewhat more complex than Yehuda Bauer had it when he caricatured it as "a God who is present and cries with you." Rather, Fackenheim recuperates God's presence in the acts of heroism, endurance, love, and faith the inmates of the camps manifested in the face of radical evil. He calls *this* the commanding voice of Auschwitz, the voice that forbids posthumous victories to Hitler.

But Fackenheim himself does not argue that this notion of a silent presence *resolves* the mystery of God's shift to silence when those who prayed to him were most massively in peril. It's just that the alternative is, to Fackenheim, intolerable. Intolerable not so much because it would mean acceding to Bauer's syllogism in which God is either Satan or nebbish, but because that accession, that dismissal or rejection of God by Jews, will have, in effect, been *dictated* by Adolf Hitler. Giving Hitler, in death, the ultimate victory over the Jews he was denied in life. An extermination of belief more complete than the extermination of believers. For Fackenheim, I believe, to give in to the stark logic of Yehuda Bauer's syllogism—if God is all-powerful, he permitted the Holocaust to happen, in effect caused it—is to make God Hitler or Hitler God.

It was Fackenheim's revolt against this impossible dead-end choice, his revolt against letting Hitler dictate what Jews believe about God, that led him to conceive of his "614th commandment." A dictum I hadn't fully understood until that afternoon in Jerusalem when he gave me a dramatic description of the moment he confronted the unbearable gravamen of the evidence for the case against God—and how he came to formulate his famous 614th commandment about Hitler as a kind of "limiting instruction" to the jury.

It was April 1967, just after Purim, a holiday celebrating Jewish deliverance from slaughter, but one that found Fackenheim sickened both physically and spiritually by the sudden cloud shadowing the future of the Jewish state.

With Egyptian president Nasser about to blockade Israel's ports, a growing threat of the three-front attack to come, with the world indifferent if not hostile, it looked to Fackenheim as if a second Holocaust was in the works.

"There was a symposium in New York on Purim, which coincided with Easter. And I was morally pressured by a friend of mine to participate. I had never written anything about the Holocaust before, because it was too frightening. And not only that, among the other participants was Elie Wiesel, and I held him in great awe. It was a real crisis moment and I knew it myself because I was sick before."

Sickened by the prospect that God could permit a second Holocaust, he says, "that was the crisis where I first put forward the 614th commandment": Jews are forbidden to grant posthumous victories to Hitler.

It's a commandment whose power I'd long felt, but the implications of which I had questioned or (as I came to feel after listening to Fackenheim describe its genesis) misinterpreted. A commandment designed to deny Hitler a certain kind of power that I'd misinterpreted as in some perverse way restoring to him another kind of power.

Think about it: Its implications are obvious and nonproblematic if one takes it to mean one should resist and combat anti-Semitism, neo-Nazism, and other manifestations of Hitler-like hatred in order to deny Hitler and Hitlerism a posthumous resurrection and life. But, on the other hand, as a habit of thought for Jews, for anyone, it paradoxically could be seen giving Hitler a continuing life, a defining *presence*, a central presence if not a commanding one— although one could almost say a commanding one by negation. If one feels compelled to refer all one's actions in relation to all significant post-Holocaust phenomena *to* Hitler—in the sense of how will such acts or stances affect Hitler's legacy—one comes close to submitting oneself to a putative Hitler's judgment: How would this or that act or stance make Hitler feel? Would Hitler consider it a posthumous victory if I chose x or y? Hitler becomes, if not the ruling principle, then the ultimate referent.

But, in fact, when Fackenheim places the genesis of the 614th commandment in the specific context of his 1967 crisis of faith, in the context of post-Holocaust theodicy, of the impulse to demand that God explain Hitler in the face of the potential advent of a second Holocaust, the commandment can be seen as an inspired gesture of defiance, a kind of Higher Stubbornness, a repudiation of Hitler as ultimate referent.

Higher stubbornness? I'd recast the impulse behind it this way: No, dammit, whatever I decide about the relationship between God and evil, between God and Jewish suffering, however unsatisfied I might be by other attempts to explain it, however much I might resent God's apparent silence or absence in the death camps, however much I reject the notion of some "larger plan" in which God required the murder of millions of children to accomplish some inscrutable end, however much I reject all the consolations and rationalizations of theodicy's attempt to explain Hitler, I refuse to allow Hitler the power, refuse to allow Hitler to be the catalyst, the defining issue over which I will reject the God my ancestors have lived with and died for, for better or worse, for three thousand years. Reject God for any other reason, for nonexistence, for silence, for death, but not for *Hitler*, don't give Hitler that power, *that* posthumous victory.

I'd come to Jerusalem saturated with the unanswered and perhaps unanswerable question of post-Holocaust theodicy, the arguments that put God in the dock after Hitler and Auschwitz. I was drawn to Yehuda Bauer's cleansing and logical syllogistic dismissal of God as Satan or nebbish because it offered at least a resolution of a tormentingly unresolved issue. But finally I found myself won over not by Fackenheim's theodicy but by what I sensed, beneath the sophisticated Hegelian ratiocinations about radical evil, as a kind of sheer *orneriness*—the stubborn refusal to let Hitler be the judge in the trial of God.

The 614th commandment as an article of faith: "That was the only way for me . . . and still is," Fackenheim told me, "to avoid the hopeless dilemma between not facing up to the Holocaust and having Judaism destroyed." Not facing up to the Holocaust: that is, not exempting God from questions of ultimate responsibility left unresolved by attempts to explain Hitler in human terms. Not having Judaism destroyed: not finding God guilty, at least not in the first degree, not abandoning God or the Jewish way of worshiping him because of Hitler's evil.

Fackenheim's 614th commandment is then, if not a plea bargain, a limiting instruction to the jury: God can be found culpably negligent, but capital punishment is ruled out. "There has to be another possibility" than the death or execution of God, Fackenheim told me. "If you face up to the Holocaust and say, 'Oh, it's just another catastrophe'—that is a blasphemy to the victims." The alternative, however, is blasphemy to the God so many of the victims worshiped: "If you face up to it and the result is that Judaism is destroyed"—because facing up to it might mean God is Satan—"then it's a posthumous victory for Hitler."

Some, like Rabbi Richard Rubenstein, suggest there is a third answer that combines continued love for the Jewish people, for Judaism in that sense, with rejection of the God who abandoned them to Hitler. But for Fackenheim, there was no middle way. "That was the first thing I said" at the 1967 symposium, Fackenheim told me. Before anything, he ruled out the ultimate guilty verdict on God, because it would make God Hitler's final victim. Issuing that limiting instruction resolved a personal spiritual crisis for him: "The moment I said what I said—making that decision—the sickness left me," he said.

Fackenheim stepped back from the brink, from where the logic of his critique of explanation was taking him. In George Steiner we see someone who, out of either intellectual courage or recklessness, steps over it.

CHAPTER 17

George Steiner:
Singling out the Jewish
"Invention of Conscience"

In which a character named A.H. escapes from its famous
literary creator—who is accused of "playing with fire"

It is, in a certain sense, a Frankenstein story: about a frightening creation that escaped from its creator. The creator is George Steiner, one of the foremost men of letters in the English-speaking world. His creation: a fictive character called "A.H.," who is transparently Adolf Hitler.

George Steiner's Hitler began life as a figure in a literary fantasy, a sophisticated "survival myth" parable about a Hitler who'd escaped the bunker in 1945, and who—thirty years later—is finally tracked down, put on trial, and forced to defend himself, to explain himself.

But something disturbing has happened with the Hitler in Steiner's fable: He explained himself far too well. He did more than escape the bunker, it seemed to some—he escaped Steiner.

Even some of Steiner's most thoughtful supporters in the bitter controversy over Steiner's Hitler novel, *The Portage to San Cristóbal of A.H.*, believe that in some way "A.H." escaped him.

"It scared the hell out of me," Steiner himself told me, recalling the first time he came face-to-face with a living embodiment of the Hitler figure he'd created. The occasion was the opening of the London stage production of his novel. It was the first time Steiner saw his Hitler character in the flesh. Until then, his Hitler character was just the barest of initials on a page. Now, suddenly, "A.H." was a charismatic, full-bodied, full-blooded figure bestriding the stage, mesmerizing an audience with words of self-justification Steiner put in his mouth. It was the first time he heard the applause.

The dispute over the nature of that applause is a deeply disturbing one to Steiner, who has both an enormous scrupulosity about—and an enormous distrust of—the power of language, of the Word.

Toward the close of our conversation in Steiner's Cambridge University study, I read him a quotation from an account in the London *Observer* of the play and the fierce controversy that surrounded the production—the pickets outside, the applause within. The *Observer* critic said the audience appeared to be applauding Hitler's speech in the play, the final epic soliloquy of self-justification Steiner had crafted for his Hitler character; the words that close the play.

"Oh no!" said Steiner, horrified. "Oh no, no, no, no, *no*," he insisted five times. The applause was not for what *Hitler* said, he told me, but for the play as a whole, which ends a moment after Hitler's speech. In other words, they were applauding *him*—or the actors—not Hitler.

Even assuming Steiner is correct about who the applause was for, he concedes he knows that the Hitler character he created might be dangerous, even on the page. He was aware of it, he told me, from the moment he put his pen down at the end of a three-day sleepless "fever dream" of composition. He was aware he'd created an entity that needed to be controlled rather than unleashed indiscriminately upon the world.

"The moment I finished it," Steiner told me, "I pledged to myself that neither in Hebrew nor in German would I allow it to be translated. I'm not going to have the Germans hear that in their own language."

"Was it because you fear Hitler's speech could escape from its context?" I asked him.

"Yes, yes," he said, "and it could be *used*. There have been pirated attempts in German, but they've been stopped," he said. They've been stopped, but it's out there in circulation, however unauthorized: Steiner's Hitler speaking German to Germans, explaining himself, excusing himself, blaming the Jews for everything including himself.

The notion of a German edition of his Hitler is troubling to Steiner, but it doesn't seem to trouble him as much as seeing his Hitler in the flesh. And even more than the sight, it was the voice: hearing his voice from the stage, "scared the hell" out of him. There is something more dangerously potent to him about the voice, the word made flesh, than the word on the page alone. Perhaps it is because Steiner's lifelong horrified fascination with Hitler began—at age five—with the sound of Hitler's voice.

The story of how one of the foremost Jewish intellectuals of the postwar era brought a Hitler figure to life and how—golemlike, Frankenstein style—this Hitler escaped to haunt him begins with Steiner as a child, sitting in front of the radio, listening to that frightening, terrifying voice.

"I was born in 1929, so from '33 on my earliest memories are sitting in the kitchen hearing The Voice [of Hitler] on the radio."

The kitchen was in Paris. "My father was from Czechoslovakia. [He met] my mother in Vienna. I was born in Paris. My father had left Vienna because he believed that Austrian anti-Semitism was going to explode one way or another. He couldn't have guessed it would be Mr. Schicklgruber that was coming. But he was always astonished that the [Eastern European] pogroms had stopped short of Austria—Austrian anti-Semitism seemed to be irremediable, as it is today."

Paris proved to be no refuge. Steiner was eleven when his family had to flee France shortly before the Germans marched in. "By great good luck we were able to get out with the last ship to sail from Genoa," one heading for the United States.

What his father felt about Austrian anti-Semitism, Steiner felt about the French variety. "It is very odd, given the Dreyfus Affair, that it [the Holocaust] didn't happen in France. In some ways, it was ghastly bad luck for Germany that Hitler—it *could* have happened in France. French anti-Semitism had a kind of systemic power and political profit which it didn't have in Germany. Had it not been for Hitler's quote unquote peculiar genius, had there been a French Hitler, he might have had an even quicker ascent to power."

"You don't agree with those who explain Hitler as somehow a product of the German soul?" I asked him.

"Not at all. Not at all. On the contrary. German distaste about the vulgarity of Hitler's racism ran very, very deep. The Prussians never bought it, the Bavarians had their own particular case against him. They never bought it. In France you can, at any time, get an explosion of French chauvinism against Jews. The Dreyfus Affairs are French. The first plan to ship Jews to Africa did not originate in Germany."

"The Madagascar Plan?"

"French," Steiner says.

If it was not the German soul, Steiner believes, there *was* something in the German language that peculiarly suited what he called "Hitler's quote unquote peculiar genius." He heard it in that voice on the radio: "The overwhelming power was there. And the ease with which he got away with the Rhineland matter suggests a reading of the weakness of the West which was somnambular, that of a man who was a political genius."

That word "somnambular," suggesting a paradoxical state of unconscious consciousness—a mind both spellbound and spellbinding, Caligari-like—is a recurrent one in Steiner's description of Hitler. A Hitler who is a kind of medium for the evil genius of the German language itself. He speaks of Hitler's language being like "antimatter" to ordinary language.

"Yes, yes, that's what my novel tries to show, among other things. It *is* antimatter. He is one of the greatest masters of the language. As are [Martin] Luther's pamphlets asking that all Jews be burned. German language has—all languages can have it—but in the German language, Hitler drew on a kind of rhetorical power which, in a way that is perhaps a little bit peculiar to German, allies highly abstract concepts with political, physical violence in a most unusual way. . . . And [Hitler] was easily a genius at that, absolutely no doubt about it."

The essence of the genius, Steiner insists, is not so much in the written word, but the embodied voice. "It's a hard thing to describe, but the voice itself was mesmeric," he says, recalling the radio addresses. It was specifically the physicality rather than the metaphysicality that mesmerized, he told me. "The physique is—the amazing thing is that the *body* comes through on the radio. I can't put it any other way. You feel you're following the gestures. [Marshall] McLuhan has a famous thesis that it [Hitler's charisma] wouldn't have worked on TV. I think that's balderdash. Hitler would have been the ultimate master on TV—all you need to look at is the Riefenstahl films of the rallies to see how he mastered every image, every gesture."

The fascination and the distrust of speech, the love and hate for the power and terror of language, has been at the very heart of Steiner's remarkable career as literary prodigy and prodigal. After earning degrees from the University of Chicago and Harvard and spending a stint at Princeton's Institute for Advanced Study, he made a decision to return to England and the Continent; he held dual professorships at Cambridge and the University of Geneva. The return was not casual, it was the fulfillment of a paternal injunction.

"It was my father's central resolution that I go back to Europe," he told me. "Because—although there were wonderful opportunities in America—for my father, for me not to have come back would have meant that Hitler had won his boast that Europe would be *Judenrein* [Jew-free]. And that he couldn't bear."

There is something in this that echoes Emil Fackenheim's injunction to post-Holocaust Jews, his commandment that Thou shalt not grant Hitler any posthumous victories. But there is also something very idiosyncratic in the way Steiner formulates it: "for *me* not to have come back" would be decisive—almost as if Hitler's posthumous victory or defeat would have been decided not by whether Europe was Jew-free but whether or not it was Steiner-free.

It's the kind of casual hubris that has made Steiner such a controversial figure, an intellectual provocateur who both dazzles and outrages. An admiring introduction to a book of essays about Steiner's work speaks of his "*greatness.* . . . The shocking massiveness of his learning . . . the prodigiousness of his competence in the major Western languages, the speculative power of his . . . reflections, the brilliance of his textual commentary; the piercing eloquence of his prose . . . [an] *oeuvre* that, in its puissant majesty, is virtually without parallel." But this same commentator nonetheless acknowledges that "an enormous amount of ill will toward him is harbored within the Anglo-American university community" because "he can seem too vehement, hortatory, overbearing; he raises his voice in public. . . . Conventional academicians cannot forgive his polymathic virtuosity."

How much Steiner's Jewishness enters into the resentment he engenders is a difficult question. The suspicion of some that his Jewishness had in the past denied him the honors in the Oxbridge academic community that his accomplishments should have commanded may be matched by the Oxbridge community's resentment of the implicit imputation of genteel anti-Semitism to it.

But it cannot be gainsaid that Steiner's speculations are often designed to be not just vehement and hortatory but profoundly provocative. Such is certainly the case with his assault on language—and civilization itself—for its guilty implication in the Hitler horror, an assault that became the central theme of his work with the publication in 1967 of *Language and Silence* and then in 1975 of *After Babel*, the nonfiction predecessor to his notorious Hitler novel.

Both works raised the question of the potential diabolism within language itself and implicitly addressed the relationship between Hitler and language: Did the evil of the Holocaust come into being because of Hitler's power to manipulate language to bad ends, or was there something perverse—something demonic and Hitlerian—in the very essence of the language and the civilization built upon it? Something that expressed itself *through* Hitler. Steiner famously challenged the notion that language and culture were "civilizing" factors with his image of a death-camp guard reading great German literature and listening to great German music and then proceeding to go out and stoke the great German crematoria.

This issue can be found at the heart of some of Steiner's most daring and provocative speculations. Consider the suggestion he made to me about the way the language of Kafka might not only have foreshadowed but somehow *created* Hitler.

I'd been struck by something Steiner had written about Kafka's *Metamorphosis*: that the word "*Ungeziefer*"—the word Kafka used in 1922 to describe the kind of insect poor Gregor Samsa found himself transformed into—was the very same word Hitler used to characterize Jews in his earliest speeches: vermin. Were you the first to point this out? I asked Steiner.

"Yes, that's in my very earliest work," he said. "That's in *Language and Silence*. And it seemed to be—and I still don't know the answer to this—such is the exactitude of Kafka's foresight in 'The Penal Colony' and *The Metamorphosis*, such is the *authority*, that it raises a ghastly question: Are prophecies self-fulfilling? I have no answer to that."

"That's an interesting idea. Do you mean—?"

"At a certain level, does a prophecy start engendering that which it has foreseen?" he asks.

"Just by its presence in the world? You can't say Hitler read Kafka, obviously."

"No, of course not, he never heard of it. But it was *there*. It was suddenly *there* as a possibility."

"Kafka as a source of Hitler?"

"As a source of the concentration-camp world, of the world of the bureaucracy of murder. In Kafka's case, we're dealing with the single most powerful act of prophecy ever. Karl Kraus is the other. Karl Kraus [the Viennese literary satirist] says in 1909, 'Soon in Europe they will make gloves out of human skin.' That's 1909! And Kraus, another Jew on the margin, saw it *absolutely clearly*, coming out of the Vienna situation."

But with Kafka, Steiner is going further than asserting the kind of prophetic foresight he attributes to Karl Kraus. With Kafka, he's coming close to an almost black-magic view of the dark power of words: that they have a spell-like power to bring into being that which had been inconceivable before they were uttered—something more radical than a prophetic relationship, a *causal* one. I don't think he believes, literally, that Kafka made Hitler possible; I think he's pressing a metaphoric correspondence to its limits, and the explicit parallels between Kafka's "Penal Colony" world and the death-camp universe have been persuasively challenged by Lawrence Langer. But it is Steiner's *need* to see them is what is most of interest. It is testimony to his awe and distrust of the power of language. It reflects his profoundly ambivalent attitude toward European civilization in relation to Hitler: Was Hitler a culmination of dark forces within European civilization or an aberration from its values? I believe this is what is behind Steiner's touching preoccupation with Hitler's recess schedule in junior high school and his obsession with the lost works of Viennese street photographers.

"I am the first to ask that we comb every photograph [of Vienna]—it hasn't been done yet—to see whether by chance we have him [Hitler] on a tramway or street with Freud and Mahler. Now, remember, he also goes to the same school as Wittgenstein."

Steiner is so obsessed with this connection that he's researched the recess hours of that school at Linz. Hitler and Wittgenstein were "two years apart at school, but I have looked into this. At eleven or eleven-fifteen, as in all European schools, there's recreation—you go out in the yard and play. There's no doubt they were in the same yard. And I find it almost impossible to believe that on the Ringstrasse [in Vienna] he didn't cross the men I've named [Freud and Mahler], Of course he did. And it *is* conceivable that a street photographer—you know, with their big tripods and the thing over their heads. . . . It's conceivable, one captured them together."

I wondered what could be the source—the point—of Steiner's peculiar fascination with the possibility that Hitler, Freud, Mahler, and Wittgenstein could be found on the same piece of photo paper or in the same recess yard. On reflection, I believe it has something to do with Steiner's uneasy wavering between the poles of that key divide in Hitler-explanation literature: the divide between the aberrationist and culminationist camps.

On the one hand, Steiner can call Hitler "a singularity," an aberrant freak of human nature with a "peculiar genius," but in Steiner's theoretical works, he comes across as a culminationist, taking the darker view that Hitler was a product, the culmination of the dark side of European civilization, of the cursedness of language which underlies and shapes that civilization. In this view, the evil is in the Word itself; Hitler is merely the somnambular medium that gave voice to it.

Thus Steiner's obsession with finding a photo that captures Hitler with such avatars of European thought as Wittgenstein and Freud: Seeing a Hitler who emerged from the same photo emulsion as these paragons of European and Jewish civilization would then symbolize, fix in silver nitrate Steiner's vision of a Hitler who emerged from the same underlying matrix of culture that produced that civilization's highest achievements. Thus, the one is inseparable from the other; the fabric of the civilization that produced Wittgenstein is implicated nonetheless in the causation of Hitler. And so, when we imbibe the distillation of civilization's finest fruits, we are inevitably also drinking from a poisoned chalice.

His preoccupation with the photo-emulsion image of Hitler, Steiner disclosed to me, was the source of what became his most notorious and controversial work, the novel in which he addressed the Hitler mystery most directly. A 1919 photograph of Hitler set him off, he says.

"That's the center of the novel," he says, "that photograph." It's a real, albeit obscure photo, he says, that shows "Hitler standing in the pouring rain like a beggar. It's 1919, I believe, when he was a discharged corporal without a penny and nobody's even stopping as they hurry by on a Munich street corner. And a year later, a hundred people [stop], a few years later ten thousand and then ten million, and this is something which I come back to and back to in my thinking. It is a terrifying proof of the omnipotence of the Word. Even if it is an *anti-Word*."

The notion of an anti-word comes from the same speculative vein in Steiner as the notion of Hitler's language as antimatter, fusing, perhaps too casually, concepts from ancient cabalistic legends and up-to-the-minute quantum physics. This was the sort of feverish speculation that gave rise, Steiner told me, to the "fever dream" in which he gave birth to the Hitler novel and the Hitler character, his Frankenstein creation.

"I was in Geneva, and it actually took only three days and nights. It was a single—total rush [in which he wrote] two things, Lieber's speech [an attempt to capture the hideous pathos of the death-camp victims in maimed and fragmented sentences] and the speech of A.H.," as his Hitler character is referred to in the text of the novel. "Matter and antimatter."

Why then? I asked him. Was there anything about the circumstances of his life that brought forth the fever dream of creation at that point?

"Possibly—a naïve guess," he says with surprising candor. "It could be that it was the point at which it became evident that my wife and children would be staying in our new home in Cambridge. She has an appointment [a professorship in history] here. And that we would have to explore the very difficult separate lives. And that may have triggered certain intensities. I wouldn't know, but it came in one extremely simple—it wrote itself. It wrote itself and then had its very complicated destiny."

Before getting into that complicated destiny, by which Steiner means the fierce attacks on it and the Frankenstein-like escape of his Hitler character, let's look more closely at what Steiner actually wrote in that three-day fever dream. Fever, in fact—in one form or another—infects the novel. Set in the feverish heat of the steamy, swampy rain forest, where almost all its characters become progressively infected with malaria and other, worse forms of fever, it is a trek through the jungle that becomes a trek back into the fever dream of twentieth-century history.

The Portage to San Cristóbal of A.H. is a philosophical novel that makes use of a pulp-fiction premise: Hitler is alive in South America. Hitler escaped the bunker, as the survival myth has it. He's been living comfortably in South America but when he hears that a search team of Israeli Nazi-hunters is on his trail, he flees to the depths of the rain forest.

The novel opens with the Nazi-hunter team catching up to him there, taking prisoner the frail, gray ninety-year-old the Führer has become, signaling their team leader back in civilization, in San Cristóbal, that they're beginning the trek back out. But Hitler's too weak to walk, and his captors become too weakened with fever to carry him. Deep in a malarial swamp, eaten alive by infectious insects, they realize they'll never succeed in making it all the way back, in bringing him to justice. And so they decide that before they all die, they'll put Hitler on trial right there in the jungle.

Meanwhile, their radio signal has been intercepted by various intelligence operatives of the Western powers who fought Hitler. In London, Sir Leslie Ryder, a caricature of Hugh Trevor-Roper, is alarmed by the political problems a Hitler trial would cause. Curiously, Steiner has chosen to put into his Trevor-Roper figure's mouth the characterization of Hitler favored by Trevor-Roper's archrival Alan Bullock. Sir Leslie specifically calls Hitler a "mountebank," the very word Trevor-Roper reviles as the symbol of what he believes was Bullock's original misapprehension of Hitler. Sir Leslie derides Hitler as "actor to the end—that's the secret of him," the Hitler-as-cynic characterization favored by Emil Fackenheim and Bullock but rejected by Trevor-Roper, who sees Hitler as unfeignedly possessed. Sir Leslie then wonders if the man found in the rain forest is the real Hitler or, in a fiendishly ironic trick of fate, the look-alike double Hitler was alleged to have used on occasion for security purposes—"the shadow, the mask of him," the Hitler actor rather than the actor Hitler.

On the other hand, Emmanuel Lieber, the commander of the Israeli team who is waiting at the San Cristóbal base camp for their return, has no doubt it is the real Hitler they have. But he expresses less triumph than dread, dread of Hitler's diabolical antimatter language. He radios his team to tell them whatever they do, don't talk to him, don't listen to him. "Gag him if necessary, or stop your ears as did the sailor. If he is allowed speech he will trick you and escape."

Don't let him speak, Lieber repeats, citing the prophecy of a medieval Jewish sage: "There shall come upon the earth in the time of night a man surpassing eloquent. All that is God's . . . must have its counterpart, its backside of evil and negation. So it is with the Word, with the gift of speech."

But weakened by disease, near death, and fearing that if they all die, Hitler will never face justice, the team in the jungle decides to disobey Lieber's warning, to put Hitler on trial, to allow him to speak in his own defense.

That speech, Hitler's own Hitler explanation, constitutes almost all of the final section of the novel. He speaks, this Hitler, with all the feverishly insidious fluency that Lieber had warned against, speaks with a force and a slippery fluidity that a summary can't convey, but the overriding theme is that whatever he was, whatever he became, he learned from the Jews—they, not he, are to blame for what he became and did.

It's a theme that expresses itself in three variations. First, he insists he learned his racism, his notion of the Master Race, from the Jewish idea of the Chosen People. He even points the finger at a specific Jew, a fellow flophouse denizen in Vienna named Jacob Grill who, he claims, read him Chosen People passages from the Bible that he merely adapted by substituting Aryan for Hebrew superiority: "My racism was a parody of yours," he tells his Jewish captors, "a hungry imitation."

Second, he claims that in seeking to exterminate the Jews, he was not imposing his will upon the world but expressing, carrying out the wishes of the rest of the world—with its willing collaboration. It was not just the Germans but the whole world who wanted to erase the Jews because "the Jew invented conscience and left man a guilty serf," forever tortured by expectations he cannot meet. Expectations Hitler summarizes as the three-fold "blackmail of transcendence": the Ten Commandments of Moses, the Sermon on the Mount of Jesus, and the demands for social justice of Karl Marx—three Jews who tormented mankind with the demands of conscience, love, and justice.

"What were our camps compared with *that?*" Hitler asks the jury in the jungle. "Ask of man more than he is, hold before his tired eyes an image of altruism, of compassion, of self-denial which only the saint or the madman can touch, and you stretch him on the rack. Till his soul bursts. What can be crueler than the Jew's addiction to the ideal?" With Moses, Jesus, and Marx, "Three times the Jew has pressed on us the blackmail of transcendence. Three times he has infected our blood and brains with the bacillus of perfection."

Steiner's Hitler denies, then, that he is some "singular demon of your rhetorical fantasies." He is not an aberration: "You have made of me some kind of mad devil, the quintessence of evil, hell embodied." No, he says, he is rather a *culmination* of human wishes: How else "could millions of ordinary men and women have found in me the mirror, the plain mirror of their needs and appetites?" The slaughter could not have happened without their active and passive complicity: "It was . . . an ugly time. But I did not create its ugliness, and I was not the worst." Here, he indulges in an excursion into exculpation through comparative evil, measuring himself against the slaughter of the Congolese by the Belgians (twenty million, he says), against the Boer War inventors of the concentration camp, and finally, against Stalin: "Our terrors were a village carnival compared with his."

Hitler's final argument is that he was, in fact, serving as an instrument of the will of the Jewish God. He was not the destroyer of the Jews but, in fact, their *savior*, because his war on them made possible the fulfillment of the messianic dream of the return to Israel. In fact, his most outrageous claim is that he, Hitler, might in fact *be* the promised Messiah.

Finally, Hitler gives his summation. "Gentlemen of the tribunal: I took my doctrines from you. I fought the blackmail of the ideal with which you have hounded mankind. My crimes were matched and surpassed by those of others. The *Reich* begat Israel. These are my last words."

His last words: Part of the problem with this astonishing speech—and I should stress it's only one cause of the rage with which many reacted to it—is that these are not only Hitler's last words but virtually the last words in the entire novel.

There is one final full paragraph appended in which a rain-forest tribes-man who has been a silent witness to the trial of Hitler leaps up, intending "to cry out, 'Proved!'" The tribesman had not understood the words Hitler spoke, Steiner writes, but their "brazen pulse carried all before it." In fact, the tribes-man's cry never escapes from his mouth, so the last *sounded* word is in fact Hitler's. But assuming the tribesman did utter it, there's an ambiguity here: What is "proved," Hitler's case for himself or the case against him? In any event, Hitler's speech is followed not by any refutation, just the sound of heli-copters descending on the clearing in which the trial has taken place. Are the copters there, as has been hinted, to silence Hitler, to execute him before he can become a terrible inconvenience to the former Allies by reminding them of their complicity in his rise, their complacency despite their knowledge of the death-camp slaughter? Or have they come to convey Hitler back where his dangerously insidious words, his antimatter language, will once again have the power to seduce and destroy? The novel ends in mid-sentence with the helicopters descending. The only thing clear is that with the conclusion of the novel, the trial of Adolf Hitler had ended—and the trial of George Steiner had begun.

The charges against Steiner were manifold and stinging, ranging from the artistic to the personal: First, it was said he'd allowed Hitler to have the last word. That long, insidious, subversive, and disturbing speech at the end of the novel is allowed to go unrefuted. While some of Steiner's defenders twisted themselves into exegetical knots trying to prove that the Hitler speech, like the speech of Satan in Milton's *Paradise Lost*, subverted, refuted *itself*—self-deconstructed, pulled the rug out from under its own rhetoric, if you looked closely at it—their efforts in this direction were undermined by Steiner's enig-matic silence on where *he* stood in regard to the Hitler speech. In fact, before speaking with him, I hadn't been able to find any published instance in which he made explicit his actual attitude toward the words he put in Hitler's mouth, much less adopted that defense.

Despite the attacks on him and his work, which escalated into public pick-eting when the novel became a stage play, he would not use the defense of irony, that he'd intended Hitler's speech to be self-subverting. And to some, even if he had, it wouldn't have been enough. To give Hitler even a semblance of cogency, of sophistication, was "playing with fire," as Steiner's most pen-etrating critic, Hyam Maccoby, put it: In a world historically receptive to any anti-Semitic argument, however crude, to put in Hitler's mouth a powerful rationale for blaming the Jews, however ironically intended, was feeding the same fires that sent Jews up the chimneys of the death camps.

The sharpest attacks of all insinuated that Steiner was not merely put-ting words in Hitler's mouth but making Hitler his mouthpiece—that Steiner's

Hitler was saying things about the Jews that Steiner himself believed. For a time after the publication of the book, this argument was carried on in small intellectual publications and Jewish journals. But when Steiner permitted the novel to be staged, when the actor Alec McCowen gave full-blooded persuasive voice to Steiner's Hitler's words, when audiences seemed to some to applaud Hitler and Jewish pickets chanted outside the theater, it became a public nightmare for Steiner. A Frankenstein nightmare: Some part of him clearly wondered whether he had in fact given birth anew to a posthumous Hitler that would haunt him, haunt Jews forever after—giving Hitler not just a posthumous victory but a posthumous life. Some part of him must have feared that the fantasy in the novel—a Hitler who had escaped—had come true, although Hitler hadn't escaped until Steiner freed him, gave him voice again. A perverse fulfillment of the warning of one of his characters: "If he is allowed speech he will trick you and escape."

I could sense Steiner's deep unease over the issue in his anguished denial that the audience at the London production had applauded Hitler and not his play. His quintuple "no, no, no, no, *no.*"

And yet I found to my surprise he was willing to answer my questions about his Hitler quite frankly, more revealingly I believe than he ever had before. I put the question very directly: Can't the unanswered Hitler speech, the novel itself, be interpreted as blaming the Jews for Hitler's crimes against them?

At first, he seemed to be distancing himself from that possibility with the it's-only-a-character-speaking ploy. "It can be interpreted that Hitler would have defended himself this way. . . . Suppose he hadn't shot himself. He's put in a glass box. And suppose his demonic power *had* been unleashed?"

In other words, Steiner was merely trying to extrapolate the reality of Hitler rather than put his own persuasive words into his mouth or endorse those words in any way. His use of the word "demonic" suggested to me that he might, in fact, be deploying the "Milton's Satan" defense of his Hitler speech. William Blake had argued provocatively that the dazzling heroic rhetoric Milton puts in Satan's mouth in Book I of *Paradise Lost* (when a speech by Lucifer rallies his fellow fallen angels with romantic rhetoric of rebellion against tyranny) proved that Milton himself was "of the Devil's party." But the thrust of the twentieth-century critical response to Satan's speech was to attempt to prove that Milton had ingeniously devised Satan's rhetoric in such a way that, examined closely, it betrayed its own diabolical meretriciousness; that the reader was designed to first be seduced, to be "surprised by sin" (the title of an excellent early study of the question by Stanley Fish), only then to realize how the glittering surface of Satan's rhetoric had ensnared him. And—shocked by the nearness of his own fall—to emerge chastened and ever more alert to the danger of taking at face value the words of the Devil.

But when I gave Steiner the opportunity to avail himself of this defense, he refused the easy way out. The questions Hitler raises in his speech are *valid*, he told me. "I think it calls for answers," he said. "Hitler's speech calls for answers," he repeats. And he means answers from Jews.

Consider the argument he puts in his Hitler's mouth that the Jewish concept of the Chosen People is the origin of the Master Race idea. Steiner defends the comparison: "The thousand-year reich, the nonmixing of races, it's all, if you want, a hideous travesty of the Judaic. But a travesty can only exist because of that which it imitates."

Almost refusing to hear Steiner's endorsement of the comparison, I kept offering him a way out from behind his Hitler.

"When Hitler calls himself Sabbatai," I began, referring to a passage in Steiner's Hitler's speech in which he invokes the name of the famous false messiah who deceived masses of Jews worldwide before recanting and converting to Islam, "I thought that was an indication of—I was looking for irony in your view of Hitler."

"There is irony!" Steiner says. "Because of the Sabbatai Zvi figure then converting, and there's mockery there." But it's localized irony. He insists the questions his Hitler asks about the implication of the Jews in their fate must be taken seriously. "I have demanded an answer [to these questions] and never got one" from his critics who condemned him for even asking. He insists on his right to ask—and on the need to answer—Hitler's questions.

Hitler's questions or Steiner's questions? Perhaps the most revealing thing Steiner said came when he reiterated to me the need for answers: "I don't think *I* even know how to answer what I say in that last speech," he told me. It wasn't until reading over the transcript of the interview that I realized I'd missed the import of that quote: "I don't . . . know how to answer what *I* say in that last speech." Not what Hitler says, what *I*, George Steiner, say. His Hitler speaks for him. He stands behind his Hitler's questions: "There were many attacks on that speech," he says, but they attacked the very notion of raising the questions rather than answering them.

"And I *want* it to be answered," he insists, raising his voice. "Where *is* the answer? Not just saying you're being an outrageous cretin for asserting such things. I'm still waiting for answers. I've debated its role often, including with Fackenheim. And no answers. He needed to malign me, that I totally misunderstood the sense of God's election [of the Chosen People]. And I then began quoting the book of Joshua and said to Fackenheim. 'You really don't get it. I *really* want an answer.'"

Struck by how impassioned he was, I asked him about the final, most outrageous question his Hitler asks: Wasn't *he*—Hitler—the Messiah who brought about the fulfillment of the messianic dream of a Jewish homeland in Palestine?

"We can show that the miracle of the recognition of Israel in 1948 is inseparable from the Shoah," Steiner replied, "so my Hitler says, 'Who created Israel?' There wouldn't have been an Israel without the Shoah."

I tried to get a sense of just how closely Steiner stands behind another assertion of his Hitler: that he was only embodying the animus of the world against the Jews, exterminating the Jews for the "blackmail of transcendence," for torturing non-Jews with the invention of, the demands of conscience.

"It seems pejorative, the phrase you use," I said, "calling it 'the blackmail of transcendence.' Is there something wrong with asking people to be better than themselves?"

"No," he says. "But they hate you for it. We hate no one as deeply as somebody who says we've got to do better and keeps saying it and rubbing it in, just rubbing our nose in our own failing. Oh boy! Who do we hate most? Those who have been generous to us in a moment of weakness, those who have seen us in abject need? And when we end up doing well, we will do anything not to look them in the eye again."

It's hard to deny that this is a truth of human nature, that, as the saying goes, no good deed goes unpunished. But is Steiner endorsing the view that the Jews deserve to be punished for asking (in the persons of Moses, Jesus, and Marx) for an ethic of good deeds? "Is transcendence something Jews should be apologetic for?" I asked Steiner.

"On the contrary," he said. "It's the highest—My *God*, if we could be—if we could love our neighbors as ourselves, oh boy."

"But aren't you saying the inevitable product of positing this as an ideal is Hitler?"

"Not just positing it," Steiner replied. "The Jews were demanding it and demanding it," he said, once again sounding as if the Jews *were* to blame.

"Should we have demanded less or—"

He sighed, "Probably we should have done better by demanding it more of *ourselves*. Now if Mother Teresa were sitting here, I'd shut up. She has the right to demand it. I've known human beings—very few—who have given up high careers to work on the Afghan border in the refugee camps, right. Or people in geriatric wards in New York, emptying the shit bowls at night, holding people shouting and shaking with drugs. *These* people have every right to say to me, 'Why don't you do something more with your life?' In fact, they don't. The other ones that don't [live those lives] do [demand] it. And until you know that you can do far better, it is very difficult to ask it of others. And Judaism has asked it of others three times."

Again, while Steiner insists these are questions he wants answers to, the way he frames the questions seems to suggest he *knows* the answers. Not that he likes the answers, but the answers do seem, if not to blame the Jews, then to implicate them in their fate. Here he seems to be saying that it's not so much the Jews' fault for demanding transcendence but rather for the implicit hypocrisy of demanding it from others without first sufficiently demonstrating it themselves. Jews don't always live up to the standards they set for everyone, therefore, supposedly, we can *understand* why the world secretly approved when Hitler slaughtered them.

Because of my admiration for Steiner's intellect and his art, I was reluctant to come around to his critics' view that he was, in his Hitler novel, devising sophisticated ways of blaming the victim. But, in fact, in my conversation with him at Cambridge that morning, he took a breathtaking leap even beyond the blame-the-victim rhetoric of his Hitler novel. He tossed out, almost casually, what might be seen as the ultimate blame-the-victim argument: the Jews' *ontological* responsibility for Hitler's crime.

It was a line of speculation so shocking, so transgressive, I later found myself wishing I hadn't heard it at all. He introduced it by referring to a startling remark in the final, posthumously published interview with Sidney Hook, the celebrated anticommunist philosopher—a remark Hook realized was so inflammatory he insisted it could not be published during his lifetime.

"It had a tremendous impact on me," Steiner tells me. "Dying, Sidney Hook gave [Norman] Podhoretz an interview. And he believed great philosophers should not be afraid to speak out, but he demanded it be kept posthumous. It says something very important. It says something roughly like this: If we [the Jews] had disappeared, assimilated, wouldn't it have been much better? Hasn't the price been too great? Now, this is a key question. And Hook was afraid to touch on that taboo until after his death, but it's there. He dictates it to Podhoretz."

It's controversial enough, but, Steiner says, "My question goes even further. I have said Auschwitz does two things: It does everything to the Jew, and it does everything to those who *do* it to the Jews." And then he delivers the unspeakable implication: "The horror of the thing is we have lowered the threshold of mankind."

"We as Jews have? By—?"

"By being the occasion of mankind's ultimate bestiality," he said. "We are that which has shown mankind to be ultimately bestial. We refused Jesus, who dies hideously on the cross. And then mankind turns on us in a vulgar kind of counter-Golgotha which is Auschwitz. And when somebody tortures a child, he does it to the child, he does it to himself, too."

"Well, true, but who are we to sympathize with—both equally?"

Steiner presses on with his extraordinary argument about Jews lowering the threshold of mankind: "Auschwitz breaks the reinsurance on human hope in a sense."

"Breaks the reinsurance on human hope?" I asked. "The sense that there is always some kind of safety net, some reason not to give in to utter despair at the evil in the world?"

"Yeah. And without us, there wouldn't have been Auschwitz. In a sense, an obscene statement and yet an accurate statement."

Again, I found myself not quite willing to believe that Steiner believed in the implications of what he was saying: It went beyond blaming the victim for giving the perpetrator an excuse, a "reason" that explained his crime against them; it blamed the victim for even *existing* in the first place and thus becoming an "occasion" for the perpetrator sinking to new levels of depravity or inventing new degrees of evil.

And so I questioned him closely about this conjecture. What was it about Auschwitz in the first place that defined it as a quantum leap in the evolution of evil, made it different from previous massacres, in the sense that this one "breaks the reinsurance on human hope"?

What made it different, he says, is its "terrible ontological comprehensiveness. There have been many other horrible massacres," he says. "And men are cruel, and they've tortured." But the ontological difference, the new, darker mode of being that came into being with Auschwitz, has to do with the ontological reason the Jews were killed: not because of their actions but because of their being.

"To kill a child because he *is*, not because he does, not because he believes, not because he belongs [to a religion]. For his being. That's what the word 'ontological' means. Because you *are*, you must die. This is not like other pursuits. If you kill a lot of Serbs, it's because you want their territory, et cetera, et cetera. Islam converts Jews, doesn't kill them. The idea that the Jew has to be eliminated because he *is*, that his existential being is inadmissible—the attempt to fulfill *that* idea probably means that humanity has no road back to certain illusions."

"No road back": What he's saying has something in common with his speculation on Kafka as the cause of the death camps: By bringing into the world the previously unthinkable *idea* of such sophisticated bestiality, Kafka might somehow have caused it. Similarly by being the victim of such previously unimaginable bestiality, the Jews may have "caused" the bottom to drop out of the world, an unmendable rent in the tenuous fabric of hope suspended over the bottomless abyss of despair.

Which is why Steiner invokes Sidney Hook's despairing posthumous question: Might the world have been better off if the Jews had stopped being Jews? Hook asks. Might the world have been better off if the Jews had never existed at all? Steiner asks.

Steiner calls this line of speculation obscene yet accurate. It's certainly obscene; is it accurate? For one thing, Hook's conjecture is belied by the fact that conversion or assimilation rarely spared Jews the ravages of anti-Semitism. Recently, Benzion Netanyahu demonstrated that in the Spanish Inquisition hatred and murder of the Jews persisted regardless of their conversion to

Christianity: It was *racial* rather than religious (in fact, especially targeted at the converts and Marranos); so, of course, was Hitler's.

In another sense, Steiner's ontological blame-the-Jews argument contradicts the gravamen of what he—or his Hitler—argues in that notorious speech in the novel. To Steiner's Hitler, Jews weren't exterminated just for "being" but for "cause"—for the torments of conscience they supposedly inflicted on the world, for instance.

Just to clarify this point, I asked Steiner about his argument that the Jews were killed because they tortured the conscience of mankind.

"You seem to be saying that something about the Jews—that this is a *rational* hatred—"

"No—it is—*no*. Call it, if you want, an intuitive [hatred]—I believe that explanations for anti-Semitism of a sociopolitcal nature are fine as far as they go, but they tell you nothing about two things. About Jew-hatred where there are no Jews [in contemporary Poland, for instance] and about the ontological decision that one must kill the human person because of its being. And hence I put forward this image, this hypothesis that our invention of God, of Jesus, our invention of Marxist utopia, has left humanity so uncertain inwardly that it is trying to banish its own bad conscience."

"Are you saying, then, that the torture of conscience is worse than the torture in the camps even?"

"Over the long run," he says, "to feel yourself at fault probably builds up unbearable hatreds, *self*-hatreds. To feel yourself found out."

Of course, there are those who believe that what is really going on here is Steiner's self-hatred, Steiner as a self-hating Jew. But I don't think so. I found Steiner deeply identified as a Jew, not anti-Zionist, as he's occasionally been portrayed—in fact, anti-anti-Zionist. But he has even more deeply identified with the Jew as the perennial outsider, with the alienating, self-lacerating, self-awareness of Jewish intellect, making the Jew so often an exile not just from a physical homeland but from metaphysical comfort in the world. He spoke in fact of his fondness for the figure of the Wandering Jew, and for Jewish wanderers and wonderers from Spinoza to Kafka and Trotsky.

But I still found it disturbing how far he was willing to wander into speculation that seemed to make Jews responsible for the ontologic scale, the ontology-shifting-and-darkening crimes against them. Unless, perhaps, there was in Steiner a willful need to place himself and his people at the ontological center of the universe. It's almost a Steinerian reinvention of the Chosen People doctrine he professes to question: the fate of the Jews as the fulcrum, the test case of Being.

But something else seemed to be going on, something more disturbing, something that may confirm Steiner's distrust of the Word, of the uncanny power of Hitler's voice. In attempting a daring act of literary ventriloquism, in attempting to speak *with* Hitler's voice, to make him mouth Steiner's own ideas (about the blackmail of transcendence, and so on), a frightening inversion seems to have taken place, one that calls into question who is really pulling the strings—who is the ventriloquist, who the marionette. An inversion that finds a Jewish intellectual talking about the world being better off had the Jews never existed—arriving at the same place, by however different a route, that Hitler did. Another case of the subtle working of the Hitler spell?

Still, as the formal interview came to a close, I couldn't help being impressed by Steiner's candor, by his willingness to take personal responsibility for ideas and questions he'd put in Hitler's mouth fifteen years previously, by his courage, or recklessness, in venturing beyond them to even more incendiary territory. While raising the notion of his Hitler as a frightening creation who'd escaped him, he ultimately was standing squarely behind his Hitler, odd as it sounds to say it.

Walking back to the porter's lodge of Churchill College, Cambridge, Steiner and I returned to the subject of the historical Hitler—in particular, his fabled charisma.

"I used to ask my students," Steiner said, "'If Hitler walked into a room, would you get up?'"

"'Would they get up' meaning—"

"Would one sit in the presence of world history?"

"And you feel that the presence would be so commanding—but didn't Beryl Bainbridge make him seem to be essentially just a slight, unimpressive figure?" I was referring to Bainbridge's challenging novel, *Young Adolf*, which postulates an apocryphal young Hitler visiting his half brother Alois Jr. in Liverpool in 1911, during the "lost years" when he was twenty-two. Bainbridge's brilliantly understated premise in limning a lazy, layabout slacker Hitler is to raise the question of the unbridgeable abyss between the youthful, inconsequential Hitler and the evil god he became. It raises the eternal question of the source of his metamorphosis: When and how did he acquire his demonic charisma?

"But you feel that had the young Adolf walked into the room, one would have immediately *known*?" I asked him.

"Many did," he says. "Many did. Speer fell in love with him and never gave up that love." (It's interesting how often Speer's love for Hitler is cited as impressive by sophisticated Hitler commentators such as Trevor-Roper and Steiner. It's as if to say, If someone as sophisticated as *I* am could fall under the Hitler spell, then he really *must* have had something.)

"Wasn't Speer falling in love with the later, charismatic Hitler, though?" I asked.

"Goebbels meets him very early, very early. And writes in his diary, 'Is he John the Baptist? Is he Jesus?'"

"Yes, but that was still about 1925," I said. "We still have him just the unimpressive corporal in the First World War."

"He's not!" Steiner exclaims. "He has the Iron Cross twice over. Three times wounded! Oh boy! In the most dangerous of all military functions—namely, courier. Where the survival rate was about a week, usually like one *hour*. Later on, he's a spotter, an artillery spotter in front of the lines. And he *volunteered* for this. And his contempt later for general staff officers who haven't been in a fighting war was fully justified. He *knew*, he knew."

"So Hitler was a genuinely brave man?"

"Immensely. You do not get three major wounds and the Iron Cross unless you are."

"So we can't get off the hook by thinking of him as cowardly, as hypocritical about—"

"Oh no."

"He was heroic and admirable in a way? Up to that point?"

"Well, his record is objectively there for anybody to see. And it's [his military courage] very important for the later politics."

I took my leave with mixed feelings. It was similarly hard to doubt Steiner's personal courage in asking explosive questions—and giving incendiary answers to them—in venturing beyond the lines of conventional thinking on the subject. Speculations that make *him* vulnerable to hostile fire.

And he has been fired upon. His most thoughtful and thoroughgoing critic, Hyam Maccoby, once said of Steiner and the words he put in Hitler's mouth: "He knew he was playing with fire."

The implication is that Steiner was being intellectually immature, a child playing with matches; that he was giving in to the seductions of his own brilliance—to the impulse to play with ideas, to push speculations to the limits without caring enough for the consequences in the hands of those less well intentioned in a world dangerous to Jews. An impulse to play that might not be dangerous in one who lacked Steiner's powerful intellect, but is in him. That, in effect, Steiner is too smart, but not wise enough, for his own good. Or ours.

But Maccoby himself—as we'll see in the next chapter—is also not averse to "playing with fire."

CHAPTER 18

Singling out Christianity: The Passion Play of Hyam Maccoby

*In which a Jewish scholar offers the explanation
that dare not speak its name*

It's the beginning of holiday season in London; the crowds bustling through the bracing December chill are exhibiting the conventional Dickensian cheer, bearing festive rolls of wrapping paper and ribbon home. But deep in the basement of the Sternberg Library of the Leo Baeck Institute for Jewish Studies, the combative scholar Hyam Maccoby was exhibiting a very different kind of holiday spirit.

"People go on about this jolly festival of Christmas," he was saying to me. "But I think Christmas is a *sinister* festival."

Sinister?

"Because what is it? The sacrifice has been born. Let us rejoice. The Christian doesn't think about Easter now, but somewhere in the back of his mind, Christmas is leading him to Easter. In the back of everybody's mind is, Why are we celebrating this birth with such joy? We are garlanding the sacrifice. Because he's due for a horrific death." A horrific death the Jews will pay for, have paid for. To Maccoby, the dark truth beneath the cheer, the skull beneath the skin of the holiday spirit, is the responsibility Christianity, even Christmas, bears for the horrific death of the Jews.

"Christians say the Holocaust is part of the evil of humanity," Maccoby remarked to me later in our conversation. "It isn't the evil of humanity. It's the evil of Christendom."

And Hitler? "He embodied a certain *aspect* of Christian civilization which in other people is diffused," he told me later on in our conversation, when he spoke of Hitler as "the boil" in which the poisons of "Christian society" came to a head.

This is extremely strong stuff, another example of how attempts to explain Hitler drive the most mild-mannered and scholarly types, like Maccoby, to rhetorical and philosophical extremes. Sitting behind his desk in the book-lined office set in the corner of the library stacks, Maccoby has the demeanor of a retired clerk, but his words carry the fiery conviction of the warrior priests, the Maccabees, whose name he bears.

Maccoby's is not the emotional partisanship of a religious fanatic. An Oxford-educated literature scholar turned historian of religion, his serious convictions arise from a lifetime of study and scrupulous research. He is, he believes, merely expressing painfully uncomfortable truths that other Jews refrain from expressing for fear of offending the primarily Christian society in which they live. But for Maccoby, the Hitler explanation that dare not speak its name *must* be expressed, the Christian roots of genocide must be exposed. When Maccoby says, "Christmas is a sinister festival," he's not saying, "Bah, humbug"; he's saying, in effect, "Bah, Holocaust."

To some extent, the dispute between George Steiner and Hyam Maccoby conjures up the great disputations of medieval Europe. Those disputations were, in fact, terrible Inquisitional torments inflicted on Jews in the guise of theological debates. The disputations could be seen as the intellectual crucifixion of Jewish faith. A prominent figure of Jewish learning or rabbinic scholarship would be compelled—often dragged—to the cathedral to take part in a "debate" with a leading Christian theologian over the crude proposition: Which religion has the truth: Judaism or Christianity?

Needless to say, the fight was fixed, the judging rigged, the Jews subjected to catcalls and verbal and physical abuse while trying to maintain with dignity beliefs they had no wish to subject to debate—often against converted, renegade Jews who claimed to know insidious and shameful fallacies and secret distortions in Jewish doctrine. Maccoby himself has written a play based on one of the most famous of these, *The Disputation*, a play one Jewish critic described as "a Jewish Passion play."

While the conflict between Steiner and Maccoby has some elements of the grand medieval disputations, it's more a battle of equals, both brilliant and impassioned partisans. But ultimately the crux of the debate comes down to the stark choice of Judaism versus Christianity. Which is more to "blame" for Hitler? Steiner finally blames Judaism's "blackmail of transcendence" for making the Jews an object of murderous hatred. Maccoby blames what he believes is the blood hate at the heart of the Christian Gospels for sanctioning, preparing the ground for, what in his view amounts to the Christian ritual murder of the Jewish people.

For Maccoby, a trim, distinguished-looking man who was close to seventy when I saw him, this has become a deeply ingrained article of faith but one he insists is the product of reason, years of painful immersion in the history of the Christian-Jewish relationship. The executive director of the Sternberg Library in the Leo Baeck Institute (a distinguished London center for the study of German Jewish culture), Maccoby is the author of half a dozen scholarly books, but he's most well known in America through his combative polemics in *Commentary*, which challenge Jews to cut through the warm fog of ecumenical hopes and cast a cold eye on the responsibility of Christian culture and Christian belief for the Holocaust.

For someone with Maccoby's views on the responsibility of Christianity, George Steiner's elaborate speculations about the responsibilities of Judaism are not merely misguided, they are patently offensive. He goes so far as to accuse Steiner of "glorifying Hitler" by giving him that final unrefuted speech of blame-the-Jews self-justification in *The Portage to San Cristóbal of A.H.* Maccoby's tone in speaking of Steiner ranges from the acidulous (he does "not consider him a charlatan," although he implies others do) to the contemptuous: He accuses Steiner of "playing with fire" in giving Hitler's incendiary speech such rhetorical power. He makes it sound as if Steiner were an irresponsible child playing with matches.

But there is a sense in which Maccoby himself can be seen as "playing with fire," burning bridges—the fragile bridges of ecumenicism that link Christians and Jews in the aftermath of the Holocaust—by insisting Christianity is irremediably infected with a murderously evil hatred in its very essence.

When I raised the question, Maccoby's response was, "Forget ecumenicism, one can't be ecumenical with a faith whose essence is sanctioned hatred of Jews."

Maccoby knows that what he's doing is breaking a taboo, that pronouncing aloud the explanation that dare not speak its name can be as troubling to Jews as it is to Christians. He'd first advanced the notion that Christianity (not just some Christians) must bear responsibility for the Holocaust—that it was not an aberration of Christian principles but a culmination of some malevolent essence—in a piece in *Commentary* that created an uproar on the Jewish magazine's letters page.

"Your position was attacked almost as if it were a breach of decorum—of an unspoken rule that Jews have to be nice about not saying such things," I suggested.

"Oh very much so," he said. "You could see the extent to which what I said *horrified* many people, Jews as well as Christians. But I felt that people were concerning themselves so much with Jewish-Christian relations they were sweeping things under the carpet which needed to be talked about. All these people will say, 'Yes, yes, there have been Christians that have been anti-Semites, and it's unfortunate that it's spread among the people as a kind of *misconception* of Christianity, but it was never really the true meaning of Christianity, it was never shared by the leaders of Christianity.' And my argument was just the contrary: that people remained for centuries unaffected by anti-Semitism. It took the indoctrination *by* the leaders over the entire course of eighteen centuries to make the people anti-Semitic enough to accept Hitler."

Maccoby is not anti-Christian per se: He speaks well of certain variants that don't emphasize "the human sacrifice" of the Crucifixion, as he calls it, and the concomitant need to scourge the Jews as the "sacred executioners" of God. But he does believe that the impulse to hate and to murder Jews, the impulse that Hitler tapped into, is not an aberration but an essence of mainstream Christianity.

It is a straight line, "a direct connection," Maccoby believes, "between Judas and Hitler." Between the hate-filled portrait of a treacherous betrayer of the Lord, who became the archetypal Jew in Christian consciousness for eighteen centuries, and the culmination of that indoctrination in Jew-hatred: the readiness of Christian nations, Christian people to become complicit in the murder of the Judas people when incited and empowered to by Hitler.

Perhaps considering his preoccupation with Judas, it should not come as a surprise that betrayal is a recurrent theme of Maccoby's discourse: One senses that part of his anger at George Steiner derives from his feeling that Steiner (like one of those medieval disputationist Jews who argued the Christian side) has betrayed his own people—become a Judas to the Jews—in the service of his intellectual vanity. And Maccoby's account of the evolution of his own personal antagonism to Christianity began with what he describes as a personal betrayal: his betrayal by T. S. Eliot.

"I come to the whole subject as a British Jew rather than, let's say, someone personally involved in the Holocaust," Maccoby told me. "My family are all part of that Russian Jewry which moved to Western Europe and America as a result of the [turn-of-the-century] pogroms. It's very possible that some of my family were lost in the Holocaust, but I don't know because we lost touch with our Russian relatives."

He was, however, personally involved in the war against Hitler. "I served in the British army, but that's the extent of my involvement." He was too young to see combat before the war ended. He speaks of the "underestimation syndrome" in Britain in the prewar era of his childhood, "which wanted to regard Hitler as a normal kind of politician who might have been extreme in one way or another, but as time went on, rational considerations would take over. I mean, people even are talking on those lines today. There's [John] Charmley now," the author of a recent biography of Winston Churchill that argues that he was too fanatically obsessed with Hitler and that the British might have been better off making a "peace of equals" with Hitler in 1940 or 1941.

"I think that's all wrong. I mean, people just didn't understand how extreme Hitler was and how mad he was." He speaks of his own first intimations of that in his first year at Oxford in 1942. "When I was a student at Balliol [College], people were beginning to hand round pictures, evidence of what was going on in Hitler's death camps. And there were one or two big meetings held at various parks in London and in Oxford to make people aware of what was going on. But people weren't aware, the general public was not aware."

His own awareness had not yet begun to affect his cultural preoccupation. He'd embraced the Western canon at the roots, the fount of Balliol. "I studied classics at Oxford—that is, Latin and Greek. And then I went on to study philosophy, and, in the end, English literature became my main study."

As much as he embraced Western literature and Western culture, he could not help but begin to feel a growing disturbance at one aspect of it. "I think the first time I encountered that was in the writings of G. K. Chesterton, which I got very interested in when I was a teenager. I loved his writing, but then there was the streak of anti-Semitism running through it. And also Hilaire Belloc. His writing was even worse." Something about the difference between Belloc's and Chesterton's anti-Semitism made Chesterton seem somehow *more* sinister to Maccoby.

"With Chesterton, it didn't seem to come too naturally to him. He seemed to pick it up from his religious belief rather than from the kind of inbred anti-Semitism that Belloc's was. I became interested in the relationship between Christian doctrine and anti-Semitism. I'd always been interested because I was brought up in a very rabbinical family. My father's father was, and my uncle was, a serious student of the Talmud. So I was brought up in the study of Judaism at its most scholarly. And I read quite deeply in the history of Christianity in my early years. And I came back to it after I started getting deeply into the study of English literature, because the author whom I was particularly interested in—whom I wrote many articles and did research on—was T. S. Eliot.

"And here we're back to the same syndrome of Christianity: an author whom I admired as a writer and who, at the same time, seemed to have anti-Semitism not just as something peripheral to his writing, but one that seemed to go right to the depth of his personality and the heart of his beliefs as a Christian."

To his dismay, Maccoby came to feel that it was the kind of writer who felt his Christianity most deeply, writers such as Chesterton and Eliot, who were more likely to feel impelled to disparage Jews and Judaism. And, Maccoby came to believe, in doing so they weren't necessarily misunderstanding Christianity; they might have been understanding the anti-Semitic impulse within it all too well.

It's an impulse Maccoby believes emanates from, above all else, the Judas story in the Gospels, the identification of Judas as the archetypal Jew and the incitement to hatred in his portrayal. While Judas isn't singled out for his Jewishness in the New Testament (all the disciples were at least nominally Jewish), the identification was made official by papal pronouncement as early as the fifth century when Pope Gelasius I denounced Judas as "a devil and the devil's workman [who] gives his name to the whole race" of Jews.

Unofficially, elements of the Judas story in the Gospels have lent themselves—or helped create—the most pernicious stereotypes of the Jew: his treachery was mercenary (he sold Jesus to the authorities for thirty pieces of silver), he was a greedy embezzler (in the Gospel of John, he's filching from the disciples' funds for the poor), and, above all, he is a dishonest, deceitful traitor, a smiling villain who kisses Jesus on the mouth while stabbing him in the back. Indeed, one can hear incendiary anti-Semitic echoes of the Judas story in the stab-in-the-back accusation Hitler manipulated to convince the German public that the heroic German army had not lost the First World War but had been betrayed, stabbed in the back, by treacherous Jews and Jewish-paid politicians on the home front. Judasness is central to the vision of Jewishness in Hitler's rhetoric.

In his focus on the Judas story, Maccoby differs from much of the previous discussion of the sources of Christian anti-Semitism, which has tended to focus more on the early "anti-Judaizing" shift in Christianity's self-definition— from a faith that saw itself fulfilling the promises of Judaism to a faith that "superseded" its Jewish origins. The focus of this school of thought is less on Judas than on the powerful anti-Judaizing supersessionist ideology of Paul, the Jewish persecutor of Christians who became the Christian purger of Jewishness from Christianity. Some see Paul's doctrinal predisposition as sanctioning popular rage against Jews for denying and crucifying Jesus.

Maccoby emphatically disagrees. While there are anti-Jewish elements in Paul's doctrine and in the rhetoric of the Pauline Epistles, "my main point is that it's not so much a question of doctrine. It's a question of the imaginative image that is produced by the Judas story itself. There's no credo in Christianity saying you have to be anti-Semites. The figure of Judas plays no part in the Christian *creed*, but in the Christian *story* it plays a very important part because he personifies the figure of the Jews."

I was somewhat skeptical of Maccoby's position initially. Having recently reread the Pauline Epistles, I'd been shocked at the kind of insidious, incendiary incitements Paul uses against the Jews in certain of them. But I made a point, after speaking with Maccoby, to look again at the Judas passages in the New Testament. In part, their anti-Semitic potential derives from the fact that Judas is not the abstract people that Paul rails against but a vividly embodied flesh-and-blood Jew—one Christians had not only heard of and read about but had actually *seen*, the sneaking, despicable betrayer familiar to centuries and centuries of Christian audiences: the Jew in the Passion play.

What struck me also in reading the Gospel accounts of Judas is the exterminationist imperative embedded at the very heart of the story in the words, the curse, of Jesus himself. Knowing, at the Last Supper, that Judas has already betrayed him, Jesus issues this curse: "Woe to that man by whom the Son of Man is betrayed. *It would have been better for that man if he had never been born*" (emphasis added). A curse that struck me more forcefully for having recently heard George Steiner speculate that it might have been better if the Jewish people had disappeared or never existed, *had never been born*. It is virtually a wish for retroactive extermination, which in Maccoby's thesis paved the way for Hitler's proactive extermination.

Perhaps the emotional power of the Judas story has something to do with its pervasive rhetoric of blood. The thirty pieces of silver Judas has taken from the temple authorities to betray Jesus becomes "blood money"; when a cravenly remorseful Judas slinks back to the temple to try to return it to his paymasters, even they reject it because it's tainted with blood. Those cursed silver coins are used by the temple authorities to buy a field that later becomes known as the Field of Blood. A place that becomes (in another variant of the story) the place where Judas meets his bloody end. It's a field he bought with his blood money and, while surveying his purchase, he suffers a violent fall— a plunge that resulted in his intestines bursting out of his body, bathing the ground in blood, turning it into a "field of blood" in fact as well as name.

The pervasiveness of blood in the Judas story finds its reflection, Maccoby believes, in the pervasiveness of blood in the most incendiary and murderous of anti-Semitic legends: the so-called blood libel—the persistent legend that Jews practice the ritual murder of Christian children (a kind of recapitulation of the Crucifixion) in order to obtain blood for use in Passover rituals.

To Maccoby, the repetition of the Judas story—centuries and centuries of Christian children being indoctrinated with that primal tale of mercenary Jewish blood-money betrayal—had, by the time of the Holocaust, cumulatively built up a profound and deeply embedded thirst for Jewish blood, a vengeful thirst once satisfied by periodic pogroms but easily manipulated by Hitler into complicity with extermination.

I asked Maccoby if there was, in the story of the "field of blood," of the blood of the Jew soaking the landscape, an anticipation of or sanction for the fields of blood that Hitler's camps became.

"It is the *story*, yes, people are much more affected by a story than they are by theology or creeds. And children who are taught a story in which from the earliest years the Jew is the hateful figure—Judas Iscariot and the Jews generally are hateful figures—will hate Jews from then onwards, *without even knowing why they hate the Jews.* And if they lose their Christian belief, that hate will still remain with them. They'll find some other reason for hating Jews. Like Hitler himself, for example."

"You feel the Judas story was directly responsible for *Hitler's* anti-Semitism?" I asked Maccoby.

He emphasizes that in two of the Gospel accounts of Judas's betrayal, he is "entered by Satan" (Luke) or "taken possession by the Devil" (John) before he betrays Jesus, forever inscribing an image of the Jews as the people of the Devil on the hearts of children who hear the story in a state of primal receptivity.

"Hitler was brought up to hate the Jews, *particularly* to hate the Jews as the people of the Devil," he insists. "He lost his Christian faith, but he retained the hatred of the Jews as the people of the Devil." Maccoby is here deliberately undercutting the argument of those who attempt to exempt or exculpate Christianity as a source of Hitler's Jew-hatred by citing various anti-Christian remarks Hitler made over the years.

An instance of this can be found in a newspaper column by Pat Buchanan. In attempting to repudiate Jesse Jackson's inflammatory remark that a "Christian coalition" in Nazi Germany provided "a suitable scientific theologic rationale" for Hitler, Buchanan declared: "Hitler loathed Christianity. In Louis Snyder's *Hitler's Third Reich: A Documentary History*, Hitler is quoted as saying 'Antiquity was better than modern times because it didn't know Christianity and syphilis.'"

Of course, Hitler was all over the map with his pontifications on Christianity, often attacking it as Judaism under another name, but just as often uttering pieties about the importance of the church to national morality.

Maccoby's point is that however many anti-Christian quotes from Hitler you find, they came from the adult Hitler; the true relevance of the anti-Jewish animus of Christianity to Hitler's psyche was its effect on Hitler's impressionable imagination as a child. That the emotional indoctrination of the Judas story was a powerful, poisonous legacy that ran deeper than any later disagreements Hitler might have over the political and social role of the Christian church in Germany. In the ongoing controversy over the origin of Hitler's anti-Semitism and the cause of its virulence, then, Maccoby seems to be envisioning a far earlier starting point than most.

"Are you saying it began at the Benedictine monastery, then?" I asked him, referring to Hitler's early schooling in the Benedictine friars' school at Lambach.

"Yeah, well, you may say lots of people who [received similar education] didn't turn into Hitlers. But it was certainly that, combined, of course, with a particularly obsessive personality, which made this the center of his thinking. I'm quite sure that his personal upbringing had a great deal to do with it—if he hadn't had a Christian upbringing he would have been probably a sick personality anyhow, but his sickness would've fastened onto some other kind of hatred. But having had that Christian upbringing, his sick personality centered on the traditional enemy. And particularly in the circumstances of the defeat of Germany, there is the need for a scapegoat—the tendency of people to turn to the traditional scapegoat in times of great distress."

I asked Maccoby what his reaction was to Hitler's own account in *Mein Kampf* of a later transformative moment in his perception of Jews: that moment in the Vienna street some ten years later than Lambach when he "first" glimpsed a Jew in alien-seeming black caftan and black earlocks.

"Well, he's kidding himself, I think," Maccoby says. Or kidding us: "Hitler has an interest in portraying anti-Semitism as something he *developed* rather than grew up with. I think he saw this figure, but *why* was he filled with such hatred for this figure? I mean, if it had been Amish, for example, and also dressed in rather unfamiliar black garb, he wouldn't have felt a sense of hatred at all."

I mentioned to Maccoby a doctoral thesis I'd seen (by Helmut Schmeller) that argued that, growing up in Linz, Hitler was most likely reading the extremely anti-Semitic newspaper the *Linzer Fliegende Blätter*, which would suggest an anti-Semitic awareness of oft-caricatured black-caftaned Jews long before the alleged revelatory encounter with that apocryphal wandering Jew in the streets of Vienna.

"So he's lying about that. Or at the very least this was something that probably went back so early in his life he can't remember when it started."

"And what about all the millions of Christians indoctrinated in the same way who *didn't* become Hitler?" I asked.

"He was very unique in a way—in the sense that he embodied a certain *aspect* of Christian civilization which, in other people, is diffused and has many other things to counterbalance it. But he struck a *chord* with that aspect in others. He was himself a human being who contained that chord. He embodied it single-mindedly. He was the focal point of a kind of evil which grew to a head, like a boil, in him." It was that common chord that united the German people with Hitler in their partnership in genocide, he believes.

"The criticism of your point of view," I said to Maccoby, "has been that Hitler's was a *racial*, not a Christian anti-Semitism. Am I right in thinking that what you're saying is that racial anti-Semitism as the Nazis and Hitler formulated it was something that had been around for maybe a century? But there were eighteen centuries of Christian—"

"Right, absolutely. The point is, you see, that you build up a fund of hatred against a certain group of people. The fact that that fund is backed by certain dogmas doesn't mean that when those dogmas left, the hatreds left. The hatred's still there. And it has to be backed up by newer theories. I mean, if the Jews are no longer hated because they are the people of Satan who killed Jesus, then some other theory works—in the case of the Nazis it was a racial theory; with Karl Marx, the Jews played the role of the archetypal capitalist. This is what I call post-Christian anti-Semitism"—a continuation of Christian anti-Semitism in a different guise, as opposed to Daniel Goldhagen's concept of "eliminationist anti-Semitism," for instance, which Goldhagen defines *against* Christian anti-Semitism.

For Maccoby, it all comes back to the Gospels, to the emotional power of the blood curse. "The Gospels really worked up this picture of the Jews as murderous deicides."

In fact, I came to think that in Maccoby's insistent emphasis on the emotional power of the blood curse and the blood rhetoric of the Gospels, he was doing something very powerful and emotional. He was reversing the poles of the notorious blood libel, so long and so murderously leveled at Jews, to say: *We* are not guilty of the bloodthirsty ritual murder of Christian children we've been accused of. But you Christians *are* guilty of, accomplices to, paved the way for, the ritual murder of the Jews. Our blood is on your hands.

In his book on the Judas question, *The Sacred Executioner: Human Sacrifice and the Legacy of Guilt*, Maccoby offered an anthropological analysis of the way the Crucifixion is transformed into the ritual murder of the Jews. "Jews are killed because of Christian guilt," he wrote. "Guilt for their [the Christians'] need for a human sacrifice to make their salvation possible" (the sacrifice of Jesus to atone for their sins).

"The fact that the powers of evil [the Jews] bring about the [necessary, redemptive] death of the sacrifice doesn't excuse [the Jews] in any way," he told me. "They're still hated. In fact, the more you hate them, the more you are saved yourself, because you therefore can wash your hands like Pilate and *you're* no longer implicated in the death [of Jesus], which was done for your sake [for your sins]. You benefit by the death of Jesus because you're saved, but you have no part in the death. Guilt for it is displaced to the Jews who can then be killed with impunity."

Jews are, in Maccoby's interpretation, dragged into the Gospel story to perform a function (killing the necessary sacrifice) and then are themselves slaughtered to absolve the guilt of those who really benefited from the killing of Christ, the Christians. The blood is really on Christian hands, Maccoby believes—they're the ones guilty of the ritual murder.

Frankly, I'm not sure Maccoby's psychoanthropological analysis is necessary or adds anything to his Judas-based case against Christianity. But he's attached to it, as he's attached to that case. Maccoby isn't unaware of how transgressive, indeed offensive, this analysis will sound to devout Christians. He's thought about the consequences of what comes close to indicting Christianity for Hitler's murder of the Jews, but he believes it has to be said, Christians have to be confronted with what he sees as the hatred at the heart of the Gospels. He also knows that his insistence on this is disturbing, even offensive, to many Jews.

He talks about a 1989 clash at a symposium at New York's City University Graduate Center with the American Jewish ecumenicist Rabbi Marc Tannenbaum. "He was very much against my whole line of approach. He was involved in Jewish-Christian relations in a very big way. And he was involved particularly with talks with the pope to try to get the Vatican to recognize Israel. And he felt that this line that I was adopting was counterproductive. But I reject that line of thought," he continued. "It's what I call pusillanimous. Here we [Jews] are, for the first time for many centuries, we're *able* to speak out. Before we *couldn't* speak out because we're going to get killed if we speak out. Now supposedly we *mustn't* speak out because it's bad taste to speak out. One way or another, there's some gag on us. I said if we don't speak out now, when *are* we going to speak out? We can't speak out in time of persecution because we'll be persecuted. But in times when we're not being persecuted, we mustn't speak out because that would show lack of gratitude to people for not persecuting us? So when do we speak out? Never?"

"On the other hand," I suggest, "your view *is* fairly bleak in the sense that it doesn't hold out *any* ecumenical hope of some reconciliation between Jews and Christianity, because you're saying at the very heart of Christianity is the sanctioned hatred and murder of Jews."

"Well, as I always say to people who say 'You're calling for the end of Christianity in the sense that it depends on the ritual murder of Jews,' I say, '*No*, I don't think so, I'm supporting a certain *strand* in Christianity against official Christianity. I'm saying that throughout the centuries there have been Christians who have actually protested against Christianity. People like Pelagius who protested against Augustine. People who believed in the humanity of Jesus, not in the divinity of Jesus. Who didn't want to think of the death of Jesus as being a sacrifice, a theological sacrifice, but simply the martyrdom of a great man in the cause of freedom. He was fighting against Rome, not against the Jews. People who think of Jesus as a model teacher. And Jesus would be in the same position then, in Christianity, that Moses is in Judaism, as Mohammed is in Islam, a human teacher. There's nothing antireligious in this."

"It's not a position, then, that Christianity, if it were self-aware, has to abolish itself? It's more that there is a kind of Christianity that does not have implicit in it hatred of the Jews?"

"Right. In other words, that instead of concentrating on Jesus' death they would concentrate on Jesus' life."

It is, however, a Christianity that would be recognized as such by only a small percentage of those calling themselves Christians, mainly Unitarians and the like.

In response, Maccoby points out that there are some post-Holocaust Christian theologians such as Rosemary Ruether who tend to agree with him—who feel so troubled by the implication of Christian anti-Semitism in paving the way for the Holocaust that they have begun to call for mainstream Christianity to reevaluate or revise its core beliefs to exorcise anti-Jewish animus.

I wondered if he was also referring to the strand of post-Holocaust German Christian theologians who have attempted to incorporate the Holocaust into the Gospel story of the Crucifixion by positing that the Jews of Europe were in some way *on* the cross, that *they* were the victims of the Crucifixion, the true body of Christ in some mystical, atemporal way.

He rejects it as pernicious. "I object very strongly to that kind of Christianization of the Holocaust by which the Jews become a kind of Christ figure suffering for the Christians' sins." He sees a tricky theological rationalization going on here which still reifies or recuperates the notion of a sacrificial crucifixion by a sacred executioner—here Hitler assumes the role of Jewish crucifier, driving the nails into the body of the Jewish people. It ends up, in effect, renewing the crucifixion story with fresh blood, so to speak, and "blaming the Jews in a more sophisticated way," Maccoby says.

Blaming the Jews in a more sophisticated way: This is exactly what Maccoby believes George Steiner is doing. Of all the attacks on Steiner following the publication of his Hitler novel, Maccoby's (which appeared in *Encounter*) was the most thoroughgoing, cut closest to the bone, and was the one Steiner's allies have gone to the greatest lengths to refute. In part, because Maccoby knows Steiner's work all too well; knew the sources of Hitler's speech in Steiner's earlier work; could cite the way Hitler in Steiner's novel "becomes a full blown Steinerian . . . expressing views taken word for word from Steiner's other writings." Maccoby's verdict is also the most severe, going so far as to characterize Steiner's novel as a "misleading piece of anti-Jewish propaganda of a regrettably contemporary kind which may prove of aid and comfort to anti-Semites for years to come." He accuses Steiner of not merely giving Hitler as a person "a cosmic dignity" but serving to "dignify Hitler by elevating him into a metaphysical principle."

Part of Maccoby's animus seems to stem from the fact he is reacting not only to the publication of the novel but to the 1981 stage production of the novel at London's Mermaid Theatre, the production staged by Christopher Hampton, the one with a Hitler who "scared the hell" out of Steiner himself.

But Maccoby's attack was on more than the speech of Steiner's Hitler character, it was on Steiner's whole oeuvre, on *Steiner*'s character, for what he called a "colossal miscalculation" produced by intellectual "vanity."

I wondered, after an attack like that, if the two had ever met and confronted each other.

"Well, I do come across him sometimes," he said. "I don't see a *lot* of George Steiner, but I do from time to time. We don't really see eye to eye very much," he says with seeming mildness before taking a rather sly swipe at him: "I've never come to criticize him in the way *some* people have and call him a charlatan and so on. I admire some of his work. But I do think when he gets into Jewish topics, he falls into a trap."

Falls into several traps, according to Maccoby. But before moving on to them, let us take note of the acidulous "*I've* never . . . call[ed] him a charlatan" remark, which has the effect of propagating the idea that the charlatan notion is widespread while distancing himself from such an uncharitable view in the guise of generosity toward his foe. Although I suspect it's a view Maccoby really *does* share.

The primal "trap" Steiner falls into, both personally and in his Hitler novel, Maccoby tells me, involves not so much his image of Hitler but his image of Jews. "He falls into a trap, which is to think of the archetype of the Jew being the Wandering Jew."

And, in fact, just a few days before, Steiner *had* spoken to me in a very heartfelt way of his identification with the Wandering Jew, with Jews who wandered, outcasts and dissidents such as Freud and Leon Trotsky—Trotsky in particular, the inventor of a system, cast out by the monster state he helped create (another kind of Frankenstein story), forced to become the haunted, controversial provocateur in exile.

But there is a profound problem, Maccoby believes, in Steiner's—in any Jew's—identification with the Wandering Jew. "The Wandering Jew is not a Jewish image but a *Christian* image." He's referring to the origin of the Wandering Jew legend in Christian apocrypha as the story of an encounter between Jesus and a Jew on the streets of first-century Jerusalem. Jesus, dragging his cross, bleeding from his crown of thorns, about to be crucified, asks the Jew for something for his thirst. The Jew rejects him and as a punishment is condemned to wander the world, forever after an outcast, condemned to a living eternity of remorse. Later, in legends and novels, the Wandering Jew becomes a more ambiguous, even heroic figure. But at its core it is, Maccoby insists, "A *Christian* image of an ideal kind of Jew"—a Jew who acknowledges his guilt over rejecting Christ and implicitly acknowledges the justness of the persecutions inflicted on him by Christians.

"It's saying that Christians would like Jews to accept the role of the people who brought about the death of Jesus," the role of murderer in effect. "And to do so in a spirit of repentance," acceptance even, of the punishments inflicted upon them. Up to and including the Final Solution?

Maccoby didn't go on to make the connection between the Wandering Jew's acceptance of his implication in his fate and Steiner's apparent argument for the Jews' implication in their genocide in his Hitler novel.

I'd argue that Steiner's image of the Wandering Jew owed much more to the modern intellectual's preference to be seen as the alienated outsider and to existentialist philosophy's elevation of guilt into something not to be ashamed of but rather something to aspire to—as a higher, more acute and authentic form of consciousness in a fallen world. But Maccoby might be onto something in the sense that Steiner may have fewer qualms about imputing guilt to the Jews for the Holocaust because this guilt gives the Jews a tragic ironic chosenness Steiner seems to relish as much as he rejects the conventional, triumphalist concept of the Chosen People.

Steiner's ideas about the triumphalist character of the Chosen People concept constitute another trap Maccoby believes Steiner's fallen into. I told Maccoby about my conversation with Steiner in which Steiner had steadfastly, repeatedly insisted that the questions he raised in his fictive Hitler's speech are questions *he* thought were valid, questions *he* wanted answers to. The question, for instance, about whether Hitler's racist doctrines were "a hungry imitation" of the alleged racism of the Chosen People idea in Judaism.

"Actually, the doctrine of the chosen race is fundamentally different from a racialist doctrine," Maccoby says. "The Jews don't say we are the chosen race because we are inherently *better* than other people, because of some racist characteristics. On the contrary, what is said is that the Jewish people were chosen not for any qualities that they had but because of the mission: that it was given that the Jews actually come up *short* all the time. The whole story is about the *defects* of this people. The whole story is about the backslidings, and it's not a glorification of the Jews at all. It's a history of how they failed on the whole to live up to the mission entrusted to them. It was the story of a failure. And you can't imagine Hitler talking about the failings of the Nordic race; on the contrary, the only failures are not their fault but the fault of traitors who are plotting against them. Whereas Jews came to be evil in the sight of the Lord: Most people turned away from God and had to be upbraided by the prophets. So it's entirely different from a racist concept. It's the story of a totally degraded people, a slave people who were chosen to develop a concept of freedom. The idea of election is at opposite poles from being a superior race."

Opposite poles from being a superior race, perhaps, but still chosen in the sense of "chosen to develop a concept of freedom." This might often have been a freedom to fail, a freedom to choose wrong, but a freedom, a power to choose that was especially important to God, even if as an object of his wrath. Maccoby might be strictly right in rejecting the notion that chosenness represents "superiority" in the sense of intellect, beauty, or nobility—the kinds of claims made for the Nordic race by Hitler—but it does reflect a perhaps even more special moral significance or responsibility.

There are two better arguments against Steiner's position than the one Maccoby advances. First, *all* religions have ways of conferring upon some of their initiates some sense of superiority over the rest of mankind: the Elect and saved in some versions of Christianity, the Enlightened of Buddhism, the Brahmans of Hinduism, the man who has made the pilgrimage to Mecca in Islam. To single out this aspect of Jewish belief as somehow implicating Jews in their own murder is uncalled for.

Another argument against Steiner (or Steiner's Hitler) is that there is little evidence that Hitler *did* adapt his doctrine of Aryan superiority from the Chosen People concept of the Jews. In fact, there's more evidence that he adapted it from an abundance of tracts and treatises available to him on the mystical superiority of the Aryan race, ones that ranged from the semipornographic *Ostara* magazine in Vienna to the multivolume "scholarly" works of Wagner's "scientific" race guru Houston Stewart Chamberlain.

Maccoby is more persuasive, I believe, in his attack on the assertion Steiner puts in the mouth of his Hitler that the source of the success of Hitler's anti-Jewish crusade was the threefold "blackmail of transcendence"—the invention of conscience by Moses, the impossible injunction to perfect love by Jesus, the impossible injunction to perfect justice by Marx.

"I disagree with this whole idea of his [Steiner's] that Judaism differs from other religions in that it sets a high moral standard which is so impossible that people have to resent it. This is a theory about anti-Semitism, that anti-Semitism consists of the resentment of Christians being forced to live up to the Judaic standard of morality. I don't think that's the case. I think, on the contrary, what is resented in Judaism is people saying morality is *possible*. That it's not all that hard, and, therefore, all the excuses people make for avoiding morality don't work. Because what the Bible says is it's not in the heavens, it's not beyond the seas, it is there before you. Morality is easy; the only thing that makes it difficult are all the excuses people make. One of those excuses is to say that morality is so difficult that the only virtue is total humility—that we cannot possibly be good people, so therefore we need a savior to come from heaven in order to suffer death on our behalf. So what's resented is not the difficulty of Jewish morality but more a notion that morality is a possibility."

It was strange, the week I spent going from Steiner to Maccoby: both brilliant, impassioned intellects; both utterly at odds; both playing with fire. While Maccoby clearly regards Steiner as having done something dangerous in giving birth to an intellectual rationale for Hitler that blames his victims, Maccoby might, in fact, be doing something equally dangerous: telling the overwhelmingly dominant Christian majority within which diaspora Jews live that its faith bears within it—inextricably entangled at its very heart—the murderous evil seeds of genocide. And that to truly exorcise the guilt of their faith, they must radically transform it or abandon it.

They're both playing with fire with their Hitler explanations, but they both also, in very different ways, could be seen as absolving Hitler of responsibility for the Holocaust. They're both shifting the focus from Hitler himself to abstract ideological and anthropological forces of which Hitler is at most a pawn, a boil, a mouthpiece. In Steiner's view, Hitler merely serves and exploits the widespread animus against Jews for the torments of conscience they invented. In Maccoby's view, it was not Hitler so much as Judas—not the real Judas but the hateful Christian representation of Judas as archetypal Jew—who is responsible for the slaughter of the Jewish people. The image of Judas made Hitler's crimes possible, fertilized the field of blood Hitler harvested. Hitler was merely the catalyst for the inevitable crystallization of Christian hatred.

And the other thing that Steiner and Maccoby might seem to do is to remove, if not completely exculpate, *Germany* from explaining Hitler. While Steiner mused about some potential for violence in the German *language*, he was emphatic about it being just "Germany's bad luck" that Hitler came along "with his peculiar genius," because, Steiner believed, France would have been more naturally receptive, more anti-Semitic at the core than Germany and the German culture of Goethe and Heidegger, which Steiner still cherishes, despite his distrust.

Maccoby's exemption of Germany or at least of German culture is even more heartfelt. At the close of our conversation, as Maccoby was gathering his papers to hurry off to a lecture he was to deliver, I raised a question I'd hesitated to ask because I sensed it might be troubling, if not offensive. A question about Leo Baeck, the tragic luminary of the German Jewish community, the Berlin rabbi Maccoby's institute is named after. It was a question raised by Richard Rubenstein, the American rabbi and one of the most outspokenly heretical of post-Holocaust Jewish theologians. Rubenstein had argued that Jews must hold God to account (if not to blame) for the Holocaust, that to worship him without questioning his silence and passivity in the face of the death camps is virtually an insult to the Jewish victims.

Rubenstein has also raised questions about the silence and passivity of some leaders of the German Jewish community in the thirties who, trusting in God, urged Jews to go about business as usual despite the fate being prepared for them. Rubenstein singled out Rabbi Leo Baeck, the revered leader of the sophisticated, cosmopolitan, assimilated Berlin Jewish community, for Baeck's final act before he was dragged off to Theresienstadt concentration camp in the final evacuation of German Jews in 1942.

What stunned Rubenstein was an apparently trivial gesture Baeck made in the moments before he went off with the SS: He paid his electric bill. Think about it, Rubenstein says: He's joining the rest of the Jews in death camps run by the Nazi regime, but he pays his electric bill to that regime before he leaves.

"For Rubenstein," I said to Maccoby, "this emblematizes Jewish passivity in the face of the Holocaust. What's your response to that?"

I was surprised at the eloquence—and the direction—of his reply.

"What he [Rubenstein] wants Baeck to do is to be a kind of token rebel against the whole system," Maccoby told me. "The point [of Baeck's act] is that Jews are *always* expecting decency from people around them. That's our trouble, really. This is really why so many Jews failed to leave Germany. They really couldn't believe that this Germany, which they loved, felt obligations toward—professionals, for instance, felt gratitude toward Germany [for giving them more opportunity for advancement and fulfillment than any other European country]. And they wanted nothing more than to express this gratitude by being good citizens."

At that point, an assistant came in and whispered something in Maccoby's ear, probably about his being late for his lecture.

"Yes, yes, we've just finished," he said. But he had something more he wanted to add, something about Baeck and his electric bill. "I'd say that Leo Baeck never lost that feeling of love for Germany, that sense of obligation toward Germany, as a place to which he had obligations. And he expressed that by acting as an obedient citizen as far as he possibly could, even at the time when Germany was taken over by someone who he felt to be against the whole spirit of Germany."

Was Hitler contrary to the spirit of Germany—if so, why did he strike such a receptive chord in Germans?—or was he an expression of that spirit? Maccoby's Leo Baeck Institute is devoted to the principle that there is a spirit of Germany Jews can still love. "Even today," he says, "you've got German refugees who have a whole German Jewish culture still going outside Germany. The *Leo Baeck Yearbook* [of scholarly articles on German Jewish culture] is an expression of the love of Jews for Germany. And that's a very real thing."

And then he returns to the culture he regards as far more responsible for the Holocaust than Germany. "Germany's one thing. The Christian side of Germany is another thing. I don't blame Germany for the Holocaust; I blame *Christendom* for the Holocaust." (Cynthia Ozick, an admirer of Maccoby's work, stressed to me her belief that Maccoby is not exculpating Germans—the German perpetrators—by blaming "Christendom" because the Holocaust was executed largely by German Christians.)

Still, it was interesting, two Jews, Steiner and Maccoby, going to great lengths to absolve Germany (if not Germans) from guilt. Two intellectuals who go to great lengths to shift responsibility from Hitler to Great Abstractions such as "the blackmail of transcendence" and "Christendom." Why are so many so reluctant to find the obvious suspects guilty or at least responsible? In fact, the argument over the centrality of Hitler's responsibility and over the proportion of that responsibility shared by the German people as a whole is one of the most contentious and unresolved disputes in the whole field of Hitler explanation. One that, not long after my encounters with Steiner and Maccoby, turned into a bitter and divisive battle of scholars over the work of Daniel Goldhagen.

CHAPTER 19

Daniel Goldhagen:
Blaming Germans

*In which we witness a scholarly wilding and
explore explanation as revenge*

By the time I had my first encounter with Daniel Jonah Goldhagen, the young scholar had already suffered much for his attempt to explain the Holocaust, and I did not wish to add to his distress. Although as it turned out, judging from the abrupt way in which Goldhagen broke off our conversation about Hitler, I must have.

Perhaps I shouldn't have been surprised at this development; I'd been witness to the first act of Goldhagen's ordeal about a month before we met: a wild and unruly symposium of scholars at the U.S. Holocaust Memorial Museum in Washington that turned into an impromptu tribunal—with Goldhagen on trial. It became an unrelenting assault on his thesis and even his character that was shocking to many who witnessed it, almost akin to a scholarly wilding.

The occasion was a four-hour-long panel discussion of Goldhagen's just-published book, *Hitler's Willing Executioners*, in early April 1996, an event that attracted a capacity crowd to the museum's Meyerhoff auditorium. More than capacity: There were long lines long before the doors opened and considerable anxious pushing and shoving to secure seats. While there were scholars and academics in the audience, most appeared to be the kind of devoted admirers among the book-buying public who had just propelled Goldhagen's book onto the national bestseller lists, a rarity for a scholarly work (the book was an expansion of Goldhagen's doctoral thesis at Harvard). Many of them had brought copies hoping to get them autographed, many crowded around him before and after the proceedings remarking on his youth (he looked younger than his thirty-five years), on his dark-haired good looks.

Few were prepared for what was to come, for the ferocity of the assault on Goldhagen by fellow scholars, a ferocity made all the more surprising and shocking by contrast with the almost unanimous acclaim by reviewers in the mainstream media who had hailed *Hitler's Willing Executioners* as an important new way of looking at the Holocaust. Yes, it was true there had been an uproar in the German press by some historians and intellectuals who accused Goldhagen of reinventing a demonic "German national character" to explain the Holocaust as an inevitable product of an intrinsically flawed Teutonic essence. But that night in the Holocaust Memorial auditorium, Goldhagen's scholarly accusers were mainly fellow Jews.

The first short, sharp, shocking hint at the tone of the proceedings that night came in the "strangling" reference. That the strangling allusion came from the evening's moderator, Lawrence Langer, made it all the more jolting. Langer is the author of a study of Holocaust literature and testimony I'd particularly admired because of its eloquently and scrupulously argued injunction against the consolation response: the tendency to take the horrifying raw material of Holocaust-survivor testimonies and attempt to find in them glib, consoling morals about the triumph of the human spirit over adversity—the kitsch sentimentality the moralizers use to console *themselves*—a betrayal, Langer argues, of the inconsolable horror of those who underwent the actual experiences.

Langer struck an ominous note in his opening remarks by calling upon the panelists to observe the "canons of civility" in their discussion, hinting there were those who thought the whole occasion ill-advised because passions ran too high and too deep to *hope* for civility. But it was Langer, too, who first signaled the tenor of the rhetorical violence to follow when—after Goldhagen had run a few minutes over his allotted time for an opening statement— Langer not only upbraided the young scholar for his time-limit transgression but indulged in a peculiar aside to the audience to the effect that, when students in his college courses transgressed in that fashion, he "often thought of strangling them."

The pointed strangling fantasy—pointed at Goldhagen—brought an audible intake of breath from the audience. It seemed rather disproportionate to the nature of the offense. But in fact, the image of strangling an impertinent, overzealous student might have inadvertently figured forth the true agenda of the evening: the attempt by some of his more senior colleagues to strangle Goldhagen's impertinent student's pretensions—if not the student himself—in the cradle.

There was more direct abuse to follow, and afterward I wondered why Goldhagen provoked such an intemperate and seemingly disproportionate response from his older colleagues. Henry Kissinger once remarked that the reason academic infighting is so bitter is that "the stakes are so small." But here I think it can fairly be said that—although professional jealousy over a younger scholar's sudden media stardom might have been a factor—the stakes in fact were not small; the stakes were very high. Goldhagen claimed to have explained the Holocaust, Hitler, the entire tragedy, in a way no one else had before, to have corrected errors, to have demolished myths unthinkingly accepted for generations.

Implicit in his claims was his belief that if he was right, then the best and brightest scholars and thinkers before him were wrong.

And what was it that made them wrong? What made Goldhagen's explanation so unique? At the heart of Goldhagen's argument is a single striking and strikingly graphic metaphor, in which can be found compressed the whole vision of his thesis: By the time Hitler came to power in 1933, he argues, the racial anti-Semitism *of* Germany was already "pregnant with murder."

It's a metaphor itself pregnant with implications: murder, the mass murder of the Jews, had been gestating within Germany (meaning within the German people and their culture) long before Hitler emerged or the Nazi Party came to power. The conception of mass murder, the seeds of genocide had been sown in the German psyche by centuries of hate literature of a peculiarly German variety, Goldhagen argues. He gives that strain of literature a name, "eliminationist anti-Semitism." He defines it as a variety of Jew-hating that goes beyond the traditional Christian antagonism toward the people who were said to have rejected or killed Jesus, beyond the hatred Hyam Maccoby sees gestating for eighteen centuries before bringing forth its murderous issue.

No, Goldhagen says, a different kind of hatred superseded Christian anti-Semitism in Germany, one whose character crystallized in the nineteenth century, one characterized first by a focus on Jews as a racial and biological evil and second by an insistence that no internal restrictions but only total elimination, either expulsion or murder, could solve or cure the Jewish problem in Germany.

It is this hatred that impregnated Germany, to use Goldhagen's metaphor, with murder, long before Hitler, that made Germans "willing executioners" of the Final Solution when they were given a chance by Hitler. Germans were thus not merely followers of orders, not colorless paper shufflers exhibiting Hannah Arendt's famous "banality of evil," but rather viciously, joyously, cruelly, zealously *willing* torturers and murderers who did not need to be whipped into a frenzy by Hitler or Nazi propaganda. It wasn't *Hitler's* willingness to murder the Jews that was crucial, Goldhagen implies, it was *Germany's*—Germans'—willingness.

If eliminationist anti-Semitism made Germany pregnant with murder long before Hitler stepped onto the public stage, pregnant at least since the nineteenth century, then Hitler is relegated to little more than a midwife role, there to assist the delivery, perhaps (to stretch the metaphor) to induce labor. But he's a facilitator of an irresistible force rather than a charismatic instigator and father of the murder being brought to birth. Germans did not need Hitler to prompt them to kill Jews. As one critic has characterized Goldhagen's thesis, Germans were already "little Hitlers." As another, Columbia's Fritz Stern (who attacked *Hitler's Willing Executioners* as "pretentious . . . shrill and simplistic"), put it, "For Goldhagen, as for the National Socialists, Hitler *was* Germany."

The "pregnant with murder" metaphor challenges a number of influential Hitler and Holocaust explanations. It challenges Hyam Maccoby's view that eighteen centuries of Christian anti-Semitism were more crucial than nineteenth-century German anti-Semitism. It challenges the view of Hannah Arendt and her epigones that Germans were for the most part indifferent bureaucratic accomplices to a Hitler/Nazi Party project. It challenges the fashionable contemporary academic attempt to look for the origin of the Holocaust in a deep-rooted Western racism of which German, Nazi anti-Semitism was merely a particularly virulent variety.

More significant, Goldhagen's pregnant-with-murder metaphor implicitly challenges Milton Himmelfarb's influential "No Hitler, No Holocaust" formulation—an argument that the Holocaust didn't *have* to happen because of abstract historical forces, Christian anti-Semitism, racial anti-Semitism, German character, and the like. It would not have happened, it wasn't inevitable, Himmelfarb insists, had not one man—Hitler—*wanted* it to happen.

The fact that Hitler wanted it is less important to Goldhagen than another causal element: ordinary Germans wanted it. Hitler didn't have to talk them into killing Jews, he gave them the license they were longing for. The best, most original sections of Goldhagen's book are those devoted to a painstaking and painful to read account of the lesser-known modes of murder in the concentration-camp universe—the obscenely euphemistic "work battalions"—instruments of murder whose operation displayed the joy the killers took in turning the killing process into merciless slow torture. And the horrific death marches of late 1944 and '45, when some of the concentration-camp guards packed up and took flight (with their prisoners) from advancing Russian troops and—despite the fact that the war was lost—zealously turned the retreat into a moving column of mass murder. His research does much to demolish the glib resort to sophisticated-sounding clichés about the banality of evil. The German killers—whose number (the number actively engaged in the execution process) Goldhagen places at over half a million—were devoted and dedicated, far from the indifferent bureaucrats Arendt depicts.

And yet it might seem puzzling at first—it was to me—that a book that argues that Germans hated Jews, really, *really* hated them and wanted to kill them, should be controversial to scholars, particularly Jewish scholars.

In part, it was the packaging. A number of Goldhagen's attackers that evening referred to the book's boast to have solved a problem that had baffled previous scholars. In part, it was the book's implicit claim to have ended the debate over explanation. In fact, however, if the Holocaust can be traced to German "eliminationist antisemitic literature," to the nineteenth-century books and pamphlets that impregnated the nation with murder, then the process of explanation is not ended but begun: *Why* were German people, why was German culture, so receptive to the seeds of genocide?

In addition, like all explanations that narrow their focus too sharply to a single point, the eliminationist anti-Semitism hypothesis inadvertently but implicitly tends to exculpate those factors it eliminates from primacy: Christian anti-Semitism, European cultural hostility to the Jews, the Nazi Party (which becomes in this view less the evil inciter and instigator of German hatred than the obedient servant of the evil wishes of an evilly conditioned German people). Even Hitler is, to an extent, exculpated. If Germany was pregnant with murder, that pregnancy was not *his* monstrous conception; he just brought the hot towels and boiling water to assist in its delivery.

And yet, one was forced to wonder, when hearing the extreme—and at times extremely personal—attacks on Goldhagen that evening, whether it was not so much the Germanness of Goldhagen's theory but its *Goldhagenness* that caused the furor. Because a persistent subtext of the attacks on his thesis were jabs at his lack of deference paid or credit given to previous scholars, at his claim to have refuted decades of misconceptions, to have overturned received wisdom—at the packaging of unremarkable ideas into mainstream marketability as some dazzling, breakthrough reconception of the past. There were expressions of resentment at his book's instant bestsellerdom and the mainstream-media coverage. There was resentment at a mere postdoctoral scholar suddenly thrusting himself into the center of a difficult conversation they'd been engaged in for decades. As if the youngest child at the Passover ceremony had decided not just to ask the traditional Four Questions (such as, Why is this night different from all other nights?) but to deliver the answers as if they'd never been answered correctly before.

And so the strangling remark, while shocking when first uttered, was just a pale portent of what was to come. A slap compared to the thunderbolt hurled at Goldhagen from on high by the next speaker. The way the symposium was structured, Goldhagen spoke first, following which he returned to his seat and attempted to maintain his composure (with relative success) as the blows began to fall from other panelists. Beginning with the charge of "worthless-ness," an epithet all the more shocking to the packed auditorium because of its source: one of the demigods in the pantheon of Holocaust scholarship, Raul Hilberg. One who did not appear in person to pronounce Goldhagen's book worthless but who relayed his angry condemnation through a panelist who proclaimed it by waving aloft a letter from Hilberg, brandishing the interdic-tion in "I have a list" fashion.

The flamboyant, red-faced, angry bearer of the bad tidings for Goldhagen was an Australian Holocaust scholar, resident fellow at the Holocaust Memo-rial Museum, Konrad Kweit. Kweit, of course, did not neglect to make his own heated attack on Goldhagen. An attack that could be summed up by the well-known barb: "What's true isn't new, and what's new isn't true."

First of all, Kweit argued, the effort to find the deep root, the ur-explanation of Hitler and the Holocaust in some intrinsic pathology of German culture was something German intellectuals themselves had been seeking for decades since the war. One version of what might be called "German exceptionalism" was the notion of the "*sonderweg*"—the special path German history and culture had taken in the centuries since the Reformation. In its more pointed, more self-lacerating form, this became the postwar "*Schuldfrage*" controversy—the blame question, in which some German thinkers contended there was some-thing not merely exceptional but deeply darkly *wrong* in German culture. That the violent extremism of thought to be found in Nietzsche and Wagner made Hitler possible if not inevitable.

Goldhagen seems to go further, as if to say that Hitler was virtually *irrel-evant* to a Germany pregnant with murder. Any midwife would do. But Kweit goes further, too, in accusing Goldhagen not merely of ignoring previous ex-plorations of the Germanness of the Nazi genocide but of resurrecting "naïve and discredited notions of German national character" and packaging it as a revolutionary new thesis. It was the packaging, Kweit declared, that was the most offensive aspect of the Goldhagen thesis: "Only those who offer extreme views can make a name for themselves," he said.

It was at this point Kweit pulled out the missive from Raul Hilberg and told the crowd, "I have a letter here" from the Vermont-dwelling sage, a letter in which "Hilberg says 'I take exception to Goldhagen's thesis, which is *worthless*, all the hype from [his publisher] Knopf notwithstanding.'"

"Worthless" is fairly strong, virtually a scholarly anathema. It's true that, in his book, Goldhagen did take more than "exception" to an essential com-ponent of Hilberg's lifework, his three-volume history of the Holocaust, *The Destruction of the European Jews*, virtually declaring *it* worthless, or at least founded on worthless misconceptions of the evidence. So it could be said that Hilberg's anathema was not without a personal agenda.

But the battle between them is a crucial one. The issue transcends the ad hominem element, and it's worth taking a look at the source of their division: the attempt to explain both the alacrity and efficiency with which the German perpetrators accomplished the task of mass murder.

It is similar to the question of excessive virulence that is at the heart of the explanatory perplexity over Hitler: Why was this anti-Semite different from all other anti-Semites? Goldhagen poses this question about the German perpetrators of the Holocaust, not the paper-shuffling middlemen but the actual executioners of the genocide: What made them not just cold-blooded killers but ones who reveled in cruelty, torture, and the degradation of their victims?

Goldhagen dismisses what he calls "the five conventional explanations" for this phenomenon: that they were coerced on pain of execution to participate; that they were blindly following orders because they were "unwavering servants of authority"; that peer pressure and conformity made them do it; that they were "like petty bureaucrats pursuing careerist self-interest"; and finally that they were not aware that their individual actions were part of a monstrous design for mass murder.

All these conventional explanations are wrong, Goldhagen says, because they assume that German citizens would otherwise be *opposed* to the mass killing of Jews, that they had to be numbed, coerced, or made unaware of the magnitude of the crimes they were participating in. No, he says, it's false to believe that Germans needed special inducements of institutionalized self-deception or peer pressure to join in the killing. As Milton Himmelfarb says of Hitler, Goldhagen says of ordinary Germans—*They wanted to.*

And then Goldhagen holds up Raul Hilberg as "an exemplar of this sort of [false conventional] thinking" because Hilberg asks: "Just how did the German bureaucracy overcome its moral scruples?"

[Hilberg] assumes that "the German bureaucracy" naturally had "moral scruples" regarding the treatment of Jews which with difficulty had to be surmounted. . . . Explanations proceeding in this manner [Goldhagen insists] cannot account for Germans taking initiative, doing more than they had to, or volunteering for killing duty when no such volunteering was necessary. . . . Such explanations cannot account for the instances in which Germans killed Jews in violation of orders not to do so. . . . [They] cannot account for the overall, indeed incredible, smoothness that characterized the execution of this far-flung program which was dependent upon so many people, people who, either through sabotage or foot-dragging, could have produced innumerable mishaps and poorly executed tasks.

In other words, Goldhagen was saying that Hilberg's explanatory work of a lifetime was not merely worthless, it was trying to answer *the wrong question entirely*, trying to find reasons why Germans were transformed into killers by Hitler and his party when, Goldhagen believed, they needed little transformation at all.

But I think something more was going on beneath the surface charges of worthlessness traded by Goldhagen and Hilberg. I think the submerged issue can be found in the word "smoothness"—the "incredible smoothness" of the execution process and how to account for it. Hilberg's massive account of the vast, continentwide, German-organized mobilization of troops, trains, guards, and resources that went into engineering the Holocaust has been criticized because Hilberg described a *Jewish* contribution to this smoothness. He argued that the cooperation, even complicity, of the *Judenräte*—the so-called Jewish councils in the ghettos—in rounding up and making available Jews for transshipment to death camps made the work of the German killers easier. Hilberg's argument on that point could be a bit unfairly caricatured by saying he saw reluctant executioners and willing victims. As the son of a Holocaust survivor, Goldhagen's animus against Hilberg might be attributed to a desire to restore the onus for the "smoothness" of the mass murder to the eager alacrity of the perpetrators—to blame the smoothness on Germans rather than Jews.

But if this submerged battle was the hidden agenda beneath Hilberg's "worthless" charge, it didn't diminish the impact of the critic's accusation, particularly on an audience most of whom had come to salute Goldhagen, seek his autograph. There were stirrings of indignation and unease. And then things got worse. The following speaker—an even more lofty member of the Holocaust-scholar pantheon than Hilberg—launched an attack that was even more harsh and sweeping.

The following speaker was none other than Yehuda Bauer, widely regarded as perhaps the most scrupulous and clear-sighted historian of the Holocaust in the world. He'd been spending the year as a fellow of the U.S. Holocaust Memorial Museum. Still wiry, vigorous, and energetic at seventy, Bauer leaped up and seized the microphone, radiating intensity and passion as he paced the stage. It came as a surprise to me since the Bauer I'd seen in Jerusalem had been so deliberate and reserved, but tonight he was like a man possessed, a man with a mission.

After offering some dutiful praise for the less controversial aspects of Goldhagen's work—the chapters on the work battalions and the death marches—Bauer moved swiftly to the attack, beginning with the packaging of Goldhagen's thesis, particularly in its claim to newness, the notion that no one had previously dared point the finger at the true source of genocide, which he, Goldhagen alone, was bold enough to name: nineteenth-century German eliminationist anti-Semitism.

Bauer expressed astonishment that Goldhagen had made his assertions about the special genocidal virulence of German anti-Semitism without placing it in the context of other national versions of anti-Semitism in Europe at that time: What about Russia, Romania, Poland? he asked. "What about France?" and he went on to substantiate George Steiner's contention to me that *French* anti-Semitism was far worse, far more virulent, deep-rooted, and bitter than Germany's in the pre–World War I period. Bauer cited the highly regarded historian George Mosse, who had done comparative studies and had said that "if someone had come to me in 1914 and told me that one country in Europe would attempt to exterminate the Jews, I would have said then, 'No one can be surprised at the depths to which the French could sink.'"

Bauer's point was that if there was something intrinsically German about the Holocaust, it is inherent not in the rhetoric or ideology of nineteenth-century German *writing*, which could be matched in violence and virulence by the products of other European nations. But rather, Bauer suggested, if there's an intrinsic Germanness to the killing, it might better be sought for in the susceptibility of Germans to the extreme authoritarian character of the Nazi Party, of the Hitler state.

But Bauer didn't stop there. Pacing the stage of the Meyerhoff auditorium (with Goldhagen sitting at a table behind him), Bauer went beyond denouncing the thesis to denouncing the person behind it. Not Goldhagen; he didn't even accord Goldhagen adult responsibility for it.

"It's not Goldhagen's fault," he told the audience. "It's his Harvard *tutor*'s fault." It was the Harvard tutorial system that failed Goldhagen, he said, since his book grew out of a Harvard Ph.D. thesis.

"It's the tutor's fault! You don't permit a study like this without comparatives, with a complete disregard for German history, which ignores the opposition—no Social Democrats, no communists. You can read Goldhagen and it seems like Hitler gained power by vote! In the last free election the Nazis had thirty-three percent of the vote! Sixty-seven percent did not vote Nazi. They came to power *because* they lost votes in that last election, because they no longer seemed dangerous to the conservative camarilla around the senile president Hindenburg."

Having reduced Goldhagen to a wayward student failed by his tutors, Bauer returned to the attack, this time chastising Goldhagen personally, without the pretense of blaming it on his tutor. Bauer spoke of the need for humility in the face of the Holocaust and added, "When you open your book by saying 'I am the first, I am the only, all others are wrong' . . . when you start off with media hype, you run the risk of ending up like Arno Mayer" (the Princeton professor whose book argued that the Holocaust was less about hatred of Jews than of Bolsheviks). "It's gone," Bauer said of Mayer's book, after its initial media hype, "and rightly so. It was the wrong way to start. You have to have humility, you don't start with p.r."

After this intellectual equivalent of a horsewhipping, Professor Langer returned to the microphone to offer Goldhagen the cold comfort that what he'd received from Yehuda Bauer was not a "death sentence" but a "life sentence" for which he should presumably feel grateful and relieved. Again, the imagery of violence and retribution (an execution!) mercifully suspended; Goldhagen was given the grim scholarly equivalent of life imprisonment.

The worst was over; yes, there were further attacks on Goldhagen's thesis: Christopher Browning, Goldhagen's archrival and frequent target, had a chance to confront him face-to-face. But Browning's remarks focused on the issue between them, not on Goldhagen's motives, the packaging of his book, or the hype surrounding it. It was almost as if the succeeding speakers had been shaken by the thunderbolt from Hilberg, the lightning strike from Bauer.

By the time of my meeting with Goldhagen several weeks later, what had begun as, if not a tempest in a teapot, then an academic furor had escalated even further, had begun to take on the dimensions of a transnational firestorm.

The book had provoked headlines in Germany as newspapers and magazines seized on Goldhagen's book as an assault on the German national character. "EIN VOLK VON DÄMONEN?" (A people of the Devil?) asked the lurid headline of the cover story in *Der Spiegel*—it was the exact same epithet Hitler used to characterize the Jews—implying that Goldhagen was using the same rhetoric of collective intrinsic evil.

Meanwhile, *Die Zeit*, a leading German weekly, was serializing the critical attacks on Goldhagen made by Jewish scholars at the Holocaust Memorial Museum and calling the controversy another *Historikerstreit*, another battle over the German past, the German identity, the German "special path" as momentous as the one that convulsed German intellectuals in the eighties. But this was deeper and more divisive. It wasn't German versus German, it was American versus German, Jew versus German (although at the Holocaust Memorial Museum it had been mostly Jew versus Jew). The American-German aspect of it (the German press implied) could result in a freeze, if not a breach, in relations between the two countries; Goldhagen's book thus becoming more than a thesis about history but a fact of it.

In fact, American reverberations from the controversy in Germany disrupted my first scheduled meeting with Goldhagen. I had arranged with his publicist at Knopf to coordinate an interview session with his visit to New York to address German scholars and writers at New York University's Goethe House about a month after the Holocaust Memorial Museum brawl. But at the last minute, Goldhagen abruptly canceled the NYU meeting and his New York trip; he'd learned that a substantial number of representatives of the German media would be present at Goethe House and he issued a statement saying he didn't want to engage in further running discourse with the German press until his book was available in German translation for the German people to read and judge for themselves. The position had its merits, but tactically it might have given some the impression that he was avoiding critical scrutiny.

By the time Goldhagen did appear in New York, the following week, he looked somewhat shaken by the sudden international dimension of the controversy, although I didn't realize *how* shaken until about a half hour into our talk, which took place in the cavernous main lounge of the Yale Club.

I also wasn't aware at first of the source of his distress. It had seemed to me that the hostile German response should have been more predictable and less disturbing to him than the attack by Jewish scholars. But, as it turned out, it was not so much the general German uproar that was upsetting to him that day as one specific manifestation of it: one German writer's intrusive psychological explanation of his thesis, an attempt to explain his explanation—to explain *him*—that had unsettled him. But I didn't become aware of all that until he broke off the interview.

Our conversation began productively enough. I was curious to hear more from Goldhagen about a figure almost absent from his book: Adolf Hitler. In Goldhagen's focus on Germans and Germanism, Hitler seemed to vanish from view. I wondered whether Hitler's Austrian origin had something to do with it, whether it posed a problem to Goldhagen's ascription of the genocidal impulse to a specifically German source.

Many scholars have argued that, in fact, Austrian anti-Semitism was something different from the German variety, that it was in many ways even more virulent. One estimate has it that Austrians made up a full 40 percent of SS officers assigned to death-camp command duty, and eight out of twelve concentration camps were headed by Austrians. And, of course, the man in charge of administering the entire extermination process was the other Austrian Adolf, Eichmann.

Sir Isaiah Berlin has written about the borderland effect in which those on the periphery of empires (as the Austrian Germans were on the periphery of the German Reich) often manifested more feverishly radical xenophobic hatreds than those securely within its borders. And Norman Cohn, the director of the International Research Project on Genocide at the University of Sussex and author of a study of *The Protocols of the Elders of Zion*, has written of the way "the völkisch-racist outlook was perhaps even stronger" in Austria, "on the periphery of the German-speaking world where, ever since the war of 1866, the German-speaking element had felt isolated and threatened by the preponderant Slav element" of the Hapsburg kingdom.

Indeed, Cohn defines Hitler's Austrianness *against* his Germanness: "He embodied a whole century of [Austrian] frustration, disappointment and insecurity, and the boundless lust for revenge which possessed him was a magnified version of something which possessed a whole stratum of Austrian society."

I asked Goldhagen if he regarded Hitler's Austrianness as something that distinguished him from the mentality of "ordinary Germans" or if he saw it as all of a piece.

"There were regional variations in anti-Semitism even within Germany," he said. "But Hitler's exemplified and brought to an apotheosis the particular form of eliminationist anti-Semitism that came to the fore in the latter part of the nineteenth century. Whatever the variations, I think Austrian and German anti-Semitism can be seen of a piece, where there was a central model of Jews and a view that they needed to be eliminated."

When he speaks of Hitler, it's this "central model" Goldhagen returns to again and again, a model that, he believes, saturates German culture and Austrian culture, a model that explains Hitler more than any personal trauma or deformation of his personality. The central model takes on the aspect of a malign, personal, prompting evil, an irresistible compulsion, whose irresistibility in a way exempts the will it usurps, in effect exculpating the individual it acts upon, making an analysis of individual psyches of Germans, of Hitler himself irrelevant.

"I'm not persuaded by the arguments of the psychohistorians," Goldhagen told me. "You understand Hitler better by seeing him as bred in a particular culture where these kinds of notions about Jews were quite common. That tells us why he became an anti-Semite better than looking at aspects of his personal biography. Now if you want to understand how he became *as* murderous as he did and why he took these ideas to their—in some sense—logical and most fatal conclusions, then of course we need to plumb the depths of psychology, and that is not my forte."

I thought there were two important—and possibly contradictory—points in Goldhagen's last remark.

"What you're saying, then, is that psychohistorians are forever searching for some disorder, some trauma or abnormality as the source of Hitler's anti-Semitism, when in fact to be an anti-Semite didn't require a departure from the norm, it *was* the norm."

"And to be willing to persecute Jews and to kill them systematically [was the norm], I think that Hitler's decision to kill the Jews is derived *logically* from his belief structure," he said. But he also seems to be saying that there *was* something about Hitler that exceeded the norm, that exceeds logic, that exceeds Goldhagen's own capacity to "plumb the depths of psychology" for an explanation of that excess.

"Clearly there was something more than that [the logic of his ideology] driving Hitler on," Goldhagen added, "because it was not just the Jews. There were many other people he killed. He was a man who leaped to murder to solve social problems biologically, by extirpating them. Of course, this is in accord

with his view of the world, his racism, his social Darwinism, the general biolo-
gism with which he viewed the world. And so I agree with your point that it
doesn't require a psychological malformation. But this doesn't of course rule
out the possibility that in Hitler's case there *was* something else driving him."

Something more, something else: He does seem to be conceding here that
something more than the "ordinary German character," something more
than the "central model" is required to explain Hitler, to explain why Hitler
went beyond the relatively passive midwife role. Something to explain what
made Hitler (to adapt a Shakespearean birth metaphor) rip murder untimely
from the womb.

I asked Goldhagen about his pregnant-with-murder metaphor in relation
to Hitler. "It invites a characterization of Hitler as mere midwife, doesn't it?"

"The analogy's imperfect," he concedes. "It implies the baby comes without the need for the midwife. But 'No Hitler, No Holocaust!'" he says, repeating
Milton Himmelfarb's phrase, the rhetorical gauntlet Himmelfarb threw down
before those who'd see the Holocaust as the inevitable product of abstract historical forces and ideologies rather than of Hitler's individual will.

Goldhagen has an uneasy relationship to Himmelfarb's formula. He
wants to embrace it, but even as he expressed agreement, he seems inexorably
to undermine it.

"So you would agree with Himmelfarb's argument?" I asked him. "No
Hitler—"

"Or if not Hitler, someone *like* Hitler," he said. "If the Nazis had never
taken power, there would not have been a Hitler. Had there not been a depression in Germany, then in all likelihood the Nazis wouldn't have come to power.
The anti-Semitism would have remained a potential, in the sense of its killing
form. It required a state. Hatreds do not issue in systematic violence unless
they're organized by governments. At most, they will produce ethnic violence,
pogroms. Hitler was a very powerful leader, and he certainly deepened and
widened the existing current of anti-Semitism in Germany, further legitimizing that, and brought people with him."

In other words, it *was* Hitler, but then again it *could* have been someone
else, someone *like* Hitler. It was not Hitler so much as the party, not the party
so much as the state; and the party took over the state because of the economy.
It's a revision of "No Hitler, No Holocaust" that is more like "No Hitler, maybe
someone else."

Goldhagen confirmed my feeling when he proceeded to attempt to recast
Max Weber's famous concept of "charismatic leadership"—the relationship
between great men and those who follow them—in this light. "Charisma, as
we know," Goldhagen began, "although it's not often treated this way, but as
Max Weber first expressed it, it is not a property of leaders, it's a property of the

people really. The extent to which the leader is charismatic as Weber discussed it depends on the belief of the *people* in his infallibility and the prophetlike nature of the leader. *They* grant him his charismatic quality."

Shortly after my talk with Goldhagen, I reread Weber's famous essay, "The Nature of Charismatic Domination," and saw the extent to which Goldhagen had recast Weber to shift the burden of responsibility for the phenomenon of mass hysteria from leaders to followers—that is, from Hitler to "ordinary Germans." Yes, the belief, the credulity of his followers is necessary to certify, to recognize the special chosenness of a charismatic leader, Weber says. But "his right to rule," Weber states explicitly, "is *not* dependent on their will, as is that of an elected leader; on the contrary, it is the duty of those to whom he is sent to recognize his charismatic qualification" (emphasis added).

There is an ambiguity or, more precisely, a dynamic in Weber's account of charisma. The best analogy is the relationship between hypnotist and subject: The subject's credulity, his willingness to submit to the mesmerist, is essential, but it is the subject who is being mesmerized and manipulated to the hypnotist's will, not the other way around. It is the hypnotist's commands that are obeyed, not the subject's. Goldhagen is here skewing what Weber said to make it better reflect his view that it was the will of the German people in thrall to the "central model" of eliminationist anti-Semitism, the will of all the "little Hitlers" who drove, who created the big Hitler to serve their genocidal appetite. They were the ventriloquists; he was their dummy. Of course, it is not an either/or matter, not either Hitler or the German people; it is a matter of where one places the emphasis in the relationship between the two.

Goldhagen pressed his point about ordinary Germans being in the driver's seat, rather than Hitler, when it came to choosing the targets of mass murder by citing the difference between the German people's reaction to the Nazi euthanasia campaign and to the extermination of the Jews.

"Hitler certainly was a charismatic figure in the sense that people had a great deal of faith and belief in his extraordinary qualities and were willing to follow him—but not on all matters." When the euthanasia program—the extermination of mental and physical defectives (regardless of religion), a program that may have resulted in one hundred thousand deaths in 1939 and 1940—became known to the German public, there were protests from churchmen, protests from ordinary Germans, and the program was halted. There were no such protests when news of the extermination of Jews began to spread. From this distinction, Goldhagen argues that it was the readiness, the willingness, the eagerness *of* the people to kill Jews that was at least, if not more, important than Hitler's desire to kill them.

On the other hand, without Hitler's summons, his bidding, *neither* program would necessarily have materialized. And, in fact, there is evidence of the difficulty some Nazi officials experienced in whipping up sufficient anti-Jewish hatred among the populace. It is rare to find any of the Nazi perpetrators complaining that the German people were pressing authorities to speed up the expulsion and extermination of the Jews because it was going too *slowly*. Rather, there are complaints that the populace is insufficiently motivated for total and final solutions. To cite one study on this point, not at random but close to home, Goldhagen's own father, Erich Goldhagen, a refugee from wartime Europe, a Harvard Holocaust scholar and lecturer, published a 1972 essay called "Pragmatism, Function and Belief in Nazi Anti-Semitism," which portrayed the demand for anti-Jewish action coming from the top down, from the Nazi Party to the German people, rather than from the bottom up.

Goldhagen *père* cites numerous instances of Goebbels and other propaganda officials of the Nazi Party feeling the need, in the midst of the war, to "increase and intensify the anti-Semitic 'enlightenment' of the populace." Noting that the Jewish question had been rather neglected in propaganda, one of Goebbels's ministry's inner circle warned that such neglect was "false and dangerous." Dangerous because there was a fear of a fatal slackening in the level of Jew-hatred, a level that needed constant bolstering.

Goldhagen's father makes the same distinction as the son between the German populace's reaction to the euthanasia program and to the genocide of the Jews. But the father describes the German people's reaction to the knowledge of genocide in far milder terms than his son: He characterizes it as "widespread indifference, approval or only mild disapproval." Even the strongest term there, approval, is reactive, a sharp contrast with the proactive alacrity of the "willing executioners" the son describes. In the father's vision, anti-Semitic ideology conditioned ordinary Germans to not *oppose* the programmatic killing of Jews—they were a people who, they thought, deserved to perish. But the impulse to commence extermination did not issue from a public demand by ordinary Germans; rather, it was accepted (indictment enough!) when imposed from above. The father is closer to "No Hitler, No Holocaust" than the son.

Who was the master, who the servant, who the mesmerist, who the subject? Goldhagen the elder seems to see the bloodthirsty Hitler Party flogging the masses along to hate the Jews more than they do; Goldhagen the younger seems to see the evil eliminationist ideology permeating the hearts and minds of the German people, compelling Hitler and the party to carry out *its* collective genocidal wishes and dreams.

Disentangling individual elements of what is a dynamic, a folie à deux between Hitler and the German people, is a tricky business, and it can be said that father and son are looking at two faces of a single process, a dynamic in which Hitler exacerbated the already implanted seeds of hatred, removed the restraints, while the responsive chord he struck in the German people liberated

Hitler from any need to restrain himself in turning a murderous fantasy into reality.

Similarly difficult to disentangle are the purely Christian and purely German strains of anti-Semitism. Hyam Maccoby wants to condemn the Christian and exempt the German (cultural) aspects of the genocide. Goldhagen seems to want to find something intrinsically German. (Saul Friedländer has recently proposed a persuasive synthesis of the Christian, racist, and Wagnerian elements in Hitler's ideology, one he calls "redemptive anti-Semitism.") When I mentioned that the critics accused him of resurrecting the concept of a demonic German national character, Goldhagen bridled.

"I do *not* believe in German national character," Goldhagen told me, quite emphatically. He was not an expositor, as some of his German opponents had implied, of an anti-Germanism to explain and replace anti-Semitism. Instead of German national character, he speaks of the character of German nationality, the precarious and insecure sense of national selfhood that Germany—a nation that did not come into existence in anything like its current form until after 1848—felt.

The newness, the precariousness, the easily threatened stability of German national identity, rather than its overweening strength, was what was crucial, Goldhagen argues. The precarious sense of self it afforded, the weakness of the new nation's internal bonds, fed an appetite for an ideology in which all Germans could define who they were by who they were *not*—an Other, an inflammatory foreign body within (the Jews), a reaction to whose foreignness defined the body surrounding it.

If Goldhagen doesn't believe in a German national character, he still seems to argue that there was a special German *receptiveness* to eliminationist anti-Semitism in the nineteenth century. If Germany was pregnant with murder by 1933, conception had taken place not when Hitler began speaking in Munich beer halls in the 1920s but when the poison was injected into German culture late in the previous century.

It is this aspect of his thesis that has come under the most persuasive attack. Yehuda Bauer had argued from firsthand acquaintance with the literature in several languages that Russian, French, Romanian, and Polish anti-Semitic literature was at *least* as virulent and violent as German. What's more, Russian, Polish, and Romanian anti-Semitic literature had little trouble in directly and repeatedly inciting actual outbreaks of murder by the populace: pogroms that killed tens of thousands of Jews in the period when Germans were reading and discussing anti-Semitic literature, at most legislating separationist measures. Perhaps the most cogent summation of the difficulties Holocaust scholars have with the Germanness of Goldhagen's thesis came from Professor Richard Breitman, Yehuda Bauer's successor as the editor of *Holocaust and Genocide Studies*, then chairman of the history department at

Washington's American University, and the author of a highly nuanced study of the Hitler/Himmler relationship, *The Architect of Genocide*, which focuses on the timing and motivation of the ultimate decision to execute the Final Solution.

I met with Breitman the day following the Holocaust Memorial Museum fracas over Goldhagen's thesis. Breitman suggested to me that what made German anti-Semitism turn to mass murder was not some special character it had in the nineteenth century but rather the special character of twentieth-century German history: the defeat in the First World War, the subsequent starvation, humiliation, and inflation, followed, after an all-too-brief interval, by a crushing depression. These national traumas that devastated the German populace banked a kind of desperation and rage that Hitler was able to channel against Jews once he gained control of the apparatus of state power. Breitman emphasizes the devastation in the twenties and the period of intense, murderous anti-Semitic propaganda Hitler saturated Germany with in the thirties as more decisive in moving the population from attitude to action than something peculiarly German about its nineteenth-century anti-Semitism.

Goldhagen does not neglect twentieth-century factors, but he's devoted enormous effort in his book to documenting the pervasiveness and unique virulence of nineteenth-century German anti-Semitism, of the pervasiveness of the eliminationist urge even among more liberal Germans who posed as friends of Jews (but who wanted them to assimilate themselves out of existence).

It was over his emphasis on nineteenth-century origins, I believe, that our conversation broke up (although other factors entered in). "Germany really *was* different from other countries, particularly in the latter part of the nineteenth century, the beginning of the twentieth," he told me, "when there was this vast outpouring of vituperative anti-Semitic literature and even the growth of avowedly anti-Semitic political parties."

There was something about that latter statement that I wanted to pursue: that remark about the "growth of avowedly anti-Semitic political parties," in the latter part of the nineteenth and beginning of the twentieth century.

I asked Goldhagen about Professor Richard S. Levy's study, *The Downfall of the Anti-Semitic Political Parties in Imperial Germany*, a book which painted a picture of both those parties and the anti-Semitic political agitators behind them suffering setbacks, failures, and virtually *disappearing* from German political life by 1912. Which would seem to argue against a prewar triumph of eliminationist anti-Semitism.

"You're familiar with the Levy thesis, I'm sure—" I began.

"Yes," he said quickly. "But, you see, there's a broader question there, which is, How do we read voting behavior?" He went into a long disquisition about voting behavior that attempted to demonstrate that the precipitous decline in voting for anti-Semitic political parties didn't necessarily mean a decline in anti-Semitic *feeling*. All of which might have been more convincing had he not just cited a *rise* in anti-Semitic political parties as a sure sign of a rise in such feeling. One can't have it both ways: If voting for anti-Semitic political parties means something, then a decline in voting means something, if not everything.

But at that point a deeper problem made itself manifest. Whether it was my somewhat pointed question about the Levy thesis (a thesis that Goldhagen had omitted mentioning in his book) or whether this relatively mild query was the straw that broke the camel's back after the onslaughts from both the German press and the Jewish Holocaust scholars, suddenly it seemed it was all too much for Goldhagen to take.

I had just asked him my next question: What were his views of the Bullock/Trevor-Roper dispute over Hitler's "sincerity"—Was Hitler a cynical manipulator of anti-Semitism or a possessed true believer?—when he suddenly interrupted his own answer in mid-sentence:

"I need to interject something here," he told me. "I didn't realize it, but I have a reservation about this [meaning about speaking to me]. Actually, I have a contractual obligation to Knopf not to produce anything that will compete in some sense with my book for them."

I assured him this book was a couple of years from appearing, much less competing.

"No, I know," he said. "But I'm very legalistic in these matters, and I would actually like to talk to Knopf before going further with this."

"You really think your contract prohibits you from talking to anyone writing a book?"

"No, I would just like to talk to my editor there, let her know what I'm doing."

"You know," I said, "I'm interviewing a lot of people who have written or are writing books. This has never—"

"I know, I go by the letter of the law."

"Have I said anything you objected to? Have my questions been belligerent?"

"No, not at all," he said. "I want to think through some of these issues. I . . . really would like to talk to her because it is actually part of the contract."

"It says you can't do an interview with someone who's writing a book?"

"It doesn't say that. It doesn't say that. It's just that Knopf has authorized this book and—"

"But I went through the Knopf publicity department to arrange—"

"I would like to talk to them about it."

The way we left things, Goldhagen was going to call me if there was some contractual problem in talking to me. He didn't call, but I felt reluctant to pursue him for further reflections and risk further upsetting someone whose impassioned scholarship I had much respect for—particularly after Goldhagen told me a little more about what he'd been through in the weeks since the Holocaust Memorial Museum attacks and the German uproar. It had taken a toll on him, he said, the attacks, the heat of the spotlight. He was experiencing stress symptoms such as short-term memory lapses. There was one thing in particular that was upsetting him that day, he said, one specific aspect of the German uproar over his book that had shaken him. Something in the *Der Spiegel* story he regarded as an intrusive attempt to explain his explanation, to explain *him* by dragging in his father.

I had come across the *Der Spiegel* cover story ("*Ein Volk von Dämonen?*") the night before I met with Goldhagen but had not had a chance to look at the sidebar interview with Erich Goldhagen, the one headlined "I'm Very Proud." It was a strange piece, one in which the author, Henryk Broder, seemed to be attempting to mask his hostility toward both Goldhagens in the guise of an elaborate, condescending psychological explanation of the son's thesis as a sublimated expression of the father's wishes and fantasies, the father's love/hate affair with German culture.

Broder (a German Jew) begins by placing the Goldhagen father/son relationship in the context of the much-discussed, highly charged paradigm of the relationship between Holocaust survivors and their children. Erich Goldhagen was in fact a Holocaust survivor born in the Ukraine. He escaped to America from wartime Europe and rose eventually to a position as a lecturer in history at Harvard, where he developed a following for his powerful and moving lectures on Holocaust issues. He's also the author of a number of scholarly articles, some of which are cited in footnotes to his son's book. Certain of these articles mention in their author-identification notes that Erich Goldhagen is working on a book on the ideology of genocide, a book that has yet to appear.

The one aspect of the Holocaust Erich Goldhagen has not written about, has never spoken of in his lectures, is his own personal experience in surviving and escaping it. His son has said his father has never discussed the experience with him. And neither has wished to discuss the influence of the father's survivor experience on the son's thesis about Germany. Onto this virtual vacuum of actual information Broder projects his own grand theory: that the son's book is a sublimation of the father's unexpressed longings, the working-out of a curious personal agenda vis-à-vis German culture.

Claiming to base his generalizations about Holocaust survivors and their children on "psychological literature," Broder argues that survivor parents demand a "price from their offspring. Demand a kind of reparational devotion to their parents' suffering." He proceeds to speculate, apparently without much firsthand information (one can see why this upset Daniel Goldhagen), about the son's childhood. He envisions the father inculcating the son with the historic magnitude of the Holocaust experience, cramming his mind with details "so that as a child Daniel knew more about Adolf Eichmann and Heinrich Himmler than Huckleberry Finn and Tom Sawyer." (There is a barely restrained suggestion of subtextual mockery in this line of Broder's that I found disturbing.)

Broder goes on to say that Daniel's father instilled in him a "mission to revolutionize Holocaust scholarship, a mission the father began too late to accomplish himself." Broder has a unique notion of what this mission was: It was not strictly a mission of revenge, he asserts, not "German bashing," not an attack on German culture, but an attempt to become *part* of it.

After Broder quotes Erich Goldhagen expounding at length to him on the best-selling success of his son's book, after quoting him attacking those who attacked his son at the Holocaust Memorial Museum (Yehuda Bauer was "only jealous of Daniel's success"), Broder quotes Goldhagen's father speaking fondly of German culture: "The Jews were the German culture bearers in Eastern Europe. . . . For me, facility with the German language came as naturally as the use of French for Russian aristocrats. My mother knew Goethe and Schiller by heart." Broder then records that (over the transatlantic phone line) Goldhagen the elder recited to him the first lines of Schiller's "*Die Glocke*" in fluent German.

All of which leads Broder to theorize, to explain the Goldhagen (father *and* son) mission as ultimately not the product of hostility to German culture but rather of a thwarted *love*: "an effort to get back in contact with a culture after fifty years' absence, a culture from which the 'German culture bearer' had been expelled. . . . This contact can only be accomplished via the story of the Holocaust, the end point of German-Jewish history, which has now become the starting point of joined scholarly activity, the only thing that binds Germans and Jews existentially."

This is a remarkably self-satisfied Germam vision of Goldhagen's thesis and of the Jewish relationship to German culture, this view of the Jews with their noses still pressed to the glass of the great German culture, using the Holocaust—their own tragedy—as a kind of ticket back to the mother ship.

But the urge to explain Daniel Goldhagen's thesis as somehow an expression of his father is not confined to Germans. I heard it the night after I spoke to Goldhagen from an American Jewish scholar, Richard S. Levy, distinguished professor of history at the University of Illinois and moderator of an Internet scholars' group discussion of Holocaust issues that had taken up, mostly critically, the Goldhagen thesis. Levy was, of course, also the author of *The Downfall of the Anti-Semitic Political Parties in Imperial Germany*, a study which at the very least casts doubt on Goldhagen's thesis that anti-Semitism had been irrevocably implanted in the German psyche by the end of the nineteenth century. Levy told me that he thought Goldhagen's book could be seen as the father using the son as vindication in the father's struggle with the Holocaust-scholar establishment for recognition of his views—vindication for the big book on the "ideology of genocide" the father himself had not produced. And that as a survivor he was using his son to punish the German perpetrators, a kind of revenge for the mass murder he barely escaped from.

One can understand how theories that depict him as a pawn of his father would upset Goldhagen. But the episode left me puzzled, wondering if in fact there might be something to the notion of explanation as revenge. It happened that shortly after I spoke to Goldhagen there arrived in the mail from Professor Berel Lang a copy of an essay he had written on "Holocaust Memory and Revenge" (for the quarterly *Jewish Social Studies*). It was an absolutely unique and fascinating exploration of a controversial and difficult theme, another example of the reason I find Lang's work so valuable: His style is cautious, not flashy, his rhetoric scholarly, not sensational. But he is willing to take on and investigate some stark, radical, even sensational questions about how to envision and respond to evil. Here he undertakes an extremely careful and considered examination of a radical question: "How could it be that revenge was *not* an element in the [Jewish] reaction to the Shoah?"

In fact, he says, there have been some isolated examples of direct vengeance—outbreaks of retaliation against German prisoners of war by Jews in charge of their camps. Then there was the ambitious plan by former Jewish partisans to poison the water supplies of German cities to punish collectively the German people for complicity in genocide, a plan that actually got as far as poisoning German prisoners' food in one detention camp. And there were and are Nazi hunters such as Simon Wiesenthal and the Klarsfelds, but Lang considers this more in the realm of justice and law rather than vengeance.

He's more interested in what he calls "displaced," indirect, forms of revenge on Germans. There was wartime U.S. Secretary of the Treasury Henry Morgenthau's ambitious plan to reduce postwar Germany to an agrarian economy to prevent a resurgence of the fevers that had twice brought the world total war in this century. There are the spontaneous, ad hoc individual boycotts of contemporary German products (such as Volkswagen and Mercedes cars) of German cultural figures (such as Wagner, whose works some Israeli orchestras refuse to play). Lang even sees Emil Fackenheim's famous commandment enjoining Jews never to give Hitler any "posthumous victories," which requires a vigilant monitoring of actions vis-à-vis contemporary Germans and Germany, as a kind of devotional, displaced revenge.

Most surprising about Lang's analysis, as I read it, is that he does not take the conventional route and disparage revenge outright. Rather, in his unique fashion, he scrupulously examines "the unusual allegiance between revenge and memory." He even goes so far as to say that revenge "is *useful* for memory and identity" (emphasis added). He contrasts two kinds of memory: the *commemoration* of the Holocaust in memorials and museums, which tends to comfort the survivors and establish their memory in the minds of those who came after. And revenge, which reinforces the memory of the crime among the heirs and successors of the *perpetrators* and solidifies the identity of those enacting the revenge.

Lang argues that, in effect, revenge is better if it comes out of the closet, so to speak, rather than disguise itself through displacements and sublimations, in which it might lose its impact and clarity for both the perpetrator of the crime and the perpetrator of revenge. But in his most cautious rhetoric, Lang asks us not to dismiss the notion of revenge as beyond the pale of legitimacy.

Can Goldhagen's thesis about the Germanness of the Holocaust be seen as a kind of displaced revenge in Berel Lang's sense of the term? As an intellectual rationale of a vengeful impulse not quite conscious of itself? If it wasn't intended vengefully, it came across that way, even to some of its most sophisticated readers, who believed Goldhagen was branding the German mind, character, and soul as irretrievably iniquitous.

Are all these readers, as Goldhagen insists, reading into his thesis something that isn't there, or are they reading in it something of which Goldhagen might not be completely aware?

I know that when I first saw the headline in *Der Spiegel* about the Goldhagen controversy—"Ein Volk von Dämonen?"—I had two conflicting reactions. At first I felt somewhat disturbed by the apparent attempt to accuse Goldhagen, a Jew, of using the same kind of demonizing rhetoric about Germans that Germans used to demonize Jews. But I must admit that there was another dimension to my reaction to it: a certain satisfaction in thinking about ordinary Germans confronting that sensational headline on their newsstand, a headline whose primal accusatory power—*A People of the Devil!*—would, for many, transcend the irony intended.

So much of recent German discussion of the Holocaust has been about how—not so much whether—one can "normalize" German history. How to see the Hitler years in the context of deeper, longer trends in Western history, how to contextualize its horrors in relative terms (compared, for instance, to the "Asiatic" horrors of Stalin). But here was a reminder that however much ordinary Germans might feel *they've* normalized, absolved themselves, explained themselves to others, to many they still need to prove they're *not* a people of the Devil.

And so I suppose it could be said that part of the satisfaction I felt from that headline did arise from a vengeful or at least punitive impulse, what Berel Lang calls "displaced revenge." A wish to impress upon ordinary Germans that even if they objected to the notion of a demonic national *character*, they shouldn't be exempt from a continuing examination of demonic national *behavior*. That the responsibility for explaining Hitler was at least as much theirs as ours, and if they couldn't explain Hitler, they ought not attempt to explain him away.

Consequently, I found I couldn't fault Goldhagen for his accusatory passion, though I also understood the irritation of some Jewish Holocaust scholars with him. They, the older generation of scholars, people like Yehuda Bauer, many far closer to the tragedy than Goldhagen, had gone to great lengths and perhaps great sacrifice to purge from their work any personal rage and vengefulness in their attempts to explain the Hitler regime's crimes and the German people's behavior. They'd held themselves to the self-effacing pursuit of the ideal of scholarly neutrality, a supposedly higher ideal. And then along comes a novice academic who restates what to them are obvious and well-known facts but casts them in the accusatory, emotionally charged tones of a new, vengeful indictment. And he's acclaimed as a knight of Jewish truth telling, his book achieves the worldwide bestsellerdom few scholarly books attain, and he's hailed for his courage in daring to say what others—what they—have not.

Still, Goldhagen's passion—whether you say it's for justice, revenge, or enlightenment—was something I respected. Clearly, he felt it, and to deny it in his prose would have been less than honest. Which made it all the more disappointing when I learned of the changes made in the German translation of his book. A second cover story in *Der Spiegel* some three months after the first (tied to the release of the German edition of Goldhagen's book and his German publicity tour), a friendlier story this time, included another curious sidebar. This one described certain crucial changes in the German translation of Goldhagen's book, dramatic softenings of key phrases, beginning with the very title. Instead of *Hitler's Willing Executioners* (usually, *Scharfrichter*) in the German translation it is closer to *Hitler's Willing Executors* (*Vollstrecker*), as in the custodians of a legacy, a will.

"Executors" is certainly a less inflammatory, less bloody vision of the role of ordinary Germans than "executioners." It's a different notion of "will" they're carrying out. "Executors" makes them sound like neutral functionaries: An executor is closer to Arendt's banal bureaucrats following orders than to Goldhagen's depiction of the perpetrators as bloodthirsty enthusiasts for torture and murder.

Consider some other changes among the many spotlighted by *Der Spiegel*: The "German conception of the Jews in the twentieth century" in the English original has become "the typical twentieth-century conception." The expulsion of the half-million Jews from Germany (the entire Jewish population) is, in the English edition, "the most radical act in centuries of Western European history." In the German edition, it's "the most radical act in decades of Western European history," which says something entirely different.

In addition, the English version tells us "the entire German elite wholeheartedly accepted eliminationist anti-Semitic measures." In the German version the German elites were merely "obliging" in their acceptance. Of the accounts I've seen of the subsequent popularity of Goldhagen's book—and Goldhagen himself—among "ordinary Germans" only Fritz Stern in *Foreign Affairs* has suggested these fairly dramatic softenings of his rhetoric may have played as much of a role as Goldhagen's widely noted personal charm with German audiences.

Was Goldhagen having second thoughts about the displaced revenge in his book? Was it vengeful in the first place? I called Berel Lang to ask him if he thought Goldhagen's thesis could be considered a kind of "displaced revenge."

"Yes," he said simply. He'd just reviewed the book for the Jewish publication *Moment*. He felt the exaggerated nature of its claim to have "discovered the necessary and sufficient" cause for explaining the Holocaust and Hitler in the ideology of eliminationist anti-Semitism "is so excessive—*nobody* can claim necessary and sufficient cause for the simplest act in history, much less one so complex"—that it suggests that something more is at work than objective historical analysis. Something that fits Lang's description of a displaced, unacknowledged revenge impulse.

Lang finds further support for his belief in what he calls Goldhagen's "extremely inconsistent" account of just how many perpetrators, how many "executioners," there were among the German people: "He says there are one hundred thousand who participated in the killing process and sometimes five hundred thousand, but he also seems to argue that the rest of the sixty million German people were as much active participants as the one hundred thousand. He ignores the opposition, and if it [genocide] was the overriding goal always, why did it not happen before it did? Why as late as 1941 was the policy still enforced expulsion but not extermination?"

Curiously, just a day after I spoke to Lang, revenge returned with a vengeance as a Holocaust issue. The front page of the lively Jewish weekly, *The Forward*, featured a story about Elie Wiesel and the impulse toward revenge, a story headlined, "The Rage That Elie Wiesel Edited Out of *Night*."

In it, Naomi Seidman, a young Jewish scholar at the Berkeley Theological Seminary, was quoted on her comparative study of the original Yiddish manuscript of *Night* (Wiesel's first impassioned book about his concentration-camp experiences) and the French translation published in 1956—the one that led to his worldwide acclaim, the one from which all English versions are derived.

Seidman argued that in the Yiddish version the young Wiesel focused his rage specifically against Germans and Germany, that he "railed against a world that was rehabilitating Germany, where the bestial sadist Ilse Koch (the Beast of Buchenwald) is happily raising her children." In the Yiddish version, Wiesel spoke of his disappointment after the war that camp survivors did *not* take vengeance on their captors and the captor nations: "The historical commandment to revenge was not fulfilled," Wiesel wrote.

But, she says, Wiesel excised these references to revenge against Germans in the French version of his book under the tutelage of the French Catholic writer François Mauriac, his patron, who brought his manuscript to the attention of the world, got him a French publisher, and wrote glowing introductions to the French and English editions.

Seidman suggests further that in revising his Yiddish manuscript for translation, Wiesel redirected his rage from Germans to an existential quarrel with God, a rage against the bleak meaninglessness of the universe. She claims Wiesel did so in order to make his memoir less offensive to Christian Europe, to existential European intellectuals. She argues his revisions of the Yiddish manuscript recast the Holocaust in the post-Christian rhetoric of "death of God" theology: that Wiesel made the tragedy as much about the death of God, of belief, as the death of Jews at the hands of Germans.

Seidman seems to imply a kind of bad faith on Wiesel's part as an explanation for the excision of thoughts about anti-German revenge; that he was attempting to make his persona more palatable to the Christian West, to curry favor. Not so, the scholars Eli Pfeffercorn and David Hirsch contend: "The quarrel with God is clearly established in the Yiddish book." And Wiesel himself denied to *The Forward* there had been any conscious agenda behind his revisions; he claimed he was merely trying to shorten his manuscript for the French edition.

This does not completely rule out a third explanation for the revisions that neither Wiesel nor Seidman advanced: that Wiesel might have had genuine second thoughts about the revenge impulse that leaped out of his pen when he first set down his feelings in memoir form. That his thinking might genuinely have *changed* between the Yiddish version and the French revision.

Perhaps the same thing could be said about Goldhagen's shift from the English to the German version of *his* thesis, from calling ordinary Germans "executioners" to calling them "executors" and the like. From blaming something specifically German to blaming history, the more abstract "twentieth century" rather than twentieth-century Germans, for the tragedy.

In any case, both Lang's reflections on revenge and the controversies over Goldhagen's and Wiesel's revisions prompted me to look a little more closely at the possible presence of a displaced revenge impulse in my own work, in the character of my preoccupation with Hitler and Hitler explanations. I looked at the nature of my own dissatisfaction with Goldhagen's thesis in that light. It was a dissatisfaction not so much with the extremity with which it pilloried Germans as with the way in which it, implicitly at least, could serve to exculpate Hitler.

If the German people were so relentlessly and inexorably driven by their eliminationist anti-Semitic ideology, then they had no choice but to act the way they did, and having no choice, they have no responsibility, any more than a schizophrenic who hears delusory voices in his head urging him to kill, voices he has no power to resist, has responsibility. By insisting on the overwhelming, irresistible power of his "central model," the abstract force he calls "eliminationist anti-Semitism," Goldhagen performs an eliminationist act himself: He eliminates from consideration, from history, those individuals and groups who *did* resist: the *Munich Post* journalists who attempted to expose Hitler, the Social Democratic Party activists whose failure does not diminish the importance of their struggle, the Germans who voted against Hitler (as the majority of Germans in every free election did).

In a very real sense, Goldhagen's fixation on the all-powerful determinism of his "central model" has the inadvertent effect of exculpating even the guilty among the German people, making them seem helpless pawns of that inexorable force, powerless to resist, powerless to choose otherwise. Perhaps this helps explain, perhaps this is the real reason for, the extraordinary popularity of his book (the German version anyway) with the German public.

Perhaps there *was*, then, "displaced revenge" at work in my reaction to Goldhagen's thesis about the German people: I did not wish to absolve them by shifting responsibility from individuals to a "central model," by blaming an abstract German character rather than the individual German characters who chose to act as they did.

And I suppose my dissatisfaction with some of Goldhagen's *critics* could be said to have sprung from the same source—displaced revenge. It might explain my reaction to Christopher Browning's critical explanation of Goldhagen's explanation.

Browning is Goldhagen's archrival among the younger generation of Holocaust scholars. Goldhagen denounced Browning's 1992 book, *Ordinary Men* (about a killing squad of German policemen), in a scathing *New Republic* review in which he accused Browning of being duped by the apologetic postwar testimony of these accused mass murderers, duped into believing that they had *trouble* making the transition from "ordinary men" to killers. The very subtitle of Goldhagen's book, *Ordinary Germans and the Holocaust*, is a deliberate shot at Browning's *Ordinary Men* title. It was the Germanness of these killers, not their ordinariness, that was most decisive, Goldhagen insisted.

I visited Browning a couple of days after the wild Holocaust Memorial pillorying of Goldhagen. Browning had been a speaker there, too, that evening, but he avoided personal attack, delivering his critique in a respectful, serious manner. However deep his disagreements, however much he'd felt injured by Goldhagen's previous attacks on him, he did not question Goldhagen's motives or good faith. In his office in the Holocaust Memorial research division, Browning, a scruffily youthful-looking scholar whose bowl-cut hair evokes both Beatle and monkish associations, filled me in—before we got to the Gold-hagen question—on the current line of research he's pursuing.

He's one of the international group of scholars who've been focusing on the decision question: the controversy over just when (and why then) Hitler made the irrevocable decision to proceed with the Final Solution. It's a fasci-nating dispute (to which I'll devote much of the next chapter) because theories about exactly when Hitler made the decision involve more than just quibbles about days and months. Almost inevitably, they turn out to be theories about the nature of Hitler's mind, about the place of Jew-hatred in his heart (the "sincerity" or opportunism of his anti-Semitism—in a way a recapitulation of the Bullock–Trevor-Roper debate), about the map of his psyche—about who Hitler really *was*. Almost always, a scholar's position on when Hitler made the decision is a reflection of his position on these larger questions.

In general, the earlier a scholar or historian locates what he or she be-lieves was Hitler's irrevocable decision to physically exterminate the Jews, the more they see a Hitler whose obsession with Jews eclipses anything else in his consciousness. The later a scholar locates the decision, the more he or she sees a Hitler with other, sometimes conflicting, concerns—lebensraum, his war aims, the practical realities of troop and train deployments—a somewhat more pragmatic, conflicted, or indecisive Hitler.

Thus, the late, much-respected historian Lucy Dawidowicz argued that Hitler had decided to devote his life to the extermination of the Jews as early as 1918. She cites a letter Hitler wrote in 1919 to a doctor in Munich declar-ing that the Jews must be eliminated to save Germany, not as some abstract prescription but as a literal goal. A goal that everything Hitler did after that, including launch a world war, was devoted to fulfilling. Which is why Dawido-wicz titled her book on Hitler *The War Against the Jews*. World War Two, she insists, was not a war against Poland, France, England, and Russia so much as it was a war against the Jews, waged to give Hitler the power to execute the decision he'd made two decades earlier.

Goldhagen emphasizes the moment just a bit later than Dawidowicz—a speech Hitler delivered in 1920, the difference between them being that, in Goldhagen's thesis, Hitler's decision, his will, plays a far less important role than the already determined, already gestating murder that nineteenth-century hate literature had impregnated Germans with.

Between the Dawidowicz/Goldhagen 1918–1920 pole and the extreme "functionalist" position, which argues that Hitler *never* really made the key extermination decision itself (he passively acceded to something which gath-ered momentum from the exigencies of harried bureaucrats who had more captive Jews on their hands than they knew what to do with), there are a num-ber of distinct gradations of decision theory on the spectrum from "moderate intentionalist" to "moderate functionalist," as the converging positions of contemporary scholars have been called.

There are those intentionalists who believe Hitler had the wish and the fantasy to exterminate the Jews foremost in his mind *before* 1939 and was waiting only till the outbreak of the war to make the fantasy reality. There are those who point out that even *after* the events of 1939 put millions of Polish Jews under Hitler's control, planning still continued in a desultory way to evacuate Jews to Madagascar or to relocate them in southern Poland. They argue that it wasn't until 1941, when Hitler conceived and executed the invasion of Russia, that he made up his mind about what to do with the Jews.

But even within 1941, current scholarship is embroiled in debates over which month, which week, which *weekend* the decision was made and why it was made then. Yehuda Bauer argues for March 1941. The moderate intentionalists, led by Richard Breitman, place the decision in May 1941, shortly *before* the Russian invasion, which makes the capture of the millions of Jews in Soviet territory an exterminationist objective of the surprise attack on Russia. Other intentionalists place the decision somewhat later—in the early euphoric days of the Russian campaign, in late June or July 1941, when, they assert, Hitler, intoxicated by victory, finally allowed his long-deferred wish-dream of extermination to emerge. And to be funded: He finally allocated the troops and trains necessary to make mass murder a massive industry.

The moderate functionalists tend to place the decision two or three months later, when the first euphoria of the Russian campaign bogged down, when Hitler had his first apprehension that victory in the east wouldn't be as swift, as complete, and as certain as it first seemed and the administrators of the captured territories pressed for a way to dispose of captive Jews. In this view, the decision for genocide was Hitler's revenge or consolation prize for a lost victory.

This had been Browning's position, although when I spoke to him he seemed to be shifting in the light of a new study by German scholar Peter Witte that seemed to narrow the moment of decision down, not to a month, but to a single weekend in mid-September 1941, the weekend of September 16–17, 1941. Witte argues that until September 1941, three months into the Russian campaign, Hitler had placed a higher priority on the anti-Soviet rather than the anti-Jewish aspects of the war on the eastern front: "For a period of six months in the spring and summer of 1941, Hitler's guidelines remained in effect, i.e., that no Jews were to be deported from the Reich and the [Polish] Protectorate before there was a successful conclusion to the Russian campaign. Hitler personally stressed this point on a number of occasions."

While this may have been a tactical decision, dictated by military considerations, Witte seems to argue that Hitler had not yet decided *whether* to transform the sporadic "special action" killing of Jews into a comprehensive program of extermination. "Hitler's decision to deport the Jews from the territory of Greater Germany while the fighting was still taking place [the decision to commence full-scale extermination] occurred quite suddenly in the middle of September 1941," Witte argues.

He cites certain decisions Hitler made on that weekend—decisions to approve allocation of trains and troops to evacuate jews from Germany and France to the east—as the orders that broke the logjam of indecision and began the uninterrupted flow of evacuees to the death factories. Interestingly, Witte's analysis places the decision after the initial euphoria of the Russian campaign *and* after the first disappointment that followed. He locates it in a brief moment after the disappointment, a blip in time in which the news on the eastern front turned temporarily good again—which makes the decision a product of both bitterness and triumph. (A recent claim by a German historian, Christian Gerlach, that the order came not until December 18, 1941, appears to be a misinterpretation of notes Himmler made about how Hitler wanted him to "spin" the leaks about the killing process already under way: The Jews were being killed because of their activities as "guerrilla partisans.")

I'll go deeper into the decision question in the next chapter, but here I'm concerned with a different aspect of Browning's thinking: with his explanation of the remarkable mainstream popularity of Goldhagen's thesis. In particular, his explanation of the disparity between its almost universal acclaim in the mainstream media and its more frequent disparagement among fellow scholars.

Browning's explanation, an unusual venture into media/cultural analysis for a scholar, focuses on what he believes is a popular reaction against some recent deeper trends in scholarship about Hitler and the Holocaust. Browning sees an impulse in the scholarly literature to look for ever-broader, allegedly deeper explanations for Hitler's crimes: deeper than Jew-hatred, deeper than Nazism, deeper than Germanism. To look for the kind of explanation that sees *all* of these as mere products of some more profound and universal flawed disposition in Western civilization. To see Nazism, Hitlerism, not as an *aberration* of Western civilization but as a *culmination* of certain of its tendencies—usually racism, eugenicism, or a racial-biological-based supremacist aesthetic. Or, as the now-fashionable academic buzzword has it: "biopolitics." Biopolitics is a vision of the World War II–era killing that includes and explains the killings of Gypsies, homosexuals, and Slavs, the euthanasia of the physical and mental "defectives" and other "inferior types," in the same inclusive racial-eugenicist drive that targeted Jews. It's an explanatory vision that sees not Jewishness but a generalized *otherness* as the target (thus denying Jewishness its special relevance). In addition, instead of seeing Hitler as some monstrous enemy of "civilized Western values," Hitler becomes a kind of perverse embodiment of the worst impulses buried in, intrinsic to, Western culture, to the Western "project," as the postmodernists like to call it.

The kind of explanation that sees Nazism as merely an extreme variation of Western racism might be called the politically correct view of the origins of the Holocaust (although Browning, who buys into some of its assumptions, wouldn't disparage it that way). It tends to broaden, to *obscure* the identity of the primary perpetrators and the primary victims of the Holocaust, Browning believes. Broadens it beyond German and Jew, tends to make the specific identity of the victims less relevant.

The mainstream popularity of the Goldhagen book, with its thesis about eliminationist anti-Semitism, the all-powerful, all-explaining central model, is, Browning argues, a reaction against this scholarly tendency. A reaction that returns the focus once again to the primal duality of German and Jew.

"People have lost *their* Holocaust," Browning told me, in the supposedly sophisticated broadening explanation of contemporary scholars. "What Goldhagen is doing," he says, using a somewhat patronizing if not deliberately offensive metaphor, "is re-ghettoizing it for them," narrowing it to a story about Jews and the Germans, rather than about the West and the generalized Other.

I suspect that Browning is overestimating the degree to which trends in contemporary scholarship have penetrated or even registered in mainstream popular consciousness, enough to provoke a counterreaction. Still, if it's true, as he says, that Goldhagen's thesis represents a kind of narrowing, my problem with it—and here is where displaced revenge might make itself manifest— is that Goldhagen does not narrow things *enough*. The eliminationist aspect of his thesis that troubles me most is its virtual elimination of *Hitler* from it.

By portraying the German people as pregnant with inevitable, inexorable murder, by reducing Hitler to a marginal midwife role, Goldhagen's thesis does what Browning's more sophisticated explainers seemed to be doing: attributing the crime to an irresistible *abstraction* that overwhelmed ordinary Germans. In effect, he makes the perpetrators themselves a kind of victim— victims of ideological poisoning which robbed them of the power to resist, robbed them of agency, of choice, any possibility of pursuing another—any other—course than the one they'd been driven to. They weren't following the orders of a Hitler, but, like Hitler, they were driven by the "orders" of an abstract impersonal idea that deprived them—deprived even Hitler—of responsibility and thus of culpability.

Goldhagen's insistence on the inevitability of the Holocaust—"if not Hitler someone like him"—on the irresistibility of the impersonal force that compelled ordinary Germans to do its bidding and made the genocide unavoidable, is challenged further by an illuminating recent book about the circumstances of Hitler's takeover. *Hitler's Thirty Days to Power*, by Yale's Henry Ashby Turner, is a close examination of the political maneuvering in January 1933, the month that ended with Hitler being called to the chancellorship by Hindenburg.

Turner follows Bullock's footsteps in examining in telling detail just how precarious, contingent, that end result was—the extent to which Hindenburg's fateful decision to call upon Hitler was the product of unpredictable factors of chance and personality, rumor and accident, rather than the inevitable product of historical abstractions. Turner focuses in particular on the rivalry between General Kurt von Schleicher, the manipulative chancellor in power before Hitler, and the even more manipulative ex-chancellor Franz von Papen, who maneuvered Hitler into power in the mistaken belief that he, Papen, would be the one pulling the strings (perhaps the single worst miscalculation, in every respect, in twentieth-century history).

Turner's account emphasizes just how much Hitler's January 1933 nomination as chancellor was (as Yehuda Bauer put it) due more to his electoral *failure* two months earlier in November 1932, to his perceived slippage, to the (very real) sense that the forces of history were leaving him behind. Such a perception made him seem less threatening, more manageable to those like Papen who schemed to get him into the job as their cat's-paw. Hitler's triumph, Turner argues persuasively, was far from inevitably determined by historical forces and central models and the like: "To explain Hitler's acquisition of power in deterministic terms is to rule out the question of responsibility for that disastrous development," Turner writes. "If his appointment as chancellor was the inexorable result of impersonal forces beyond the control of the individuals involved, *then it would obviously be unjust to hold any of them responsible*" (emphasis added).

Indeed, it could be said that if that was true, it diminishes Hitler's responsibility: He becomes a cat's-paw of historical inevitability. And I suppose that is where displaced revenge may well enter into my preference for Turner's own contingent vision, which makes individual schemers, flesh-and-blood immoral agents—Hitler himself—responsible for Hitler's crimes, rather than impersonal, inexorable forces of history.

It's not that I don't feel an intellectual rationale for the critiques I've made, in the course of this book, of abstract inevitability theories (and I'm aware that historical causation always involves a complex interaction of factors, of abstract ideas and forces as well as personal agency). But I suspect that *some* of my predisposition to take a critical attitude toward the more abstract class of explanation—my drive to devote a book to the questions and agendas embedded in Hitler explanations and the ways in which some seem to permit Hitler to escape—may derive from a displaced-revenge impulse. Although I wouldn't call it revenge upon Hitler so much as doing him *justice*. Not so much forbidding him a posthumous victory but forbidding him a posthumous *escape*.

It's not that the name "Hitler" needs to be blackened further in the popular imagination, although there *has* been a strain of misguided argument about

Hitler's "greatness" that tries to separate the history-making magnitude of the man from the kind of history he was making. And there are myths still about Hitler as a kind of supply-side economic genius—the way he is supposed to have solved the German unemployment problem as soon as he came into office. One additional virtue of Henry Ashby Turner's book is that he demolishes that myth: He points out that the massive public-works program that reduced German unemployment by a full two million in the first half of 1933 was devised by Chancellor von Schleicher and signed just forty-eight hours before he was forced out to make way for Hitler's appointment. Hitler, with his uncanny luck, still reaps the credit for it.

But there is a different, perhaps more insidious strain of argument that emerges in even the most sophisticated recent Hitler-centered scholarship—particularly in the moment-of-decision controversy over when and why Hitler made the choice to proceed with total extermination. This line of thought doesn't exculpate Hitler's decision as the product of abstract historical forces, but rather gives us a Hitler who was almost too indecisive to make the decision at all. A Hitler whose mind defies explanation because he truly did not know his mind himself. A Hitler who allows himself to be pushed and pulled by conflicting advisers, conflicting forces of expediency, military exigency, and uncertain conviction. A Hitler who postpones for as long as possible making up his mind on the Final Solution. A figure I'll examine in the following chapter. One who might be called, in caricatured terms, the Hamlet Hitler, or even the nebbish Hitler.

CHAPTER 20

Lucy Dawidowicz:
Blaming Adolf Hitler

In which the dithering, Hamlet Hitler of Christopher Browning meets the contemptuous, laughing Hitler of Lucy Dawidowicz

Did Adolf Hitler feel *shame* about his decision to murder the Jews? Is it possible to conceive of a Hitler capable of shame? Did he feel trepidation, doubt? Was he scared? These are some of the questions that emerged in my conversation with Christopher Browning about his account of Hitler's decision. An account that represents the cutting edge of much contemporary scholarship on the question, scholarship that has given us the nebbish Hitler, the Hamlet Hitler, a Hitler who could not make up his mind.

The question of Hitler's "shame" emerged when I attempted to explore with Browning his surprising use of the word "enormity." Less as a description of the murder of the Jews than as an attempt to describe Hitler's *feeling*—his trepidation, his personal apprehension—about his decision to murder the Jews, as Browning conceived it. I'd asked Browning where he stood in the touchstone dispute between Hugh Trevor-Roper and Alan Bullock over Hitler's "sincerity."

"I think he *was* a true believer," Browning told me. "That he does believe Jews were the source of all evil in the world. But I also think he was aware of the *enormity* of what he was doing, and so what you get in fact is a kind of series of hesitations. My tracing of the final decision to go over the brink in the fall of 1941 shows that this is not a big-bang decision. That there are, in fact, a series of decisions. And that there is even hesitation at the end."

It's an end, a final decision Browning still wants to place much later than even some of his "moderate functionalist" fellow scholars. One senses that in his heart of hearts Browning doesn't see Hitler in *his* heart of hearts *ever* truly reconciled to the "enormity" of the decision. He sees a Hitler always shying away, retreating from the decision: Hitler as Hamlet.

"People in August 1941 have come to Hitler and said 'Can we begin the deportations?'" Browning is telling me. "And Hitler says, 'No, not until the war is won.'" The deportations in question are, of course, the removal of Jews "to the East," to their death.

"Then," Browning says, "in the middle of September 1941, you get Himmler's letter to [regional leader Arthur] Greiser in the Warthegau [the captured Polish territory formally integrated into the German Reich]. In that letter, Himmler says Hitler has now agreed to deport all the Jews by the end of the year. You see, before that, both Heydrich and Goebbels have gone to Hitler in August and said, 'Can't we begin the deportations [of the Jews in Germany to the East]?' Hitler says, 'No, not yet.' But finally, on September 18, you get the letter from Himmler to Greiser [signaling Hitler's assent to deportation]. In the recent article by Peter Witte, he traces Hitler's decision to the weekend of September 16 to 17."

Browning makes a bow to the notion of Witte's article establishing a kind of end point for Hitler's decision-making process—an end point for those who believe he *was* having trouble making up his mind. But clearly Browning believes the process of hesitation, of dithering, did not end even then, on that fateful weekend: "Himmler and others meet with Hitler that weekend. The meeting takes place at east-front headquarters. The letter to Greiser follows. The letter to Greiser may *appear* to be unequivocal. In it, Himmler informs Greiser, 'The Führer wishes that the Old Reich and Protectorate be emptied and freed of Jews from West to East as quickly as possible.'"

But having said the weekend before the Greiser letter was *the* moment of decision, Browning begins to adduce evidence of further hesitation, further wavering *after* that supposedly decisive weekend of September 16–17.

The following weekend, Browning points out, "Hitler meets with Himmler and Goebbels and Heydrich on the twenty-third and twenty-fourth [of September 1941]. He says he wants to clear the cities out [of Jews]. We can begin *as soon as the military situation clarifies*. He's still hesitating! Even after Kiev falls, after the complete encirclement of Vitebsk and Bryansk on October 6, Hitler says we can go ahead with this—*as soon as we have the transportation*. In other words, even after he's supposedly made the decision, he still seems to be hesitating. . . . In principle he's agreed, but he *still* hasn't given the green light to implement it. The decisions are piecemeal ever since he begins talking about a 'war of destruction' with Goebbels in February [1941]. The final green light doesn't seem to come until October 10.

"My sense," Browning concludes, "is he hedges and he *wants* to [begin exterminating the Jews], but it's not a big-bang goal; it's this extraordinary slow process of edging up to the brink."

At this point, I tried to probe what Browning considered the source of these hesitations; was he suggesting a Hitler contending with a *conscience?* "You say it's a sense of the 'enormity' of the decision. 'Enormity,' you know, has two meanings: magnitude, bigness, and also great, horrific transgressiveness, right?" I asked him.

"Well, those two are not mutually exclusive. But enormity, here it does seem to mean it was not a *casual* decision. It was not a decision he had set out *long* before, as others say, so that when the opportunity came, he just said, 'Go with it.' It's a decision, I think, he didn't make until he was confident of the victories in hand, thinks there's no more inhibitions in the way, so he really *can* turn fantasy into reality. The enormity inheres into the fact he realizes this isn't an everyday decision, this isn't like the Nuremberg Laws. I mean, even the earlier decision to approve the systematic mass murder of the Russian Jews by setting up the Einsatzgruppen [special killing squads]—they get *vague* orders.

"My feeling is that they're told . . . Everybody who goes to Russia knows they're not going to get in *trouble* for killing Jews, but there isn't an explicit order saying kill *every* last Jew down to women and children. You can kill Jews and communists, you can kill Jews in party and state positions, but no one quite yet says, *'Kill every last Jew. Down to the infants.'* And that signal *seems* to come in mid-July 1941 when Hitler gives this euphoric speech about [how] we're going to turn this land into a Garden of Eden.

"And my feeling is that at that point, he turns to Himmler and says, *'My dear Heinie, what about the rest of them? Would it be possible?'* And Himmler goes back and has to create a feasibility study. This is what the Göring letter basically says. You know, when Heydrich goes in to Göring, the Göring *Auftrat* [memo/order] at the end of July then says, 'You're authorized to draw up the study to coordinate things and to come back to me with a plan as soon as possible.' This isn't an *order.* This is an authorization to draw up a plan."

"My dear Heinie . . . Would it be possible?" There is something arresting about Browning's evocation of a Hitler pleading, imploring, overwhelmed by the magnitude of a dawning opportunity to realize a dream he'd never dared contemplate, yet humbled by the vast implications and consequences. "My dear Heinie . . ." Here is the voice of the nebbish Hitler brought to life. A kind of comic-pathetic Hitler, almost a comic-*opera* Hitler.

"My dear Heinie . . . Would it be possible?" Browning's Hitler is a man of

Hamlet-like procrastination. "There are these hesitations, there is this uncertainty," he says. "And then there's this 'Yes, but,' this 'Yes, if only,' and finally—'Yes.'" He makes it sound like Molly Bloom's soliloquy of graduated surrender to a longed-for, yet feared, final yes.

"Now, what does that mean?" Browning asks me. "To me, that means there *was* hesitation. There was . . ." He pauses and hesitates himself, not willing to go over the threshold to attributing it to self-doubt or scruples of conscience. " . . . a sense that in the end he was *scared* of what he was doing. Now I interpret that as he didn't think it was *wrong*, but he was aware that he was now doing something that had never been done before. Stepping into new territory. Could it be done?"

My dear Heinie . . . Would it be possible?

"It's in that sense I use the word 'enormity,' not was it right or wrong—because he ultimately believed it was right—but could it actually be *done?*"

"You're suggesting his trepidation is not moral but—?"

"Well, part of it's logistical and practical—will it work?—you know, in August of 1940 he had to call off the euthanasia program because of popular reaction against it. So he can't not be aware there might be some problems: Will the German people do it? Will others do it? Will he reach a point [where] others don't rush to do it anymore? And what he finds out, unfortunately, is that they *do* rush to do it. And that is one of the most humanly devastating things about this, that where there ought to have been a bump in the road, there doesn't appear to have been one. But he couldn't have *known* that, given what had happened with the euthanasia program.

"So he had to be concerned about that: *Can* he in fact carry this off? I think that—imagining here again—he must also have realized that this, in a sense, was going to define his destiny. This was how Hitler was going to go down in history. And it must have been intoxicating in one sense, but it had to have been scary on the other hand."

Scary? Trepidation? Hesitation and doubt? Is this der Führer or Hitler, Prince of Denmark? There are (at least) two troubling aspects of Browning's vision of the nebbish Hitler, beyond its problematic status as a historical portrait of Hitler's hesitant inwardness.

The first disturbing element lies in the unstated, unexpressed corollary of Browning's nebbish-Hitler analysis: This is a Hitler who just as easily might *not* have gone ahead. A Hitler whose indecision could have been resolved otherwise. A Hitler who might finally have shrunk from the enormity of what he contemplated. That, in other words, even as late as October 1941, the Holocaust as we know it, in its totality *didn't have to happen!*

It does what some might have thought impossible: It makes the phenomenon of the Holocaust even more painful to contemplate because it suggests powerfully an alternate possibility: that it could just as easily have been avoided if a wavering, indecisive Hitler had wavered back rather than forth. It's painful to contemplate because in a sense it once again puts us in Hitler's power, in Hitler's hands, as he purportedly weighs the possibility of the act against the enormity of it. When we hear Browning impersonate such a Hitler's conflicted contemplation of the possibility—"*My dear Heinie . . . Would it be possible?*"— when we hear Hitler wonder *if* it could be done, it is in a certain sense undone, made contingent again. And then, even more sickeningly, done again.

In fact, however, the degree to which it is more or less painful or uncomfortable to contemplate should not confirm or disqualify Browning's Hamlet-like conception of Hitler. A better way of assessing Browning's Hitler is to see how it holds up under challenge from a powerful rival vision of Hitler.

The most powerful and direct challenge to Browning's vision of Hitler and his decision comes from a predecessor, the late Lucy Dawidowicz. In her important but now somewhat neglected 1975 study, *The War Against the Jews*, she fastens on exactly the same language, exactly the same moments of decision, of action and inaction, that Browning sees betraying hesitation, trepidation, a sense of enormity, a sense of doubt—and comes to the opposite conclusion. She finds Hitler using "esoteric language" and euphemism to create the *false* impression of hesitation and calculation, a false impression that concealed an unswerving, relentless, decades-long determination to exterminate the Jews. A decision she believes he made as early as 1918, rather than the fall of 1941, where Browning puts it. A decision, finally, that Dawidowicz believes was *never* in doubt.

Reading Lucy Dawidowicz after listening to Christopher Browning on the subject of Hitler's alleged dithering is the equivalent of a therapeutic slap in the face. In forceful but carefully footnoted prose, she makes the case that those who believe Hitler had not made up his mind as late as 1941 are ignorant of the true nature of Hitler's intentions, have been taken in by a cunning con game Hitler played on all but his innermost circle when it came to the question of the Final Solution. Her challenge to the tendency of contemporary scholarship to give us a Hitler who dithered over his decision is not one of degree, not an argument about difference of months, even years; it's an argument over decades. But more than that, it's an argument about Hitler's mind.

So much has been written about Hitler and the Holocaust, so many arguments and controversies have come and gone since the publication of Dawidowicz's book, that the importance of her argument may have been overlooked of late, even if its thrust has not been convincingly refuted or superseded. Her argument about Hitler's mind, about Hitler's decision, remains an extreme but powerful conjecture against which other interpretations must be measured and tested. One of the reasons I was driven to write this chapter was to try to restore the case she makes—the vision of Hitler, the method to his madness—to the place it deserves in the forefront of the explanatory wars.

In her vision, beneath the esoteric language of concealment—the language of trepidation and hesitation, the "*My dear Heinie . . . Would it be possible?*" that Browning hears—is not a nebbish or a Hamlet Hitler but a Hitler crafty enough to *create* a hesitant persona to conceal his true intent, to cloak himself in deniability: an actor Hitler scripting himself as a Hamlet of indecision while ruthlessly and decisively stage-managing the drive to extermination.

She sees, in other words, an actor Hitler, but one who is not precisely the same *kind* of actor postulated by Emil Fackenheim. He saw a Hitler whose act covered up an *absence* of conviction (like the cynical-actor Hitler Alan Bullock initially intuited). No, for Dawidowicz, Hitler's acting inheres not in insincerity but in *disguising his sincerity*—in the counterfeit of indecision, in concealing his murderous intention under a cloak of hesitant, opportunist calculation. An important difference. And what's more, she has painstakingly reconstructed the creation of the act, the process, the method, the language of the charade. It's an extraordinarily well crafted act, she believes, an act that still has the power to persuade and deceive today.

The truth concealed beneath the act, she insists, with a conviction powerful and virtually unique in the literature about Hitler's decision, is that Hitler conceived a mission to murder the Jews en masse—not drive them out, expel, harass, exile, defeat them, but murder and exterminate them—as early as November 1918, in the sanitarium at Pasewalk. Conceived it in that feverish moment he learned of the German defeat and then made it his mission to avenge the Jewish stab in the back he believed responsible. Thus, all his apparent hesitations, his zigs and zags, his doubts and trepidations, were an actor's Machiavellian disguise—tactical shifts to further the esoteric strategy, to conceal his own responsibility.

But before proceeding to Dawidowicz's remarkable and powerful conception of Hitler's mission and his method, let's briefly look at how she came to her mission, a rather remarkable story in itself. She was, first of all, an American Jew who made an unusual reverse pilgrimage that brought her to Hitler's Berlin in the fateful, world-shaking month of September 1939. Born in 1915 in New York City, she was initially a resolutely secular New Yorker, "an English major who read Wordsworth and wrote poetry," she told Diane Cole, a writer who interviewed her in 1983. (Dawidowicz died in 1990.)

But then there came a moment in 1937, when, as a graduate student, she was sitting in a Columbia University seminar, "hearing the professor drone on about Wordsworth. It was a time when it seemed that the world and in particular my Jewish world was going up in flames. I looked out the window and thought, 'What is Wordsworth to me at this time?'"

She did more than think about it; she radically changed her life. She began what she called "a reverse journey, reverse in the sense of the track of history," to Vilna, the impoverished, dilapidated, but still-thriving heart and repository of the centuries-old "golden tradition" of Yiddish learning and literature in Poland. She went there to immerse herself in that past, to help preserve it, and to share the terror of the onrushing future.

"I was there for a year, and that experience changed everything," she told Cole. She was speaking of experiencing Vilna's glory and its impending eradication, of being there in the final moments before the Final Solution exterminated all but the memory of that golden civilization. It changed everything for her by focusing her attention ever after on its existence and those who exterminated its existence.

But there was another experience on her journey home from the doomed city that might have "changed everything" in a different way, shaped the very way she looked upon the perpetrators of the war against the Jews—shaped in particular the almost surgical precision with which her historical analysis biopsied the malignant tissue of their language and their lies.

In August 1939, as the shock of the Hitler-Stalin pact and preparation for war and invasion caused turmoil in Poland, Lucy Dawidowicz, then twenty-four, began a dangerous and difficult journey west from Warsaw to Copenhagen, a journey that would take her into the heart of the beast: into Berlin.

"Leaving Warsaw was a journey of great drama," she told Diane Cole. "Poland was mobilizing everything that moved. . . . The Polish port of Gdynia was closed. So I decided to go to Copenhagen, but to get there I had to change not only trains but stations in Berlin. And then somewhere near the Polish/German border, probably at Posen, a German consul got on the train and sat in my compartment. We started talking in English. I told him I was an American; he didn't know I was Jewish. When we arrived in Berlin, a frightening city—everywhere soldiers, the military—he helped me get a taxi."

That taxi ride between stations, along boulevards draped with blood-red swastika flags, was her closest brush with Hitler's war machine as it prepared the war against the Jews.

There seems to be—particularly in light of her later distinctive take on Hitler—something paradigmatic in this still-strong memory of her encounter with the German consul. Something in the tenor and subtext which left a lasting impression.

Consider the contrast between the spoken and unspoken levels of their encounter: polite and civil on the surface, yet deceptive on both sides. Dawidowicz concealing her Jewishness (as well, we can intuit, as her contempt and hostility), the German consul concealing . . . We cannot be sure exactly how much he knew, but his return to Berlin from Poland the week before the invasion suggests he knew the horror that was about to happen: the invasion, the beginning of the extermination.

Their double-leveled conversation—the polite, euphemistic surface concealing the bitter truths—is an instance of the kind of euphemistic bilevel "esoteric" communication Dawidowicz came to believe was the signature, the method of those Hitler insiders who knew but concealed the plan to murder the Jews.

Dawidowicz's esoteric-language thesis begins with an underlying argument about the timing of Hitler's decision. One that places her at the earliest edge of the decision-theory continuum.

"The Final Solution had its origins in Hitler's mind," she writes.

> In *Mein Kampf* he tells us that he decided on his war against the Jews in November 1918, when, at the military hospital in Pasewalk, he learned, in rapid succession, of the naval mutiny at Kiel, the revolution that forced the abdication of the Emperor, and finally the armistice. "Everything went black before my eyes," he wrote. In the ensuing "terrible days and even worse nights," while he pondered the meaning of these cataclysmic events, "my own fate became known to me." It was then that he made his decision: "There is no making pacts with Jews; there can be only *the hard*: *either-or*. I, for my part, decided to go into politics" [emphasis added].

She suggests that Hitler decided "then, in November 1918, on the destruction of the Jews as his political goal," but she allows the possibility that "the idea remain[ed] buried in his mind until it took shape in *Mein Kampf*, which he wrote in 1924." She thus makes 1924 the terminus ad quem, the date beyond which we needn't go, but returns to the matter to argue that it could "indeed go back to November 1918, as Hitler himself claimed." Clearly she favors the belief that when Hitler referred to the "hard: either-or" back then, he was referring explicitly to extermination, either of the Aryan race by the Jews or the Jews by the Aryans.

If, as she believes, Hitler had made that decision as far back as November 1918, she also believes that he made another decision when he entered politics the following year: the decision to *conceal* his ultimate goal. She asks,

> How does one advocate publicly an idea or a program whose novelty lies in its utter radicalism? No matter how anti-Semitic the Munich of 1919 and 1920 was, the explicit transformation of a slogan like "*Juda verrecke*" [The Jews must perish] into a practical political program would have brought on the censorship of the local authorities and

discredited the incipient National Socialist movement even among conventional anti-Semites. In this situation Hitler availed himself of a time-honored device—the use of *esoteric language*. In all periods of history, when government or society has put limits on public discussion, those who wish to circumvent censorship resort to the use of esoteric language. Exoterically understood, the text is unexceptional, but to the insiders who know how to interpret the words, the message is revolutionary and dangerous to the status quo [emphasis added].

She is in effect applying to Hitler the kind of analysis of esoteric communication that the influential philosopher Leo Strauss became famous for applying to philosophers and thinkers such as Plato and Machiavelli. In doing so, she is staking out two rather heretical positions on Hitler, heretical certainly in the light of the contemporary consensus Christopher Browning represents. First, she argues that Hitler made his decision to murder the Jews en masse far earlier than almost anyone else has him making it, nearly a quarter century earlier. Second, she makes a case that what others see as Hitler's fitful, wavering, opportunistic commitment to Jew-hatred (the term Dawidowicz favors over anti-Semitism) did not reflect absence of conviction or the presence of conflicting priorities, as later, more "sophisticated" interpretations of his behavior have it. Rather, she argues the apparent dithering was a deliberate disguise adopted to shield an absolutely unwavering commitment.

Let's look first at her belief that Hitler conceived of *murdering*—not opposing, expelling, restricting, or harassing but *murdering*—the Jews, all of them, as early as 1918. Almost no other scholar or historian makes such a strong claim, and she is unable to offer conclusive proof—eyewitness testimony, an overheard conversation—unless one counts Hitler's own words pinpointing Pasewalk in 1918 as the moment he conceived his "mission." So her conjecture is often cited as defining the extreme (subtext: impossible) end of the spectrum of debate on the decision question.

Almost every other decision-theory conjecture envisions a Hitler who *evolved*, a Hitler whose aims became more radical the more power he acquired, a Hitler whose solution to the Jewish question was "radicalized" finally by the opportunity the 1941 eastern-front war created. That until the exigencies of the battlefield forced him to solve the "problem" of the millions of Jews who were suddenly in his power, he was still thinking of forced expulsion, forced emigration to Madagascar, that kind of thing. Until suddenly in 1941 it *dawned* on him: He could murder them all. Dawned on him first as a glimmer of fantasy—"*My dear Heinie . . . Would it be possible?*"—and then, only after many hesitations and trepidations, as a reality.

The seminal book of the functionalist scholars, the ones who believe that the Holocaust was in effect forced on Hitler from below, from bureaucrats who pressed for a decision on what to do with the Jews on their hands, is Karl Schleunes's *The Twisted Road to Auschwitz*. Even most intentionalists who believe Hitler himself made the decision, imposed it from above, believe there was in effect a twisted road *within* Hitler, within his psyche, a twisted road around his own doubts, competing demands, conflicting impulses, and, above all, caution signs.

But those who advance this purportedly more sophisticated model of Hitler's decision have no more solid evidence than Lucy Dawidowicz does for her model. Perhaps even more treacherously, they rely on taking Hitler at his word about the meaning of his apparently hesitant steps up to the decision. Taking Hitler at his word is a risky proposition, particularly when, as Dawidowicz has adduced, there are occasions when Hitler disclosed his deliberate use of disingenuous and deceptive language.

And when we know the enormity of what Hitler actually did, is she really asking us to believe the impossible when she suggests that in November 1918 a feverish, gas-blinded, shell-shocked Corporal Hitler, perhaps in the midst of some full-blown hysterical nervous breakdown, reacted to the news of the shattering defeat by vowing to make the Jews—all the Jews—pay for his suffering? Is it too much to believe that he could have said to himself: I will make the Jews pay, pay with their lives, every one of them.

Of course, he could have said this in a metaphoric way—it could have been a passing fantasy, a feverish wish, not a plan. He could have thought it but not meant it literally, not thought of translating it into a long-range plan to accomplish it (as Dawidowicz believes he did).

On the other hand, considering the fact that he *did* accomplish it, can we rule out the possibility that he said it and meant it literally and that he dedicated the rest of his life to making it come as true as it did?

I'd suggest that the fairly widespread dismissal of Dawidowicz's notion of a 1918 origin of Hitler's extermination decision is not as carefully considered as it might be. That it's a rejection that comes less from evidence to the contrary than from a preference for seeing historical figures as complex, as sensitive to conflicting forces, as historians themselves. A preference for believing that people don't act "that way"—don't conceive an enormity of an idea and spend a quarter century creating the circumstances to enact it. And it's true, people in general don't. Ordinary people don't orchestrate mass murder. But some fanatics have. And Adolf Hitler did.

Still, historians prefer to imagine that extermination was an idea that dawned on Hitler slowly. This requires them to ignore the occasional obtrusive outburst, such as the comment Hitler made to one Josef Hell in Munich in 1922 in which he spoke of hanging Jews from lampposts until he exterminated them all. Or the reference to the "stab in the back" Hitler made in 1921 in which he argued that "gassing tens of thousands" of Jews back in 1918 might have saved Germany from that betrayal. Or if such excrescences are acknowledged, they are seen as exceptions to the more moderate mainstream of Hitler's thought process about the fate of the Jews, a mainstream that muddled along on a more temperate, pragmatic course, often ignoring the Jewish question for long periods, or speaking mainly of legislative remedies, restrictions on immigration and citizenship rights, or expulsion at most. Never swerving to mass murder, at least as a practical "solution," until 1941.

The fact that Dawidowicz's thesis is not easily or intuitively disprovable does not mean it is easily provable either. But I found her attempt to make a very serious case for a 1918 or 1924 Hitler decision (in her heart of hearts, I think she believed 1918) fascinating, and, at the very least, one of the most powerful and polarizing conjectures in the Hitler literature, well worth close scrutiny in itself. And particularly important because buried in her analysis of the question, buried in a long footnote, there lurks a remarkable latent image. A unique image she surfaces for other reasons, a surprising specter I'd never seen adumbrated before, but one that's haunted me ever since: the figure of the laughing Hitler.

Recall that, in first defining her thesis about Hitler's esoteric language, Dawidowicz proposed both that Hitler had made up his mind for extermination early—and that he'd begun the process of concealing it early as well.

"How does one advocate . . . an idea . . . whose novelty lies in its utter radicalism?" she asks of Hitler's radical extermination idea. "One disguises it."

The rhetorical inquiry raises a question about her method: How does *she* advocate a position (hers, on the decision) whose radicalism makes it so novel? In part, it requires her to argue from an absence: that Hitler's *failure* to advocate extermination openly in the early twenties means he was concealing, esoterically, something that *was* there, rather than the alternative—that it *wasn't* there in the first place.

She adduces the necessity of concealment in the years immediately after 1918 from Hitler's concern over the "anxiety" of the Reichswehr, the largely demobilized German army with whom Hitler was still affiliated as a "political education officer" after his return to Munich in 1919: "Hitler's oratorical talents and anti-Semitic presentations to the recruits were much admired by his superiors, [but] there was anxiety that these speeches would be characterized as 'anti-Jewish agitation.' Instructions were consequently given [by army superiors] for a cautious treatment and the avoidance of 'plain references' to the Jews."

She looks at Hitler's earliest speeches through this lens of enforced esoteric language, where, she argues, "the code words he used for Jews outnumbered the plain references. Code words like 'usurers,' 'profiteers,' 'exploiters,'

'big capitalists,' 'the international money power,' 'communists,' 'social democrats,' 'November criminals.'" She is, in effect, saying the fact that he *doesn't*
call them Jews is proof that he *was* referring to the Jews.

Intuiting Hitler's inwardness is a tricky business, particularly when she
seems to be arguing from an absence. But one could also say she's arguing
from a deferred presence, the terrible reality of what Hitler ultimately did. And
similarly, her opponents are forced to intuit from an absence as well, an absence of evidence that he did *not* conceive back then of what he would do so
ruthlessly later.

I became fascinated by the often brilliant lengths to which Lucy Dawidowicz
would go, the conjectural leaps she'd take, in her impassioned drive to vindicate
her esoteric language thesis about Hitler and his decision. By the way she applied the literary-critical techniques from her English-major period—the search
for subtextual ambiguities she pursued in studying Wordsworth—to the prose
of Adolf Hitler. Agree or disagree, it's a dazzling performance. As is her entire
book, which, it should be noted, is not exclusively concerned with explaining
Hitler, although that aspect of it is my concern here. In fact, more than half her
book is devoted to the experience of Hitler's victims, to the range of responses
embattled Jewish communities of Europe mustered in the face of overwhelming and murderous force. As her friend and colleague Harvard professor Ruth
Wisse pointed out to me, Lucy Dawidowicz felt strongly, at the time she wrote
The War Against the Jews, that too much of the literature was dedicated to the
war, too little to the Jews—a state of affairs her eloquent book helped alter.

She begins her analysis of Hitler's duplicity about his plan for the fate of
the Jews with an analysis of the words Hitler initially used to describe his "solution" to the Jewish problem: *"Entfernung," "Aufräumung,"* and *"Beseitigung,"*
which mean "removal," "cleaning up," and "elimination," with increasing degrees of finality. She argues that "Hitler had from the beginning" resorted to
language whose meaning he intentionally made ambiguous; to be understood
both exoterically and esoterically. "'Removal' or 'elimination' could be understood to mean 'expulsion,' and no doubt some of Hitler's followers thought"
that's all he meant.

But when Hitler wrote in a 1919 letter to a Munich man named Gemlich
that "rational anti-Semitism . . . must lead to a systematic legal opposition and
elimination [*Beseitigung*] of the special privileges that Jews hold. . . . Its final objective must unswervingly be the removal [*Entfernung*] of the Jews altogether,"
Dawidowicz insists the "final objective" was clear in Hitler's mind: extermination, however ambiguous or less drastic it might have seemed to some readers
and listeners.

She cites a passage from a Hitler speech in which it seems he was, in a joking fashion, explicitly *disclaiming* extermination as a goal and finds, through

her "esoteric" analysis, evidence that he was, in fact, *communicating* the intent to exterminate to those in the know.

In August 1920, for instance, Hitler told an audience he favored "removal [*Entfernung*] of the Jews from our nation, not because we would begrudge them their existence—we congratulate the rest of the whole world on their company [great merriment], but because the existence of our own nation is a thousand times more important to us than that of an alien race." Dawidowicz insists that the true import of the remark is the opposite of its face-value meaning. She suggests that the irony and the "merriment," the laughter at it reported by the witness to the speech, was not at the ostensible "joke"—"We congratulate the rest of the whole world on their [the Jews'] company"—but actually at the *previous* phrase, "We do not begrudge them their existence." This Dawidowicz suggests is an "inside joke" for party members who know the secret meaning: that in fact they do "begrudge," they *are* dedicated to eradicating the Jews' existence. To Dawidowicz, "the ambiguity is calculated." Hitler was not disclaiming designs on the Jews' existence, he was posing an either/or dichotomy: "their existence" versus "the existence of our own nation."

Dawidowicz goes to impressive lengths of ratiocination to find, even in the denial or the elision of a reference to extermination, a determination to exterminate. For example, she cites an April 1922 speech in which Hitler declared, "there can be no compromise—there are only two possibilities: either victory of the Aryan or annihilation of the Aryan and the victory of the Jew." Noting that Hitler omitted from the paired antitheses "annihilation of the Jews," Dawidowicz argues this very elision was a "signal to the cognoscenti" of what Hitler *meant* to say. Then she reconstructs Hitler's actual quote to read what she believes is being said esoterically: "Either victory of the Aryan *and annihilation of the Jew* or annihilation of the Aryan and the victory of the Jew." While it might seem at times she is striving to find evidence for her thesis in the very absence of it, Ruth Wisse emphasized to me that Lucy Dawidowicz's contention about Hitler's intent and concealment of it does not depend on the ingenuity of Straussian esoteric analysis. "She understood, as a historian," Wisse wrote me, "that events as enormous as the destruction of one people by another have their roots *in history* and must be the culmination of an extended process." Her thesis grew out of history, Wisse argues, and her esoteric analysis was a way of exposing "that which Hitler and others had been keen to obscure" with esoteric duplicity.

The Dawidowicz argument gathers strength as she analyzes the self-conscious language Hitler used to describe his methods and his intentions once he assumed power.

Consider a fascinating address Hitler made to party insiders in April 1937 (about the very same time Lucy Dawidowicz was staring out her college seminar-room window at Columbia and realizing Wordsworth was not enough, with her world in flames). In his speech to a regional Nazi Party meeting, Hitler "addressed himself to the Jewish question [and] referred contemptuously to the insistent demands within the party for more action against the Jews, Dawidowicz writes. He assures them no one is more qualified to think about the disposition of the Jews—he knows where he's going, but he must employ Machiavellian tactical considerations to make sure he gets there: "The *final* aim of our whole policy is quite clear for all of us" (emphasis added), Hitler says,

> Always I am concerned only that I do not take any step from which I will perhaps have to retreat, and not to take a step that will harm us. I tell you that I always go to the outermost limits of risk, but never beyond. For this you need to have a nose more or less to smell out: "What can I still do." . . . In a struggle against an enemy[,] I do not summon an enemy with force to fight. I don't say: "Fight!" because I want to fight. Instead I say, "I will destroy you! And now, Wisdom, help me to maneuver you into the corner that you cannot fight back, and then you get the blow right in the heart."

It's a passage in which Hitler seems to be confiding to his insiders exactly the exoteric-esoteric two-track strategy Dawidowicz has conceived of him employing. There is no doubt, no hesitation, no wavering around his final goal: the destruction of the enemy. But he discloses to his confidants his intention to conceal from outsiders, from the enemy, the ultimate goal in order to take, one after another, cautious, intermediate steps toward it. Steps that will appear hesitant only to those not in the know; caution that will seem like trepidation only to those it's designed to deceive.

It is in this light, I believe, that the chief objection to the Dawidowicz thesis must be examined: the apparent seriousness with which Hitler allowed lower-echelon Nazi officials to proceed with plans for forced emigration and expulsion (rather than outright murder) of German Jews up until the time of the invasion of the Soviet Union in June 1941. As her literary executor Neal Kozodoy (now editor of *Commentary*) suggested to me in a discussion of this question, Lucy Dawidowicz was not portraying Hitler as oblivious to the need for caution, for craftiness, but as someone who sought the most radical solution feasible while carefully nurturing and often disguising his unchanging ultimate goal.

Of course, one could raise the question, Is Lucy Dawidowicz picking up on Hitler's *actual* master plan and his carefully calculated Machiavellian method of achieving it, or is she accepting at face value his self-aggrandizing posturing as a grand strategist—in which he tries to present what actually might be a less disciplined or decisive way of proceeding to his associates—*as if* he had a carefully calibrated grand design? But her account of the events of the year that follow that 1937 talk, the series of gradually escalated restrictions, deprivations, and indignities visited upon Germany's Jews (culminating in what she rightly regards as the deeply sinister decree requiring all Jews to assume the first names of Israel or Sarah—a constriction and extermination of individual Jewish identity to the point at which all Jews become the *same* Jew), paints a picture not of haphazard hostility and hesitant half-measures but rather of a relentless, carefully calibrated death by a thousand cuts.

It was a process she sees culminating in November 1938 in the notorious Kristallnacht nationwide mass pogrom. It's an event that some historians still see as a spontaneous outbreak of anti-Semitic violence, or one that was incited by Hitler's underlings without his full knowledge or approval. It's an event Dawidowicz sees as a perfect paradigm for the way Hitler's decisive but partially hidden role in the Holocaust was shrouded in deniability. As with the extermination to come, there was no written Hitler order for the Kristallnacht pogrom and no direct testimony of a verbal Hitler order either. But she sees the purportedly unexpected/unplanned outbreak of bloody violence against Jews in November 1938 serving a strategic purpose in Hitler's long-range calculations. And she sees his carefully hidden hand controlling the supposedly out-of-control violence.

Dawidowicz puts Kristallnacht in the context of the Munich Agreement two months earlier, in September 1938. Widely regarded as a diplomatic triumph for Hitler, it nonetheless meant that his undiminished drive for war as a final solution had stalled—"misfired," as she put it. She sees him seeking an opportunity for taking "drastic, but less visible, action against the Jews" when "an unexpected opportunity . . . opened up with the assassination on November 7, 1938, of Ernst vom Rath, a third secretary in the German embassy in Paris, by a seventeen-year-old Polish Jewish student, Herschel Grynszpan." Grynszpan's parents had been expelled into a stateless no-man's-land between Germany and Poland, where they were held in virtual concentration-camp conditions, a cruel imprisonment that drove their son to violence.

Just as with the absence of an extermination order, there is an absence of a Kristallnacht order: "Hitler himself never uttered a word publicly on vom Rath's assassination or on the events of the Kristallnacht," Dawidowicz notes. But while some have taken that public silence to indicate Hitler's ignorance, detachment, or disapproval of the violence that followed, while others have focused on conflicts among Göring and Goebbels and Himmler over how much to license or limit the destruction, Dawidowicz finds in Hitler's absence the hidden hand of a guiding presence.

She locates him in Munich at the Nazi Party's anniversary celebration of the 1923 putsch, having dinner on the night of Kristallnacht "with his old comrades . . . seen in prolonged conversation with Goebbels. Hitler usually delivered the main speech on this occasion, but this evening he left early. He had been overheard to say that 'the SA should be allowed to have a fling.'"

But she finds, once again, proof in absence: "His absence from the festivities was planned to exculpate him—and the government—from responsibility for the subsequent events. . . . Goebbels delivered an inflammatory exhortation to the assemblage, calling for 'spontaneous' demonstrations . . . and SA men took Goebbels' hints as he intended them to be taken: Jewish blood was to flow for the death of vom Rath."

The pattern, to Dawidowicz, is clear: Hitler's absence, the absence of a Hitler order, concealed beneath an official exculpating surface the esoteric truth: Hitler's instructions to Goebbels to see to it that Jewish blood was spilled. Most historians have taken the exculpatory scenario at face value and have focused on a cabinet meeting in Berlin shortly thereafter, where, in the face of outraged world reaction at the primal violence, Göring and others express how shocked, *shocked* they were at the extent of the damage, the irrationality of the violence. The finger-pointing among underlings in the aftermath masked, Dawidowicz argues, Hitler's decisive role as instigator and his little-known but decisive intervention as the violence spread: When SS chief Himmler sought to intervene to moderate Goebbels's incitement of the thuggish SA, Hitler stopped Himmler from interfering and permitted Goebbels to continue to fan the flames, fulfilling Hitler's deniability-screened desires.

With Kristallnacht's absent presence as a model, Dawidowicz proceeds to examine the deadly chain of euphemism that has similarly, she believes, continued to deceive historians about Hitler's intentions and Hitler's role in the Final Solution decision. She proceeds to make her case that the war Hitler prepared to launch in 1939 was not a war against the Poles but the first step in his larger objective: the war against the Jews. She begins with a little-known private declaration she's unearthed in her search of the archival and memoir sources: a remarkable quote from Hitler, a declaration he made privately in early January 1939 to Foreign Minister Chvalkovsky of the Nazi-puppet Czech government, in which Hitler flatly stated: "We are going to destroy the Jews." A remark which Hitler follows by tracing his determination to do so to the decision date Dawidowicz favors: "They [the Jews] are not going to get away with what they did on November 9, 1918. The day of reckoning has come." This is a remark made in confidence, an esoteric disclosure that did not come to light until after the war.

It must be remembered that there is a powerful school of thought (best exemplified in A.J.P. Taylor's book *The Origins of the Second World War*) that seeks to see Hitler as a somewhat more fanatic but still basically conventional

European statesman whose goals in the period leading up to the 1939 war were "traditional ones": power, expansion of territory and influence, and access to markets. But here in Hitler's remark to the Czech minister is the key linkage Dawidowicz clearly believes vindicates her belief that Hitler formed his intention in 1918—and that his real goals were not traditional foreign policy ones, with war as a last resort. But rather, that his goal was *always* war—war against the Jews.

The esoteric truth he confided to his Czech puppet was confidential, but twenty-nine days later, she points out, Hitler made a now-famous speech in which he made public a threat to destroy the Jews, a destruction he linked to the beginning of a war about to come, one that focused on, of all things, the Jews' laughter.

In a speech to the Reichstag in Berlin on January 30, 1939, the sixth anniversary of his assumption of power, Hitler made what Dawidowicz calls his "declaration of war against the Jews":

> And one more thing I would like now to state on this day memorable perhaps not only for us Germans. I have often been a prophet in my life and was generally *laughed* at. During my struggle for power, the Jews primarily received with *laughter* my prophecies that I would someday assume the leadership of the state and thereby of the entire Volk and then, among many other things, achieve a solution of the Jewish problem. *I suppose . . . the then resounding laughter of Jewry in Germany is now choking in their throats.*
>
> Today I will be a prophet again: If international finance Jewry within Europe and abroad should succeed once more in plunging the peoples into a world war, then the consequences will be not the Bolshevization of the world and therewith a victory of Jewry, but on the contrary, the destruction of the Jewish race in Europe [emphasis added].

One senses in this focus on laughter something very *close* to Hitler, something at the heart of the way he personalized his war against the Jews. It's there in the savage satisfaction he feels in imagining, quite graphically, the "resounding laughter of Jewry . . . now choking in their throats."

And, one wonders, which Jews were laughing at Hitler? Some might have underestimated him, thinking of him as a provincial pogromist rather than a world-bestriding figure. But was there, really, a lot of laughter among Jews, whom all-too-recent history had taught that even provincial pogromists (like those in Poland and Russia) can succeed in slaughtering innocent families?

Can we imagine Hitler genuinely wounded by the imagined laughter of the Jews? Or is it the counterfeit of outrage? And is the laughter he conjures up so obsessively when he discusses the extermination of the Jews not so much the Jews' laughter but his own?

In an absolutely brilliant, utterly fascinating, nearly page-long footnote to her account of that speech—to my mind the single most thought-provoking footnote in Hitler-explanation literature—Dawidowicz, with her eagle eye for explicatory resonances, adduces no fewer than three further instances in which Hitler links the laughter of the Jews to their extermination. Instances in which, over a period of two years, Hitler paints the ongoing story of the extermination process in the esoteric language of laughter.

It's a portrait that emerges almost unremarked upon explicitly by Dawidowicz in her pursuit of one of her most impressive feats of explication. In it, she finds Hitler betraying the central truth about himself, the inmost motive for his war, in a series of curious "slips," as she calls them. She adduces the slips to deal with a potentially troubling challenge to her grand thesis—that the war Hitler waged against the nations he invaded was really a cover for his real objective: the war against the Jews.

The specific problem she's addressing is again an apparent absence: In Hitler's September 1, 1939, speech to the Reichstag, his declaration of war against Poland hours after the blitzkrieg had begun, he doesn't declare war against the Jews. In fact, as she notes, "It was one of the few speeches in which he failed to mention Jews."

At this point, Dawidowicz discloses a remarkable strategy for explaining this absence: the "slips" in his *future* references to that September 1939 speech that disclose what he was really doing. No less than four times in the three years following the September 1939 declaration of war, "Hitler fixedly and repeatedly referred to *this* speech on *this* day [the one in which he omitted mention of the Jews] as the speech in which he had threatened the Jews with destruction in the event of a war, though he had made *that* speech on January 30, 1939."

She then proceeds to quote in that footnote from those four "slips" and goes on to conclude that "in [Hitler's] mind he associated his declaration of war on September 1, 1939, with his promise to destroy the Jews."

But what stayed with me in the footnote, in which she quotes extensively from the "slips," is not merely Hitler "fixedly and repeatedly" referring to the Jews in that speech when they weren't there, but Hitler fixedly and repeatedly returning to their *laughter.*

And so, on January 30, 1941, Hitler told an audience, "And I should not like to forget the indication that I had already given once, on September 1, 1939 . . . to wit, that if the rest of the world would be plunged into a general war by Jewry, then the whole of Jewry would have finished playing its role in Europe!" A threat he actually made seven months earlier, on January 30,

1939, when he threatened the Jews with extermination *if* there was a war. That seems to matter less to Hitler in this 1941 address than the laughter he still seems to hear echoing: "They may still laugh today at that, exactly as they laughed at my [other] prophecies. The coming months and years will prove that I also saw correctly here."

Then once again, a year later, on September 30, 1942, he fuses or confuses the date of the threat against the Jews and the declaration of war against the Poles:

> On September 1, 1939, I stated . . . at the meeting then of the Reichstag: . . .
>
> That if Jewry would plot an international world war for the annihilation of the Aryan peoples of Europe, then not the Aryan peoples would be annihilated, but on the contrary Jewry. . . . The Jews laughed once also in Germany at my prophecies. I do not know if they are still laughing also today, or if their laughter has not already subsided. But I can also now only assert: Their laughter everywhere will subside.

And then, finally, a third time, the exact same slip, the obsessive reference to the laughter, the final, most chilling in a series of passages in which the dying of the Jews can be traced in the subsiding and dying of the laughter in Hitler's ironic image of the slaughter. Here, once again, he refers to the Reichstag speech in which he says he

> declared: If Jewry perchance imagines that it can bring about an international world war for the annihilation of the European races, then the consequence will be not the annihilation of the European races, but on the contrary, it will be the annihilation of Jewry in Europe. I was always laughed at as a prophet. *Of those who laughed then, countless ones no longer laugh today, and those who still laugh now will perhaps in a while also no longer do so* [emphasis added].

It is possible, then, to reconstruct Hitler's personal portrait of his extermination of the Jews in the progression of his chilling images of laughter—the extermination of the Jews in the extermination of their laughter.

We begin with his January 30, 1939, speech, in which the "resounding" laughter of the Jews is now resoundingly choking in their throats. In 1941, he imagines the laughter of the Jews still sounding, if not resounding, but "the coming months" will change that. And twelve months later, he professes no longer to *know* if the Jews "are still laughing." But whether they are or not, he says he's confident "if their laughter has not already subsided," it soon "will subside" everywhere. And, finally, he confirms for us that not only the laughter but those who once laughed have been exterminated: "Countless ones no longer laugh today, and those who still laugh now will perhaps in a while also no longer do so."

Dawidowicz cites these passages for the "slips," not for the laughter, for Hitler's retrospective fusion of the January 30, 1939, threat to annihilate the Jews with the September 1, 1939, declaration of war that launched his armies east and made Auschwitz possible. But it might be argued that the laughter imagery is itself a kind of slip, the kind of slip that vindicates Dawidowicz's thesis about Hitler more powerfully than his confusion or conflation of dates of declarations and speeches. It seems to vindicate her vision of Hitler as someone who knew always what he wanted to do with the Jews, not someone who hesitated and doubted and suffered nervousness about the enormity of the idea. Rather someone who knew what he was doing and laughed about it.

The unspoken displacement in these passages is, I'd suggest, not so much from one speech date to another, but from one species of laughter to another. The laughter Hitler incessantly conjures up dying in the Jews' throats is reborn in his own. The laughter suffusing those passages is not the Jews laughing but Hitler laughing. It's not the laughter of someone suffering from trepidation about what he's doing. It's not the laughter of someone who still, at an even later date, could think, "*My dear Heinie . . . Would it be possible?*"

It's the laughter of someone who knows what he's doing and relishes it to the bone, relishes the coded way he speaks of it, relishes the fact that the relish of the joke is only shared by an esoteric few. It's the very same relish with which he and Heydrich and Himmler, the three architects of the Final Solution, relish their ostensible dismay at the scurrilous "rumor" that the Jews are being exterminated, in that passage in the Table Talk in which the chief perpetrators of the Holocaust share a private joke about both their complicity and their cover-up.

Nor is this the laughter of someone "convinced of his own rectitude," as Trevor-Roper would have it. It's the laughter of someone savoring a secretive triumph, whose pleasure is clearly enhanced by an awareness of its profoundly *illicit* nature, whose pleasure can only be truly savored by the cognoscenti aware of the magnitude of the illicit acts that are concealed by esoteric references to mass murder as "subsiding laughter." This is not something whose "enormity" Hitler feared, but something he relished, with obscene gleefulness.

Once, I heard a parable about a Jew going into battle who asks a rabbi what he should do if he's captured by the enemy and his only alternative to starvation is to eat pork. The rabbi counsels him that, yes, to save his life he can do what would otherwise be a transgression, an enormity: He can eat the pork. But don't, the rabbi adds, relish it: "Don't suck the bone." With his laughter, the laughter he sucked from the dying Jews' throats, Hitler was expressing his obscene relish at the enormity of his transgression. With his laughter, Hitler reveals extermination is not a matter of rectitude to him, a difficult task done for a stern ideal. With his laughter, Hitler reveals he is both aware of and wallowing in the illicitness of his transgression, his conscious evil. With his laughter he is "sucking the bone."

And what exactly is he relishing so deeply? Not merely the thing in itself, the mass murder, but the delicious—to him—irony of it, the exquisite—to him—literary irony that those who laughed are now having their murders measured out in the sound of their subsiding laughter by the very one they laughed at. In a way, it is a confirmation of Berel Lang's thesis that it is in the savoring of the slaughter as an aesthetic experience, in the perpetrators' relishing its piquant artful ironies, that the highest degree of conscious evil discloses itself.

This chapter began with the question, Did Hitler feel shame, or did he at least, as Browning seems to believe, display an awareness of the enormity of his decision, an awareness that expresses itself in "sincere" hesitation, trepidation? In fact, one comes away from immersion in Lucy Dawidowicz's powerful argument feeling that shamelessness rather than shame, that shameless laughter rather than trepidation, is what Hitler experienced inwardly (and outwardly as well: The Goebbels diaries are replete with entries reporting how the two of them shared laughter at the fate of their enemies). And that it might not be an exaggeration to think that, had he known how some scholarship a half century after his death had come to portray him—as a sensitive, trepidatious soul—he might enjoy one final shameless laugh.

How does one react to the laughing Hitler, to the degree of shamelessness and knowingness, the obscene delight he appears to take in relishing the prospect of extermination, one strangled laugh at a time?

It might be argued that a half century's attempts to "explain" Hitler have served in some sense to avoid confronting the specter of that Hitler, the laughing Hitler, a Hitler fully conscious of his malignancy. A half century of efforts have added to, broadened, deepened, contextualized, historicized our vision of Hitler in many valuable—though also contradictory—ways. But in doing so, they may also have distanced and distracted us from his person, from his personal responsibility, his desire, the fact that, as Milton Himmelfarb put it, he didn't *have* to kill the Jews, he wasn't merely compelled by abstract forces—rather, he chose to, he *wanted* to.

The tendency of contemporary explanation has been to explain away Hitler's personal responsibility, his conscious agency (as academics like to call it these days), to explain it away by postulating either that his will wasn't decisive (if he hadn't done it, deep forces in history would have compelled someone else

like him to do it). Or that he didn't really *have* the will. He didn't make the decision, or he wasn't sure of the decision, or he shrank from making the decision,
or he felt conflicted, awed into Hamlet-like impotence by the enormity of the
decision. Or that the decision was "produced" or spontaneously "generated"
somehow by "others," by "his inner circle," by the "bureaucracy," or by the
exigency of underlings who forced it on him "from below."

All are sincerely held beliefs, and I've found many of them at times more or
less persuasive on their own terms. But stepping back from them, one could also
say they serve as consolations, ways of avoiding having to face the inexplicable
horror of a knowing, laughing Hitler. By diminishing Hitler, by explaining him
as a pawn of "deeper," more abstract forces, as an automaton programmed
by ideology, bureaucracy, or dialectical materialism, programmed to embody
and carry out "the inevitable," his laughter at our expense is less woundingly
triumphal, more the deluded laughter of the ventriloquist's dummy whose
strings are being pulled by abstract forces—who gives the false impression of
being in control. Alternately, a more hesitant, conflicted Hitler might be easier
to live with because we "know" he suffered doubts, was racked by indecision,
tormented by trepidation. He couldn't *really* be laughing so triumphantly,
aware as he was of the enormity of what he was doing, more fearfully awed
than laughingly exhilarated by the crime he was committing.

It may not be that those who diminish Hitler and Hitler's agency do so *in
order* to comfort themselves. It might just be that the tendency of intellectual
effort expended on any enigmatic subject will always be to complexify until
everyone and everything is responsible and no one person, not even Hitler, is.

One response to this is Claude Lanzmann's extreme rejection of *all* explanation as ultimately exculpating. Another might be the employment of Emil
Fackenheim's "double move": to pursue explanation as far as it takes us but at
the same time, at another level, to *resist* explanation, or at least the kind of explanation that would give Hitler a "posthumous victory" by exculpating him,
blaming his evil on a bad family, a bad society, a Jew in his past, a perversion in
his sexuality, malignant ideas, malign historical forces.

Fackenheim's notion of "posthumous victory" suggests that, much as
we would like to understand Hitler, it is important to realize that we should in
some sense also still be at war with him. And there might be some value to continuing to resist, even to hate, the enemy. Is hatred of Hitler still a legitimate
response, or is it the kind of crude, debased emotional reaction that explanation and understanding should ideally lead us upward from? Is it bizarre, out-
of-bounds, a sign of an unevolved sensibility, for a civilized, educated citizen of
the post-Holocaust world to hate Adolf Hitler? Put another way: Would it be a
bizarre moral failure *not* to hate Hitler?

The notion of hatred, the question of whether hating Hitler and explaining Hitler are mutually contradictory, arose in a fascinating conversation I had with Milton Himmelfarb, whom I sought out after discovering the laughing Hitler figure in Lucy Dawidowicz's footnote.

Ever since I came upon it back in 1984, I had been impressed by the thought-provoking power of Himmelfarb's "No Hitler, No Holocaust" polemic in *Commentary*. It was responsible, as much as any work, for impelling me to look more closely at how we conceive of Hitler, and I'd wanted to ask him what had prompted him to take that stance—Hitler killed the Jews not because he had to, not because he was driven by "deeper" forces, but because he *wanted* to—at that particular time.

In the living room of his White Plains, New York, home, in his characteristically earthy, no-nonsense manner, which masks a subtle and discerning intellect, Himmelfarb told me he'd been troubled back then by an emerging tendency in the Hitler literature, even—particularly—among Jews. A tendency to downplay Hitler's personal animus against Jews as the motive engine of the Holocaust, to "broaden" and "universalize" the tragedy. He thought that what was really at work beneath this was a kind of embarrassment among Jews at being singled out for such murderous hatred, a reluctance to accept explanations that were, in Himmelfarb's colorful phrase, "too Jewy." There was, he believed, a desire instead to conceive of it as a more universal tragedy, Hitler's hatred as another horrific instance of man's inhumanity to man, as the saying goes—rather than a very personal, very specific hatred of Jews.

The question of whether Jews, whether anyone, should hate Hitler arose toward the end of our conversation in the context of a larger discussion of the question of "exceptionalism": the deep divide in Hitler-explanation literature between those who argue that Hitler can be explained by or integrated into systems of explanation we're already familiar with, systems used to explain other tragedies in history. And those who believe Hitler is a singularity, an exception not explicable in terms of what has been experienced before. The argument over "exceptionalism" can be found throughout intellectual history. "American exceptionalism" is the belief or the sentimental hope that the American experience would not have to recapitulate the sorrows of European history, become a predetermined consequence of that past, but could be a fresh start. Shakespearean exceptionalism is the argument that there is something distinctive about Shakespeare that elevates his work above the rest of great literature.

Emil Fackenheim, as we've seen, makes an exceptionalist argument about Hitler and human nature: You cannot locate Hitler on the ordinary continuum of human nature; you cannot merely say that he is a very, very, very, very, very bad man, perhaps the most wicked yet, but still explicable as the product of the same human nature, the same psychological forces that produced, say, the next-worst human being and the next and the next until we reach ourselves.

No, Fackenheim says, Hitler is off the charts, off that grid, in another category of radical evil entirely.

Himmelfarb arrived at the subject of exceptionalism—and hatred—in the course of a discussion not of Hitler but of Stalin, the historical figure many place next to Hitler on that continuum of evil. Stalin remains a figure of some importance in Himmelfarb's own political evolution. When I spoke with him, he was seventy-six, still scrappy, still intellectually combative in the inimitable manner of that famous core group of Jewish leftists in the thirties, the Trotsky-ites and Stalinists who later renounced their dialectical materialism and be-came the core group behind the anticommunist liberalism of the 1950s and the neoconservatism of the seventies and eighties. Himmelfarb had been a Marxist as a youth, although he later joined his sister Gertrude Himmelfarb, now an influential social historian, and her future husband, Irving Kristol, in the ranks of the neocons.

Himmelfarb had been even more of an enthusiastic leftist partisan than his future brother-in-law, he told me. He had been a devotee of the ultimate abstract system of "scientific" historical explanation, dialectical materialism, in which nothing could be considered an exception. Every phenomenon in his-tory and human consciousness was an almost mathematically determinable product of its place in the dialectic of the class struggle. Hitler, then, was a nec-essary stage of the consolidation and ultimate collapse of capitalism, which would inevitably produce, or midwife, the dictatorship of the proletariat whose advance guard was embodied in Stalin's Russia.

Himmelfarb and I were sipping tea in the chilly kitchen of his large, drafty frame house in White Plains (a hardy sort, he kept the house largely unheated despite the deep freeze outside). His wife was kind enough to hook up a port-able heater for us between the kitchen table and the stove, where he brewed tea. The afternoon light was dying, and the talk was about Stalin, and the scene had a kind of Russian, even Dostoyevskian, feel as we approached the question of hatred.

We were discussing comparative evil, the relative status of Hitler and Stalin on the continuum, and what criteria one used to judge such impossible ques-tions. I had recently read the historian Robert Conquest's powerful account of Stalin's crimes. No historian has been harsher in his judgment of Stalin. But Conquest would later tell me that—if forced to make a comparison between the two—he'd have to say, however hesitantly and subjectively, that Hitler's degree of evil "just feels worse" than Stalin's. While Himmelfarb is unsparing of Hitler, to say the least, he spoke scathingly that afternoon of those who still resist seeing the full dimensions of Stalin's near Hitler-like level of evil.

"The reason people refused to see Stalin for what he was," Himmelfarb said, "may have been a question of professional deformation [Himmelfarb's rather harsh translation of the more forgiving French phrase for a character-istic habit of thought—*deformation professionelle*]. They wanted to apply the universal political-science categories, economics categories, to what was going on, so that it was left to the Solzhenitsyns to tell you what the gulag was. But he was kind of dismissed—'His books don't have the methodological rigor,' they said. 'It's anecdotal, it doesn't tell us about the *system.*'"

"Because what Solzhenitsyn was saying," I suggested, "was something so much darker than 'It's a flawed system,' or 'Stalin wasn't being true to Marx-ism.' Solzhenitsyn was saying, 'No, this is hell on earth,' and the gulag, like the concentration camps, doesn't fit into the explanatory categories which take the system seriously?"

In response, Himmelfarb tells me a story of meeting "a poet named Shlomo Dykman, a Hebrew poet and a classicist who translated into Hebrew the *Aeneid*. And it wasn't easy, because Hebrew doesn't lend itself to—" He begins reciting from memory the opening lines of that epic (a tale of escape from a kind of ancient-world holocaust), in perfectly inflected classical Latin. "Dykman came to Israel as a refugee from a Soviet gulag, where he'd been imprisoned since the Russians took over eastern Poland. He spent many, many years in the gulag. He quoted to me the words of a Lubavitch Hasid whom he met in the gulag. The Hasid said in Yiddish, 'This country is such a country! *It would be a mitzvah to leave it by train, on a Yom Kippur that fell on a Saturday!*'"

Himmelfarb laughed. "I'm not sure how you translate this for a political scientist." (It's a dual violation to travel on a holy day Sabbath.)

"It's an exceptionalism he's talking about, isn't it?" I suggest. "It's the kind of country so irredeemably horrible you make exceptions to the holiest com-mandments to leave it behind. And I guess that's what you are saying about Hitler in 'No Hitler, No Holocaust': He was not just the product of a bad system or a bad country, he's not just a manifestation of forces we're familiar with—"

"And it isn't even that the Germans were an especially evil people or espe-cially disposed to killing Jews," he says.

"It wasn't that the *Germans* were the exception, it was that *Hitler* was the exception?"

"Yeah," he said, "that's my take on it. And I think it's yours, isn't it?"

A good question. Until that moment I might not have been ready to ac-knowledge my allegiance to one party or another in this most primal of Hitler-explanation controversies—the exceptionalism question. But the moment Himmelfarb said that—"I think it's [your position] too"—I sensed there was some truth to his observation. With some modifications: I might argue that if I'm an exceptionalist, it's more by default than a metaphysical conviction that Hitler could never be explained by rational means. After spending nearly a decade examining the often ambitious and often inadequate claims by rival schools and scholars to have explained Hitler, I don't think he *has* been explained, but, on the other hand, I'm not convinced he is, categorically, inexplicable. I tend to agree with Yehuda Bauer that we suffer from an absence of sufficient evidence on most key questions. Although I'm not sure I have Bauer's confidence that if we did have sufficient facts we *would* be able to explain Hitler. I wouldn't rule out the possibility that even with all the evidence in hand we still might find ourselves as mystified by Hitler as Emil Fackenheim believes we would be.

I'd take a more cautious position, steeped in the doctrine of "negative capability" and epistemological skepticism: that we cannot be sure that, even with all the facts in the world in our hands, Hitler might not still in some way escape us, escape comprehension. That there's no way for us to know whether Bauer or Fackenheim is correct about Hitler's knowability. That we may forever be consigned to a deeply disturbing sense of doubt, forever haunted by Hitler's elusiveness.

Still, if we can't say for sure whether Hitler is metaphysically explicable, it's hard to deny he is exceptional, in the sense that, as of now, he has not been pinned to anyone's grid.

How does one react to an exception like Hitler? I asked Himmelfarb his thoughts on the question of demonization. The failure, the impossibility of explaining Hitler in terms of human nature led Fackenheim to characterize Hitler as "an eruption of demonism into history." Certain scholars have disparaged what they call a tendency to "demonize" Hitler, to make him an ultimate exception to historical explanation. The charge of demonization is sometimes hurled at any attempt to examine Hitler's personal responsibility, which is sometimes regarded as an unsophisticated response, one that ignores powerful systemic, historical explanations that make Hitler less a powerful figure of evil than a pawn of those forces.

I asked Himmelfarb what he thought of those who disparage "demonizing."

"What do you mean 'demonize'?" he exclaimed. "You mean he's a run-of-the-mill bad guy and we give him a tail and horns?"

In a sense, I said: "It means putting Hitler in some unique exceptional category of evil, beyond precedent."

"Well," he said, "those who call that demonizing are simply accepting some version of A.J.P. Taylor's thesis that Hitler was a statesman with goals like any other. Or the political scientists who say he was an accidental agent of the necessary transformation of German society. And that to focus on him personally is to lose sight of the larger truth, don't be distracted by personalities. But I don't think he *was* a statesman. I don't think he was an accidental agent. I think he was an evil man, an evil genius."

"Some people are reluctant to use the word 'evil.'"

He responds by telling me a story about Leo Strauss, the political philosopher. "I was not a disciple of Strauss, just met him a few times, but a philosopher friend of mine told me this story. How he'd told Strauss he was going to Germany—this was after the war. And he told Strauss he was going to see—what's his name?" Himmelfarb asks me, feigning (I think) forgetting the name in order to take malicious delight in phrasing the question this way: "You know, Hannah Arendt's Nazi boyfriend?"

"Heidegger?"

"Yes. My friend told Strauss that Heidegger had written him inviting him to visit." This was even before the full extent of Heidegger's Hitler-era sycophancy and his unrepentant stance after the war were fully known. "And Strauss told my friend, '*Don't go!*' Now, there was no more subtle mind than Leo Strauss. But *he hated Nazis!*" says Himmelfarb, voice rising nearly to a shout. "He wasn't sophisticated about it. *He hated Nazis!* He was a Jew. That was one very important reason why he hated Nazis. He was a political philosopher, but he was a Jew, and *he hated Nazis!* That doesn't detract from his sophistication."

Himmelfarb almost seems to be saying that it is, in fact, the culmination of a *truer* sophistication to be able to hate Hitler, a sophistication that doesn't fall prey to the pseudosophisticated snares of explanation as exculpation, of explanation as abstraction away from Hitler's personal agency. Hatred as not that which one *starts* with, rather as something one ends up with: the product of a *deeper* understanding. A less inflammatory word than "hatred" might be "resistance." It's the word Emil Fackenheim used when he described the "double move" one must make in attempting to explain Hitler: to seek explanation but also to resist explanation.

Not to resist all or any inquiry, not to resist thought, but to resist the misleading exculpatory corollaries of explanation. To resist the way explanation can become evasion or consolation, a way of making Hitler's choice to do what he did less unbearable, less hateful to contemplate, by shifting responsibility from him to faceless abstractions, inexorable forces, or irresistible compulsions that gave him no choice or made his choice irrelevant. To resist making the kind of explanatory excuses for Hitler that permit him to *escape*, that grant him the posthumous victory of a last laugh.

AFTERWORD TO
THE UPDATED EDITION

Why Hitler Lost the War. Or Did He?

The debates over the "true nature" of Hitler and Hitler's crimes may never come to rest. They haven't in the fifteen years since *Explaining Hitler* was first published. But if I had to choose the most significant—and dramatic—recent contribution to the most central debate, it would be an essay on Hitler's war aims by Sir Richard Evans, author of *The Third Reich at War,* who has become one of the most authoritative sources on the subject.

Published in the December 12, 2013, issue of the *New York Review of Books,* Evans's essay reasons its way back from Hitler's conduct of the war, and the German military defeat, to say something important about who Hitler was. Something that had been, in essence, argued by Hugh Trevor-Roper and Lucy Dawidowicz, as one can read in this book. But Evans sharpens the point and reminds us of what I think some historians and intellectuals have lost sight of.

Evans's essay is entitled "What the War Was Really About" and you could think of it as Evans's Hitler explanation. One that puts him at one side of what has been perhaps the longest-running schism in "Hitler studies" as Don DeLillo called the field.

Ostensibly it's a review of a book by Yale's Paul Kennedy—one that claims the key to the Allied victory had less to do with some flaw within Hitler, in the Nazis, or in their war plans, than with Allied superiority in technology (Kennedy's title: *Engineers of Victory: The Problem Solvers Who Turned the Tide in the Second World War*). Evans offers respect to many of Kennedy's observations but advances a very different thesis, one that takes us to the very cutting edge, the state of the art of the argumentation about Hitler.

Evans goes beyond the Kennedy thesis to look at other, rival, explanations for Hitler's military defeat, and in so doing reveals just how unresolved so much about the interpretation of Hitler and the Holocaust still is. Was it the Allies' superiority in economic resources that gave them victory? Evans joins Kennedy in rejecting "the crude economic determinism" of that claim. Was it the Allies' remarkable success in cracking the German military codes with the now famous "Enigma" machine? Again, that played a part, Evans believes, but code-breaking has been given a glamorous triumphalist history which, he points out, ignores Allied intelligence failures and German intelligence successes. Was it the Allies' weapons and technological superiority, as Kennedy suggests? "In the end this made little difference," Evans asserts. "German science and technology were second to none in their capacity to innovate," Evans argues.

Then what was it? Evans points to one factor more than any other: the often misunderstood nature of Hitler's war aims. He states his conclusion with finality: For Hitler this was not an ordinary war, "This was a racial war in which the extermination of six million European Jews, not dealt with at all in Kennedy's book because it did not seem to belong to the normal arsenal of military strategy, was a paramount war aim."

"A racial war": In other words, what the late Lucy Dawidowicz called "the war against the Jews" (in her book of that title) was of greater importance to Hitler than the war against the Allies. That was "what the war was really about." And that, according to Evans, more than anything was why Germany lost the war.

The most cited instance of the practical effect of this assessment of Hitler's mind-set was Hitler's continued refusal to allow redeployment (to resupply his crumbling front lines) of the trains crammed full of Jews rolling ceaselessly, relentlessly, to the death camps. (An affirmation of the remarkably prescient insight of the late historian Raul Hilberg: that so much of the truth of what went on can be found in the railway schedules.)

For Hitler, it was not a matter of making the trains run on time so much as making the trains never stop running to Auschwitz and Treblinka. One relatively new aspect of Holocaust study is the horror that happened when the trains finally did have to stop running because the Russians were about to overrun the mainly Polish-based camps. The full story, much of which was new to me, can be found in Daniel Blatman's 2011 work, *The Death Marches: The Final Phase of Nazi Genocide* (Harvard University Press).

When the camps were disbanded, the large SS and native Polish and Ukrainian guard troops feeding the gas chambers were not redeployed to stave off the Russians. Instead they were ordered to take all the living and half-dead captives on the road in what became the final phase of the Final Solution: the Death Marches. Hundreds of thousands closely guarded, mercilessly beaten, and shot when they couldn't keep up, starved to death while being harried along icy roads to . . . where? There was no sanctuary left safe for killing, but the killing had to continue at all costs. In some ways at least as, if not more, disgusting than at the camps themselves, the Death March commanders didn't have to "follow orders." They had incorporated Hitlerism so deeply, they *wanted* to follow orders. As Evans argues, killing Jews was more important than military objectives. They risked their own lives to continue the murder.

What's worse, Blatman reports, is that not just military men but civilians along the way who gleefully took part in murdering the half-dead Jews. For those, like me, who thought it impossible to be further shocked by Hitler's willing accomplices, reading about the Death Marches introduced a new level of horror.

It is a testament to how deeply dyed the souls of the killers were. Hitler was possessed, some might say, but he was the cause of possession in others. It seems to me a remarkable vindication of what Trevor-Roper argued in the immediate aftermath of the war when he described Hitler as more than anything a messianic "true believer" in his anti-Semitism. A position at first countered by Alan Bullock and others (such as A.J.P. Taylor), who tried to see him as more a cynical "mountebank," an actor, a charlatan, a "realist politician" even (Taylor), who merely used his Jew-hatred opportunistically for popular support.

Though Bullock conceded to me that he had eventually come round to a version of Trevor-Roper's position: Hitler was an actor who came to be possessed by his own act to the point of self-destruction. Bullock also adduced a connection between Hitler's messianic vision of himself as racial savior and the loss of the war. Hitler's suicidal prohibition against even a tactical retreat, such as the one that might have saved his Sixth Army from capture at Stalingrad, was—Bullock believed—a self-inflicted defeat entirely due to his delusion of a messianic destiny that would not be denied or even countenance the idea of a minor tactical retreat. He fell under his own spell.

Yet astonishingly there are those such as Kennedy who somehow think the Jew-hatred—the continent-wide messianic project of extermination "not dealt with at all in Kennedy's book"—was irrelevant to Hitler's conduct of the war.

There is one respect in which I would take Evans's characterization further. A point that Lucy Dawidowicz makes in Chapter 20: Hitler *didn't* lose the war. Not the war Evans, I'd say persuasively, argues was most important to him: the racial war. He won that war. Six million to one. Yes, he committed suicide at the end. (And yes, 50 million others lost their lives so he could win the part of the war he cared about most. Collateral damage.)

Thinking about that suicide now, in the light of 9/11 and the subsequent exaltations of suicide bombing on messianic, theological grounds, does in fact offer a radical new way of characterizing Hitler. In retrospect at least, it's tempting to argue that Hitler was, if not the first, then by far history's *greatest* single suicide bomber. He blew up Europe to kill the Jews in it, even if it meant killing himself and tens of millions of others in the end.

Thinking about Evans's essay, I couldn't help recall a watershed moment for me in writing this book, the one that made me realize how the attempt to explain Hitler involves the attempt to explain evil itself.

It was in the midst of my conversation with Trevor-Roper at the Oxford and Cambridge Club. Trevor-Roper's *The Last Days of Hitler* has remained a landmark early study of the man. It was a retrospective view built upon the physical evidence and the eyewitness testimonies to Hitler's "spell"—what fatal magnetism kept so many down in the doomed bunker to the bitter end? In the process of interviewing the survivors (scouring the bunker and Berlin in the immediate aftermath of the defeat), he conjured up a vision of a strange mesmeric talent and a single unshakable mission. He found, among other documents, Hitler's "Last Will and Testament," which he described as a defining document. It called on the German people to never cease fighting "the eternal poisoners of the world," the Jews, thus defining himself with his last words as a man who held one mission above all else.

In any case, I decided to ask Trevor-Roper what I feared might seem a simplistic question but turned out to be a gateway to the entire realm of the philosophy of evil and its theodicy: "Do you think Hitler knew," I asked Trevor-Roper, "that he was doing wrong when he committed his crimes?"

"Absolutely not," Trevor-Roper said with asperity. "He was convinced of his own rectitude." The logic of this, traceable back to Socrates, is that evil is impossible because those who commit evil *acts* always believe they are doing good, however mistaken they might be. Only in literature, in Iago ("motiveless malignancy"—Coleridge) or Richard III, do we find those who commit evil for the pleasure of it, for the hell of it. Many of my encounters in the book are taken up with the ramifications of this question. Since writing the book, I've come to believe more strongly that evil is not a concept to be dispensed with, but that what we call evil inheres in ideas, in ideologies that motivate the commission of evil acts, under the guise of providing for the collective good. The real question is what heightens susceptibility to evil ideas? More on this, but first:

What We Can Learn from the *Downfall* Parodies

One critic described *Explaining Hitler* as, in part, about "the cultural processes by which we try to come to terms with history." How have we succeeded and failed since *Explaining Hitler* was published? How has the image of Hitler (and our perception of the reality) evolved? Forgive me, but I must begin with what can only be called a meme.

I'm speaking of what may be the single most replicated moving image of Adolf Hitler on the planet. For the past five years, for better or worse, it has been the most frequent way that Adolf Hitler has been brought back to life in the new century: as a YouTube parody meme, the one based on a four-minute clip from the German film *Downfall*, featuring Bruno Ganz as Hitler in a raving, demented, and deluded rant delivered in the Berlin bunker when he finally realizes all hope for military survival is lost.

If you're not among the half billion or so viewers of one of the scores of variations of this meme, the parody aspect comes from the fake subtitles Photoshopped onto the clips. The new subtitles have Hitler raging, not about the crumbling of the Russian front, but about, shall we say, lesser things. Things of more contemporary and trivial relevance. To cite a few examples, there are parodies with titles like "Hitler Rants About New PlayStation 4 Defects," "Hitler Rants About Being Taken by a Nigerian E-mail Scam," and "Hitler Rants About Kanye West Interrupting Taylor Swift's VMA Acceptance Speech."

The demonic reduced to the trivial. But the genius of the parodies is that *they trivialize the trivialization.* For their effect they depend on Hitler occupying a preeminent place in the hierarchy of evil, and in some peculiar but effective way they restore "the real Hitler" to a place beyond capture by pop culture or web snark. Even Bruno Ganz has praised their "creativity."

"The Real Hitler." Of course, that is the problem. That is the question without out a satisfying answer. Something we may not fully know but something upon which we project our worst conception of humanity. Even if we know not the explanation, we know there is something there that has to be contended with, incorporated into our view of history and human nature. But at a perhaps irrecoverable distance from ourselves. In its place, the place of a purported "real Hitler," we project upon him, as in a Rorschach, "a cultural self-portrait in the negative," I'd called it.

The YouTube parodies are not a trivial development. Cultural processing is going on here! The parodies are no mere "viral" memes, most of which have the lifetime of mayflies. The *Downfall* parodies have, on the contrary, become a sturdy go-to trope, a communal way of perpetuating a running commentary on how trivial so many of the concerns of our culture are. A virtual medium unto itself. Which paradoxically, it seems to me (some may disagree), doesn't diminish Hitler. They depend on, for their apparently robust continued effect, placing Hitler in a separate category, thus preserving him as a category of one.

They've lasted decades in Internet time. The fact that they are so robust may be less an example of processing than of our culture's continuing inability to "process" Adolf Hitler. Just the fact that we can somehow contain him by caricaturing him and caricaturing the caricature demonstrates a desire to distance ourselves from facing whoever the "real" Hitler might be.

Which, in a way, is a good thing. That Hitler still resists "processing," resists being made an exemplar of some system, whether psychological, sociological, ideological, hypnotic, or epidemiological (the post-encephalitic syndrome). That he has not been successfully subject to reductionism, the real target of my skeptical analysis of Hitler explanations.

The Spell

The recent (non-parodic) history of Hitler explanations has been mixed. Evans's essay, which restores to primacy a way of looking at Hitler that has been obscured of late, is important. But as far as learning more about Hitler himself, his "thought world," there have been valuable, massive biographical/ historical studies, all worthy, by Ian Kershaw, Saul Friedländer, and Evans himself, all of which add depth of detail but, as they often admit, leave a black hole in the center, a Hitler-shaped shadow.

There are a few works I'd like to single out among those I've read (by no means a comprehensive survey). Timothy Ryback's *Hitler's Private Library*, an especially thoughtful study, adds to the familiar list of Henry Ford's *The International Jew* and its source, *The Protocols of the Elders of Zion*, another name whose prominence I'd missed.

In an admiring review of Ryback, Jacob Heilbrunn cites "the one book among Hitler's extant prison readings that left a noticeable intellectual footprint in '*Mein Kampf*': a well-thumbed copy of '*Racial Typology of the German People*' by Hans F. K. Günther, known as 'Racial Günther' for his fanatical views on racial purity."

Add to this one unexpected, almost forgotten, work. I'd been asked to write an introduction to a fiftieth-anniversary edition of William Shirer's *The Rise and Fall of the Third Reich*, a longtime bestseller when published in 1961, that had shaped my and subsequent generations' picture of Hitler and the war for some time thereafter. (It was completed just before Eichmann's capture.) It was a work I had read long before writing this book and, probably would not have reread it if I hadn't been asked by its publishers to contribute an introduction. But I found myself impressed with Shirer's reporter's eye. For Hitler. For the still inexplicable power of the "spell."

Even for Eichmann before he became Eichmann, the icon of evil, and of controversy over evil. Before his capture, when he was known to Shirer as Karl—his rarely used first name. Shirer had his number in a way Hannah Arendt never would. He found the key damning document that recorded the testimony of a fellow officer who quoted the Lord High Executioner of the Final Solution toward the end of the war. Eichmann not experiencing any regret or any of the misattributed "banality." Instead, with a vengefully triumphant snarl (he knows who's really won the war), Eichmann declared "he would leap laughing into the grave because the feeling that he had five million people on his conscience would be for him a source of extraordinary satisfaction." O happy Eichmann.

Of course, not the Eichmann of Hannah Arendt ("the world's worst court reporter," as I've described her), who credulously bought into his "poor schlub" pen pusher defense—just following orders, moving things along deep within the bureaucracy, "nothing against the Jew" facade. Just doing a job, according to Professor Arendt, equally credulous about her feverishly devoted "ex-Nazi" lover Heidegger, for whom she used her influence to help in his sham postwar "de-Nazification."

Subsequent definitive discrediting of the "banality of evil " cliché by David Cesarani' s *Becoming Eichmann* and by Bernard Wasserstein's revelations in the *Times Literary Supplement* on how often Hannah Arendt depended on overtly anti-Semitic sources in her work should have put to bed that antiquated and meretricious "banality of evil" phrase. (Although it does deepen the mystery of how someone as brilliant as Arendt undeniably was could have been so willingly misled.) Not that banality doesn't exist, it just didn't exist in any respect in Eichmann's case.

But the larger lesson of Shirer's prescience here is that somehow those who were eyewitnesses, those who were ear witnesses as well (like George Steiner, who tells me in Chapter 17 that he was so transfixed just from hearing Hitler's voice on the radio in 1930s Vienna, that he *knew*); they all somehow knew something beyond the ken of those who experienced it secondhand.

There is a phrase I neglected to use in the first edition: *Führerkontakt.* The transformative personal charisma that turned his rival, Berlin-based Goebbels, into a gibbering sycophant in a single meeting, according to Goebbels's own diary. *Führerkontakt* that had mind-scrambling effects on august German General Staff strategists and radiated out from the inner circle to all those tens of thousands in Sportzplatz- and Nuremberg-style rallies within the sound of his voice, the access to his appearances in real time. Different, almost incomprehensible, to those of us consigned to a remote viewing.

This is one reason why I found the first-person perspective of the courageous Cassandra-like reporters of the anti-Hitler *Munich Post* (to whom I pay my respects in the "Poison Kitchen" chapter) so invaluable. Sifting through the crumbling original issues of the paper I found in the basement of a Munich archive, seeing the rise of Hitler through their eyes, I felt an almost palpable sense of that spell. I still feel not enough recognition has come to their efforts to investigate and publish the truth about Hitler, particularly from the world of journalism for whom there are few greater models of heroism. I still recall the chill I felt when I came across their September 9, 1931, issue that published excerpts from a secret Nazi Party document that first used the word for "Final Solution": *Endlossung*. The fact that few seemed to realize its implications does not excuse ignoring their achievement. It's true that has begun to change—one of the things I'm most proud of about this book. Indeed, a former mayor of Munich did his Ph.D. thesis on them and at least one entire book (albeit in Portuguese) has been inspired by my account. Yes, Woodward and Bernstein took on Nixon, but those reporters took on Adolf Hitler and the entire Nazi Party.

Distance does not always give wisdom but can create a fog of obfuscation as the once fashionable, bureaucratic, or "functionalist" school of the relation between Hitler and Hitler's Holocaust was reduced to calling the murder of the Jews a mere matter of logistics. More economically efficient to work them to death and then dispose of them than to feed them or relocate them.

Comparative Evil

Moving beyond Hitler, there are concentric circles of controversies about the consequences of Hitlerism and how to put the Holocaust in perspective. Consider for instance two books that deal not with *what* happened but with how to integrate—or separate—two overlapping mass murders. Hitler's murders of the Jews and Stalin's murders of just about everyone.

Two of the most interesting writers on these questions, Alvin Rosenfeld and Timothy Snyder, have differing, though not necessarily contradictory, ways of talking about the Holocaust, its centrality, and its uniqueness.

Timothy Snyder's *Bloodlands* expands the timeline of what is conventionally known as the Holocaust years, usually thought of as 1939 to 1945.

Snyder contends that the time span should be extended back to the early thirties, and defined more geographically than ethnically. Which means including what is now regarded as Stalin's deliberate mass starvation of the Ukrainian peasant populace (the "kulaks") beginning in 1931. A series of decrees caused mass starvation in the millions and even cannibalism among the desperate, decrees most historians have come to characterize as deliberate attempts to murder the recalcitrant "bourgeois" peasant farmers of the Ukraine.

The Ukrainian atrocity has become a major subject of historical study and has been given by some its own Holocaust-related name: "the Holodomor." The darkness of the crime still shadows that bloody land.

Synder places this slaughter on the continuum of subsequent Stalinist mass-murder frenzies including the Great Purges of the mid-'30s, which cost millions their lives in summary executions and gulag starvation. And then the meshing of two mass-murdering nations in the wake of the Hitler-Stalin Pact of 1939, which led to the almost immediate murder of hundreds of thousands of Poles and the beginning of the murder of millions of Jews.

It is hard not to read Snyder's work without trying to deny that human nature could give rise to such insane, relentless slaughter. But one can't.

It is true that Snyder's conflation of the Holodomor, the Purges, and the murder of the Poles tends to make the Holocaust of the Jews part of a continuum rather than a stand-alone horror. It raises profound questions about how we establish a hierarchy of evil acts. Is an order about agricultural administration that seems to deliberately seek starvation the same as rounding up and gassing Jews in a hands-on way?

Alvin Rosenfeld has some concerns about this. Not about Snyder's work specifically, but about whether the Holocaust should be conflated with other mass murders. And about the denatured domestication of the Holocaust. In the way its memory is transmitted. In his dramatically titled but always incisive work *The End of the Holocaust,* Rosenfeld takes on what might be called the ahistorical cultural assimilation of the Holocaust into the anodyne language of "man's inhumanity to man," "intolerance," and the like. Formulations that manage to elide the rather significant and distinct aspect of Hitler's extermination: anti-Semitism.

I've called this sense of the dilution of the particular meaning of the Holocaust a kind of Faustian bargain, in which the sometimes specious "universalizing" of the Holocaust, or incorporation into a generic "mass murder" category, is achieved by denaturing its actuality.

Rosenfeld is not afraid to contend with the fact that, as he writes, "with new atrocities filling the news each day and only so much sympathy to go around, there are people who simply do not want to hear any more about the Jews and their sorrows. There are other dead to be buried, they say." The sad, deplorable, but, he says, "unavoidable" consequence of what may be the necessary limits of human sympathy is that "the more successfully [the Holocaust] enters the cultural mainstream, the more commonplace it becomes. A less taxing version of a tragic history begins to emerge, still full of suffering, to be sure, but a suffering relieved of many of its weightiest moral and intellectual demands and, consequently, easier to be . . . normalized."

What are those weighty moral and intellectual demands? For one thing, I think the Holocaust demands of us that we not lose sight of the fact that it was not just another tragedy in war-torn Europe and clashing nationalisms. At the heart of Rosenfeld's argument is that anti-Semitism has a two-millennium-long history (at least), one that has produced a continuous slaughter of Jews, and Hitler's holocaust should be seen in that light, as not an aberration but a culmination of a disease of Western civilization that transcends ordinary violence. And that the Holocaust portended not an end but a beginning.

Rosenfeld quotes Imre Kertész, the Hungarian Holocaust survivor and novelist: "Before Auschwitz," Kertész writes, "Auschwitz was unimaginable. That is no longer so today. Because Auschwitz in fact occurred, it has now been established in our imaginations as a firm possibility. What we are able to imagine, especially because it once was, can be again."

That chilling last sentence tempts me into a discussion of the contentious "second Holocaust" controversy, one I stirred up when I wrote an essay essentially saying what Kertész was saying: No matter how many times and how many Jews (and non-Jews) aver "never again," it *can* happen again. The only thing that has changed is that now we know that it can happen at all.

But when I wrote the words "second Holocaust" (a phrase I found in Philip Roth's novel *Operation Shylock*), some were horrified that anyone could imagine—even utter—such a phrase. "Ethnic panic," shrieked Leon Wieseltier, who regards himself as the Holocaust discourse police. A fear of facing the possibility, of even uttering the phrase, a fear I characterized as "second Holocaust denial."

In fact Rosenfeld, a far more learned figure on the subject, devotes the final section of his book to taking up and elaborating upon the necessity of confronting the potential for such an atrocity. As has the Israeli historian Benny Morris, who mordantly observed that "this time" a second holocaust would be much easier to accomplish: A single thermonuclear weapon could kill 6 million Israeli Jews in six seconds with a strike on Tel Aviv, rather than the six years it took Hitler.

One recurrent question the Snyder and Rosenfeld books cause us to face again is the question of comparative evil. Hitler vs. Stalin: It's not a competition, but it can be a way for us to evaluate what we think is worst about what human beings are capable of. What we talk about when we talk about evil.

Do we measure it by body count? A case could be made that Stalin's death toll (and indeed Mao Zedong's) is greater than Hitler's (unless we add to Hitler's ledger the 50 million deaths from the war he started in 1939). Or do we also have to factor in the question of deliberation, intent, "agency"? Hitler's murder of the Jews could be said to be more "hands-on" (machine-gunning and gassing, the Death Marches), while Stalin's engineered starvation of the Ukraine (like Mao's massive famines during "The Great Leap Forward") was more a remote-control manipulation (and denial) of resources that caused a populace to shrivel and die (amidst the horror of cannibalism) without hands-on killing. Hands-off killing can be just as bad or worse. But as the first great exposer of Stalin's crimes, Robert Conquest, one of the first English writers to document even in a preliminary way the massive death tolls from Stalin's purges and starvations, said to me, "Hitler's just feels worse." After reading Snyder's *Bloodlands,* one acolyte of Conquest said to me that it still "feels" a little worse, but by a little less.

I've tended to believe that it doesn't diminish Hitler's evil or the horror of the Holocaust to acknowledge crimes of equal magnitude but of different methods. Indeed I believe that if we err we should err on the side of seeking commonality with victims of other genocidal horrors, mass murders, and the like (Rwanda, Native Americans, African slavery, etc.) rather than seek to find differences that separate us from their suffering.

I would reject, however, one argument put forward in the comparative-evil discourse by apologists such as the postmodern Marxist-sophist Slovoi Žižek. He has argued that Stalin's crimes are less deplorable than Hitler's because they sprang from communism's "good intentions" gone awry while Hitler's were merely from racism. Alas, Hitler, too, saw himself as someone with "good intentions," someone "convinced of his own rectitude" as Trevor-Roper put it. He saw himself as a savior of the human race from a plague, a disease. The Jews were "a bacillus" and he was a heroic Dr. Pasteur. Himmler called the SS exterminationists not an army of racist genocidal murderers but "courageous" for having to do the "hard task" of eliminating the infection. Žižek's arguments are that of a rationalizer of mass murder.

If the question of comparative evil is a worthy if perhaps unresolvable one, the search for the origin of Hitler's evil, as adumbrated in the subtitle, has not turned up much that can be called illuminating since publication of the book. In fact, I've felt as though I've had to play a kind of "whack-a-mole" with old discredited Hitler theories that kept resurfacing.

For a time after this book's publication it seemed like I'd become the designated default debunker for various documentaries on cable channels about "new" Hitler theories. Yes, I spoke about the questions I thought important on the BookTV channel, on *Charlie Rose,* on NPR, and in a Peter Jennings documentary on the twentieth century that I remember as particularly well done.

But every year or so, one of the Hitler myths would crop up and I'd go on a cable doc to discredit it: the "Jewish blood," the "gay Hitler," the "one-testicle theory," the "survival in Argentina myth"—the evergreen tale that took new life from some declassified FBI documents from the late '40s, which seemed to take seriously an "eyewitness" who thought he'd seen Hitler and Eva Braun holed up in a hotel in Argentina. (As I've written, some of these tales, like the survival myth, are of emblematic or anthropological value: Hitler *has* survived in some respects, but as a dark presence in some southern hemisphere of our brain.)

Someone has to do it. But I do draw the line. As I was writing this Afterword I was contacted by a French documentarian who said he was preparing a Hitler film that he said would examine, "with great prudence," the myth that as a youth Hitler had spent a year in Liverpool, England, with his half-sister, a myth based on a fabrication by Hitler's "black sheep" half-nephew William Patrick Hitler. One that had been utterly discredited. I sought to explain to the French documentarian that this would be like examining "with great prudence" the belief the earth was flat.

Perhaps the most poignant consequence of a misreading (or mythreading) of an aspect of my book was the case of Norman Mailer and Geli Raubal. According to Mailer's biographer, J. Michael Lennon, "Rosenbaum's book turned Mailer's head." He quotes Mailer as saying that "long after the details had faded from my mind the feeling of the book remained." Until then "I was absolutely intrigued with the idea of Montaigne as a Jungian." I suppose it's possible to say that I should feel some satisfaction in sparing us Mailer's unlikely attempt to prove Montaigne was a Jungian. But here is where the story gets poignant. Mailer decided on the basis of reading *Explaining Hitler* that he would focus on the murky Geli Raubal relationship (about which, I should reiterate, I concluded there was unlikely to have been a sexual relationship nor did Hitler murder or have her murdered, though he may have driven her to suicide). Nonetheless, this was going to be the core of a vast three-novel Mailer trilogy, the first of which, *The Castle in the Forest,* he completed before his death, the second of which he was working on when he died. As it happened, Mailer and I had shared an editor at Random House, David Ebershoff, who was up in Provincetown when Mailer passed away and told me he'd discovered, on Mailer's writing desk the day he died, an open copy of *Explaining Hitler* next to Mailer's reading glasses. Sad.

The Baby Picture

If explanations—or most—were unsatisfying, incomplete, or reductive, it can be said they were often worth examining for the fears they projected and reflected: what they told us about ourselves and our culture.

And all were really seeking an explanation for the Baby Picture.

I'll never forget Claude Lanzmann, the director of *Shoah,* the nine-and-a-half-hour Holocaust documentary, shouting at me, accusatorially, in his Parisian flat: "There is even a baby picture of Hitler!" Virtually aghast at the very idea that there could be such a picture, because it would insidiously ensnare people into the evil enterprise of trying to explain why—why that innocent infant evolved into a genocidal monster.

Lanzmann rejected any such "understanding," preferring a Hitler who sprang full-blown like a demon in our midst. Almost like Macbeth, not "of woman born," Hitler not of human formed. A hostility to the baby picture, almost disclaiming the picture's right to exist because of its misleading potential. All of which led, after the French publication of the book, to my clash with Lanzmann, which the Parisian magazine *Le Figaro* called "L'Affair Rosenbaum."

Of course, it is true, many explanations become exculpations, but I would suggest that does not deny, prima facie, the validity of the search to know more than we do. Or entail forgiveness no matter how much we know. Maybe we will never know all, never know enough, but it won't necessarily be because we're dealing with a supernatural creature beyond human explanation. It may be because human nature has more profound depths than we imagined. Or it may be that we lack some crucial piece of his personal history.

But *something* or some things made Hitler want to do what he did. It wasn't a concatenation of impersonal, external forces, a kind of collective determinism. It required his impassioned desire for extermination, even at the potential cost of defeat for Germany. It required him to choose evil. It required free will.

It required Hitler to make a continuous series of choices, the ultimate source of which may always be shrouded in mystery. We will likely never know, for instance—barring some discovery in a "lost safe-deposit box"—what went on between Hitler and the alleged hypnotist, Dr. Forster, said to have treated him at the time of the World War I German surrender. We have only Ernst Weiss's fascinating novelistic speculation to go on, and it can't be counted as proof, although it may be my favorite unsolved Hitler mystery (see Introduction). In fact, we lack proof, and the most salient clues might be lost in the mists of history. We just may never know with certainty what made Hitler *Hitler*. And worse, we may never know why we don't know: whether it's because of a missing piece of biographical evidence, or an inability to evaluate the evidence we have. It's beyond frustrating not knowing whether we might. Yes, the phrase made famous by Donald Rumsfeld: "unknown unknowns."

A phrase that must make us content with what Keats called "negative capability"—the ability to live with uncertainties without an "irritable" reaching for certainty. That word "irritable": such a stroke of genius in characterizing the doggedness the most single-minded explainers display in defense of their certainties. (A phrase, by the way, that Fitzgerald cribbed from Keats when he declared "the test of a first-rate intelligence is the ability to hold two opposed ideas in the mind" without needing to embrace one or the other. Only two? With Hitler, there are dozens, or at least a dozen worth holding in mind and considering.)

A Regret

One regret I have about the original edition: I did not deal with the deeply misguided regard for Charlie Chaplin's *The Great Dictator*, perhaps the most fraudulent aspect of the conventional wisdom about what might be called "Hitler culture."

Chaplin's meretricious and in fact genuinely, historically damaging *The Great Dictator* is a film I'd seen long before focusing on this book and had taken for granted the conventional wisdom and knee-jerk approbation. And forgotten it. But its "courage" is one of those myths that really needs re-examining because it persists to this day. The myth that *The Great Dictator* was a bold challenge to Hitler or that it somehow damaged his cause. Quite the opposite.

It may be too late, but I feel an obligation to set the record straight. I'm recalling now how shocked I was when, after being invited to "present" a showing of it at the Harvard Film Archives, I actually watched it for the first time in years.

It was shocking on two levels. First, the fact that in his alleged anti-Hitler satire, who does Chaplin blame for the hostility his Hitler character has for the Jews? Jewish bankers! Jewish bankers turned down the Great Dictator and it's all about getting even with those Jews. The Jews' misfortune was their own fault, in effect. That's Charlie Chaplin's Hitler explanation. That's what he told America at that crucial moment in October 1940 when the film was released. People seem to forget this when they get all misty-eyed about how great *The Great Dictator* is. Which is why I believe it needs to be dealt with, and what better place than here?

It's fascinating that the film-buff community is so blinkered by apolitical estheticism they never speak of this when heaping unwarranted praise on this mendacious film. Or do they just not want us to notice the "Jewish banker" moment so we can appreciate the great genius without reservation?

They must know. The Chaplin groupies have seen it all too many times. It's shocking in another way if you consider it in the context of history. When I tried to point out Chaplin's "Jewish banker" Hitler theory on a "social media" thread, the film's defenders *didn't* seem disturbed by this. When I pointed it out at the Harvard Film Archives, the emblematic response was from a film theory–addled questioner who posited that the entire film was really about Chaplin's resistance to the end of silent films. Seriously!

But the real damage of this alleged satire was done at the time of its release, in its successful trivialization of Hitler. Chaplin trivialized his "Great Dictator" by "revealing" what a sentimental, foolish softy he was, dancing with a globe balloon. Nothing to be seriously alarmed by. Not a threat that required resistance. Just the Little Tramp being a little bit mean to the Jews.

The film was released at a time when the appeasers and America Firsters, many of them anti-Semitic and pro-fascist, were trying to keep the United States out of the struggle against Hitler. Another fact overlooked by the Chaplin groupies: The film won an award from the right-wing pro-appeasement Daughters of the American Revolution, because of Chaplin's mistakenly celebrated "pro-peace" speech, a speech, which was really at that time, in that context, an argument not for peace but instead for not fighting Hitler. It called on the soldiers and workers of the world not to take up arms against anyone (including Hitler), which was why it was also celebrated by the Communist Party, then promoting the odious Hitler-Stalin pact, which also argued against the anti-fascist struggle (until the Soviet Union was attacked, of course). Hitler was murdering people, and Chaplin was telling the world not to resist, the Stalinist line at the time.

Godwin's Law and "Feel-Good" Holocaust Stories

One of the fascinating things I discovered in the course of writing this book was the reluctance of scholars and savants to use the word "evil" in regard to Hitler. Some years after writing the book and studying the question of evil, on a fellowship at Cambridge where I got to converse with scientists and theologians on this tormentingly complex matter, I ended up writing a long essay I called "Rescuing Evil." It was an attempt to find a rationale for rescuing the idea of freely chosen "wickedness" (the technical philosophical term) from the determinists and materialists who would instead explain away evil as the purely neurochemical, physiological product of the brain.

"Neuromitigation" the great contrarian writer Raymond Tallis called it in an essay in the London *Times Literary Supplement,* and alas that is the way "scientific" studies of evildoers are heading. Blame it all on a brain defect. Neuroscientists would have a field day with their fMRI machines and Hitler's brain. Sooner or later they'd claim to find some fragment of gray matter responsible for it all. Instead, we have a gray area, a fog, a *Night and Fog,* to cite Alain Resnais's groundbreaking Holocaust movie, that we may never penetrate, and physics alone my never explain.

Does Hitler's apparently unequalled evil entail certain linguistic obligations? That is the question raised by Godwin's Law, whose Internet ubiquity I was not aware of when writing the initial edition.

Godwin's Law is something that's come into prominence with debate about the devolution of discourse on websites. For those unfamiliar, Godwin's Law has now entered the *Oxford English Dictionary,* but here since it is an Internet phenomenon is a somewhat more expansive (and net-native) Wikipedia entry: "Godwin's Law (also known as Godwin's Rule of Nazi Analogies or Godwin's

Law of Nazi Analogies) is an assertion made by Mike Godwin in 1990 that has become an Internet adage. It states: 'As an online discussion grows longer, the probability of a comparison involving Nazis or Hitler approaches 1.'"

I'm sure you've seen examples of such comparisons: bans on high-fructose sodas are "just like Nazi Germany," so-and-so politician "adopts Hitler's technique of the big lie." As I write, a bill has been introduced into the Israeli Knesset, of all places, to ban the use of the words "Hitler," "Nazi," or their variants as disparagement because they denature the reality. While I can see the logic of the proponents—that the usage has trivialized the originals—I just find it wrong in most cases to ban speech of any kind.

No Hitler analogies then? Yes, they can trivialize, but on the other hand, a blanket, ironclad rule denying the use of Hitler or Nazi analogies removes them from significance in contemporary discourse entirely. It consigns Hitler to the YouTube parody realm and virtually sacralizes Hitler analogies by prohibiting them, like Claude Lanzmann prohibiting Hitler explanations. Yes, such comparisons are most often hyperbole, but the value of a concept like hyperbole is that it at least acknowledges that there may in fact be some *ultima Thule*, some distant but real mark of the existence of ultimate evil. A dark pole star.

Godwin's Law may suggest that no comparison to Hitler or Nazis is ever valid, which removes them from referentiality entirely. Removes them from having any validity as comparison, when for instance in fact the reason the world does have plutonium atomic clocks (or however they keep Greenwich Mean Time now) attests to the value of having some absolute standards by which we can measure things.

Another way of dematerializing Hitler's crime, another development, another means of "cultural processing" I had not anticipated when I wrote this book is the rapid growth of what might be called the "Feel-Good Holocaust Genre." Ones that may not have you leaving the movie theater humming the tunes, so to speak, but which "lift the spirit," demonstrate the noble side of human nature in the face of evil. Do we need these demonstrations if they end up giving us the message that Hitler shouldn't disturb our faith in human nature? That Holocaust stories should somehow make us think better of our fellow human beings? Dammit, Hitler *should* disturb our faith in human nature. If he doesn't, he's not Hitler, or you've erased and effaced him and made him serve as a convenient talisman for your self-congratulatory, self-serving "humanity."

The shock of the moral and historical idiocy of Roberto Benigni's *Life Is Beautiful* "heartwarming" Holocaust fantasy still remains with me. (I wrote an essay about Chaplin and Benigni, whose triumphalist clowning at the Oscars, dancing not just on the chairs but, metaphorically, on the graves of the dead, I still find disgusting beyond belief. I called it "The Arrogance of Clowns.") It was probably Spielberg's *Schindler's List* that opened the floodgates for teary, uplifting Holocaust tales. As someone put it, Spielberg made a movie about one Christian saving 400 Jews instead of a movie about a continent of Christians killing 6 million. Not that the Schindler story shouldn't be told, but that one, the one that climaxed with a teary, colorful celebration of the Schindler survivors in the land of Israel, was given preeminence. A happy ending to a Holocaust movie!

Afterward, the cheap and tawdry feel-good Holocaust books and movies came surging in like a flood. Some were complete fabrications. Some, like *The Boy in the Striped Pajamas,* trivialized the reality of the death camps to create a "Holocaust Lite," a Child's Garden of the Death Camps.

And then, to cap it off, there was the pop-sophistry of Malcolm Gladwell's uplifting Holocaust story. The world's leading purveyor of oversimplifications about human nature offers us, in *David and Goliath,* a supposedly heartwarming story of poor villagers who protected some Jews during the war. Gladwell's lesson: "It was not the privileged and the fortunate who took in the Jews in France. It was the marginal and the damaged, which should remind us that there are real limits to what evil and misfortune can accomplish."

You know what we need reminding of, Malcolm Gladwell? Setting aside the ahistorical generalizations about who did and didn't do what for the Jews under what circumstances. What we need to be reminded of, what the French people finally needed to remind *themselves* of, is how most of them happily collaborated with the Nazis in serving up the Davids to the German Goliath. That this fact is more important than some spurious lesson about "the limits of evil" you toss in as if we know what "the limits of evil" are.

The Holocaust wasn't *It's a Wonderful Life,* an event to be exploited for heartwarming anecdotes. Life was not beautiful and human nature, if anything, exceeded all imaginable expectations of evil's limitlessness. The lesson of the Holocaust should be to question whether there *are* any limits to human evil.

In this connection, I would like to add a corrective, or rather an extension, of a remarkable defining statement about the Holocaust by the German writer W. G. Sebald. He's most well-known for his book about the firebombing of Dresden—someone I had thought was part of the exculpatory "moral equivalence" tendency in postwar German culture. But then I came upon that remarkable statement. When asked whether it was possible to think too much upon the Holocaust, Sebald said, "No serious person thinks of anything else." A line meant to shock, yet shock value is not always valueless. It was a kind of hyperbole, of course. We all think about lunch and dinner, too, but it's clearly meant to signify that this was an overwhelming change in how we should think about human nature, a change whose nature and extent need careful if not constant consideration from those who take the nature of human nature seriously. To which I would add, "No serious person takes these pathetic little reassurances about human nature (such as Gladwell's) seriously. They are the consolations of fools, and those who peddle them should be ashamed of themselves."

The Rise and Rise of Holocaust Denial

But the appeal of these false hopes for human nature cannot be denied. All these moments of micro-compassion, these stories, might be true locally, but they are false globally; they are the moral equivalent of Holocaust denial.

Which brings us to the subject of Holocaust denial and the ongoing argument about the history of evil.

The continued rise of Holocaust denial: that may well be the most remarkable Hitler-related development since the first publication of this book. And not just the massive Internet-bred tidal wave of toxic filth that washes up on websites worldwide along with instant access to *Mein Kampf* (17 million copies printed by some estimates—even before Internet distribution) or the *Protocols of the Elders of Zion*. Judging from Google hits and chat room stats, there are more people who believe in the *Protocols of the Elders of Zion* than ever.

When the first edition of *Explaining Hitler* came out, Holocaust denial was mainly the province of skinhead neo-Nazis, addled pseudo-intellectuals, and one individual whose anti-Semitic pseudo-history one can observe in my David Irving chapter. (In April 2000, a British judge issued a ruling in a libel trial involving the courageous writer Deborah Lipstadt which said Irving was "an active Holocaust denier; that he is anti-Semitic and racist, and that he associates with right-wing extremists who promote neo-Nazism.) But now Holocaust denial has not only the allegiance of the addled and Machiavellian anti-Semites but a vast new audience who have endowed it with a geopolitical rationale. An ideological agenda for anti-Semitic anti-Zionism: The Jews invented the Holocaust in order to guilt-trip the world into giving them sovereignty over Israel. You would be surprised (or perhaps not) to discover how prevalent some variety of this narrative has become among those who want to de-legitimize and ultimately erase the state of Israel (and usually "remove" its Jews, as well).

An entire nation, Iran, has seen its leadership endorse this version of Holocaust denial. Even, notoriously, sponsoring a worldwide conference of Holocaust-denying "scholars" to substantiate this fabrication. A nation which, of course, denies that the original Holocaust happened but nonetheless has leaders who have endorsed the idea of perpetrating another one. As early as 1999, Ali Akbar Hashemi Rafsanjani, the former president of Iran, announced that he did not fear a nuclear exchange with the state of Israel, because, although Iranians might lose millions of lives, there would be millions left alive and a billion and half Muslims in the world, but in Israel, there would be "nothing left on the ground." Something that's useful to remind those who quibble that a later Iranian leader, Ahmadinejad, who expressed his fervent hope that Israel would be "wiped off the map," merely meant that the state, the regime, the lines on the map would be erased. It was just a metaphor. . . .

Hitler lives in threats to repeat his crime.

And it is worth remembering, as well, when there is talk about how the new "moderate" Iranian leader, Hassan Rouhani, has backed off the official state stance of Holocaust denial. No, rather he has said that he would just "leave it to the historians" ("let the historians reflect") as to how many, if any, Jews had been killed by Hitler. This "not taking a position," applying the much-derided "he said/she said" doctrine to the question of the Holocaust's facticity, is one of the subtle new guises Holocaust denial has taken.

Meanwhile, if you want the final word on the matter, the true position of the state from the mouth of Supreme Leader Ali Khamenei, the one who truly rules Iran, there's a sickening statement posted on his English-language website as I write that denounces "the myth of the massacre of the Jews known as the Holocaust." Case closed.

Holocaust Inconsequentialism

But more subtle and more insidious versions of Holocaust denial have continued to emerge in the decade or so since this book was first published. I'd like to talk about the varieties of Holocaust denial by expanding upon the discussion I had in the book about "the history of evil" with philosopher Berel Lang.

Lang is one of the most brilliant and courageous thinkers I encountered in writing this book. Emeritus Chairman of the Philosophy Department at New York State University's Albany campus, he is an exacting writer who tangles with the most complex and perplexing questions. I was fortunate to come upon a brief essay he wrote on the question of whether there could be "a history of evil," which means: did evil evolve? Beginning with the first murder, Cain and Abel, and reaching an end point in Hitler. Is it possible to imagine an evil greater, more malignant than Hitler's? How does one measure evil? By quantity—body count? By intent? Is there an algorithm? The technical philosophical term for the *ultima Thule*, the endpoint of evil, is "malignant wickedness," which means the conscious desire to do evil knowing that it's evil. Not with Trevor-Roper's conviction of rectitude.

Can we envision a qualitative point beyond that, beyond Hitler, or merely a quantitative one?

In my conversation with Lang, I had suggested Holocaust denial might be considered a further step in the evolution of evil because it owned the evil of the Holocaust—amongst themselves, most deniers know it's a cruel anti-Semitic game—yet demonstrated that it was possible to torment the souls of the dead beyond the grave. Holocaust denial not only robbed the graves of their bodies but condemned those who had been murdered to characterization as liars and fabricators, twisted the knife into their already violated souls.

Lang had countered by saying he thought he'd come upon a subtler, more insidious sort of Holocaust denial: "Holocaust indifference." It was a phrase he used when writing about the postwar career of Martin Heidegger, once a world-renowned philosopher for his almost incomprehensible, some said incoherent, meditations on Being, Time, the World Spirit, and human identity. Heidegger had also shown himself an eagerly sycophantic Nazi follower once Hitler came to power, getting himself appointed rector of the University of Freiburg where he gave pro-Hitler lectures wearing a Nazi uniform, denounced Jews, and got the Jews on the faculty fired forthwith.

After the war, after exploiting his prewar love connection with Hannah Arendt (as credulous and deceived about Heidegger, it seems, as she was about Eichmann) to obtain de-Nazification, he settled into a quiet, bucolic existence, occasionally issuing polemics mainly about the evils of industrialized agriculture. Sounding, as some have mocked him, like a locavore *avant la lettre.* Industrialized agriculture was evil. Nothing about industrialized murder or what it might have meant for the World Spirit. It might as well not have happened, but he's okay that it did. Holocaust indifference.

Indeed, as Lang found to his incredulity, not once did this man who pronounced on history and human nature with such sweeping majesty find it in him to utter or indite a single word about the murder of 6 million Jews in which he shared complicity with all others who wore the Nazi uniform and saluted (and enabled) Hitler. Holocaust indifference! Worse than denial because the knowledge is there and yet it doesn't make a difference.

I found myself thinking of another variation on this, which I call "Holocaust inconsequentialism." It was Cynthia Ozick who called my attention to the phenomenon. Five years after the publication of *Explaining Hitler* I published a five-hundred-page compilation of essays on contemporary anti-Semitism to which Ms. Ozick contributed a stunningly powerful afterword, in the course of which she singled out for particular scorn a remark made by Ian Buruma, the British journalist.

In writing about the 1981 Israeli raid on Saddam Hussein's nuclear reactor at Osirak, Buruma, in a caustic aside, called it shameful and unnecessary that Menachem Begin, the prime minister who ordered the raid, had alluded to the Holocaust as one of his justifications for preventing the development of weaponizable nuclear fuel at the reactor. What Begin had said at the time was that in making a terribly difficult decision he knew would be (initially) condemned by most of the world, but he was thinking about the million and a half children murdered in the Holocaust. And how much it weighed on his mind that a single Iraqi nuclear weapon derived from Osirak fuel enrichment (the whole purpose of the plant) would put an entire new generation of Israeli children and citizens in peril of a Second Holocaust. Was it shameful, as Buruma contended? No, it was Buruma, Ozick argued, who exhibited a shamefully "obstinate indifference to the moral realities of human behavior and motivation."

Holocaust indifference. For some reason, Buruma felt the need to scold Begin. For what? For acting on the basis of history, a history that made Begin's forebodings more, rather than less, likely, as Kertész pointed out. That something so incomprehensible and unimaginable had actually happened once meant it was no longer unimaginable that it could happen again.

Buruma was shaming Begin for the crime of making a historical analogy. "Is the imagination's capacity to connect worthy of such scorn?" Ozick wrote.

Thus the more inclusive category of "Holocaust inconsequentialism." The Holocaust happened in history but for one reason or another one is not allowed to use or allude to its facticity in making judgments about how to act in the future (Godwin's Law of Geopolitics?). No denial it existed, just denial it should have any consequences. One can see Holocaust inconsequentialism even—or especially—in those like Claude Lanzmann who attempt to sacralize the Holocaust, to privatize it for their own personal construal, denounce anyone who deviates from his approach.

And it is here we come to what I believe is the most urgent mission of this Afterword: to set the record straight on Lanzmann's blatant misinterpretation of one of the great writers on the Holocaust, Primo Levi.

"L'Affair Rosenbaum"

It wasn't my idea of a Parisian affair, but that was the banner headline—"L'AFFAIR ROSENBAUM"—across two facing pages of an issue of the Parisian glossy news magazine *Le Figaro* that appeared shortly after the French publication of this book. A debate on facing pages between me and Claude Lanzmann over the issue of Hitler explanation, the legitimacy of which (as you can see in chapters 6 and 7) Lanzmann has declared himself Final Arbiter and Lord High Executioner of all others. A debate that came down to my exposure of his misreading of the words of Primo Levi. If I risk repetition, so be it, for all I know some may only read this Afterword and Primo Levi deserves justice.

Levi, you probably know, is an Auschwitz survivor, one of the most highly regarded writers and thinkers about the Holocaust. At issue were the chilling words Levi heard harshly thrown in his face on his first day in Auschwitz, the words Lanzmann utterly misread to support his war against the question "Why?"

I have made it my mission, in homage to Levi (such a more complex and interesting thinker than Lanzmann), to distinguish what Levi was actually trying to say on this crucial question from Lanzmann's opportunistic obfuscation, since Lanzmann's misrepresentation of Levi is still quoted as if it were gospel. And he conspicuously avoided the challenge I made to the reading in his contribution to *Figaro*'s "L'Affair Rosenbaum." So let me briefly compress the way Lanzmann distorts the Primo Levi aphorism. It is no small point; it is at the heart of the debate of the question of explanation, the very epistemology of it.

In his book, *If This Is a Man,* Levi tells the story of his first day at Auschwitz. No food or water for days. Freezing cold, but dying of thirst, he opened a window in his confinement hut to break off an icicle outside for water. An SS Camp guard shouted at him to stop. *Verboten!*

To which Levi had the temerity to ask "Why?"

In response to which, Levi writes, the SS guard harshly told him, *"Hier ist kein warum"* ("Here there *is* no why"). Which Levi takes as meaning "Here—in the Auschwitz/death camp world, a world ruled by SS mass murderers—there is no why, no asking questions." Because any question was a challenge to authority. The power of the guard is absolute—one could be executed simply for asking why a guard asks one to do something.

And so yes, in the death camps there was no "Why," no one was permitted to ask for explanation. But Levi did not wish to deny "Why" to everyone outside of Auschwitz. Not to himself or others. He devoted the rest of his life and his eloquent words to seeking an answer to the question "Why" and if he did not find one (there is a dispute about whether he died from an accidental fall or killed himself), it is tragic to see a central tenet of his thought misrepresented.

But Lanzmann—either out of obtuseness or opportunism—misuses Levi's quote to indict all explanation—all attempts to ask "Why"—even by Jews, even by Auschwitz survivors. Indeed I describe in chapter 15 how he uses it as a verbal club to personally denounce and cruelly insult an actual Auschwitz survivor in a public forum—for wishing to explore the question. In *Le Figaro* I once again taxed him with the misappropriation of an SS death camp guard's words to assail Jews who ask "Why" as well as appropriating the moral authority of Primo Levi to do so. And then demanding that we follow his command, the Lanzmann variation of the SS command as if it were a Commandment writ on a stone tablet: No "Why," Now and Forever.

Instead, he bloviates with immense self-sacralizing self-importance: "The Holocaust is first of all unique in that it constructs a circle of flames around itself," he says, "the limit not to be broken because a certain absolute horror is not transmittable." Because the horror is not utterly and totally transmittable, we must not attempt to transmit *anything* about it! We must be content just to know it exists. But how do we know it exists if it is not "transmittable"? By watching *Shoah,* Lanzmann's film! Seriously! That seems to be the only permissible way. By putting a circle of flame around the "untransmittable," Lanzmann succeeds in doing what the inconsequentialists and the deniers also do—removing the Holocaust from history, from a search for origins, from the scrutiny of, and effect upon, subsequent history.

It's madness. But Lanzmann exploits the unexamined moral seriousness he ascribes to himself—and has ascribed to him—for having made a nine-and-a-half-hour film about it. Intellectually he has little more going for him than that epic running time, a length that people have unfortunately mistaken for wisdom. It's a disgrace that he is allowed to get away with his high-flown sophistry to silence all others on the subject.

Someone needs to speak up for the traduced spirit of Primo Levi. If not now, when?

The Degenerate Artist

I'd like to add a final thought that came to me only recently about the nature of Hitler's evil, whether it can even be called evil, and whether we believe evil exists. A question that is intimately bound up in the question of whether we believe free will exists. The specific impetus for this final thought, not a final solution but a possible one, was the discovery in Munich in early November 2013 of a huge collection of stolen or "appropriated" art that had been hidden in a house by a Nazi specialist in "degenerate art."

You're probably familiar with the story. Most of the pieces seemed to have come from the notorious 1937 Hitler-inspired exhibit. It was a treasure trove of work by artists now recognized as some of the greatest of the twentieth century. Picasso, Renoir, Munch, Chagall, and the like. The kind of art Hitler hated and he commissioned a museum exhibit entitled "Degenerate Art" to prove to the German people the dangers of Jewish-inspired modernism. Apparently some 1,500 pieces of this now priceless treasury were found hidden in the Munich home of a man named Gurlitt, who had gathered them and supported himself by periodically selling them.

The whole affair made me think about the relationship between Hitler and art and evil again. The problem with calling Hitler evil is the problem of consciousness and free will. The trend of late has been to deny free will's ability to choose evil. (Denial again!) Evil choices and evil acts are now said to be the product of a defect to be found in the *DSM-V* or locatable on an fMRI scan. The product of determinism, not choice. I had advanced a notion in the book that one of the most heuristic ways of looking at Hitler was to see him as he saw himself from the very beginning in Vienna: as an artist. A failed artist, but one who was then able to put himself in a position where he could create a kind of art of evil.

"Art of evil" in this context is not an empty phrase. In one sense, he was using genocidal means to re-sculpt the human genome by carving off entire chunks (Jews, gypsies, homosexuals, Slavs). Ascribing to Hitler an artistic consciousness is important in the discourse about the very possibility of evil. In an age when neuroscience is replacing evil with neural-defect diagnoses like psychopath and sociopath, which see evil as the result of brain defect or malformation. With free will considered an illusion, there is no evil because there is no choice, only determinism. Artistic consciousness may be its last validation, the last refuge from determinism. It is hard to ascribe every efflorescence of artistic consciousness, every brush stroke or musical note or poetic image, to some materialist or behaviorist syndrome in the brain.

The "Degenerate Art" collection reminded me of something Berel Lang had said about the connection between the artistic consciousness and the Holocaust. Not surprisingly, he began by quoting Primo Levi: "Primo Levi used the phrase 'needless violence' to describe the death camp experience. It's the element of gratuitousness but it's more than gratuitousness. There seems to be this imaginative protraction, elaboration one finds best exemplified in art forms and which in art we usually take to be indicative of a consciousness, an artistic consciousness."

I thought of the sign on the gate above the entrance to Auschwitz: *Arbeit Macht Frei.* A deliberate work of artistic (demonic ironic) artistry. My response then was to think that the notion of an art of evil implies a knowing, conscious choice to turn evil into art. Not convinced of one's rectitude but of one's evildoing. And so it came to me, something I hadn't thought of before. Perhaps one illuminating way to characterize Hitler's evil is to think of him in his own terms, to use his own rubric against him: Adolf Hitler: "Degenerate Artist." A degenerate artist of evil.

Postscript

Noted without comment:

On April 13, 2014, a long-time Ku Klux Klan hate monger shot three dead at a Jewish Center complex in Kansas City on the eve of Passover. From the *New York Times* story the following day: "[the suspect] Mr. Miller was taken into custody on Sunday afternoon at a local elementary school near Village Shalom, the police said. In video taken by KMBC, a local television station, the suspect yelled 'Heil Hitler!' while sitting in a police car."

NOTES

Introduction: The Baby Pictures and the Abyss

p. xi.   "the survival myth." See Donald M. McKale's fascinating study. *Hitler: The Survival Myth* (New York: Stein and Day, 1981).

p. xi.   "Similarly suggestive . . . remains of Hitler's cranium." See the persuasive if not conclusive analysis in Ada Petrova and Peter Watson, *The Death of Hitler* (New York: W. W. Norton, 1995).

p. xii.   "The mountebank Hitler of Alan Bullock's initial vision." See chapters 4 and 5 for an extended discussion of these differences.

p. xii.   "Dawidowicz . . . Browning." See chapter 20.

p. xii.   "a controversial Russian autopsy." This was first disclosed in Lev Bezymenski, *The Death of Adolf Hitler* (New York: Harcourt, Brace and World, 1968).

p. xiii.   "culture, which produced Goethe . . ." Bill Clinton, speech at dedication of U.S. Holocaust Memorial Museum, April 22, 1993.

p. xiii.   "Milton Himmelfarb." See "No Hitler, No Holocaust," *Commentary* 76.3 (March 1984): 37–43.

p. xiii.   "All that history . . ." Ibid., p. 37.

p. xv.   "remains a frightening mystery." H. R. Trevor-Roper, interview with author.

p. xv.   "The more I learn . . ." Alan Bullock, interview with author.

p. xv.   "no representations of Hitler." Alvin H. Rosenfeld, *Imagining Hitler* (Bloomington: Indiana University Press, 1985), p. xx.

p. xvi.   "theologian of the Holocaust." See Hyam Maccoby, "Theologian of the Holocaust," *Commentary* 74.6 (June 1982): 33–37.

p. xvi.   "There are some pictures of Hitler as a baby." Claude Lanzmann, address to Western New England Institutes of Psychoanalysis, April 1990, published as "The Obscenity of Understanding: An Evening with Claude Lanzmann," *American Imago* 48.4 (1991): 473–95.

p. xvi.   "a Hitler without victims." Rosenfeld, *Imagining Hitler*, p. 40.

p. xvii.   "*The Hitler Nobody Knows.*" Heinrich Hoffmann, *The Hitler Nobody Knows* (Berlin: Zeitgeschichte Verlag, 1932), p. 3. The picture is identified as Hitler's "first photograph."

p. xvii.   "backshadow." Michael André Bernstein, *Foregone Conclusions: Against Apocalyptic History* (Berkeley and Los Angeles: University of California Press, 1994).

p. xviii.   "You can take all the reasons . . ." Claude Lanzmann, interview with author.

p. xx.   "They sent to his widow, Sophie . . ." Johannes Steiner, statement to author.

p. xxi.   "near-ultimate evil." Yehuda Bauer, interview with author.

p. xxi.   "If *he* isn't evil . . ." Alan Bullock, interview with author.

p. xxii.   "transworld depravity." See, for instance, Alvin Plantinga, "God, Evil, and the Metaphysics of Freedom," in *The Nature of Necessity* (Oxford: Clarendon Press, 1974), pp. 164–93.

p. xxii.   "Hitler was convinced . . ." H. R. Trevor-Roper, interview with author.

p. xxii.   "a tendency first articulated." Plato, *Protagoras*, trans. W. C. Guthrie (New York: Penguin Books, 1956), 345e–346a.

p. xxii.   "Hitler thought he was a doctor!" Efraim Zuroff, interview with author.

p. xxiii.   "If evil is defined as conscious wrongdoing." Dr. Peter Loewenberg, interview with author.

p. xxiv.   "thought-world." Albert Schweitzer, *The Quest of the Historical Jesus*, trans. W. Montgomery, from the first German edition [1906] (New York: Macmillan, 1948).

p. xxv.   "Gordon Craig and John Lukacs." See Gordon A. Craig, *The Germans*, rev. ed. (New York: Meridian Books, 1991), and "The War of the German Historians," *The New York Review of Books*, January 15, 1987 (on the *Historikerstreit*); and John Lukacs, *The Hitler of History* (New York: Alfred A. Knopf, 1997), particularly chapter 3, "Reactionary and/or Revolutionary."

p. xxv.   "Saul Friedländer and Ian Kershaw." See Saul Friedländer, *Nazi Germany and the Jews*: Volume 1, *The Years of Persecution, 1933–1939* (New York: HarperCollins, 1997); and Ian Kershaw, *The Hitler Myth* (Oxford: Oxford University Press, 1987) and *Hitler* (London: The Longman Group, 1991).

p. xxv.   "David H. Fischer." See David H. Fischer, *Historians' Fallacies* (New York: Harper and Row, 1970).

p. xxv.   "Steiner describing with great candor." George Steiner, interview with author (see chapter 17).

p. xxvi.   "Hyam Maccoby . . . sinister festival." Hyam Maccoby, interview with author (see chapter 18).

p. xxvi.   "Emil Fackenheim . . . posthumous victory." Emil Fackenheim, interview with author (see chapter 16).

p. xxvi.   "Gertrud Kurth." Gertrud Kurth, interview with author (see chapter 8).

p. xxvi.   "Berel Lang." Berel Lang, interview with author (see chapter 11).

p. xxvi.   "clean as a newborn babe." David Irving, quoting Christa Schroeder, interview with author (see chapter 12).

p. xxvii.   "why not take a look." Don DeLillo, *White Noise* (New York: Viking Penguin, 1985).

p. xxvii.   "Howard noted the tendency." Michael Howard, in conversation with Thomas Powers, cited to author.

p. xxvii.   "In 1948, less than three years." Irving Kristol, "The Study of Man: What the Nazi Autopsies Show," *Commentary* (September 1948): 271–82.

p. xxviii.   "gone too far." Friedländer, *Nazi Germany and the Jews*, p. 3.

p. xxviii.   "His long-untranslated doctoral thesis." Albert Schweitzer, *The Psychiatric Study of Jesus* [1913] (Boston: Beacon Press, 1948).

p. xxix.   "*Unsolved Mysteries.*" "Diabolic Minds," *Unsolved Mysteries*, show 423 (Burbank: Cosgrove Meurer Productions, November 1991).

p. xxx.   "Deadly Routine." Dietrich Güstrow, *Tödlicher Alltag* (Berlin: Severin and Seidler, 1981).

p. xxxi.   "Consider the attempt." Alice Miller, *For Your Own Good*, trans. Hildegarde and Hunter Hannon (New York: Farrar, Straus and Giroux, 1983), pp. 142–97.

p. xxxii.   "In his retrospective psychoanalysis." Erich Fromm, *The Anatomy of Human Destructiveness* (New York: Holt, Rinehart and Winston, 1973).

p. xxxiii.   "A 1975 paper." John H. Walters, "Hitler's Encephalitis: A Footnote to History," *Journal of Operational Psychiatry* 6.2 (1975): 99–112.

p. xxxiii.   "The post encephalitic moral imbecile." A. Wimmer, "Zur Kriminalitaet der Encephalitiker." *Acta Psychiatrica* (Copenhagen) 5 (1930): 2343, cited in Walters, "Hitler's Encephalitis."

p. xxxiv.   "Wiesenthal's persistent if quixotic effort." See Simon Wiesenthal, *Justice Not Vengeance: Recollections*, trans. Ewald Osers (New York: Grove Press, 1990).

p. xxxiv.   "Her Jewishness then becomes." See Alan Levy, *The Wiesenthal File* (London: Constable, 1993).

p. xxxv.   "Seductive Jewish Grandfather Explanation." See chapters 1 and 2.

p. xxxv.   "Seductive Jewish Music Teacher Theory." See chapters 7 and 10.

p. xxxv.   "Bungling Jewish Doctor Theory." See chapter 13.

p. xxxv.   "Hitler's own disingenuous effort." Adolf Hitler, *Mein Kampf*, trans. Ralph Manheim (Boston: Houghton Mifflin, 1943, 1971), p. 56.

p. xxxvi.   "the scholar Helmut Schmeller has pointed out." Helmut Schmeller, "Hitler's View of History" (Ph.D., Kansas State University, 1975).

p. xxxvi.   "A most recent instance." Lukacs, *Hitler of History*, pp. 53–75.

p. xxxvi.   "*Hitlers Wien.*" Brigitte Hamann, *Hitlers Wien* (Munich: Piper, 1996).

p. xxxvii.   "the claim by . . . Lanz von Liebenfels." See Nicholas Goodrick-Clarke, *The Occult Roots of Nazism: The Ariosophists of Austria and Germany, 1890–1935* (Wellingborough: Thorson Publishing Group, 1985). This is the most responsible (and virtually the only) scholarly work in a field—Hitler and the occult—that is cluttered with myth and superstition. Goodrick-Clarke examines the evidence skeptically and concludes: "it seems most probably that Hitler did read and collect the *Ostara*, although Liebenfels's 1951 claim of a personal encounter cannot be conclusively corroborated" (p. 198).

p. xxxvii.   "One piece of evidence." See the ZDF documentary produced (in association with Arte and the History Channel) by Guido Knopp, *The Rise and Fall of Adolf Hitler*, vol. 1, 1995.

p. xxxvii.   "All of which leads Lukacs to argue." Lukacs, *Hitler of History*, p. 59.

p. xxxviii.   "the threefold 'blackmail of transcendence.'" George Steiner, *The Portage to San Cristóbal of A.H.* (New York: Washington Square Press, 1983), p. 185.

p. xxxix.   "Ford's contribution to Hitler's success." See the valuable discussion in Albert Lee, *Henry Ford and the Jews* (New York: Stein and Day, 1980), on the charge made by the vice president of the Bavarian Diet in a report to the German President in 1922: "The Bavarian Diet has long had the information that the Hitler movement was partly financed by an American anti-semitic who is Henry Ford." Lee says the question of whether and how Ford supported Hitler financially (aside from lending the prestige of his name to Hitler's anti-Semitic ideology) "may never be answered completely," but he believes that Ford did so is "highly likely" (p. 57).

p. xxxix.   "I would be very happy . . ." See Levy, *Wiesenthal File*, pp. 17–18.

p. xli.   "The Nazi genocide is somehow central . . ." Michael André Bernstein, *TLS*, March 7, 1997, p. 3, in a review entitled "The Lasting Injury."

p. xli.   "So many modernist thinkers wish . . ." Robert Grant, "No Conjuring Tricks," review of *Enemies of Hope*, by Raymond Tallis, *TLS*, November 14, 1997, p. 3.

p. xlii.   "an article . . . for *The New Yorker.*" Ron Rosenbaum, "Explaining Hitler," *The New Yorker*, May 1, 1995, pp. 50–70.

p. xliii.   "According to the postwar biography." Erwin von Aretin, *Fritz Michael Gerlich: Ein Martyr unserer Tage* (Munich: Schnell and Steiner, 1949).

p. xliv.   "There was a state's-attorney inquiry . . ." Karl-Ottmar Freiherr von Aretin, statement to author.

p. xliv.   "in thinly veiled fictional form." Ernst Weiss, *The Eyewitness* (Boston: Houghton Mifflin, 1977).

p. xliv.   "the German historian Ernst Deuerlein." "There just had to be fact behind Weiss's fiction about Hitler at Pasewalk, Deuerlein remarked" to Rudolph Binion; cited in Binion's foreword to ibid., p. v.

p. xlv.   "the most important part [of Forster's] records . . ." Ibid., pp. 184–85.

p. xlv.   "Hitler's alleged pornographic drawings of Geli Raubal." Ernst Hanfstaengl, *Hitler: The Missing Years* [1957] (New York: Arcade Publishing, 1994), p. 163.

p. xlv.   "the rumored 'Austrian secret-police dossier.'" See, among others, Charles Wighton, *Heydrich* (London: Odhams Press, 1962), p. 132.

p. xlv.   "a smooth-talking 'metabolic technician.'" Ron Rosenbaum, "Tales from the Cancer Cure Underground," in *Travels with Dr. Death* (New York: Viking Penguin, 1991).

Chapter 1: The Mysterious Stranger, the Serving Girl, and the Family Romance of the Hitler Explainers

p. 4.   "People must not know who I am." William Patrick Hitler, cited in John Toland, *Adolf Hitler* (New York: Doubleday, 1976), citing *Paris-Soir*, August 5, 1939.

p. 4.   "scion of the seigneurial house of Ottenstein." Werner Maser, *Hitler: Legend, Myth, and Reality*, trans. Peter and Betty Ross (New York: Harper and Row, 1973), p. 2.

p. 5.   "In all probability, we shall never know . . ." Alan Bullock, *Hitler: A Study in Tyranny*, rev. ed. (New York: Harper and Row, 1964), p. 24.

p. 6.   "It was in 1590." Mark Twain, *The Mysterious Stranger and Other Stories* [1916] (New York: Signet, 1989), p. 161.

p. 6.   "We had two priests . . ." Ibid., p. 162.

p. 7.   "Sir Isaiah Berlin . . . borderland theory." Sir Isaiah Berlin, *Against the Current: Essays in the History of Ideas*, ed. Henry Hardy (New York: Penguin Books, 1982), p. 258.

p. 8.   "*other blood* must have entered." Helmut Heiber, *Adolf Hitler*, trans. Lawrence Wilson (London: Oswald Wolff, 1961), p. 8.

p. 8.   "Family romance." Sigmund Freud, "Family Romances" (1909), in *The*

Standard Edition, vol. 9, ed. James Strachey (London: Hogarth Press, 1959), pp. 237–41.

p. 10.   "Gestapo officers made no less than four expeditions." See Robert G. L. Waite's summary of the *Gestapo-Berichte* in *The Psychopathic God: Adolf Hitler* (New York: Basic Books, 1977), pp. 149–50n.

p. 10.   "an ingenious journalist published . . ." Rudolf Olden, *Hitler* (New York: Covici-Friede, 1936), pp. 9–10. (The ingenious journalist seems to have been Willi Frischauer. See his letter to the London *Sunday Telegraph*, Dec. 17, 1972.)

p. 10.   "It is difficult to imagine . . ." Toland, *Adolf Hitler*, p. 5.

p. 11.   "Not two months after Hitler invaded . . ." Franz Jetzinger, *Hitler's Youth* (London: Hutchinson, 1958), p. 24.

p. 11.   "Maser . . . argues that it was the Russians." Maser, *Hitler*, pp. 7–8. But see the statement by Wehrmacht General Knittersched, the commanding general of the Döllersheim Military District, who described preparations for a 1938 bombardment of Döllersheim, in Waite, *Psychopathic God*, p. 186.

p. 13.   "As John Toland describes it." Toland, *Adolf Hitler*, p. 6.

p. 14.   "Hitler's peculiar ecstasy over . . . the Hirsch case." Waite, *Psychopathic God*, p. 149.

p. 14.   "the bastard son of a Jew . . ." Ibid., citing Gerhard L. Weinberg, ed., *Hitlers zweites Buch* (Stuttgart, 1961). Waite points out that Hitler's "facts" about Erzberger's Jewish father were incorrect, making his obsession all the more peculiar.

Chapter 2: The Hitler Family Film Noir

p. 16.   "One translation of Jetzinger's." Maser, *Hitler*, p. 8.

p. 17.   "those who are obviously uncomfortable . . . such as . . . Fest." See Joachim Fest, *Hitler*, trans. Richard and Clare Winston (New York: Harcourt, Brace and Jovanovich, 1974). Fest doubts the credibility of Frank's factual discovery but calls his report of his findings to Hitler "psychologically of crucial importance."

p. 17.   "Bullock." Interview with author.

p. 18.   "a thousand years shall not suffice." Nuremberg statements cited in Joseph Persico, *Nuremberg: Infamy on Trial* (New York: Penguin Books, 1995), pp. 323–25.

p. 18.   "a secular confessor, the American psychologist." See G. M. Gilbert, *Nuremberg Diary* [1947] (New York: Da Capo Press, 1995).

p. 19.   "These people must not know . . ." W. P. Hitler, *Paris Soir*, August 5, 1939, cited in Toland, *Adolf Hitler*.

p. 20.   "One day, it must have been . . ." Hans Frank, "In the Shadow of the Gallows," typescript, English translation in John Toland Papers, the Franklin Delano Roosevelt Library, Hyde Park, N.Y. (pp. 330–31 in original German manuscript).

p. 23.   "admonitory stories in *Der Stürmer.*" See, for instance, those cited by Randall L. Bytwerk, *Julius Streicher* (Briarcliff Manor, N.Y.: Stein and Day, 1983), p. 145.

p. 23.   "The first products of such cross-breeding . . ." Adolf Hitler, *Mein Kampf*, p. 400.

pp. 24–25.   "an archivist named Nikolaus Predarovich." See Maser, *Hitler*, p. 352, n. 51.

p. 25.   "a different version of Frank emerges." Niklas Frank, *In the Shadow of the Reich*, trans. Arthur S. Wensinger with Carole Clew-Hoey (New York: Alfred A. Knopf, 1994).

p. 25.   "the tape of the interview Gilbert gave." The Toland Papers, FDR Library, Hyde Park, N.Y.

p. 26.   "While he was prone to exaggerate . . ." Ibid.

p. 26.   "That Adolf Hitler certainly had no Jewish blood . . ." Ibid.

p. 27.   "Walter C. Langer . . . seized on the Rothschild rumor." Walter C. Langer, *The Mind of Adolf Hitler* (New York: Basic Books, 1972), pp. 107–9.

p. 27.   "partly spurious memories of industrialist Fritz Thyssen." Typescript of a critique of the Thyssen memoirs sent to author by Henry Ashby Turner, Jr.

p. 27.   "Chancellor Dollfuss had ordered." Langer, *Mind of Adolf Hitler*, p. 107.

p. 28.   "certainly a very intriguing hypothesis . . ." Ibid., pp. 108–9.

p. 29.   "The psychoanalyst Norbert Bromberg." Norbert Bromberg and Verna Volz Small, *Hitler's Psychopathology* (New York: International Universities Press, 1983), p. 29.

p. 29.   "a rather wild story." Fest, *Hitler*, p. 15.

p. 29.   "These facts were so well known . . ." Miller, *For Your Own Good*, p. 150.

p. 30.   "Was Hitler a Jew?" Letter to the Saudi *Gazette*, cited in the *Jewish Press*, 1984.

p. 31.   "The two great figures . . ." George Steiner, interview with author.

p. 32.   "the Caligari Hitler." *The Cabinet of Dr. Caligari*, dir. Robert Wiene (Germany, 1919). It should be noted that at the end of the film there is ambiguity over whether Dr. Caligari is a brilliant doctor or a mountebank, but the name "Caligari" has come to embody the dark Gothic expressionism of Weimar romanticism.

p. 33.   "The debriefing took place." "OSS Sourcebook," National Archives, Washington, D.C., pp. 926–27.

p. 33.   "John Toland hinted." Phone conversation with the author, 1984.

Chapter 3: The Poison Kitchen

p. 37.   "the Poison Kitchen." See, for instance, the front page of the *Völkischer Beobachter*, the official Nazi Party newspaper, on the morning of the Munich Beer Hall Putsch, November 9, 1923. Beneath a headline that read DESTRUCTION OF THE MUNICH POST, the lead sentence proclaimed, "The Poison Kitchen at Altheimereck was destroyed."

p. 38.   "The eternal poisoners of the world." See H. R. Trevor-Roper, *The Last Days of Hitler*, 3d ed. [1962] (Chicago: University of Chicago Press, 1992). Trevor-Roper prefers the phrase "universal poisoners of all nations," while Waite, in *Psychopathic God*, uses "poisoners of all peoples." When the Geli Raubal story broke, Hitler raged against "poisonous details" in the *Munich Post*.

p. 38.	"An argument can be made." Lucy S. Dawidowicz, *The War Against the Jews: 1933–1945* (New York: Holt, Rinehart and Winston, 1975), pp. 142–46.
p. 39.	"This poison-pen polemic." "Adolf Hitler-Verrater," *Munich Post*, August 8, 1921.
p. 40.	"HITLER GEGEN DIE MÜNCHENER POST." *Munich Post*, December 7, 1921, p. 5.
p. 41.	"ON HIS BELLY AGAIN!" *Munich Post*, November 9, 1932.
p. 41.	"he could not look at a paper . . ." Frank, *In Angesicht des Galgens* (In the shadow of the gallows) (Munich: Alfred Beck Verlag, 1953), p. 97.
p. 42.	"the exposé of 'Cell G.'" See "The Tsechka in the Brown House," *Munich Post*, April 8, 12, and 19, 1932.
p. 42.	"They even glimpsed." "The Jews in the Third Reich," *Munich Post*, December 9, 1931 (trans. by Alexander Stengel, revised by author).
p. 43.	"the Prussian Nightingale." Hans Dollinger, *Edmund Goldschagg, 1886–1971*, foreword by Rolf Goldschagg (Munich: Süddeutscher Verlag, 1986).
p. 44.	"'No,' the son insisted." Rolf Goldschagg, interview with the author.
p. 45.	"WARM BROTHERHOOD IN THE BROWN HOUSE." *Munich Post*, June 22,1931, with follow-ups on June 23, 24, and 26, 1931.
p. 48.	"Roehm and the Hitler Party responded." Ibid., June 24, 1931.
p. 48.	"Roehm withdrew his charges." Ibid., April 16, 17, 1932.
p. 49.	"many (not all) historians believe." Henry Ashby Turner, Jr., dissents in *Hitler's Thirty Days to Power: January 1933* (Reading, Mass.: Addison Wesley, 1996).
p. 50.	"photographs of General Blomberg's new young wife." Toland, *Adolf Hitler*, p. 427.
p. 50.	"Bavarian Joe." Ibid., pp. 427, 429.
p. 52.	"Hitler's murder beasts." *Munich Post*, January 2, 1933.
p. 52.	"a teenage SA recruit named Herbert Hentsch." *Munich Post*, December 27, 28, 29, 30, 1932; January 2, 3, 4, and 21, 1933.
p. 53.	"THE NOVEMBER CRIMINALS." *Munich Post*, February 13, 18–19, and 20, 1933.
p. 54.	"'Stab-in-the-Back Swindle' trial." The *Munich Post* series called "Stab-in-the-Back Swindle" began April 25, 1924, and continued in the issues of April 26, 27, 28, and May 2, followed by a report on the trial and the court judgment on November 21, 22, and December 9, 1925. It was a response to Nikolaus Cossman's article "Der Dolchstoss," in *Süddeutsche Monatschefte*, April 1924.
p. 54.	"transcript of the epic 1924 'Stab-in-the-Back Swindle' trial." Institut für Zeitgeschichte, microfilm collection, Munich.
p. 55.	"A forgery that one historian called . . ." Norman Cohn, *Warrant for Genocide* (London: Serif Press, 1996).
p. 56.	"the regrettably neglected vision." Konrad Heiden, *Der Fuehrer* (Boston: Houghton Mifflin, 1944), pp. 1–20, 141.
p. 57.	"The act that launched." Toland, *Adolf Hitler*, p. 567.
p. 58.	"to find counterfeiting the essential metaphor." Karl Robert (pseud.), *Hitler's Counterfeit Reich*, foreword by M. W. Fodor (New York: Alliance Books, 1941).

Chapter 4: H. R. Trevor-Roper

p. 63.   "It was from the Stern Gang." H. R. Trevor-Roper, interview with author.

p. 64.   "In September 1945." Trevor-Roper, *Last Days of Hitler*.

p. 66.   "I have been accused . . ." H. R. Trevor-Roper, "Hitler Revisited: A Retrospective," *Encounter*, December 1988, p. 19.

p. 66.   "The fiction writer within the scholar . . ." Rosenfeld, *Imagining Hitler*, p. 23.

p. 67.   "The fascination of those eyes . . ." Ibid., p. 23 (citing Trevor-Roper, *Last Days of Hitler*).

p. 72.   "his most illuminating essay . . ." H. R. Trevor-Roper, "The Mind of Adolf Hitler," in *Hitler's Secret Conversations* (New York: Farrar, Straus and Young, 1953), pp. vii–xxx.

p. 72.   "The Ten Commandments . . ." Ibid., p. 70.

p. 73.   "From the rostrum . . ." Ibid., p. 72.

p. 75.   "The ideological school." See J. P. Stern, *Hitler: The Führer and the People* (Berkeley and Los Angeles: University of California Press, 1975), and Eberhard Jäckel, *Hitlers Weltanschauung* (Tübingen, 1969).

p. 76.   "Murdoch's response." Robert Harris, *Selling Hitler* (New York: Pantheon, 1986), p. 315.

p. 76.   "I took the bona fides . . ." Ibid., p. 260.

p. 76.   "The directors of *Stern*." Ibid., p. 302.

Chapter 5: Alan Bullock

p. 78.   "If you ask me what I think evil is." Alan Bullock, interview with author.

p. 79.   "was in love." Bullock, *Hitler*, p. 393.

p. 80.   "The Soviet autopsy findings." See Bezymenski, *Death of Adolf Hitler*, and Petrova and Watson, *Death of Hitler*.

p. 80.   "On Stalin's orders . . ." Alan Bullock, *Hitler and Stalin* (New York: Vintage Books, 1993), p. 888.

p. 81.   "Waite . . . built an elaborate castle." Waite, *Psychopathic God*.

p. 85.   "the philosopher Berel Lang." See chapter 11.

p. 86.   "Emil Fackenheim." See chapter 16.

p. 94.   "a review article." Alan Bullock, "The Evil Dream," review of *The Path to Genocide* and *Ordinary Men*, by Christopher R. Browning, *TLS*, February 5, 1993, p. 5.

p. 94.   "since no written order." See David Irving, *Hitler's War* [1977], rev. ed. (New York: Avon Books, 1990). Also see chapter 12, below.

p. 95.   "the address . . . Bullock's final testament." "Hitler and the Holocaust" at the London Yad Vashem Institute, subsequently published in pamphlet form (London: The Sidney Burton Center for Holocaust Studies, 1994).

Chapter 6: Was Hitler "Unnatural"?

p. 99.   "Chief Archivist Weber." Dr. Reinhard Weber.

p. 99.   "The document he's been reading from." Munich police document,

"Report of Det. Sauer." September 28, 1931, Bavarian State Archives, Munich.

p. 101.   "None of them had heard a shot." Ibid.

p. 102.   "His niece was a student . . ." Ibid.

p. 105.   "everybody in Munich knew." Nachum Tim Gidal, interview with author.

p. 105.   "reeking miasma of furtive unnatural sexuality . . ." Hermann Rauschning in *The Voice of Destruction* (New York: G. P. Putnam, 1940), p. 263.

p. 105.   "Hitlerism as a Sex Problem." Rodney Collin, "Hitlerism as a Sex Problem," *The Spectator*, January 19, 1934.

p. 106.   "*Male Fantasies.*" Klaus Theweleit, *Male Fantasies* (Minneapolis: University of Minnesota Press, 1987).

p. 106.   "The Kronor document." "Adolf Hitler's Blindness: A Psychological Study." OSS Document 31963, National Archives, Washington, D.C. (Intelligence Division, Office of Chief of Naval Operations: Intelligence Report 24–43).

p. 107.   "His own niece . . ." Ibid.

p. 108.   "Regarding this mysterious affair." "A Mysterious Affair," *Munich Post*, September 21, 1931.

p. 108.   "a survey of the newspaper archives." Typescript prepared for author by Dr. Waltraud Kolb, University of Vienna.

p. 109.   "Hitler's private life . . ." *Die Fanfare*, September 1931.

p. 110.   "The idea that Hitler had a sexual perversion . . ." Waite, *Psychopathic God*, p. 288.

p. 110.   "The Mimi Reiter story." Günter Peis, "The Unknown Lover," *Stern*, no. 24, 1959.

p. 111.   "He was wearing breeches . . ." Ibid., trans. Dr. Waltraud Kolb.

p. 111.   "a study of Hoffmann's portraits." See Rudolf Herz, *Hoffmann and Hitler: Fotografie als Medium des Führer-Mythos* (Munich: Fotomuseum im München Stadtmuseum, 1994).

Chapter 7: Hitler's Songbird and the Suicide Register

p. 118.   "a ledger of lost souls." Munich's *Selbstmörder* register for 1931, Bavarian State Archives, Munich.

p. 121.   "the son of a colleague." Karl-Ottmar Freiherr von Aretin, statement to author.

p. 121.   "the not always reliable memoirs of Otto Strasser." Otto Strasser, *Hitler and I* (Boston: Houghton Mifflin, 1940).

p. 121.   "Gürtner is his bête noire." Dr. Reinhard Weber, interview with author.

p. 121.   "Heiden . . . the Munich-based reporter." Heiden, *Der Fuehrer*.

p. 122.   "Heiden depicts Geli disconsolately wandering." Ibid., p. 387.

p. 122.   "I was walking down the street . . ." Frau Braun, interview with author.

p. 123.   "One has to take on trust . . ." Jenny Diski, *London Review of Books*, August 18, 1994.

p. 123.   "This cranky but useful volume." Anton Joachimsthaler, *Korrektur einer Biographie: Adolf Hitler, 1908–1920* (Munich: Herbig Verlag, 1989).

p. 124.   "I'm glad you said she had *been* shot." "Anna," interview with author.

p. 125.   "immense crown of blond hair." Louis L. Snyder, *Encyclopedia of the Third Reich* (New York: Paragon House, 1989), p. 282.

p. 125.   "an empty-headed little slut . . ." Hanfstaengl, *Hitler: The Missing Years*, p. 162.

p. 126.   "Henrietta Hoffmann . . . told John Toland." Toland, *Adolf Hitler*, p. 229.

p. 126.   "riding through the countryside . . ." Heiden, *Der Fuehrer*, p. 279.

p. 127.   "Toland suggests that it was Geli's jealousy." Toland, *Adolf Hitler*, p. 254.

p. 128.   "Heiden calls the story he tells." Heiden, *Der Fuehrer*, pp. 384–86.

p. 129.   "In Hanfstaengl's version." Hanfstaengl, *Hitler: The Missing Years*, pp. 162–63.

p. 130.   "the highly respectful *New York Times* obituary." July 20, 1966.

p. 131.   "Binion . . . contends that Heiden." Interview with author.

p. 133.   "*this* version of the perversion story." See Langer, *Mind of Adolf Hitler*, p. 29. All five "collaborators on this study agree" that the Strasser version of the perversion "is probably true in view of their clinical experience and their knowledge of Hitler's character."

p. 133.   "Strasser told a German writer." Wulf Schwarzwäller, *The Unknown Hitler*, trans. Aurelius von Kappau (New York: Berkley Books, 1990), pp. 122–23.

Chapter 8: The Dark Matter

p. 136.   "someone *like* Hitler." Daniel Jonah Goldhagen, interview with author.

p. 136.   "when Einstein specifically addressed the question." Albert Einstein, *Cosmic Religion, with Other Opinions and Aphorisms* (New York: Covici-Friede, 1931).

p. 137.   "Freud . . . did not pronounce." Telephone conversation with Frederick Crews.

p. 137.   "the only book-length purely psychoanalytic study." Bromberg and Small, *Hitler's Psychopathology*.

p. 138.   "'Around 1928,' they write." Ibid, pp. 285–86.

p. 138.   "a work . . . known as *Hitler's Secret Book*." Adolf Hitler, *Hitler's Secret Book*, trans. Salvatore Attanasio (New York: Grove Press, 1961).

p. 139.   "addressed to a Munich man." Letter to Adolf Gemlich, cited in Fest, *Hitler*, p. 114.

p. 141.   "The forensic description of Hitler's remains." Bezymenski, *Death of Adolf Hitler*, p. 47.

p. 142.   "Klara was not only worried . . ." Waite, *Psychopathic God*, p. 173.

p. 142.   "the work of . . . Dr. Peter Blos." Peter Blos, "Comments on the Psychological Consequences of Cryptorchism," *Psychoanalytic Study of the Child* 15 (1960): 408–20.

p. 142.   "playing cowboy-and-Indians." Bromberg and Small, *Hitler's Psychopathology*, p. 219.

p. 143.   "See I do have two powerful (potent) testicles." Waite, *Psychopathic God*, p. 182.

p. 143.   "a previously unpublished passage from Hitler's wartime Table Talk." Ibid., p. 183.

p. 144.   "Freud cited Gloucester in *Richard III.*" Sigmund Freud, "Some Character Types Met with in Psychoanalytical Work" (1916), in *Standard Edition*, vol. 14, ed. James Strachey (London: Hogarth Press, 1957), pp. 314–15.

p. 144.   "another Freudian study." W. G. Niederland, "Narcissistic Ego Impairment in Patient with Early Physical Malformations," *The Psychoanalytic Study of the Child* 20 (1965): 518–34.

p. 145.   "Fear of his father's imagined castration threat." Bromberg and Small, *Hitler's Psychopathology*, p. 254.

p. 145.   "a communiqué from . . . Gertrud Kurth." Letter to author.

p. 145.   "The novel, called *One for Many.*" Betty Kurth, *One for Many, Confessions of a Young Girl by "Vera,"* trans. Henry Britoff (New York: J. S. Oglivie, 1903).

p. 147.   "her influential 1947 paper." Gertrud Kurth, "The Jew and Adolf Hitler," *Psychoanalytic Review* 16 (1947): 11–32.

p. 147.   "Hitler's conscious and unconscious attitudes [to the doctor]." Ibid., 27.

p. 147.   "It is not about blame." Gertrud Kurth, interview with author.

p. 149.   "That was my big scoop." Kurth, "The Jew and Adolf Hitler," pp. 28–31.

p. 149.   "in the redaction of Hitler's words." Waite, *Psychopathic God*, p. 188.

p. 151.   "Hans Gatzke, threw cold water." Hans W. Gatzke, "Hitler and Psychohistory," *American Historical Review* 78.2 (April 1973): 394–401.

p. 151.   "Kurth herself now has second thoughts." Interview with author.

p. 151.   "one assertion in Kurth's 1947 paper." Kurth, "The Jew and Adolf Hitler."

p. 152.   "his book-length study of the Hitler-Churchill relationship." John Lukacs, *The Duel* (New York: Ticknor and Fields, 1990).

p. 152.   "In my considered view." Ibid., p. 43.

Chapter 9: Fritz Gerlich and the Trial of Hitler's Nose

p. 155.   "DOES HITLER HAVE MONGOLIAN BLOOD?" Fritz Gerlich in *Der Gerade Weg*, July 17, 1932.

p. 157.   "Hitler's favorite quack racial theorists." Hans F.K. Günther, *Rassenkunde des deutschen Volkes* (Racial characteristics of the German people) (Munich: J. F. Lehman, 1923).

p. 158.   "Schaber takes a lively if also melancholy interest." Walter Schaber, interview with author.

p. 158.   "Alfred Kazin told me of his disappointment." Interview with author.

p. 161.   "Something strange happened to Gerlich and this little group." See Von Aretin, *Fritz Michael Gerlich.*

p. 163.   "his reverent biography of Therese Neumann." Johannes Steiner, *Therese Neumann* (Staten Island, N.Y.: Alba House, 1967), pp. 89–90.

p. 163.   "Graef's summation of the evidence." Hilda Graef, *The Case of Therese Neumann* (Westminster, Md.: Newman Press, 1951). The fact that both this and the Steiner book were published by Catholic religious houses indicates a continuing split in the Catholic Church over the validity of the stigmatic girl.

p. 163.   "Gerlich 'became acquainted' . . ." Steiner, *Therese Neumann*, pp. 89–90.

p. 164.   "What you have to remember." Interview with author.

p. 166.   "that final image of Gerlich." Johannes Steiner, statement to author.

p. 167.   "The resultant composite perplexed me greatly." *Der Gerade Weg*, July 17, 1932 (trans. Alexander Stengel, revised by author).

p. 168.   *"The Hitler Nobody Knows."* Hoffmann, *The Hitler Nobody Knows.*

p. 168.   "a 1923 issue of *American Monthly* magazine." George Viereck, "Hitler, the German Explosive," *American Monthly* 15.8 (October 1923).

p. 169.   "Tim Gidal's contention." Interview with author.

p. 169.   "He showed me the photo." Published in *Nachum Tim Gidal: Photographs, 1929–1991* (Jerusalem: The Open Museum, 1992), p. 59.

p. 170.   "two illustrations of persons with Nordic noses." Günther, *Racial Characteristics.*

p. 173.   "a follow-up article." Fritz Gerlich, *Der Gerade Weg*, July 24, 1932.

p. 174.   "Richard Breitman's study of the Himmler-Hitler relationship." Richard Breitman, *The Architect of Genocide: Himmler and the Final Solution* (New York: Alfred A. Knopf, 1991).

p. 174.   "a two-volume biography of Genghis Khan." Michael Prawdin, *Tschingis-Chan Der Sturm aus Asien* and *Das Erbe Tschingis-Chan* (Stuttgart: Deutsche Verlags-Anstalt, 1934, 1935), cited in Breitman, *Architect of Genocide*, pp. 39–43.

p. 175.   "a famous 'secret speech' Hitler gave." Cited in Breitman, *Architect of Genocide*, p. 43.

p. 176.   "In a 1942 speech to SS troops." Ibid., p. 177.

p. 176.   "a member of the Iranian Parliament." *The New York Times*, January 26, 1991, p. 1.

p. 177.   "Abraham Foxman, was quoted." *The Forward*, January 26, 1996.

Chapter 10: The Shadow Hitler, His "Primitive Hatred," and the "Strange Bond"

p. 179–80. "The raw files of what's known as the 'OSS Sourcebook.'" "The OSS Sourcebook on Adolf Hitler," National Archives, Washington, D.C.

p. 180.   "The Shadow Hitler." Thomas Powers, *Heisenberg's War: The Secret History of the German Bomb* (New York: Alfred A. Knopf, 1993), p. 479.

p. 180.   "the report by Hitler's parole officer." "OSS Sourcebook," Bavarian State Police doc. IV #2427 (September 22, 1924) predicts Hitler "will remain a continual danger for the inner and exterior security of the State" and, as "the soul" of the "racial movement," should be deported rather than released.

p. 180.   "cozy chats in wartime Hollywood with émigré directors." "OSS Sourcebook," interview with A. Zeissler, pp. 921–25.

p. 181.   "the more widely known book-length analysis." Langer, *Mind of Adolf Hitler.*

p. 181.   "Under the heading of women." "OSS Sourcebook," p. 1i.

p. 182.   "a Munich student who'd become Geli's fiancé." "OSS Sourcebook," p. 639.

p. 183.   "a copy of the extremely curious article." "Adolf Hitler," New York *American*, November 30, 1930.

p. 183. "the son of a cousin of Adolf's father." Ibid.

p. 183. "the OSS analyst's memorandum of a debriefing." "OSS Sourcebook," interview with Princess Stephanie von Hohenlohe, pp. 656–62.

p. 183. "extracts from the memoirs." Frederick Oechesner, *This Is the Enemy*, cited in "OSS Sourcebook," pp. 665–97.

p. 184. "a figure of a very real interest to American intelligence agencies." Charles Higham, *Trading with the Enemy: An Exposé of the Nazi-American Money Plots, 1933–1949* (New York: Delacorte Press, 1983), has extracted a fascinating narrative of her ambiguous role from various agency files.

p. 184. "Princess Stephanie appears to have been." Ibid.

p. 184. "Wiedemann had been close." Snyder, *Encyclopedia of the Third Reich*, p. 380.

p. 184. "according to Princess Stephanie." "OSS Sourcebook," Hohenlohe debriefing, pp. 657–58.

p. 184. "some intelligence analysts believed." Higham, *Trading with the Enemy*, pp. 188–209.

p. 185. "as Lord Rothermere's personal representative." "OSS Sourcebook," Hohenlohe debriefing, p. 657.

p. 185. "The anonymous OSS interviewer." Ibid., pp. 667–68.

p. 185. "Hitler at one point confesses." Ibid., p. 658.

p. 186. "have never reached the intimate stage of *brüderschaft*." Ibid.

p. 186. "*A strange bond seems to hold these two together*." Ibid.

p. 186. "Oechsner's report on Hitler's alleged nose job." Ibid., pp. 685–86.

p. 187. "a primitive hate typical of half civilized." Ibid., p. 697.

p. 187. "Der Führer is always greatly quickened in his anti-Jewish feelings." Ibid.

p. 189. "Even Daniel Jonah Goldhagen." See Daniel Jonah Goldhagen, *Hitler's Willing Executioners* (New York: Alfred A. Knopf, 1996), and discussion in chapter 19, below.

p. 189. "Toland frames this remark." Toland, *Adolf Hitler*, p. 125.

p. 190. "Hitler had an unexpected answer." Ibid., pp. 125–26.

p. 190. "like the philosopher Berel Lang and the historian Lucy Dawidowicz." See chapters 11 and 20, respectively.

p. 191. "the final paragraph of the Princess Stephanie debriefing." "OSS Sourcebook," p. 662.

p. 191. "corroborates the analysis . . . by Lucy Dawidowicz." See Dawidowicz, *War Against the Jews*, pp. 100–104.

p. 192. "Ronald Hayman . . . uses all three of these quotes." Hayman, *Hitler and Geli* (London: Bloomsbury, 1997), p. 215.

p. 192. "the change must have been substantial." Ibid.

p. 192. "appetite for carnage grew monstrously." Ibid., p. 216.

p. 192. "Hayman even seems to fault Eva Braun." Ibid.

p. 194. "they were used to mood changes in Geli." Frau Schaub, cited in ibid., p. 182.

p. 195. "Hayman uses the fabricator of a missing year." Waite, *Psychopathic God*, pp. 501–3, was the first and most thorough to discredit Bridget Hitler's missing-year claim, which was first discovered and promoted by Robert Payne in *The Life and Death of Adolf Hitler* (New York: Praeger, 1973).

p. 195.   "in our safe deposit box at the bank." *The Memoirs of Bridget Hitler*, ed.
               Michael Unger (London: Duckworth, 1979), p. 185.
p. 196.   "the evidence accumulated by Dr. Gerlich's investigation." Ibid., p. 102.
p. 196.   "In the summary of Gerlich's . . . pamphlet." Ibid., p. 103.
p. 197.   "Schaub's two-decade-later recollection." Cited in Hayman, *Hitler and Geli*, p. 182.

Chapter 11: To the Gestapo Cottage

p. 202.   "Bormann announced with great fanfare." *The Obersalzberg and the Third Reich* (Berchtesgaden: Verlag Plenk, 1982), p. 61.
p. 207.   "The German psychiatrist Helm Stierlin." *Adolf Hitler: Familien Perspektiven* (Frankfurt: Suhrkamp, 1978).
p. 208.   "something both new and important being suggested." Berel Lang, *Act and Idea in the Nazi Genocide* (Chicago: University of Chicago Press, 1990).
p. 208.   "The History of Evil and the Future of the Holocaust." Berel Lang, in *Lessons and Legacies: The Meaning of the Holocaust in a Changing World*, ed. Peter Hayes (Evanston: Northwestern University Press, 1991), pp. 90–105.
p. 209.   "Saul Friedländer . . . Cynthia Ozick." Quoted on the back cover of Lang, *Act and Idea*.
p. 209.   "I wondered about that, too." Berel Lang, interview with author.
p. 210.   "Socrates' insistence in the Protagoras." Specifically, "nobody does wrong willingly" because "virtue is knowledge." Plato, *Protagoras*, 345b–e.
p. 210.   "one of the most famous statements." Himmler's secret address to SS officers at Poznan [alternatively Posen], June 10, 1943, cited in Lang, *Act and Idea*, p. 3.
p. 211.   "As early as 1919, Hitler wrote." Adolf Hitler, letter to Adolf Gemlich, cited in Dawidowicz, *War Against the Jews*, pp. 16–17.
p. 212.   "The discovery of the Jewish virus." *Hitler's Secret Conversations*, p. 269.
p. 212.   "Another key objection." See Bullock, address to Yad Vashem Institute.
p. 213.   "He begins his journey." Lang, *Act and Idea*, pp. 199–200.
p. 213.   "Which leads Lang to argue." Ibid., p. 210.
p. 214.   "Many philosophers question whether this degree of evil." A useful discussion of the degrees of conscious evil can be found in S. I. Benn, "Wickedness," *Ethics* 95 (July 1985): 795–810.
p. 214.   "a passage from Hitler's Table Talk." *Hitler's Secret Conversations*, p. 72 (October 25, 1941).
p. 217.   "As Gordon Craig points out, Thomas Mann." Thomas Mann, "Brother Hitler," cited in Gordon Craig, *The Germans* (New York: Meridian Books, 1982), p. 67.
p. 217.   "a study of the architecture of Auschwitz." Debórah Dwork and Robert Jan van Pelt, *Auschwitz: 1270 to the Present* (New York: W. W. Norton, 1996).
p. 217.   "as Yale's George Hersey argues." George L. Hersey, *The Evolution of Allure* (Cambridge, Mass.: MIT Press, 1996).

p. 218.	"Hitler and Kafka were fellow artists." D. M. Thomas, *Pictures at an Exhibition* (New York: Scribner's, 1993), p. 228.
p. 220.	"the recent book on the German neo-Nazi movement." Ingo Hasselbach with Tom Reiss, *Führer-Ex* (New York: Random House, 1996).
p. 220.	"Heidegger . . . knew it happened." See Berel Lang, *Heidegger's Silence* (Ithaca, N.Y.: Cornell University Press, 1996).

Chapter 12: David Irving

p. 221.	"He's a real rabble-rouser." Bullock, interview with author.
p. 222.	"1991 dispatch by Gitta Sereny." Gitta Sereny, *The Independent*, November 27, 1991.
p. 222.	"an interview with the *Telegraph*." London *Sunday Telegraph*, January 12, 1992.
p. 222.	*"Hitler's War."* Irving, *Hitler's War*, p. 1.
p. 223.	"The Jewish community in Argentina." Irving, interview with author.
p. 224.	"A Munich court convicted him in 1992." Verdict of the Munich District Court, Criminal Proceedings, no. 432, case 113, main hearing, May 5, 1992. Upheld on appeal, 1993.
p. 224.	"A spokesman at the Koblenz archives." "Zu den 'Eichmann Memoiren,'" statement to author, January 17, 1992, Bundesarchiv, Koblenz.
p. 225.	"I tried to apply the three criteria." Irving, interview with author.
p. 226.	"According to a London paper." London *Sunday Telegraph*, January 19, 1992.
p. 227.	"I wrote a book on the Dresden air raid." David Irving, *The Destruction of Dresden* (London: William Kimber, 1963).
p. 229.	"the last sentence of the book." Ibid., p. 257.
p. 232.	"no traces of cyanide compounds in the walls." See the thoroughgoing refutation of Leuchter's "science" in *Truth Prevails*, ed. Shelly Shapiro (New York: Beate Klarsfeld Foundation, 1990).
p. 234.	"'Traditional enemy' is Irving's name." See David Irving, *Action Report*, March 5, 1996, p. 1.
p. 234.	"in the somewhat schizoid biography of Goebbels." David Irving, *Goebbels: Mastermind of the Third Reich* (London: Focal Point Publications, 1996).
p. 234.	"Auschwitz was not a place." Ibid., p. 426.
p. 236.	"If this biography were simply a history . . ." Irving, *Hitler's War*, p. 17.

Chapter 13: A Tale of Three Kafkas

p. 239.	"Kafka moved in for the kill." Rudolph Binion, interview with author.
p. 240.	"Bradley Smith's 1967 study of Hitler's childhood." Bradley F. Smith, *Adolf Hitler: His Family, Childhood, and Youth* (Stanford, Calif.: Hoover Institution, 1967).
p. 240.	"his book *Hitler Among the Germans*." Rudolph Binion, *Hitler Among the Germans* (New York: Elsevier, 1976).

p. 240.   "Binion's most recent work." Rudolph Binion, *Love Beyond Death: The Anatomy of a Myth in the Arts* (New York: New York University Press, 1993).

p. 241.   "Holocaust-literature scholar Lawrence Langer." See Lawrence Langer, "Kafka as Holocaust Prophet: A Dissenting View," in *Admitting the Holocaust* (New York: Oxford University Press, 1995), pp. 109–24.

p. 241.   "George Steiner, who, as we'll see." See chapter 17.

p. 241.   "Claude Lanzmann." The cover band across the front of *Les temps modernes* 555 (October 1992), on which Lanzmann as editor promoted an essay attacking Binion by Sabine Prokhoris, read, "Rudolf [sic] Binion et Adolf Hitler: La Psychohistoire cache-misere du revisionisme?" (roughly, "Binion and Hitler: Psychohistory as Fig Leaf for Revisionism?" See chapter 14.

p. 242.   "Gertrud Kurth." Kurth, "The Jew and Adolf Hitler," pp. 11–32.

p. 244.   "Several decades of medical warnings were defied." Binion, *Hitler Among the Germans*, p. 16.

p. 244.   "Such a Hitler." Ibid., p. 16.

p. 244.   "Bloch would say later." In the Bundesarchiv, Koblenz, cited in ibid., p. 18.

p. 244.   "Hitler's experience of his mother's last illness." Binion, *Hitler Among the Germans*, p. 18.

p. 244.   "He cites telling examples from Hitler's rhetoric." Ibid., pp. 24–35.

p. 245.   "Abusing 'the Jew.'" Ibid., p. 19.

p. 245.   "Dr. Kafka brought to my attention." Dr. John Kafka, telephone interview with author.

p. 245.   "the advance description of . . . Binion's thesis." Flyer read to author by Dr. John Kafka. I came to admire Dr. Kafka's impassioned defense of his uncle.

p. 246.   "a scholar in his own right." See Dr. John Kafka, *Multiple Realities in Clinical Practice* (New Haven: Yale University Press, 1989).

p. 248.   "a terrifyingly complicated . . . response." Photocopy provided to author by Rudolph Binion.

p. 249.   "One German researcher." Ernst Günter Schenck, *Patient Hitler* (Düsseldorf: Droste, 1989).

p. 249.   "George Kren." See, for instance, George M. Kren and Rodler F. Morris, "Race and Spirituality: Arthur Dinter's Theosophical Antisemitism," *Holocaust and Genocide Studies* 6.3 (1991): 233–52, a valuable study of a now nearly forgotten early shaper of Nazi Party anti-Semitic consciousness; and George M. Kren and Leon Rappoport, *The Holocaust and the Crisis of Human Behavior* (New York: Holmes and Meier, 1980).

p. 249.   "Kren's mother had called Binion's book." Cited by George M. Kren, interview with author.

Chapter 14: Claude Lanzmann and the War Against the Question Why

p. 251.   "He called the filmmaker's behavior." Dr. Louis Micheels, interview with author.

p. 252.   "There is no why here." Primo Levi, *Survival in Auschwitz* [1947] (New York: Collier Books, 1993), p. 29, cited by Lanzmann in "Hier Ist Kein Warum," *Nouvelle revue de psychoanalyse* 38 (Autumn 1988).

p. 252.   "Consider the introductory description." Remarks by Shoshana Felman recorded in "The Obscenity of Understanding," 473–95.

p. 252.   "Lanzmann's unquestioning adoption." Lanzmann's most dramatic survivor-witness testimony in *Shoah* comes from the barber at Treblinka who shaved the heads of the women in the camp about to be gassed. He made a point of not letting them know they were being prepared for death rather than for delousing, thus denying these women the choice of how they might wish to react to the truth. It was a decision defended on implicitly paternalistic grounds—the barber knew what was best for the women (keeping them in ignorance of their imminent fate). A policy that is presented as noble—and perhaps it was, although the element of self-interest is never alluded to: namely, the barber preserved his job and *his* life by keeping the women in the dark, sparing the camp administration any possible disruption of the killing process that telling the truth might provoke. Lanzmann's refusal to see any complexity in the barber's choice might also have a component of self-interest—he has made it clear in interviews that the barber of Treblinka is the "star" of *Shoah*, one who gave Lanzmann as a filmmaker his most memorably dramatic moment.

p. 253.   "his published attack on Steven Spielberg's film." Claude Lanzmann, review of *Schindler's List, Le Monde,* March 3, 1994.

p. 253.   "No, my researcher insisted." Author's conversation with Alexander Stengel.

p. 254.   "Thou shalt not grant Hitler posthumous victories." In Emil Fackenheim, *To Mend the World: Foundations of Future Jewish Thought* (New York: Schocken Books, 1982).

p. 254.   "some disturbing transcripts and memoirs of that episode." See "The Obscenity of Understanding," and letter from Dr. Louis Micheels to Cathy Caruth, redactor of the event.

p. 254.   "According to the laudatory introduction." "The Obscenity of Understanding," p. 474.

p. 254.   "One observer of the crusades." Dr. Sean Wilder, telephone interview with author.

p. 254.   "His reply to a questioner at a seminar at Yale." *Yale French Studies* 79 (1991): 94.

p. 255.   "an acolyte's vituperative assault on Binion's book." Sabine Prokhoris, "Une histoire en quête de Führer," trans. Masha Belenky, *Les temps modernes* 555 (October 1992): 92–109.

p. 255.   "A blood-red banner across the otherwise sedate cover." *Rudolf Binion et Adolf Hitler: La Psychohistoire cache-misère du revisionisme?* Ibid., cover.

p. 255.   "Binion believes the misspelling." Rudolph Binion, interview with author.

p. 256.   "Binion . . . had to drop the suit." Ibid.

p. 256.   "the ruling enterprise of Binion is obscene." Claude Lanzmann, interview with author.

p. 256.   "The obscenity of this question is stressed by Claude Lanzmann." Prokhoris, "Une histoire en quête de Führer," 93.

p. 256.   "catalogue of insults." Ibid., pp. 93–109, trans. for author by Masha Belenky.

p. 257.   "method *as* final solution." Ibid., p. 109.

p. 258.   "There are some pictures of Hitler as a baby too." "The Obscenity of Understanding," p. 480.

p. 259.   "I don't say that the Holocaust is an enigma." Claude Lanzmann, interview with author.

p. 260.   "the question of 'why' is a fundamental human function." Dr. Sean Wilder, interview with author.

p. 261.   "deploring the 'mystification' of the Holocaust." See Yehuda Bauer, "Is the Holocaust Explicable?" *Holocaust and Genocide Studies* 5.2 (1990): 145–55.

p. 262.   "described in a *New York Times* story." Roger Cohen, "Book on Nazi Murder Industry Stirs French Storm," *The New York Times*, October 28, 1993, p. 3.

p. 262.   "Klarsfeld . . . called the Pressac book." Ibid.

p. 263.   "Lanzmann wrote in the weekly *Le Nouvelle Observateur*." Cited in ibid.

p. 263.   "his own staged and crafted catharsis." In *Shoah*, Lanzmann persuaded the long-retired barber from Treblinka to cut hair in a barbershop setting while Lanzmann hectored him into tearful recollections.

p. 263.   "(The *Times* reporter told me he stood by his story . . .)." Author's phone conversation with Roger Cohen.

p. 263.   "Yehuda Bauer told me." Interview with author.

p. 264.   "in an essay entitled." Yehuda Bauer, "On the Place of the Holocaust in History," *Holocaust and Genocide Studies* 2.2 (1987): 209–20, at p. 210.

p. 264.   "a collection of essays on *Shoah*." *Au sujet de Shoah* (Paris: Belin, 1990).

p. 265.   "the locus classicus of his attack on explanation." Lanzmann, "Hier Ist Kein Warum."

p. 265.   "a story he takes from Primo Levi's memoir." Levi, *Survival in Auschwitz*, p. 29.

p. 265.   "here is what Lanzmann makes of this story." Lanzmann, "Hier Ist Kein Warum."

Chapter 15: Dr. Louis Micheels

p. 268.   "Micheels's . . . memoir." Dr. Louis J. Micheels, *Doctor #117641: A Holocaust Memoir* (New Haven: Yale University Press, 1989).

p. 268.   "a documentary film about Dr. Wirths." Produced in the Netherlands by Rolf Orthel and Hans Fels.

p. 268.   "Our feeling of love." Micheels, *Doctor #117641*.

p. 269.   "I thought Munch was important." Micheels, interview with author.

p. 269.   "These are questions Robert Lifton addresses." Robert Lifton, *The Nazi Doctors: Medical Killing and the Psychology of Genocide* (New York: Basic Books, 1986).

p. 269.   "Dr. Micheels's wife told me." Interview with author.

p. 270.	"I've read the transcript of the public clash." "The Obscenity of Understanding."
p. 270.	"Lanzmann conceded that he was 'violent, very violent.'" Ibid., p. 480. (He means verbally.)
p. 270.	"began with Dr. Micheels speaking about." Interview with author. His speech was not reprinted in "The Obscenity of Understanding."
p. 271.	"Lanzmann told the audience." "The Obscenity of Understanding," pp. 479–80.
p. 272.	"He cites a discussion between Elie Wiesel." Ibid., pp. 481–82.
p. 273.	"the film was . . . a hoax." Dori Laub, ibid., p. 494.
p. 273.	"one member of the audience rose." Ibid., pp. 489–90.
p. 274.	"He confined himself that night." Ibid., pp. 490–93.
p. 275.	"I found I had an ally in Tzvetan Todorov." Tzvetan Todorov, *Facing the Extreme* (New York: Metropolitan Books, 1996).
p. 275.	"Primo Levi spent forty years . . ." Ibid., p. 277.
p. 275.	"something he's written on the subject." Micheels, letter to Cathy Caruth, cited to author.

Chapter 16: Emil Fackenheim and Yehuda Bauer

p. 279.	"For Bauer, Hitler's murderousness." Yehuda Bauer, interview with author.
p. 281.	"a couple of powerfully argued polemics." Bauer, "Is the Holocaust Explicable?" and "On the Place of the Holocaust in History."
p. 281.	"an increasing number of commentators." Bauer, "Is the Holocaust Explicable?" p. 145.
p. 283.	"no way that there can be an all-powerful." The classic statement of the problem of omnipotence for theodicy can be found in J. L. Mackie, "Evil and Omnipotence," *Mind* 64 (1955): 200–212.
p. 284.	"Notre Dame philosopher Alvin Plantinga." Plantinga, "God, Evil, and the Metaphysics of Freedom," and Plantinga, telephone interview with author.
p. 284.	"a survey of the debate." Bill Bruinooge, "The Holocaust as a Challenge to Belief," *Journal of the American Academy of Religion* (1989): 192–200. The phrase "does not remove God from the dock" comes from John Roth in *When God and Man Failed*, ed. Harry Cargas.
p. 285.	"How do you explain a person anyway?" Emil Fackenheim, interview with author.
p. 285.	"It was there, Fackenheim has written." Fackenheim, *To Mend the World*, pp. 206–7.
pp. 285–86.	"The fiction was still maintained." Emil Fackenheim, interview with author.
p. 286.	"His theory of 'radical evil.'" Fackenheim's vision of radical evil differs from both Martin Buber's and Hannah Arendt's uses of the term in that it does not have an origin within man; it takes a force beyond psychology or therapy to ameliorate a being as powerful and inexplicable as God. See Laurie McRobert, "Emil Fackenheim and Radical Evil," *Journal of the American Academy of Religion* 58.339 (summer 1989): 325–39.

p. 287. "Jews are forbidden . . ." Though first expressed in print as "Jews are forbidden to grant posthumous victories to Hitler," later, in *God's Presence in History*, Fackenheim expresses it, "Jews are forbidden to *hand* Hitler posthumous victories."

p. 287. "An exchange of letters with writer Terrence Des Pres." Terrence Des Pres, *The Survivor* (New York: Oxford University Press, 1976).

p. 288. "I read people like the Auschwitz commandant." Rudolf Höss, *Death Dealer* (Buffalo: Prometheus Books, 1992).

p. 289. "J. P. Stern . . . took issue." Stern, *Hitler*.

p. 289. "You know Robert Waite's book?" Waite, *Psychopathic God*.

p. 289. "What Waite actually wrote." Ibid., p. 482.

p. 291. "as one commentator on Fackenheim describes it." McRobert, "Emil Fackenheim and Radical Evil," p. 339.

p. 291. "The insistence on the Holocaust's uniqueness." Elizabeth Domansky, "'Kristallnacht,' the Holocaust, and German Unity," *History and Memory* 4.1 (Spring/Summer 1992): 60–84, at p. 79.

p. 293. "Heinz Höhne, the historian of the SS." Heinz Höhne, *The Order of the Death's Head* (New York: Coward-McCann, 1970), pp. 182–84.

p. 293. "a League of Nations official." Carl Burckhardt, cited in ibid., p. 184.

p. 293. "Fackenheim cites Himmler's belief." Fackenheim, *To Mend the World*, p. 211.

p. 294. "the masseur Felix Kersten." Felix Kersten, *The Memoirs of Dr. Felix Kersten*, ed. Herma Briffaut, trans. Dr. Ernst Morwitz (Garden City, N.Y.: Doubleday, 1947).

p. 294. "Waite's formulation." Fackenheim, *To Mend the World*, pp. 232–33.

p. 295. "Herbert Luethy's 1954 *Commentary* essay." Reprinted in Norman Podhoretz, ed., *The Commentary Reader* (New York: Atheneum, 1966).

p. 295. "Fackenheim goes on to declare." Fackenheim, *To Mend the World*, pp. 232–33.

p. 296. "Elie Wiesel is famous for a stunning image." Elie Wiesel, *Night* [1960] (New York: Random House, 1973).

p. 296. "In a Yom Kippur 1997 essay." Elie Wiesel, "A Prayer for the Days of Awe," *The New York Times*, October 2, 1997, p. A19.

p. 298. "Some, like Rabbi Richard Rubenstein." See Richard L. Rubenstein, *After Auschwitz*, rev. ed. (Baltimore: Johns Hopkins University Press, 1992).

Chapter 17: George Steiner

p. 300. "a fictive character called 'A.H.'" Steiner, *Portage to San Cristóbal*.

p. 300. "It scared the hell out of me." George Steiner, interview with author.

p. 301. "an account in the London *Observer* of the play." London *Observer*, February 21, 1982. The reviewer, Victoria Radin, spoke of "a storm of applause and shouts of 'bravo.' I think they were in some measure for Hitler as much as [Alec] McCowen [the actor who played Hitler]."

pp. 303–4. "An admiring introduction . . ." Nathan A. Scott, Jr., in *Reading George Steiner*, ed. Nathan A. Scott, Jr., and Ronald A. Sharp (Baltimore: Johns Hopkins University Press, 1994).

p. 304. "*greatness.* . . . The shocking massiveness." Ibid., p. 1.

p. 304. "the honors in the . . . academic community." Steiner has since been appointed to a special chair in Comparative Literature at Oxford.

p. 304. "*Language and Silence* and . . . *After Babel.*" George Steiner, *Language and Silence* (New York: Atheneum, 1967), and George Steiner, *After Babel* (New York: Oxford University Press, 1975; rev. ed. 1992).

p. 305. "persuasively challenged by Lawrence Langer." L. Langer, *Admitting the Holocaust*, pp. 109–24.

p. 308. "Sir Leslie specifically calls Hitler." Steiner, *Portage to San Cristóbal*, p. 12.

p. 308. "actor to the end." Ibid., p. 10.

p. 308. "Don't let him speak." Ibid., pp. 47–48.

p. 308. "Hitler's own Hitler explanation." Ibid., pp. 179–89.

p. 308. "My racism was a parody." Ibid., p. 182.

p. 309. "The Jew invented conscience." Ibid., p. 184.

p. 309. "What were our camps compared with that?" Ibid., pp. 184–85.

p. 309. "some 'singular demon.'" Ibid., p. 186.

p. 309. "Our terrors were a village carnival." Ibid., p. 188.

p. 309. "Gentlemen of the tribunal." Ibid., p. 189.

p. 310. "One final full paragraph." Ibid., pp. 189–90.

p. 310. "playing with fire." Hyam Maccoby, interview with author. See chapter 18.

p. 311. "when Steiner permitted the novel to be staged." An adaption by Christopher Hampton, at the Mermaid Theater, London, February 1982.

p. 311. "excellent early study of the question." Stanley Fish, *Surprised by Sin: The Reader in Paradise Lost* [1967] (Cambridge, Mass.: Harvard University Press, 1998).

p. 314. "Sidney Hook gave [Norman] Podhoretz an interview." Sidney Hook, "On Being a Jew," *Commentary* 88.4 (October 1989): 28–36.

p. 314. "he demanded it be kept posthumous." Hook said: "This part I don't want published until I'm dead." Ibid., p. 36.

p. 314. "If we [the Jews] had disappeared." Hook's words were "I've found myself thinking about the crazy Zealots . . . what if the whole Palestine Jewish population of that time had gone down fighting? Just think what we would have been spared, two thousand years of anti-semitic excess. . . . Under some circumstances I think it's better not to be than to be." Ibid., p. 36.

p. 315. "Benzion Netanyahu demonstrated." In *The Origins of the Inquisition in Fifteenth Century Spain* (New York: Random House, 1995).

p. 317. "Bainbridge's challenging novel." Beryl Bainbridge, *Young Adolf* [1978] (New York: Carroll and Graf, 1995).

Chapter 18: Singling out Christianity

p. 319. "People go on about this jolly festival." Hyam Maccoby, interview with author.

p. 321. "combative polemics in *Commentary*." In particular, Hyam Maccoby, "Theologian of the Holocaust," *Commentary* 74 (December 1982), ostensibly about Emil Fackenheim, provoked a furor by suggesting that

Jews are unwilling to place the full share of the blame for the Holocaust on Christian anti-Semitism. See also Hyam Maccoby, "Christianity's Break with Judaism," *Commentary* 78.2 (August 1984).

p. 321.   "a piece in *Commentary* that created an uproar." Maccoby, "Theologian of the Holocaust," and "Letters from Readers," *Commentary* 75 (March 1983).

p. 323.   "There's [John] Charmley now." John Charmley, *Churchill: The End of Glory* (London: Hodder and Stoughton, 1993).

p. 324.   "a devil and the devil's workman." Pope Gelasius I, cited in Hyam Maccoby, *Judas Iscariot and the Myth of Jewish Evil* (New York: Free Press, 1992), p. 6.

p. 325.   "Woe to that man." Mark 14:21.

p. 325.   "field of blood." Matthew 27:3–10.

p. 325.   "intestines bursting out of his body." Acts 1:18–19.

p. 326.   "entered by Satan." Luke 22:3.

p. 326.   "taken possession by the Devil." John 13:2.

p. 326.   "a newspaper column by Pat Buchanan." Pat Buchanan, *New York Post*, December 14, 1994, p. 25.

p. 327.   "a doctoral thesis I'd seen." Schmeller, "Hitler's View of History."

p. 328.   "Daniel Goldhagen's concept of 'eliminationist anti-Semitism.'" See discussion in chapter 19. Goldhagen defines this against Christian anti-Semitism in the sense that Christian anti-Semites at least profess to be satisfied with conversion of Jews. Racial, eliminationist anti-Semites are satisfied only by Jews' deaths.

p. 328.   "In his book on the Judas question." Hyam Maccoby, *The Sacred Executioner: Human Sacrifice and the Legacy of Guilt* (New York: Thames and Hudson, 1982).

p. 328.   "Jews are killed because of Christian guilt." Ibid.

p. 330.   "theologians such as Rosemary Ruether." See, for instance, Rosemary Ruether, *Faith and Fratricide* (San Francisco: Seabury Press, 1974).

p. 330.   "Of all the attacks." Hyam Maccoby, "George Steiner's Hitler," *Encounter*, May 1982, pp. 27–34.

p. 330.   "Hitler . . . 'becomes a full blown Steinerian . . .'" Ibid., p. 31.

p. 330.   "misleading piece of anti-Jewish propaganda." Ibid., p. 30.

p. 331.   "colossal miscalculation." Ibid., p. 30.

p. 334.   "Richard Rubenstein." Rubenstein, *After Auschwitz*.

p. 334.   "Rubenstein singled out Rabbi Leo Baeck." Rubenstein, phone conversation with author.

p. 335.   "Cynthia Ozick . . . stressed to me." Cynthia Ozick, letter to author.

Chapter 19: Daniel Goldhagen

p. 337.   "Goldhagen's just-published book." Goldhagen, *Hitler's Willing Executioners*.

p. 338.   "Langer is the author of a study." Langer, *Admitting the Holocaust*.

p. 338.   "often thought of strangling them." Lawrence Langer, author's notes, U.S. Holocaust Memorial Museum forum, April 8, 1996.

p. 339.   "pregnant with murder." Goldhagen, *Hitler's Willing Executioners*, p. 75.

He goes on to say: "The only matter that cannot be ascertained is . . . how many Germans subscribed to it" at what point. But, certainly, state-encouraged murder began as early as 1933.

p. 340.   "Columbia's Fritz Stern." Fritz Stern, "The Goldhagen Controversy," *Foreign Affairs*, November–December 1996, pp. 128–38.

p. 340.   "pretentious . . . shrill and simplistic." Ibid., p. 138.

p. 340.   "For Goldhagen . . . Hitler *was* Germany." Ibid., p. 131.

p. 341.   "the book's boast to have solved a problem." According to Goldhagen, "explaining why the Holocaust occurred requires a radical revision of what has until now been written. This book is that revision," cited in ibid., p. 128.

p. 342.   "a letter from Hilberg." This letter was actually written to Henry Friedländer. Friedländer is the author of *The Origins of Nazi Genocide* (Chapel Hill: University of North Carolina Press, 1995).

p. 342.   "Kweit goes further, too." Author's notes, Holocaust Memorial Museum forum.

p. 342.   "Hilberg says, 'I take exception . . .'" Kweit, citing Hilberg's letter to Friedländer, ibid.

p. 342.   "Hilberg's lifework, his three-volume history." Raul Hilberg, *The Destruction of the European Jews*, rev. ed. (New York: Holmes and Meier, 1985).

p. 343.   "Goldhagen dismisses . . . the 'five conventional explanations.'" Goldhagen, *Hitler's Willing Executioners*, pp. 379–85.

p. 343.   "Hilberg as 'an exemplar . . .'" Ibid., p. 385.

p. 345.   "Bauer cited . . . George Mosse." Author's notes, Holocaust Memorial Museum forum.

p. 345.   "It's not Goldhagen's fault." Ibid.

p. 345.   "the risk of ending up like Arno Mayer." Arno Mayer, *Why Did the Heavens Not Darken?* (New York: Pantheon, 1988). Mayer's book does have its defenders, although it seems to me a peculiar backhanded way of recuperating Marxism by portraying Jews as martyrs more for their "Bolshevism" than their Jewishness.

p. 346.   "the lurid headline . . . in *Der Spiegel*." *Der Spiegel* 21, May 20, 1996.

p. 346.   "*Die Zeit*." The weekly ran a series on the Goldhagen debate from April 11 through June 24, with a reply from Goldhagen to his critics on August 2.

p. 346.   "Goldhagen abruptly canceled the NYU meeting." "Forum on Holocaust Canceled After Author Withdraws," *The New York Times*, May 7, 1996.

p. 347.   "Sir Isaiah Berlin has written." Berlin, *Against the Current*.

p. 347.   "Norman Cohn . . . author of a study." Cohn, *Warrant for Genocide*, p. 194.

p. 347.   "Cohn defines Hitler's Austrianness." Ibid., p. 194.

p. 348.   "There were regional variations in anti-Semitism . . ." Daniel Goldhagen, interview with author.

p. 350.   "I reread Weber's famous essay." Max Weber, "The Nature of Charismatic Domination." In *Weber: Selections in Translation*, ed. W. G. Runciman, trans. Eric Matthews (New York: Cambridge University Press, 1978), pp. 226–50.

p. 350.   "his right to rule." Ibid., p. 227.

p. 351.   "Erich Goldhagen . . . a 1972 essay." Erich Goldhagen, "Pragmatism, Function and Belief in Nazi Anti-Semitism," *Midstream*, December 1972, pp. 52–62.

p. 351.   "Goldhagen *père* cites numerous instances." Ibid., p. 57: In May 1943, Goebbels's office distributed "secret circulars" ordering "the Propaganda officials of the party . . . to increase and intensify the anti-Semitic 'enlightenment' of the populace," which, by the son's thesis, should scarcely have been necessary.

p. 351.   "in far milder terms than his son." Ibid., p. 59.

p. 352.   "Saul Friedländer . . . 'redemptive anti-Semitism.'" In Friedländer, *Nazi Germany and the Jews*.

p. 353.   "Breitman suggested to me." Richard Breitman, interview with author and later telephone conversation.

p. 353.   "Professor Richard S. Levy's study." Richard S. Levy, *The Downfall of the Anti-Semitic Political Parties in Imperial Germany* (New Haven: Yale University Press, 1975).

p. 355.   "I'm Very Proud." Henryk Broder, *Der Spiegel* 21, May 20, 1996, pp. 58–59.

p. 355.   "Broder . . . begins." Ibid., p. 59.

p. 356.   "Levy told me that he thought." Levy, phone interview with author.

p. 357.   "mail from Professor Berel Lang." Berel Lang, "Holocaust Memory and Revenge: The Presence of the Past," *Jewish Social Studies* 2 (Winter 1996): 1–20.

p. 357.   "How could it be that revenge was *not*." Ibid., p. 2.

p. 357.   "An ambitious plan by . . . partisans." Ibid., pp. 4–5.

p. 357.   "what he calls 'displaced.'" Ibid., pp. 9–10.

p. 359.   "A second cover story in *Der Spiegel*." *Der Spiegel* 33, August 12, 1996, pp. 40–55.

p. 359.   "another curious sidebar." Ibid., p. 42.

p. 359.   "Consider some other changes." Ibid. (trans. Alexander Stengel).

p. 360.   "He'd just reviewed the book." Berel Lang, review of *Hitler's Willing Executioners*, by Daniel Jonah Goldhagen, *Moment*, May 1996.

p. 360.   "[Lang] felt the exaggerated nature of its claim." Berel Lang, interview with author.

p. 360.   "The Rage That Elie Wiesel Edited Out of *Night*." E. J. Kessler, *The Forward*, October 4, 1996, pp. 1, 10.

p. 360.   "Seidman argued that in the Yiddish version." Naomi Seidman, "The Scandal of Jewish Rage," *Jewish Social Studies* 3.1 (Fall 1996): 1–19.

p. 361.   "Not so, the scholars Eli Pfeffercorn and David Hirsch contend." Eli Pfeffercorn and David Hirsch, "Elie Wiesel's Wrestle with God," *Midstream* 43.8 (November 1997): 21ff.

p. 361.   "And Wiesel himself denied to *The Forward*." *The Forward*, October 4, 1996, p. 10.

p. 362.   "Goldhagen denounced Browning's 1992 book." Daniel Jonah Goldhagen, "The Evil of Banality," review of *Ordinary Men*, by Christopher R. Browning, *The New Republic*, July 13–20, 1992, pp. 49–52.

p. 363.   "the late . . . Lucy Dawidowicz argued." See extensive discussion of her thesis in the following chapter.

p. 363.   "Goldhagen emphasizes the moment." Hitler's speech, "Why Are We Anti-Semites," August 13, 1920, cited in Goldhagen, *Hitler's Willing Executioners*, p. 134.

p. 364.   "Yehuda Bauer argues for March 1941." Yehuda Bauer, interview with author.

p. 364.   "Breitman . . . May 1941." Breitman, *Architect of Genocide*.

p. 364.   "a new study by German scholar Peter Witte." Peter Witte, "Two Decisions Concerning the 'Final Solution to the Jewish Question': Deportations to Lodz and Mass Murder in Chelmno," trans. B. Richardson, *Holocaust and Genocide Studies* 9.3 (Winter 1995): 318–45.

p. 364.   "For a period of six months . . ." Ibid., p. 320.

p. 364.   "Hitler's decision to deport the Jews . . ." Ibid., p. 321.

p. 365.   "A recent claim by . . . Christian Gerlach." See *The New York Times*, November 21, 1998, p. 4.

p. 365.   "appears to be a misinterpretation." Author's conversation with Richard Breitman. Breitman does not explicitly call it a misinterpretation: that's my interpretation of his tentative comments.

p. 366.   "People have lost *their* Holocaust." Christopher Browning, interview with author.

p. 366.   "an illuminating recent book." Turner, *Hitler's Thirty Days to Power*.

p. 367.   "Hitler's triumph, Turner argues." Ibid., p. 176.

Chapter 20: Lucy Dawidowicz

p. 369.   "my conversation . . . about his account of Hitler's decision." See especially Christopher Browning, "Beyond Intentionalism and Functionalism: The Decision for the Final Solution Reconsidered," in *The Path to Genocide* (New York: Cambridge University Press, 1992).

p. 369.   "I think he *was* a true believer." Browning, interview with author.

p. 370.   "the recent article by Peter Witte . . ." Witte, "Two Decisions."

p. 373.   "In her important . . . study." Dawidowicz, *War Against the Jews*.

p. 373.   "She finds Hitler using 'esoteric language.'" Ibid., p. 151ff.

p. 374.   "an English major who read Wordsworth . . ." Diane Cole, interview with Lucy Dawidowicz, *Present Tense*, autumn 1983, pp. 22–25.

p. 376.   "The Final Solution had its origins . . ." Dawidowicz, *War Against the Jews*, p. 150.

p. 376.   "How does one advocate publicly . . ." Ibid., p. 151.

p. 378.   "the comment Hitler made to one Josef Hell." Cited in Toland, *Adolf Hitler*, p. 116n, from notes by Hell in the Institut für Zeitgeschichte, ZS 640, folio 6. Hell's description of Hitler's vision of his plans is worth quoting at length as a counterweight to those who argue that Jew-hatred was a secondary or tactical matter for Hitler: "If I am ever really in power," he told Hell, "the destruction of the Jews will be my first and most important job. . . . I shall have gallows after gallows erected. . . . the Jews will be hanged one after another, and they will stay hanging until they stink. . . . As soon as they are untied the next group will follow and that will continue until the last Jew . . . is exterminated."

p. 379. "Hitler's oratorical talents and anti-Semitic presentations . . ." Dawidowicz, *War Against the Jews*, p. 151.

p. 379. "the code words he used for Jews . . ." Ibid., p. 152.

p. 380. "her friend and colleague . . . Ruth Wisse, pointed out." Ruth Wisse, interview with author.

p. 380. "She begins her analysis." Dawidowicz, *War Against the Jews*, pp. 152ff.

p. 380. "1919 letter to a Munich man." Ibid., pp. 16–17.

p. 381. "In August 1920 . . . Hitler told an audience." Hitler, "Why Are We Anti-Semites," cited and discussed in ibid., pp. 17–20.

p. 381. "she cites an April 1922 speech." Ibid., p. 154.

p. 381. "She understood, as a historian." Ruth Wisse, letter to author.

p. 381. "Consider a fascinating address Hitler made." Ibid., p. 93.

p. 382. "her literary executor Neal Kozodoy." Neal Kozodoy, telephone conversation with author.

p. 383. "Dawidowicz puts Kristallnacht in the context." Dawidowicz, *War Against the Jews*, p. 93.

p. 383. "A seventeen-year-old Polish Jewish student." For an important sympathetic reconsideration of Herschel Grynszpan's role, see Michael Marrus, "The Strange Story of Herschel Grynszpan," *American Scholar* 57.1 (Winter 1988): 69–79.

p. 384. "a little-known private declaration." Dawidowicz, *War Against the Jews*, p. 106, citing Hans Bucheim in Helmut Krausnick et al., *Anatomy of the SS State*, p. 44.

p. 384. "A.J.P. Taylor's book." A.J.P. Taylor, *The Origins of the Second World War* [1961] (New York: Macmillan, 1982).

p. 385. "his 'declaration of war against the Jews.'" Dawidowicz, *War Against the Jews*, p. 106.

p. 386. "an absolutely . . . fascinating . . . footnote." Ibid., pp. 110–11n.

p. 386. "on January 30, 1941, Hitler told an audience." The following Hitler speech extracts are all from ibid.

p. 391. "in Himmelfarb's colorful phrase." Milton Himmelfarb, interview with author.

p. 392. "Robert Conquest's . . . account of Stalin's crimes." Robert Conquest, *The Great Terror: A Reassessment*, rev. ed. (New York: Oxford University Press, 1990).

p. 392. "just feels worse." Robert Conquest, telephone conversation with author, citing a remark he originally made to a French newspaper.

p. 392. "The reason people refused to see Stalin." Himmelfarb, interview with author.

ACKNOWLEDGMENTS

My father died in 1990, before this book took its final form, but it was something he disclosed to me several years earlier that might have, as much as anything else, set me on the path I've taken. His parents were Hungarian Jews who came to America before the First World War. The Holocaust was something he rarely if ever spoke of. Few did in the fifties and sixties when I was growing up in suburbia. But at a family gathering late in 1982, not long before a stroke incapacitated him, he told me something that surprised and puzzled me: a cousin from a French branch of his family had died in the Nazi genocide. This puzzled me in two ways: why hadn't he mentioned it before; and why did he mention it then? A mystery I never really resolved. Not that the tenuous family connection should have made a difference, but I think it did mark a moment when I came to feel that all Hitler's victims were, in a sense, part of my (very) extended family. And at a time in my life when I felt somewhat adrift both as a person and a writer, in retrospect my father's words surely played a role in my decision to begin investigating the man who murdered them. But even if it hadn't, I'd want to pay tribute to that gentle man Henry Rosenbaum with his unique sense of humor, of melancholy and absurdity, for all he's meant to my life. And I'd like to thank as well my mother, Evelyn, indefatigable spark plug and beloved teacher, for putting up with both of us with grace and tolerance. I owe an immense, immeasurable debt of gratitude and love to my sister, Ruth, without whose moral support, wisdom, and advice I could not have survived the crises that plagued me while working on this book.

I began discussing writing something about this question more than a dozen years ago with Kathy Robbins. Through every week of every month of that time, through every permutation in the evolution of the eventual book, through every other writing project I've engaged in, she has been a rock and a jewel. An absolutely invaluable presence of matchless clarity, intelligence, and fierce integrity: thoughtful, tough minded, and tender hearted. I can never thank her enough. I'd also like to thank the many bright and talented people who have worked for her and on my behalf over the years, including the current sterling crew of Bill Clegg, David Halpern, Elizabeth Oldroyd, Rick Pappas, Chlöe Sladden, Robert Simpson, and Cory Wickwire.

Ever since my first conversation with Harry Evans about this book, I've felt I've been in good hands. I'm grateful to Harry for his infectious enthusiasm and his critical intelligence and to his impressive successor, Ann Godoff, for the support she's shown for the book throughout the process of bringing it to publication.

I owe a special debt to my editor, Jonathan Karp, without whose intelligence and discernment I could not have seen my way through the unique challenges a subject like this presents. He's the kind of editor every writer hopes to find, one who really cares about writing and one whose dedication was both inspiring and calming. Thanks as well to his assistant, Monica Gomez, for all her help.

I feel much gratitude as well for the care with which Benjamin Dreyer, Random House production editor, shepherded the manuscript through the system, and I was especially fortunate to have in Timothy Mennel a copy editor who went beyond the call of duty in his attentiveness, acuity, and erudition. Thanks as well to managing editor Amy Edelman for her enthusiasm.

I also want to thank my English editor, Clare Alexander, at Macmillan; her early enthusiasm for my manuscript made a world of difference to me.

Another important point in the process for me was the publication of a fifteen-thousand-word excerpt from my work in progress in *The New Yorker* in 1995, and I'd like to thank the people there, beginning with Tina Brown, who took the time to carefully read the twenty-thousand-word chunk of manuscript from which the excerpt was carved. Robert Vare, my editor there, was both insightful and relentless in raising the draft to another level. Thanks also to some of the others there who made a difference, including the famous Miss Gould (whose copyediting proof I still treasure), to Virginia Cannon and Rick Hertzberg, to Peter Canby, Emily Eakin, and Liesel Schillinger.

In Vienna and Munich, I was blessed by finding two young scholars, Waltraud Kolb and Alexander Stengel, respectively, whose research and translation efforts made an extraordinary contribution to my book and who compensated for my less-than-successful struggle with the German language.

I'd like to mention as well a number of people who were particularly important in the evolution of the book from its early stages. Robert Silvers's critical comments about an early draft of an essay on the ancestry question was an important catalyst in shifting my focus from the perhaps irretrievable Ultimate Explanation to the agendas and obsessions of the explainers. Nan Graham's belief in the idea for this book, when she was my editor at Viking, was important, even though we both ended up elsewhere. Tom Powers's encouragement of the kind of investigation into the meanings projected upon uncertainty and ambiguity in historiography was vital in giving me the confidence to take on the uncertainties embedded in the Hitler question. The encouragement I got from Jack Rosenthal and his colleagues at *The New York Times Magazine* to spend nearly a year exploring the question of what we mean when we use the word *evil* was of crucial importance. I'm grateful as well to three people—Alfred Kazin, Cynthia Ozick, and Frederick Crews—to whom I sent an earlier version of the manuscript and whose challenging comments and criticisms were helpful in clarifying and improving it (although they should in no way be held responsible for the ultimate result).

For research and fact checking, I have benefited from the hard work and persistence of a number of people over the years, including Elise Ackerman, Peter Wells, Bonnie Pfister, Anne Gilbert, Jill Tolan, and, in supervising the final stages of the fact checking, Mervyn Keizer. Any errors that may have slipped through their nets are my responsibility.

Now comes what is both the most pleasurable and the most terrifying section of any acknowledgments. Pleasurable because it gives me a chance to express some slight measure of the gratitude due to a wide array of friends and colleagues and others who have helped me in all sorts of ways in the course of writing this book. Terrifying because I've been working on this book so long, and I've benefited from so many, I fear I might foolishly neglect to name some people, and so I preemptively ask the forgiveness of those unintentionally slighted.

But to begin with, Betsy Carter and Gary Hoenig, and proceeding in random order, Helen Rogan and Alfred Gingold, Stanley Mieses, Anne and Michael Mandelbaum, Richard Ben Cramer and Carolyn White, Liz Hecht, Michael Berger, Kathy Rich, Errol Morris, Dan Kornstein, Larissa MacFarquhar, Craig and Allison Karpel, Susan Kamil, the late Duncan Stalker, my godmother, Hortense Greenberg, Sheldon Piekny, Boris Piekny, Katie Karlovitz, Peter Kaplan, Noah Kimerling, George Dolger, David Livingstone, Linda Healy, Ed Fancher, the late Dan Wolf, Clio Morgan, John Roche, Dr. Reinhard Weber at the Bavarian State Archives, Gail Ganz of the Anti-Defamation League, Louise Jones at the Yale Club library, Sarah Kernochan, Michael Caruso, Deirdre Dolan, Nancy Donahoe, Steven Weisman, Caroline Marshall, Virginia Heffernan, the late Veronica Geng, Arthur Carter, Steven Varni and Jeannette Watson of the late great Books and Company, my childhood pals Richard Spivak and Richard Molyneux, my college buddies Richard Burling and Richard Bell, Amy Gutmann, Judi Hoffman, Glenn and Georgia Greenberg, Steve and Myrna Greenberg, Deb Friedman, Jay Matlick, Faye Beckerman for taking care of Smooch and Stumpy, Cynthia Cotts, Abbie Ehrlich, the guys in my once-regular poker game (David Hirshey, Gil Schwartz, Peter Herbst, David Blum, Michael Hirschorn, Bob Asahina, Gene Stone), Jesse Sheidlower and Elizabeth Bogner, Adrienne Miller, David Granger, Cheryl Tanenbaum, Virginia Wing, Lauren Thierry, Jim Watkins, Carole Ann Smith, Mike Drosnin, Liz Ferris, Richard Horowitz, and Dora Steinberg.

Extra special thanks to Marianne Macy.

Finally, I want to express my appreciation to all those I interviewed and consulted for the time they spent talking to me on this difficult subject, and I want to express my admiration for those writers and thinkers, even those I've been critical of, for their courage and dedication in taking up the impossible challenge of explaining Hitler.

Acknowledgements for the Updated Edition

I'd like to thank Prof. Alvin Rosenfeld who suggested the need for a new edition, David Halpern for acting upon it with speed and dexterity, Robert Pigeon, my editor at Da Capo Press, for his valuable suggestions on the new material, Amber Morris for her production skills, Christine Arden for her deft copyediting touch, and Justin Lovell, a part of the team. And—I don't care if I'm repeating here—the great Harry Evans for commissioning the book in the first place.

INDEX

Abend, Der, 109
Act and Idea in the Nazi Genocide (Lang), 208–9
Acta Psychiatrica, xxxiii
Action Report, 234
"Adolf Hitler" (Alois Hitler, Jr.), 183
"Adolf Hitler, Traitor" (Nazi Party), 39
Adorno, Theodor, 253
After Babel (Steiner), 304
Albert Speer: His Battle with Truth (Sereny), 222
American Imago, 258–59
American Jewry and the Holocaust (Bauer), 280
American Monthly, 168
Anatomy of Human Destructiveness, The (Fromm), xxxii
Andreas-Salomé, Lou, 240
Anna (Raubal's niece), 123–26
Anti-Defamation League, 177
anti-Semitism, xiii, xiv, 172, 304, 353
    Austrian, 302, 347–48
    blackmail culture and, 51
    blood-libel and, 325, 328
    borderland effect and, 347
    Christian, 339–41, 352
    Christian doctrine and, 322–23
    eliminationist, *see* eliminationist anti-Semitism
    French, 302, 334, 345
    hatred and, 187–89, 190, 198, 316
    Judaic standards and, 333–34
    in literature, 323–24
    post-Christian, 328
    Protocols of the Elders of Zion and, 55–57
    as racial vs. religious, 315–16
    "redemptive," 352
    sexual pathology and, 137–39, 151
    see also Hitler, Adolf, anti-Semitism of
Architect of Genocide, The (Breitman), 174, 353
Architecture of Doom, The (film), 217
Arendt, Hannah, 216, 287, 291, 339, 340, 395
Aretin, Erwin von, xliii, xliii–xliv, 162
Aretin, Karl-Ottmar Freiherr von, xliii
Argentina, 223–24
argumentum ad Hitlerum, xxii
Aristotle, 83

Association for Applied Psychoanalysis, 258
atomic bomb, 180
Auer, Erhard, 42
Aufbau, 157–58
Augustine, Saint, 329
Auschwitz, 38, 75, 215, 217, 218, 232, 234, 262, 268, 291, 314–15
    "bearers of secrets" in, 270
    fictive "work battalions" at, 285–86
    God's presence and, 284
    Levi's "no why here" experience at, 252, 265–66, 275–76
    see also Final Solution; Holocaust
Austria, 147
    Anschluss of, 50
    anti-Semitism of, 302, 347–48

Baeck, Leo, 334–35
Bainbridge, Beryl, 317
Barbie, Klaus, 262
Bauer, Yehuda, vii, xv, xxi, xxiv, xl, 85, 94, 259, 261, 263–64, 279–85, 298, 352, 356, 359, 364, 367, 393
    God-is-Satan-or-nebbish syllogism of, 283–85, 295–96
    Goldhagen criticized by, 344–36
    mystifiers opposed by, 281–82, 284
    theodicy problem and, 283–85
    work of, 280–81
Baumann, Emil, 182–83
Beauvoir, Simone de, 254
Belloc, Hilaire, 323
Berlin, Isaiah, 7, 347
Bernadotte, Folke, 63
Bernstein, Michael André, xvii, xli, 240–41
Bezymenski, Lev, 80
Binion, Rudolph, xliv, 131, 146, 147, 239, 260, 264–65
    background of, 239–42
    iodoform gauze research of, 246, 248–49
    on Jewish doctor episode, 242–48
    John Kafka and, 245–46, 247–50
    Lanzmann's criticism of, 242, 255–57, 264
Black Front, 133
Blake, William, 68, 311

ABOUT THE AUTHOR

Ron Rosenbaum was born in Manhattan and grew up in Bay Shore, Long Island, New York. He graduated Phi Beta Kappa from Yale, in English Literature, specializing in the 17th-century metaphysical poets, and went on to study English literature on a Carnegie Fellowship at Yale Graduate School before leaving to take up writing full time.

He began at the *Village Voice* and *Esquire* at the end of their respective Golden Ages. (He did not personally cause the end.) He went on to write for *Harper's*, *New York Times Magazine*, the *New Yorker*, the *Atlantic*, and *Vanity Fair*, among many other periodicals. His nonfiction has been collected in four separate volumes, most recently *The Secret Parts of Fortune*, and more of his past work can be found on the long form site, Byliner.com.

He wrote "The Edgy Enthusiast" cultural affairs column for the *New York Observer* for twelve years. Among his proudest achievements was writing columns that got the four out-of-print novels by Charles Portis (including *The Dog of the South*) back into print. And helping to save the last unfinished manuscript of Vladimir Nabokov from burning.

His most recent books include *The Shakespeare Wars* (about genuine scholarly controversies, not the foolish "authorship" question); and *How the End Begins* (about the continued peril of nuclear war). He also edited a collection of essays about contemporary anti-Semitism, *Those Who Forget the Past*. He has taught writing seminars at Columbia Journalism School, NYU, and the University of Chicago.

Currently a cultural columnist for Slate.com, he is also the National Correspondent for *Smithsonian Magazine*, serves on the editorial board of *Lapham's Quarterly* and the Publications Advisory Board of the Royal Shakespeare Company. He lives in Manhattan.